HITLER'S FOREIGN DIVISIONS

FOREIGN VOLUNTEERS IN THE WAFFEN-SS 1940–1945

SS HITLER'S FOREIGN DIVISIONS

FOREIGN VOLUNTEERS IN THE WAFFEN-SS 1940–1945

CHRIS BISHOP

amber
BOOKS

First published in 2005 by Amber Books Ltd

Copyright © Amber Books Ltd 2005

ISBN 1-904687-37-7

Published by
Amber Books Ltd
Bradley's Close
74–77 White Lion Street
London N1 9PF
United Kingdom
www.amberbooks.co.uk

Project Editor: Michael Spilling
Design: EQ Media
Picture Research: Natasha Jones

Printed in Italy

PICTURE CREDITS
Aerospace/Art-Tech: 13, 28, 37, 49, 61, 69, 77, 82, 86, 91, 100, 102, 105, 111, 117,
118, 119, 139, 144, 145, 153, 157, 160, 166;
AKG Images: 8, 18;
Amber Books: 14, 15, 116, 167;
Cody Images: 9, 10, 11, 16, 20, 23, 24, 25, 27, 30, 32, 34, 35, 38, 39, 41, 43, 44, 46, 47,
50, 52, 54, 55, 56, 60, 71, 78, 87, 93, 94, 96, 99, 107, 112, 114, 123, 124, 125,126, 129, 130,
132, 137, 147, 148, 150, 154, 163, 164, 165, 170, 172, 173, 175, 176, 178, 179, 185;
Ian Baxter: 6, 53, 65, 83, 98, 121, 122, 128;
Popperfoto: 59;
Private collection:155;
Süddeutscher Verlag: 17, 22, 29, 66, 67, 72, 73, 75, 79, 80, 84, 85, 88, 109, 115, 134, 135,
141, 142, 151, 158, 168, 180, 182;
Ukrainian State Archive: 7, 62, 76.

CONTENTS

INTRODUCTION

Even today, more than six decades after the outbreak of World War II, it still seems incredible that thousands of men whose countries had been conquered by the Nazis should have volunteered for service with the SS. Hundreds of thousands more volunteered or were conscripted into the *Wehrmacht*, the *Kriegsmarine* and the *Luftwaffe*. Many had no choice in the matter, but a significant number were willing members of the German armed forces, and those who served with the SS were mostly volunteers. But why did the SS recruit them and, having done so, trust them in battle?

Above: Cossacks in German service ride across the steppe. The German invasion of the USSR in 1941 was seen as a liberation by many minorities which had been suppressed under Stalin, and huge numbers flocked to the Nazi colours.
Left: A ski trooper attached to the 6th *SS-Gebirgs Division Nord* is seen on patrol, armed with a Soviet Tokarev self-loading rifle. The more accomplished skiers in the division came from the *Skijäger Bataillon Norge*.

Above: Although Adolf Hitler was the founder of the SS, it was Heinrich Himmler who gave it a structure. Himmler's desire to expand the fighting SS led to recruitment beyond the borders of the Reich, after Army opposition restricted available manpower in Germany.

During the course of World War II, the *Waffen*-SS grew from an elite force of four regiments composed solely of Germans meeting Heinrich Himmler's exacting physical and racial standards, into a polyglot force of 900,000 men in 39 divisions, with over half of its troops foreign volunteers or conscripts. Even so, at its peak the *Waffen*-SS represented only one-tenth of the strength of the *Wehrmacht* – although it provided a quarter of German panzer strength.

Few people realize just how international were the German forces in World War II. It is estimated that nearly two million foreign nationals served under the Swastika. Although towards the end of the war many

were transferred to the SS, large numbers served with the Army, particularly on the Eastern Front. The most committed of the foreign volunteers found a home in the SS, until parts of it were more like a German equivalent of the French Foreign Legion than the elite of the German race. *Waffen*-SS equipment and organization were the same as those of the Army. Units were interchangeable with Army units, and senior *Waffen*-SS officers adopted Army ranks.

The *Waffen*-SS

Although the SS did not welcome non-German volunteers until midway through the conflict in Russia, the idea of recruiting such men dated back to before the war. In his quest for a pan-Germanic Europe, *Reichsführer*-SS Heinrich Himmler had decreed in 1938 that non-Germans of suitable 'Nordic' origin could enlist in the *Allgemeine*-SS. At that point in time the distinction between the civilian 'general' SS, or *Allgemeine-SS*, and the 'armed' SS, or *Waffen-SS*, did not exist. By the outbreak of war in 1939, however, the armed SS had emerged in its own right, as a separate entity from the *Allgemeine-SS* and from the *Totenkopf* units which guarded the concentration camps. The *Waffen-SS* played a small but important part in Germany's early campaigns. Its fighting reputation pleased Himmler greatly, and he wanted to increase the organization's importance. Established primarily as a security force, it would have to become much bigger if it was to play its part in the

Below: Himmler's recruitment drive was made easier by the growth of right-wing nationalist parties in Europe in the 1930s, members of which could easily be persuaded to join a 'crusade' against communism. Here, Staf De Clercq of the *Vlaamsch Nationaal Verbond* addresses members of the Flemish Volunteer Legion before their departure for the Eastern Front.

pan-Germanic future which would come after the war was won. But expansion did not come easily.

The explosive wartime growth of the *Waffen-SS* reflected Himmler's desire to create an instrument of political power that would safeguard the National Socialist revolution inside Germany. In the process, it would provide a counterweight to the influence of the Army. Although a number of former SS officers claimed after the war that the *Waffen-SS* was a purely fighting force, in truth the organization was never completely free of its political origins. As late as 1943, the preface to an SS panzer training manual contained a paragraph which read: '... The SS fulfils a requirement to provide an unflinching force at the disposal of the leadership of the Reich in any situation. This includes the maintenance of order at home by the use of any and all methods.'

The main stumbling-block to this expansion was the Army. With good reason, the generals had feared

the establishment of a powerful party organization answerable only to Hitler. Before the war, the General Staff had blocked SS acquisition of artillery, and had forbidden the formation of an SS field division. Above all, the Army controlled the number of men the SS could recruit. Each year, the *Oberkommando der Wehrmacht* (OKW), or Military High Command, laid down the proportion of men to be conscripted to each arm or service. All men of recruitable age were registered with the local *Wehrbezirkskommando* (WBK), or Military District Headquarters. No volunteer could join a military unit until he had been released by his local WBK, and the Army made sure that as few men as possible were released to join the SS.

Conditions for the SS improved slightly with the outbreak of war. In spite of the rigorous selection process, German volunteers were plentiful. Many were attracted to Himmler's romantic dream of a race of blue-eyed, blond heroes, an elite formed according to 'laws of selection' based on criteria of physiognomy, mental and physical tests, character and spirit. His 'aristocratic' concept would combine charismatic authority with bureaucratic discipline. The SS man

would represent a new human type – warrior, administrator, scholar and leader, all in one – whose messianic mission was to repopulate Europe. The SS played on its status as an elite force by using its Nazi connections to recruit the cream of the Hitler Youth movement and the *Reichsarbeitsdienst* (RAD), or Reich Labour Service, before they could be snatched up by the *Wehrmacht*.

Himmler's plans received a major boost when an energetic Swabian SS-*Brigadeführer* named Gottlob Berger was given responsibility for SS recruitment. With recruitment blocked by the Army, it was Berger who suggested to Himmler that he should make use of his control of the concentration camp guards and the police to form two new formations, the *Totenkopf* and the *Polizei* Divisions. As the SS expanded, these were eventually to become the 3rd SS-*Panzer Division Totenkopf* and the 4th SS-*Panzergrenadier Division SS-Polizei*.

Volunteers were still coming in, but early public approval of the *Waffen*-SS was beginning to diminish, and the armed SS began to acquire some of the sinister reputation of other branches of the organization. Heinz Höhne, in his seminal work *The Order of the Death's Head*, quoted a *Sicherheitsdienst* (SD – the SS Security Service) report written in March 1942:

'... it may be stated that by its achievements the *Waffen*-SS has won its place in the popular esteem. Particular reference is made to the good comradeship and excellent relations between officers, NCOs and men ... Unfortunately voices are also to be heard saying that the *Waffen*-SS possesses no trained officers and that therefore SS men are "recklessly sacrificed" ... Critical voices are to be heard saying that the *Waffen*-SS is a sort of military watchdog. SS men are trained to be brutal and ruthless, apparently so that they can be used against other German formations if necessary ... The *Waffen*-SS is a most ruthless force.'

Left: Members of the *SS-Freiwilligen Verband Danemark*, also known as the *Freikorps Danmark*, are sworn in as members of the SS after completing their training at Hamburg in the autumn of 1941. Unlike German SS recruits, the Danish volunteers swore an oath to Adolf Hitler as the commander of the *Wehrmacht*, not the personal oath of absolute loyalty to the *Führer*.

Nordic volunteers

Continually looking for fresh sources of manpower that the Army could not block, Berger now began looking outside Germany's borders for troops. In part, this followed Himmler's romantic vision of a pan-Germanic Europe, in which Germany would annex the 'Nordic' states with the aid of right-wing collaborationist governments.

Himmler believed that once exposed to German propaganda, volunteers from northern and northwestern Europe would flock to the Swastika to take part in a crusade in the East against the 'Judaeo-Bolshevik' enemy. In his dreams, Himmler saw his multi-national SS supplanting the German Army in a new German empire stretching from the Atlantic to the Urals. Curiously his master, Adolf Hitler, was much less excited about such ideas, wanting to win the war before going full speed ahead with reconstructing

Above: Members of an *SS-Polizei Schützen* regiment on the march early in the war. Partially absorbed into the SS in 1940, police regiments were not as highly regarded as *Waffen*-SS units, and many of the early eastern volunteers were assigned to them rather than regular SS units.

Europe in the Nazi image. After the May 1940 *Sieg im Westen*, or 'Victory in the West', the SS began an active programme to recruit suitably 'Nordic' or 'Germanic' volunteers from northern and western Europe to join a number of *Waffen*-SS *Freiwillige* (volunteer) legions. This effort intensified after June 1941, as the SS exhorted volunteers to join the campaign in the Soviet Union.

Norway, Denmark, Holland and Belgium all had their own fascist parties, which in some cases modelled themselves on Germany, while others took their inspiration from Rome. Initially it was Nazi racial doctrine which determined the level of acceptance of volunteers. Danes, Norwegians and Flemish (Dutch-speaking) Belgians were considered 'Aryan', and could volunteer for the *Waffen-SS*, while Frenchmen, Spaniards and Walloons (French-speaking Belgians) were not considered racially pure. Walloon volunteers for the great anti-Bolshevik crusade preached by the Nazis had to join a volunteer legion in the German Army, and the *Légion des Volontaires Français* (LVF) also came under Army control.

However, the LVF was just a small portion of the French contribution to the war effort. Tens of thousands of French speakers became German citizens when the Nazis annexed Alsace and Lorraine. As a result, they became eligible for conscription into the *Wehrmacht*, the *Kriegsmarine* and the *Luftwaffe*. Later in the war some were conscripted directly into the *Waffen-SS*, as Himmler's private army increasingly became a fully fledged member of the *Wehrmacht*.

Racial standards

As the war progressed and manpower grew scarcer to find, the SS lowered its racial standards. Nazi propaganda also changed as more and more 'non-Aryans' joined the *Wehrmacht* and the *Waffen-SS*. Instead of talking about a Germanic empire, the posters, books, magazines, films and radio broadcasts generated the myth of the 'New European Order', which extolled the unification of a continent divided for millennia, and which made much of the battle to overthrow Bolshevik Russia.

However, all this was still in the future, and standards were still high when in September 1940 Hitler consented to the raising of a new *Waffen-SS* division. The formation was originally to be named *SS-Division Germania*, and the backbone of the unit was to be provided by the experienced and combat-tested *Germania* Regiment of the SS-*Verfügungstruppe* (VT) Division (the pre-war forerunner of the *Waffen-SS*). However, the bulk of its strength would be provided by Dutch and Flemish volunteers from the *SS-Regiment Westland* and Norwegians and Danes from *SS-Standarte Nordland*.

Early 1941 saw the addition of a volunteer unit of Finns, the *Finnisches Freiwilligen-Bataillon der Waffen-SS Nordost,* which had been raised in February 1941.

On 20 December Hitler ordered that the division should be known as the *SS-Division Wiking*.

The invasion of the Soviet Union

By the time *Wiking* was formed, the most important boost to the recruitment of foreign volunteers was well under way – the German attack on the Soviet Union. Launched on 22 June 1941, Operation *Barbarossa* was the largest military operation in history. Three huge army groups smashed across the border, punching through the weak Soviet defences with ease. The German plan called for a lightning advance by the *Wehrmacht* to destroy the forward-deployed Red Army, followed by a general pursuit along three main axes: towards Leningrad, towards Moscow, and south to seize the productive wheatfields of the Ukraine and from there on to the oilfields of the Caucasus. It was expected that the onset of winter should see the Red Army completely defeated and Germany in control of much of European Russia. A rump Soviet state might still exist beyond the Urals, but German possession of Russia's major cities and industrial and agricultural regions would secure the resources necessary for the Third Reich to prosper. In the long run, it was to be Hitler's most fatal miscalculation, but the initial stages of the great gamble brought the *Wehrmacht* perilously close to success.

The campaign in Russia was the main driving force in the recruitment of foreign volunteers. Depicted as a crusade against communism, the war in the East attracted many right-wing idealists. Between the wars, politics in Europe had strongly polarized political viewpoints all over the continent, and Soviet support for local communist movements had made the USSR something of a pariah in Europe. It was that attitude which was exploited by German propagandists, who depicted the ongoing struggle as a battle to rid Europe of the 'Red Menace' for ever.

Apart from the volunteers serving with the multi-national *Wiking* Division, early European recruits were incorporated into national volunteer units. These 'legions' could be sponsored and recruited by local collaborationist parties and governments. Nobody knows just who was responsible for the idea: it was probably a spur-of-the-moment plan with a strong propaganda element, inspired by local organizations

keen to be seen taking part in the fight against communism. The first legions were mooted even before Hitler's approval of the use of foreign troops, which came on 28 June 1941.

However, Hitler's approval came with some caveats. The SS would only accept those with 'Nordic' blood, which in essence meant that the only 'Germanic' legions would be those recruited in Scandinavia, Holland and Flanders. However, that did not mean rejecting anti-communist volunteers flocking in from France, Wallonia, Croatia and Spain: these would be assigned to the *Wehrmacht*, which would oversee their equipment and training. To further the image of a multi-national crusade, Germany also persuaded Axis allies to fight alongside the Germans. Troops from Italy, Romania, Hungary and Slovakia were sent to the Eastern Front. Neutral Spain also sent a large volunteer force, the Blue Division. Nominally manned by members of the *Falange*, the local fascist organization,

Above: Members of an SS *Feldgendarmerie* unit take Soviet men into custody. Known as *Kopf Jäger*, or 'Head Hunters', the SS field police worked closely with the death squads of the *Einsatzgruppen* and with volunteer police units recruited in the Baltic states.

the Blue Division was in fact a mix of regular soldiers, civil war veterans and *Falange* militia. Most of the officers were regulars.

Erratic performers

Although the early volunteer formations in the Army and *Waffen*-SS had strong political motivations for fighting, their performance on the field of battle did not match their initial enthusiasm. The Spanish Blue Division was large enough to have some real military value, and could be considered the equivalent of a second- or third-line German infantry division. However, the much smaller French Legion was not a

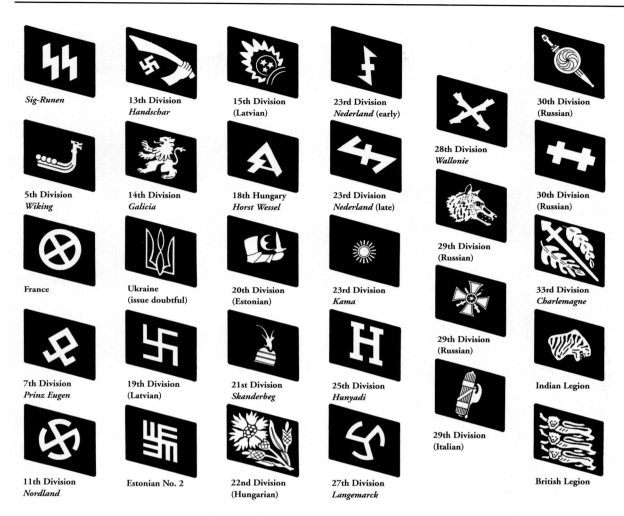

Sig-Runen

13th Division
Handschar

15th Division
(Latvian)

23rd Division
Nederland (early)

28th Division
Wallonie

30th Division
(Russian)

5th Division
Wiking

14th Division
Galicia

18th Hungary
Horst Wessel

23rd Division
Nederland (late)

29th Division
(Russian)

30th Division
(Russian)

France

Ukraine
(issue doubtful)

20th Division
(Estonian)

23rd Division
Kama

29th Division
(Russian)

33rd Division
Charlemagne

7th Division
Prinz Eugen

19th Division
(Latvian)

21st Division
Skanderbeg

25th Division
Hunyadi

29th Division
(Russian)

Indian Legion

11th Division
Nordland

Estonian No. 2

22nd Division
(Hungarian)

27th Division
Langemarck

29th Division
(Italian)

British Legion

Opposite: Germany invested a great deal in the recruitment of suitably 'Nordic' volunteers into the Waffen-SS. This Dutch recruiting poster is typical of the striking graphic style used to present the SS in an heroic light.

Above: Foreign volunteer units in the Waffen-SS did not wear standard 'Sig-rune' collar tabs. Instead, they wore tabs bearing emblems indicating their origins. Foreigners also wore a sleeve shield with their national colours.

success at the front line, and it took considerable effort to make it efficient enough for rear-area security operations. The even smaller Walloon Legion fought reasonably well, but it was too limited in capability to have much effect. The 6000–7000 SS volunteers who served in the various SS legions were more effective. Most were used to man static defences or to carry out rear-area security duties. They did occasionally see brief but intense fighting in mopping-up operations. However, the Danish Freikorps saw intense action when used to reinforce the Totenkopf Division in the

vicious fighting in the Demyansk pocket in 1942. The Dutch regiment and the Norwegian and Flemish battalions joined the 2nd SS Infantry Brigade in the siege lines of Leningrad, and were eventually incorporated into the SS proper.

In contrast to the legions, the Wiking Division was a true elite formation. Commanded by Felix Steiner, one of the most influential officers in the Waffen-SS, Wiking was the first 'international' Waffen-SS division. It proved to be an excellent fighting unit, and as the 5th SS-Panzer Division Wiking it gained a combat

Above: A patrol from the 5th *SS-Division Wiking* moves through the Russian snow. The prototype of the multinational SS division, *Wiking* gained an excellent reputation as a fighting unit in its four years on the Eastern Front.

Opposite: *Obergruppenführer* Felix Steiner, the original commander of the 5th *SS-Division Wiking*, is seen here awarding the Knight's Cross to an Estonian volunteer, *Obersturmführer* (First Lieutenant) Harald Riipalu.

reputation second to none. In the process, it served as the progenitor of a number of other SS divisions.

However, Germans outnumbered Germanics in its ranks, and a sluggish Germanic replacement system kept the proportion of Germans to Germanics quite high. *Wiking* operated exclusively on the Eastern Front, serving as a spearhead unit for Operation *Barbarossa* in 1941, for the drive on the Caucasus in 1942, and for the *Citadel* offensive at Kursk in 1943. The division served in the Cherkassy pocket and in Hungary as the war turned against Germany. Despite at least one allegation of war crimes, *Wiking* earned a tough but fair reputation – or as fair a reputation as

any unit on the Eastern Front could have. Before the withdrawal of the Legions from the Eastern Front in 1943, Himmler had already compromised the exclusive status of his foreign auxiliaries by combining them with each other and with German units. Thus, in September 1942, Himmler reported to Hitler that he would merge the legions with the formerly all-German SS brigades in Army Group North. The Danish volunteers joined one regiment of the 1st SS Brigade, and the Dutch and Norwegian Legions formed a regiment in the 2nd SS Brigade. The reason for this consolidation was straightforward: as individual, independent units the legions were simply too small

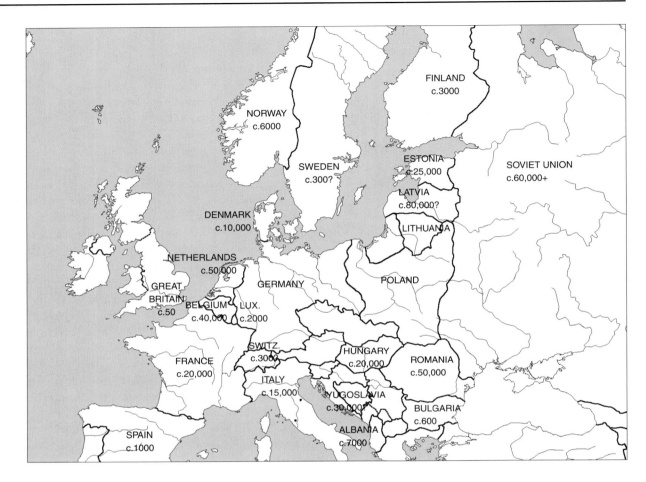

Above: Foreign volunteers serving in the *Wehrmacht*, the *Kriegsmarine* and the *Waffen*-SS came from almost every country in occupied Europe, as well as from Allied nations and from neutrals like Sweden and Switzerland. By the end of the war over half of the *Waffen*-SS was non-German.

to have any effect on operations over the vast distances and in the huge scale of combat on the Russian Front. Additionally, it was proving increasingly hard to recruit volunteers for the legions, since any European enthusiasm for the anti-communist crusade had gradually melted away as the volunteer units began to suffer heavy casualties in the bitter fighting on the Eastern Front.

Himmler now decided to combine the available Germanic volunteers in a new multi-national division modelled on the successful SS *Wiking* Division, as part of the *Waffen*-SS expansion programme which had

begun in 1942. Formed in July 1943, the 11th *SS-Freiwilligen Panzergrenadier Division Nordland* absorbed the SS *Nordland* Regiment from *Wiking*, the remnants of the volunteer legions, and new replacements recruited in Norway, Denmark and Holland under Berger's refurbished recruitment programme.

Western European volunteers who joined the *Waffen*-SS were not treated the same as their German counterparts. They did not take the oath of allegiance to Hitler, most being motivated by their own idealistic beliefs in the fight against communism. They were certainly exposed to less political and racial indoctrination than Germans. However, there were many problems, not least being the fact that in the early days they were treated with some disdain by their German cadres. Communications were also a problem, with units from several different countries speaking different languages often being brigaded together for combat. In the later stages of the war, the Western and Nordic *Freiwillige* divisions were among the most disciplined and fanatical of all SS units. This was possibly because as the war turned against Germany, they realized that their countrymen back home would look on them as traitors, and that their only hope would be to fight as hard as possible for an unlikely Nazi victory.

The *Volksdeutsche*

Although more than 125,000 Western Europeans volunteered for the *Waffen*-SS, it was still not enough to satisfy the organization's ever-growing need for manpower. Once again, it was Gottlob Berger, by now an *Obergruppenführer* in charge of the SS-*Hauptamt* (SS Main Office), who came up with a solution. He proposed expanding SS recruitment to include the *Volksdeutsche* – ethnic Germans scattered in communities all over Central and Eastern Europe.

The origins of many of the German-speaking communities dated back to the Middle Ages. Others were remnants of the former Austro-Hungarian Empire and of the Kaiser's empire. As well as the loss of Germany's colonial empire, the Versailles Treaty of 1919 had seen German border territory ceded to Denmark, Poland and Belgium. Closer to home, Germany lost the important coalfields of Alsace-Lorraine, which went back to France after having been captured by Prussia in 1871. The desire to undo the perceived iniquities of Versailles and to bring the Germanic territories of Europe from their current foreign control into a greater German state was an article of faith for Hitler and the Nazis.

In Europe there were several countries and regions with large populations for whom German was their first language. Poland, Hungary, Transylvanian Romania and the Sudeten area of Czechoslovakia had German-speaking communities of between one and five million, while in Yugoslavia there were up to a million German speakers. Within Europe the Nazis were actively engaged in political and propaganda activities in Hungary and Yugoslavia, while pro-Nazi political movements of varying sizes existed in almost every other country. For Hitler and his pan-German mentors, a long-term goal was the creation of Greater Germany, a country that united those people who were ethnically German, or *Volksdeutsche*, into one nation. As far back as November 1937 Hitler explained his plans: 'The aim of German policy is to secure and preserve the racial community – and to enlarge it.'

For many Germans or German communities living abroad, Hitler's Third Reich seemed a dynamic and vigorous nation that had grown out of defeat and the decadence of the Weimar Republic. It was exciting to be involved as *Auslandsdeutsche*, whether at a distance or as close neighbours. When the SS began recruiting *Volksdeutsche*, that attitude led to a flood of new recruits. However, there were problems. Despite their ethnic background, many of the *Volksdeutsche* recruits had only a rudimentary command of German, and the hard discipline typical of SS training meant that their motivation and commitment to the cause often failed to match that of members of the western legions. Some *Volksdeutsche* units fought well, but as a whole the ethnic Germans had a mixed reputation. Many of the *Reichsdeutsche* members of the SS felt that the *Volksdeutsche* were cowardly and untrustworthy. The flood of volunteers also began to dry up fairly quickly, and Germany leaned heavily on the governments of various puppet states to allow the conscription of men of the right age straight into the SS.

New divisions

The next two SS divisions to be formed made extensive use of *Volksdeutsche* volunteers to fill out their respective orders of battle. The *Waffen*-SS had started the war as the most poorly equipped troops in the German armed forces. Most SS formations had gone into battle on foot, with horse-drawn transport. SS equipment was procured through the Army, and as long as the Army saw the SS as a potential rival, it refused to supply the latest weapons. Even though the big-name units like the *Leibstandarte* and *Das Reich* were grudgingly supplied with the latest weaponry, less favoured SS units were much less well equipped.

The 7th *SS-Freiwilligen Gebirgs Division Prinz Eugen* was one such unit. Created for anti-partisan operations in the Balkans, the bulk of its strength consisted of *Volksdeutsche* volunteers and conscripts from Romania, Hungary and Yugoslavia. Formed as a mountain division, *Prinz Eugen* was equipped with

Above: A propaganda picture of Cossacks in German service. In the original French magazine article it was captioned, 'Fighters for a New Europe: Gathered in their hundreds and commanded by German officers, Cossacks hunt down partisan bandits behind the lines.'

obsolete and captured equipment such as Czech machine guns and French light tanks.

Despite this poor equipment, it was one of the most effective counter-insurgency units the Germans fielded in Yugoslavia, and was greatly feared by the partisans. However, that reputation was gained primarily by brutality and utter ruthlessness. The conflict in Yugoslavia combined guerrilla war with civil and tribal warfare, and neither side was prone to giving quarter. The 8th *SS-Kavallerie Division Florian Geyer* was also used on anti-partisan operations, and quickly gained an equally unsavoury reputation. The origins of the unit dated back to the formation of cavalry units

within the *Allgemeine*-SS *Totenkopf Standarten* late in 1939. These cavalry units were then consolidated under the command of the *Kommandostab-RFSS* (Command Staff *Reichsführer*-SS) for Operation *Barbarossa*. Their primary function was security, being used behind the front lines to mop up bypassed Soviet Army units.

Gradually, their main function became the waging of an extremely ruthless anti-partisan campaign. Formed in 1942, the *Florian Geyer* Division continued with these security duties but did see some front-line service. The Soviet Army destroyed the division during the siege of Budapest in February 1945.

The success of his troops in Russia prompted Himmler to expand the *Waffen*-SS still further. Four new divisions were authorized, three of them armoured. These were the 9th *SS-Panzer Division Hohenstaufen,* the 10th *SS-Panzer Division Frundsberg,* the 11th *SS-Freiwilligen Panzergrenadier Division*

Nordland and the 12th *SS-Panzer Division Hitlerjugend*. All began forming in 1943, but none were ready to take part in the summer offensive that year. Only the *Nordland* Division made extensive use of foreign volunteers.

In the spring of 1944 the SS Panzer Corps was a shadow of the powerful force that had spearheaded Operation *Citadel* at Kursk the previous year. Most units had been withdrawn to Western Europe to rest and refit, becoming fully fledged panzer divisions in the process. However, the 9th and 10th Divisions had now completed their training, and went into action at Tarnopol in April 1944. By now, the SS could no longer sustain itself on volunteers alone, and conscripts manned the two divisions. Nevertheless, they had been given full SS-style training, and they fought at least as well as the original divisions. By accepting conscripts, the SS solved at least part of its manpower problem. Even *Volksdeutsche* volunteers could not fill out the rest of the manpower needs of the SS, so Himmler began looking for volunteers from beyond the German 'race'.

The bulk of the early non-Germanic volunteers fighting for Hitler served with the *Wehrmacht*. Those from Eastern Europe were initially used in secondary roles, serving in police battalions or as prison camp guards, working as labourers or moving supplies on the long lines of communication. But gradually, as the pressure on German manpower increased, they were used more and more often as combat troops. Some fought extremely well, while others were worthless in battle. Some of the auxiliary units, particularly those employed by the *Einsatzgruppen* and as camp and ghetto guards, were among the worst perpetrators of war crimes.

Later, as manpower demands grew apace with Himmler's ambitions, SS racial standards were relaxed still further and units were formed from Muslims, Slavs, Indians and other 'Asiatics'. The first such division was raised in 1943. The 13th *Waffen-Gebirgs Division der SS Handschar* was a *Waffen*-SS division of Bosnian Muslim volunteers. Most had joined the division in order to protect their homes and families from *Ustase/Chetnik* and partisan attacks. The fascist Croat puppet government disapproved of the formation, since they felt that the SS recruitment in

Bosnia violated their sovereignty. A small-scale mutiny during training in France was instigated by partisans who had infiltrated the ranks.

Enter the Slavs
Following the defeats at Stalingrad and Kursk, Himmler began to reappraise the SS attitude towards the 'subhuman' Slavs of Eastern Europe. The 14th *Waffen-Grenadier Division der SS* was formed in Galicia in mid-1943. The region of Galicia, covering southeastern Poland and western Ukraine, was colonized by German settlers in the fourteenth century. It had became a province of Maria-Theresa's Austro-Hungarian Empire by the 1770s, with the provincial capital at Lemberg (L'vov). Although the region was considered Germanic by the Nazis, the main cultural influence there was in fact Ukrainian, as were most of the troops in the division.

The next major units came from the Baltic. In June 1940, the Soviet Union annexed the republics of Estonia, Latvia and Lithuania. Stalin claimed the take-over had been at the instigation of the three countries themselves, but it was in effect a military conquest. The communists moved large forces into the area, and immediately enacted repressive measures against opposition and liberation groups. As a result, the Balts welcomed the 1941 German invaders as liberators, and when the SS formed a Latvian unit there was no problem with recruitment. Early in 1943, the *Lettische SS-Freiwilligen Legion* was formed from several SS-linked Latvian internal security units, known as *Schutzmannschaft* battalions

The largest number of foreign volunteers in German service came from the Soviet Union, although it was not until late in the war that SS racial standards were relaxed to permit Russian SS units to be formed. Almost from the beginning of the campaign in Russia, huge numbers of individual Soviet Army prisoners and deserters offered their services to the Germans. Known as *Hilfswillige* – literally 'willing helpers' but more often known as 'auxiliary volunteers' and generally nicknamed '*Hiwis*' – these men served in non-combat and support units in such roles as drivers, cooks, labourers and medical orderlies. Initially serving in their Soviet uniforms, many were later issued with basic German uniforms.

Left: An instructor holds a Soviet DT light machine gun. The first volunteers to rally to the Germans after the *Barbarossa* invasion were local defence units that had risen against the Soviets. Armed with Soviet weapons at first, many of these *Selbstschutz* formations were incorporated into police and later into SS formations.

centuries, and gained a reputation as skilled horsemen. However, like other Russian minorities, they had been persecuted under the communist regime, and initially welcomed the Germans as liberators. They were recruited in small squadrons and served as local auxiliaries, but their numbers grew as the war progressed until an entire division was formed in 1943.

Allied recruits

Not all of the foreign volunteers in the SS served in the SS divisions. One of the most interesting units, given Himmler's racial obsessions, was the *Indische Freiwilligen Legion der Waffen-SS*. It was founded by the Indian nationalist leader Subhas Chandra Bose, whose dream it was to raise a German-sponsored Indian Legion that would be in the vanguard of the German advance in the Caucasus. The Indian Legion would then push on through Persia, Afghanistan and onward to liberate their homeland. The *Indische Freiwilligen Legion* (transferred to

More significant to the conduct of the war were the *Osttruppen*. These were former Soviet units incorporated into the German forces, the bulk of which were non-Russians from the Baltic, the Ukraine and other Soviet republics. These were armed units, but were mainly used for security behind the lines. However, they were never entirely trusted, and as a result thousands were sent to the West. As early as 1942 there were more than 72 *Ost-Bataillonen* doing occupation duty in Western Europe, which freed up large numbers of German troops for service in the East. The Cossack communities, or 'hosts', had provided light cavalry for the armies of the Tsars for

the *Waffen*-SS in 1944) never did fulfil the martial dreams of its founder, the polyglot force of Sikhs, Muslims and Hindus being relegated to garrison duty.

Less successful was Himmler's attempt to recruit SS members from British prisoners of war. John Amery, son of Conservative minister Leo Amery and a pre-war fascist, suggested the idea of a volunteer legion of British POWs soon after being captured in 1940. It was not until 1943 that the *Waffen*-SS expressed interest in the project, creating the 'Legion of St George'. Despite promises of cash bonuses, limited freedom and access to prostitutes, the SS recruitment efforts were essentially a failure, with less than 50 men volunteering. This was too few to have any military value, and the men were too unreliable to have any propaganda impact. The British Freecorps (BFC) spent most of its existence in training, but apart from half a dozen individuals who volunteered for the front in 1945, it never saw action. After the war, Amery was hanged for treason.

The foreign volunteer programme remained central to the development of the *Waffen*-SS, but the value of the non-German contribution to the war in the West and in Russia ranged from excellent to very poor. In the case of the Western European volunteers, the SS was able to tap a useful source of high-grade manpower, which the German armed forces would otherwise have found unavailable. After a generally poor start, the western volunteers fought well. The SS had one major criticism levelled against it, as far as the western volunteers were concerned, however, which was the inability of its training grounds and officer and NCO schools to readily accommodate non-German recruits, a systemic weakness that was corrected far too slowly.

With regard to the Eastern European volunteers, SS policy can only be seen as an almost unmitigated disaster. Given the wide range of nationalities involved, the German suggestion that the invasion of the Soviet Union was a 'European' undertaking to rid the world of communism was valuable propaganda. But the military evaluation is more critical. The small Finnish SS detachments were obviously good soldiers, but would have fought just as well in their own national uniforms. Some of the Baltic divisions also fought well, especially in the defence of their homelands, but the remaining units ranged from poor to appalling.

Right: Himmler's search for manpower took some exotic turns as the war progressed. He hoped – erroneously – that an Indian Legion would be the nucleus of a force that could be used to overthrow British rule in India.

The programme might have made sense even as late as 1942, if only for its propaganda potential. However, the fortunes of war changed considerably from 1943 onwards, after Soviet successes at Stalingrad and Kursk forced the Germans onto the defensive. In such difficult circumstances it made no sense to keep expanding the SS with units of questionable value – units which generally needed an experienced German cadre for training. Deploying combat-tested German officers and NCOs desperately needed elsewhere was not a good idea at a time when manpower and material shortages began to bite.

WESTERN EUROPE

The SS had high expectations that European volunteers would provide a real boost to German fighting power. In particular it was hoped that troops of northern European origin, considered racially Germanic, would be able to fit into the *Wehrmacht's* fighting plans with little trouble. In the event, the early volunteers performed badly. Too few came forward to join, and those that did were unhappy with German discipline. However, as the war progressed, several Western European formations became effective combat units. Some of the toughest of the defenders of Berlin in 1945 were members of these divisions.

Above: An SdKfz 232 heavy armoured car of the 11th *SS-Panzergrenadier Division Nordland,* bearing the division's *Sonnenrad,* or 'Sunwheel', variant of the Swastika on the front (next to the headlamp).
Left: SS men on parade in Brussels at the end of July 1944. Even at this late stage in the war, with the Nazis on the defensive everywhere, fresh volunteers were sought to fill the ranks of Himmler's ever-expanding SS.

NETHERLANDS

DATE OF OCCUPATION: MAY 1940
NUMBER OF VOLUNTEERS: 50,000
MAIN SS UNITS INCLUDING VOLUNTEERS: 23rd SS-Freiwilligen Panzergrenadier Division *Nederland* (niederlandische Nr. 1); 34th SS-Freiwilligen Grenadier Division *Landstorm Nederland*

Although the Netherlands is related linguistically and culturally to its much larger neighbour, Germany, a strong sense of independence has meant that Holland has never been overwhelmed by Germanic power. During the 1930s the *Nationaal Socialistische Beweging* (NSB, or National Socialist Movement), led by Anton Mussert, tried to emulate the success of the Nazi Party in Germany, but the people of the Netherlands never rallied to its support in any great numbers.

On 10 May 1940, Germany invaded, and Holland was swiftly overrun and occupied. Mussert and the NSB saw this as their chance to seize control of the nation, but their lack of popular or political support meant that they had little value to, and hence little influence with, their masters. One way of trying to increase what little influence they had was by fighting for the Germans. After the fall of the Low Countries in June, the SS began to recruit new members from Holland and Flanders, the Dutch-speaking part of Belgium. Seen as suitably 'Aryan' by the Nazis, the Dutch volunteers were funnelled into the SS *Westland* Regiment, a counterpart to the *Nordland* Regiment which was recruiting in Norway and Denmark. Mussert initially dreamed that the Dutch volunteers would fight in their own uniforms under their own colours, but the Germans would have none of it. The Dutch volunteers were inducted into the *Waffen*-SS. The Nazis made it clear that the Netherlands would eventually be integrated into Greater Germany, and to

The Netherlands provided more recruits for the Waffen-SS than any other European country. Most had been influenced by Anton Mussert's home-grown national socialist party, the NSB.

that end Himmler insisted on the formation of a Dutch *Allgemeine*-SS. This organization was intended to help to Nazify the Dutch people and make them ready for the final integration.

Although Mussert had urged closer ties with the Nazis, he was primarily a Dutch nationalist, and did not want to see his country absorbed into the Reich. However, opposition to German plans would have meant the marginalization of the NSB. Mussert chose to collaborate, and on 11 September 1940, shortly after a meeting with Hitler, he established the *Nederlandsche*-SS. Although almost identical with the German *Allgemeine*-SS, the Dutch version was officially a part of the NSB. In September 1940, Hitler approved Himmler's request to form a fifth SS division. Centered on the *Germania* Regiment, which had been withdrawn from the SS-VT Division (which later became *Das Reich*), it was intended that the bulk of its strength would come from the Nordic volunteers of the *Westland* and *Nordland* Regiments. The division, then named *SS-Germania*, would be equipped as an Army motorized division. Late in 1940, the division was renamed *SS-Division Wiking*, to avoid confusion with the *Germania* Regiment.

The German occupation forces established recruiting centres in all the major cities of Holland. Many Dutchmen volunteered to join, and in May 1941, a contingent of 631 Dutch recruits with a cadre of German personnel were incorporated into the *Wiking* Division. Many of the volunteers knew exactly what they were doing when they signed up.

However, quite a few were tricked: hundreds thought that they were signing on for political, police or sports education in Germany. They only found out the truth when they arrived at the SS barracks. However, *Wiking* was multi-national more in theory

Above: *SS-Standarte Westland*, **made up from suitably 'Germanic' volunteers from the Low Countries, was formed in July 1940 even before the war in the West had ended. These Dutch members wear the 'Wolfshook' insignia above their 'Deathshead' cap badge.**

than in practice. In June 1941, as the division formed up to cross the Soviet border, it numbered only 1564 foreign volunteers in a total strength of 19,377 men. The remainder consisted of German SS men, with a scattering of *Volksdeutsche*. However, those 1500 volunteers provided grist to the German propaganda mill as the *Wiking* Division amassed a combat record

second to none. The coming war with Russia saw the SS needing more volunteers to enable it to expand further, and in April 1941 Hitler gave Himmler permission to recruit up to 2500 Flemings and Dutch nationals for a new volunteer regiment, *SS-Nordwest*. By 25 May, some 920 Dutchmen had arrived in Hamburg-Langenhorn, and they were joined by a further 560 Dutch, Flemish and Danish volunteers over the next three months.

SS planners foresaw separate battalions of Flemish and Dutch volunteers, but too few volunteers meant that the SS had to scrap the scheme. It was decided to form a purely Dutch formation on the lines of the *Nordwest* Regiment, but without the 'Greater Dutch' ethos which permeated that Flemish/Dutch formation.

A contingent of 2000 volunteers entrained for the SS basic training camp at Debica in Poland, and by the end of August 1941, two battalions of volunteers were formed into the Dutch Legion. The volunteers wore SS uniforms with a sleeve shield in the Dutch national colours of red, white and blue. Command was given to the former chief of staff of the Dutch Army, 69-year-old Lieutenant-General H.A. Seyffardt. Although the Dutch provided one of the

Below: Dutch SS volunteers arrived in the East in the winter of 1941. They made their combat debut on the Volkhov front around Lake Ilmen, being thrown into battle against the Soviet winter offensive.

largest of all the volunteer legions, most of the officers and NCO cadre were German. In September, the legion was moved to East Prussia for further training. Later that month, it absorbed the Dutch contingent of the *Nordwest* Regiment, and was declared operational as the *Freiwilligen Legion Niederlande*.

The Dutch Legion blooded

Like many of the foreign legions, the Dutch Legion had very little of the order and discipline inculcated into the German units of the *Waffen*-SS. Partly this was due to the curiously mixed nature of the Dutch recruits, who included in their number volunteers ranging from political idealists and true believers to thrill-seekers and criminals. *Waffen*-SS training personnel had little regard for their Dutch charges, and relations were bad from the beginning.

Sent to the Volkhov front early in 1942, the legion arrived at Lake Ilmen at the height of the Soviet winter offensive, and suffered 80 per cent casualties in its first major combat in March of that year. After refitting, in June 1942 it was attached to the German 2nd SS (Motorized) Infantry Brigade. In spring of 1943, the legion was withdrawn to Grafenwohr, Germany, and disbanded.

By 1943, the experiment with the European 'Germanic' legions had pretty much failed, since such small units were simply not effective in the titanic conflict which had evolved in Russia. Mussert then suggested that a Dutch SS division be formed, but finding 20,000 men in the time scale envisaged proved to be impossible. However, a brigade-sized formation was possible, and the *SS-Freiwilligen Panzergrenadier Brigade Nederland* was formed in

Above: New recruits for the *Waffen*-SS take the oath of loyalty to Adolf Hitler. After the loss of so many men on the Eastern Front, the organization was forced to scour Europe for suitable replacements.

October 1943 as part of the further expansion of the *Waffen*-SS. Some 2500 veteran legionnaires joined with an additional 3000 volunteers from the *Nordland* Regiment. This brigade was composed of two regiments: the *General Seyffardt* (named after the first legion commander, who had been assassinated by the Dutch resistance earlier that year) and the *De Ruyter* Regiment (named after the seventeenth-century Dutch admiral Michael de Ruyter). Renamed 4th *SS-Freiwilligen Panzergrenadier Brigade Nederland*, it saw action in Yugoslavia. In December 1944 the brigade was expanded to become the 23rd

SS-Freiwilligen Panzergrenadier Division Nederland (niederlandische Nr. 1), though it was never brought up to full divisional strength.

One further Dutch unit should be mentioned. On 1 January 1942 the SS raised the *SS-Wachbataillon Nordwest*. Although nominally part of the *Waffen*-SS, the *Wachbataillon* had much lower physical entry standards and accepted recruits up to the age of 40. It also included a company of Ukrainian volunteers transferred from the Eastern Front.

The reason for the lower standards was simple: *Wachbataillon Nordwest* was responsible for guarding German concentration camps in the Netherlands. The new *Wachbataillon* consisted of six companies:

Below: Flemish volunteers in the SS prepare to fire an MG34 machine gun during training. Belgian members of the *Waffen*-SS reflected the divided nature of the country, coming as they did from both Dutch-speaking Flanders and French-speaking Wallonia.

two companies served at the police detention camp at Amersfoort; one was based at St Michielsgestel, which was a camp for intellectuals and hostages from prominent families; two more were responsible for the concentration camp at Vught; the sixth company was based at Haaren. One further company was intended to take up guard duty at Westerbork concentration camp, but this unit was transferred to the garrison at Scheveningen, where it became an anti-tank company.

Criminals and conmen

The irregular nature of its duties and the poor quality of its recruits meant that *Wachbataillon Nordwest* was 'an irregular lawless mess' in the words of Dutch World War II historian Lou de Jong. The *Wachbataillon* was also an attractive option for those who wished to avoid German forced labour, which was starting to make increasing demands of the male population of the Netherlands. Poor-quality recruits

who were less than honest meant that it was not long before the military police began to receive regular complaints about the unit. *Nordwest* men were accused of large numbers of thefts, burglaries and episodes of looting. The unit commander was held responsible for the incidents, but he claimed that it was not his fault. He claimed that since his men had not been provided with enough alcohol or with decent food, they had simply gone crazy.

A senior SS investigating judge was to recall after the war that 'the battalion had a very high crime rate, without even considering purely military crimes such as desertion, absence without leave, abandoning sentry duties, and disobedience. The men of the Wachbataillon committed every single crime that is known in common criminal law: crimes like theft, looting, fraud, and blackmail.'

Landstorm Nederland

In November 1944 the *SS-Wachbataillon Nordwest* was transferred to the Ardennes front, where it was combined with two *Landstorm* battalions to form the *SS-Freiwilligen Grenadier Brigade Landstorm Nederland*. The *Landstorm* had been formed (originally as the *Landwacht Nederland*) on 12 March 1943 as a territorial defensive unit. The name was changed to *Landstorm Nederland* in October 1943. The unit consisted of Dutch volunteers and was stationed in Den Bosch, Vught, Roermond and Hoogeveen.

Some took part in the Arnhem campaign. Many of the volunteers joined simply because the *Landstorm* was a source of employment, shelter and food (the latter in short supply in Holland in 1944). Also, by joining the force workers escaped the *Arbeitseinsatz* – the all-embracing German forced labour programme. In February 1945, the *Brigade Landstorm Nederland* was expanded, in name only, to become a division. The 34th *SS-Freiwilligen Grenadier Division Landstorm Nederland*, like most of the late-war *Waffen*-SS divisions, was smaller than brigades had been less than a year before.

BELGIUM

DATE OF OCCUPATION: JUNE 1940
NUMBER OF VOLUNTEERS: 40,000
MAIN SS UNITS INCLUDING VOLUNTEERS: 27th SS-Freiwilligen Grenadier Division *Langemarck* (flämische Nr. 1); 28th SS-Freiwilligen Grenadier Division *Wallonien*

Adjectives like 'plucky' and 'courageous' are often used to describe Belgium in World War II, but there was a darker side to the nation's experience between 1940 and 1944. Although the government had set itself up in exile in London, most of the civil service remained, along with the king, and continued to run the country under the Germans. However, pre-war rivalries between the Dutch-speaking Flemings and French-speaking Walloons added a great deal to the tension.

How much the government and local police helped the Germans identify Jews for deportation is difficult to say, but certainly some right-wing organizations collaborated actively with the Nazis. It is known that in Antwerp, the German Army and SS battalions staffed with Flemish volunteers relied on local police units to help catch Jews earmarked for deportation. Those same organizations provided much of the volunteer manpower who fought alongside the German Army on the Eastern Front.

On 27 June 1941 the *Führer* approved the establishment of national legions from the occupied nations which would take part in the struggle against communism. Belgium would provide two legions. One was to be a Flemish unit, which being considered Aryan would be attached to the *Waffen*-SS. The other, to be manned by Walloons, was not considered to be suitably Nordic, and as such would come under the aegis of the German Army. The right-wing parties in the Flemish region of Belgium,

Above: Belgian SS men on parade. Belgian volunteers fought hard for Germany, most notably in the struggle to hold back the Red Army in the fierce battles on the Narva River, where both Flemish and Walloon elements were under the command of III *Germanisches Korps*.

from which the Germans expected to recruit racially acceptable volunteers, were far from united. Some wanted an independent state, some a union with Holland, while the more extreme parties were believers in the pan-Germanic ideal of a Nordic super-state. Differences between these parties meant that Flemish volunteers were not forthcoming in any great numbers when in 1940 the SS sought to form the *Westland* Regiment of the *Wiking* Division.

Nordwest Volunteers

In an attempt to tap into Flemish manpower, the *Nordwest* volunteer unit was created. Manned by both

Dutchmen and Flemings, the regiment used the *Vlaamsch Nationaal Verbond* led by Staf De Clercq as the nucleus of Flemish participation. De Clercq encouraged party members to volunteer, and three companies were formed in April 1941. However, not all German commanders were keen on the 'Greater Dutch' sentiments which were common in *SS-Nordwest*, and a more broadly based Flemish volunteer unit was established in September 1941. The *Legion Flandern* benefited from anti-communist feeling engendered by the invasion of Russia, and over 1000 men (including a cadre of 150 German professionals) reported for training at Radom in Poland. The legion was the foundation of the Flemish SS units which were to fight on the Eastern Front and which will be covered in more detail later in this volume.

The formation of Flemish volunteer units caused considerable concern in the French-speaking part of Belgium. To counter any influence the separatist

Flemings might have gained with their German masters, Belgian unionist forces announced that a *Corps Franc Wallonie* would be recruited for service in the great crusade against the Russians. This would draw its strength from the fascist Rexist Party, led by the charismatic Léon Degrelle. Although they had made some political gains in the 1930s, the largely Catholic Rexists had fallen into disarray mainly due to internal rivalries. The German campaign in Russia allowed Degrelle to use anti-communist sentiments to force the party in a new direction. Up to that point, the occupying authorities had seen little value in the Rexists, who in spite of their pro-German stance had minimal support among the Belgian people.

However, control of the new volunteer units was seized by Fernand Rouleau, Léon Degrelle's deputy and head of the Rexist militia, the *Formations de Combat*. Because the Walloons were considered to be non-Aryan, the volunteers were taken into the German Army rather than the SS, where they were designated the *(Wallonische) Infanterie Bataillon 373*. On 8 August 1941, 869 Walloon volunteers embarked at Brussels for the long rail trip to a training camp at Meseritz, near the Polish border. Volunteer number 237 was Léon Degrelle, serving as a private soldier but acting as political leader. He had been forced to volunteer to prevent Rouleau from seizing control of the legion, and had announced his intention at a Rexist meeting in Liège on 20 July.

The name *Corps Franc Wallonie* was intended to echo the name of a volunteer *Freikorps* which had operated in the Baltic after the end of World War I, but it was quickly changed to the *Légion Belge Wallonie*. It was hoped that this title would foster a unionist spirit in the Belgian troops operating in the East, but the Flemish separatists would have no part of it. Eventually the name was changed to the more accurate *Légion Wallonie*. The legion included three members of the Belgian nobility and a handful of White Russians who had fought the Bolsheviks in the Russian Civil War. A small cadre of professional officers was joined by a number of reserve officers,

Initially considered to be non-Germanic, French-speaking volunteers from France and Wallonia were recruited by the German Army in 1941. They were incorporated into the Waffen-SS late in 1943.

most of whom were veterans of World War I. It was agreed that the legion was to be employed as a light infantry unit, with no front-line duties. In fact, the only combat it was intended to see would be mopping-up operations well back behind the lines. Degrelle was more ambitious, however, and sought a more active role for his Walloons, secretly fearing that the fighting would all be over before he and his men could take part. However, he found matters difficult to arrange from his position as a private soldier. Repeated requests to be made an officer were refused on the grounds that he lacked military experience.

Training was completed on 15 October, and the next day the 373rd Infantry Battalion of the German Army set off by train for the Ukraine, where it would join Army Group South. The battalion commander was Captain Georges Jacobs, a former officer of Belgian colonial troops. The legion was really too small to have any independent existence, and the Germans deployed it on security duties on lines of communication around Dnepropetrovsk. For the next six months, the *Légion Wallonie* was attached to various units in the First Panzer Army and the Seventeenth Army. The Germans did not regard it with any respect and morale plummeted. Relations went from bad to worse in December, when the Germans took most of the Walloons' heavy weapons for redistribution to 'real combat units'.

A report by the operations section of the Seventeenth Army noted that: 'We are having some difficulties with the Walloon Battalion. Members of the battalion complain about unfair treatment by our command to OKW, while IV Corps reports that the behaviour and non-cooperation of the Belgian troops borders on treason. The only use we can see is to transfer them to the rear areas of LII Corps.' At the beginning of 1942 the Germans tried to correct matters by appointing a new commander and a new German liaison officer. But before any reorganization could take effect the Walloons found themselves directly in the path of a Soviet counter-attack through the Donetz basin.

Opposite: Léon Degrelle, leader of Belgium's fascist Rexist Party, joined the Walloon Legion as a common soldier. In three years of combat in the East he rose to command the 28th *SS-Freiwilligen Grenadier Division Wallonien*.

Above: The Walloons fought alongside the *Wiking* Division in the Cherkassy pocket. Surrounded by overwhelming Red Army forces, the beleaguered SS men led a breakout in February 1944, losing half their number in the process.

Combat experience

The legion was ordered to eject Soviet troops from the village of Gromovayabalka. Having done so, on 28 February the Walloons, stiffened by an SS company attached from the *Germania* Regiment of the *Wiking* Division, fought off a counter-attack by two Soviet infantry regiments supported by tanks. After fierce house-to-house fighting, the legion was relieved by German forces on 2 March, by which time only two officers and some 250 men were still in action. Léon Degrelle, slightly wounded, won promotion to sergeant for bravery on the field of battle. In spite of their losses, proof that they could fight meant that morale in the legion improved. Sent to the rear to recuperate, the Walloons awaited reinforcements from Belgium. However, these were

hard to find. The legion had little popular appeal in Belgium, and replacements had to come from Rexist Party members alone. Men were drafted from the political leadership of the party and from its youth corps. These recruits reported to Meseritz for training in April 1942, and by May the legion was nominally up to strength.

On 21 May 1942, the Walloon Legion was assigned to the 97th Light Infantry Division. Lucien Lippert, a professional artilleryman, assumed command, and combat-tested NCOs, including Léon Degrelle, became junior officers. On arrival at the front, the Walloons were initially restricted to the reserve, where they carried out security duties until true unit cohesion could develop. The battalion was moved to the front lines in June, holding a supporting position on the Donetz River during the German summer offensive. The Walloons stayed at the rear, securing lines of communication as German panzer units smashed through the Don Basin and into the Caucasus.

Their first major action, a mopping-up operation in the village of Cheryakov, took place on 21–22 August. It was something of a milk run, assigned to the Walloons for propaganda purposes. The legion cleared Cheryakov by the end of the 22nd, capturing 35 Russians and an anti-tank gun. Walloon casualties were light, with only one man killed and 10 or so wounded. Minor though the fighting was, the action report was passed up through division, corps and onwards up to OKW.

The Walloon Legion was commended, and much was made of Lieutenant Léon Degrelle's leadership and bravery. Eventually it emerged as a press release which was widely distributed by the German propaganda organs.

However, the true combat value of the Walloons is a matter for conjecture. Within a week of the battle at Cheryakov the legion was withdrawn from the front after mounting casualties. Restricted to flank security duties, the Walloon Legion was briefly

attached to the elite *SS-Division Wiking*. Degrelle was deeply affected by the leadership qualities of *Gruppenführer* Felix Steiner, and the Rexist leader started trying to build SS-style ideological zeal into his men after orders came for their withdrawal for rest and refitting. In September Degrelle was sent to Berlin to help organize the formation of a second battalion, made up from Rexist volunteers among the Belgian POWs held by the Germans since 1940. Most of the rest of the legion returned to Belgium, apart from one company which remained with *Wiking* through the withdrawal from the Caucasus after the disaster at Stalingrad.

The legion began to reassemble at Meseritz in March 1943. Its strength had grown rapidly, with surviving veterans being joined by released POWs and men recruited from Belgian civilians working in Germany. As many as 2000 men were now serving under German colours, but their future was no longer with the Army. Degrelle, using his new-found celebrity, was negotiating with Himmler and SS personnel chief Berger to transfer the legion to the *Waffen*-SS, where it would form the nucleus of an SS *Sturmbrigade*, eventually growing to become the 28th *SS-Freiwilligen Grenadier Division Wallonien*.

FRANCE

DATE OF OCCUPATION: JUNE 1940
NUMBER OF VOLUNTEERS: 20,000
MAIN SS UNITS INCLUDING VOLUNTEERS: 8th Französische SS-Freiwilligen Sturmbrigade; 33rd Waffen-Grenadier Division der SS *Charlemagne*

The defeat of France in 1940 and the one-sided armistice which followed fostered a pessimistic and cynical spirit in the French people. The octogenarian Philippe Pétain, Marshal of France and lionized as the 'Victor of Verdun', was called upon by President Lebrun to form a government on 17 June 1940. The 84-year-old marshal consented, signing an armistice with Germany on 22 June. Under the terms

of this agreement, the only one Hitler ever signed with a defeated enemy, only part of France was to be occupied. The rest would be free of the enemy's presence – but in both occupied and unoccupied zones the authority of the French Government would apply … theoretically. Vichy, in the unoccupied zone, became the seat of the new government after it had established itself in the city.

Right-wing parties in both zones of France would become fertile recruiting grounds for the Nazis. The outbreak of war with Russia had a similar effect on anti-communists in France as it had elsewhere in Europe. The war in the East brought the prospect of the destruction of communism; at the same time

active combat over a huge area might reduce German pressure upon France. The war strengthened the positions of the collaborationist parties, since it fostered the idea that a German victory was far more acceptable than the 'Bolshevization' of Europe. However, Vichy France was never allowed an official role in the war in the East, unlike Germany's allies and satellites such as Italy, Finland, Hungary, Slovakia, Romania and Bulgaria. That is not to say that the French did not play a part in the German war effort. In fact, more Frenchmen worked directly for the Germans than did any other Western European nationality.

Not all were volunteers, however. Over 140,000 men from Alsace and Lorraine were conscripted into the German armed forces after their territories were annexed by Hitler. The Nazis believed that Alsace and Lorraine were rightly part of Germany, so their citizens were considered to be Aryan, unlike the rest of

Above: Right-wing recruits for the *Légion des Volontaires Français* depart to become part of the German Army. In common with other legion units, French volunteers who continued to fight were transferred to the SS in 1943.

the French population. At least another 150,000 men were conscripted into the *Organisation Todt* to help build the massive defences of the Atlantic Wall, and a further 25,000 worked for the *Kriegsmarine* in the Breton and Biscay ports. Many thousands of former POWs were forced to work in factories in Germany, where they were joined by members of the *Service du Travail Obligatoire* (STO), who were labourers conscripted on the Germans' behalf by the Vichy government.

But not all of those who served in German uniform were unwilling conscripts: about 45,000 Frenchmen volunteered to serve in the branches of Germany's armed forces and in various paramilitary arms. As in other countries, the early volunteers chose to fight for political or idealistic reasons, primarily to fight against communism. More than 6000 served with the *Légion des Volontaires Français* (LVF), while a company of some 212 men, *La Phalange Africaine*, fought with the 754th Panzergrenadier Regiment against the British in North Africa.

The Paris *Fronde*

The idea of a French legion to fight at the side of the Germans came neither from Vichy nor the Germans. Rather, it was the creation of the group of Paris collaborationist parties known collectively as the Paris *Fronde*. The main collaborationist political parties included *le Rassemblement National Populaire* (RNP),

Below: Not part of the German forces, but extremely active alongside the *Gestapo* in Metropolitan France, the collaborationist *Milice*, or 'Militia', hunted down Jews and resistance fighters for the Nazis in Vichy France.

founded in February 1941 by Marcel Déat, a former socialist who admired the order and discipline of European fascists; *le Francisme*, an overtly fascist pre-war movement led by Marcel Bucard that received financial support from Mussolini in the 1930s and which enjoyed a new lease of life in occupied France; the *Mouvement Social Revolutionnaire* (MSR), led by Eugene Deloncle; and the *Parti Populaire Français* (PPF), established by Jacques Doriot with the backing of numerous financiers and industrialists. Doriot was formerly a leading member of the French Communist Party, who had been expelled in 1934 after disagreeing with the party leadership.

An admirer of the achievements of Mussolini's Fascists, he formed the PPF soon afterwards, and through the remainder of the pre-war years used *Le Cri du Peuple*, the party newspaper, to advocate collaboration with Germany. Support for these Parisian collaborationist parties in France was limited. Historian Yves Durand estimates that less than one

Right: French volunteers in the German Army featured strongly in German propaganda photos, but they were not highly regarded by the *Wehrmacht*. However, those that stayed in German service after 1943 were much more highly motivated, and French SS units fought to the death in the defence of Berlin in 1945.

per cent of the French population ever became members. Even so, they were the driving force behind the formation of the French volunteer legion to fight against the Soviets on the Eastern Front.

Hitler (who despised the French) reluctantly approved the recruitment of a volunteer anti-communist legion in July 1941, though he denied the collaborationist request to form a full division. Public meetings, propaganda campaigns, and the formation of symbolic committees of party leaders and intellectual notables all took place through July and August, amid a feverish anti-Bolshevik atmosphere. The usual *Wehrmacht* health and racial regulations were applied to the recruits raised by this campaign, but the more stringent racial and physical strictures of the SS did not apply. Even so, there is some evidence that the Germans rejected many otherwise passable recruits to ensure that the French volunteer unit remained small.

Volunteers

Records indicate that some 3600 legionnaires enlisted and were accepted by the German Army through February 1942, and a further 3000 through May 1943. Those accepted were mainly members of the right-wing parties which had supported the formation of the LVF; others were veterans of the *Légion Etrangère* (Foreign Legion), including some of White Russian, Georgian and Armenian origin, as well as Arab and black colonials and veterans of the Spanish Civil War – both those who had fought under the 'Jeanne d'Arc' banner for the Nationalists and disenchanted ex-Republican International Brigade members.

The *Légion des Volontaires Français contre le Bolchevisme* mounted their first parade on 27 August 1941 at the Borguis-Desbordes Barracks at Versailles. Unfortunately, an assassination attempt carried out by an infiltrator, from within the ranks of the legion, wounded ministers Pierre Laval and Marcel Déat.

Nationalsocialistische Kraftfahrkorps

Less well known than the LVF, but offering far more to the German war effort, was the 4th NSKK Regiment, part of the NSKK *Motorgruppe Luftwaffe*. The NSKK, or *Nationalsocialistische Kraftfahrkorps*, was the original Nazi motorized organization, and during the war it provided logistic support to the *Wehrmacht*. The 4th NSKK Regiment was a logistics unit of some 2500 French drivers and engineers attached to the *Luftwaffe*. Formed in July 1942, it saw service on the Eastern Front and in the Balkans before returning to France in 1944 to provide motor support to the V-1 missile sites being built in the Pas de Calais. Later the unit was to see service in Italy, Denmark and Hungary before finally surrendering in Austria.

This unlucky beginning proved to be an omen for the legion's experiences in Russia. Sent by train from Paris, the LVF began training at Deba, Poland, through September and October. The unit swore fidelity to Adolf Hitler, but only as overall commander of the forces fighting against communism. By the end of October the legion was ready to be shipped to Smolensk as the *Französisches Vestartktes Infanterie Regiment 638* (French Reinforced Infantry Regiment 638) of the German Army. The regiment was reinforced only in name: the LVF would never be deployed as more than a light regiment with only two battalions.

The members of the LVF were a strange mixture of idealists, adventurers, political opportunists and professional soldiers. Doriot himself had joined as an NCO. Command had been given to Colonel Roger Henri Labonne, formerly military attaché to Turkey. Labonne, a veteran of World War I and a former commander of a French colonial regiment, was, at 65, far too old for the rigours of a winter campaign in Russia. Without adequate leadership and with incomplete training, the Germans held out little hope that the LVF would be of any use in combat. That judgement appeared to be vindicated when they were attached to the German 7th Infantry Division near Smolensk.

First blood
The LVF's baptism of fire came at the end of November during the advance towards Kubinka. The unit performed poorly, but did much better a few days later in a series of small engagements during which they inflicted casualties on the Russians but suffered heavy losses themselves. The weakened unit had no answer to the heavy Soviet counter-offensive which began on the night of 5 December. The battalion was so heavily mauled that it had to be withdrawn after only a few hours of combat. In just two weeks the LVF had lost 150 men in battle – with another 300 killed or severely frost-bitten by the icy Russian weather.

In January 1942 the LVF was withdrawn to Smolensk for reorganization. Incompetent officers were removed and Russian *Hilfswilliger* (volunteer auxiliaries) were attached. Even though it was assigned to relatively easy security duties, the LVF's performance remained poor, and after the Germans decided that the regiment had zero combat capability, it was pulled back to Poland. The two existing battalions were merged, while a new battalion was raised after reinforcements arrived from France. However, the French were considered the worst of all the foreign volunteer units serving with the *Wehrmacht*, and the LVF was destined to remain on anti-partisan duties for the remainder of its existence. Surviving members of the legion were transferred to the SS in 1943. Under SS tutelage the French proved vastly more capable, and by the time they returned to front-line duty in 1944 they were able to earn the respect which had never been offered to the LVF.

Smaller units worked for organizations as diverse as the 21st Panzer Division, which had a French logistics company, and the *Kriegsmarine*, which employed some 4000 sailors, shore workers and policemen.

There were also 180 Frenchmen in the 8th Company of the 3rd Regiment of the Brandenburg Division. They were used in anti-partisan actions, but their primary mission was to infiltrate resistance groups in the South of France.

Police units

There were approximately 10,000 French members of German police units, who controlled as many as 30,000 civilian auxiliaries and informers. Many of the more active collaborators worked directly for the German intelligence services, including the *Abwehr*, the *Sicherheitspolizei* (Security Police), the *Gestapo* and the SD. The Germans also operated alongside the right-wing Vichy militia, the *Milice*.

Up to 20,000 Frenchmen served in the *Waffen*-SS, the majority after Himmler's men had taken control of most foreign volunteer units in the last two years of the war. However, individuals served in a number of

SS units before that, including at least two members of the *Leibstandarte*, Hitler's SS bodyguard. By late 1943, the remaining French volunteers were inducted into the *Waffen*-SS *Französische SS-Freiwilligen Grenadier Regiment*, which was later upgraded to the 8th *Französische SS-Freiwilligen Sturmbrigade*. At the end of the war the *Sturmbrigade* saw considerable action, suffering 90 per cent losses in Galicia and in the Carpathians.

The survivors were absorbed into the 33rd *Waffen-Grenadier Division der SS Charlemagne*. This too suffered heavy losses, initially in Pomerania and then in the final battle for Berlin.

Below: In spite of the impression of comradeship between *Luftwaffe*, SS, *Wehrmacht* and the LVF suggested by this photo, the early French volunteers in Russia did not perform well, and the German high command withdrew them from combat.

ITALY

DATE OF OCCUPATION: 1943
NUMBER OF VOLUNTEERS: 15,000
MAIN SS UNITS INCLUDING VOLUNTEERS: Waffen-Grenadier Brigade der SS (italienische Nr. 1); 29th Waffen-Grenadier Division der SS (italienische Nr. 1)

Italian troops had fought alongside the *Wehrmacht* in North Africa, the Balkans and on the Eastern Front since 1940. After the disaster at Stalingrad, where the Italian Eighth Army was among German satellite forces, Mussolini formed a new government in February 1943, *Il Duce* personally taking over from Ciano as foreign minister. Two months later, after Axis troops capitulated in North Africa and the Germans were being driven back through the Ukraine, Mussolini visited Hitler at Salzburg and urged him to make a settlement with the USSR.

By July 1943, Italy had lost all of its colonies in Africa, and most of its army, and was being invaded. Mussolini was deposed by a revolt within his own Fascist Grand Council, and Victor Emmanuel III, the king of Italy, who had been reduced to a figurehead by Mussolini, appointed Marshal Badoglio to be the new prime minister. Arrested as he was leaving the palace, *Il Duce* was bustled off in an ambulance to a succession of heavily guarded hiding places, ending at an isolated hotel located in the highest mountains of the Apennines, the Gran Sasso d'Italia. Badoglio told the Germans that he was going to continue to fight, while at the same time beginning to negotiate in secret with the Allies. Even though Hitler knew nothing of the Italian plans, he suspected that they might be about to surrender, and so pushed forward his own plans to occupy the country.

On 3 September, as the British Eighth Army crossed the Straits of Messina and landed in Calabria, the Italians signed an armistice to become effective on 8 September. Some Italian troops were able to surrender to the Allies, but although their leaders slipped away to comfortable exile, the surrender was

a disaster for most ordinary soldiers. Across Italy, the Balkans and Greece, German garrisons turned on their erstwhile allies. Italian units were disarmed and hauled off to Germany for use as slave labour. In some cases, as depicted in Louis de Bernières' novel *Captain Corelli's Mandolin*, they were massacred.

Meanwhile, Adolf Hitler had plans for *Il Duce*. The *Führer* maintained his high regard for Mussolini long after it became clear that Italy could offer little to the Axis cause, and ordered his friend's rescue. A specially picked team of SS and *Luftwaffe* parachutists commanded by Otto Skorzeny made a daring descent on the Gran Sasso on 12 September. After his dramatic rescue, Mussolini was bundled into a tiny Fieseler Storch reconnaissance plane and flown off the mountain. Once in German-occupied territory he was flown immediately to see Hitler.

To occupy his friend, the *Führer* set up a fascist puppet state in northern Italy, which would continue to fight alongside the Germans. He installed the 'cardboard Caesar' under heavy SS protection as head of the 'Salo Republic'. Its seat was the village of Gargnano on the western shore of Lake Garda. As an early item of business Mussolini established a tribunal to avenge the *coup d'état* of 1943. His son-in-law Count Ciano was among those ordered executed on 11 January 1944. Although a titular head of state, Mussolini remained a somewhat pathetic figure for the remainder of his life. He continued to inspect military formations, and went about the business of running his republic with the aid of Marshal Graziani. But he was a broken man.

New formations

However, Italian troops still had a considerable part to play in the Axis war effort. Nominally

Opposite: Long after Mussolini had been overthrown, Hitler continued to treat him as a head of state. However, surviving Italian Fascist troops were incorporated into the *Wehrmacht* structure under German control.

Prima Brigata d'Assalto della Legione SS Italiana – the Italian SS

Some Italian Fascists came under direct German control. After the 1943 armistice, the SS began recruiting for an Italian Volunteer Legion among the 800,000 disarmed and 250,000 interned members of the former Italian Army. In November 1943 the *Italienische Freiwilligen Legion* was established after more than 15,000 Italians volunteered to join the *Waffen*-SS. Many of the would-be recruits had been members of the 'Fortunato' *Bersaglieri* unit which had fought hard as part of the Italian Army on the Eastern Front. In January 1944 the unit was renamed 1st *Sturmbrigade Italienische Freiwilligen Legion*. It was also known as the 1st *Italienische Freiwilligen Sturmbrigade Milizia Armata*, while to the Italians themselves it was the *Prima Brigata d'Assalto della Legione SS Italiana*.

Of the SS but not actually part of it, the Italian Legion wore a similar uniform but with green rather than black trimmings. However, following a hard-fighting contribution to the struggle around Anzio in the spring of 1944, the Italian SS men received a sign of approval from Heinrich Himmler, who in June wrote: 'For valour and devotion to Duty, the Sturmbrigade Italienische Freiwilligen Legion shall hereafter adopt the black collar and rank insignia of the German SS, and shall be eligible for all duties and rights thereto.'

In September 1944 the unit was renamed the *Waffen-Grenadier Brigade der SS (italienische Nr. 1)*. Early in March 1945 the unit was nominally expanded to divisional size, becoming the 29th *Waffen-Grenadier Division der SS (italienische Nr. 1)*. It was a 'second-hand' divisional number, which was applied to the Italians after the 29th *Waffen-Grenadier Division der SS (russische Nr. 1)* was disbanded. It was intended to be brought up to strength by fresh drafts of German and Italian troops but the war ended before the formation could approach its planned strength.

Those divisional members – in fact, almost any Italian in SS uniform – who surrendered to the partisans at the end of the war were almost invariably executed.

independent, the former Fascists were actually under *Wehrmacht* control, and were treated as part of the German armed forces. In July 1943, the German high command ordered the formation of a new Italian Army.

By March 1944 four new divisions had been formed, the 1st Infantry Division *Bersaglieri*, the 2nd Infantry Division *Camice Nere*, the 3rd Infantry Division *Granatieri* and the 4th Infantry Division *Alpini*. These were joined by Fascist militiamen from the *Milizia Voluntaria Sicurezza Nationale* (MVSN), which by the end of 1944 had put seven Blackshirt battalions into the field.

Opposite: A poster that circulated through northern Italy at the end of 1943 calls for volunteers to join the Italian SS, claiming that the only way for Italy to escape defeat is through a real fighting force – the *Waffen*-SS.

Nominally under the command of Marshal Graziani, the four infantry divisions were actually under the control of *Oberbefehlshaber* Southwest. The 1st Division was attached to the German Fourteenth Army, and went into action around Parma at the end of 1944. Early in 1945 it was in action in the Parma/Fidenza/Salsomaggiore area alongside the 162nd (Turkistani) Infantry Division. The 2nd Division, by now renamed the *Littorio* Division, went into action near Parma in November before being transferred to the Alps in December 1944. The 3rd Division was renamed the *San Marco* Division. Most of its personnel had been transferred from the Italian Navy. In July 1944 it was sent to the Ligurian coast, where it was used for coastal security and anti-partisan duties. One infantry regiment was later detached and sent to the Alps where it became part of a *Kampfgruppe* of the German Army's 4th

Left: The German Army and the SS oversee the disarmament of Italian forces in German occupied Italy after Badoglio's government switches to the Allies in the autumn of 1943. Many Fascist units remained loyal to Mussolini, however, and were soon rearmed and under German control.

to Garfagnana where it was thrown into battle against the US 92nd Infantry Division. The 8th *Kampfgruppe* stayed in Liguria until March 1945, when it was also sent to join the 5th German *Gebirgsjäger* Division in the Alps.

The four infantry divisions were only the tip of the iceberg, however. Early in 1944, a *Wehrmacht* report recorded 18 Italian coastal fortress battalions under German orders or forming. Most of these had German officers or NCOs. These units were supplemented by six coastal artillery battalions. In addition, six German-led pioneer battalions were in service, and another 38 wholly Italian labour battalions were being formed. These were supported by up to 15 signals, transportation and supply units, and by 42 medical units distributed around northern Italy. More Italian units served in the Balkans under *Oberbefehlshaber* Southeast. Seven Blackshirt battalions were used on anti-partisan and security operations in the Balkans.

The *San Marco* Legion was formed in Croatia in 1943 under the aegis of the V SS Mountain Corps. Other Italian volunteer legions were formed by committed Fascists on the Greek islands of Crete, Samos and Rhodes, after Germany disarmed the Italian garrisons there in 1943.

Gebirgsjäger Division. The 4th Infantry Division was formed at Munsingen between March and May 1944. It too was sent to Liguria, where it suffered heavily in the anti-partisan war.

In September two battalions were disbanded after losing most of their men in the guerrilla campaign, and a mountain regiment and an artillery regiment were transferred to the 5th German *Gebirgsjäger* Division in the Alps. Much of the rest of the division was reorganized by the Germans into two *Kampfgruppen*. The 7th *Kampfgruppe* was transferred

DENMARK

DATE OF OCCUPATION: APRIL 1940
NUMBER OF VOLUNTEERS: 10,000
MAIN SS UNITS INCLUDING VOLUNTEERS: 5th SS-Panzer Division *Wiking*, 11th SS-Panzergrenadier Division *Nordland*

In April 1940, the Germans invaded Denmark and conquered the country after encountering virtually no resistance. Denmark was looked on as a Nordic nation with suitably Aryan bloodlines, so on 23 April 1940 – just two weeks after the invasion – Himmler ordered a recruiting drive to be mounted in both Denmark and Norway (rather presumptuously, as parts of the country at that time had yet to fall to the Germans). As has already been seen, the German Army's stranglehold on recruiting in Germany proper blocked Himmler's ambitions to increase the size of the SS, so northern European volunteers were seen as a way around the problem.

Suitable volunteers from Denmark and Norway between the ages of 17 to 23 were encouraged to sign on for a minimum enlistment of two years. By doing so, they would receive German citizenship, with all the rights and privileges of *Reichsdeutsche*, while also retaining their Danish citizenship.

However, only some 200 Danes initially volunteered, not the flood into German service that Himmler had hoped for, but ethnic Germans from Schleswig, on the German border, provided enough manpower, along with the Norwegians, to establish the *SS-Standarte* (Regiment) *Nordland*, which was to become one of the constituent parts of the *SS-Division Wiking*. Over 1000 German Danes also joined the SS individually, most serving with the *Totenkopf* Division and with the 1st SS Brigade, which gained a sinister reputation on the Eastern Front. As in other European nations, Operation

Above: Three brothers from Copenhagen take a break from physical training as they prepare to join the *Nordland* Regiment. Soon to become part of the SS Division *Wiking*, *Nordland* numbered several hundred Danes and Norwegians in its strength.

Barbarossa in June 1941 provided the impetus for a much more successful recruiting drive. By now, both the SS and the German Army were recruiting foreign volunteers into a new kind of formation: the legion. These units tried to avoid association with out-and-out Nazis, an anti-communist theme being used to attract members of right-wing political groups who were not necessarily national socialists.

Most of the SS legions – those from Norway, the Netherlands and Flanders – were the result of a combined effort between the SS *Hauptamt* in Berlin and local national socialist or Nazi-inspired parties. The local parties expected to gain political capital with the Germans, which could be used in the post-war 'New Order' which at that time, in 1941, they expected to be in place within a year. In Denmark, the DNSAP (Danish National Socialist Workers Party) were willing helpers of the SS. Party leader Frits Clausen used the *Barbarossa* offensive to call upon Danes to fight for Europe against the *Weltfeind* or 'World Enemy'. In a speech on 23 June 1941, he urged Danes to join *SS-Standarte Nordland*. Other party officials, however, recommended that a new, all-Danish unit be established. It was to be a national legion, similar to one which had fought for the Finns against the Russians during the Winter War.

The Danes raised the only volunteer legion that had the full backing of the government of their country; legions elsewhere in Europe were usually inspired by local right-wing nationalist political parties.

Clausen and the DNSAP needed a military man to help set up the new unit, so they called on Artillery Lieutenant-Colonel Christian Peder Kryssing for assistance. Kryssing, a well-known Danish nationalist, did more than the Nazis expected. He sought and obtained the acceptance of the Danish Government for the legion's formation, and got permission for Danish citizens, including regular military officers, to take service under a foreign power. The War Ministry passed a regulation to that effect on 8 July, some weeks after the initial recruiting drive started. The new formation would differ from other volunteer legions in two main ways. Firstly, since it was officially sanctioned by the Danish Government, serving members of the Danish armed forces were free to volunteer. Indeed, regular soldiers were to retain their Danish ranks, and service with the *Waffen*-SS would count equally with their Danish military service when it came to pension rights. Secondly, the new unit was to be officially sponsored by the Danish Government, unlike other legions whose primary support was from local fascist parties like Vidkun Quisling's *Nasjional Samling* in Norway, or Léon Degrelle's Rexist Party in Belgium.

Danish Legion formed

The formation of the legion was officially announced by the Danish Government on 28 June 1941. Press releases and public notices giving details of the new legion were posted on 8 July 1941, and recruiting offices were opened all over Denmark. The legion was to be open to men between 17 and 35, preferably serving soldiers or reservists who had completed their national service in the previous 10 years. The new legion received the official German designation of *SS-Freiwilligen Verband Danemark*, or SS Volunteer Group *Denmark*. However, it was more generally known as the *Freikorps Danmark*.

An initial draft of 430 volunteers was placed under the command of Colonel Kryssing, and the new battalion was sent to Hamburg for training in July. Most volunteers still wore Danish uniforms, but once in Germany they were issued with *Waffen*-SS equipment. The members of the *Freikorps* wore standard *Waffen*-SS uniforms, with a '*FREIKORPS DANMARK*' cuff-band worn on their lower left tunic sleeve and a shield above this title bearing a white cross on a red background, the Danish national flag. SS flashes were worn on all ranks' collar tabs. More volunteers, together with a cadre of 200 Danes who had been transferred from *SS-Standarte Nordwest*, arrived in August to form a second battalion. By the end of 1941, the legion had grown to more than 1200 men.

Some 40 per cent of the *Freikorps* members had some previous military experience, but only 30 or so had recent combat experience, having served as

volunteers with the Finns during the Winter War. Like German SS members, they had to prove their 'Aryan' racial heritage before being accepted. A criminal record meant automatic rejection, as did being in debt. The motives of Danes for volunteering were varied. A few joined because they were professional soldiers and the Germans had the only war going at that time. Others were simply adventurers, who were looking for excitement in the thrill of combat. However, over three-quarters of the 6000 Danes who were to serve in the SS over the next four years did so because they were anti-communist, pro-German, or were connected with the Danish Nazi Party. As with the pre-war SS in Germany, the

Above: SS troops escorted by a Panzer 38(t) move across the Russian steppe in the winter of 1941–42. While many of the volunteer legions served in the north, the Danes of the *Wiking* Division were in action in the Ukraine.

bulk of the other ranks were working class, many being unskilled labourers or farmhands.

As the Danish volunteers gathered in Hamburg to begin their training, SS headquarters issued orders to organize them as an independent motorized battalion of three infantry companies and one weapons company. Sent to Russia in the spring of 1942, *Freikorps Danmark* was thrown into the battle of the Demyansk pocket, suffering heavy casualties.

NORWAY

DATE OF OCCUPATION: MAY 1940
NUMBER OF VOLUNTEERS: 6000
MAIN SS UNITS INCLUDING VOLUNTEERS: 5th SS-Panzer Division
Wiking, **Den Norske Legion**

The driving force behind Norwegian collaboration with the Germans during World War II was Vidkun Quisling, whose name has since become synonymous with treasonous collaboration with an enemy. Born in Fyresdal, Telemarken, Quisling joined the Norwegian Army in 1905 and was commissioned as an artillery officer. He spent long periods abroad as a military attaché and diplomat, before becoming war minister in 1931. Quisling resigned in 1933 to form the Nazi-style *Nasjional Samling* (NS, or National Unity Party). On 9 April 1940 Quisling gave orders that no NS member should participate in armed resistance against the German invasion, but most ignored this order, among them his own 'minister of defence', Major Ragnvald Hvoslef. Following the German conquest Quisling declared himself prime minister, but his regime had no popular support, which made him useless to the Nazis, and he was replaced by a German administration.

Below: Vidkun Quisling (centre right) accompanies
***Reichsführer*-SS Heinrich Himmler (left) during a visit to**
Germany. Quisling had formed a pro-German government
in Norway, but the Nazis did not trust him and later
replaced Quisling with a German administration.

Even before the conquest of Norway had been completed, the SS began seeking recruits for the *SS-Standarte Nordland*. Initial numbers volunteering were not great, most of the few hundred signing on being members of the NS. Late in 1940, *Nordland* combined with the Dutch/Flemish *SS-Standarte Westland* and the German *SS-Standarte Germania* as the nucleus of what was to become the *SS-Division Wiking*. Quisling was rather disappointed, since he had had visions of a 50,000-strong Norwegian Army serving alongside the Germans.

Formation of the DNL

As in other occupied countries, the invasion of Russia brought an increase in the numbers volunteering. On 29 June 1941 *Reichskommissar* Josef Terboven announced the creation of a Norwegian legion to fight against the USSR. Known as *Den Norske Legion* (DNL), or *Legion Norwegen* in German, the first battalion carried the name *Viken*, after a historical Norwegian Army unit from Oslo. The Germans carefully orchestrated a call for volunteers based upon the 'flood of requests ... to take part in the opposition against Bolshevism'. The *Legion Norwegen* formed at

the end of July under the command of Major Joergen Bakke. Several thousand men volunteered, many being members of the *Hird*, the NS militia. About 1000 of these volunteers were accepted.

Quisling supported the effort, and assumed that the unit would fight in Finland. He also believed it would form the core of a new Norwegian Army after the expected German victory. Many Germans favoured this idea, since it would inspire the spirit of Scandinavian solidarity which had arisen during Finland's Winter War with the Russians. However, OKW squashed the notion, saying that there was not enough transport available. The DNL would have to go wherever they said it would go. Training began near Kiel. The men wore standard SS uniforms, but with the Norwegian lion replacing the 'Sig-runes' on collar patches, and the uniform carried an arm patch of the Norwegian flag. *Hird* members also wore a silver-on-black version of the St Olaf's Cross on their left sleeve.

Early in 1942, the legion was moved up to the front, but not to Finland. It was sent to take part in the siege of Leningrad. By this time, Adolf Hitler had declared war on the USA, which did not sit well with many of the Norwegian volunteers, many of whom

SS-Skijäger Kompanie Norge

Another unit was the *SS-Skijäger Kompanie Norge*, formed in 1943 by the Danish-born Gust Jonassen, who was the leader of the sports section of the NSUF, the NS equivalent of the Hitler Youth. A keen skier, he had fostered the sport within his organization. The 6th *SS-Gebirgsdivision Nord*, fighting in central Finland, had a requirement for a specialised ski company, and Jonassen proposed the formation of a Norwegian ski unit which would be used for reconnaissance and long-range patrolling. Jonassen was sent on an officer training course at the SS officer school at Bad Tolz, and began to recruit 120 skiers from the NSUF. Late in the spring of 1943, the unit joined *Nord*. Jonassen was killed soon afterwards when he stepped on a mine, but the ski company had proved its worth, and it was decided to

expand it to battalion size. Unlike other volunteer units, the ski battalion had no difficulty in finding volunteers. Most of the Norwegians in the *Waffen*-SS had originally expected to serve in Finland, and a number transferred from the *Norge* Battalion and from the *Luftwaffe*. In October 1943 it was joined by a company raised from the Norwegian police. The ski battalion distinguished itself in the fighting against the Soviets over the next two years. On 4 September 1944 Finland signed an armistice with the Russians, and the Norwegians retreated through Finnish Lappland towards Norway, often providing the rearguard for the 20th *Gebirgsarmee*. They reached Narvik by mid-December, where the battalion was reformed into a security police unit, in which form it fought until the end of the war.

had relatives in America. On 10 March 1942, the Norwegians entered the German siege lines around Leningrad, part of a mixed Army/SS battle group. It was intended to free up first-line divisions for a counter-attack on the Volkhov pocket. The legion at this time numbered about 1150 officers and men. Even though static operations called for less military skill than other forms of combat, SS headquarters was not satisfied with the Norwegian Legion.

Towards the end of 1942 the SS removed Major Bakke and his second-in-command, Major Andersen, from the legion. The Germans described Bakke as obstinate, and his fiercely nationalist attitude also made co-operation difficult. SS Personnel Chief Berger instructed his staff not to employ him in any other role, saying that 'his unpleasant personality and

independent character combined with his age make him of little value in a political or training role'. Bakke was replaced by Major Arthur Quist, a much more diplomatic former Norwegian Army officer.

The Norwegian Legion remained at Leningrad until the spring of 1943. Whether it was because of the appalling conditions under which they served, or the poor quality of their leaders, most Norwegian legionnaires declined to extend their enlistments. The *Reichsführer*-SS ordered the replacement of the Norwegian Legion with the Latvian Legion at the front in February 1943. Because of the legion's bad experiences, the Germans encountered problems in the recruitment of Norwegian volunteers for the rest of the war. In 1943, the *Nordland* Regiment was removed from the *Wiking* Division to form the nucleus of a new multi-national SS division. The 11th *SS-Freiwilligen Panzergrenadier Division Nordland* incorporated its Norwegian troops into a new unit, the *SS-Panzergrenadier Regiment 23 Norge*. Organized in September 1943, the regiment included those

Below: Norwegian volunteers are sworn in as members of the SS. *Waffen*-SS recruitment in Norway lagged significantly after an initial outburst of enthusiasm, and only with the war against the USSR did it pick up again.

Above: The *Den Norske Legion* was thrown into action on the Leningrad front. Poor leadership and heavy casualties meant that only one in five surviving volunteers re-enlisted after their two-year terms expired at the beginning of 1943.

members of the DNL who had been persuaded to re-enlist, together with surviving Norwegian members of the *Nordland* Regiment – about 700 men in all.

The regiment was brought up to strength with Hungarian *Volksdeutsche*. *Norge* was to be the second infantry regiment of the *Nordland* Division, but the Danish Government was slow to approve the formation of *SS-Panzergrenadier Regiment Danmark*, so *Norge* took its place. Again the number of Norwegian volunteers was to disappoint Quisling, who had expected more than 3000 recruits. However, those that served gained a much better reputation than their predecessors. Training was far more intense, and its core of combat veterans made *Norge* a far tougher unit than the Norwegian Legion.

Serving the cause

Not all of the Norwegian volunteers fighting for the Nazis were members of the *Waffen*-SS. The German administrators of occupied Norway did not trust the ambitious Quisling, and so they formed a branch of the *Allgemeine*-SS as a counter to Quisling's NS. Established in May 1941, it was renamed the *Germanske SS Norge* (GSSN) in 1942. The GSSN attracted those more fanatical and often younger members of the NS who saw Norway as a part of a Greater Germanic Europe. Most of them considered the NS to be an old-fashioned organization that placed the good of Norway ahead of the good of Europe as a whole. Officially Quisling approved of the GSSN, though in private he must have been less than delighted.

The only purely Norwegian unit in the SS, and one of the most controversial, was the *SS Vaktbataljon Norge*, also known as the *SS-Wachbataillon Norwegen*. Like the Dutch *Wachbataillon*, it was set up to provide

Left: By the second winter of the war in the Soviet Union, German troops had been issued with more effective winter uniforms. This Norwegian NCO of the *Wiking* Division is seen at Cherkassy, wearing *Waffen*-SS winter camouflage parka.

force, manned exclusively by older men beyond the normal age of military service. Also, after the occupation of Norway in 1940, a number of members of the Norwegian Air Force volunteered to join the *Luftwaffe*, but most were diverted into the *Waffen*-SS. About 100 men joined the *Luftwaffe* individually, with two serving as pilots (including Alf Lie, who had previously served in the *Wiking* Division), and about 500 Norwegians served as individuals or small groups in the German *Kriegsmarine*. Some are known to have served on the old pre-dreadnought battleship *Schlesien* in the Baltic. Some of the younger recruits were provided by the *Unghirdmarinen*, the naval youth movement of the NS. Many thousands more Norwegians served in the *Germansk Landtjeneste*, a labour organization, and in the *Organisation Todt*. They were employed all over Europe on the building of roads, forts and other military structures: large numbers of Norwegians worked on the building of the *Westwall* fortifications in Germany and the Atlantic Wall in France, the Low Countries and Norway. Some also served with the *Reichsarbeitsdienst*, or Reich Labour Service.

Over 350 Norwegian women served as front-line nurses. *Frontsisters* over the age of 21 saw duty in Finland, the Baltic States, the USSR, Poland, Croatia, Italy and France. Those under 21 generally served in Norway and Germany. At least 13 *Frontsisters* were killed in action, and one, Anne Moxness, was the only non-German woman to be awarded the Iron Cross.

guards for concentration camps. Manned by older NS members, its training grounds were at Holmestrand. Some 360 men served as *Konzentrationslager* guards, mostly in northern Norway.

Norwegians also served in the other German armed forces. As many as 1500 Norwegians served in the German Army, most having joined independently as individuals. Some had been students in Germany at the outbreak of war in 1939. The German Army actually established an all-Norwegian unit in 1942, though it was far from being a true combat unit. The *Wachdienst Norwegen* was a kind of home defence

FINLAND

DATE OF OCCUPATION: ALLY – NOT OCCUPIED
NUMBER OF VOLUNTEERS: 3000
MAIN SS UNITS INCLUDING VOLUNTEERS: SS-Regiment
Nordland; Finnisches Freiwilligen-Bataillon der Waffen-SS

The Winter War of 1939–40 began when Finland, formerly a Russian province, refused Soviet demands for border adjustments. Germany gave moral support to the Finns in their disagreement with Stalin, but would not give material support, Adolf Hitler being as yet unready to take on the USSR.

The Soviets attacked Finland on 30 November 1939, launching half a million men with massive armoured and air support against a Finnish Army less than half as strong. But the Finns proved to be ferocious fighters, and the Soviets made no headway until they committed a further 500,000 men under Marshal Timoshenko. Battered by sheer numbers in a war of attrition they could not win, the Finns signed an armistice in March 1940, after losing some 25,000 men. Soviet losses were at least 10 times higher, many soldiers freezing to death in the Arctic cold which on occasion fell to –50°C (–58°F). Finnish stubbornness and the sheer fighting qualities of Finnish soldiers meant that Moscow did not treat the Finns as they

Below: Although vastly outnumbered, the Finns had fought overwhelming Soviet strength almost to a standstill in the Winter War, 1939–40. Most Finns served in their own units, but a few joined the *Waffen*-SS.

had the other Baltic States, leaving Finland a measure of independence that was denied to Latvia, Lithuania and Estonia. The Soviet failure to dominate Finland convinced many Germans – Adolf Hitler and the high command included – that the Soviet Union was a paper giant, and would be easy to conquer.

The Finns had impressed the Germans with their fighting qualities, and Himmler sought to include Finnish volunteers when he accelerated the expansion of the *Waffen-*SS in 1941. Moreover, the Finnish government was in secret negotiations with the Germans to join in the forthcoming invasion of Russia, Operation *Barbarossa*. But there was a clause in the agreement that while Finnish troops would take part in the Axis campaign, no Finns would be used against Britain or Greece, who were the only nations actively fighting against Germany at that time.

Wiking volunteers

Several months before this, however, the first 1000 Finnish volunteers for the *Waffen-*SS had been assembled. In an effort to avoid complications with the Russians, the volunteers were described as industrial workers taking up employment in Germany, but it would be several months before the Finns actually arrived in Germany: they were delayed by details, including the refusal of many individual soldiers to take the SS oath of unquestioning obedience to Adolf Hitler.

Eventually these problems were settled, and between May and June 1941, somewhere in the region of 125 officers, 110 NCOs and 850 other ranks joined the SS on the Eastern Front, ready for Operation *Barbarossa*. Because most of the volunteers had recent military training and combat experience, they were assigned directly to the *Wiking* Division, which by now was a fully motorized formation.

Two more groups of volunteers, this time made up from those who lacked a military background, were sent to Vienna for full *Waffen-*SS training. These would form the nucleus of a new battalion, the *SS-*

Opposite: The Finns were respected by the Germans, since they were masters of Arctic warfare. However, the Finnish Government insisted that Finns enlisting in German units must only be used to fight against the Soviets.

Freiwilligen Bataillon Nordost. As more recruits arrived for training, the unit was renamed the *Finnisches Freiwilligen-Bataillon der Waffen-SS.* The Finns considered themselves an elite light infantry unit, and described themselves as *Jäger* (literally 'Hunters', the north European term for light infantry). In August 1941, the battalion transferred for advanced training to the *Truppenlager* Gross Born. Training was completed by the middle of October, and the unit was declared combat ready. It was eventually sent by rail to the Eastern Front early in December 1941.

Although the Finns were good soldiers, they had some problems integrating with their German counterparts. Admittedly, they looked like any other *Waffen-*SS unit, but they were very much their own men. Unlike other volunteer legions, the Finns would only accept their own officers and NCOs. They made that point clear by refusing to accept any orders given in German. The legendary Finnish stubbornness eventually prevailed over German parade-ground discipline, and the Finns got their way.

Disbandment

The Finnish volunteers came to the end of their two-year enlistments in March 1943, and the Finnish Government made it clear that it expected its men to be returned home. In May 1943 they were pulled from the front lines, and after rest and recuperation at Grafenwohr, were sent by rail to Tallinn, from where they were shipped back to Finland. There, on 2 June 1943 the men of the *Finnisches Freiwilligen Bataillon der Waffen-SS* were sent on a month's leave. The unit was officially disbanded on 11 July 1943, and its members were transferred back into the Finnish Army. The last official ceremony, commemorating those members of the battalion who had fallen in action, was held in Helsinki on 19 September 1943.

There was now no Finnish unit in the official *Waffen-*SS order of battle. However, a number of Finnish troops were still serving in the *SS-Standarte Nordland*, which in July 1943 was detached from the *Wiking* Division to become part of the 11th *SS-Freiwilligen Panzergrenadier Division Nordland*. These men were allowed to remain in German service, and the Finns were still in action with the division when hostilities ceased in May 1945.

LUXEMBOURG

DATE OF OCCUPATION: MAY 1940
NUMBER OF VOLUNTEERS: 2000
MAIN SS UNITS INCLUDING VOLUNTEERS: Not known –
Luxembourgers were classed as German and served in all
branches of the _Wehrmacht_

The Grand Duchy of Luxembourg, the tiny country southwest of Belgium, had retained its independence for centuries. However, its strategic position on the Belgian and German borders meant that it stood astride the _Wehrmacht_'s invasion route in the West, and it was overrun on 10 May 1940, the first day of the Western campaign.

Like Alsace and Lorraine, Luxembourg was looked on by the Nazis as an integral part of Greater Germany. There had been some attempts to establish a German-style national socialist party after Hitler's accession to power in 1933, but without success. It was not until July 1940, after the German occupation, that the _Volksdeutsche Bewegung_ (VDB) was formed under the leadership of 62-year-old Professor Damian Kratzenberg. The VDB's motto was _Heim ins Reich_, or 'Home to the Reich'. This was not strictly accurate: Luxembourg had been an independent member of the German Confederation between 1815 and 1867, but it had never officially been part of the German Reich.

After the campaign in the West ended, on 28 June 1940, Luxembourg was formally linked to _Gau_ Koblenz-Trier. _Gaue_ were the main Nazi territorial units, corresponding to the old _Reichstag_ electoral districts and civil defence regions. _Gaue_ were also set up after 1938 in Austria and Czechoslovakia, and by the outbreak of war there were 43 – the 43rd being the _Auslands_ organization for overseas Germans which was administered from Berlin by _Gauleiter_ Ernst Wilhelm Bohle. Territories like Luxembourg, which were annexed into the Reich proper rather than simply being occupied were attached to existing _Gaue_. In February of 1941 _Gau_ Koblenz-Trier was renamed _Gau_ Moselland.

A rigid policy of Germanization was forced on Luxembourg. German organizations were set up and rapidly made compulsory. From January 1941, manual and industrial workers had to join the _Deutsches Arbeits Front_ (DAF) or face dismissal. Compulsory service in the _Reichsarbeitsdienst_ (RAD) was introduced for school-leavers of both sexes. By 1942 a German report showed that 110 Luxembourgers were in the _Allegemeine_-SS, 1100 had joined the _Sturmabteilung_ (SA, or 'Brownshirts'), nearly 1500 were members of the NSKK and as many as 60,000 had joined the DAF.

More than 14,000 Luxembourgers fought for the Germans as part of the _Wehrmacht_ between 1940 and 1945, but since Luxembourg was regarded by the Germans as an integral part of the Reich, there was no 'Luxembourger Legion'. However, the _Wehrmacht_ mounted an intensive recruitment campaign in the tiny Duchy soon after the victory in the West was completed at the end of June 1940.

Volunteers and conscription

The spectacular German triumph over France made finding volunteers for the unit relatively easy, and the first German recruitment drive brought in as many as 2000 volunteers from a total population of only 290,000. In August 1942 Luxembourg was officially made a part of the German Reich, and all of its citizens were subject to conscription into the armed forces of the Reich. Soon afterwards, all of the classes of (that is to say, men born in the years) 1920 to 1926 were drafted. In the two years before liberation at the end of 1944, the Germans called up 12,035 men from Luxembourg.

Over 2750 Luxembourgers were killed or missing in action, 1500 were severely wounded or disabled, and 3516 deserted. Luxembourg volunteers and conscripts served in various units of the Army, _Luftwaffe_, _Kriegsmarine_ and _Waffen_-SS, but since they were classed by the _Wehrmacht_ as Germans they were not identified by their origin.

SPAIN

DATE OF OCCUPATION: NEUTRAL
NUMBER OF VOLUNTEERS: 1000
MAIN SS UNITS INCLUDING VOLUNTEERS: Spanische Freiwilligen Kompanie der SS 101; 3rd (Spanish) Company of the 1st Battalion, 28th SS-Freiwilligen Panzergrenadier Division *Wallonien*

Despite Adolf Hitler's best efforts, the wily Spanish dictator Francisco Franco refused to bring his nation into the war on Germany's side. 'Dealing with Franco is like pulling teeth,' the *Führer* is reported to have said, after one particularly difficult meeting. Hitler wanted Franco's help in eliminating the key British naval base at Gibraltar, but the Spaniard could not be persuaded.

That is not to say that Spain did not contribute to the Axis war effort. Franco knew that he owed Germany and Italy a debt for the aid which they had provided during the Spanish Civil War – and he had a score to settle with Stalin, who had supported the Republicans in the same conflict. It was after the German invasion of the USSR that he saw the chance to repay some of that debt, without actually becoming a belligerent. Within a day of the launch of Operation *Barbarossa*, the Spanish Government

Below: Many of the Spanish volunteers who served with the *Wehrmacht* on the Eastern Front were veterans of the Spanish Civil War. However, their free-and-easy ways infuriated the German instructors who had to train them.

Aged 45, he had been a successful corps commander in the Civil War, and was a former secretary general of the *Falange*. He oversaw the raising of four infantry regiments at Madrid, Seville, Valladolid, Valencia, Barcelona, Zaragoza, Corunna, Burgos and at Ceuta in Spanish Morocco. Divisional artillery and support services were formed from veteran Spanish Army units.

It took less than four weeks to assemble the new division, and it was sent to Grafenwohr training ground in Bavaria in the middle of July 1941. The division arrived at Grafenwohr on 17 July. There, the four regiments were reduced to three to match German Army practice. Soon afterwards, the Spanish volunteer contingent was included into the German Army order of battle as the 250th Infantry Division. Total strength in August 1941 was 641 officers, 2272 NCOs and 15,780 other ranks.

As with most of the foreign volunteer formations, the ferocious discipline of the instructors at Grafenwohr caused problems. The German NCOs in particular felt that the Spanish soldiers were slovenly and lacked respect for parade-ground routines. To the Spaniards, most of whom were veterans of one of the most bitterly fought civil wars of the century, what mattered was what was done on the battlefield, not the parade ground. Nevertheless, training proceeded quickly, and by the end of August the division was classified as combat-ready.

From the beginning, the German high command regarded the Spanish Volunteer Division more as a political and propaganda symbol than as a real contribution to the *Wehrmacht*. In the war diary of the Ninth Army for September 1941, it was said that '... the deployment of the division from Spain is less a military advantage than a political and propaganda

offered to raise a unit of volunteers to fight alongside the Germans in the East. The plan was to call for volunteers from the regular army and from members of the ruling fascist party in Spain, the *Falange*. Response was enthusiastic: only three years before, the Spanish fascists had been fighting a bitter civil war against an enemy backed by the international communist movement, and the thought of playing a part in bringing down the home of communism was exciting. The idea was to form a full infantry division of volunteers, some 18,000 men, which would become known as the *Azul*, or 'Blue', Division – a reference to the blue shirts worn by *Falange* members.

The Blue Division formed

So many potential fighters appeared at the recruiting stations set up in army barracks and at *Falange* offices that they could have manned several divisions, not just one. Many of the recruits were ex-Civil War combatants, and a number of flyers also volunteered which enabled an *Esquadra Azul* to be formed to serve with the *Luftwaffe*. Franco appointed General Agustin Munoz Grandes to command the volunteers.

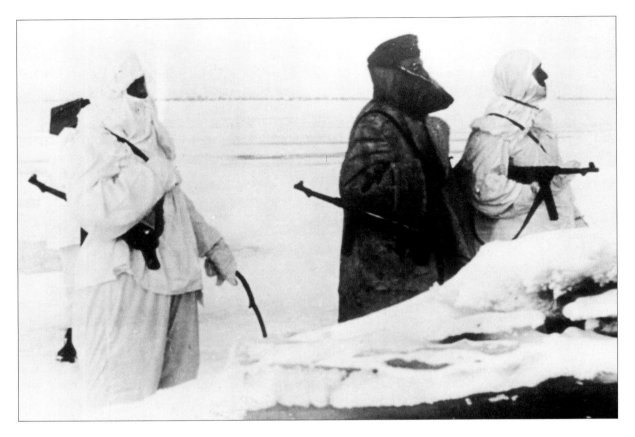

Above: Although Spanish troops were fighting in unfamiliar terrain, and under extremely unfamiliar weather conditions, the Blue Division performed about as well as a second-line German division on the Eastern Front.

effect. Therefore, despite any lack of ability, they should be welcome as comrades in the struggle.'

Delivered by train to Sulwalki in Poland, the *Division Azul* now began a gruelling 1000km (621 mile), 40-day march to Vitebsk in northern Russia. Setting out on 29 August, they had no mechanized transport, and their problems were compounded by having been issued with the worst of the *Wehrmacht*'s horses. Nevertheless, the exhausted division reached Vitebsk in October. There they were assigned to the XVIII Army Corps of Army Group North. The Spanish/German difficulties which had emerged during training continued during the long march. German liaison officers with the division reported that the Spaniards were 'stealing chickens on the march; associating with persons of Jewish race; threatening civilians; they lack march discipline; they do not care for their horses, nor their weapons, nor their equipment. Above all, junior officers and non-commissioned officers seem to be unable to enforce their orders to the troops.'

Over the next month the Spaniards saw considerable action along the Volkhov front, and were the recipients of several 'human wave' attacks by the Red Army. Far from the sun of Spain, the division also had to face the horrors of a Russian winter, made even worse by continual Soviet attacks. On Christmas Eve 1941, a company of Spanish grenadiers at Lubkovo was overrun. The position was retaken, but the Spaniards found the stripped and mutilated bodies of one platoon which had been cut off. Their comrades had been nailed to the frozen ground with their own bayonets. A revenge attack by two companies of the *Azul* ripped through a Soviet battalion, who were slaughtered to a man.

In spite of the Spaniards' capacity to fight with a ferocity which should have gone down well with their allies, German documents concerning the Spanish are filled with criticism of their attitudes and skills. While their sacrifices on the Volkhov front were recognized, the Germans did not like what they saw as excessive Spanish pride and a reluctance to accept German orders. In a note to Field Marshal von Leeb in November 1941, Chief of the General Staff Franz Halder commented that 'Spanish troops do not measure up to German norms of general discipline and care of horses, weapons, and equipment'.

> **'Russia is guilty of causing our civil war and our pain, and the destruction of Russia can only be for the well-being of Europe.'**
>
> *Spanish Foreign Minister Serrano, 1941*

Heavy losses

In June 1942, after several months of rebuilding, the Blue Division again suffered heavy losses during the final mopping-up of the Volkhov pocket. According to the *Kampfgruppe* commander, the Spaniards should not have suffered such losses in a simple mopping-up operation, and the reason that they had was down to Spanish ineptitude and inexperience.

The two German battalions taking part in the operation suffered around one-fifth of the losses sustained by the two Spanish battalions involved. The Spanish, by contrast, claimed that their losses were because they had failed to receive promised support from the Germans. Ultimately, the military value of the early volunteer formations of the Army and *Waffen*-SS must be measured at the time of their withdrawal in the summer of 1943. The large Spanish division had shown itself capable of performing as a second-line German infantry unit in limited offensive and static defensive missions. Thanks to its size, its employment of regular army officers and its replacement system, it performed reasonably well under a harsh climate and in a demanding military situation. The changing face of the war in 1943 saw Franco seeking to distance himself from the Axis cause, which was clearly on a downwards slide. In October, he changed Spain's status from non-belligerence to strict neutrality.

As a neutral, the Spanish could not be seen to provide any support to one of the warring factions, so Franco ordered the withdrawal and disbandment of the Blue Division. Several thousand hard-line anti-communists refused to leave, and they formed the last of Germany's foreign legions, the *Legion Espanola de Voluntarios*, more commonly known as the *Legion Azul*, or Blue Legion. This did not last long, since it was disbanded six months later on 15 March 1944.

New recruits

Even as the Blue Legion was returning home, however, hundreds of young Spaniards were crossing the Pyrenees clandestinely to join the *Waffen*-SS.

Einheit Ezquerra – the last Spanish survivors

Miguel Ezquerra, a veteran of the Blue Division and then a captain in the *Waffen*-SS, led another small Spanish unit, later to be called the *Einheit Ezquerra*, or 'Unit Ezquerra'. This had originally been formed as part of the Brandenburger, or special forces, organization, and had worked for the *Gestapo* in France, fighting the French resistance (which included many Spanish exiles in its numbers).

After taking part in the Battle of the Bulge, Ezquerra was instructed to gather up all the Spanish survivors he could to form a single unit. By mid-April, he had about 100 men left out of three companies which had been cobbled together in January. After being attached to 11th *SS-Freiwilligen Panzergrenadier Division Nordland*, the men of Unit Ezquerra were amongst the last troops fighting the Russians in the rubble of Berlin.

Some were adventurers, but many were young Falangists, idealists who wanted to play their part even now in the anti-communist crusade.

More volunteers were found among the tens of thousands of industrial workers and labourers Franco had sent to Germany. By 6 June 1944, the day the Allies launched Operation Overlord, over 400 Spaniards were in training at Stablack-Sud camp in East Prussia.

By the middle of July numbers of this 'ghost battalion' had risen to 550. After rapid training, they were formed into two companies, the *Spanische Freiwilligen Kompanie der SS* 101 and 102. Other small units of Spaniards, left as flotsam after the retreating tide of the war, were attached to German units in northern Italy and Yugoslavia.

Over a hundred Spanish volunteers joined Léon Degrelle's 28th *SS-Freiwilligen Panzergrenadier*

Opposite: A StuG III assault gun and a motorcycle combination of the *Wiking* Division move through Hungarian mud in the last months of the war. By this time, about a third of the neutral Swiss and Swedish volunteers who had joined the unit had died for the *Reich*.

Division Wallonien where they formed the 3rd (Spanish) Company of the 1st Battalion. Some Spanish platoons were attached to the 3rd Mountain Division and the 357th Infantry Division.

The 101st Company of Spanish Volunteers served against the Red Army in Romania until the Romanians switched sides on 27 August 1944. What was left of the 101st began a slow, painful retreat northwest, eventually joining up with the equally mangled remains of the 102nd Company at Holabrunn, north of Vienna, which had been fighting partisans in northern Italy and Yugoslavia.

SWEDEN

DATE OF OCCUPATION: NEUTRAL
NUMBER OF VOLUNTEERS: 300
MAIN SS UNITS INCLUDING VOLUNTEERS: 5th SS-Panzer Division *Wiking*; 11th SS-Freiwilligen Panzergrenadier Division *Nordland*

Unlike Spain, Sweden was strictly neutral during World War II, and did not allow the belligerent powers to recruit from amongst its population. However, the government did allow some 10,000 men to fight for Finland against the USSR during the Winter War, and when Germany launched Operation *Barbarossa*, the Swedes allowed Finland to recruit a further 1500 volunteers. A few individuals are known to have joined the *Wehrmacht* between 1939 and 1941. After the invasion of Russia, the *Waffen*-SS began a clandestine recruitment programme, working through the German Embassy in Stockholm and funnelling any such volunteers through Norway.

There are several estimates of the number of Swedes who fought for the Germans, ranging from 150 to 330. Swedes are known to have served with the 5th *SS-Panzer Division Wiking*, the 11th *SS-Freiwilligen Panzergrenadier Division Nordland*, and the 23rd *SS-Freiwilligen Panzergrenadier Division Nederland*. It is known that 11 Swedish SS men went through the SS Officer School at Bad Tolz. Several Swedes worked as SS war correspondents. One unit, the 3rd Company of *Nordland*'s Armoured Reconnaissance Battalion, had a large proportion of Swedes; so many that the 4th *Zug* (platoon) of the company was known unofficially as the *Swedenzug*.

The *Swedenzug*, along with the other Swedes in the *Nordland* Division, were among Hitler's last defenders in the Battle of Berlin. After seeing action in the Baltic and Courland late in 1944, it was withdrawn to the Oder front early in 1945. It was practically wiped out in an attempt to break out of Berlin on 2 May 1945.

SWITZERLAND

DATE OF OCCUPATION: NEUTRAL
NUMBER OF VOLUNTEERS: 300
MAIN SS UNITS INCLUDING VOLUNTEERS: 5th SS-Panzer Division *Wiking*; SS-Standarte *Kurt Eggers*

L
ike Sweden, Switzerland was strictly neutral during World War II. As a neutral, it could not allow a belligerent power to recruit among its citizens. To the Nazis, the German-speaking Swiss would have made natural recruits for both the *Waffen*-SS and for the *Wehrmacht*, but official Swiss disapproval meant that no real recruiting effort, open or clandestine, was made. Nevertheless, without official approval, a small number of Swiss citizens volunteered for service in the East, primarily in the ranks of the SS. Between 700 and 800 Swiss volunteers are thought to have become members of

the *Wehrmacht* during World War II. Of these, at least 300 are thought to have been killed in action.

No single national unit of Swiss volunteers was formed during World War II since all Swiss volunteers had joined the *Wehrmacht* individually. The vast majority of Swiss volunteers found themselves in the ranks of the *Waffen*-SS, most of these being assigned to the 5th *SS-Panzer Division Wiking*, although a number were assigned to the *SS-Standarte Kurt Eggers*.

This was the SS *Kriegsberichter*, or war reporters' unit. It was named after the former editor of the SS magazine *Das Schwarz Korps*, who had been killed in action near Kharkov while serving with *Wiking* in 1943. Many non-Germans were attached to the unit, usually being assigned to report on the activities of their own national formations.

EASTERN EUROPE

From the very beginning of the German invasion of the Soviet Union in June 1941, the *Wehrmacht* made extensive use of 'native' volunteer and conscript units in the front line and in rear-area security roles. Many were volunteers who had actually approached the Germans first, reflecting the internal opposition to Stalin's regime. Communist oppression had been fiercest in areas with long and proud national histories, and the German invasion gave them hope that they might eventually throw off the Soviet yoke.

Above: On a Silesian plain, a Latvian SS man prepares to fire a *Panzerfaust* 30 or *Faustpatrone* 2 recoiless anti-tank rocket in the last days of the war.
Opposite: Soviet Central Asian *Freiwillige* – 'volunteers' – served the *Wehrmacht* in large numbers. It was not until late in the war that the SS relaxed its racial standards and recruited from such nationalities.

SOVIET UNION

DATE OF OCCUPATION: JUNE 1941
NUMBER OF VOLUNTEERS: 60,000+
MAIN SS UNITS INCLUDING VOLUNTEERS: 29th Waffen-Grenadier Division der SS (russische Nr. 1); 30th Waffen-Grenadier Division der SS (russische Nr. 2); XV SS Kosaken-Kavallerie Korps

Although Adolf Hitler's primary racial hatred was directed at the Jews, he also despised Slavs. Slavs occupied the land into which the Greater German Reich must expand; Slavs had spawned world communism; Slavs were seen as *Untermenschen* ('Subhumans'). Given that such ideas filtered down from the very top of the *Führer* state, eventually they permeated every corner of Nazi society. It is all the more surprising, then, to discover that more Slavs fought on Germany's side than any other racial group, and that Soviet citizens made an essential contribution to the *Wehrmacht* war machine on the Eastern Front. From very early in the German occupation of Russia, which began in June 1941, the *Wehrmacht* made extensive use of local volunteers and conscripts. Originally employed to provide labour, they were also used later in combat roles. Mostly they provided rear-area security, but they were also sent out to hunt down partisans, and occasionally they found themselves fighting on the front line.

First volunteers

The first volunteers were employed by German front-line units on their own initiative. As the *Wehrmacht* pushed ever deeper into Soviet territory, it became clear that the sheer size of Russia meant that lines of logistics would be strained almost to the limit. Although the men of the *Wehrmacht* were greeted as liberators by many of the non-Russian populations of the USSR, any initial good feeling was quickly squandered. Germany intended to have European Russia for itself and its people. German administrators arrived soon after the armies, and proceeded to loot the Nazi Party's victims, and the SD, SS and the *Gestapo*

instituted a reign of terror. Welcome quickly turned to hatred, and partisan activity grew at an increasing rate. However, the manpower resources of the Reich, even at this early stage of the war in the East, were strained almost to breaking point.

Unable to divert enough of their front-line units to combat partisans in the rear, the Germans had to draw manpower from somewhere, and the 'Eastern peoples' seemed to provide the perfect answer. Anything which freed German soldiers from such mundane (but vital) tasks as protecting supply routes gave the Army a reinforcement of reliable, trained troops who could then be used in combat. Then someone remembered the prisoners in POW cages.

The original German estimate of the number of Soviet prisoners that would be taken during Operation *Barbarossa* was far too low. OKW had made plans to deal with prisoners by the tens of thousands. What they got after the great battles of encirclement of the summer of 1941 were prisoners by the hundreds of thousands, often taken in a single day. By the autumn of 1941, the number of Soviet soldiers in POW camps had reached the millions. Official German contempt for Slavs meant that they were kept in overcrowded barbed-wire pens, with little food and even less shelter. The arrival of the Russian winter would see many of these POWs dying of starvation or disease. The POWs represented a huge potential labour force, which could be used for slave labour back in Germany. However, by the time the German authorities realized that fact, millions had died from neglect. Among those who died were many from non-Russian ethnic minorities, who would have been all too willing to fight against Stalin's oppressive and murderous regime. The whole question of POW treatment was an huge waste of a usable resource for the Germans, as well as an immense tragedy and, for the wider world, a criminal act.

Hilfswillige

With the manpower shortage starting to bite, divisions, regiments and even battalions organized

Left: Germany's triumphant advance through Soviet territory in the summer of 1941 created a major problem for the *Wehrmacht*. Nobody on the General Staff had anticipated the sheer numbers of Soviet prisoners that would be taken.

(*Schutzmannschaft*, or self-defence units) were formed. These were intended primarily for border and rear-area security in their own Baltic states. In the event, they served all over the Eastern Front, eventually being converted into regular police battalions. They had an unsavoury reputation, since many such units were used by the SS and SD as 'hands-on' thugs when committing atrocities. By the spring of 1942, there were at least 200,000 Russians serving in the German rear areas. By the end of that year, the numbers of Russians in German uniform or taking German orders has been estimated variously as between 800,000 and one million.

The next step taken by the German commanders in the East – again behind Hitler's back, since the *Führer* would never have approved – was the organization of volunteer armed units, known as *Osttruppen*. Wearing German uniforms, they were recruited or conscripted to guard lines of communication, to fight partisans in the rear of the German armies, and sometimes even to reinforce and hold positions along the front line. Volunteers were plentiful, since the Germans were able to capitalize on the real hatreds generated among ethnic minorities by the brutality and oppression of Stalin's regime. Most *Osttruppen* units were of battalion size or smaller. By the summer of 1942, there were six *Ost-bataillonen* in Army Group Centre alone.

Osttruppen volunteer units

Cossacks, Turkomans, Kalmyks, Estonians, Latvians and many other groups which had been absorbed into the USSR or the preceding Russian Empire had

their own support units. They acquired the necessary manpower by taking in Soviet deserters, drafting in prisoners and calling for volunteers from among the local population. Known as *Hilfswillige* ('volunteer helpers'), commonly shortened to '*Hiwi*', the Russian auxiliaries were employed in non-combat posts such as drivers, porters, orderlies, storesmen and labourers. Obviously, given Nazi racial policies and the attitude of senior German authorities towards Slavs and Asiatics, those units that chose to employ *Hiwis* initially kept quiet about the fact. But by the autumn of 1941 the reality of combat on the Eastern Front forced a grudging change of attitude on the part of the high command. In October 1941, the first semi-official groups of Soviet prisoners were allowed to be used in road construction behind German lines, and during the winter the first Baltic *Schumas*

distinctive cultures, histories and national identities. Such individualism was not tolerated in the USSR, and most were victimized by communist rule. Serving with the Germans, they believed, offered a chance at getting revenge on the Russians. Also, they hoped that the defeat of the Soviet Union might give them the chance of gaining independence. The *Osttruppen* were organized roughly on the basis of ethnicity, the majority of a battalion's personnel being drawn from a single nationality. Command and cadre positions were usually filled by German officers and NCOs.

There were two main types of unit as defined by the German Army. These were generally known as *Ost-Bataillone* and *Turk-Bataillone*. *Ost-* units were drawn from European Russia, and their personnel were mostly a mix of Russian and Byelorussians, with a few Ukrainians thrown in for good measure. *Turk-*battalions generally referred to units formed from the 'Asiatic' Turkic peoples of the Caucasus and beyond, such as Turkomans and Kalmyks. Eastern battalions attached directly to a corps staff used the number of the corps plus 400 as their designated number, so a battalion belonging to the XXXIV Corps would be known as the 434th *Ost-Bataillone*. Battalions answering to army headquarters and operating in rear areas received a number in the 600 series. Battalions assigned directly to a division used the number of the division, combined with *Ost-Bataillon* (or other appropriate title) as their designation. All of these battalions were referred to as the *Osttruppen*, although by 1943 many had been given designations reflecting their main ethnic component – typically, units with a majority of Cossacks would be known as *Kosaken-Bataillone*.

The organization of the *Osttruppen* was co-ordinated by the *Fremde Heere Ost*, the Foreign Armies East section of the Intelligence Department of the Army General Staff. It was clear to much of the German Army that an anti-Soviet Russian army fighting on the German side could be a serious contribution to victory in the East. Many senior commanders were keen to establish such an army. In

The German invaders were greeted as liberators by many of the subject peoples of the USSR, but any good feelings were quickly negated by the brutal and short-sighted way in which the occupiers went about their business.

the autumn of 1941, Field Marshal Fedor von Bock sent the OKW a proposal to create a liberation army of around 200,000 men. He also suggested giving the area around Smolensk some form of independent local anti-communist government. But nobody told the *Führer*. The proposal was returned in November 1941 with the comment that 'such thoughts cannot be discussed with the *Führer*', and that 'politics are not the prerogatives of Army Group Commanders'. Field Marshal Keitel, who lacked the spine to present anything remotely controversial to the Nazi leadership, knew what Hitler's feelings about the Russians were, and he did not present such a radical idea to his leader.

Russian National Army of Liberation

One of the first Russian volunteer formations was the *Russkaya Osvoboditelnaya Narodnaya Armiya* (RONA, or the Russian National Army of Liberation). In the autumn of 1941, the mayor of Lokot, a town with about 6000 inhabitants just south of Bryansk, raised a small militia unit to defend the town against partisans. The mayor and most of his staff were later killed in a partisan attack, and the unit was taken over by Bronislav Vladislavovich Kaminski. Born to a Polish father and a German mother, Kaminski expanded the militia from its original strength of some 400 men. In June 1942, the unit took part in Operation *Vogelsang*, a major German anti-partisan operation in the Bryansk Forest.

His 'army' – which in fact never exceeded the strength of a division – at first fought against Soviet partisans, and later at the front. In the summer of 1944, after considerable losses, RONA was withdrawn to East Prussia, It was renamed *Volksheer-Brigade Kaminski* shortly before being taken over by the Waffen-SS in July 1944, as *Waffen-Sturm-Brigade RONA*, with Kaminski himself receiving the rank of *Waffen-Brigadeführer der SS*. The SS had plans to expand the brigade to a full division, the 29th *Waffen-Grenadier Division der SS (russische Nr. 1)*. The unit was used during the obliteration of the Warsaw Rising, committing numerous atrocities. Later, Kaminski was

Eastern legion shields

Because of the increasing numbers of foreign volunteers entering the service of the Third Reich from all over Europe, the Germans authorized and issued national insignias to be worn on *Wehrmacht* uniforms. Most foreign volunteers served in the German Army and the *Waffen*-SS, and the majority of such insignias were issued by these organizations.

During the early stages of Operation *Barbarossa*, which commenced in June 1941, many of these foreign contingents wore their own home-made patches to distinguish their nationality. Eventually German regulations prohibited their use, and the intention was to replace them with standardized badges of German manufacture. By 1943, most of the foreign volunteer legions had been disbanded and incorporated into the *Waffen*-SS.

Manufacture

The SS shields were machine embroidered onto black wool base cloth – earlier badges issued to units serving the German Army had been made in the BeVo machine-woven style. BeVo was the abbreviation for *Bandfabrik Ewald Vorsteher*, a principal maker of wartime woven insignia. The later SS shields and SS collar insignia are commonly referred to as 'DACHAU' issues because many were made – and many were found unissued – at the SS clothing depots at Dachau. Another firm that made these shields was Troltsch & Hansemann of Berlin. Shields were at first worn above the cuff title, and later beneath the SS arm eagle.

A variety of armshields were worn by members of the *Ost-Legionen*, which were the administrative

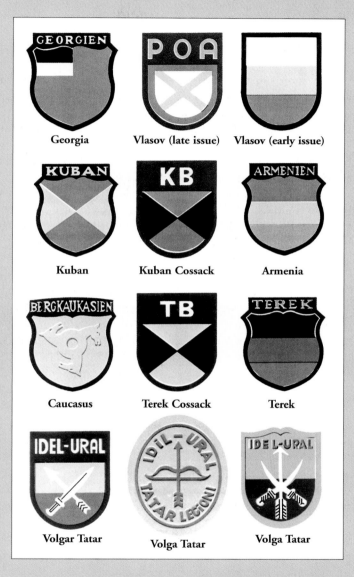

Georgia   **Vlasov (late issue)**   **Vlasov (early issue)**

Kuban   **Kuban Cossack**   **Armenia**

Caucasus   **Terek Cossack**   **Terek**

Volgar Tatar   **Volga Tatar**   **Volga Tatar**

centres for the eastern units. These were worn on either the upper left or upper right arm. Initially, they were the same shape as those worn by other foreign legions, and bore the name of the region of the Soviet Union from which the unit was recruited. Many units, especially those formed late in the war, had shields designed and made but never issued.

Above: Russian volunteer cavalrymen on patrol are watched warily by local civilians. Such units were used primarily on anti-partisan duties, though German manpower shortages meant that more and more were sent to the front line.

called to Lodz to attend an SS leader's conference. What happened next is not entirely clear. The official version was that he was killed by Polish partisans in an ambush, but some sources say that the activities of his troops in Warsaw had sickened even the SS; placed in front of a military tribunal, he was then shot by a firing squad. Others claim that he was arrested and shot out of hand by the *Gestapo*.

Rodionov's SS

In April 1942 the Fighting Union of Russian Nationalists, or BSRN (*Boyevogo Soyuza Russkaya*

Naroda) was formed in the town of Suvalki. It was headed by the former chief of staff of the Soviet 229th Rifle Division, V.V. Gil, who took the pseudonym 'Rodionov'. This was the first Russian national unit to be taken into the SS, and was known as the *Druzhina* (which is the Russian word for militia unit). With a strength of some 500 men, the *Druzhina* was formed to provide rear-area security and to fight partisans. In December 1942 a second Russian SS detachment was formed under the command of former NKVD (Soviet secret police) Major E. Blazhevich. In March both detachments were combined into the 1st Russian SS Regiment with Gil-Rodionov as its commander.

In May the regiment, some 2000 strong, was deployed to the town of Luzhki in Byelorussia, where it was again expanded, becoming 1st Russian SS Brigade. Although the brigade took part in many anti-partisan operations, it was never particularly effective, and the change in the tide of war after the Battle of Kursk in 1943 convinced many of its members that they had chosen the wrong side. On 16 August 1943 the brigade destroyed their German liaison headquarters and deserted *en masse* to the partisans.

Also in the autumn of 1941, a White Russian émigré, S.N. Ivanov, suggested to the *Abwehr* chief Admiral Canaris that he should form a unit made up of Soviet prisoners of war and deserters. Its mission would be to infiltrate deep behind Soviet lines. The unit came into existence in March 1942. It wore Soviet uniforms with the addition of the old Tsarist colours, and it used Soviet equipment.

The unit's Russian members believed that they would be the nucleus of a future great Russian 'liberation' army, and called themselves the *Russkaya Natsionalnaya Narodnaya Armiya* (RNNA, or Russian Nationalist Patriotic Army). By the end of 1942 it had grown to be a brigade-sized unit some 7000 strong. It

saw considerable action in 1942, and was attached to Army Group Centre as the 'Experimental Formation Centre'. However, in accordance with Hitler's orders that no Russian unit in German service should be larger than a battalion, the unit was broken up by Field Marshal von Kluge and its battalions assigned to reinforce German units. This, together with the order that they should be re-equipped with German uniforms and weapons, caused considerable dissension in the ranks, and after numerous desertions and several near mutinies, the unit was disbanded.

Many other volunteer battalions, companies and squadrons were formed. The majority of them, composed of volunteers of Russian nationality, were later incorporated into the Russian Army of Liberation

Below: Azerbaijani volunteers served in both the SS and the German Army. Most of the original *Osttruppen* volunteers were transferred to the SS in 1944, but many remained under Army control, serving in France and Poland.

– the name given to all Russian volunteer formations which recognized General Vlasov as their leader.

The Germans also formed a number of *Ost-Legionen* (eastern legions), largely from POWs held in the *Generalgouvernement* in Poland and organized by ethnicity. The legions were not tactical formations, but were created as administrative centres where national units, mostly battalions, were organized and trained. The region of the Caucasus in particular was home to several of the ethnic groups fighting on the side of the Germans. In order to promote better unit cohesion and loyalty, the German Army attempted to divide some of the Caucasian peoples into units according to their religion.

In 1942, in addition to the various *Ost-Legionen*, the German Army used the staff of the disbanded 162nd *Infanterie-Division* to supervise the training of Turkic-manned eastern battalions in the territory of the *Generalgouvernement*. The division was itself reactivated on 21 May 1943 as the new 162nd *Infanterie-Division (turk.)*. The original German 162nd *Infanterie-Division* had been destroyed at Stalingrad. A second division of eastern troops, the 1st *Kosaken-Division*, was also formed during 1943, by using several pre-existing Cossack cavalry regiments organized under brigade-level command staffs. On 13 December 1942 the position of *Inspekteur der*

Opposite: An officer inspects members of a *Turkverband*, one of the early *Osttruppen* units formed on the Eastern Front in 1941. 'Turk' units were manned by Asiatic volunteers from the Caucasus and Central Asia.

Eastern legions

By the end of 1942, the following eastern legions had been created:
• *Armenische Legion:* established by an order of 30 December 1941, but not actually created until 4 July 1942 in the *Generalgouvernement*, to serve units composed of Armenians.
• *Aserbeidschanische Legion:* this unit was created on 22 July 1942 by renaming the original *Kaukasisch-Mohammedanische Legion* to serve (Muslim) Azerbaijani formations. This legion was converted into the staff of *Infanterie-Regiment* 314 of the 162nd *Infanterie-Division (turk)* on 1 June 1943.
• *Georgische Legion:* established by an order dated 30 December 1941, but not actually formed until 24 February 1942 in the *Generalgouvernement*, to serve Georgian units.
• *Kaukasisch-Mohammedanische Legion:* formed 24 March 1942 in the *Generalgouvernement* from parts of the *Turkestanisch-Kaukasisch-Mohammedanische Legion*. Renamed *Aserbeidschanische Legion* on 22 July 1942.
• *Nordkaukasische Legion:* formed 5 August 1942 at *Truppenübungsplatz Rembertow* in the *General-*

gouvernement to serve (Orthodox Christian) North Caucasian units.
• *Turkestanisch-Kaukasisch-Mohammedanische Legion:* formed on 13 January 1942 out of *Abwehr-Unternehmen Tiger* B, a special forces unit operated by *Amt Ausland/Abwehr* of the OKW, composed of Germans from *Brandenburg-Regiment z.b.V.* 800 and Caucasian volunteers from the POW camps. On 24 March 1942 the legion was broken up into three separate elements: *verstärkt Turkestanisches Infanterie-Bataillon* 450, the *Kaukasisch-Mohammedanische Legion*, and the *Turkestanische Legion*.
• *Turkestanische Legion:* formed 24 March 1942 in the *Generalgouvernement* from parts of the *Turkestanisch-Kaukasisch-Mohammedanische Legion*, to serve Turkoman units
• *Wolgatatarische Legion:* formed in January 1942 in the *Generalgouvernement* to serve Volga-Tartar and Volga-Finn units.

Other ethnic groups from the Soviet Union, such as the Cossacks and Kalmyks, did not have their own ethnic legions, although they did form a significant number of volunteer combat units.

Osttruppen im OKH was created within the German Army high command. The eastern troop command staff was designated *General der Osttruppen* in early 1943, and was renamed *General der Freiwillige-Verbände* on 1 January 1944. In May 1943 there were 10 regiments, 170 battalions, 221 companies and 11 platoons/sections of *Osttruppen* operating under the authority of the *General der Osttruppen*.

Police units

Even before the German Army was forming its *Ost-Bataillone*, the SS and *Ordnungspolizei* were forming their own 'native' units in the Baltic and the Ukraine, mainly for police and security duties. The *Schutzmannschaft* (*Schuma*) battalions were police units under control of the local HSSPF (*Höhere SS und Polizei Führer* – Higher SS and Police

Commander), and were given designations based on the duties they were intended to perform: '*Wach-*' for installation and depot guard duty; '*Ersatz-*' or '*Stamm-*' for replacement or training service respectively; '*Pionier-*' for units mainly made up from engineers and '*Front-*' for front-line combat duty.

In addition to the *Schuma* battalions, the SS and *Ordnungspolizei* used Byelorussian, Ukrainian, Latvian and Estonian volunteers to form several police rifle regiments for front-line and anti-partisan service. In May 1943 the *Schuma* designation, in use since early 1942, was dropped in favour of '*Polizei-*'. At the same

Below: Russian auxiliaries race through a burning village on the southern Russian steppe. Many volunteers from the Ukraine and southern Russia were more than willing to carry out atrocities on behalf of the Germans.

time, the police regiments which were formed from mainly non-German personnel became '*Polizei-Schützen-*' regiments.

The native police battalions continued to serve in anti-partisan and front-line combat roles to the end of the war, but by 1944 more and more of their personnel were being drafted unwillingly into the 'volunteer' *Waffen*-SS divisions such as the 14th *Waffen-Grenadier Division der SS (ukranishe Nr. 1)*, 15th *Waffen-Grenadier Division der SS (lettische Nr. 1)* and 20th *Waffen-Grenadier Division der SS (estnische Nr. 1)*.

Cossack volunteers

Possibly the largest group of former Soviet citizens to fight for the Germans was the Cossack nation, who wanted to use the Germans to help build their own independent state, Kazakia. German commanders had great sympathy for the Cossacks, as their bravery and their hatred of the Soviets produced quick results for the Germans. As early as mid-1942, a Cossack cavalry

Above: The largest contingent of volunteers fighting for the Germans was provided by the Cossacks. They had a long and proud warrior tradition, and saw service with the *Wehrmacht* as a means to an end: the establishment of the independent state of Kazakia.

formation existed in Mohylev, under the command of a former Soviet major, Kononov, who had crossed over to the Germans at the first opportunity with the greater part of his regiment. In the summer of 1942 the German armies entered territories inhabited by the Cossacks. During the civil war which followed the Bolshevik revolution, they had formed six federated republics: the Cossacks of the Don, of the Kuban, of Terek, of Orenburg, of the Ural, and of Astrakhan.

After the communist victory these had been liquidated by the Bolsheviks with extreme cruelty. The Cossacks, therefore, greeted the Germans as liberators. The entire populations of towns, villages and settlements went out to meet the German troops with flowers and gifts of all kinds, singing their national anthems. Cossack formations of the Red Army came over to the Germans almost to a man. Thousands of Cossacks in POW camps offered their services in the fight against the Soviets. The scattered remnants of the Kalmyk tribe, numbering no more 80,000 men, women and children, formed and equipped 16 cavalry squadrons which cleared the steppes of the remaining Soviet units, showing no mercy in return for years of terror at the hands of the NKVD.

In the summer of 1943, the 1st Cossack Division was formed under the command of General von Pannwitz. It had six cavalry regiments. Shortly

afterwards the division was expanded into the XV SS Cossack Cavalry Corps, which numbered some 50,000 men. This was part of Himmler's plan to take over all foreign formations from the Army. Two further Cossack brigades and 12 Cossack reserve regiments were formed, and a number of smaller units were attached to German formations.

In all, Cossack troops on the German side numbered about 250,000 men. The Germans used the Cossacks to fight Soviet partisans, to cover the rear of their armies, and sometimes for action at the front. Later on, some Cossack formations were moved to France and Yugoslavia. The Cossack command objected, on the ground that the Cossacks should fight only against the Soviets, but in vain.

Vlasov and the Russian liberation movement

The success of some of the former Soviet troops fighting on the side of the *Wehrmacht*, together with

Below: Andrey Vlasov (right) was a charismatic Soviet military leader who after his capture in 1942 was persuaded by a faction in the German General Staff to switch sides. However, Vlasov was never given the freedom he needed to build up a true Russian liberation army.

**Left: Formed early in 1944, the
*Mussulmanischen SS-Division
Neu-Turkistan* took part in the brutal
suppression of the Warsaw Rising,
serving alongside the murderous thugs
who made up the *SS-Sturmbrigade
Dirlewanger*.**

Seventh and Twentieth Soviet
Armies, and later deputy commander
of the Volkhov front, was captured.

Vlasov was the son of a Russian
smallholder from Nizhni Novgorod.
Originally a theological student, in
1919 he was conscripted into the
Red Army and saw service against the
'Whites' in the Ukraine, the
Caucasus and the Crimea. Joining
the Communist Party in 1930, he
rose swiftly through the ranks of the
Red Army, serving in China as
military adviser to Chiang Kai-Shek
in 1938. In the early stages of the war
with Germany he commanded a
division, escaping the encirclement
of Kiev and playing a major part in
the defence of Moscow. He was
captured in July 1942 after the
Germans had encircled a large part of
the Volkhov front in the previous
month. Taken to a camp for
prominente, or important prisoners,
he was persuaded by the Germans to
switch sides, mainly because of his
distaste for Stalin and the communist

the counter-productive effect of harsh German policies
in the occupied territories, convinced a faction in the
German Government and *Wehrmacht* high command
that the only way to guarantee German success in the
East would be to create a genuine Russian liberation
movement, but Hitler's opposition to any such
movement meant that they had little success.

However, a small group of civil servants and officers
continued in their efforts. They gained a glimmer of
hope when on 12 July 1942 General Andrey
Andreyevich Vlasov, former commander of the Thirty-

system. Vlasov argued that Germany should create a
Russian provisional government and a Russian army of
liberation to be under his command.

In September 1942, while still in the POW camp,
General Vlasov wrote a leaflet for the Propaganda
Section of the *Wehrmacht*, WPrIV. In it he called on
the officers of the Red Army and the Russian
intelligentsia to overthrow Stalin, whom he blamed for
all the disasters which had befallen Russia. Hundreds
of thousands of copies of the leaflet were dropped over
Soviet lines by the *Luftwaffe*. Within days, thousands

of deserters from the Red Army were coming over to the Germans. Most asked to serve under General Vlasov and wanted to fight against the Soviets. But Hitler was not amused. The last thing he wanted was a powerful Russian liberation movement. He wanted European Russia for the German race. At the *Führer's* command, Field Marshal Keitel forbade everybody, up to and including the General Staff, to present any kind of memorandum or report on the subject of General Vlasov and Russian formations.

The Russian National Committee

In spite of this prohibition, in December 1942 the German promoters of the Russian anti-Soviet movement decided to sponsor the Russian National Committee, headquartered at Smolensk, with General Vlasov as chairman. Vlasov's personal charm, his talents and his ability to inspire confidence made him the obvious choice. However, opposition from non-Russian anti-communists together with inefficient dissemination of the new committee's manifesto meant that it had little effect on Soviet citizens living in the occupied areas. Nevertheless, in March 1943 the commanders of Army Groups Centre and North invited General Vlasov, on their own initiative, to go on a tour of their areas and deliver speeches to prisoners of war, Soviet volunteers and the local population.

In the second half of April Field Marshal Keitel demanded to know who had allowed General Vlasov to issue a political proclamation; he also threatened grave consequences if it proved true that General Vlasov was appearing in public, and was being called 'the future leader of the Russians'. Keitel issued an order on behalf of the *Führer* which stated that: 'Vlasov is only a prisoner of war. His shameless speeches have infuriated the *Führer*, who has forbidden

> **'The Führer has forbidden mentioning the name Vlasov in his presence ... If in future Vlasov appears anywhere in public, he will be arrested and handed over to the Gestapo.'**
>
> *Order issued by Keitel*

mentioning the name Vlasov in his presence. Vlasov is immediately to be sent back to the POW camp, and will be kept under special surveillance. If, in future, Vlasov appears anywhere in public he will be arrested and handed over to the Gestapo.'

Soon all army groups and some of the armies reported that the publication of a political declaration and a change of attitude towards the anti-Soviet volunteers were a necessity, otherwise the occupation of the Eastern territories would prove to be an impossible task. Vlasov abandoned his previous stand of the 'one and undivided Russia', consented to the principle of self-determination of the non-Russian peoples and agreed that Russia, in a peace settlement, would renounce her claims to the Ukraine and the Caucasus.

Hitler once more intervened. On 8 June, he declared that the Liberation Army was a dangerous folly. He would never consent to its organization. The setting-up of any states in the occupied territories was out of the question. Instead of forming volunteer units, Russians would be sent to Germany to work in coal mines, replacing Germans. He accepted that Vlasov might be needed for propaganda work at the front, but any other activity would not be permitted. Hitler's *diktat* reduced the Russian National Committee and its proposed Liberation Army to a propaganda tool, controlled by Germans and working through Russian-language newspapers and pamphlets. Even so, the committee and the Liberation Army became symbols of the Russian nation's fight against Soviet tyranny.

'Treacherous' behaviour

By the summer of 1943, it is estimated that anything from 800,000 to one million Russians were serving the German Army in the East. However, the success of the Soviet autumn offensives that year were blamed on the treacherous behaviour of the Russian volunteer formations on the front line. Hitler was enraged, and ordered that all eastern formations be immediately disbanded, and that 80,000 of their men, as a first

Opposite: Members of the Georgian Legion undergo training in the summer of 1943. Although they have been issued with German uniforms, they are armed with captured Soviet Degtyarev DP light machine guns.

contingent, immediately be sent to France to dig coal. After three days Hitler modified his order when it became clear that such an action would leave a massive hole in the *Wehrmacht*'s manpower on the Eastern Front. Only formations from the broken sector of the front were disbanded. Some days later, Hitler appeared to have calmed down, and he ordered that rather than disband, the *Osttruppen* were to be sent to other

Below: The complex ethnic mix of the Soviet Union ensured that there would always be a sizeable number of minority peoples willing to fight against the Russians, even if that meant accepting having to fight under the control of the German *Wehrmacht*.

theatres of operations. By the end of 1943 several hundred thousand eastern volunteers had been transferred to France, Italy and the Balkans.

One exception to Hitler's policy came with the formation of a Ukrainian SS division, 14th *Waffen-Grenadier Division der SS (galizische Nr. 1)*. Part of Himmler's expansion of the SS, the division was formed on the understanding that it would only be used to fight the Soviets. It suffered heavy losses in June 1944 during the massive Soviet summer offensive, and was reformed as the 1st Ukrainian Division in the autumn. However, Himmler was not a complete convert, nor did he realize the scale of Russian involvement in the *Wehrmacht*.

In October 1944, the General of Eastern Troops informed the *Reichsführer*-SS that in June 1944 there were more than 800,000 eastern volunteers serving in the German Army, with a further 100,000 in the *Kriegsmarine* and *Luftwaffe*. Himmler simply could not believe it. Nor could Hitler. As late as the end of March 1945, he could still exclaim at a staff conference: 'We just don't know what is floating around. I have just heard for the first time, to my amazement, that a Ukrainian SS Division has suddenly appeared. I don't know a thing about this.'

The enforced captivity of the Russian National Committee, and of General Vlasov, continued in spite of many efforts on the part of the German sympathizers of the anti-Soviet movement. By the middle of 1944, the Russian Army of Liberation was still not a true military organization. Units which bore its name were mostly commanded by German officers and were dispersed all over Europe; General Vlasov and the Russian National Committee had no influence whatsoever, and were not recognized by the German Government.

KONR formed

However, Soviet advances in the East persuaded Himmler, previously a confirmed opponent of the ROA (*Russkaya Osvoboditelnaya Armiya*), to change his mind. After a meeting with Vlasov, *Reichsführer*-SS Himmler proposed that a new committee be created – the KONR (*Komitet Osvobozhdeniya Narodov Rossii*, or Committee for the Liberation of the Peoples of Russia) – along with a KONR army under General Vlasov's command. The committee and army were to embrace all Soviet citizens living under German rule, in order to unite their political and military activities in the fight against Bolshevism.

Initially, five divisions were to be organized from the millions of Russian prisoners and forced labourers who had been brought to Germany. These would gradually be reinforced by ROA units currently serving all over Europe. The KONR met strong opposition from the non-Russians, who felt that it was mainly a Russian enterprise and controlled by Russians whom they did

Above: *Waffen*-SS instructors teach Ukrainian volunteers how to use a 50mm (2in) 50-PM 30 light mortar. The Ukraine had suffered dreadfully under Stalin, and large numbers enlisted with the Germans. Others, however, fought against both the Germans and the Soviets.

not trust. The formation of the KONR army also met with difficulties. The German Army did not want to give up its *Ost-Bataillonen*, and delayed their transfer. German industrialists objected to the raid on their slave labour force for personnel. As a result, only two divisions were formed. The first units were operational by February 1945.

After a series of actions against the Soviets, the 1st Division retreated on its own initiative back towards Prague, reaching the city on 2 May. In the city, Czech nationalists had risen against the Nazis, but were in danger of being wiped out. Since most of the nationalists were also anti-Soviet, the Red Army had stopped to allow the SS to do their work for them, as

Above: Volunteers from Josef Stalin's homeland, Georgia, on parade. The Georgian Legion consisted of at least 12 infantry battalions, and the 822nd Georgian Infantry Battalion served on the Atlantic Wall during the Allied invasion of Normandy.

they had at Warsaw. The Czechs appealed to Vlasov's men for aid. Vlasov despised the SS, so he attacked his former allies, routing them and preserving the Czech city.

Vlasov and the rest of his force, desperate to escape the vengeful Red Army, retreated westwards to surrender to the British and the Americans. During the flight, however, many were shot by Soviet troops, the majority were captured by the Red Army, and others were handed over by the Americans. Some 17,000 of

Vlasov's men are said to have been deported to Russia, where many were executed and the remainder imprisoned in the *Gulag* for life. Their fate was shared by most of the members of the Cossack Corps (handed over to the Russians by the British to whom they had surrendered), by the 162nd Turkoman Division and by most other members of the *Osttruppen*. Among their number was General Vlasov.

On 2 August 1946 the first mention of the Vlasov movement appeared in the Soviet press. The last page of *Pravda* announced the death by hanging of the following: Vlasov, Malyshkin, Zhilenkov, Trukhin, Zakutny, Blagoveshchenski, Meandrov, Maltsev, Bunyachenko, Zverev, Korbukov and Shatov. 'All accused admitted their guilt in the charges made against them ... The sentence has been executed.'

LATVIA

DATE OF OCCUPATION: JULY 1941
NUMBER OF VOLUNTEERS: 80,000
MAIN SS UNITS INCLUDING VOLUNTEERS: 15th Waffen-Grenadier Division der SS (lettische Nr. 1); 19th Lettische SS-Freiwilligen Division

As with the other Baltic States, Latvia fought for its independence from the Soviet Union after World War I, and came under pressure from both Germany and the USSR during the 1930s. In common with Lithuania and Estonia, Latvia was forced to accept a Soviet garrison in 1940, and in 1941 the country itself was absorbed by Stalin's Russia. The Soviets took Latvia's small army into the Red Army, and political opponents and nationalists quickly came to the attention of the NKVD. Many were arrested and executed, while others were transported to labour camps in Russia. The German attack on Russia in 1941 saw the *Wehrmacht*'s Army Group North smashing through the Baltic States in its drive towards Leningrad. German intelligence had previously initiated ties with Latvian nationalist organizations to promote a mutiny in Latvian units of the Red Army. Riga was besieged by the beginning of July, and by the 10th the entire country was in German hands.

Below: Latvian volunteers in the *Waffen*-SS are seen manning an artillery piece in the summer of 1943. At that time the 1st SS Motorized Brigade, by now a largely Latvian formation, was in intense action around Smolensk.

Above: Women and children are ordered to strip prior to execution. Baltic police units were used to support German anti-partisan operations in 1942 and 1943 – operations which were often little more than massacres of unarmed civilians accused of 'harbouring bandits'.

Latvian nationalists

The Germans were seen as liberators by many Latvians, and initially had the full support of Latvian right-wing nationalists. Although a minority in Latvia, these groups had been an important factor in the nation's politics from the early 1920s. The *Aizsargi*, or 'Guards', was created in 1919. A paramilitary organization along the lines of the SA, it had been used by K. Ulmanis, the Peasants' Union Party leader, in a military coup which took place in May 1934.

Once he established his dictatorial state, Ulmanis made the *Aizsargi* a part of the police. Another nationalist group, the Lettish National Club, was banned soon after being formed in the early 1920s. However, its members were the core for a new extreme

nationalist group, the 'Fiery Cross', formed in 1927. It was renamed the *Perkonkrust*, or 'Thunder Cross', Lettish People's Association in 1933. Although membership never rose above 5000, the Thunder Cross advocated the disenfranchisement and persecution of non-Letts, particularly the Jews. Ulmanis and his government were Latvian nationalists, who immediately enacted laws against all minorities in the state, closing German, Russian and other minority language schools and declaring non-Latvian-speaking organizations to be illegal.

Assisting the *Einsatzgruppen*

Former members of Latvian nationalist organizations resumed their activities right after the Red Army withdrawal, and offered their willing assistance to the SD's *Einsatzgruppen* who instituted the massive Nazi slaughter of Jews in the wake of the advancing *Wehrmacht*. Former *Aizsargi* and *Perkonkrust* members, together with former Latvian Army and police members, formed voluntary 'self-defence squadrons' in the summer of 1941. These were used by the *Gestapo* and the SD for searches, arrests, raids and mass shootings of Jews, communists, Soviet activists and sympathizers. Tens of thousands of Jews and communists were slaughtered in the autumn of 1941 at places like Riga, Daugavpils and Liepaja. However, the Latvian irregulars were soon to expand their areas of operations.

Partisan activity quickly forced the *Wehrmacht* to set up units to provide rear-area security all along the Eastern Front. To free German soldiers for front-line duty, as many of these as possible were to be formed from local volunteers. On 25 August 1941, Army Group North formally authorized the formation of volunteer battalions of Baltic citizens.

In autumn 1941 regular police battalions were organized out of the irregular self-defence squadrons, and in October of that year the first Latvian police battalion went into action just over the Russian border

in the area of Pskov. Over the next three years over 40 Latvian police battalions were formed, ranging in size from 200 to 600 men. Latvian battalions saw action in Latvia itself, but were also deployed in the Ukraine, in Byelorussia and as far away as the Caucasus. Some battalions gained an unsavoury reputation for atrocity as they supported the *Einsatzgruppen* in their attempts to eliminate the Jews.

Heavy losses incurred by the German Army during the Red Army's winter counter-offensive (1941–42) in the environs of Moscow forced OKW to attach many of the Latvian police units to the German Army as reserve units. Later they were used to fill gaps in the front line, but were most actively involved in the fierce

Below: *Reichsführer*-**SS Heinrich Himmler visits Latvian SS artillery units on the Narva River. The Latvian SS divisions were to be heavily involved in the fierce fighting which took place in this area in 1944.**

partisan war. By 1942, German manpower resources were being stretched to breaking point. German troops were in action from North Africa to Norway and from the Bay of Biscay to the Caucasus. The legion programme was an SS attempt to increase numbers by calling for non-German volunteers to fight the communists. Volunteers came from all over Europe, but the largest legion by far was the Latvian Legion.

Latvian SS

The first large unit of the new Latvian Legion was formed at the Leningrad front from three police battalions, later reinforced by three further battalions. Initially known as the 2nd *SS-Infanterie-Brigade (mot)*, it was redesignated as the 2nd Lettish *Freiwilligen* SS Brigade. It was to be expanded as the 19th *Waffen-Grenadier Division der SS (lettische Nr. 2)* in the summer of 1944. In the meantime, the first Latvian division, the *Lettische SS-Freiwilligen Division*, had been authorized in September 1943. Renamed the 15th *Waffen-Grenadier Division der SS*

(lettische Nr. 1) soon after, it was formed from the new recruits in Latvia. Only partially trained, the division was transported to the front at the end of November 1943. Some regiments had not even received winter clothing. Dispersed for further training among the German 83rd and 205th Infantry Divisions, the Latvians were treated with contempt, and many of their new German-issued weapons were taken by their 'allies'. In German eyes, it was a waste of resources giving modern weapons to people who could only serve as cannon fodder.

Opposite: A Latvian volunteer in full winter gear, 1943. Latvian SS units fought hard at the end of the war. In spite of early doubts, Himmler stated that the Latvians and other Balts were essential to the defence of the Eastern Front.

Conscription introduced

Appearances can be deceiving, however. Although the Letts served in greater numbers than any other nationality, probably less than 20 per cent were volunteers. Initially, German authorities organized genuine volunteer recruitment campaigns, but when desired results were not obtained, further steps had to be taken. At the end of 1942, the German Labour Administration notified those Letts born between 1919 and 1924 to report for registration on 26 February 1943.

The draftees were supposed to be given a choice between serving with the legion, serving with the German *Wehrmacht* as auxiliaries, or working in important war industries – which in other words meant being transported to Germany to work as forced labour. They had to sign a declaration that they were volunteering, and those who refused were sent to the Salaspils concentration camp. Draftees wore SS uniforms, but since they were neither fully Aryan nor true volunteers, they were not considered to be true SS men. Rather than serving in SS divisions, the Latvian units (and other similar non-Germanic formations) were designated 'divisions of the SS'. The two SS

divisions were not the only Latvian forces fighting in the front. Police regiments and battalions were being used in front-line combat on top of their rear-area security duties. Additionally, tens of thousands of Latvian auxiliaries had been pressed into service by the German units to which they were attached. Although attempts were made to transfer these auxiliaries to the Latvian Legion, German commanders in the field refused; one German commander replied that 48 per cent of his men were Latvians and to comply with the request would fatally weaken his division. Ultimately both the Latvian police battalions and the grenadier divisions were considered part of the legion. As a result, the Latvian Legion, with a peak strength in excess of 87,000 men, was more than 10 times as large as any of the other volunteer legions.

When the Soviets pushed the Germans back in the last year of the war, Courland in western Latvia remained in Axis hands, and the Latvian 19th SS Division fought fiercely in the defence of its homeland. Part of the 15th SS Division, forced back by the Soviets, retreated westwards to try to surrender to the Americans or the British. Cut off by advancing Soviet armies, the unit found itself in Berlin, where it unwillingly played its part in the defence of Hitler's bunker in the last days of the war. It later surrendered to the Americans at Güterglück near the Elbe River. In all, more than 150,000 Latvians served more or less willingly with the German forces during World War II.

ROMANIA

DATE OF OCCUPATION: ALLY
NUMBER OF VOLUNTEERS: 50,000
MAIN SS UNITS INCLUDING VOLUNTEERS: 7th SS-Freiwilligen Gebirgs Division *Prinz Eugen*; 8th SS-Kavallerie Division *Florian Geyer*

As in many other countries of Eastern Europe, Romania had a large ethnic German population, though many of these *Volksdeutsche* were indistinguishable from their Romanian neighbours. Concentrated in the Banat region (which straddles the Romanian and Serbian border) and in Transylvania, there were over 500,000 Romanians who claimed German descent.

Recruiting the *Volksdeutsche*

When Gottlob Berger, head of the SS recruiting office, sought to find manpower to expand the SS late in 1940, he looked to the more 'Aryan' of the *Volksdeutsche* as well as to the Nordic countries for volunteers. In the winter of 1940 and 1941, the SS launched a recruitment drive in Transylvania, successfully reaching its target of 1000 volunteers who were trained and then sent as replacements to the elite SS-*Reich* Division, which later became the 2nd SS-*Panzer Division Das Reich*. The Romanians, who were Germany's allies in the Axis pact, were not pleased with the SS poaching on their patch. In fact, under Romanian law it was illegal for Romanian nationals to serve in foreign armies, so further recruits were invited to visit Germany where they could join the SS as individuals.

The next SS recruitment drive took place early in 1942 with the formation of the *SS-Freiwilligen Gebirgs Division*, later known as the 7th *SS-Freiwilligen Gebirgs Division Prinz Eugen*. Volunteers in this instance mainly came from the Banat, as well as from Serbia and Croatia. Formed as a mountain division, *Prinz Eugen* was equipped with obsolete and captured equipment such as Czech machine guns and French light tanks. Its first commander was SS *Brigadeführer*

und Generalmajor der Waffen-SS Artur Phleps. Phleps had served in the Imperial Austrian Army, and had commanded a mountain corps in the Romanian Army until 1941. Despite its poor equipment, the *Prinz Eugen* Division was one of the most effective counter-insurgency units the Germans fielded in Yugoslavia during the war, and was greatly feared by the partisans. However, that reputation was gained primarily by brutality and utter ruthlessness. The conflict in Yugoslavia combined guerrilla war with civil and tribal warfare, and neither side was prone to giving quarter.

Although Germany was still on the offensive in 1942, it was becoming increasingly difficult to find enough manpower to replace combat losses on the Eastern Front. Berlin put pressure on the government of Marshal Antonescu, and the Romanians eventually gave permission for Germany to actively recruit among Romanian *Volksdeutsche*. By 1943, over 60,000 had joined the *Waffen-SS*. They did not serve in individual Romanian formations, but large numbers served in the 8th *SS-Kavallerie Division Florian Geyer*, the 11th *SS-Freiwilligen Panzergrenadier Division Nordland*, and in the newly formed 17th *SS-Panzergrenadier Division Goetz von Berlichingen* and the 18th *SS-Freiwilligen Panzergrenadier Division Horst Wessel*.

However, not all of the Romanian *Volksdeutsche* served in SS fighting units. In August 1942, an agreement between the Romanian governor of Transnistria and the SS authorized the *Volksdeutsche* to organize a *Selbschutz*, or self-defence, force, eventually growing to be 8000 strong. As with other *Selbschutz* forces elsewhere in Eastern Europe, its main role was intended to be to fight partisans, but in reality its main use was as an anti-Jewish force. In addition to killing Jews, the force also liaised with and profited from German companies moving in to take over Jewish businesses.

Waning enthusiasm

Ethnic Romanians did not join German units in any numbers until the last year of the war. Romanians began losing enthusiasm for the conflict in 1943 after the tide began to turn against the Axis. The military dictatorship which had run the country was overthrown by a coup in August 1944. A fascist government in exile led by Horia Sima was set up in Vienna, and the SS initiated plans to create a Romanian National Army. Troops for the new force would come from POWs taken after Romania switched sides, from members of the fascist Iron Guard which had fled Romania after the coup and from regular Romanian soldiers who were opposed to the idea of a communist regime. Two regiments of two battalions each were operational early in 1945. *Waffen-SS Grenadier Regiment Rumänische Nr. 1* saw action in Pomerania, north of Stettin, where it was almost

completely destroyed. The second regiment was made into an anti-tank unit, *Waffen-SS Panzer Zerstörer Regiment Rumänische Nr. 2.* A third regiment never got beyond training.

Romanians also provided the personnel for several small special operations units at the end of the war. Seventy volunteers trained near Vienna and joined a Brandenburg unit, the *Brandenburg Streifkorps Karpaten.* After further training in guerrilla warfare at Korneuberg, they were to be dropped behind Soviet lines to perform intelligence gathering and sabotage. Another 175 Romanian men transferred from other SS divisions for training at Stockerau. These were intended to join Otto Skorzeny's commandos in the largely mythical 'Alpine Redoubt' tasked with supporting the Sixth SS Panzer Army's offensive at Balaton in Hungary.

In the event, the expected breakthrough failed, and the *Jägdeinsatz Rumanien* retreated through Austria into the Alps, eventually surrendering to the Americans a month after the end of the war.

Below: An SS *Reiter* (cavalry trooper) of the SS Cavalry Division *Florian Geyer* moves through a burning village in the Balkans. Romanian *Volksdeutsche* served with this formation, which acquired a brutal reputation in the partisan war in Yugoslavia.

ESTONIA

DATE OF OCCUPATION: JULY 1941
NUMBER OF VOLUNTEERS: 25,000
MAIN SS UNITS INCLUDING VOLUNTEERS: Estnische SS-Legion;
20th Waffen-Grenadier Division der SS (estnische Nr. 1)

The origins of the involvement of Baltic soldiers in the war in the East can be found in the difficult position in which the three states of Estonia, Latvia and Lithuania found themselves in 1939 – trapped between Nazi Germany to the west and communist Russia to the east. The rapid destruction of Poland in 1939 and the partition of the country between Germany and the USSR came as a severe shock to the Estonian Government, particularly when it became clear that Adolf Hitler was going to give the USSR a free hand in the Baltic.

At the end of September, the Soviets demanded that Estonia allow Soviet troops to be based on its territory, and 35,000 Red Army troops had arrived by 18 October. For the moment, the Soviets demanded little more – they were fully involved in preparing for the invasion of Finland. However, by June 1940, with the *Wehrmacht* triumphant in the West, the Soviets presented an ultimatum. The Estonian Government must resign, a new government acceptable to Moscow must be formed, and Soviet military forces must be allowed to occupy the country.

Soviet occupation

In spite of considerable anti-Soviet sentiment among the Estonian population, the government caved in on 17 June, and within days the Red Army was on the move. Lessons learned in fighting the Finns meant that they moved in strength: 160,000 men were supported by over 500 tanks and were also able to call on more than 1100 aircraft deployed to cover the occupation of all three Baltic States. To prevent any escape by sea the coast was blockaded by the Soviet Baltic Fleet. Along with the armies were the NKVD security units, who had instructions to prepare for nearly 60,000 political and military detainees. Among the first victims of the

Russians were the 12,000 ethnic Germans living in Estonia. Over 2000 were executed over the next 12 months, and most of the rest were deported to Germany, while 35,000 ethnic Estonians were conscripted to work as forced labourers in Russia. The Estonian Army was absorbed into the Red Army as the 22nd Territorial Rifle Corps (though the 16,000 Estonians were outnumbered by 20,000 Russians). Most Estonian officers were imprisoned or executed. By June 1941 Estonian numbers in the unit had dropped to 5500, and most deserted to the Germans after the launch of Operation *Barbarossa*.

When the Germans launched their invasion on 22 June 1941, Army Group North, attacking out of East Prussia, had Leningrad as its objective. But to reach the cradle of the communist revolution, it would have to force its way through the Baltic States. Within two weeks, Field Marshal Ritter von Leeb's forces had driven through Lithuania to reach Riga, Latvia's capital, and were approaching the Estonian border. The German Eighteenth Army began crossing the Estonian border over a wide front on 7 July. Over the next six weeks, the Germans smashed Soviet forces in the region, and the capital Tallinn was taken by the end of August. The Germans were assisted in their task by approximately 12,000 Estonian irregulars, who were known as the 'Forest Brothers'. These became the nucleus of an Estonian 'Home Guard', which had reached a strength of 25,000 men by 1 September.

Security units

Soon after the occupation of Estonia, the Germans began to allow the formation of Estonian units, variously called security, police or defence battalions or companies. Their primary purpose was to provide security in German rear areas, which came to mean fighting partisans. Volunteers were plentiful, and by March 1942 there were 16 Estonian battalions and companies with 10,000 men on active service in Russia. Eventually more than 50 such units were to be formed, with as many as 25,000 Estonians under arms.

Above: Detached from the *Estnische SS-Freiwilligen Brigade* in 1943, the *Estnisches SS-Freiwilligen Bataillon Narva* was assigned to the crack SS Panzer Grenadier Regiment *Nordland*, part of the *Wiking* Division.

Their experience of Soviet oppression at first hand meant that the Baltic States were seen by the SS as potentially valuable recruiting grounds for foreign volunteer legions to take part in the 'crusade' against communism. On 28 August 1942 the *Waffen*-SS announced the intended formation of the *Estniches Freiwilligen SS Legion*.

Estonian SS units formed

By the end of the year, 1280 men were under training at Debica in Poland as the 1st *Estnisches SS-Freiwilligen Grenadier Regiment*. In March 1943, one battalion was detached as the *Estnisches SS-Freiwilligen Bataillon*

Narva, replacing the disbanded Finnish battalion as the third battalion of the *Nordland* Regiment of the *Wiking* Division.

At the same time continuing manpower shortages led to reinforcements being conscripted in Estonia, some 12,000 men being called into service. Of these, 5300 were sent to the legion battalions training at Debica, which were reinforced and organized as the

Right: Haralt Nugiseks, *Waffen-Unterscharführer der SS* and recipient of the Knight's Cross on 9 April 1944. Nugiseks, an Estonian volunteer, was an NCO in the 1st *SS-Volunteer-Grenadier-Regiment 46*, which was part of the 20th *Waffen-Grenadier Division der SS (estnische Nr. 1)*.

3rd *SS-Freiwilligen Brigade*. The remaining conscripts were sent to German Army units. Five thousand more Estonians were mobilized in the winter of 1943–44. They were used in the expansion of the Estonian SS brigade into a full division, which was authorized on 24 January 1944. The 20th *SS-Freiwilligen Division* was renamed in June 1944, becoming the 20th *Waffen-Grenadier Division der SS (estnisches Nr. 1)*.

On 1 February, as the advancing Soviet armies approached the Narva River, another 45,000 Estonians were called up. Some 20,000 were used to form six new *Schutzmannschaft* and *Polizei Front* battalions. About 60,000 men were serving in these border guard units by the end of February, with a further 10,000 in the Estonian SS division. A further 37,000 men were deployed as home guard battalions, while 3000 teenagers served in anti-aircraft defence units. By the autumn of 1944 more than 100,000 Estonians were in German service.

Fighting as part of Field Marshal Walter Model's Army Group North, the Estonian units spent most of February fighting to destroy Soviet bridgeheads across the Narva River. Their success enraged the Soviet high command, which threw nine full corps against the Axis forces in March and April. In one of the largest (and least known) battles of the war, seven Axis divisions fought the Russians to a standstill. Soviet casualties exceeded 120,000, while the Germans and their Estonian and other European allies lost 20,000 men killed or wounded.

The end

After a period of regrouping, the Soviets threw two armies of 205,000 men against five understrength German divisions with just 27,000 men. Unable to stand up to such overwhelming strength, the Axis forces retreated through a series of defensive lines when the Soviets attacked on 24 July. Further attacks came south of Lake Peipus in August, Russian tanks smashing through the lightly armed Estonian border regiments and battalions. However, the attack was blunted by the arrival of German panzers.

Finland's armistice with the Russians in September 1944 left the entire north of Estonia open to attack, and OKW decided to evacuate. With the retreating Germans went 43,000 Estonian soldiers and 24,000 civilians. The Estonian battles probably cost the Soviets something under 200,000 dead; the Germans probably lost between 40,000 and 50,000.

Over 80,000 Estonians fled the country in 1944, mostly to Sweden or Germany. More than 6500 Estonian citizens were executed by the Germans, including 929 Jews and 243 gypsies.

HUNGARY

DATE OF OCCUPATION: ALLY
NUMBER OF VOLUNTEERS: 20,000
MAIN SS UNITS INCLUDING VOLUNTEERS: 25th Waffen-Grenadier Division der SS *Hunyadi*; 26th Waffen-Grenadier Division der SS *Hungaria*

At the beginning of the twentieth century, Hungary was a large, ethnically diverse nation with a population of more than 18 million. Some two million of those were ethnic Germans, or *Volksdeutsche*. After the fall of the Hapsburg Empire at the end of World War I, Admiral Miklós Horthy, the one-time *aide-de-camp* of Emperor Franz Josef, was appointed regent to the vacant Hungarian throne. In common with all the losing states of the Great War, Hungary suffered major territorial losses, the country losing a third of its area under the terms of the Treaty of Trianon. The Trianon treaty had the same kind of effect on the Hungarians as the Treaty of Versailles had on the Germans. The country had lost a third of its territory, and three million Hungarians suddenly became minority citizens in neighbouring and traditionally hostile countries. Between the wars, Hungary grew economically, but the lost territories remained a painful subject. Any party which promised to regain Hungarian territory was likely to succeed.

After the Great Depression, the government of Prime Minister Gyula Gombos signed a trade agreement with Germany which began to pull Hungary into the Axis camp. After Germany's annexation of Czechoslovakia, Hungary got back some of its lost territory. In 1940 the Germans gave back parts of Poland which had been conquered the previous year, and in 1941 the Hungarians received part of Yugoslavia. The membership of the Axis alliance and the apparent German generosity in handing back former Hungarian territory meant that the Hungarian Government felt honour-bound to join the war. After taking part in the invasion of Yugoslavia, the Hungarians provided an army to fight with the Germans in the invasion of Russia in June 1941.

The experience was not kind to the Hungarians, especially after the Hungarian Second Army was wiped out in the Don Bend after the fall of Stalingrad. The Hungarian Government was also coming under pressure from the Germans, who wanted a free hand to conscript the two million or more Hungarian *Volksdeutsche*. The Germans were also pressuring the Hungarians to give up their large Jewish population for 'resettlement'. In a 1943 meeting with Hungarian prime minister Miklos Kallay, Hitler leaned on the Hungarians to allow the recruitment of 80,000 ethnic Germans. Soon afterwards, German teams were moving through Hungary drafting *Volksdeutsche*. *Volksdeutsche* had already been volunteering individually in some numbers since the beginning of

the war, and many of the new SS divisions formed after 1942 had Hungarian troops in their number. The Nazis recruited Hungarian Germans by bringing them into Germany for youth camps, summer schools and sports programmes, where they were indoctrinated with propaganda. The German Army encouraged those who had Magyarized their names to change them back to their Germanic form.

However, the new draft was not voluntary, and anti-German feeling, already high after severe losses on the Eastern Front, grew more intense.

First SS units

After it became clear that the Germans were on the retreat in Russia, Admiral Horthy and Prime Minister Kallay sought to negotiate a separate armistice for Hungary with the Western Allies. To keep Hungary (and its vital oil reserves) in the Axis fold, the Germans occupied the country on 19 March 1944. Horthy was permitted to remain regent, but Kallay was replaced by General Dome Sztojay, head of the Hungarian Arrow Cross fascists and fanatically pro-German. Under the new regime, more than 500,000 Jews were rounded up and deported to the death camp at Auschwitz, a move which had been resisted by the previous government. Sztojay's appointment freed the SS to recruit actively among the Hungarian population.

The first Hungarian SS unit was *SS-Kampfgruppe Deák*, raised by *SS-Oberführer* László Deák. Consisting of 1000 men in three companies, the *Kampfgruppe* was raised on 15 August 1944, from Hungarian Army and police volunteers. Declared operational in September, the unit went into action in the Banat soon afterwards. Absorbed into the 25th *Waffen-Grenadier Division der SS Hunyadi (ungarische Nr. 1)* early

'World War II brought heavy losses to Hungary: during the Battle of Stalingrad and the offensive on the Don, 40,000 soldiers of the Second Hungarian Army were killed and 70,000 were captured by the Red Army.'

Opposite: *Standartenführer* Gustav Lombard, commander of the *Florian Geyer* SS Division, is awarded the Knight's Cross, March 1943. The previous year, 9000 Hungarian *Volksdeutsche* had been assigned to the division.

in November 1944, the *Kampfgruppe* was later used to form the 61st *Waffen-Grenadier Regiment der SS (ungarische Nr. 1)*.

In October 1944, *Kampfgruppe Ney* was formed by Hungarian SS-*Obersturmbannführer* Dr Károly Ney. Established in Budapest from former Hungarian Army soldiers – members of the KABSZ, or Eastern Front Comrades' Federation – the unit's recruitment was organized under the auspices of the *SS-Ersatz Kommando/Ungarn* (SS Replacement Command/Hungary) at Budapest. Weapons, uniforms and equipment were provided by the 22nd *SS-Freiwilligen Kavallerie Division Maria Theresa*, with which it was to serve as a security company. By the end of October the unit had grown to battalion size. Two months later it had grown to regimental size, and battalions were detached to serve with 3rd *SS-Panzer Division Totenkopf*, and with 5th *SS-Panzer Division Wiking*. In the last months of the war it saw extensive combat.

At about the same time, the 800-man complement of the Hungarian *Honvéd* Mountain Training Battalion transferred to the SS, swearing allegiance to Adolf Hitler under the designation of the 1st *Ungarische SS-Schibataillon*. Transferred to Neuhammer Camp in Germany for training, it was almost disbanded and absorbed into the newly forming 25th *Waffen-Grenadier Division der SS Hunyadi*. However, the SS *Führungshauptamt* changed its mind, and on 1 December it was reinstated. Equipped with the latest small arms, heavy machine guns and anti-tank weapons, the Ski Battalion saw continuous action against the Russians in the last five months of the war.

Towards the end of October 1944, the SS and police commander in Hungary asked the Hungarian Government to provide the manpower for two SS divisions. The Hungarians agreed – on condition that they would only fight in Hungary, and only against the Russians. In November 1944 Himmler ordered that the 25th *Waffen-Grenadier Division der SS Hunyadi* be raised. By the end of November, strength had been

Above: SS troops retreat west through Hungary towards the Austrian border. Most preferred to surrender to American forces; every member of the SS knew his likely unpleasant fate should he ever fall into Soviet hands.

raised to 16,700 men, most being former members of the 13th *Honvéd* Light Infantry Division. Transferred to the Neuhammer training ground in Germany, the division was followed by many of the families of its members, fearful of the approaching Red Army. By December divisional strength was over 22,000 men – but its total weaponry came to just 50 machine guns and 2000 rifles. More equipment arrived over the next month, but the approaching Russians meant that the training ground had to be abandoned early in February 1945. The division, little more than a rabble, retreated to Austria where it surrendered to the Americans.

The second SS division raised in Hungary was the 26th *Waffen-Grenadier Division der SS Hungaria*. Its formation was ordered at the end of November 1944, based around a battalion of former Hungarian Army mountain troops which had been redesignated as the 26th *Waffen-Schibataillon der SS*. By Christmas 1944,

some 8000 men had been mustered, the majority – about 5000 – being civilian recruits or draftees with no prior military experience. In January 1945 around 15,000 men were transferred to Poland for training. Short of supplies and food but issued with weapons, the troops clashed with Polish partisans before the massive Soviet winter offensive forced the still untrained division to make a headlong retreat towards southern Germany.

On 8 January, a Hungarian assault unit was formed by merging the remnants of two ski battalions. The 1st *Ungarische SS-Sturmjäger Regiment* was assigned to the IV SS Panzer Corps and saw action with the 5th *SS-Panzer Division Wiking* and the German Army's 3rd Panzer Division. Fought to a standstill and without ammunition or supplies, the regiment split up into small battlegroups which retreated into Austria.

The German Army was finally driven out of Hungary by the Soviets in April 1945. The war cost the lives of half a million Hungarians, and 40 per cent of the nation's material resources were destroyed. The provisions of the Treaty of Trianon were reinstated and Hungary was forced to pay a large indemnity.

CROATIA

DATE OF OCCUPATION: APRIL 1941
NUMBER OF VOLUNTEERS: 20,000
MAIN SS UNITS INCLUDING VOLUNTEERS: 13th Waffen-Gebirgs Division der SS *Handschar* (kroatische Nr. 1); 23rd Waffen-Gebirgs Division der SS *Kama* (kroatische Nr. 2)

Germany's assault on Yugoslavia, launched on 6 April 1941, was the first step in Adolf Hitler's determination to take his revenge on a state which had stood out against Nazi political pressure. Yugoslavia was an artificial state, formed out of fragments of the Austro-Hungarian and Ottoman Empires. Internal rivalries between Serbs and Croats,

Orthodox Christians and Catholics, Muslims and Christians, and communists and nationalists made breaking the nation into its constituent parts a relatively easy task. Croatia, largely Catholic, had designs on parts of Serbia and Bosnia-Herzegovina. It already had a pro-German nationalist/fascist party in the shape of the *Ustase*, led by Ante Pavelič. Following the German victory, Yugoslavia was dismembered and

Below: The German puppet state of Croatia provided two infantry divisions to fight under German Army control on the Eastern Front, but as the partisan war in Yugoslavia grew, the units had more than enough work to do at home.

Chetniks, fought with either side depending on circumstances. The Croatian *Ustase* set up a concentration camp system every bit as harsh as their German mentors. Paveliç and the *Ustase* now launched a genocidal campaign against the Serbian and Jewish populations under his control throughout Croatia and Bosnia-Herzegovina. *Ustase* thugs slaughtered tens of thousands of Serbs in Croatia, often forcing them into their Orthodox churches and burning them alive. Other Serbs were given the choice of conversion to Roman Catholicism or death. On 17 April, Croatia declared war on the British, thus making Croatia a formal Axis partner. Following the German invasion of the USSR, Paveliç and his government offered the services

divided among the victors – Germany, Italy, Hungary and Bulgaria. Croatia was granted independence as an Axis puppet state under Paveliç. As a reward for supporting the Axis, Hitler ceded Bosnia-Herzegovina to Croatia.

The Germans might have thought that they had conquered the Balkans, but nobody had told the locals. The transfer of Germany's élite combat troops to the Russian Front was the signal for the start of one of the most brutal, most bitterly fought partisan campaigns the world has ever seen. Part of the problem was that it was several wars in one. The Croat puppet state was heavily involved, as were large numbers of German troops. Fascists from Croatia were on the side of the Germans, while Tito's communist guerrillas were on the other. The Serbian royalist forces, called

of Croatian troops to the *Wehrmacht*. Hitler and the German high command agreed to the offer, requesting that ground troops be recruited and sent to join the 'battle of freedom-loving nations against Communism', with air and naval units following once they could be trained to an adequate level. On 2 July, Paveliç called for volunteers, hoping for around 4000 to make up an infantry regiment. But in less than a fortnight, nearly 10,000 Croats had stepped forward, and it was easy for the Germans to select the best volunteers to make up a large infantry regiment.

Kroatischen Infanterie-Regiment 369

Established on 16 July 1941, the volunteer regiment was given the German Army title of *Verstarken Kroatischen Infanterie-Regiment 369*, or 369th

Reinforced Croatian Infantry Regiment. The regiment had 3895 officers, NCOs and men. The unit was issued with German uniforms and used German rank insignia. The only national insignia was a red and white chequered armshield surmounted with the title *Hrvatska* (Croatia), and a similar helmet badge. A training and replacement battalion was also set up at Stokerau in Austria. After three weeks of training and equipping at Dollersheim in Germany, the regiment entrained for Dongena in Bessarabia, from where it began a 35-day, 750km (466 mile) forced march to reach the front lines at Budniskaja in the Ukraine. Assigned to the 100th *Jäger* Division early in October, the regiment went into action on the 13th of that month. Over the next year the regiment fought in all of the German campaigns in the Ukraine. The first major reinforcements arrived on 26 August 1942, and the regiment was withdrawn to rest and refit.

Debacle at Stalingrad

At the end of September, the Croatian regiment received orders to join the German Sixth Army, then fighting through the suburbs of Stalingrad. The 369th Regiment was the only non-German *Wehrmacht* unit to take part in the battle through the city. Losses were heavy – by 13 October it was down to 983 men in one weak battalion and two weak companies. Losses grew even worse as the Croats took part in the ferocious, no-quarter, hand-to-hand fighting around the *Krasny Oktyabr* (Red October) tractor factory. By 3 November, numbers had dropped to under 200, with nine machine guns and six anti-tank guns. Although some reinforcements arrived from Stokerau, these were not enough to take the regiment up to even battalion strength. On 16 January 1943, the Soviets launched a major attack on the Croatian position. On 23 January, 18 wounded Croats were flown out of Stalingrad – the last to leave alive. The rest of the regiment's surviving members were killed in battle, or sent as prisoners on the long death march to Siberia after Stalingrad's fall.

Those lucky enough to have been sent back wounded in the previous months were used as a core around which a new Croatian formation would be built. Its origins dated back to 1941, following the success of the 369th Regiment in German service. The

Wehrmacht decided to raise a Croatian division, which began to form on 21 August 1942. Training battalion personnel and about 1000 former members of the 369th Regiment were joined by fresh volunteers from Croatia. The division took the German Army title 369.*Infanterie-Division (kroat.)*, but was more commonly known by its members as the *Vrazja*, or 'Devil's', Division.

Partisan war

Instead of heading for the Eastern Front, however, it was sent back home to Croatia, where the partisan war had become a major factor in German planning. In January 1943 it was decided that the situation in Croatia was becoming critical due to the communist partisan uprisings in the region, and the division was instead to be used in the Balkans rather than on the Eastern Front. Upon arrival in Croatia, the division had approximately 14,000 men in its ranks. Over the next year, the division was heavily engaged in northern Bosnia, taking part in a number of major anti-partisan battles. Tens of thousands of partisans were killed, but losses on the Axis side were also heavy, and the operations were unable to destroy the guerrilla movement. Late in January 1945, the partisans launched a major offensive against Mostar, and in February the 369th was forced to make a fighting retreat through Croatia towards Austria. On 11 May 1945, the 1000 or so survivors surrendered to the British, who promptly handed them back to the partisans. Most were executed immediately.

In January 1943, the German Army formed a second Croatian division at Dollersheim in Germany. Intended to fight in the partisan war in the Balkans, it had a German officer and NCO cadre. Designated the 373.*Infanterie-Division (kroat.)*, it was known as the *Tigar*, or 'Tiger', Division by its members. Sent to northern Bosnia in the summer of 1943, it was deployed in an operational area between the Adriatic coast of Croatia and Sarajevo. Most of its combat operations took place around Banja Luka and Bihac. By December 1944, the 373rd had lost heavily in the defence of Knin, and in January 1945 it retreated towards Bihac, were it became part of the German XV Mountain Corps. At the end of the war survivors surrendered to the partisans west of Sisak.

Above: The Croatian Naval Legion operated with the *Kriegsmarine*'s light naval forces in the Black Sea. By 1943, however, the legion had been broken up and its members had been drafted as replacements aboard German vessels in the Adriatic.

Eight months after the Tiger Division had been established, the *Wehrmacht* formed a third Croatian division, again at Dollersheim. Given the title of 392. *Infanterie-Division (kroat.)*, it was given the nickname *Plava*, or 'Blue', Division. As with the 373rd Division, the officers were mainly Germans, as were the bulk of the NCOs. The 392nd Division operated from southern Slovenia along the Adriatic coast as far south as the city of Knin. The division fought mostly in northern Croatia, both on the mainland and on the many islands along the coast. Like the other German/Croat divisions, the 392nd suffered severely at partisan hands in the last three months of the war. On 24 April, the Germans released all Croatian nationals from service before surrendering to the partisans north of Fiume (now Rijeka).

Air units

Part of Croatia's initial offer to the Nazis in April 1941 were air and naval volunteer units. Croats who had formerly served in the Yugoslav Air Force volunteered for the air legion in large numbers, and on 15 July its recruits set off for Germany for training. Two fighter flights were established at Furth and Herzogen airfields. By September 1941, pilots and groundcrew had completed training. The unit was issued with Messerschmitt Bf 109s, and on 6 October arrived at Poltava, where they became part of *Jagdgeschwader* (JG) 52.

Over the next two and a half years, 15.*(kroatische)*/JG 52 fought over southern Russia and the Ukraine. Its one thousandth mission was flown on 21 June 1942, by which time the unit had accounted for 53 Soviet aircraft. The score had risen to more than 280 when the squadron was recalled to Croatia in the summer of 1944. Losses incurred were an incredibly low two planes and five pilots. Equipped with Dornier Do 17s, the legion's bomber squadron was attached to *Kampfgeschwader* (KG) 53. Trained at *Kampfflieger*

Schule 3, in Greifswald, it was sent to the front at the end of October 1941. The bombers were attached to Army Group North, and in just over a year of operations flew nearly 1250 sorties. The squadron was dissolved at the end of 1942, its personnel and aircraft being transferred from the *Luftwaffe* back to the Croatian Air Force.

Himmler's Muslim experiment

During the dismemberment of Yugoslavia following the German invasion of 1941, Croatia claimed the former Austro-Hungarian province of Bosnia-Herzegovina. Something of a melting pot of history, the province was a volatile ethnic and religious mix, including Catholic Croats, Orthodox Serbs as well as Muslims of Croatian, Bosnian and Albanian ancestry. Himmler was fascinated by Islam. He believed that Muslims would make excellent shock troops, since he understood their faith offered them a place in paradise if they gave their lives against an enemy. He also supported the crackpot Nazi theory that Croatians were not Slavs, but were descended from the Aryan Goths. As a result of his beliefs, Himmler advocated the formation of a European Muslim division, which was approved by Hitler on 13 February 1943. It was not approved of by Ante Paveliç, who felt that the SS was poaching on his preserves, but there was little that the Croatian Government could do.

The division began forming on 5 March 1943, and reached its full strength of at least 20,000 men by July. Not all were Muslim volunteers, however. Several thousand *Volksdeutsche* and Catholic Croats were included, and initial Muslim enthusiasm quickly fell off, so numbers had to be made up by conscription.

Originally known as the *Kroatische SS-Freiwilligen Division*, it was turned into a mountain unit and became known as the *Kroatische SS-Freiwilligen Gebirgs Division*. In an attempt to appease the Bosnian members (who did not like Croats), it was renamed the 13th *SS-Freiwilligen Bosnien-Herzogowina Gebirgs Division (Kroatien)*, before eventually receiving its final name of 13th *Waffen-Gebirgs Division der SS Handschar (kroatische Nr.1)* in May 1944.

The name came from the Croat word for a curved scimitar-like sword traditionally associated with Bosnia, the *Handzar* (spelt *Handschar* in German). The division wore regular SS-issue uniforms. The divisional collar patch showed an arm holding a *Handschar* over a swastika. A red and white Croatian shield was worn on the left arm, and the divisional headgear was a traditional Muslim fez. Non-Muslims wore standard SS mountain caps.

In spite of Himmler's belief that Muslims would make good shock troops, the *Handschar* Division had a poor disciplinary record. However, the division could fight – as long as they were in Bosnia, protecting their

The Croatian Naval Legion

The Croatian Naval Legion was formed at the same time as the air legion. The Italians opposed a Croatian naval force operating in the Adriatic, so the naval volunteers became part of the *Kriegsmarine*. The 350-strong Croatian Naval Legion arrived at Varna on the Black Sea on 17 July 1941, and began training on German minesweepers and U-boats. On 30 September 1941 the unit moved to Gensicek in the USSR, where it became operational as the *Kriegsmarine*'s 23rd Minesweeping Flotilla. Unable to man their ships over the winter, the sailors dug trenches and fought as infantry to defend the town

against a number of Russian attacks. They eventually put to sea in April 1942, and were operational until the end of the year, when they went home to Croatia for rest and recuperation, before returning to Varna in Bulgaria. During their tour of duty in the Crimea, the Sea of Azov and the Black Sea, the Croatians managed to recruit several Ukrainians, former Soviet sailors, some of whom brought their ships with them. In October 1943, the legion was sent to Trieste, where it was broken up and used as drafts to reinforce the crews of *Kriegsmarine* vessels operating in the Adriatic.

homes against communist forces. In spite of the less than outstanding performance of the *Handschar* Division, Himmler persisted in trying to form Muslim fighting units.

In June 1944 Hitler approved the raising of a second Croatian *Waffen*-SS division, which would be given the honour title *Kama* after another type of Turkish sword. The 23rd *Waffen-Gebirgs Division der SS Kama (kroatische Nr. 2)* began to take shape in July and August of 1944. Officer and NCO cadres were German, to which were added several units transferred from the *Handschar* Division. It was sent to the Bachska region (annexed by Hungary in 1941) for training. In September 1944, with the formation's basic training barely complete, the advancing Red Army moved perilously close to the training area. The SS decided to disband the division late in September, and its units began to disperse. The official disbandment took place in October 1944, and most of the divisional elements went to the 31st SS Division. Muslims were ordered to report to the *Handschar* Division, and a large minority deserted on the way.

On 15 July 1943, a German-Croatian police force under German police and SS command was announced. Intended for internal security operations, the force grew rapidly until by the spring of 1944 there were 15 battalions organized into five *Polizei Freiwilligen-Regiments*. A further 15 independent *Polizei-Freiwilligen Kroatien* battalions were raised, eventually combined, nominally, as the *Gendarmerie Division Croatia*. However, they were scattered all over the Balkans and were never gathered into a single unit. A total of 32,000 Croatians served in these German police units.

Some Croatians fought in the Italian Army. On 26 July 1941, the Croatian Army established the 'Light Transport Brigade' which was to serve in the Italian Eighth Army in Russia. It was wiped out on 21 December 1942.

After the destruction of the brigade, the Italian-sponsored 'Croatian Legion', an 1800-man infantry regiment, was established near Lake Garda. With the Italian surrender, its personnel were transferred to the Croatian divisions in the German Army.

SERBIA

DATE OF OCCUPATION: APRIL 1941
NUMBER OF VOLUNTEERS: 10,000
MAIN SS UNITS INCLUDING VOLUNTEERS: Serbisches Freiwilligen Korps

The war in the Balkans was one of the most fiercely fought and merciless campaigns of the war, and it was also one of the most complex. The Croat puppet state was heavily involved, as were large numbers of German troops. At its most simplistic, the Italians, Germans and fascist Croats were on one side, while Tito's communist guerrillas were on the other. The Serbian royalist forces, called *Chetniks*, fought either side depending on circumstances. Croat fought Serb, communist fought royalist, and Muslim fought Christian. The Croatian *Ustase* killed hundreds of thousands of Serbs, Roma and Jews, running a

concentration camp system every bit as harsh as that established by the Germans.

The *Waffen*-SS played a major role in the anti-partisan and pacification campaigns, which were conducted with a medieval level of brutality. This was in part caused by the frustration of not being able to identify the attackers from among the population, but also by a sadistic streak that exists in many people and to which war often gives licence. Most of the local troops who fought under German colours were Croats or Bosnian and Albanian Muslims, but a number of Serbs also fought directly for the Germans.

Serbian Volunteer Command
In September 1941, Dimitri Ljotiae, head of the fascist *Zbor* movement, formed a volunteer body to fight communist partisans. The unit was known initially as

the *Srpska Dobrovoljacki Komanda*, or Serbian Volunteer Command, and most of its fighters were *Zbor* members, but the unit also numbered some nationalist *Chetniks* on its roster. Renamed the *Srpski Dobrovoljacki Korpus* (SDK, or Serbian Volunteer Corps) in 1943, it consisted originally of five 500-man battalions, usually divided into three companies, to which were added an armoured car battalion, a cavalry squadron and an air flight with six light aircraft which were used for reconnaissance.

Equipment was mixed – the armoured car unit operated about 20 obsolete or war-weary vehicles, including pre-war Czech and French light tanks.

SS Serbian Volunteer Corps formed

By the middle of 1944 the SDK had grown to include five 1200-man infantry regiments and an artillery battalion. A sixth regiment, the 2.*gvozdeni puk*, or 2nd

Above: Uniforms gave little indication of loyalties in the Balkans. Serbian SS units wore pre-war royalist uniforms, while *Chetniks* often wore a mixture of German and Yugoslav gear, depending on who they were fighting against.

Iron Regiment, was raised in June, increasing total strength to approximately 9000 men. In November 1944, the unit was taken over by the *Waffen*-SS, and was renamed the *Serbisches Freiwilligen Korps*, or Serbian Volunteer Corps. Although armed by the SS, the unit continued to fight in Royal Yugoslav Army uniforms.

In March 1945, surviving members of the corps retreated into Slovenia with the *Chetnik Shumadia* Division. Retreating further into Austria, the corps surrendered to the British. Most of the corps members were returned to Yugoslavia, where they were executed by the communists.

ALBANIA

DATE OF OCCUPATION: **1943**
NUMBER OF VOLUNTEERS: **7000**
MAIN **SS** UNITS INCLUDING VOLUNTEERS: **21st SS Waffen-Gebirgs Division der SS** *Skanderbeg* **(albanische Nr. 1)**

Albania's contribution to Germany's war effort differed somewhat from that of any other nation. Part of the Muslim Ottoman Empire for five centuries, Albania declared its independence in 1912, after the First Balkan War. During the Paris Peace Conference of 1912, a plan to divide the country among its neighbours was defeated by American opposition. The collapse of the Ottoman Empire left the Balkans in chaos, however, and the Albanians asked Italy for assistance in maintaining their country's independence. They got more than assistance, however, once Mussolini's Fascists came to power. Italian interference in Albanian affairs grew over the next decade, in spite of the efforts of King Zog, a Muslim clan chief who came to the throne in 1928 when the country became a monarchy. In 1939, Italian troops occupied Albania, overthrowing the king, and soon afterwards the kingdom was annexed by the Italians.

War declared

Albania became a war front with the Italian attack on Greece in 1941. Germany had to intervene when the Italians became bogged down by dogged Greek resistance, in the process occupying Yugoslavia. The Axis powers planned to dismember Yugoslavia, setting up puppet regimes in Croatia and Serbia. As part of the process they intended to create a 'Greater Albania' by transferring the Kosovo-Metohija region of Serbia, along with territory in southwest Montenegro and southern Serbia (now part of Macedonia), to Albania.

During the occupation of Kosovo-Metohija, the Germans recruited a local paramilitary police force consisting of 1000 Kosovar Albanians and a similar number drawn from the Albanian paramilitary force known as the *Vulnetara*. These assisted the Germans in the 'ethnic cleansing' which followed, during which tens of thousands of Serbs, Jews, gypsies and other non-Albanians and non-Muslims were arrested, interned, deported or murdered. The Serbs were a particular target for the paramilitaries: Serbian homes and Orthodox Christian churches were looted and destroyed. Albanian nationalists, members of the *Balli Kombetar* (BK, or National Union), were encouraged by the Germans and Italians to think of Albanian Kosovo as part of a Greater Albania.

With the overthrow of Mussolini, communist and nationalist partisans rose against the Fascist regime. Italian military positions and police units were overwhelmed by partisan attacks, and the communists seized most of southern Albania's cities while nationalists seized control of the north. A brief truce between the factions was swiftly broken, and a bitter civil war began – a civil war which was made more complicated by German occupation.

German occupation

In September 1943, following Italy's surrender to the Allies, Germany occupied Albania. *Fallschirmjäger* seized the capital, Tirana, before the guerrillas could, and the German Army marched into the country, swiftly driving the guerrilla forces into the hills. The Germans sent the 100th *Jäger* Division from Greece, the 297th Infantry Division from Serbia and the 1st Mountain Division. However, the Germans were fully occupied defending the coastline, and more troops were needed for operations in the interior. Berlin organized an Albanian government, police and military, and sought to win over the nationalists by supporting the annexation of Kosovo. Large numbers of BK paramilitaries fought on the German side against the communists, though matters were complicated further at the end of 1943 by the rise of a third major guerrilla force in the north. Known as 'Legality', this group wanted to continue the annexation of Kosovo, and was opposed to the communists, the nationalists and the Germans.

**Left: An SS man is
captured by Serbian
partisans. The SS were
targets for partisan groups
all over Europe, and
prospects for an SS man
taken prisoner were not
good. Many of the foreign
volunteers who surrendered
to partisan groups at the
end of the war were
summarily executed.**

studies carried out by
Italian Fascists claimed
to have proved that the
Ghegs, the people who
occupied   northern
Albania and Kosovo-
Metohija, were Aryans.
The 21st *Waffen-Gebirgs
Division   der   SS
Skanderbeg (albanische
Nr. 1)* was formed in
April 1944. It included
300 Albanian Muslims
who had been transferred
from   the   *Handschar*
Division, joined by 6500
new Albanian recruits

One of Himmler's beliefs was the Muslims would make good shock troops. The 13th *Waffen-Gebirgs Division der SS Handschar* was raised from Bosnian Muslims in 1943. However, the division had a poor record – its troops mutinied in training, killing several of their German cadre members. Most had joined the division in order to protect their homes and families from *Ustase/Chetnik* and partisan attacks. The fascist Croat puppet government disapproved of the formation, since they felt that the SS recruitment in Bosnia violated their sovereignty. Needless to say, the division had a patchy combat record.

Nevertheless, Himmler persisted in his attempts to create an Islamic SS unit. Himmler wanted to use Albanian manpower to form two *Waffen*-SS divisions. He was especially keen, on this since anthropological

(two-thirds of whom were from Kosovo). To this Albanian core were added German troops and *Kriegsmarine* sailors who no longer had ships to crew. Leadership was provided by a cadre of *Volksdeutsche* officers, NCOs and enlisted men transferred from the 7th *SS-Freiwilligen Gebirgs Division Prinz Eugen*, which at that time was carrying out anti-partisan operations in Bosnia-Herzegovina. The majority of the division's Albanians were Bektashi and Sunni Muslims, but several hundred Albanian Catholics also served.

Unit markings

The SS *Hauptamt* designed a distinctive arm patch for the division, consisting of a black double-headed eagle on a red background, the national symbol of Albania. The division was named after George Kastrioti

Skanderbeg (1405–68). Brought up as a hostage in the court of Sultan Murat II, Kastrioti was named Iskander Bey for his prowess in battle. Breaking away from the Turks and becoming a Christian, Skanderbeg led Albania's ultimately unsuccessful fight for independence from the Ottoman Empire.

Albanian recruits wore a white fez-style cap, the national attire of the Ghegs of northern Albania. The SS also issued grey headgear in the same style, with the *Totenkopf* sewn on the front below the Nazi eagle and swastika.

Ethnic cleansing

Ostensibly intended to fight partisans, the division was in fact used to clear Kosovo of 'undesirables', defined as Orthodox Serbs, Jews, gypsies – in fact, anybody who was not Albanian. Many were killed or driven from their homes, while a large number of Kosovo's estimated 500 Jews were deported and died at Belsen. However, although many of *Skanderbeg*'s members enthusiastically played their parts in atrocities against Serbs and Jews, a large number proved to be very reluctant recruits. There were as many as 3500 desertions in the unit's first three months of existence.

By the beginning of October, divisional strength had fallen to just 3504 men, and it was disbanded in December. The remaining troops fought as *Kampfgruppe Skanderbeg* before the German cadre was transferred back to *SS-Gebirgsjäger Regiment* 14 of the *Prinz Eugen* Division.

BULGARIA

DATE OF OCCUPATION: ALLY
NUMBER OF VOLUNTEERS: 600?
MAIN SS UNITS INCLUDING VOLUNTEERS: Waffen-Grenadier Regiment der SS (bulgarisches Nr. 1); SS-Panzer Zerstörer Regiment (bulgarisches)

Bulgaria was a full member of the Axis, but it played no real part in the war on the Eastern Front. Bulgaria had been enticed into an active role initially by the return of territory from Romania in 1940. On 1 March 1941, Bulgaria signed on to the Tripartite Treaty. As a result, the Bulgarian Government permitted the Germans to use its naval facilities, air bases and rail network. A day later, German troops bound for Yugoslavia and Greece began staging through the country. Bulgarian troops were primarily used on anti-partisan operations in the occupied Balkans.

Ultimately, seven Bulgarian divisions were employed in Yugoslavia. As a reward, Bulgaria was ceded the Greek territory of Thrace and much of Macedonia. In December 1941, Bulgaria declared war on Britain and the United States – but refused German pressure to participate in the war against Russia. This was because there was considerable pro-Soviet sentiment in

Bulgaria, and not exclusively from the communists. In August 1943, the death of Tsar Boris saw power being transferred to a council of regents who were in most respects German puppets, but by 1944 it was obvious that Germany was losing the war and the regime began to look for a way out. In August the rapidly advancing Soviet Army prompted Bulgaria to announce its withdrawal from the war. German troops were asked to leave and Bulgarian troops serving in Greece and Yugoslavia were called home. On 16 September, the Soviet Army entered Sofia. Less than a week before, Bulgaria declared war on Germany and took an active part in operations against the Germans in Yugoslavia, Hungary and Austria.

At the same time several hundred Bulgarians working in Germany, most of whom had been supporters of the old regime, offered their services to the *Wehrmacht*. Up to 600 were accepted and went into training as the *Waffen-Grenadier Regiment der SS (bulgarisches Nr. 1)*. It was hoped that this would form the core of a Bulgarian *Waffen-Grenadier* division, but this was never achieved. The unit participated in some of the final battles of the war, being renamed the *SS-Panzer Zerstörer Regiment (bulgarisches)* in April 1945.

LITHUANIA

DATE OF OCCUPATION: JUNE 1941
NUMBER OF VOLUNTEERS: 50,000 (MAINLY NON-SS POLICE UNITS)
MAIN SS UNITS INCLUDING VOLUNTEERS: NONE

Lithuania, the southernmost of the three Baltic States, had a different relationship with Germany than did Latvia and Estonia. Lithuania shared a frontier with Germany, and had been engaged in a long dispute with the Germans over possession of the port of Memel (Klaipeda in Lithuanian). In the 1930s Lithuanians imprisoned ethnic German Nazis. By

1938, most of these had been released ready to welcome the Germans who seized the port in 1939.

In the wake of the Nazi-Soviet pact which had carved up Poland, the Baltic States were declared to be in the Soviet sphere of influence, and there was little opposition when on 15 June 1940 the Soviets took complete control of Lithuania, including the capital, Vilna (Vilnius), which had been part of Poland until October 1939. Numerous underground groups formed in reaction to the Soviets, one of the most extremely nationalist of which was the *Lietuviu Aktyvistu Frontas* (LAF, or Lithuanian Activist Front).

The Lithuanian Activist Front

Strong supporters of the Nazis, the LAF also were violently anti-Semitic, claiming that the Jews in Lithuania were profiting from the Soviet occupation. Some 150,000 Jews lived in Lithuania between the wars, in a community which had been in existence since the fourteenth century. Another 100,000 were added to the total when Vilnius was returned from Polish control in 1939. Jews had gained some freedoms under the Soviets, but their cultural and economic activities were deemed to be anti-Soviet, and 7000 Jews were arrested and deported to Siberia in June 1941, along with 10,000 other Lithuanians.

Soviet oppression caused real hatred in the Lithuanian population, which

Left: A Lithuanian member of a *Polizei Bataillon*. Although there were no Lithuanian SS formations, some 38 Police Battalions were formed. A few Lithuanian *Volksdeutsche* served in German units, but they joined as individuals.

meant that when the Germans invaded on 22 June 1941, over 100,000 Lithuanians took up arms against the retreating Soviets. Much of Lithuania was liberated even before the arrival of the Germans. Unfortunately, organizations like the LAF were prominent in these guerrilla groups, and they saw no difference between attacking Jews and attacking Russians.

Even before the Germans were in control of the country, Lithuanian nationalists were carrying out anti-Jewish pogroms. These nationalists were soon joined by *Einsatzkommando 3*, and between them the Lithuanians and the Nazis managed to kill the majority of country Jews. City Jews, being more important to the economic life of the country, were herded into ghettos to be dealt with later. By the end of 1941, only 40,000 out of a quarter of a million Jews remained in Lithuania. Some 20,000 had fled abroad, and a similar number had escaped to the Russians. The rest had been liquidated.

Lithuanians served as auxilliaries to the Ordnungspolizei *in the occupied areas of the Soviet Union, where they often supported the Einsatzkommandos'* murderous 'cleansing' operations.

Police battalions

There was considerable support for the Germans in the early months of the occupation. Large numbers of young men came forward to join the fight against the hated Russians. Many had served with the Soviet 29th Light Infantry Corps – the former Lithuanian Army, which had been absorbed into the Red Army in 1940, and which had deserted *en masse* on the outbreak of war. As in the other Baltic States, the first units to come under German control were the irregular groups who had formed to fight the Soviets.

The first unit to be formed was known as the *Lituanische Hunterschaften*. This provided the basis for the formation of the self-defence units known *Selbschutz-Bataillonen*. Renamed as *Schutzmannschaft-Bataillonen*, or *Schumas*, when they came under German police control, they were reformed into regular *Polizie-Bataillonen* in May 1943. A total of 35 such battalions were formed, usually with a strength of between 500 and 600 men. They were initially used for security duties, but later in the war were used increasingly in combat roles. They were primarily

assigned to rear areas, but as the Soviets drew nearer to Lithuania, they also saw service fighting the Soviets directly.

Lithuanian police battalions served all over the Eastern Front, from the Baltic to the Black Sea. They saw combat at Demyansk, Volkhov, Lake Ilmen, Opotschka and in the Courland. One battalion, the 7th, even managed to break out from Stalingrad, losing half their number in the process. Since they served as auxiliaries to the *Ordnungspolizei* in the occupied areas of the Soviet Union, the Lithuanian police battalions were often used to support the *Einsatzgruppen* of the SD. Rather than working for the Army, units engaged in these murderous actions took their orders from the *Reichsicherheits-hauptamt* (RSHA, or Reich Main Security Office), or from the *Höhere SS-Polizei Führer* (HSSPF) of the *Ostland* regions.

The Lithuanian Defence Corps

Unlike its Estonian and Latvian neighbours, Lithuania never provided Germany with a national SS legion during World War II. This was in part because Himmler considered that the Lithuanians were the least reliable of the Baltic races. Unlike Protestant Latvia and Estonia, who had a long history of relations with Germany, Lithuania was largely Catholic, like the despised Poles with whom the Lithuanians had been allied many times over the centuries. The Lithuanian authorities would not agree to allow any unit to be formed which was not Lithuanian-led, and they also insisted that any such unit must only be used within Lithuania. The Germans finally agreed in February 1944, and a Lithuanian defensive force was formed, though not as part of the SS. It was known as the *Schutzkorps Litauen*, or Lithuanian Defence Corps. On

Opposite: A *Polizei* patrol takes a suspected 'bandit' – the standard propaganda term for a partisan – into custody. Lithuanians served with such units in Poland, Byelorussia and the Ukraine, and they also provided rear-area security in the Baltic region.

Above: SS men enter a Soviet village. Although not part of the *Waffen*-SS, Lithuanian police units sometimes came under SS control when they were thrown into combat in the desperate struggle to hold back the Red Army in the last year of the war.

16 February an appeal went out for volunteers, and although none were too keen to serve the Germans, the Lithuanians were still eager to fight the Russians. Over 19,000 men volunteered, rather than the expected 5000.

Rebellion and desertion

The Germans wanted to use the volunteers to reinforce *Wehrmacht* units, but Lithuanian opposition meant that they were formed into 13 police battalions instead. The *Schutzkorps* began training in March 1944. Less than three weeks later, on 22 March, the Lithuanians were again offended when Field Marshal Walter Model, commander of Army Group North, requested Lithuanian units to protect *Luftwaffe* airfields in Russia.

The last straw came in May, when the Germans announced a general mobilization, and 14 Lithuanian police battalions were placed under *Wehrmacht* command. Near mutiny was followed by massive desertion – 16,000 out of the original 19,000 in the *Schutzkorps*.

The *Schutzkorps* was disbanded and the remaining 3000 men were drafted into *Luftwaffe* Flak batteries. Five armed construction battalions were also formed in 1943, attached to German pioneer units in Army

Group North. These were asked to join the *Waffen*-SS, and something under a half actually joined up as individuals.

Soviet pressure

As the Soviets approached the Baltic States towards the end of 1944, the Germans formed three Lithuanian regiments by grouping three or four Lithuanian police battalions into regimental-sized units known as *Lituanische Freiwilligen Infanterie Regimenter*. Later, as Soviet forces began to enter Lithuania, the Germans formed the Fatherland Defence Force. This was an amalgamation of small groups of retreating Lithuanian

troops organized into two *Kampfgruppen*, under overall German command.

After heavy fighting and crippling losses, the 1000 or so survivors were gathered in East Prussia to form a new unit known as the Lithuanian Engineer Battalion. Caught in the path of the oncoming Soviet juggernaut, the battalion was totally destroyed in February and March 1945.

After World War II ended, tens of thousands of armed Lithuanians remained active, waging a guerrilla war against the Soviet occupation forces well into the 1950s. The last of the Lithuanian partisan forces are thought to have been wiped out in 1956.

POLAND

DATE OF OCCUPATION: SEPTEMBER 1939
NUMBER OF VOLUNTEERS: NONE
MAIN SS UNITS INCLUDING VOLUNTEERS: NONE

Poland suffered more under German occupation than any other country bar the Soviet Union, and proportionately it suffered even more than the Soviets. After the conquest of 1939, Poland was dismembered. The west was annexed directly into the Greater German Reich, the area around Danzig being absorbed into West Prussia and the rest becoming part of *Gau* Posen. The east came under Soviet control under the secret non-aggression pact between Hitler and Stalin. The remaining central portion of the country was controlled by the *Generalgouvernement*, which also took over the Soviet-controlled areas after Operation *Barbarossa* in 1941.

Poland suffered cruelly. One in every six Poles died, mostly as a result of brutal repression by German security forces. The Poles take pride in the fact that they did not collaborate with the Germans – possibly the only occupied country not to do so. However, there were some Polish citizens who volunteered to work for the enemy. The largest group were the *Volksdeutsche*, people of ethnic German descent whose ancestors had lived all over Eastern Europe for centuries. The Nazis

looked on the *Volksdeutsche* as potential citizens of the coming Greater Germany – and as a source of man-power for the expanding *Wehrmacht* and *Waffen*-SS.

Volksdeutsche formations

As early as the first crossing of the border by German troops on 1 September 1939, small groups of *Volksdeutsche* in western Poland (which had been part of Germany until the end of World War I) formed local militia groups. These were later organized into self-protection units known as *Selbschutz*, these being the prototype for similar units set up in the Baltic and elsewhere in occupied Europe after June 1941.

Controlled by the SS, the *Selbschutz* units came under the direct control of the SS-*Hauptamt* and of Heydrich's infamous RSHA. They earned an unsavoury reputation in their few months of existence, and they were disbanded from the end of 1939 through until April 1940. Some 45,000 ethnic German Poles served in the *Selbschutz* units before they were ordered to be disbanded. Many of their members took service in other paramilitary organizations, including the NSKK, the *Generalgouvernement*'s labour office (the *Baudienst*) and in the police forces. Few, if any, Slavic Poles volunteered or were allowed to work as anything but slave labourers.

THE FOREIGN SS DIVISIONS

From its earliest days, the SS was a volunteer organization which saw itself as an elite within the Nazi state. Troops of the first SS divisions were exceptionally fit, and the first foreign recruits were expected to be of the same standard. However, by the middle of the war manpower shortages meant that to fill out newly forming units like the *Prinz Eugen* and the *Florian Geyer* divisions the SS had to accept recruits of a considerably lower standard.

Above: Russian volunteers man an anti-tank gun on the Eastern Front. By this time, in the winter of 1943, foreigners in Army units were being transferred to the SS to help fill out the large numbers of newly created *Waffen*-SS divisions.
Left: Before the war, the SS would only accept mature recruits. However, wartime needs meant that younger volunteers were sought, many of whom went straight from the *Hitler Jugend* after their seventeenth birthdays.

5th SS-Panzer Division *Wiking*

• *Nov 1940 – Jan 1941:* SS-Division (motorisierte) *Germania*   • *Jan 1941 – Nov 1942:* SS-Division (motorisierte) *Wiking*   • *Nov 1942 – Oct 1943:* SS-Panzergrenadier Division *Wiking*   • *Oct 1943 – May 1945:* 5th SS-Panzer Division *Wiking*

Wiking has not been accused of any war crimes, but the infamous Joseph Mengele served (briefly) in the Pioneer Battalion (where he was also awarded the Iron Cross) during his time in the *Waffen*-SS.

Initially authorized in May 1940 as *SS-Division (motorisierte) Germania*, the division was renamed within days, becoming the *SS-Division (motorisierte) Wiking*, to avoid confusion with the *Germania* Regiment of the SS-VT Division. The *Germania* Regiment would form the core of the new division, but it was intended that the bulk of the formation's personnel would be provided by Scandinavian volunteers – hence the name *Wiking*.

Joining the *Germania* Regiment in the division would be the *Nordland* and *Westland* SS Regiments. The first truly international division of the *Waffen*-SS, *Wiking* numbered Dutch, Danes, Norwegians, Finns, Walloons and Flemings among its personnel, together with a smattering of *Volksdeutsche* from the Balkans. However, in spite of the propaganda, which made much of its international nature, the bulk of the division's personnel (as much as 90 per cent) was German. Formation of the division began in the autumn of 1940, and by the time of the German invasion of Russia in June 1941 (Operation *Barbarossa*), *Wiking* was a fully fledged, fully trained SS motorized infantry division.

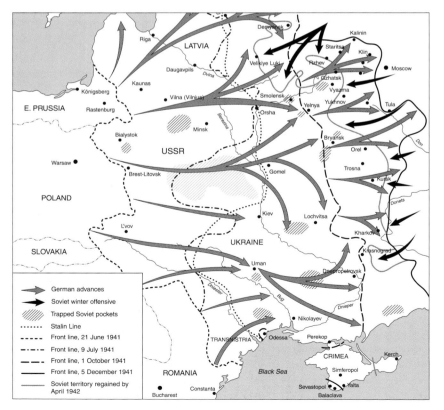

German advances
Soviet winter offensive
Trapped Soviet pockets
Stalin Line
Front line, 21 June 1941
Front line, 9 July 1941
Front line, 1 October 1941
Front line, 5 December 1941
Soviet territory regained by April 1942

Left: A map showing Operation *Barbarossa* and the subsequent Soviet counter-offensive of the winter of 1941–42. *Wiking* gained its first combat experience as part of Army Group South, attacking through the Ukraine. Following the invasion, the Germans' need for additional manpower led them to recruit foreign volunteers by employing anti-communist propaganda. The glamorous, hard-fighting image of the *Waffen*-SS attracted many 'Germanic' volunteers.

Opposite, right: A Tiger commander of the *Wiking* Division, April 1944. *Wiking* was created as a motorized infantry division, but was successively upgraded into a *Panzergrenadier* division and then into a fully fledged panzer division.

First battles

Wiking first saw action on 29 June 1941. Assigned to Army Group South, it took part in the fighting for Tarnopol in Galicia. In August 1941, the division was at the head of the army group as it fought to establish a bridgehead across the Dnieper River. Continuing the drive, *Wiking* fought its way through Dnepropetrovsk and on to Rostov. When the Germans were pushed out of Rostov by the first truly successful Red Army counter-attack, *Wiking* moved back to the line of the Mius River where it spent the winter months.

Although it suffered heavy losses, it achieved an excellent reputation, even earning the grudging respect of the Soviets in several battle reports for its pugnacious fighting spirit. Soviet commanders were always concerned to learn that their troops were facing the soldiers of the *Wiking* Division. When the Germans launched their major offensive in the summer of 1942, *Wiking* was again one of the spearhead divisions. It fought its way into and through the Caucasus, and would remain in the area until von Kleist's Army Group was forced to pull back after the fall of Stalingrad early in 1943. By this time it had been converted from a motorized infantry division to a *panzergrenadier*, or armoured infantry, division.

Individual elements of the *Wiking* Division were added and removed many times in its existence. As a replacement for the disbanded Finnish battalion of the *Nordland* Regiment, the Estonian *Narwa* Regiment was transferred to *Wiking*. The *Nordland* Regiment itself was detached to help establish another *Waffen*-SS division, providing the nucleus of the new *Nordland* Division.

The Korsun salient

Wiking avoided the cataclysmic battles at Kursk, serving further south with Fourth Panzer Army on the Don, fighting a defensive campaign through the summer and autumn of 1943. In October 1943, the division was again upgraded, being converted from a *panzergrenadier* division to a fully armoured panzer division. In the summer and autumn of 1943, the division fought in defensive operations in the area of Kharkov and the Dnieper River. By the end of 1943, *Wiking* was one of six divisions occupying a 96km (60 mile) salient at Korsun, on the east of the Dnieper.

Hitler had the highly unrealistic belief that the 56,000 men in the salient could thrust in an offensive towards Kiev. He had not reckoned on the Russians. General Konev's 2nd Ukrainian Front punched through the bridgehead lying between Kremenchug, which lay far to the southwest of Kharkov, and Dnepropetrovsk to the east of Kremenchug. Konev's objective was to form a wedge between First Panzer Army and Eighth Army. The latter was no match for the strong Soviet forces and was forced to pull back in the face of the steady advance of the 2nd Ukrainian Front.

In the north, things were no better, with ever more powerful Russian forces throwing the Germans out of Kiev on 6 November after they had established a bridgehead there. Russian pride was further restored with the recapture, after a temporary loss, of the town of Zhitomir on 20 November. Buildings there were reduced to rubble and the streets were littered with the burnt-out hulks of vehicles. Of considerable

compensation were the large supply dumps and foodstuff depots of Fourth Panzer Army which the Germans had established in the high summer of triumph two years before.

For all the efforts of the panzer units and the *Waffen*-SS, the truth was that the Soviet advance had become a flood, with the great winter offensive dealing the decisive blow. Not the least disastrous event was the overwhelming of Army Group Centre when, in mid-December, the Soviets burst out of the salient at Nevel in their progress southwest. Another knockout blow was delivered the following month by the Red Army in the north, forcing Army Group North to give up its encirclement of Leningrad.

The men of *Wiking* were assigned to territory where the prospects were bleak for the Germans. Four divisions were encircled in this flat countryside under snow with the temperature in Kirovograd itself at –20°C (–4°F). On 5 January 1944, Konev's 2nd Ukrainian Front launched its attack and took the city. A breakout was eventually achieved by 3rd Panzer Division with covering fire from the artillery; engineers and *panzergrenadiers* followed while the Russians were pinned down in local fighting. The recapture of Kirovograd still left unfinished business for the Russians. To the north lay the salient around Korsun

and Cherkassy which Hitler was determined to hold and which was defended by six and a half divisions with around 56,000 men. Manstein wanted to open the pocket, but Hitler insisted contact must be established with the beleaguered forces: the Dnieper line would be held, no matter the cost.

The German positions south of the Korsun bulge took the full bombardment. The Russian Fourth Guards and Fifty-Third Armies, soon followed by Fifth Tank Army, struck at the heart of the German line. From the north of the bulge came 1st Ukrainian Front with its massive armoured forces. By 28 January it had joined Konev's 2nd Ukrainian Front, which had advanced from the south. Men of *Wiking* were among the 60,000 trapped there. Being the only panzer unit in the pocket, *Wiking* spearheaded an attempt to break out. At the time, an independent foreign formation, *Wallonien*, was a part of *Wiking*. The division managed to break out, but casualties were heavy, and *Wiking* lost all of its armour and a great deal of other equipment in the process.

The end

The remnants of the division fought on as a *Kampfgruppe*, before being transferred to Poland where it would form the nucleus of a new 5th *SS-Panzer Division Wiking*. Because it was out of the line, it missed the massive Soviet summer offensive, perhaps the most powerful military attack in history, which smashed the German Eastern Front and virtually destroyed Army Group Centre. By the time *Wiking* was again in action, the Soviets had pushed all the way to the Vistula River and to Warsaw.

Along with the 3rd *SS-Panzer Division Totenkopf* and the Army's 19th Panzer Division, *Wiking* fought to stem the Soviet advance, stabilizing the front along the line of the Vistula. *Wiking* was withdrawn from Warsaw in December 1944 and transferred south to relieve 60,000 German soldiers and over 800,000 civilians trapped in the city of Budapest. *Wiking* pushed forward for two weeks, but could not penetrate the massed Soviet armies which were besieging the city. When this operation failed the division was withdrawn into Austria, where it fought in the final battles to defend Vienna in 1945. The division surrendered to the Soviets in May 1945.

Right: Waffen-SS soldiers advance through the smoke and flames rising from a Soviet T-34/76 tank and Zil truck, destroyed during the fighting near Cherkassy in the spring of 1943.

Opposite, left: A *Wiking* officer aims a Kar 98K rifle. On the defensive, *Wiking* remained in the Kharkov area into the winter of 1943. When the Soviets launched their winter offensive, *Wiking* was one of the units cut off in the Cherkassy pocket.

DIVISIONAL INFORMATION

Commanders
SS-Obergruppenführer Felix Steiner
(Jan 1940 – Jan 1943)
SS-Obergruppenführer Herbert Gille
(5 Jan 1943 – 8 Jun 1944)
SS-Oberführer Edmund Deisenhofer
(8 Jun 1944 – 8 Aug 1944)
SS-Standartenführer Rudolf Mühlenkamp
(8 Aug 1944 – 10 Sep 1944)
SS-Oberführer Karl Ullrich
(10 Sep 1944 – 5 May 1945)

Order of Battle
Stab der Division
SS-Panzergrenadier-Regiment 9 Germania
SS-Panzergrenadier-Regiment 10 Westland
SS-Panzergrenadier-Regiment Nordland
(Withdrawn from division in 1943)
Estnisches SS-Freiwilligen-Panzergrenadier-Bataillon
Narwa (Withdrawn in 1944)
Finnisches Freiwilligen-Bataillon der Waffen-SS

SS-Sturmbrigade Wallonien
SS-Panzer-Regiment 5
SS-Panzerjäger-Abteilung 5
SS-Sturmgeschütz-Abteilung 5
SS-Sturmgeschütz-Batterie 5
SS-Panzer-Artillerie-Regiment 5
SS-Flak-Abteilung 5
SS-Werfer-Abteilung 5
SS-Panzer-Nachrichten-Abteilung 5
SS-Panzer-Aufklärungs-Abteilung 5
SS-Panzer-Pionier-Bataillon 5
SS-Dina 5
SS-Instandsetzungs-Abteilung 5
SS-Wirtschafts-Bataillon 5
SS-Sanitäts-Abteilung 5
SS-Feldlazarett 5
SS-Kriegsberichter-Zug 5
SS-Feldgendarmerie-Trupp 5
SS-Feldersatz-Bataillon 5
I./SS-Panzergrenadier-Regiment 23 Norge
I./SS-Panzergrenadier-Regiment 24 Danmark

6th SS-Gebirgs Division *Nord*

- *Feb 1941:* SS-Kampfgruppe *Nord* • *Sep 1941:* SS-Division *Nord*
- *Sep 1942:* SS-Gebirgs Division *Nord* • *Oct 1943 – May 1945:* 6th SS-Gebirgs Division *Nord*

Although not a volunteer formation in the classic sense, the 6th SS Division, known as *Nord*, did have a significant foreign volunteer component.

In June 1940, the capitulation of Norway left the border with Finland and the USSR unguarded. To replace the two Norwegian infantry battalions in the area, the Germans decided to deploy SS units rather than regular army formations. The 9th *SS Totenkopf* *Standarte*, commanded by *SS-Obersturmbannführer* Ernst Deutsch, was ordered north, with the first unit – *SS Bataillon Reitz*, under the command of *SS-Obersturmbannführer* Wilhelm Reitz – arriving at Kirkenes in the late summer. In February 1941, two further SS regiments arrived in northern Norway: the 6th and 7th *SS Totenkopf Standarten*. Soon afterwards most of the 6th *Standarte* reinforced by elements of the 9th moved forward to defensive positions at Salla in

DIVISIONAL INFORMATION

Commanders

SS-Brigadeführer Karl Herrmann   (28 Feb 1941)
SS-Obergruppenführer Karl-Maria Demelhuber
                                          (15 May 1941)
SS-Obergruppenführer Matthias Kleinheisterkamp
                                          (1 Apr 1942)
SS-Oberführer Hans Scheider   (20 Apr 1942)
SS-Obergruppenführer Matthias Kleinheisterkamp
                                          (14 Jun 1942)
SS-Gruppenführer Lothar Debes   (15 Jan 1943)
SS-Obergruppenführer Friedrich-Wilhelm Krüger
                                          (14 Jun 1943)
SS-Brigadeführer Gustav Lombard   (23 Aug 1943)
SS-Gruppenführer Karl Brenner   (9 Jan 1944)
SS-Standartenführer Franz Schreiber
                              (3 Apr 1945 – 8 May 1945)

Divisional Strength

Jun 1941	10,373
Dec 1942	21,247
Dec 1943	20,129
Jun 1944	19,355
Dec 1944	15,000

Order of Battle

Stab der Division
SS-Gebirgsjäger-Regiment 11 Reinhard Heydrich
SS-Gebirgsjäger-Regiment 12 Michael Gaissmair
SS-Polizei-Grenadier-Bataillon (mot) 506
    (formed from the *SS Skijegerbataljon Norge* after
    the arrival in Oslo late in 1944)
SS-Gebirgs-Artillerie-Regiment 6
SS-Sturmgeschütz-Batterie 6
SS-Infanterie-Regiment (mot) 5
SS-Infanterie-Regiment 9 (until 1943)
SS-Schutzen-Abteilung (mot) 6
SS-Gebirgs-Panzerjäger-Abteilung 6
SS-Flak-Abteilung 6
SS-Gebirgs-Nachrichten-Abteilung (mot) 6
SS-Gebirgs-Aufklärungs-Abteilung (mot) 6
SS-Gebirgs-Pionier-Abteilung 6
SS-Dina 6
SS-Bekleidungs-Instandsetzungs-Kompanie 6
SS-Sanitäts-Kompanie 6
SS-Veterinär-Kompanie 6
SS-Kriegsberichter-Zug 6
SS-Feldgendarmerie-Trupp 6
SS-og Politikompani (two companies of Norwegian
    SS volunteers)

northern Finland. However, the German commander in Norway, General von Falkenhorst, was not impressed with the SS men. Although well equipped, the *Totenkopf Standarten* were not made up of highly trained *Waffen*-SS men but of volunteers transferred from the *Allgemeine*-SS.

With the attack on Russia in June 1941, the units, now brigaded as *SS-Kampfgruppe Nord*, were launched into battle against veteran Soviet troops on the Finnish border at Markajärvi-Salla. The poorly trained SS men made a poor showing, suffering 300 killed and more than 400 wounded in two days. In July and August 1941, units of *Nord* were rested and re-equipped, and their shortcomings were addressed by a period of intensive training. Between July and September *Nord* was gradually moved from the front to the Kiestinki-Uhtua area, 140km (87 miles) to the south. In September 1941, the *Kampfgruppe* acquired an artillery regiment, and further reinforcements were planned to bring the *Kampfgruppe* up to divisional status. Hitler directed that 'a new SS-*Gebirgsbrigade* is

to be formed by volunteering Norwegians and Finns. An Austrian SS-regiment is to be attached, and the remaining units are to be deployed from *Kampfgruppe Nord*'. Although the promised Finnish regiment was not to appear, the new *SS-Division Nord* did take into its ranks the *Freiwilligen-Schikompanie Norwegen,* later enlarged to a battalion. In the meantime, the unit was placed under the temporary command of the veteran Finnish General Siilasvuo – the only time an SS unit was placed under foreign command. As part of the temporary 'Division J', it was assigned to Siilasvuo's III Finnish Army Corps.

In January it was decided that the *Nord* Division should be redesignated as a mountain division in the near future, and plans were set afoot to create new units for the division. These arrived in September

Below: Specializing in mountain and Arctic warfare, the SS-Division Nord numbered in its strength the accomplished skiers of the *Freiwilligen-Schikompanie Norwegen*, who were used to mounting long-range Arctic reconnaissance patrols.

Left: Members of the *Nord* Division were mountain troops, classed as *Jäger*, or light infantrymen. As with all such soldiers, they were very fit as well as being highly trained, but they were also lightly equipped.

deployed to hold the line around the Kiestinki area, where it would remain until autumn 1944. It became 6th *SS-Gebirgs Division Nord* on 22 October 1943.

On 2 September 1944, the Finns withdrew from the war. The next day, all German units received the message: '*Birke anschlagen*', or 'Cut the birch'. This was a warning to prepare the evacuation of Finland. Two days later the message '*Birke fällen*' ('Birch has fallen') ordered the evacuation to begin. During August and September the Germans had activated two temporary units called *Kampfgruppe West* and *Ost* to secure their southern flank. Units from *Nord* together with *Divisions-Gruppe Kräutler* formed the bulk of these two groups. At the end of September, the two *Kampfgruppen* fought several short engagements with their erstwhile Finnish allies, but the retreat was not slowed to any great degree.

Nord reached Norway in October 1944. At the end of the year it was transferred to Germany, where it took part in the abortive offensive mounted south of the Ardennes designed as a diversion for the main Ardennes offensive. *Nord* fought mainly against US forces, and the survivors surrendered to the Americans in May 1945.

1942, and the division was redesignated *SS-Gebirgs Division Nord*. By now detached from 'Division J', *Nord* was assigned to fight alongside the Army's 7th Mountain Division in the new German XVIII Mountain Corps, which had arrived in Finland during the winter of 1941 and spring of 1942. *Nord* was

---

7th SS-Freiwilligen Gebirgs Division *Prinz Eugen*

• *Mar 1942:* Freiwilligen-Gebirgs Division   • *Apr 1942:* SS-Freiwilligen Division *Prinz Eugen*   • *Oct 1942:* SS-Freiwilligen Gebirgs Division *Prinz Eugen*   • *Oct 1943 – May 1945:* 7th SS-Freiwilligen Gebirgs Division *Prinz Eugen*

The 7th *SS-Freiwilligen Gebirgs Division Prinz Eugen* was created for partisan operations in the Balkans, and the bulk of its strength consisted of *Volksdeutsche* volunteers and conscripts from Romania, Hungary and Yugoslavia.

Named after the great eighteenth-century commander Prince Eugene of Savoy, *Prinz Eugen* was equipped with obsolete and captured equipment such as Czech machine guns and French light tanks. It was one of the most effective counter-insurgency units the Germans

fielded in Yugoslavia during the war and was greatly feared by the partisans. However, that reputation was gained primarily by brutality and utter ruthlessness.

The origins of the *Prinz Eugen* Division can be found in Himmler's desire to form entire SS units from the massive manpower resource that was the large *Volksdeutsche* community living outside Germany's borders. Many *Volksdeutsche* were already serving in the *Wehrmacht*, but primarily as individual volunteers. Gottlob Berger, head of the SS recruiting office,

Right: Mountain troopers from the *SS-Division Prinz Eugen* prepare weapons to be loaded onto a pack mule. In the Balkans this was often the most effective means of moving supplies across the rugged terrain.

proposed to form a new SS division early in 1942. It was to be made up of volunteers from the large *Volksdeutsche* community living in Serbia, Croatia and the Banat.

The new *Freiwilligen-Gebirgs Division* was initially established in March 1942. At its core were two Croatian units, an SS *Selbstschutz* (a locally recruited SS protection force) and a unit known as the *Einsatz-Staffel Prinz Eugen*. Early hopes that there would be a flood of volunteers to make up the numbers proved unrealistic. The SS was forced to introduce conscription from among the *Volkdeutsche* community to reach a target divisional strength of 21,500 members. This did not please the Pavelíç government in Croatia, who felt that their German allies were poaching Croatian manpower.

Anti-partisan warfare

The new SS division was intended from the start for use in anti-partisan warfare in the Balkans. In October 1942, the division saw its first major action in the south of Serbia, in mountainous terrain east of the Ibar River, near the Montenegro border. By now it had been reclassified as a mountain division, and its designation had been changed to *SS-Freiwilligen Gebirgs Division Prinz Eugen*. Late in 1942, *Prinz Eugen* was transferred to the Zagreb-Karlovac area, where it was one of the units taking part in the massive anti-partisan operation known as Operation 'White'. This was one of a series of major anti-partisan operations in the region, whose primary aim was to destroy the communist resistance movement led by Tito. Although some partisans were killed, the operation was in the main a failure, since the bulk of Tito's forces managed to evade the German offensive.

In 1943, *Prinz Eugen* was assigned to the *Wehrmacht*'s Army Group E. In May of that year the division took part in another major anti-partisan campaign, known as Operation 'Black'. Later in the year elements of the division were sent to Bosnia, operating to the north of Sarajevo. After that, it was

deployed around Mostar where it would continue to play its part in the fiercely fought, no-quarter partisan war for the next year. In the summer of 1943 *Prinz Eugen* was sent to the Dalmatian coast, where in September it disarmed Italian units in the region after the Badoglio government signed an armistice with the Allies. It was then used to occupy former Italian positions on Brac, Hvar and Korcula Islands and on the Peljesac Peninsula. In October 1943 *Prinz Eugen* officially became the 7th *SS-Freiwilligen Gebirgs Division Prinz Eugen*. In December, the division once more moved inland, where operations against Tito's forces, as before, proved to be less than effective.

In January 1944, the division was transferred to the area around Split and Dubrovnik for training, recuperation and re-equipment. In March it was back in Bosnia, where it again took up the fight against Tito's partisans, with a major battle being fought at Drvar in May. The Red Army's summer offensive was unleashed in June 1944, and the Soviet steamroller threatened to smash through the Axis forces without stopping. In August *Prinz Eugen* was transferred north

Left: A *Sturmbannführer* (Major) of the *Prinz Eugen* Division poses proudly for a portrait photograph. Most of the officers and cadre were German, though large numbers of Eastern European *Volksdeutsche* served in the unit.

to Bulgaria, where it suffered great losses fighting against the Red Army. The Soviet advance threatened to cut off Army Group E in Greece, so in September *Prinz Eugen* and other *Waffen*-SS units were moved south to Macedonia. There they were ordered to hold open a corridor to allow 350,000 German soldiers to escape from possible encirclement by the advancing Soviets. Once again, *Prinz Eugen* was badly mauled, but the operation succeeded in its main aim. Once the trapped German troops had escaped through the Macedonian corridor, the division was free to retreat from Cacak to Brcko and over the Drina.

In January 1945, the division fought partisans near Otok, and later was sent to the area of Vukovar where it fought again against advancing Soviet forces and Tito's partisans. From February to April 1945, the division was in action against the partisans and the Soviets, finally ending the war in Slovenia and being taken by the Yugoslav government.

DIVISIONAL INFORMATION

Commanders

SS-Obergruppenführer Artur Phleps   (30 Jan 1942)
SS-Brigadeführer Karl Reichsritter von Oberkamp
                                            (15 May 1943)
SS-Brigadeführer Otto Kumm   (30 Jan 1944)
SS-Brigadeführer August Schmidthuber (20 Jan 1945)

Divisional Strength

Dec 1942	19,835
Dec 1943	21,120
Jun 1944	18,835
Dec 1944	20,000

Order of Battle

SS-Freiwilligen-Gebirgsjäger-Regiment 13 Artur Phleps
SS-Freiwilligen-Gebirgsjäger-Regiment 14 Skanderbeg
SS-Freiwilligen-Gebirgs-Artillerie-Regiment 7

SS-Sturmgeschütz-Abteilung 7
SS-Panzerjäger-Abteilung 7
SS-Flak-Abteilung 7
SS-Pionier-Bataillon 7
SS-Gebirgs-Aufklärungs 7
SS-Feldersatz-Abteilung 7
SS-Kavallerie-Schwadronen
SS-Gebirgs-Nachrichten-Abteilung 7
SS-Freiwilligen-Gebirgs-Aufklärungs-Abteilung (mot) 7
SS-Panzer-Aufklärungs-Zug
SS-Radfahr-Abteilung
SS-Kradschützen-Bataillon 7
SS-Nachschub-Kompanie 7
SS-Werkstattkompanie
SS-Sanitäts-Abteilung 7
SS-Freiwilligen-Gebirgs-Veterinär-Kompanie
SS-Freiwilligen-Gebirgs-Kriegsberichter-Zug

8th SS-Kavallerie Division *Florian Geyer*

- *Jul 1941:* SS-Kavallerie Brigade/SS-Reiter Brigade • *Jun 1942:* SS-Kavallerie Division
- *Oct 1942:* 8th SS-Kavallerie Division • *Mar 1944 – Feb 1945:* 8th SS-Kavallerie Division *Florian Geyer*

The *Florian Geyer* Division was one of several SS units that started out as purely German-based formations but which during the course of the war increasingly numbered non-Germans, or *Volksdeutsche,* among its units. It was named after Florian Geyer (1490–1525), a Franconian knight. Geyer was a supporter of Martin Luther and led the German Peasants' War of 1522–25.

The origins of the *Florian Geyer* Division date back to the original SS cavalry units. The cavalry components of the SS *Totenkopf Standarten*, or regiments, were formed in the winter of 1939. In the summer of 1941, they were combined as an *SS-Kavallerie Regiment* under the aegis of the *Kommandostab* RFSS. The cavalry so gathered were formed into an official unit in August 1941, known variously as the *SS-Kavallerie Brigade* or the *SS-Reiter Brigade*. It was commanded by Hermann Fegelein, and therefore it was often referred to as the *Fegelein Brigade* or *Kampfgruppe Fegelein*. Fegelein began his career in Middle Franconia as a groom and then became a jockey.

A chance contact with a horse fancier who was a Nazi led him into the party. Fegelein's knowledge of horses led the *Waffen*-SS to select him as the commanding officer of the *SS-Kavallerie* units, becoming commander of the new brigade on its formation in 1941. He was

Right: The *Wehrmacht* used horses and horse transport throughout the war. Here, members of the *SS-Kavallerie Brigade* ride down a dusty Russian road in the summer of 1941. The brigade would eventually be expanded to become the *8th SS-Kavallerie Division Florian Geyer*.

wounded in September 1943 south of Kharkov and posted to the *Führer*'s HQ as Himmler's official SS liaison officer.

Anti-partisan operations

In June 1942 the *SS-Kavallerie Brigade* was upgraded to divisional status with the addition of 9000 Hungarian *Volksdeutsche* volunteers. Their primary function was security, being used behind the front lines to mop up bypassed Soviet Army units. Gradually, their main function became the waging of an extremely ruthless anti-partisan campaign. One month later the division went into action with the Ninth Army, part of Army Group Centre.

It was used to destroy pockets of Soviet resistance around the Vyazma-Bryansk-Rzhev salient. It continued to fight under Ninth Army control until

Above: The pro-German Hungarian defence minister Marshal Károly Beregfy (wearing glasses) visits the *Florian Geyer* Division at Budapest late in 1944. By February 1945 the division had been wiped out by the Red Army.

December 1942, when most of the division was sent south to Army Group South. In the Don Basin it was assigned to the Second Panzer Army as *Kampfgruppe Fegelein*. In January and February 1943 the division was again under the control of Ninth Army, where it saw extensive combat south of Orel. In March it was part of XXXXVII Panzer Corps. In April 1943 it was withdrawn to Bobruyal for refitting.

Croatia

In May 1943 the *SS-Kavallerie Division* began the anti-partisan operations which it would fight until the end of the war. Successful in this brutal form of combat, the division was again transferred to Army Group South in July 1943. It was ordered to Croatia, where it would be used in the Brod area for combat against Tito's communist partisans.

As a mounted unit the division was effective against the partisans since on horseback it could operate more rapidly over terrain impassable to vehicles than could partisans on foot. The division saw a considerable

amount of action at Bespalowka and Bol-Gomolscha before being withdrawn for rest and refitting.

On 23 October, the unit was redesignated as 8th *SS-Kavallerie Division*. At the end of the year the division had over 9300 men on strength, the bulk being Hungarian *Volksdeutsche*.

In January and February 1944, the division continued anti-partisan operations. In March, the divisional units were dispersed, being used for further anti-partisan operations in the Balkans, Hungary and Poland. On 12 March the division received the honour title *Florian Geyer*, becoming the 8th *SS-Kavallerie Division Florian Geyer*. On 19 March, elements of *Florian Geyer* became part of *Kampfgruppe Streckenbach* under *SS-Gruppenführer* Bruno Streckenbach. The unit was transferred north from

Osijek, Yugoslavia, to Budapest. In April, one of the division's regiments – *SS-Kavallerie Regiment 17* – was sent to Kisber, Hungary, for rest and refitting. From there it would form the nucleus of 22nd *SS-Freiwilligen Kavallerie Division Maria Theresa.*

Budapest

In November 1944 the division became part of the Budapest garrison. By December, the Red Army had reached the shores of Lake Balaton, Hungary. By Christmas Eve, Budapest had been surrounded by 250,000 Soviet troops from the 2nd and 3rd Ukrainian Fronts. In the ensuing siege, 800,000 civilians were trapped in the city. SS units were pulled back to Buda on the west bank of the Danube. After several weeks of bitter fighting, the Buda pocket had been reduced to a semi-circle about 1000m (1093 yards) across.

On 11 February 1945, the remnants of the division attempted a last-ditch breakout along with what was left of the 22nd *SS-Freiwilligen Kavallerie Division Maria Theresa* and the 33rd *Waffen-Kavallerie Division der SS.* Budapest fell the next day. The division was annihilated. Only 170 survivors managed to reach German lines. The divisional commander, *SS-Brigadeführer* Joachim Rumohr, committed suicide; the remaining survivors were transferred to the 37th SS Cavalry Division.

Hermann Fegelein, the unit's original commander, did not long survive the division. Having become one of Hitler's inner circle, he had married Margarete Braun, Eva Braun's sister, on 3 June 1944. Fegelein was in the *Führerbunker* in Berlin in the last days of the Reich. As Berlin fell, he tried to escape with a mistress who may have been an Allied spy. He was captured by the *Gestapo*, and Hitler had him shot for desertion.

DIVISIONAL INFORMATION

Commanders

SS-Brigadeführer Gustav Lombard	(Mar 1942)
SS-Gruppenführer Hermann Fegelein	(Apr 1942)
SS-Obergruppenführer Willi Bittrich	(Aug 1942)
SS-Brigadeführer Fritz Freitag	(15 Feb 1943)
SS-Brigadeführer Gustav Lombard	(20 Apr 1943)
SS-Gruppenführer Hermann Fegelein	(14 May 1943)
SS-Gruppenführer Bruno Streckenbach	(13 Sep 1943)
SS-Gruppenführer Hermann Fegelein	(22 Jan 1943)
SS-Gruppenführer Bruno Streckenbach	(1 Jan 1944)
SS-Brigadeführer Gustav Lombard	(14 Apr 1944)
SS-Brigadeführer Joachim Rumohr	(1 Jul 1944 – 11 Feb 1945)

Divisional Strength

Dec 1942	10,879
Dec 1943	9326
Jun 1944	12,895
Dec 1944	13,000
Feb 1945	170

Order of Battle

SS-Kavallerie-Regiment 15
SS-Kavallerie-Regiment 16
SS-Kavallerie-Regiment 17
SS-Kavallerie-Regiment 18
SS-Artillerie-Regiment 8
SS-Panzerjäger-Abteilung 8
SS-Aufklärungs-Abteilung 8
SS-Nachrichten-Abteilung 8
SS-Pionier-Bataillon 8
SS-Flak-Abteilung 8
SS-Feldersatz-Bataillon 8
SS-Sturmgeschütz-Abteilung 8
SS-Radfahr-Aufklärungs-Abteilung 8
SS-Ski-Bataillon
SS-Verwaltungstruppen 8
SS-Sanitäts-Abteilung 8
SS-Veterinär-Kompanie 8
SS-Feldpostamt
SS-Kriegsberichter-Zug (mot) 8
SS-Feldgendarmerie-Trupp 8
SS-Krankenkraftwagenzug

11th SS-Freiwilligen Panzergrenadier Division *Nordland*

- *Feb 1943:* Kampfverband *Waraeger*   • *Feb 1943:* Germanische-Freiwilligen Division
- *Apr 1943:* SS-Panzergrenadier Division 11 (Germanische)   • *Jul 1943:* SS-Panzergrenadier Freiwilligen Division *Nordland*   • *Oct 1943 – May 1945:* 11th SS-Freiwilligen Panzergrenadier Division *Nordland*

The 11th *SS-Freiwilligen Panzergrenadier Division Nordland* had its origins in an OKW order to activate a new SS panzer corps in early 1943. This new corps was to be designated III (Germanische) SS-Panzerkorps, and it was to include as many Germanic volunteers as possible.

Nordland was to include the SS *Wiking* Division, together with a new German-Scandinavian division yet to be formed. The corps headquarters was activated

Below: Cold and weary, *Waffen*-SS men occupy a hastily dug trench near the city of Narva in Estonia. In the city, the *Nordland* and *Nederland* Divisions of the SS were fighting a bloody street battle with the Red Army.

on 30 March 1943, but it proved impossible to withdraw *Wiking* from the Eastern Front and the plan to field the new corps was delayed.

However, plans to create the new SS volunteer division went ahead. Himmler wanted to give the new division the name *Waraeger* in reference to the Swedish Viking Varangian Guard, which saw service as the bodyguard of the Byzantine emperors in the Dark Ages. Hitler, more practical than his mystical SS henchman, considered the name too obscure and decided that the name of the veteran volunteer regiment *Nordland* deserved to be honoured, and ordered the division to be so named in July 1943. *Nordland* was to differ from the prototype volunteer

**Right: An *Oberstumbann-*
führer (Lieutenant-Colonel)
from the *Nordland* division
on the Narva front. The
battles against the Soviet
forces in the Baltic area saw
foreign SS units from all
over Europe participating
in fierce action.**

division *Wiking* in its
makeup. Although much
had been made of the
multi-national nature of
the elite *Wiking* Division
by Nazi propaganda, in
truth the bulk of its
strength and nearly all of
its senior NCOs and
officers were German. In
the new division, the
Germans hoped to utilize
a far greater proportion
of foreign volunteers,
especially in the more
senior ranks. Much use
was made of the remnants of the disbanded Germanic
legions in staffing the division, and it certainly carried
the widest range of nationalities to be found in any
Waffen-SS division. By the end of the war, troops from
Denmark, Estonia, Finland, France, the Netherlands,
Norway, Sweden, Switzerland and even a handful of
British volunteers had either served in the division or
been attached to it. The principle combat units were
made up of combat veterans of the *Legion Norwegen*
and the *Freikorps Danmark*. The ranks were filled out
with *Volksdeutsche* and with *Reichsdeutsche*. The first
division commander was *SS-Brigadeführer und
Generalmajor der Waffen-SS* Friedrich 'Fritz' von
Scholz, who had been commander of the *Nordland*
Regiment of *Wiking*.

The Battle of Narva

After completing training, *Nordland* and III
(*Germanische*) *SS-Panzerkorps* were posted to Croatia
to gain combat experience in the war against Tito's
communist partisans. Going into action on 28 August,
Nordland fought several vicious actions against an
equally cut-throat enemy. Just before *Nordland* was
reassigned, on 12 November 1943, it was upgraded to
full *panzergrenadier* status. Along with III
(*Germanische*) *SS-Panzerkorps Nordland* it began
transferring to the Eastern Front on 25 November and
was fully deployed with Army Group North by 22
December 1943.

The division arrived in the Leningrad sector to take
part in the unsuccessful German attempt to fight off a
massive Soviet breakout from the Oranienbaum
pocket, a breakout which succeeded in relieving the
900-day siege of Leningrad. Over the next three
months of continuous combat the Germans were
driven back over the Narva. In fact, so many volunteer
units saw action at Narva that it became known as the
'Battle of the European SS'.

Although the Germans had been forced to retreat,
the long period of combat had also exhausted the

Above: *SS-Gruppenführer* **Friedrich 'Fritz' Scholz, Elder von Rarancze, commander of the** *Nordland* **Division, makes a tour of inspection. On 28 July 1944, Scholz died of wounds received in the Narva battles.**

Soviets. The impetus had run out of the Red Army's advance and the battle for Narva became a battle of snipers. During this period the battered first battalions of both the *Norge* and *Danmark* Regiments were withdrawn to Germany for rest and rebuilding. They would never again be assigned to *Nordland*. After being brought up to strength, in December 1944 both battalions were assigned to the *Wiking* Division. Early in 1945 they were transferred south for the failed attempt to relieve Budapest.

Back on the Baltic front, Soviet pressure began to increase in early June 1944 and it soon became apparent that a major Soviet thrust was in the making. Then, on 22 June, the third anniversary of Operation *Barbarossa*, Operation *Bagration* was launched against

Army Group Centre. This was the long-awaited Soviet summer offensive and it tore a 400km (249 mile) wide gap in the German lines, annihilating the entire German army group in the process. The rapid Soviet advance threatened to isolate the hundreds of thousands of German troops in the Baltic States. To avoid being cut off, the Germans began planning for the withdrawal from the Narva bridgehead to the Tannenberg Line. Through July and August, the troops of III (*Germanische*) *SS-Panzerkorps* took part in some of the most vicious fighting ever seen on the Eastern Front.

The Battle for Berlin

On 14 September 1944 the German forces in Estonia were ordered to fall back into Latvia. By the morning of the 22nd *Nordland* had taken up positions 30km (18.6 miles) to the northeast of Riga, the Latvian capital. By the evening, *Nordland* had been relocated to the southeast of the city. Its arrival prevented the encirclement of the German Eighteenth Army by Soviet forces. As the Red Army's advance continued, *Nordland* slowly withdrew into the Courland pocket, fighting doggedly all the way, from where it was evacuated to Germany in early 1945. At this time III (*Germanische*) *SS-Panzerkorps* included *Kampfgruppen* from the 27th *SS-Freiwilligen Grenadier Division Langemarck*, 28th *SS-Freiwilligen Grenadier Division Wallonien*, elements of 10th *SS-Panzer Division Frundsberg*, and *Nordland,* and was subordinated to the newly created Eleventh Panzer Army, commanded by *SS-Obergruppenführer* Steiner.

By 21 February the conclusion was reached that no more useful gains could be made against an increasingly powerful enemy without undue casualties so Steiner ordered a general withdrawal back to the north bank of the Ihna. Between 23 and 28 February III (*Germanische*) *SS-Panzerkorps* made a slow withdrawal to the area around Stargard and Stettin on the northern Oder River.

It saw heavy fighting around Danzig, Stettin and Stargard, before becoming part of the force defending Berlin. At 20:00 on 30 April the *Norge* and *Danmark Kampfgruppe* commander, *SS-Sturmbannführer*

Ternedde, was given the news of Hitler's death. Ternedde was ordered to take the survivors and break out of the ruined city. In the event, very few of them made it to safety.

Others were caught up in the last few hours of the defence of the *Reichstag* and other government buildings. By 1 May 1945 the Soviets had overcome the last defenders of the *Reichstag,* and organized resistance in the ruined city had ceased. As night fell on 2 May the few survivors of *Nordland* and the rest of the exhausted Berlin garrison, some 130,000, marched into Soviet captivity.

Unit markings

Soldiers of the division wore a special collar patch showing a so-called curved swastika (*Sonderrad*). The members of *SS-Panzergrenadier-Regiment 23* wore the title *Norge*. Members of the *SS-Panzergrenadier-Regiment 24* wore the title *Danmark*. Members of *SS-Panzer-Abteilung 11* were given the title *Herman von Salza*. All other members of the division wore the cuff title *Nordland*. Generally speaking, soldiers of the division also wore their own particular national insignia as an arm patch.

DIVISIONAL INFORMATION

Commanders
SS-Brigadeführer Franz Augsberger	(22 Mar 1943)
SS-Gruppenführer Fritz von Scholz	(1 May 1943)
SS-Brigadeführer Joachim Ziegler	(27 Jul 1944)
SS-Brigadeführer Gustav Krukenberg	(25 Apr 1945)

Divisional Strength
Dec 1943	11,393
Jun 1944	11,749
Dec 1944	9000

Order of Battle
SS-Panzergrenadier-Regiment 23 Norge
SS-Panzergrenadier-Regiment 24 Danmark
SS-Panzer-Abteilung11 Herman von Salza
SS-Panzer-Artillerie-Regiment 11
SS-Panzer-Aufklärungs-Abteilung 11
SS-Sturmgeschütz-Abteilung 11
SS-Panzerjäger-Abteilung 11
SS-Nachrichtung-Abteilung 11
SS-Pionier-Bataillon 11
SS-Nachrichtung-Abteilung-Truppen 11
SS-Nachschub-Truppen 11
SS-Instandsetzungs-Abteilung 11
SS-Wirtschafts-Abteilung 11
SS-Kriegsberichter-Zug 11
SS-Feldgendarmerie-Trupp 11
SS-Feldersatz-Bataillon 11
SS-Bewährungs-Kompanie 11
SS-Sanitäts-Abteilung 11
SS-Werfer-Bataillon 521
SS-Jäger-Regiment 11

13th Waffen-Gebirgs Division der SS *Handschar* (kroatische Nr. 1)

- *Mar 1943:* Kroatische SS-Freiwilligen Division • *Jul 1943:* Kroatische SS-Freiwilligen Gebirgs Division
- *Oct 1943:* SS-Freiwilligen Bosnien-Herzegowina Gebirgs Division (Kroatien) • *13th* SS-Freiwilligen Bosnien-Herzegowina Gebirgs Division (Kroatien) • *May 1944 – May 1945:* 13th Waffen-Gebirgs Division der SS *Handschar*

When Croatia proclaimed its independence on 10 April 1941, part of the land it claimed was the former Austro-Hungarian province of Bosnia-Herzegovina. The province was a volatile ethnic and religious mix, including large numbers of Catholic Croats, Orthodox Serbs and Muslims.

It was these Muslim inhabitants of Bosnia that Himmler and the SS would target in their recruitment of a Croatian SS Division. Hitler approved the formation of the division on 13 February 1943, and grudging approval was given by the Croatian leader, Ante Paveliç, on 5 March 1943. The division was at full strength, in excess of 20,000 men, by the summer of 1943, though not all were volunteers. Nearly 3000 of the recruits were Catholic Croats. The uniform worn by the division was regular SS issue, with a divisional collar patch showing an arm holding a scimitar, over a Swastika. On the left arm was a red and white chequerboard shield, the Croatian colours. Standard headgear for Muslim members of the division was a fez, in field grey (normal service) or red (walking out), with the SS eagle and death's head emblazoned on it. Non-Muslim members were allowed to wear the normal SS *Feldmutze*. The oval

DIVISIONAL INFORMATION

Commanders
SS-*Oberführer* Herbert von Obwurzer (1 Apr 1943)
SS-*Gruppenführer* Karl-Gustav Sauberzweig
(9 Aug 1943)
SS-*Brigadeführer* Desiderius Hampel (Jun 1943)

Divisional Strength
Dec 1943   21,065
Jun 1944   19,136
Dec 1944   12,793

Order of Battle
SS-Waffen-Gebirgsjäger-Regiment 27
SS-Waffen-Gebirgsjäger-Regiment 28
SS-Waffen-Artillerie-Regiment 13
SS-Panzerjäger-Abteilung 13
SS-Aufklärungs-Abteilung (mot) 13

Waffen-Gebirgs-Pionier-Abteilung der SS 13
Waffen-Gebirgs-Nachrichten-Abteilung der SS 13
Waffen-Flak-Abteilung der SS 13
SS-Nachrichten-Abteilung 13
Kroatische SS-Radfahr-Bataillon
Kroatische SS-Kradschützen-Bataillon
SS-Divisionsnachschubtruppen 13
Versorgungs-Regiment-Stab 13
SS-Verwaltungs-Bataillon 13
SS-Sanitäts-Abteilung 13
SS-Krankenkraftwagenzug
SS-Freiwilligen-Gebirgs-Veterinär-Kompanie 13
SS-Feldpostamt 13
SS-Kriegsberichter-Zug 13
SS-Feldgendarmerie-Trupp 13
SS-Feldersatz-Bataillon 13
SS-Kraftfahr-Lehr-Abteilung 13

Opposite: The commander of the Croatian Army, General Stanzer, inspects an anti-tank gun of a new Bosnian Muslim regiment. When the SS began raising similar units, it allowed members to retain the traditional fez headgear.

Edelweiss patch signifying mountain troops was worn on the right arm.

Mutiny
The division departed for training in occupied France, all personnel having arrived there by September 1943. While at Villefranche, it became the only SS division to mutiny, the rising being incited by communist partisans who had infiltrated the recruitment process. Several German officers were killed during the mutiny, though most of the troops did not take part. Fourteen soldiers were executed.

By February 1944, after further training at Neuhammer in Germany, the division was declared operational. It was transferred back to Bosnia for active service against the partisans. Its area of operation was northeastern Bosnia and western Serbia. The division participated in several anti-partisan campaigns, including Operations *Wegweiser*, *Save*, *Osterei*,

Maibaum and *Maiglockchen*. Some successes were achieved, and overall the *Handschar* proved itself as a competent anti-guerrilla unit, as long as its men were fighting their hereditary enemies. Atrocities were committed, but atrocity was not unusual in the Balkans, and the *Handschar* was no worse than many other SS divisions.

In more conventional action against the Soviets it was far less effective. With the penetration of the Red Army up to the Croatian borders in late 1944, the division was transferred to southern Hungary and became involved in front-line fighting. Desertions plagued the division from this point on, as many of the Muslims decided to return to Bosnia to protect their homes and families.

The 9000 German personnel of the division were used as an SS battlegroup, known as *Kampfgruppe Henke*. This fought in southern Hungary, joining combat against the Russians near the Yugoslav border. On 7 May 1945, the remnants of the division surrendered to the British in Austria. All remaining Muslim volunteers were handed over to Tito's forces after the capitulation and most were executed at Maibor on the Drava.

14th Waffen-Grenadier Division der SS (ukrainische Nr. 1)

• *Apr 1943:* SS-Freiwilligen Division *Galizien*   • *Summer 1943:* SS-Schützen Division *Galizien*   • *Oct 1943:* SS-Freiwilligen
Division *Galizien*   • *Jun 1944:* 14th Galizische SS-Freiwilligen Division   • *Nov 1944:* 14th Waffen-Grenadier Division der SS
(ukrainische Nr. 1)   • *Apr 1944 – Apr 1945:* 1st Ukrainische Division der Ukrainischen National-Armee

The 14th *Waffen-Grenadier Division der SS* was authorized as the *SS-Freiwilligen Division Galizien* in April 1943, the name being changed briefly to *SS-Schützen Division Galizien*. Volunteers were largely from the western Ukraine.

The historical name of the area was Galicia, and the title was applied to the new division, possibly to avoid alerting Hitler that the SS was forming a division from the despised Slavs. Training of the troops began at the *Truppenübungsplatz der SS* Heidelager in Debica in

September 1943 before the division was moved to Silesia in April 1944 for further training. The recruits were mainly *Volksdeutsche* and Ukrainians from the area around Lemberg. On 22 October 1943 the division name was changed back to *SS-Freiwilligen Division Galizien*.

First combat

It was sent to the front at Brody in the Ukraine in June 1944. Inadequately armed, poorly trained, and with troops lacking in motivation, it was no match for the powerful Soviet assault which was launched as part of the Red Army's massive summer offensive. The division was quickly encircled and smashed, with only about 3000 of its 15,000 members managing to reach the German lines.

It was soon rebuilt as the 14th *Waffen-Grenadier Division der SS*. After the completion of basic training at *Truppenübungsplatz* Neuhammer, it was sent into Slovakia at the end of August, where it was used to help suppress the Slovak National Uprising. From there the division was deployed into northern Yugoslavia to fight partisans. In January 1945 it was again redesignated, now being known as the 14th *Waffen-Grenadier Division der SS (ukrainische Nr. 1)*. In January 1945 it

Left: A Ukrainian volunteer in the 14th *Galizische SS-Freiwilligen Division* poses with his Soviet-manufactured Degtyarev DP light machine gun. The 'Galician' designation was chosen partly to avoid alerting Hitler that Slavs were being recruited into the SS.

DIVISIONAL INFORMATION

Commanders

SS-Gruppenführer Walther Schimana   (30 Jun 1943)
SS-Brigadeführer Fritz Freitag   (20 Nov 1943)
SS-Brigadeführer Sylvester Stadler   (22 Apr 1944)
SS-Brigadeführer Nikolaus Heilmann   (Jul 1944)
SS-Brigadeführer Fritz Freitag   (5 Sep 1944)
SS-Brigadeführer Pavlo Schandruk   (24 Apr 1945)

Divisional Strength

Dec 1943	12,634
Jun 1944	15,299
Dec 1944	22,000

Order of Battle

Waffen-Grenadier-Regiment der SS 29
Waffen-Grenadier-Regiment der SS 30
Waffen-Grenadier-Regiment der SS 31

Waffen-Artillerie-Regiment der SS 14
SS-Waffen-Füsilier-Bataillon 14
SS-Waffen-Panzerjäger-Kompanie 14
SS-Freiwilligen-Panzerjäger-Kompanie 14
SS-Freiwilligen-Flak-Abteilung 14
Waffen-Nachrichten-Abteilung der SS 14
SS-Radfahr-Bataillon 14
Waffen-Pionier-Bataillon der SS 14
SS-Versorgungs-Kompanie 14
SS-Divisionsnachschubtruppen 14
SS-Sanitäts-Abteilung 14
SS-Veterinär-Kompanie 14
SS-Feldpostamt 14
SS-Kriegsberichter-Zug 14
SS-Feldgendarmerie-Trupp 14
SS-Feldersatz-Bataillon 14

was transferred to Pressburg (now Bratislava in Slovakia) where it took part in anti-partisan operations in the Untersteiermark (now Slovenia).

In April 1945, the unit was officially transferred to the newly forming Ukrainian National Army as the 1st *Ukrainische Division der Ukrainischen National-Armee*. Although still strong numerically, the division was short of weaponry and supplies. Retreating into the Austrian Alps north of Klagenfurt, the division surrendered to the Americans between the towns of Tamsweg and Judenberg.

Since 1945, there has been a good deal of controversy about the record of the division. Supporters claim that they were exceptional soldiers, who were not involved in the concentration camps and did not commit war crimes. To others, however, they were a sinister legion of bloodthirsty murderers. As always in such cases, the truth probably lies somewhere between the two extremes.

Right: A volunteer from the Ukraine prepares a meal in a dugout. He is wearing the Galician Division's unique collar patch, a lion rampant, reflecting the blue and gold lion rampant worn on the divisional armshield.

15th Waffen-Grenadier Division der SS (lettische Nr. 1)

- *Feb 1943:* Lettische SS-Freiwilligen Division • *Oct 1943:* 15th Lettische SS-Freiwilligen Division
- *Jun 1944 – May 1945:* 15th Waffen-Grenadier Division der SS (lettische Nr. 1)

The origins of the 15th *Waffen-Grenadier Division der SS (lettische Nr. 1)* date back to 1943, when the *Lettische SS-Freiwilligen Legion* was upgraded to divisional status. The legion had been formed in the spring of 1943, when three infantry regiments were raised.

Along with the Latvian SS Volunteer Brigade (formerly 2nd SS Infantry Brigade) the Latvian Legion served under the VI SS Volunteer Corps. In November 1943, the Latvian Legion saw action at Novo-Sokolniki, northern Russia, as part of the Sixteenth Army, Army Group North. The legion was taken out of combat in October 1943 to become the kernel of a new volunteer division, the 1st Division of the SS Latvian Legion (renamed 15th *Lettische SS-Freiwilligen Division*). The division later became the 15th *Waffen-Grenadier Division der SS (lettische Nr. 1)* and it was assigned to the XXXXIII Corps of the German Sixteenth Army.

A fighting withdrawal

The Soviet winter offensive which was launched at the end of December continued until February 1944. The fighting was furious, and both sides suffered heavy casualties. The 15th *Lettische SS-Freiwilligen Division* was assigned to the VI SS Corps, where it fought alongside the 19th Latvian SS Division which had been formed around the 2nd SS Infantry Brigade (the Latvian SS Volunteer Brigade). In March 1944 both Latvian divisions fought to control strategic points along the Velikiye River. Although the VI SS Corps faced 11 Russian Army divisions, the Soviet offensive was contained at great cost.

The launch of the great Soviet summer offensive in June 1944 saw the 15th SS Division being forced back from its defensive positions along the line of the Sanukha River. A month later, the Latvian division was fighting yet another attack, near Ostrova in Estonia.

DIVISIONAL INFORMATION

Commanders

SS-Brigadeführer Peter Hansen	(25 Feb 1943)
SS-Gruppenführer Carl Graf von Pückler-Burghauss	(May 1943)
SS-Brigadeführer Nikolas Heilmann	(17 Feb 1944)
SS-Brigadeführer Herbert von Obwurzer	(21 Jul 1944)
SS-Oberführer Arthur Ax	(26 Jan 1945)
SS-Oberführer Karl Burk	(15 Feb 1945)

Divisional Strength

Dec 1943	20,291
Jun 1944	18,413
Dec 1944	16,870

Order of Battle

Waffen-Grenadier-Regiment der SS 32
Waffen-Grenadier-Regiment der SS 33
Waffen-Grenadier-Regiment der SS 34
Waffen-Artillerie-Regiment der SS 15
Waffen-Füsilier-Bataillon der SS 15
Waffen-Flak-Abteilung der SS 15
Waffen-Nachrichtung-Abteilung der SS 15
Waffen-Pionier (motorisierte) der SS 15
Waffen-Panzerjäger-Abteilung der SS 15
SS-Sanitäts-Abteilung 15
SS-Nachschub-Truppen 15
SS-Feldpostamt 15
SS-Veterinär-Kompanie 15
SS-Wirtschafts-Bataillon 15
SS-Bau-Regiment 1 der 15. SS-Division
SS-Bau-Regiment 2 der 15. SS-Division
SS-Feldersatz-Bataillon 15
SS-Waffen-Feldgendarmerie-Trupp 15
SS-Kriegsberichter-Trupp

**Right: A Latvian SS man sends up a
signal from a Walther LP flare gun.
The first Latvian SS division, the
15th, fought long and hard against
the Soviets as part of Army Group
North; some stragglers were still in
action as Berlin fell in May 1945.**

The power of the offensive meant
that the Latvians could pull back
only at the cost of two regiments all
but wiped out. Surviving infantrymen and the divisional artillery
were transferred to the 19th SS
Division while NCO and officer
cadres were shipped to the
Truppenübungsplatz der SS West
Prussia. In September, conscripts
from Latvia and engineers from the
SS Training and Replacement
Battalions at Dresden were used to
reform the 15th *Waffen-Grenadier
Division der SS (lettische Nr. 1).*

Final act

Although training was far from
complete, in January 1945 the
division was ordered to positions
along the Oder–Vistula Canal. By
end of February, the Red Army had
broken through to the Baltic at
Kolberg, cutting off large German
forces including the 15th SS
Division. As part of *Kampfgruppe
Tettau*, the division broke through
the Soviet lines to reach German-
held territory, its 33rd Grenadier
Regiment acting as rearguard.
Survivors were sent to the town of
Neubrandenburg, north of Berlin,
for refitting.

As the Soviets pushed on towards the German
capital, a battle group drawn from the 32nd and 33rd
Regiments was dispatched towards Berlin to help in
the defence of the city. On 24 April 1945, after
fighting off Russian attacks in the south of the city, the
Kampfgruppe began to withdraw westwards to
surrender to the Americans. A week later, the rest of
the division also moved west from Neubrandenburg
and reached the American lines near Schwerin, where
it too surrendered.

18th SS-Freiwilligen Panzergrenadier Division *Horst Wessel*

- *Jan 1944:* 18th SS-Panzergrenadier Division
- *Jan 1944 – May 1945:* 18th SS-Freiwilligen Panzergrenadier Division *Horst Wessel*

In January 1944, Hitler ordered Himmler to raise a *Waffen*-SS division from a cadre of SA reservists. In fact, the 18th *SS-Freiwilligen Panzergrenadier Division Horst Wessel* was cobbled together from a *Totenkopf Standarte* motorized brigade and 1st *SS-Infanterie-Brigade,* together with elements from the 6th *SS-Gebirgs Division Nord* and numerous Hungarian and Yugoslav *Volksdeutsche.*

The division was named after one of the Nazi Party's heroes, portrayed in National Socialist mythology as a young Berlin stormtrooper who was killed in a streetfight with communists before the Nazis came to power. In fact, although Horst Wessel was indeed an SA man killed by a communist, he was actually a street thug and pimp who was killed in a fight over who would benefit from the income of Wessel's prostitute girlfriend.

The division was assembled at the Stablack training aree in East Prussia. In January 1944 it was transferred to Zagreb in Croatia. From there it was deployed to the Agram area on the Hungarian-Yugoslav border where it went into action against Tito's partisans. In March the division was moved into Hungary alongside the *Florian Geyer* SS Cavalry Division where it was used as a threat to control the Hungarian Government, at that time showing signs of trying to find a way out of the war.

In July, the bulk of the division was sent to form a *Kampfgruppe* under XXIV Panzer Corps in the Ukraine. The unit took under its command elements of the 8th *SS-Sturmbrigade Frankreich,* formed after the dissolution of the *Légion des Volontaires Français.*

Slovakia and Budapest

Under intense Soviet pressure the *Horst Wessel Kampfgruppe* retreated through Podhajce and Lipica to the Dniester River, then back through Baliezne, Podrozne and Siechow. One unit was detached in August, and for the next three months it was used in the crushing of the Slovak National Uprising. In

DIVISIONAL INFORMATION

Commanders
SS-Brigadeführer Wilhelm Trabandt   (25 Jan 1944)
SS-Gruppenführer Josef Fitzthum   (3 Jan 1945)
SS-Oberführer Georg Bochmann   (10 Jan 1945)
SS-Standartenführer Heinrich Petersen   (Mar 1945)

Divisional Strength
Jun 1944   8530
Dec 1944   11,000

Order of Battle
SS-Panzergrenadier-Regiment 39
SS-Panzergrenadier-Regiment 40
SS-Artillerie-Regiment 18
SS-Panzerjäger-Abteilung 18

SS-Panzer-Aufklärungs-Abteilung 18
SS-Panzer-Abteilung 18
SS-Sturmgeschütz-Abteilung 18
SS-Panzerjäger-Abteilung 18
SS-Flak-Abteilung 18
SS-Nachrichten-Abteilung 18
SS-Pionier-Bataillon 18
SS-Verwaltungstruppen-Abteilung 18
SS-Wirtschafts-Bataillon 18
SS-Nachschub-Truppen 18
SS-Instandsetzungs-Abteilung 18
SS-Feldgendarmerie-Abteilung 18
SS-Feldersatz-Bataillon 18
SS-Sanitäts-Abteilung 18

September the rest of the division was moved into Hungary, where it fought the advancing Soviets in the area around Jasz and Ladany.

At the end of the war *Horst Wessel* was used in the abortive attempt to break the Soviet siege of Budapest. Then it was split into two *Kampfgruppen*. One was used around Karlsbrunn and Ratibor before surrendering to the Red Army at Mährisch-Ostrau. The other *Kampfgruppe* moved to Zobten in April,

Above: SS troops on the outskirts of Budapest. In common with many SS units, the *Horst Wessel* Division saw its last major action in the abortive German attempt to relieve the besieged defenders of the Hungarian capital.

where it came under the control of VIII Army Corps. There was no serious fighting in the area, and after the final German surrender the unit tried to move westwards to surrender to the Americans.

19th Waffen-Grenadier Division der SS (lettisches Nr. 2)

- *April 1941:* SS-Brigade (mot) 2 • *May 1943:* Lettische SS-Freiwilligen Brigade
- *Oct 1943:* 2nd Lettische SS-Freiwilligen Brigade • *Jan 1944:* 19th Lettische SS-Freiwilligen Division
- *May 1944 – April 1945:* 19th Waffen-Grenadier Division der SS (lettisches Nr. 2)

The 19th *Waffen-Grenadier Division der SS* was the second division of Latvian volunteers raised by the *Waffen*-SS. Like its sister unit the 15th *Waffen-Grenadier Division der SS*, German troops formed the nucleus of the formation, the *SS-Brigade (mot) 2* also providing the bulk of the NCO and officer cadre.

Numbers were made up by the addition of Latvians who had been serving in the SS *Schutzmannschaft* battalions. Although not formed until May 1944, the division found itself in combat less than a month later when the Soviet summer offensive got under way. Over the next six months it formed part of the heavily outnumbered German force in the Baltic States which managed to hold back the assault of vastly superior Red Army forces.

Battle of Narva

The division fought at the Battle of Narva along with many other Germanic and volunteer SS units. It was later trapped in the Courland pocket as the German forces in the Baltic States retreated from the advancing Soviet juggernaut. Little has been documented about the division's record in the last months of the war, but there are rumours that some divisional units may have mutinied at the end of 1944.

Unlike other volunteer *Waffen*-SS divisions the Latvian divisions were known for their fighting ability and for their commitment to the Nazi cause. In 1945, after being smashed by the advancing Soviet Army, the remaining elements of the two Latvian SS divisions regrouped under the command of *Waffen-Standartenführer* Villus Janums for the defence of Berlin. They later surrendered to the Americans at Güterglück near the Elbe River.

Opposite: A Latvian machine-gunner with the tools of his trade: an MG42 general-purpose machine gun and fifty-round belts of 7.62mm (0.3in) ammunition.

DIVISIONAL INFORMATION

Commanders

SS-Brigadeführer Heinrich Schuldt	(7 Jan 1944)
SS-Standartenführer Friedrich-Wilhelm Bock	
	(15 Mar 1944)
SS-Gruppenführer Bruno Streckenbach	(15 Apr 1944)

Divisional Strength

Dec 1943	8033
Jun 1944	10,592
Dec 1944	9396

Order of Battle

Waffen-Grenadier-Regiment der SS 42 Voldemar Veiss
Waffen-Grenadier-Regiment der SS 43 Heinrich Schuldt
Waffen-Grenadier-Regiment der SS 44 (lettische Nr. 6)
Waffen-Artillerie-Regiment 19
SS-Füsilier-Bataillon 19
SS-Panzerjäger-Abteilung 19
SS-Flak-Abteilung 19
SS-Pionier-Bataillon 19
SS-Nachschub-Truppen 19
SS-Sanitäts-Abteilung 19
SS-Feldpostamt 19
SS-Veterinär-Kompanie 19
SS-Wirtschafts-Bataillon 19
SS-Nachrichten-Abteilung 19

20th Waffen-Grenadier Division der SS (estnische Nr. 1)

• *Oct 1942:* Estnische SS-Legion • *May 1943:* Estnische SS-Freiwilligen Brigade • *Oct 1943:* 3rd Estnische SS-Freiwilligen Brigade • *Jan 1944:* 20th Estnische SS-Freiwilligen Division • *May 1944 – May 1945:* 20th Waffen-Grenadier Division der SS (estnische Nr. 1)

The 20th *Waffen-Grenadier Division der SS (estnische Nr. 1)* was formed from the 3rd *Estnische SS-Freiwilligen Brigade*, and directly descended from the Estonian Legion, authorized by Adolf Hitler in August 1942.

The regiment-sized legion took some time to organize, becoming operational in the spring of 1943. Formed as a motorized infantry regiment, the legion was referred to in German orders as the 1st *Estnische SS-*

Freiwilligen Grenadier Regiment. It quickly grew to brigade size, however. The 20th *Estnische SS-Freiwilligen Division* was formed in January 1944. Difficulties in forming the division while its component units were fully engaged in action at the front meant that formation took longer than expected.

On 14 May 1944 it was 5000 men under strength, and Himmler ordered it up to full strength by 15 June. It was not, in fact, completely up to strength until July

1944. Units of the division were in action during the three-month campaign known as the Battle of the Narva, which took place early in 1944. The remnants of the division were later evacuated from Estonia along with the rest of the German forces. The division was reconstructed at *Truppenübungsplatz* Neuhammer from October 1944.

New division

By now it had been given the title 20th *Waffen-Grenadier Division der SS (estnische Nr. 1)*; in Estonian it was known as the 20th *SS-Relvagrenadieride Diviis (Eesti Esimene)*. In February 1945 the formation was so weakened that it had to be referred to as a battle group (SS-*Kampfgruppe*), possibly named *Augsberger* after its commander. The unit continued fighting in Silesia and later Czechoslovakia until the end of the war when parts surrendered to the Western Allies while the main body of the division surrendered to the Russians north of Prague.

Opposite: Estonian SS volunteers aboard a captured Soviet T-34 tank. The Germans captured so much Soviet materiel in 1941 and 1942 that entire units were equipped with Soviet weapons, armour, artillery and vehicles.

DIVISIONAL INFORMATION

Commanders
SS-Brigadeführer Franz Augsberger
(24 Jan 1944 – 19 Mar 1945)
SS-Brigadeführer Berthold Maack
(20 Mar 1945 – 8 May 1945)

Divisional Strength
Jun 1944	13,423
Dec 1944	15,382

Order of Battle
Waffen-Grenadier-Regiment der SS 45 Estland
  (estnische Nr. 1)
Waffen-Grenadier-Regiment der SS 46 (estnische Nr. 2)
Waffen-Grenadier-Regiment der SS 47(estnische Nr. 3)
Waffen-Artillerie-Regiment der SS 20
SS-Waffen-Füsilier-Bataillon 20
SS-Waffen-Pionier-Bataillon 20
SS-Feldersatz-Bataillon 20
SS-Waffen-Nachrichten-Abteilung 20
SS-Ausbildungs-und-Ersatz-Regiment 20

21st Waffen-Gebirgs Division der SS *Skanderbeg* (albanische Nr. 1)
(Apr 1944 – May 1945)

On 17 April 1944, Himmler approved the formation of an Albanian *Waffen*-SS division. It was named *Skanderbeg* after Iskander Bey, a fifteenth-century Kosovan hero.

The governments of Albania, of Albanian Kosovo and of Bosnia submitted the names of 11,398 recruits. Of these, 9275 were adjudged to be suitable for drafting. Of this number, 6491 ethnic Albanians were actually drafted into the *Waffen*-SS. A reinforced battalion of approximately 300 ethnic Albanians serving in the Bosnian Muslim 13th *Waffen-Gebirgs Division der SS Handschar* were transferred to the newly forming division. To this Albanian core were added veteran German troops from Austria and *Volksdeutsche* officers,

NCOS, and enlisted men, together with a number of *Kriegsmarine* sailors. The total strength of the Albanian *Waffen*-SS division would be 8500–9000 men.

The *Skanderbeg* Division did not have a good reputation. Intended to fight partisans, in its earliest days it was used to massacre Orthodox Serb civilians in Kosovo-Metohija. Over 10,000 Serbian families were forced to flee Kosovo. Albanian colonists and settlers from northern Albania took over their lands and homes. The goal of many members of the *Skanderbeg* Division was not to fight for the Germans: rather it was to advance Albanian nationalism by deporting and killing the non-Albanian populations of Western Macedonia, creating an ethnically pure and homogenous region of

Greater Albania, free of Serbs, Jews and Roma (gypsies). *Skanderbeg* targeted all of these groups when the division occupied Tetovo and Skopje and other towns and cities in Western Macedonia.

However, the Red Army was advancing in ever-increasing strength. In October 1944, *Skanderbeg* occupied Skopje, the capital of Macedonia. By November 1944, the Germans were withdrawing their forces from the Aegean islands and from Greece. Called on to fight in something other than their own private war, many of the division's members deserted. The remnants of the division were reorganized into *Regimentgruppe 21.SS-Gebirgs Skanderbeg* which was concentrated at Skopje. The *Kampfgruppe Skanderbeg*, with the *Prinz Eugen* Division, defended the Vardar River valley in Macedonia to allow Alexander Löhr's Army Group E to retreat from Greece and the Aegean.

By January 1945, remnants of the *Skanderbeg* Division retreated to Kosovska Mitrovica in Kosovo and then to Brcko in Bosnia-Herzegovina. They reached Austria in May, 1945, when Germany surrendered, following the collapse of the regime.

Above: The *Skanderbeg* Division committed numerous atrocities in Kosovo, aimed at driving the Serbs out of what the Albanian Muslims considered their historical territory.

DIVISIONAL INFORMATION

Commanders
SS-Brigadeführer Josef Fitzhum   (April 1944)
SS-Oberführer August Schmidthuber   (1 May 1944)

Order of Battle
Waffen-Gebirgs-Regiment der SS 50
Waffen-Gebirgs-Regiment der SS 51
Waffen-Gebirgs-Artillerie-Regiment 21
SS-Aufklärungs-Abteilung 21
SS-Panzerjäger-Abteilung 21
SS-Gebirgs-Pionier-Bataillon 21
SS-Versorgungs-Abteilung 21
SS-Nachrichten-Abteilung 21
SS-Sanitäts-Abteilung 21

22nd SS-Freiwilligen Kavallerie Division *Maria Theresa*

(May 1944 – Feb 1945)

The *Maria Theresa* Division was formed in May 1944. Assembled at Kisber, Hungary, it was based on a nucleus provided by the 17th *SS-Kavallerie Regiment* transferred from the 8th *SS-Kavallerie Division Florian Geyer*.

The bulk of the strength of the division was provided by Hungarian *Volksdeutsche*, who had originally been drafted by the Hungarian Army but had been transferred to the *Waffen*-SS following an agreement between the German and Hungarian Governments. The symbol of the division was a cornflower, adopted as it was the favourite flower of the Empress Maria Theresa of Austria, after whom the division had been named.

In September 1944 a detachment from *Maria Theresa*, consisting of *SS-Kavallerie Regiment 52*, was assigned to a *Kampfgruppe* commanded by *SS-Haupt-*sturmführer Toni Ameiser. *Kampfgruppe Ameiser* was deployed to Romania where it was intended to reinforce the *Wehrmacht*'s LVII Panzer Corps. It was unable to reach its designated positions because of the advance of the Red Army, and after fighting alongside Hungarian troops it was encircled by the Soviets.

One section of the *Kampfgruppe*, commanded by *SS-Hauptsturmführer* Harry Vandieken, fought its way to the Harmas River, swimming across to safety on the German-held bank. The second part of the *Kampfgruppe*, commanded by Ameiser, remained in the

Below: SS cavalrymen await a Soviet attack on the Eastern Front. The second SS cavalry division to be formed, *Maria Theresa* lasted less than a year before being wiped out during the battles for Budapest early in 1945.

trap for a month, eventually fighting its way through to the German lines south of Budapest on 30 October.

The rest of the division was still in training when it was sent to reinforce Budapest in November 1944. It was still in the city when the Red Army closed a ring of iron around the Hungarian capital, and it was destroyed along with most of the rest of the German defenders.

Only 170 men managed to make it through the Soviet lines to safety. The survivors, along with those parts of the *Maria Theresa* Division which had not been sent into Budapest, were used as the core of the newly formed 37th *SS-Freiwilligen Kavallerie Division Lützow*. What was left of the divisional flak units were transferred to 32nd *SS-Freiwilligen Grenadier Division 30 Januar*.

DIVISIONAL INFORMATION

Commanders
SS-Brigadeführer August Zehender   (21 Apr 1944)

Divisional Strength
Jun 1944   4914
Dec 1944   8000

Order of Battle
SS-Kavallerie-Regiment 52
SS-Kavallerie-Regiment 53

SS-Kavallerie-Regiment 54
SS-Kavallerie-Regiment 17
SS-Artillerie-Regiment 22
SS-Panzer-Aufklärungs-Abteilung 22
SS-Panzerjäger-Abteilung 22
SS-Pionier-Bataillon 22
SS-Nachrichten-Abteilung 22
SS-Divisionsnachschubtruppen 22
SS-Verwaltungstruppen-Abteilung 22
SS-Sanitäts-Abteilung 22

23rd Waffen-Gebirgs Division der SS *Kama* (kroatische Nr. 2)

- *June 1944 – October 1944:* Waffen-Gebirgs Division
- *October 1944:* 23rd Waffen-Gebirgs Division der SS *Kama* (kroatische Nr.2)

Approval was given for the raising of a second Croatian *Waffen-SS* division on 17 June 1944. The 23rd *Waffen-Gebirgs Division der SS Kama (kroatische Nr. 2)* was recruited from Croatian volunteers – including both *Volksdeutsche* and anti-communist Croats – and Bosnian Muslims.

In common with many volunteer divisions, the unit was stiffened by a cadre of German senior NCOs and officers. Further strength was supplied by its sister formation, the *Handschar* Division, which provided its reconnaissance battalion and a number of Croat officers and NCOs.

Like the *Handschar*, the unit was named after a traditional weapon from the region – in this case, a short Turkish sword or long fighting knife known as a *kama*. *Kama* never reached anything like its planned

strength. At its peak, in September 1944, it had a total of 3793 men in training to play their part in the anti-partisan war. That training was taking place at Backa in Hungary, far enough from the main areas of partisan action as to be safe from attack. They were not safe from the Red Army, however, which by the end of September was advancing perilously close to the divisional training grounds in southern Hungary. The SS wanted the division to be ready for combat by the end of September, but as the troops had not completed basic training this was never a realistic prospect.

On 1 October 1944, as the Red Army advanced into Hungary, the SS decided to disband the unit, transferring already formed units as replacements to other divisions. Most of the division's personnel were used to form the 31st *SS-Freiwilligen Grenadier*

Division. The Muslims of *Kama* were transferred to the *Handschar* Division. Most reported for duty, but a large minority deserted *en route*. The divisional number 23 was assigned to the newly forming *Nederland Panzergrenadier Division.*

Above: Himmler's persistent attempts to form Muslim SS divisions did not pay off. The fez-wearing SS men of the *Handschar* and *Kama* Divisions were effective when fighting for their homes, but were otherwise almost completely unreliable.

DIVISIONAL INFORMATION

Commanders
SS-Standartenführer Helmuth Raithel   (1 Jul 1944)
SS-Oberführer Gustav Lombard   (28 Sep 1944)

Divisional Strength
Jun 1944   2199
Sep 1944   3793

Order of Battle
Waffen-Gebirgsjäger-Regiment der SS 55 (kroatische Nr. 3)
Waffen-Gebirgsjäger-Regiment der SS 56 (kroatische Nr. 4)

Waffen-Gebirgs-Artillerie-Regiment der SS 23
SS-Aufklärungs-Abteilung 23
SS-Flak-Abteilung 23
SS-Panzerjäger-Abteilung 23
SS-Nachschub-Abteilung 23
SS-Pionier-Bataillon 23
SS-Nachrichten-Abteilung 23
SS-Feldlazarett 23
SS-Feldersatz-Bataillon 23
SS-Sanitäts-Abteilung 23
SS-Verwaltungs-Abteilung 23

23rd SS-Freiwilligen Panzergrenadier Division *Nederland*

• *Jul 1941:* SS-Freiwilligen Verband *Niederlande* • *Aug 1941:* SS-Freiwilligen Legion *Niederlande* • *Oct 1943:* 4th SS-Freiwilligen Panzergrenadier Brigade *Nederland* • *Oct 1944:* SS-Freiwilligen Panzergrenadier Brigade *Nederland* • *Feb 1945 – May 1945:* 23rd SS-Freiwilligen Panzergrenadier Division *Nederland* (niederlandische Nr. 1)

The 23rd *SS-Freiwilligen Panzergrenadier Division Nederland* consisted of Dutch volunteers and was formed on 10 February 1945, when *SS-Freiwilligen Panzergrenadier Brigade Nederland* was upgraded to divisional status.

The *Nederland* Brigade had been in action in the Baltic States since the end of 1943, and had shared in the retreat from Leningrad to the Narva line and back to the Courland pocket. Along with the rest of III *SS-Korps*, *Nederland* was evacuated by sea to Stettin, where they were to form part of the defensive line on the Oder. The SS had originally intended for the Dutch soldiers to be assigned to the *Nordland*

Division but after protests from the Dutch Nazi party, the NSB, it was decided that they would form their own division. *Nederland* was given the number 23 when the *Kama* Division was disbanded. The 23rd *SS-Freiwilligen Panzergrenadier Division Nederland* had little more than 1000 effective combatants when it fought its last battles on the Eastern Front.

Below: The first parade of the SS-*Freiwilligen Legion Niederlande* took place in the historic Rittersaal Square in The Hague. The legion would eventually provide the nucleus for a *Panzergrenadier* brigade and then for a *Panzergrenadier* division.

DIVISIONAL INFORMATION

Commander   *SS-Brigadeführer* Jürgen Wagner

Divisional Strength   Dec 1944   6000

Order of Battle
SS-Freiwilligen-Panzergrenadier-Regiment 48
SS-Freiwilligen-Panzergrenadier-Regiment 49
SS-Artillerie-Regiment 23
SS-Nachrichten-Abteilung 23
SS-Panzerjäger-Abteilung 23
SS-Pionier-Bataillon 23
SS-Flak-Abteilung 23

Nederland, together with the SS divisions *Nordland*, *Wallonien* and *Langemarck*, was responsible for the defence of the Oder front between the towns of Stettin and Neustadt. In April 1945 *Nederland* was split up. The *General Seyffardt* Regiment headed south. It was destroyed near Hammerstein while fighting alongside the 15th *Waffen-Grenadier Division der SS*. The 13 soldiers who were captured were executed by the Russians.

At the end of April the *De Ruyter* Regiment, which had remained on the Oder front, withdrew to the west, around the north of Berlin. On 3 May 1945, near the village of Parchim, the regiment destroyed an attacking Red Army tank unit, and then its members heard more tanks approaching. These were American, and the regiment was happy to surrender to them.

24th Waffen-Gebirgs Division der SS (*Karstjäger*)

• *1942:* SS-Karstwehr-Bataillon • *Aug 1944:* 24th Waffen-Gebirgs (*Karstjäger*) Division der SS • Dec 1944:
Waffen-Gebirgs Brigade der SS (*Karstjäger*) • *10 Feb 1945 – May 1945:* 24th Waffen-Gebirgs Division der SS (*Karstjäger*)

The *SS-Karstwehr-Bataillon* had been fighting partisans in northern Italy and the Dolomites since 1942. On 1 August 1944, it was upgraded to become the 24th *Waffen-Gebirgs (Karstjäger) Division der SS*, though it was never more than brigade-sized.

Since it was impossible to build the *SS-Karstwehr-Bataillon* into a true division, in December 1944 it was redesignated as the *Waffen-Gebirgs Brigade der SS (Karstjäger)*. However, it was redesignated as a division

on 10 February 1945. Originally under the control of the HSSPF *Adriatisches Meer* (Higher SS and Police Commander Adriatic), it was manned mainly by Italian volunteers, but it also included volunteers from Slovenia, Croatia, Serbia and the Ukraine. *Karstjäger* mainly fought partisans in Istria, with considerable success, but at the end of the war it found itself in action with the Western Allies advancing through Italy. On 8 May 1945 *Karstjäger* surrendered to the British.

DIVISIONAL INFORMATION

Commanders
SS-Obersturmbannführer Karl Marx (Aug 1944)
SS-Sturmbannführer Werner Hahn (5 Dec 1944)
SS-Oberführer Adolf Wagner   (10 Feb 1945)

Divisional Strength
June 1944   1831
Dec 1944   3000

Order of Battle
Waffen-Gebirgsjäger-Regiment der SS 59
Waffen-Gebirgsjäger-Regiment der SS 60
Waffen-Gebirgs-Artillerie-Regiment 24
SS-Panzerkompanie
SS-Gebirgsbatterie
SS-Gebirgs-Sanitäts-Kompanie 24
SS-Gebirgs-Nachrichten-Kompanie 24
SS-Gebirgs-Pionier-Kompanie 24

25th Waffen-Grenadier Division der SS *Hunyadi* (ungarische Nr. 1)
• *Oct 1944:* 25th SS-Freiwilligen Grenadier Division • *Nov 1944:* 25th Waffen-Grenadier Division der SS *Hunyadi* (ungarische Nr. 1)

The 25th *Waffen-Grenadier Division der SS Hunyadi (ungarische Nr. 1)* consisted of Hungarian volunteers. Authorized in October and set up in November 1944, it included 1000 Hungarians from *Kampfgruppe Deák*, who were used to form the 61st SS-*Grenadier Regiment*.

Waffen-Schi-Bataillon der SS 25 was raised from Hungarian Army mountain troops. Some divisional troops were transferred from *Waffen*-SS training schools, but the bulk of the troops were provided by Hungarian recruiting depots.

Training camp
Transferred to the Neuhammer Training Ground in Germany, the division was still far from operational when the Red Army entered Silesia. With over 22,000 men in the camp, together with many wives and families, Neuhammer was seriously overcrowded, and it was a relief when orders were given that the division should retreat to Bavaria. The division surrendered to the Americans after a brief firefight at Salzkammergut in Austria.

DIVISIONAL INFORMATION

Commanders
SS-Standartenführer Thomas Müller   (Nov 1944)
SS-Gruppenführer Josef Grassy   (Late Nov 1944)

Divisional Strength
Dec 1944   15,000

Order of Battle
Waffen-Grenadier-Regiment der SS 61
Waffen-Grenadier-Regiment der SS 62
Waffen-Grenadier-Regiment der SS 63
Waffen-Artillerie-Regiment der SS 25
Waffen-Schi-Bataillon 25
SS-Divisions-Füsilier-Bataillon 25
SS-Panzerjäger-Abteilung 25
SS-Veterinär-Kompanie 25
SS-Feldersatz-Bataillon 25
SS-Versorgungs Regiment 25

Left: German and Hungarian soldiers retreat from the city of Budapest, having narrowly avoided being caught in the vast Soviet encirclement in the spring of 1945. All German attempts to break the siege would ultimately fail.

26th Waffen-Grenadier Division der SS *Hungaria* (ungarische Nr. 2)
(Dec 1944 – May 1945)

The 26th *Waffen-Grenadier Division der SS Hungaria (ungarische Nr. 2)* was formed under the authority of the Hungarian defence minister, at the request of Himmler. *Waffen-Schi-Bataillon der SS 26* from the Hungarian Army was ordered to join the new division.

Late in December 1944, 5000 civilian draftees brought the strength up to 8000. By January divisional strength was up to more than 16,000, and the formation had been moved to Siederatz in Poland for training. Weapons were issued early in January – just in time to allow foraging parties to fight off attacks by Polish partisans.

Forced to retreat by the Soviet winter offensive (minus mortars and machine guns, which had been taken by the German Ninth Army), the partially trained division reached the Oder after suffering over 2500 casualties. Plans to refit at Neuhammer were dashed when on 8 February the Soviets attacked the training ground. The more experienced members of the division served as a rearguard while the rest of the formation retreated westwards. As part of XVII *Waffen-Armee Korps der SS (Ungarisches)* the *Hungaria* Division retreated into Austria, where it surrendered to the Western Allies at Attersee. Many of the division's surviving troops were turned over to the Soviets, and were destined for the *Gulag* or the firing squad.

Below: The last great battles of the *Waffen*-SS were fought in Hungary, from where the Sixth SS Panzer Army was driven back into Austria. By this time, the majority of SS troops were foreign-born.

DIVISIONAL INFORMATION

Commanders

SS-Sturmbannführer Rolf Tiemann	(Nov 1944)
SS-Oberführer Zoltan Pisky	(Nov 1944)
SS-Oberführer László Déak	(Jan 1945)
SS-Oberführer Berthold Maack	(29 Jan 1945)
SS-Gruppenführer Josef Grassy	(21 Mar 1945)

Divisional Strength

Dec 1944	8000
Jan 1945	c.15,000

Order of Battle

Waffen-Grenadier-Regiment der SS 64
Waffen-Grenadier-Regiment der SS 65
Waffen-Grenadier-Regiment der SS 85
Waffen-Artillerie-Regiment der SS 26
SS-Waffen-Panzerjäger-Abteilung 26
SS-Waffen-Artillerie-Regiment 26
SS-Waffen-Flak-Abteilung 26
SS-Waffen-Schi-Bataillon 26
SS-Waffen-Pionier-Bataillon 26
SS-Waffen-Nachrichten-Abteilung 26
SS-Waffen-Versorgungs-Regiment 26
SS-Waffen-Ausbildungs-und-Ersatz-Regiment 26

27th SS-Freiwilligen Grenadier Division *Langemarck* (flämische Nr. 1)

• *Jul 1941:* SS-Freiwilligen Legion *Flandern* • *May 1943:* SS-Sturmbrigade *Langemarck* • *Oct 1943:* 6th SS-Freiwilligen Sturmbrigade *Langemarck* • *Oct 1944 – Apr 1945:* 27th SS-Freiwilligen Grenadier Division *Langemarck* (flämische Nr. 1)

The division was formed on 19 October 1944, when the 6th *SS-Freiwilligen Sturmbrigade Langemarck* was upgraded to divisional status. The *Langemarck* Division, named after a village near Ypres which saw some of the bloodiest fighting in World War I, was descended directly from the SS Flanders Legion, the original Flemish volunteer unit in the *Waffen-SS*.

The Flemish Legion had been less than impressive in its early actions on the Eastern Front, but experience had shown that the volunteers from Flanders could fight, and fight hard. Although the legion had been withdrawn from combat by the beginning of 1943, it was expanded to form the *Sturmbrigade Langemarck* by the addition of fresh recruits from Flanders, a Finnish battalion and some German artillery and support units.

The *Sturmbrigade* was attached to the *Das Reich* Division in the Ukraine, before being sent to the Leningrad front as part of Felix Steiner's III *SS-Germanische Panzerkorps*. The *Langemarck* Brigade took part in the fighting retreat from the Baltic, and played its part in the long sequence of fierce battles on the Narva. In the autumn of 1944, the brigade was

Opposite: An SS sharpshooter takes aim with an advanced Gewehr-43 self-loading rifle. On the Oder front in February 1945, even the possession of improved weapons could do little against the sheer weight of numbers of the Red Army.

refitting on the Lüneburg Heath when it was upgraded to become the 27th *SS-Freiwilligen Grenadier Division Langemarck (flämische Nr. 1)*, though it never really approached divisional size.

At the end of 1944, the 27th Division was assigned to the 3rd SS Panzer Corps, part of the Eleventh Army. On 15 February, the Eleventh SS Army launched a counter-attack, known as Operation *Sonnenwende*. Three corps were nominally involved, but only the 3rd SS Panzer Corps (*Nordland* and *Langemarck* Divisions) were ready. They attacked southwards towards Arnswalde, about 30km (18.6 miles) southeast of Stargard. The operation was finally brought to a close in the face of more and more powerful Red Army attacks.

Most of the division surrendered at Mecklenburg, though a small battlegroup took part in the last-dich defence of Berlin.

DIVISIONAL INFORMATION

Commanders

SS-Obersturmbannführer Conrad Schellong
(19 October 1944)

SS-Oberführer Thomas Müller
(Late October 1944)

Divisional Strength

Dec 1944   7000

Order of Battle

SS-Panzergrenadier-Regiment 66
SS-Panzergrenadier-Regiment 67

SS-Panzergrenadier-Regiment 68
SS-Artillerie-Regiment 27
SS-Panzerjäger-Abteilung 27
SS-Nachrichten-Abteilung 27
SS-Pionier-Bataillon 27
SS-Div. Versorgungs Regiment 27
SS-Feldersatz-Bataillon 27
SS-Sanitäts-Abteilung 27
Verwaltungs-Kompanie
Propaganda-Kompanie
Kampfgruppe Schellong

28th SS-Freiwilligen Grenadier Division *Wallonien*

- *1941:* Wallonisches-Infanterie-Bataillon 373 (Heer) • *Jun 1943:* SS-Sturmbrigade *Wallonie* • *Oct 1943:* 5th SS-Freiwilligen Sturmbrigade *Wallonien* • *Oct 1944 – May 1945:* 28th SS-Freiwilligen Grenadier Division *Wallonien*

The 28th *SS-Freiwilligen Grenadier Division Wallonien* was formed when 5th *SS-Freiwilligen Sturmbrigade Wallonien* was upgraded to divisional size (in name only; it was never to have the strength of an early-war division).

Walloon (French-speaking) Belgian volunteers had originally served in *Wallonisches-Infanterie-Bataillon 373* of the German Army, but with the disbandment of most of the European legions in 1943, many of its members were transferred to the *Waffen*-SS.

The new *Sturmbrigade*, consisting mainly of Belgian volunteers but including some Frenchmen and Spaniards, fought on the Dnieper bend and was trapped in the Cherkassy pocket while serving with the *Wiking* Division. The unit's commander, *Obersturmbannführer* Lucien Lippert, was killed at Nowo-Buda on 15 February 1944 and he was replaced by *Hauptsturmführer* Léon Degrelle. The Walloons escaped from the pocket with 632 men of the

approximately 2000 who had originally been trapped by the Red Army. Degrelle became a hero to the Nazi propaganda machine, and he was appointed commander of the new 28th *SS-Freiwilligen Grenadier Division Wallonien* in October 1944. While still being formed in Hanover and Brunswick, the unit was ordered to be converted to a 'Type 45' division (reduced in size from three to two regiments, with the regiments themselves reduced to two battalions each).

In February 1945 the division was assigned to III *SS* (*Germanisches*) *Korps* in Pomerania, where it fought until the end of the war. Some divisional units managed to retreat to Denmark; most of the rest surrendered to the Soviets in Brandenburg in May 1945.

Below: Léon Degrelle (foreground) and survivors of the Walloon *Sturmbrigade* after their escape from Cherkassy. The rebuilt unit formed the basis of the 28th SS Division, placed under Degrelle's command in October 1944.

DIVISIONAL INFORMATION

Commanders

SS-Standartenführer Léon Degrelle
                    (19 Oct 1944 – Apr 1945)

Divisional Strength

Dec 1944   4000

Order of Battle

SS-Panzergrenadier-Regiment 69
SS-Panzergrenadier-Regiment 70
SS-Artillerie-Regiment 28

SS-Panzerjäger-Abteilung 28
SS-Panzeraufklärungs-Abteilung 28
SS-Nachrichten-Abteilung 28
SS-Pionier-Bataillon 28
SS-Nachschub-Kompanie 28
SS-Flak-Kompanie 28
SS-Verwaltungskompanie 28
SS-Sanitäts-Kompanie 28
SS-Veterinär-Kompanie 28
SS-Ersatz-Bataillon 28
Kampfgruppe Capelle

29th Waffen-Grenadier Division der SS (russische Nr. 1)

The 29th *Waffen-Grenadier Division der SS (russische Nr. 1)* was
to be formed from *Waffen-Sturm-Brigade RONA*. This unit,
descended from one of the first Soviet formations to fight for the
Germans, had possibly the worst reputation of any SS unit.

Manned by thugs and murderers, the *RONA* Brigade
had gained an unsavoury reputation during the
partisan war, and its members committed numberless
atrocities during the suppression of the Warsaw Rising
– so many, in fact, that even the SS were appalled. The
unit's commander, Bronislav Kaminski, was killed –
most likely by the *Gestapo* – in August 1944.

In December 1944 the *RONA* was absorbed by
General Vlasov's ROA. Vlasov ordered Colonel Sergei
K. Bunyachenko to form the first ROA division, using
the Kaminski Brigade as its core. When Bunyachenko
saw the men from *RONA* he shouted to the German
liaison officer: 'So that's what you're giving me, bandits,
robbers and thieves! You'll let me have what you can no
longer use!'. The division was disbanded before its
formation got under way, and the number 29 was given
to *Waffen-Grenadier Division der SS (italienische Nr. 1)*.

**Right: Bronislav Kaminski (right), receives orders from
SS-*Gruppenführer* Heinz Reinefarth, the SS commander
detailed to suppress the Warsaw Uprising, August 1944.**

DIVISIONAL INFORMATION

Commanders

Waffen-Brigadeführer der SS Bronislav Kaminski
                                (17 Jun 1944)
SS-Brigadeführer Christoph Diehm
                                (19 Aug 1944)

29th Waffen-Grenadier Division der SS (italienische Nr. 1)

• *Nov 1943:* Italienische-Freiwilligen-Legion • *Late 1943:* 1st Sturmbrigade Italienische Freiwilligen Legion • *Sept 1944:* Waffen-Grenadier Brigade der SS • *Mar – May 1945:* 29th Waffen-Grenadier Division der SS (italienische Nr. 1)

The 29th *Waffen-Grenadier Division der SS (italienische Nr. 1)* was descended from the Italian volunteer legion formed by Italian fascists after the fall of Mussolini and the Italian armistice with the Allies.

It came into existence in September 1944, when the *Waffen-Grenadier Brigade der SS (italienische Nr. 1)* was upgraded to a division.

The formation was given the number 29 when *Waffen-Grenadier Division der SS (russische Nr. 1)* was disbanded before ever being formed. The Italian SS division never reached full divisional strength, though it came closer than many of the other foreign SS divisions formed late in the war. It was primarily used on anti-partisan operations in northern Italy, but at the end of the war it saw some action against the British and the Americans.

Some parts of the Italian division surrendered to the Allies; those members of divisional units foolish enough to surrender to the Italian resistance were mostly executed.

DIVISIONAL INFORMATION

Commanders
SS-Oberführer Constantin Heldmann
(10 Feb 1945)
SS-Oberführer Erwin Tzschoppe
(Late Feb/early Mar 1945)

Divisional Strength
Dec 1944   15,000

Order of Battle
Waffen-Grenadier-Regiment der SS 81
Waffen-Grenadier-Regiment der SS 82
Waffen-Artillerie-Regiment der SS 29
Füsilier-Bataillon 29
Panzerjäger-Abteilung 29
SS-Pionier-Kompanie 29
SS-Nachrichten-Kompanie 29

30th Waffen-Grenadier Division der SS (russische Nr. 2)

(Aug – Dec 1944)

The 30th *Waffen-Grenadier Division der SS (russische Nr. 2)* was formed in August 1944 in Poland from *Schutzmannschaft-Brigade Siegling*. This in turn had been assembled from several small Russian volunteer formations withdrawn from the front following the Soviet summer offensive.

Germans provided the officer cadre for the unit. Most of the rest of the division was Russian, though it also counted Byelorussians, Ukrainians, Armenians, Tartars, Poles and at least one Czech among its number.

Never considered reliable, the division suffered from many desertions, and at the end of August troops of two infantry battalions mutinied, killing a number of German officers and NCOs. The second battalion of the 1st Regiment was disbanded, and 2300 men regarded as unreliable were transferred to construction units. The division transferred to France over the last two weeks in August, where it immediately came under attack by the French resistance.

Combat losses

Some divisional units avoided action, though others did engage the resistance fighters with enthusiasm. Strength dropped rapidly through combat losses and

DIVISIONAL INFORMATION

Commanders
SS-Obersturmbannführer Hans Siegling
(18 Aug 1944)

Divisional Strength
Dec 1944   4400

Order of Battle
Waffen-Grenadier-Regiment der SS 75
Waffen-Grenadier-Regiment der SS 76

Waffen-Grenadier-Regiment der SS 77
SS-Artillerie-Abteilung 30
SS-Aufklärungs-Abteilung 30
SS-Füsilier-Kompanie
SS-Pionier-Kompanie
SS-Nachrichten-Kompanie
SS-Sanitäts-Kompanie
SS-Panzerspäh-Kompanie
SS-Feldersatz-Bataillon

desertions. Over the next months it joined in the general retreat of the *Wehrmacht*, eventually being assigned to guard bridges on the Rhine.

Losing many men in battles with the French First Army, the division was driven to the Swiss border, where it was disbanded in December 1944. Officers were transferred to the *Nibelungen* Division, the last SS 'Division' of the war; reliable Russian troops were used

Above: A mixed force of Germans and Russian auxiliaries move through Kovel in 1942. A large number of varied Soviet volunteer units were combined, eventually becoming the 30th *Waffen-Grenadier Division der SS*.

in *Waffen-Grenadier Division der SS (weissruthenische Nr. 1)*, while the unreliable volunteers were sent to Vlasov's *Russkaya Osvoboditelnaya Armiya* (ROA).

30th Waffen-Grenadier Division der SS (weissruthenische Nr. 1)

• *Jul/Aug 1944:* Schutzmannschaft-Brigade *Siegling* • *Dec 1944:* Waffen-Grenadier Brigade der SS (weissruthenische) • *Mar 1945:* 30th Waffen-Grenadier Division der SS (weissruthenische Nr. 1)

Authorized in February 1945, with wholly unrealistic plans to complete formation by June 1945, the 30th *Waffen-Grenadier Division der SS (weissruthenische Nr. 1)* was an expansion of the *Waffen-Grenadier Brigade der SS (weissruthenische).*

The formation began gathering its troops at Grafenwohr on 9 March 1945. Why the SS felt it necessary to convert an understrength brigade which had already been downgraded from divisional status – it had originally been the 30th *Waffen-Grenadier Division der SS (russische Nr. 2)* which had been broken up in December 1944 – is a matter for conjecture. The unit was far too weak and poorly equipped to be able to function as a division.

The unit never reached any great size, and saw no action. Like its predecessor, the White Russian division was disbanded very shortly after its formation began. The German cadre were assigned to the newly formed 38th *SS-Grenadier Division Nibelungen.*

DIVISIONAL INFORMATION

Commanders
SS-Obersturmbannführer Hans Siegling
(10 Feb 1945)

Order of Battle
Waffen-Grenadier-Regiment der SS 75
Artillerie-Abteilung
Panzerjäger-Abteilung
Reiter-Schwadron

Below: Russian volunteers in service with the *Wehrmacht* go into action. Those who survived two years of warfare in the East found themselves forced into SS units at the end of the war, few of which were of any value militarily.

31st SS-Freiwilligen Grenadier Division

(Oct 1944 – May 1945)

Orders for the formation of the 31th *SS-Freiwilligen Grenadier Division* were issued in October 1944, and by the beginning of December 1944 some 11,000 recruits were in training. Many of the recruits were Czech or Slovak *Volksdeutsche.*

The civilian recruits were bolstered by the attachment of parts of the disbanded 23rd *Waffen-Grenadier Division der SS Kama (kroatische Nr. 2)* and by the addition of the *Polizei Regiment Brixen.*

The division fought briefly against the Red Army around its Hungarian training area, but was soon forced to retreat into Germany, where it was intended to complete its formation at Marburg. However, in January 1945, the division was converted into a much reduced-strength 'Type 45' unit. In February it was assigned to Army Group Centre as part of its general reserve.

By war's end, a divisional *Kampfgruppe* was operating around Königgrätz, where survivors surrendered to the Russians. According to some sources this division was to be given the name *Böhmen-Mähren* (Bohemia-Moravia).

DIVISIONAL INFORMATION

Commanders
SS-Brigadeführer Gustav Lombard   (1 Oct 1944)
SS-Brigadeführer Wilhelm Trabandt   (Apr 1945)

Divisional Strength
Dec 1944   11,000

Order of Battle
SS-Freiwilligen-Grenadier-Regiment 78
SS-Freiwilligen-Grenadier-Regiment 79
SS-Freiwilligen-Grenadier-Regiment 80
SS-Artillerie-Regiment 31
SS-Füsilier-Bataillon 31
SS-Nachrichten-Abteilung 31
SS-Nachschub-Truppen 31
SS-Panzerjäger-Abteilung 31
SS-Pionier-Bataillon 31
SS-Kranken-Transport-Kompanie 31
SS-Veterinär-Kompanie 31
Feldpostamt

33rd Waffen-Kavallerie Division der SS (ungarische Nr. 3)

(Dec 1944 – Jan 1945)

Formed in December 1944, he 33rd *Waffen-Kavallerie Division der SS (ungarische Nr. 3)* was intended to be formed from Hungarian volunteers, mostly from the scattered remnants of Hungarian Army cavalry units. It never reached anything close to divisional size and was destroyed in the fighting near Budapest in January 1945. The number 33 was given to the *Charlemagne* Division.

DIVISIONAL INFORMATION

Commanders
SS-Oberführer László Deák   (27 Dec 1944)

33rd Waffen-Grenadier Division der SS *Charlemagne*

- *Mar 1943:* Légion Volontaire Française (Heer) • *Oct 1943:* Französisches SS-Freiwilligen Grenadier Regiment
- *Nov 1943:* Französisches SS-Freiwilligen Regiment 57 • *Jul 1944:* Französisches-Freiwilligen Sturmbrigade
- *Aug 1944:* Waffen-Grenadier Brigade der SS *Charlemagne* (französische Nr. 1) • *Feb – May 1945:* 33rd Waffen-Grenadier Division der SS *Charlemagne* (französische Nr. 1)

The 33rd *Waffen-Grenadier Division der SS Charlemagne (französische Nr. 1)* was formed on 2 February 1945 when it was decided to expand *Waffen-Grenadier Brigade der SS Charlemagne (französische Nr. 1)* to full divisional status.

The extra manpower would be provided by volunteers from among the French collaborationists who had fled France ahead of the Allied advances.

The unit was given the number 33 when *Waffen-Kavallerie Division der SS (ungarische Nr. 3)* was destroyed while being formed. As might be expected from the name, the *Charlemagne* Division was a largely French formation, but it also had on its strength transfers from the *Horst Wessel* Division and volunteers from other countries. Some French sources suggest that the division had Swedish, Swiss, Laotian, Vietnamese and even Japanese members.

On deployment to Pomerania on 25 February, the division came under attack just as the trains bearing most of the unit's 7500 troops pulled into Hammerstein. Tanks of the Soviet 1st Byelorussian Front scattered the Frenchmen, who gathered into three *ad hoc* battlegroups. One group under General Krukenberg made it to the Baltic coast, eventually being shipped via Denmark to Mecklenburg. A second group, commanded by General Puaud, ran straight into one of the main axes of the Soviet winter offensive, and was never seen again. The third group took heavy casualties at the railhead before making a fighting retreat westwards to the German lines.

About a third of the 1100 survivors were released from their SS vows of allegiance. The remainder were enough to make up a single *Waffen-Grenadier* regiment. This was among the last units to enter Berlin before the Soviets completed their enclosure of the German capital. Supported by the few remaining *Sturmgeschütze* and Tiger II heavy tanks of *s.SS-Pz. Abt. 503* (Heavy SS Panzer Detachment 503), they mounted brief but ferocious counter-attacks at Hasenheide and around Tempelhof Airfield. The Frenchmen then continued to mount rearguard fights along the *Leipzigerstrasse*, in and around the *Luftfahrtministerium*, and into the *Potsdamerplatz*. On 2 May 1945, after the general order of surrender announced by General Weidling, some 30 surviving Frenchmen went into Soviet captivity near the Potsdamer Station.

Left: The last defenders of Berlin prepare to receive Soviet armour. Among those defenders were *Waffen*-SS men of many nationalities, including the 7500 men of the *Charlemagne* Division. Few would survive the war.

DIVISIONAL INFORMATION

Commanders
SS-Oberführer Edgard Puaud (Feb 1945)
SS-Brigadeführer Gustav Krukenberg (1 Mar 1945)
SS-Standartenführer Walter Zimmermann (24 Apr 1945)

Divisional Strength
25 Feb 1945 — 7500
23 Apr 1945 — 1100
2 May 1945 — 30

Order of Battle
SS-Waffen-Grenadier-Regiment 57
SS-Sturm-Bataillon 58
SS-Waffen-Grenadier-Regiment 58
SS-Artillerie-Abteilung 33
SS-Panzerjäger-Abteilung 33
SS-Pionier-Kompanie 33
SS-Nachrichten-Kompanie 33
SS-Feldersatz-Kompanie 33
SS-Nachschub-Bataillon 33

34th SS-Freiwilligen Grenadier Division *Landstorm Nederland*

- *Oct 1943:* Landstorm Nederland • *Nov 1944:* SS-Freiwilligen Grenadier Brigade *Landstorm Nederland*
- *Feb – May 1945:* 34th SS-Freiwilligen Grenadier Division *Landstorm Nederland*

The 34th *SS-Freiwilligen Grenadier Division Landstorm Nederland* came into existence when *SS-Freiwilligen Grenadier Brigade Landstorm Nederland* was upgraded to a division. A division in name only, since it was smaller than many infantry brigades, it was formed from Dutch stormtroopers, the *Landwacht Nederland* and other Dutch collaborationist organizations.

The division saw little conventional action against Allied forces. Earlier, *Landstorm Nederland* troops fought against the Dutch resistance in northwest Holland, and played a small part in the battle against British paratroopers at Arnhem in September 1944. *Landstorm Nederland* troops even saw combat with fellow Dutchmen, in an encounter with the 'Princess Irene Brigade', a unit of Dutch volunteers serving with the Allies.

The *Landstorm* was renamed *SS-Freiwilligen Brigade Landstorm Nederland* in November 1944, before being nominally made into a division in February 1945. The last strong resistance mounted by *Landstorm Nederland* was against the advancing Canadians around the villages of Oosterbeek and Otterlo in March 1945. The 3000 or so members of the *Landstorm* included

DIVISIONAL INFORMATION

Commanders
SS-Oberführer Martin Kohlroser (10 Feb 1945)

Order of Battle
SS-Freiwilligen-Grenadier-Regiment 83
SS-Freiwilligen-Grenadier-Regiment 84
SS-Artillerie-Regiment 60
SS-Versorgungs-Regiment 60
SS-Pionier-Kompanie 60
SS-Nachrichten-Abteilung 60
Werkstattkompanie

fanatical Nazis who used terror to persuade the population to acquiesce to their demands. Troops from the 84th Regiment in particular, the former prison camp guards of *SS-Wachbataillon Nordwest*, were happy to shoot Dutch civilians who refused to obey their commands. The *Landstorm* also fought against the Dutch resistance right up to 7 May, when the division was disarmed by the British 49th Infantry Division.

36th Waffen-Grenadier Division der SS

- *15 Jun 1940:* Wilddiebkommando *Oranienburg* • *1941:* SS-Sonderkommando *Dirlewanger*
- *10 Aug 1944:* SS Regiment *Dirlewanger* • *19 Dec 1944*: SS-Sturmbrigade *Dirlewanger*
- *20 Feb 1945:* 36th Waffen-Grenadier Division der SS

The 36th *Waffen-Grenadier Division der SS* was formed in February 1945 when *SS-Sturmbrigade Dirlewanger* was upgraded to a division. With an even worse reputation than the Kaminski Brigade, the 36th *Waffen-Grenadier Division der SS* was the most notorious of *Waffen*-SS units, serving under perhaps the cruellest of all commanders of World War II.

The unit's brutal commander, *Oberführer* Dr Oskar Dirlewanger, was a highly decorated veteran of World War I, but he was also a drunk and a sadist, who had been imprisoned in the 1920s for sexual assaults on children. A protégé of Gottlob Berger, Dirlewanger suggested the creation of a special punishment unit that would allow SS men convicted of crimes to atone for their deeds.

Poachers and thieves

Dirlewanger formed his first unit in 1940 from former Oranienburg concentration camp inmates convicted of poaching. On the Eastern Front, casualties were replaced with Soviet turncoats and criminals.

Sonderkommando Dirlewanger went into action behind the front lines during Operation *Barbarossa*, the Nazi invasion of the Soviet Union. The unit quickly earned a reputation for atrocity in counter-insurgency operations, with a speciality of 'pacifying' an area by slaughtering every man, woman and child. The unit, never large, spent almost all of its career raping, looting and killing in the Soviet Union, but cemented its reputation for barbarity with the murderous part it played in the brutal suppression of the Warsaw Rising in the autumn of 1944.

Reclassified as a 'paper' division in February 1945, the unit was never more than the size of an understrength brigade. Soviet troops all but annihilated the 36th Division in April, and from the middle of the month desertions meant that what was left of the division melted away.

Dirlewanger escaped to surrender in the West, but did not live long. Recognized in June 1945 by Polish troops serving with the French, Dirlewanger was attacked and beaten to death.

DIVISIONAL INFORMATION

Commanders
SS-Oberführer Dr Oskar Dirlewanger
(20 Feb 1945)

Unit Strengths

1 Jul 1940	84
1 Sep 1940	300
4 Feb 1943	700
30 Dec 1943	259
19 Feb 1944	1200
17 Apr 1944	2000
30 Jun 1944	971
15 Aug 1944	648
16 Oct 1944	4000
29 Dec 1944	6000

Order of Battle
Waffen-Grenadier-Regiment der SS 72
Waffen-Grenadier-Regiment der SS 73
Pioneer-Brigade 687 (Heer)
Grenadier-Regiment 1244 (Heer)
Schwere-Panzerjäger-Abteilung 681 (Heer)
Artillerie-Abteilung 36
Füsilier-Kompanie 36
Panzer-Abteilung Stansdorf I

37th SS-Freiwilligen Kavallerie Division *Lützow*

(Feb – May 1945)

The 37th *SS-Freiwilligen Kavallerie Division Lützow* was formed near Marchfeld on the Hungarian–Slovakian border in February 1945. Raw material for the division came from the remnants of the *Florian Geyer* and the *Maria Theresa* Divisions, shattered in the battles around besieged Budapest, which were brought up to strength as far as possible by drafts of Hungarian *Volksdeutsche*.

In March 1945 the division was far from combat-capable. However a *Kampfgruppe* from *Lützow*, consisting of all veteran and battle-ready elements of the division, was sent to Sixth SS Panzer Army. Commanded by *SS-Obersturmbannführer* Karl-Heinz Keitel (son of OKW chief *Generalfeldmarschall* Wilhelm Keitel), the *Kampfgruppe* arrived on 4 April.

Subordinated to I *SS-Panzerkorps Leibstandarte Adolf Hitler*, *Kampfgruppe Keitel* experienced some fierce combat in the retreat from the advancing Soviet Army through Hungary to Austria. In May 1945, a number of units were taken by the Russians, while others moved west to surrender to the advancing Americans.

Some men from the division took part in a mass breakout from the Altheim POW camp on 13 May after watching the release of regular *Wehrmacht* units while they and other SS men remained in custody.

Left: Members of an SS cavalry unit move along a Hungarian minor road in the Spring of 1945. Although cavalry units were important in the war against the partisans on the Eastern Front, by the time the *Lützow* Division was formed there were few horses available, together with little ammunition and supplies.

THE FOREIGN SS BRIGADES

With the notable exception of the *Wiking* Division, the first SS formations made up from foreign volunteers were regiment-sized legions and brigades. These were not successful in the East, as they were too small to serve independently on a battlefield of the scale encountered in the USSR, and linguistic and national differences meant that when they were brigaded into larger formations they did not match the performance of German units. However, they did provide the basis for more successful SS units that appeared later in the war.

Above: Men of the notorious *Dirlewanger* Brigade in Warsaw in 1944. Originally manned by poachers and convicts, the brigade quickly proved to be little more than than a collection of thugs and murderers.
Opposite: The SS tried to form a British unit using volunteers from POW camps, but the *Britisches Freikorps* was never more than 50 strong.

1st and 2nd SS Motorized Brigades

Left: A group of Soviet civilians are executed accompanied by a sign that reads: 'We are partisans and we shot at German soldiers'. The 1st SS Brigade was used mainly as an anti-partisan unit behind the front lines, supporting police battalions and the notorious *Einsatzgruppen*.

Opposite, bottom: A flag showing the colours of the 1st Grenadier Regiment, Estonian Legion.

1st SS Motorized Brigade was originally formed in the summer of 1941 from the 8th and 10th *SS-Totenkopf Standarten*. The *Totenkopf* regiments had been formed on the outbreak of war by calling up *Allgemeine-SS* reservists. As such, they were not part of the *Waffen*-SS, being more closely related to Theodor Eicke's concentration camp guards.

However, by 1941, Himmler had merged the *Totenkopf Standarten* with the *Waffen*-SS. However, they were not front-line soldiers. The SS Brigades were used to follow the *Wehrmacht*'s advance eastwards into Russia, providing rear security and being used to deal with isolated pockets of resistance. From May 1941 to December 1943 1st Brigade was controlled by *Kommandostab Reichsführer-SS*. It fought for almost three years with Army Group Centre, mostly on anti-partisan operations behind the lines. In 1941 and 1942 it was used to provide support and personnel for *Einsatzgruppen* murder squads.

Most of the personnel of this brigade were *Volksdeutsche*, and in April 1943 it took in a sizeable number of Danish recruits form North Schleswig. Later in 1943 Himmler announced that he was going to form a *Volksdeutsche* brigade. This new formation was sent into action but suffered heavy losses during

the fighting for Smolensk and was reduced to the size of a battlegroup.

It was in action in December 1943 around Bobruisk and on the Dnieper as part of the Ninth Army, Army Group Centre, its total strength being 4125 officers, NCOs and men. In January 1944 the brigade was upgraded to become the 18th *SS-Freiwilligen Panzergrenadier Division Horst Wessel*.

2nd SS Motorized Infantry Brigade was formed from the 4th, 5th and 14th *Totenkopf Standarten* at the same time as the 1st Brigade. It was deployed with Army Group North, taking part in the fighting

UNIT INFORMATION

Commanders
SS-Brigadeführer Karl von Treuenfeld
(24 Apr 1941 – July 1941)
SS-Standartenführer Gottfried Klingemann
(5 Jul 1941 – Jan 1943)
SS-Brigadeführer Friedrich von Scholz
(26 Jan 1943 – 30 Apr 1943)
SS-Standartenführer Heinrich Schuldt
(early May 1943 – 18 May 1943)

around Leningrad. This brigade was an international formation that included Dutch, Flemish and Norwegian volunteer legions.

In late 1942, the 19th and 21st Latvian Security Battalions from the Latvian Legion were attached to the brigade. The 18th, 24th and 26th Latvian *Schuma* Battalions serving in Leningrad were used to form the brigade's 2nd SS Volunteer Regiment. On 18 May 1943, these Latvian battalions along with the other three Latvian Legion battalions were incorporated into the 2nd SS (Motorized) Brigade, and converted into the 2nd *Waffen-Grenadier SS Lettische Brigade*. The Dutch, Flemish and Norwegian formations were removed from the 2nd SS Brigade. The 2nd SS Latvian Brigade was deployed with Army Group North.

Estonian SS Legion/Brigade

Immediately after the occupation of Estonia by the Germans, Estonian military units began to be formed to play their part in the war against the hated Russians. Individual *Schutz-*, *Ost-* and *Polizei-* companies and battalions were formed – by March 1942 there were 16 Estonian units with 10,000 men in Russia and 1500 men in a depot battalion at home in Estonia.

Eventually, up to 54 such units were to be formed. Most served along the lines of communication of Army Group North, providing security and fighting partisans.

In August 1942 the SS called for volunteers to form the *Estnische SS-Legion*. By the end of the year over 1200 men had been found acceptable and had been sent to Debica, Poland, for training. The sheer number of volunteers made it possible to expand the unit from a regiment to a brigade, and it was redesignated *Estnische SS-Freiwilligen Brigade* in May 1943. After the *Finnisches Freiwilligen-Bataillon der Waffen-SS* was stood down in March of 1943, the *Estnisches SS-Freiwilligen Bataillon Narwa* was used to replace the Finns as the third battalion within the *SS-Panzergrenadier Regiment Nordland*.

UNIT INFORMATION

Commanders
SS-Obersturmbannführer Franz Augsberger
(20 Oct 1942 – 21 Jan 1944)

Order of Battle (Estnische SS-Legion)
I Bataillon
II Bataillon
III Bataillon
Pionere-Kompanie
Panzerjäger-Kompanie
Artellerie-Kompanie

Order of Battle (Brigade)
SS-Freiwilligen-Regiment 42
SS-Freiwilligen-Regiment 43
SS-Flak-Abteilung 53
SS-Panzerjäger-Abteilung 53
SS-Nachrichten-Kompanie 53
SS-Feldersatz-Bataillon 53
SS-Ausbildungs-und-Ersatz-Regiment 33
SS-Artellerie-Abteilung 53

The Estonians still had sufficient manpower to form a two-regiment brigade, which became 3rd *Estnische SS-Freiwilligen Brigade* in October 1943. It was upgraded to a division by absorbing the other Estonian formations in the German military, and it also added some Estonian police formations. It was designated 20th *Waffen-Grenadier Division der SS (estnische Nr. 1)* in January 1944.

Lettische SS-Freiwilligen Legion
Lettische SS-Freiwilligen Brigade

The *Lettische SS-Freiwilligen Legion* was raised in February 1943. It saw action at Novo-Sokolniki in November 1943, under the command of Sixteenth Army.

In December 1943 it was withdrawn from the front to be expanded to divisional size. It was redesignated 15th *Waffen-Grenadier Division der SS (lettische Nr. 1)*. The *Lettische SS-Freiwilligen Brigade* was formed in late January 1943, using the Latvian battalions from the 2nd SS Brigade.

The existing 18th, 24th and 26th Latvian *Schuma* (or *Schutzmannschaft*) Battalions serving on the Leningrad front were used to form the brigade's 2nd SS Volunteer Regiment. It was redesignated 2.*Lettische SS-Freiwilligen Brigade* in October 1943. The brigade was upgraded to a division and redesignated 19th *Waffen-Grenadier Division der SS (lettisches Nr. 2)* in January 1944.

UNIT INFORMATION

Commanders
SS-Standartenführer Heinrich Schuldt (18 May 1943)
SS-Oberführer Fritz Freitag   (Jul 1943)
SS-Oberführer Heinrich Schuldt   (3 Sep 1943)

Order of Battle (Estnische SS-Legion)
SS-Freiwilligen Grenadier Regiment 39
SS-Freiwilligen Grenadier Regiment 40

Order of Battle (Brigade)
SS-Freiwilligen-Regiment 1
SS-Freiwilligen-Regiment 2
Artillerie-Bat 52
Panzerjäger-Bat 52

Right: Latvian volunteers in a police unit pose for the camera during a mission to hunt down partisans. In January 1943, Latvian security units were combined with the Latvian Legion to form the Latvian SS-Volunteer Brigade.

Finnisches Freiwilligen-Bataillon der Waffen-SS

The *Finnisches Freiwilligen-Bataillon der Waffen-SS* was formed in 1941. Initially known as *SS Freiwilligen-Bataillon Nordost* it was manned by Finnish volunteers who had signed on for a fixed term of two years.

They had also insisted that they would only fight the Soviet Union, and would refuse any orders to fight against the Western Allies. The notoriously independent Finns also refused to take the oath of loyalty to Hitler, and insisted on being commanded by Finnish officers. This demand was mostly met, though some German officers had to be used to make up for shortages. The Finnish battalion did its *Waffen-SS* training at Gross-Born, before being sent to Army Group South at the end of 1941. At the Mius River it was attached to the *Wiking* Division.

It fought in the offensive battles along the Mius River, through the German summer campaign of

UNIT INFORMATION

Commanders
SS-Obersturmbannführer Hans Collani

Order of Battle
1. Kompanie   2. Kompanie
3. Kompanie   4. Kompanie (MG)

1942 and continued on to the Caucasus. In May 1943 it was transferred away from the front, as the two-year enlistment period of the volunteers was at an end, and it was disbanded in July 1943. Those who wanted to remain in the *Waffen-SS* joined *SS-Freiwilligen Panzergrenadier Division Nordland* or *SS-Standarte Kurt Eggers*.

SS-Freiwilligen Verband *Danemark*/Freikorps *Danmark*

Freikorps Danmark was founded in 1941 at the request of the Danish Nazi party (the DNSAP) and with the approval of the Danish Government. There was some trouble recruiting officers until it was decided that they would keep their Danish rank (and pension) when they joined the *Waffen-SS*.

The Danish soldiers swore an oath to the commander of the *Wehrmacht* and not the usual oath to Adolf Hitler. Christian Peder Kryssing became the first commander of the unit even though he was not a member (or even supporter) of the DNSAP. Kryssing was soon replaced by Christian Frederick von Schalburg (who at the time was attached to the *Wiking* Division), who finished their training.

First blood

In May 1942 the *Freikorps* was airlifted into the Demyansk salient in northern Russia. They were attached to the *SS-Panzer Division Totenkopf*, then holding a position where the Lovat and Robja Rivers converged. On 27 May the Danes under the

command of *Sturmbannführer* von Schalburg mounted an assault on a Soviet bridgehead. On 2 June 1942, von Schalburg was with an assault group pinned down by enemy fire when he tripped a mine and was badly injured. As his men came to assist they were hit by mortar fire: the commander and two others were killed instantly. The Danes lost 28 men in the failed assault. The replacement commander, von Lettow-Vorbeck, was killed on 11 June at Bolschoje Dubowizy. He was one of more than 70 men killed that day.

At the end of August 1942, after suffering 121 killed and several hundred wounded, the *Freikorps* returned to Denmark with a combat strength of 299 out of the original force of 1200. After taking on new recruits it returned to the Eastern Front in October. The *Freikorps* was withdrawn from the front in March 1943. The unit was disbanded on 20 May and those volunteers who remained in service transferred to *SS-Panzergrenadier Regiment 24 Danmark* of the *Nordland* Division.

UNIT INFORMATION

Commanders

Legion-Obersturmbannführer Christian Peder
   Kryssing   (19 Jul 1941 – 23 Feb 1942)
Legion-Obersturmbannführer Knud Børge-
   Martinsen   (23 Feb 1942 – 1 Mar 1942)
Legion-Obersturmbannführer Christian Frederick
   von Schalburg   (1 Mar 1942 – 2 Jun 1942)
Legion-Obersturmbannführer Knud Børge-
   Martinsen   (2 Jun 1942 – 9 Jun 1942)

SS-Obersturmbannführer Hans von Lettow-Vorbeck
   (9 Jun 1942 – 11 Jun 1942)
SS-Obersturmbannführer Knud Børge-Martinsen
   (11 Jun 1942 – 20 May 1943)

Unit Strength

31 Mar 1942	900
May 1942	1386
Nov 1942	1800

Freiwilligen Legion *Norwegen* (Den Norske Legion)

The *Freiwilligen Legion Norwegen* (*Den Norske Legion*) was formed on 29 June 1941. Volunteers were assured that it would be a Norwegian unit with Norwegian officers, uniforms and language, and that its area of operations would be Finland.

These promises were quickly broken – instead of fighting in Finland, the Norwegians found themselves in Russia, taking part in the bloody stalemate on the Leningrad front.

Coming under the control of the 2nd SS Infantry Brigade, the Norwegians occupied positions at Krasnoye Syelo near Pushkin in February 1942. For the next two months the legion took part in the siege warfare around Leningrad. In May 1942 the legion was withdrawn for a rest, returning to the front lines in June 1942. It again became involved in major combat in February 1943, as the Soviets mounted an offensive across Lake Ladoga. The legion left the front line in the spring of 1943, having suffered over 180 casualties in a year. During that period it had been reinforced by the 1st *SS und Polizei-kompanie*, under the command of the head of the Norwegian *Allgemeine-SS*, Jonas Lie.

The legion was disbanded in March 1943. Although it had fought reasonably well, relations between the Norwegians and the Germans had not been good – a problem common to most of the

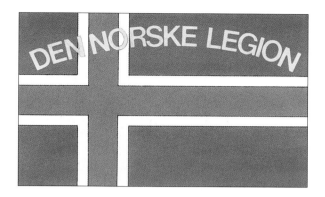

Left: Featuring the Norwegian colours (blue and white cross on a red background), the *Den Norske Legion* flag was one of the simplest used by foreign volunteer units.

UNIT INFORMATION

Commanders
Legion-Sturmbannführer Finn Hanibal Kjelstrup
(Jun 1941 – 1 Dec 1941)
Legion-Sturmbannführer Jorgen Bakke
(Dec 1941 – 15 Dec 1941)
SS-Obersturmbannführer Arthur Quist
(Dec 1941 – Mar 1943)

Unit Strength
Aug 1941	700
Dec 1941	1218
1 Dec 1942	1000
May 1943	600

Order of Battle (Brigade)
1. *Infanterie-Kompanie*
2. *Infanterie-Kompanie*
3. *Infanterie-Kompanie*
4. *Panzerjäger-Kompanie*

legions fighting on the Eastern Front. Legionnaires returned to Norway with little good to say about the Germans, which was to cause the SS some difficulty when it tried to recruit Norwegians later in the war. Most survivors of the legion who wanted to continue fighting transferred to the 23rd *SS-Panzergrenadier Regiment Norge (Norw.Frwg.1)*, one of the regiments of the newly formed 11th *SS-Freiwilligen Panzergrenadier Division Nordland*.

Opposite: A 17-year-old volunteer (foreground) in the *Legion Norwegen* helps to manhandle an artillery piece in the field. Service in the SS appealed to such idealistic youngsters, who believed wholeheartedly in the German 'crusade' against the communists.

SS-Freiwilligen Legion *Niederlande*
SS-Freiwilligen Panzergrenadier Brigade *Nederland*

The *SS-Freiwilligen Legion Niederlande* originated when the Dutch/Belgian *SS-Freiwilligen Standarte Nordwest* was split into *SS-Freiwilligen Verband Flandern* and *SS-Freiwilligen Verband Nederland* in July 1941. It was redesignated *SS-Freiwilligen Legion Niederlande* on 24 September 1941.

The legion was sent to the Eastern Front at the end of 1941. Serving with Army Group North, it went into action against a Soviet bridgehead on the west bank of the Volkhov River in January 1942. On 10 February the legion fought off a major Soviet infantry attack, the first of several over the next weeks. Although it held its positions, combat fatigue and increasing losses

affected morale badly. In the summer of 1942 the legion was attached to the 2nd SS Infantry Brigade and transferred to the Leningrad front. At the end of July the legion fought in the abortive assault on Leningrad, Operation *Nordlicht*. Over the winter of 1942–43 the legion fought around Lake Ladoga. In January 1943, operating alongside the *Legion Norwegen*, the Dutch Legion fought off a major Soviet armoured offensive.

In April 1943 the legion was pulled out of the Leningrad front. After rest and recuperation, it was upgraded to brigade size, becoming the *SS-Freiwilligen Panzergrenadier Brigade Nederland*. The former Dutch legionnaires, strengthened with new recruits from the Netherlands and Romanian *Volksdeutsche*, were assigned to III *SS-Panzerkorps* in Croatia in September 1943. The Dutch played a full part in the no-quarter war against Tito's partisans, committing numerous atrocities. The brigade was numbered 4th *SS-Freiwilligen Panzergrenadier Brigade Nederland* in October 1943 before reverting to its numberless designation on 1 August 1944.

The brigade was ordered to the Eastern Front on Christmas Day 1943, and returned to the Leningrad front. The Dutch brigade was thrown into the fierce battles around Oranienburg as the Red Army launched a major offensive to relieve the besieged city. Soviet successes meant that the brigade now had to pull back to the Narva River. In the fierce fighting on the Narva, the Dutch suffered heavy losses: between 1 January and 13 April 1944 the brigade had 87 officers, 502 NCOs and 3139 men killed, wounded or missing. In the summer of 1944 the Dutch brigade retreated into the Courland pocket along with the rest of the German Army Group North, but not before the *General Seyffardt* Regiment had been destroyed by overwhelming Soviet forces. The rest of the brigade was evacuated to the Stettin area, where it became the 23rd *SS-Freiwilligen Panzergrenadier Division Nederland (niederlandische Nr. 1)* in February 1945.

Above: Members of the *SS-Freiwilligen Legion Niederlande*, seen here in the winter of 1942–43, are congratulated after having been awarded the Iron Cross. Many of the members of the legion would die in the battle for Narva.

UNIT INFORMATION

Commanders (*Standarte Nordwest*)
SS-Oberführer Otto Reich (Apr 1941 – Jul 1941)

Commanders (Legion)
SS-Sturmbannführer Herbert Garthe   (Nov 1941)
SS-Oberführer Otto Reich   (Feb 1942)
SS-Obersturmbannführer Arved Theuermann
                                      (1 Apr 1942)
SS-Standartenführer Josef Fitzthum (10 Jul 1942)

Commanders (Brigade)
SS-Brigadeführer Jürgen Wagner
               (20 Apr 1944 – 10 Feb 1945)

Order of Battle (Legion)
I. Bataillon; II. Bataillon; III. Bataillon
13. Kompanie (Artillerie)
14. Kompanie (Panzerjäger)

Order of Battle (Brigade)
SS-Freiwilligen-Panzergrenadier-Regiment 48
SS-Freiwilligen-Panzergrenadier-Regiment 49
SS-Artillerie-Regiment 54
SS-Nachrichten-Abteilung 54
SS-Panzerjäger-Abteilung 54
SS-Pionier-Bataillon 54
SS-Flak-Abteilung 54
SS-Feldersatz-Bataillon 54

SS-Grenadier Regiment 1 *Landstorm Nederland*
SS-Freiwilligen Grenadier Brigade *Landstorm Nederland*

SS-Grenadier Regiment 1 Landstorm Nederland was formed in March 1943 as *SS-Grenadier Regiment 1 Landwacht Niederlande* and renamed on 26 April 1944. *Landwacht Nederland* was a home defence force not intended for foreign service.

SS-Freiwilligen Grenadier Brigade Landstorm Nederland was formed when *SS-Grenadier Regiment 1 Landstorm Nederland* was upgraded to brigade size, incorporating in the process personnel from *SS-Wachbataillon 3*, *SS-Flak-Batterie Glingendaal*, other Dutch *Waffen*-SS units and members of the Dutch Nazi party, the NSB.

The *Landstorm* Brigade saw action against British paratroopers at Arnhem, serving as part of the battlegroup formed by the 9th *SS-Panzer Division Hohenstaufen*. It was upgraded to 34th *SS-Freiwilligen Grenadier Division Landstorm Nederland* early in February 1945.

Above: SS troops captured by British paratroopers at Arnhem during Operation Market Garden pose for the camera, September 1944.

UNIT INFORMATION

Commanders (Regiment)
SS-Oberführer Viktor Knapp (1 Mar 1943)
SS-Obersturmbannführer Albert Doerheit (1 Apr 1944)
SS-Standartenführer Martin Kohlroser (27 May 1944)

Commanders (Brigade)
SS-Standartenführer Martin Kohlroser (2 Nov 1944 – 10 Feb 1945)

Unit Strength (Brigade)
Dec 1944   7000

Order of Battle (Regiment)
Stabskompanie
I./1. Rgt. Landstorm Nederland
II./1. Rgt. Landstorm Nederland
III./1. Rgt. Landstorm Nederland
Flak-Batterie

Order of Battle (Brigade)
SS-Freiwilligen-Regiment 83 Landstorm Nederland
SS-Freiwilligen-Regiment 84 Landstorm Nederland
Feld-Ersatz-Bataillon Landstorm Nederland

SS-Freiwilligen Legion *Flandern*
6th SS-Freiwilligen Sturmbrigade *Langemarck*

SS-Freiwilligen Verband Flandern was formed July 1941 when *SS-Freiwilligen Standarte Nordwest* was split in two. It was redesignated *SS-Freiwilligen Legion Flandern* on 24 September 1941 and assigned to Army Group North. On 10 November 1941, the Legion moved up to the front near Novgorod. Strength at that time was 1112 men, 950 of whom were Flemish.

From November 1941 the Flanders Legion was in action in the Volkhov region, fighting off Soviet attempts to raise the siege of Leningrad. From August 1942 it occupied trenches around Leningrad, before being sucked into the fighting around Lake Ladoga. In March 1943 it was pulled back from the front, returning to Debica in Poland for rebuilding.

Combat experience

On 31 May 1943 the *SS-Freiwilligen Legion Flandern* was redesignated *SS-Freiwilligen Sturmbrigade Langemarck*, becoming 6th *SS-Freiwilligen Sturmbrigade Langemarck* on 22 October 1943. The *Sturmbrigade* was assigned to operations in the Ukraine, coming under the control of 2nd *SS-Panzer Division Das Reich*. Trapped in the action at Zhitomir, the brigade fought its way out, suffering heavy casualties in the process.

After refitting in Bohemia, a *Kampfgruppe*, given the name *Kampfgruppe Rehmann*, was detached to reinforce III *SS-Germanische Panzerkorps Steiner* in Estonia. Along with many other foreign volunteer units of the SS, *Kampfgruppe Rehmann* fought through the Narva campaign and back to the Courland pocket, from where it was moved by sea to Swinemünde. On 19 October 1944, 6th *SS-Freiwilligen Sturmbrigade Langemarck* was upgraded to divisional status, becoming the 27th *SS-Freiwilligen Grenadier Division Langemarck (flämische Nr. 1)*. The new division was formed around the original 3000 men of the *Sturmbrigade*. They were augmented by up to 15,000 former Flemish *Luftwaffe* personnel as well as members of the *Kriegsmarine* without ships to crew and conscripts from the *Organisation Todt*.

UNIT INFORMATION

Commanders
SS-Oberführer Otto Reich   (Jul 1941)
SS-Sturmbannführer Michael Lippert   (Jul 1941)
SS-Obersturmbannführer Hans Albert von
   Lettow-Vorbeck   (2 Apr 1942)
SS-Hauptsturmführer Hallmann
                     (Jun 1942)
SS-Obersturmbannführer Josef Fitzthum
                (20 Jun 1942)
SS-Sturmbannführer Conrad Schellong
                (11 Jul 1942)
SS-Obersturmbannführer Conrad Schellong
     (31 May 1943 – 19 Oct 1944)

Order of Battle (Legion)
1.Komp./SS-Freiw.Legion Flandern
2.Komp./SS-Freiw.Legion Flandern
3.Komp./SS-Freiw.Legion Flandern
4.Komp./SS-Freiw.Legion Flandern
5.Komp./SS-Freiw.Legion Flandern

Order of Battle (Sturmbrigade)
Brigade Stab
I. Bataillon
II. Bataillon
Infanteriegeschütz-Kompanie
Panzerjäger-Kompanie
Sturmgeschütz-Kompanie
Fla.Kompanie
Fla.Kompanie
Marsch-Kompanie

SS-Sturmbrigade *Wallonien*
5th SS-Freiwilligen Sturmbrigade *Wallonien*

Léon Degrelle's experience while serving with Felix Steiner's *Wiking* Division convinced the Belgian Rexist leader that his *Légion Wallonie* should become part of the SS. He convinced Himmler that the French-speaking Walloons of Belgium in fact had Germanic blood, and the *Reichsführer*-SS supported his proposal.

On 1 June 1943 *Infanterie Bataillon 373* of the German Army officially became *SS-Sturmbrigade Wallonien*. The Walloon Brigade completed its *Waffen-SS* training at Wildflecken, and was redesignated as the 5th *SS-Freiwilligen Sturmbrigade Wallonien*. On 11 November it began a move to the Ukraine, where it would come under the command of the *Wiking* Division. In January 1944, the brigade cleared a Soviet salient projecting from the Teklino. Success was short-lived, however. On 26 January, the Soviet Sixth Tank Army smashed the German front, and encircled some 56,000 German troops in the Korsun area, near the town of Cherkassy. The Germans tried to relieve the pocket, but the trapped troops had to fight their way out by themselves.

The Walloon Brigade fought through the breakout with the *Wiking* Division. Its commander, Lucien Lippert, was killed, and Degrelle (who two years before had been a private) took command. Some 30,000 of the 56,000 German troops escaped without weapons

UNIT INFORMATION

Commanders
SS-Sturmbannführer Lucien Lippert
(1 Jun 1943 – 13 Feb 1944)
SS-Standartenführer Léon Degrelle
(13 Feb 1944 – 18 Oct 1944)

Unit Strength

6 Dec 1943	1972
30 Jun 1944	1188
Late Jan 1945	c.4000
1 Apr 1945	950

Order of Battle (Summer 1944)
I. Bataillon
II. Bataillon
Panzerjäger-Kompanie
Sturmgeschütz-Kompanie

or equipment. The Walloon Brigade lost 1100 out of 1750 men killed or captured. Degrelle became a German propaganda hero, being awarded the Knight's Cross by Hitler. Returning to training camps in Germany, the brigade was gradually brought back up to strength. During the process the brigade sent a *Kampfgruppe* to reinforce the III Germanic Corps in Estonia. Led personally by Degrelle, it fought for three weeks before being evacuated to rejoin the Walloon Brigade. In the autumn a flood of new recruits arrived, drawn from factories, POW camps and Rexist paramilitary formations. The brigade was upgraded to become the 28th *SS-Freiwilligen Grenadier Division Wallonien* in October 1944.

Left: Seen here in Brussels in 1943 after being transferred from German Army control, members of the Walloon Legion pledge allegiance to Hitler as they are sworn in as members of the *Waffen-SS Sturmbrigade Wallonien*.

Französische SS-Freiwilligen Grenadier Regiment
Französische SS-Freiwilligen Sturmbrigade
Waffen-Grenadier Brigade der SS *Charlemagne* (französische Nr. 1)

The *Französische SS-Freiwilligen Grenadier Regiment* was formed in August 1943 from French volunteers, many of whom had been members of various right-wing militias. It was enlarged and redesignated on 18 July 1944, becoming the *Französische SS-Freiwilligen Sturmbrigade*.

Also known as the *Brigade Frankreich* and the *Brigade d'Assaut des Volontaires Français*, it was sent directly to the front in Galicia to fight under the control of the *Horst Wessel* Division. On 10 August 1944, it was engaged with advancing Soviet armies in the foothills of the Carpathians. The newly formed brigade took extremely heavy casualties in a rearguard fight near Sanok. It was transferred to Schwarnegast near Danzig in East Prussia where it was merged with former members of the *Légion des Volontaires Français* in August 1944 to become the *Waffen-Grenadier Brigade der SS Charlemagne (französische Nr. 1)*.

The *Légion des Volontaires Français* (LVF), or *Infanterie Regiment 638*, as it was known to the German Army with which it served, had been formed in July 1941. It had suffered heavy losses during the Soviet winter offensive of 1941–42, during which the 2nd Battalion was almost destroyed; but a 3rd Battalion was formed from new volunteers – including some 200 colonial troops. After these losses it operated as individual battalions against the partisans. It continued fighting the partisans during 1943, but the battalions were again brought together when the LVF was attached to 286th *Sicherungs Division*.

In 1942 an attempt was made to make the LVF an official French formation, but the German Army would not release its French troops. Almost as soon as the *Charlemagne* Brigade was formed, it was reinforced with members of French collaborationist groups fleeing the Western Allies, and the remainder of 1944 was taken up with organizing a French SS division. The *Charlemagne* Brigade was upgraded to become the 33rd *Waffen-Grenadier Division der SS Charlemagne (französische Nr. 1)* on 2 February 1945.

Above: Members of the 638th German Infantry Regiment, otherwise known as the *Légion des Volontaires Français*, march to the front in Russia. As with other Army legions, the LVF was incorporated into the *Waffen*-SS in 1943.

UNIT INFORMATION

Commanders (LVF)

Major Roger Labonne	(Aug 1941)
Oberst Edgar Puaud	(Jun 1943 – 1 Sep 1944)

Commanders (Brigade)

SS-Obersturmbannführer Paul Gamory-Dubourdeau	(Aug 1943)
Oberst Edgar Puaud	(Late Aug 1944)

Unit Strength (*Charlemagne* Brigade)

Dec 1944	7340

Italienische-Freiwilligen Verband
SS-Bataillon *Debica* • Waffen-Grenadier Brigade der SS (italienische Nr. 1)

The rescue of Benito Mussolini in 1943 inspired Italian supporters of *Il Duce* to volunteer to join the SS. Over 1500 officers and men were sent to the training ground at Munsingen, where they formed the *Italienische Freiwilliger Verband*.

They were then sent to northern Italy as the *Italienische-Freiwilligen Legion*, where they were used on anti-partisan operations. The 1st *Sturmbrigade Italienische Freiwilligen Legion* (also known as the 1st *Italienische Freiwilligen-Sturmbrigade Milizia Armata* or *Prima Brigata d'Assalto della Legione SS Italiana*) was formed from the *Italienische SS-Freiwilligen Legion* in the summer of 1944. A second Italian SS unit was formed at the SS Heidelager training ground in Debica in Poland. The *SS-Bataillon Debica* drew its recruits from former Italian soldiers who had served with the *Lombardia* Tank Division and the *Julia* Alpine Division.

Becoming operational in March 1944, the battalion mounted anti-partisan operations south and west of Turin, before being moved south to the Anzio front, going on to fight north of Rome and on the Gothic Line at Florence. On 7 September, the *Debica* Battalion joined with the 1st *Sturmbrigade* as constituent parts of

UNIT INFORMATION

Commanders
SS-Obergruppenführer Karl Wolff (Mar 1944)
SS-Brigadeführer Peter Hansen (Summer 1944)
SS-Standartenführer Gustav Lombard (Oct 1944)
SS-Oberführer Constantin Heldmann (Nov 1944)

Order of Battle (Brigade)
Waffen-Grenadier-Regiment der SS 81
Waffen-Grenadier-Regiment der SS 82
Waffen-Artillerie-Regiment der SS 29
Füsilier-Bataillon 29
Panzerjäger-Abteilung 29
SS-Pionier-Kompanie 29
SS-Nachrichten-Kompanie 29

the new *Waffen-Grenadier Brigade der SS (italienische Nr. 1)*. It was upgraded to the 29th *Waffen-Grenadier Division der SS (italienische Nr. 1)* on 10 February 1945.

SS-Sonderkommando *Dirlewanger*
SS-Regiment *Dirlewanger* • SS-Sturmbrigade *Dirlewanger*

SS-Sonderkommando Dirlewanger (also known as *SS-Sonderbataillon Dirlewanger* and *Sonderkommando der Waffen-SS Lublin*) was formed from *Wilddiebkommando Oranienburg*. This was a small anti-partisan unit made up from poachers and SS disciplinary prisoners trained by *SS-Totenkopf* members.

After the invasion of the USSR, numbers were increased by recruiting former Soviet soldiers, convicts and concentration camp volunteers. The unit was used in anti-partisan operations in Poland and Byelorussia, where it gained a murderous reputation. *SS-Regiment Dirlewanger* was formed in August 1944 when *SS-*

Sonderkommando Dirlewanger was upgraded to a regiment. It took part in fighting against the Polish Home Army in Warsaw, where its brutality and general criminal behaviour shocked even other SS units.

SS-Sturmbrigade Dirlewanger was formed in December 1944 when *SS-Regiment Dirlewanger* was enlarged. The brigade was intended for anti-partisan and security operations, but the advancing Red Army meant that it soon found itself in front-line combat. Some sections of the unit had fighting ability, but many deserted. The unit was nominally upgraded to 36th *Waffen-Grenadier Division der SS* in February 1945.

Its brutal commander, Oskar Dirlewanger, tried to escape to western Europe after the end of the war, but he was recognized by former Polish POWs in France, and was subsequently beaten to death.

Above: An SS man executes a suspected 'partisan' while a crowd of SS and *Werhmacht* soldiers look on. Dirlewanger and his men were brutal participants in the savage struggle between Soviet partisans and the German invaders.

UNIT INFORMATION

Areas of Operations

Poland	(Sep 1940 – Feb 1942)
Byelorussia	(Feb 1942 – Aug 1944)
Warsaw Uprising	(5 Aug 1944 – 15 Aug 1944)
Slovak National Uprising	(Oct 1944)
Hungary	(Dec 1944)
Germany (Silesia)	(Feb 1945)

Commanders

SS-Obersturmbannführer (later *Oberführer*) Dr
   Oskar Dirlewanger   (1940 – 20 Feb 1945)

Order of Battle (Brigade)

SS-Regiment 1 SS-Sturmbrigade Dirlewanger
SS-Regiment 2 SS-Sturmbrigade Dirlewanger
SS-Aufklärungs-Abteilung SS-Sturmbrigade
   Dirlewanger
Nachrichten Kompanie SS-Sturmbrigade
   Dirlewanger
SS-Sanitätskompanie SS-Sturmbrigade Dirlewanger
SS-Verwaltungs-Kompanie
SS-Ersatz-Kompanie

Waffen-Gebirgs Brigade der SS (Tatar Nr. 1)

The *Waffen-Gebirgs Brigade der SS (Tatar Nr. 1)* began forming in May 1944 with the merger of Crimean Tatar *Schuma* (security) battalions.

However, there was little equipment to spare, which delayed completion of the operation. Unit formation was abandoned at the end of 1944 and the men who had already been gathered were transferred to the *Osttürkischen Waffen-Verbände der SS*.

UNIT INFORMATION

Commanders
SS-Standartenführer Fortenbacher

Unit Strength
Dec 1944   3518

Osttürkischen Waffen-Verbände der SS

The *Osttürkischen Waffen-Verbände der SS* was originally formed in 1944 as the *1st Ostmussulmanische SS-Regiment*. Heinrich Himmler's fascination with Islam was encouraged by the Grand Mufti of Jerusalem, Hajj Amin al-Husseini.

The Mufti sponsored the regiment, with the hope that it might eventually grow to be a division. The core of the *Mussulmanischen SS-Division Neu-Turkistan* was provided by troops transferred from Turkic *Osttruppen*

and *Hilfswillige* units under Army command, filled out by prisoners of war and labourers working in Germany. It was trained for anti-partisan operations,

Below: The pro-Nazi Grand Mufti of Jerusalem visits a Muslim unit of the *Waffen*-SS. In 1940, he requested that Hitler 'Settle the question of Jewish elements in Palestine and other Arab countries … along the lines similar to those used to solve the Jewish Question in Germany and Italy'.

but was not reliable: the German commander executed 78 men suspected of inciting mutiny. After serving in Byelorussia from February 1944, the division was one of the SS units attached to the *SS-Sturmbrigade Dirlewanger* which was used to put down the Warsaw Rising. Transferred to Slovakia in the autumn of 1944 after the Slovak National Uprising, it was renamed the *Osttürkischen Waffen-Verbände der SS*.

In December 1944 a large number of men deserted, although some 300 later returned. The Azerbaijani regiment was transferred to the *Kaukasischer Waffen-Verbände der SS* on 30 December 1944. Troops from the disbanded *Waffen-Gebirgs Brigade der SS (Tatar Nr. 1)* were assigned as replacements early in 1945. The *Waffen-Verband* was sent to Austria for further training, which remained uncompleted at the war's end.

UNIT INFORMATION

Commanders

SS-*Obersturmbannführer* Andreas Meyer-Mader
(Jan 1944)
SS-*Hauptsturmführer* Billig   (28 Mar 1944)
SS-*Hauptsturmführer* Hermann   (27 Apr 1944)
SS-*Sturmbannführer der Reserve* Franz Liebermann
(Jun 1944)
SS-*Hauptsturmführer* Reiner Olzscha   (Sep 1944)
SS-*Hauptsturmführer* Fürst   (Jan 1945)

Unit Strength

Feb 1944	3000
Sep 1944	4000
Apr 1945	8500

Order of Battle

Waffen-Gruppe Turkistan
Waffen-Gruppe Idel-Ural
Waffen-Gruppe Aserbaijan
Waffen-Gruppe Krim

Kalmüken Verband

Kalmüken Verband Dr Doll was formed in October 1942 from Kalmyk volunteers. At its core was a nucleus of special troops used by the *Abwehr* – German Army intelligence – known as *Abwehrtrupp* 103. At that time it consisted of two cavalry squadrons.

As with many of the early Russian units on the German side, its creation was authorized by a front-line commander – in this case, the commanding general of 16th *Infanterie-Division (mot)* – who needed mobile troops to cover his vulnerable supply lines. The *Kalmüken Verband* was also referred to as the *Kalmüken Legion* or the *Kalmüken Kavallerie Korps*. 'Dr Doll' was the codename of its first commander, *Sonderführer* Othmar Rudolf Werba. In January 1945, it was

Right: The Kalmyks were nomadic Mongols from central Asia who had settled in the Volga delta in the seventeenth century. They suffered greatly under Stalin in the 1930s and volunteered for German service in some numbers.

intended that the Kalmyks should be assigned to the *Kaukasischer Waffen-Verband der SS*, but as its constituent units were scattered in the face of the advancing Red Army, this never occurred. The *Kalmüken Verband* was eventually concentrated at the Neuhammer training area, where it was to be reorganized as a reinforced cavalry regiment. In March,

it was transferred to Croatia were it was subordinated to the XV *SS-Kosaken Kavallerie Korps*. However, the war was pretty much lost, and so the units retreated towards Austria. Many troopers were captured by the partisans, and those that reached Austria to surrender to the British were handed over to the USSR after the war. Most were executed or sent to the *Gulag*.

Waffen-Grenadier Brigade der SS (weissruthenische Nr. 1)

Waffen-Grenadier Brigade der SS (weissruthenische Nr. 1) was formed out of the more reliable troops left over after the 30th *Waffen-Grenadier Division der SS (russische Nr. 2)* was disbanded in December 1944.

Although it was not of divisional size, it was redesignated as the 30th *Waffen-Grenadier Division der SS (weissruthenische Nr. 1)* in February 1945. The name change from 'Russian' to 'White Russian' has not been satisfactorily explained, but possibly it was to differentiate the unit from its earlier incarnation, which had almost mutinied.

UNIT INFORMATION

Commanders
SS-*Standartenführer* Hans Siegling (Dec 1944)

Order of Battle
Waffen-Grenadier-Regiment der SS 75
Artillerie-Abteilung
Panzerjäger-Abteilung
Reiter-Schwadron

Waffen-Sturm Brigade *RONA*

Bronislav Kaminski, a former engineer who had fallen foul of the Soviet system and was an ardent anti-communist, took command of the local pro-German militia in the town of Lokot, south of Bryansk, when the mayor and council were massacred by partisans.

Kaminski offered his militia for partisan operations, pointing out their local knowledge could be useful to the Germans. In June 1942 they were used in Operation *Vogelsang*, in the forest near Bryansk. The Kaminski militia was split up into company-sized units

UNIT INFORMATION

Unit Strength

Dec 1941	400 – 500	Aug 1943	6000
Jan 1942	800	Sep 1943	12,000 – 15,000
Feb 1942	1200	Jul 1944	4000 – 5000
Mar 1942	1650		
Jul 1942	5000	**Order of Battle**	
Dec 1942	8000 – 10,000	*Stab*	*Panzer-Kompanie*
Feb 1943	9000 – 10,000	*1. Regiment*	*2. Regiment*
Mar 1943	8000	*3. Regiment*	*4. Regiment*
		5. Regiment	

Above: One of the many thousands of *Osttruppen* who fought for the German Army on the Eastern Front. RONA, commanded by Bronislav Kaminski, was one of the few former Soviet units which was eventually to join the SS.

serving as translators, guides and auxiliary combat troops for the German force. The official results of this operation, the first major one in which Kaminski's troops participated, were 1193 partisans killed, 1400 wounded, 498 captured, and 12,531 civilians 'evacuated'. The Axis troops suffered 58 killed and 130 wounded. Kaminski renamed his forces RONA – *Russkaya Osvoboditelnaya Narodnaya Armiya*, or Russian National Army of Liberation. It is sometimes referred to as POHA – which is what RONA looks like in Cyrillic script. The Germans referred to it as the Kaminski Brigade. Anti-Soviet volunteers flooded in.

During the summer of 1943 the Kaminski Brigade was targeted by the partisans, and desertions became more frequent. Nevertheless, it took part in numerous actions on the fringes of the great battle of Kursk. However, Soviet advances after Kursk meant that Kaminski and his men had to leave their home area, fleeing westwards on foot. The unit was renamed *Volksheer-Brigade Kaminski* shortly before being taken over by the *Waffen*-SS July 1944. The SS renamed it *Waffen-Sturm-Brigade RONA*, with Kaminski himself receiving the rank of *Waffen-Brigadeführer der SS*.

The brigade took part in several anti-partisan operations during 1944, but it is notorious for the wave of drunken looting and murder which it perpetrated during the crushing of the Warsaw Rising. Too much even for the Nazis, Kaminski was shot, possibly by the Gestapo, in August 1944.

Waffen-Grenadier Regiment der SS (bulgarisches Nr. 1)

Waffen Grenadier Regiment der SS (bulgarisches Nr. 1) was formed when Bulgaria left the Axis and joined the Allies in September 1944. It was made up of up to 600 Bulgarian workers and soldiers who did not agree with their government's decision.

Most of the volunteers were in Germany at the time or were attached to German military units, and all were willing to keep fighting with Germany against the communists.

The unit was re-equipped with anti-tank weaponry in April 1945 and was renamed the *SS Panzer Zerstörer Regiment (bulgarisches)*. The Germans hoped the regiment would provide the nucleus of a *Waffen-*

UNIT INFORMATION
Commanders
SS-Standartenführer Günter Alhalt (13 Nov 1944)
SS-Oberführer Heinz Bertling (1945)
SS-Oberführer Bogosanow (1945)
SS-Oberführer Rogosaroff (1945)

Grenadier Division der SS (bulgarische Nr. 1), but manpower was lacking and nothing could be done before the end of the war.

1st Ungarische SS-Sturmjäger Regiment

The 1st *Ungarische SS-Sturmjäger Regiment* is believed to have been made up of approximately 5000 Hungarian volunteers who joined the SS after Germany occupied the country in 1944.

Raised on 8 January 1945 by the merging of 1st and 2nd *Ungarische Schibataillons*, the regiment was attached to IV *SS Panzerkorps* at the end of the war, serving under the command of the 5th SS Panzer Division *Wiking*. The panzer corps had been transferred from France to Hungary, but could do little to stop the advancing Soviet armies.

Losses and retreat

After suffering heavy losses in January, the *Sturmjäger Regiment* was transferred to 3rd Panzer Division of III *Korps*, where it was used as infantry. Over the next weeks the regiment was switched between commands several times. During the repeated retreats which took place in spring 1945, the different parts of the

UNIT INFORMATION
Order of Battle
Stab
I. Ungarische SS-Sturmjäger-Bataillon
II. Ungarische SS-Sturmjäger-Bataillon
Dolmetscher-Zug
Nachrichten-Zug
Kradmelder-Zug
Feldgendarmerie-Zug
Stab-Sicherungs-Zug

regiment lost contact with each other, but the combat units continued fighting independently. In the last days of the war, some members of the regiment reached Austria, where, once more attached to *Wiking*, they surrendered to the Americans.

Waffen-Grenadier Regiment der SS (rümanisches Nr. 1)

The *Waffen-Grenadier Regiment der SS (rumänisches Nr. 1)* was formed out of members of the 4th Romanian Infantry Division, which had been refitting in German territory when Romania signed a ceasefire agreement with the Russians.

The regiment also included members of the fascist Iron Guard, which had always had a close relationship with the SS. It was attached to the III Germanic Panzer Corps, and fought on the Oder front until the beginning of March. It was then transferred to the eastern approaches to Berlin, where it was smashed by the Soviet offensive which was launched against the city on 16 April. Most of those regimental personnel who escaped fled westwards, where a number managed to reach the Americans to surrender.

Construction battalions

It was hoped by the Germans that this unit would form the basis of a *Waffen-Grenadier Division der SS (rumänische Nr. 1)*, and to that end a second regiment

UNIT INFORMATION	
Commanders	
(*Nr. 1*) *SS-Sturmbannführer* Gustav Wegner	
	(Nov 1944)
(*Nr. 2*) *SS-Standartenführer* Albert Ludwig	
	(Jan 1945)
Order of Battle	
I. Bataillon	*II. Bataillon*

was raised. *Waffen-Grenadier Regiment der SS (rumänisches Nr. 2)* began forming up at Dollersheim in Austria. However, by this stage in the war there was no fuel for vehicles, little food, and no weapons or ammunition for the new regiment. In April 1945 the two battalions which had been formed were used as construction battalions.

SS-Standarte *Kurt Eggers*

SS-Standarte Kurt Eggers was formed in January 1940. Originally known as the *SS Kriegsberichter Kompanie*, it was the parent unit of all SS combat correspondents. Its *Züge* – or detachments – were assigned to the four *Waffen*-SS units that fought in the Low Countries and France in 1940, and in the Balkans in 1941.

The unit was upgraded to the battalion-sized *SS-Kriegsberichter Abteilung* in August 1941, after the first major expansion of the *Waffen*-SS created more units for the *Kriegsberichter* (war correspondents) to cover. It was further enlarged to regimental size in 1943.

SS-Standarte Kurt Eggers was named after the former editor of the SS magazine *Das Schwarze Korps*.

Eggers was serving with the *Wiking* Division when he was killed in action near Kharkov in 1943. *SS-Standarte Kurt Eggers* was an all-volunteer formation, which placed a premium on press skills but which also had a requirement for multi-lingual members. Several foreign volunteers served with the regiment, usually attached to their national formation.

However, a number of correspondents were from nations with no national SS formations, and they were treated just like their German colleagues, being assigned to one of the regular *Waffen*-SS units. At least two US citizens served in this unit, as well as several from the UK and one from New Zealand.

UNIT INFORMATION

Commander
SS-Standartenführer Günther d'Alquen

Unit Strength
Dec 1943   141
Jun 1944   1180

Order of Battle
Abteilung Verwaltung
Gruppe Wort
Gruppe Bild
Gruppe Rundfunk
Abschnitt Russland-Nord

Abschnitt Russland-Süd
Abschnitt Lettland und Lettische Einheiten
Abschnitt Südost
Abschnitt West
Sonderunternehmen Südost
Kommando Oslo
Kommando Kopenhagen
Kommando Frankreich
Kommando Brüssel
Kommando Südost
Kommando Adria
Gruppe Kampfpropaganda
Sonderunternehmen 'Südstern'

Britisches Freikorps

The *Britisches Freikorps* was formed in January 1943 as *St. Georgs-Legion* (Legion of Saint George). It was made up of British and Commonwealth volunteers recruited from amongst the POWs captured in Norway, Belgium, France, Greece and North Africa.

The forming of such a British volunteer force was the idea of John Amery, son of Leo Amery, Secretary of

State for India in Winston Churchill's war cabinet. Amery, who had been in Paris when it was occupied by the Germans in 1940, managed to find just one volunteer. Himmler became interested in the concept and a renewed attempt to find volunteers was made. Around 300 soldiers expressed an interest, but the Germans felt that most of these were simply looking for a way to get out of their POW camps for a while.

Eventually, 58 volunteers were accepted as genuine (including three Canadians, three Australians, three South Africans and one New Zealander).

Some were former members of the British Union of Fascists and were genuinely committed to the fight against communism. Others were simply bored with life as a POW and were looking for excitement. The legion was renamed the *Britisches Freikorps* in January 1944, and it was nominally attached to III *SS-Panzerkorps* in February 1945, primarily for propaganda purposes. The unit never saw any action, but a handful of British SS men are believed to have fought with 11th *SS-Freiwilligen Panzergrenadier Division Nordland* in the battle of Berlin. Amery was arrested in Milan at the end of the war. He was found guilty of treason and hanged.

Indische Freiwilligen Legion der Waffen-SS

Infanterie-Regiment 950 (indische), or *Legion Freies Indien*, was formed on 26 August 1942 from Indian Army soldiers who had been captured while fighting for the British in North Africa.

Trained in Germany, the legion was used for garrison duty in Holland before being sent to man coastal defences in the Bordeaux area. The unit was transferred to the *Waffen*-SS in August 1944, where it received a new name, becoming the *Indische Freiwilligen Legion der Waffen-SS*. Allied advances out of Normandy threatened to cut off German troops in the south, so the legion was ordered to move from southern France to Germany, travelling by road from 15 August onwards. The unit was harassed by French resistance fighters and regular French troops *en route*. The Indians remained in German training facilities until March 1945. With Allied victory imminent, the legion tried to reach neutral Switzerland but eventually was compelled to surrender to American and French troops.

> **UNIT INFORMATION**
>
> **Commanders (SS)**
> SS-*Oberführer* Heinz Bertling
> (8 Aug 1944 – 8 May 1945)
>
> **Order of Battle**
> *I. Bataillon; II. Bataillon; III. Bataillon*
> *13. Infanteriegeschütz-Kompanie*
> *14. Panzerjäger-Kompanie*
> *15. Pionier-Kompanie*
> *Ehrenwachkompanie*

Right: Indian SS men undergo training in the handling of the 7.5cm (3in) LeFh Model 16 light field gun. The Indian volunteers were followers of nationalist leader Subhas Chandra Bose, who wanted to rid India of British rule.

FOREIGN *WAFFEN*-SS DIVISIONS, KNIGHT'S CROSSES AWARDED

Title (nominal divisional strength, 1945)	Knight's Crosses awarded
5th SS-Panzer Division *Wiking* (14,800)	55
6th SS-Gebirgs Division *Nord* (15,000)	4
7th SS-Freiwilligen Gebirgs Division *Prinz Eugen* (20,000)	6
8th SS-Kavallerie Division *Florian Geyer* (13,000)	22
11th SS-Freiwilligen Panzergrenadier Division *Nordland* (9,000)	25
13th Waffen Gebirgs Division der SS *Handschar* (*kroatische* Nr. 1) (12,700)	4
14th Waffen Grenadier Division der SS (22,000)	1
15th Waffen Grenadier Division der SS (16,800)	3
18th SS-Freiwilligen Panzergrenadier Division *Horst Wessel* (11,000)	2
19th Waffen Grenadier Division der SS (9000)	12
20th Waffen Grenadier Division der SS (15,500)	5
21st Waffen Gebirgs Division der SS *Skanderbeg* (5000)	0
22nd SS-Freiwilligen Kavallerie Division *Maria Theresa* (8000)	6
23rd Waffen Gebirgs Division der SS *Kama*	0
23rd SS-Freiwilligen Panzergrenadier Division *Nederland* (6000)	19

Title (nominal divisional strength, 1945)	Knight's Crosses awarded
24th Waffen Gebirgs Division der SS (3000)	0
25th Waffen Grenadier Division der SS *Hunyadi* (15,000)	0
26th Waffen Grenadier Division der SS (13,000)	0
27th SS-Freiwilligen Grenadier Division *Langemarck* (7000)	1
28th SS-Freiwilligen Grenadier Division *Wallonien* (4000)	3
29th Waffen Grenadier Division der SS (*russische* Nr. 1) (not known)	0
29th Waffen Grenadier Division der SS (15,000)	0
30th Waffen Grenadier Division der SS (*russische* Nr. 2) (4500)	0
30th Waffen-Grenadier Division der SS (*weissruthenische* Nr. 1) (not known)	0
31st SS-Freiwilligen Grenadier Division *Böhmen-Mähren* (11,000)	0
33rd Waffen Kavallerie Division der SS (not known)	0
33rd Waffen Grenadier Division der SS *Charlemagne* (7000)	2
34th SS-Freiwilligen Grenadier Division *Landstorm Nederland* (7000)	3
36th Waffen Grenadier Division der SS (6000)	1
37th SS-Freiwilligen Kavallerie Division *Lützow* (not known)	0

SS RANKS

German	British Army	US Army
Anwarter	Private	Private
Sturmann/Mann	—	Private First Class
Rottenführer	Lance-Corporal	Corporal
Unterscharführer	Corporal	Sergeant
Scharführer	—	Staff Sergeant
Oberscharführer	Sergeant	Technical Sergeant
Hauptscharführer	Staff Sergeant	Master Sergeant
Sturmscharführer	Regimental Sergeant Major	Warrant Officer
Untersturmführer	Second Lieutenant	Second Lieutenant
Obersturmführer	Lieutenant	First Lieutenant
Hauptsturmführer	Captain	Captain
Sturmbannführer	Major	Major
Obersturmbannführer	Lieutenant-Colonel	Lieutenant-Colonel
Standartenführer	Colonel	Colonel
Oberführer	Brigadier	Brigadier-General (1 star)
Brigadeführer	Major-General	Major-General (2 star)
Gruppenführer	Lieutenant-General	Lieutenant-General (3 star)
Obergruppenführer	General	General (4 star)
Oberstgruppenführer	Field Marshal	General of the Army (5 star)
Reichsführer-SS	—	—

SS UNIT ORGANIZATION TERMS & DEFINITIONS

German term

English equivalent

INFANTRY
Divisionen
SS-Divisionen
SS-Panzergrenadier-Divisionen
SS-Grenadier-Divisionen
SS-Gebirgs-Divisionen

Brigaden
SS-Brigaden
SS-Panzergrenadier-Brigaden
SS-Grenadier-Brigaden
SS-Gebirgs-Brigaden
SS-Sturm-Brigaden

Regimenter
SS-Standarten
SS-Regimenter
SS-Infanterie-Regimenter
SS-Polizei-Regimenter
SS-Panzergrenadier-Regimenter
SS-Grenadier-Regimenter
SS-Gebirgsjäger-Regimenter

Abteilungen/Bataillone
SS-Bataillone
SS-Panzergrenadier-Bataillone
SS-Gebirgsjäger-Bataillone
SS-Schi-Bataillone
SS-Jäger-Bataillone
SS-Fallschirm-Jäger-Bataillone
SS-Fla-MG-Bataillone
SS-Jagdverbände
SS-Sonderverbände
SS-Begleit-Bataillon 'RFSS'
SS-Legionen
SS-Freikorps
SS-Waffengruppen
SS-Waffenverbände
SS-Kampfgruppen

ARMOURED AND MOTORIZED TROOPS
Divisionen
SS-Panzer-Divisionen
SS-Kavallerie-Divisionen
SS-Kosaken-Kavallerie-Divisionen

Brigaden
SS-Panzer-Brigaden

Regimenter
SS-Panzer-Regimenter
SS-Schützen-Regimenter
SS-Kradschützen-Regimenter
SS-Kavallerie-Regimenter
SS-Kosaken-Reiter-Regimenter

Abteilungen/Bataillone
SS-Panzer-Abteilungen
SS-Panzerabwehr-Abteilungen
SS-Panzerjäger-Abteilungen
SS-Panzer-Aufklärungs-Abteilungen
SS-Aufklärungs-Abteilungen
SS-Radfahr-Aufklärungs-Abteilungen
SS-Radfahr-Bataillone

Divisions
SS Divisions
SS Armoured Infantry Divisions
SS Grenadier Divisions
SS Mountain Divisions

Brigades
SS Brigades
SS Armoured Infantry Brigades
SS Grenadier Brigades
SS Mountain Brigades
SS Assault Brigades

Regiments
SS Regiments
SS Regiments
SS Infantry Regiments
SS Police Regiments
SS Armoured Infantry Regiments
SS Grenadier Regiments
SS Mountain Regiments

Battalions
SS Battalions
SS Armoured Infantry Battalions
SS Mountain Battalions
SS Ski Battalions
SS 'Hunter' Battalions
SS Paratroop Battalions
SS Anti-Aircraft Machine gun Battalions
SS 'Hunter' Groups
SS Special Units
SS Escort Battalion 'RFSS'
SS Legions
SS Free Corps
SS Combat Group
SS Combat Group
SS *Ad hoc* Combat Groups

Divisions
SS Armoured Divisions
SS Cavalry Divisions
SS Cossack Cavalry Divisions

Brigades
SS Armoured Brigades

Regiments
SS Armoured Regiments
SS Mot. Rifle Infantry Regiments
SS Motorcycle Regiments
SS Cavalry Regiments
SS Cossack Rider Regiments

Battalions
SS Armoured Battalions
SS Tank Destroyer Battalions
SS Anti-Tank Battalions
SS Armoured Reconnaissance Battalions
SS Reconnaissance Battalions
SS Bicycle Reconnaissance Battalions
SS Bicycle Battalions

GLOSSARY

Einsatzgruppen: Mobile armed units, consisting of military police, SS and *Gestapo* personnel, used to round up and execute enemies in the conquered territories in the East. Their main targets were Jews, communist officials – such as commissars – gypsies, political leaders, and the intelligentsia. Each unit was made up of a number of companies known as *Einsatzkommando*.

Freiwillige: Literally, 'volunteer'. Used mainly by the *Waffen*-SS to denote units composed of foreign volunteers. For a time it was applied to non-German but Germanic volunteers (e.g., *Volksdeutsche*, Norwegians, Danes, etc.), but was later applied to denote non-Germanic units (Ukrainians, etc.) as well.

Hilfswillige: Auxiliary volunteers. After the invasion of the Soviet Union, many thousands of Soviet citizens volunteered to fight the Soviet regime. At first, the German Government refused to use them, but later relented (no doubt in the face of mounting casualties) and allowed the German Army to use them in non-combat roles. *Hilfswillige*, or *Hiwis*, served as auxiliaries to the front-line troops on various support tasks such as construction or carrying ammo.

Legion: Often used for units composed of foreigners in German service. Used by both the German Army and *Waffen*-SS. A legion had no fixed size and usually ranged in size from a battalion to a brigade.

Osttruppen: Eastern troops. Initially the Germans refused to arm Soviet citizens who volunteered to fight the Soviet regime after the German inviasion in 1941. Later in the war as German casualties continued to soar the official German stand changed. Eastern troop units were formed *en masse*. An *Ost-Bataillon* meant an infantry battalion of Eastern troops.

Reichsführer-SS: Heinrich Himmler's title as the supreme commander of the SS and *Gestapo*.

Schutzstaffel (SS): Meaning 'Protection Squad', the SS was originally the bodyguard of Adolf Hitler. Himmler transformed them into an army within the Army. Up to 40 SS divisions were created, especially as the war on the Eastern Front accelerated.

Volksdeutsche: This term was used for ethnic Germans living outside and east of Germany. This is in contrast to the *Reichsdeutsche* (literally 'Germans of the realm'), who were citizens of eastern German lands. Prior to World War II, well above 10 million ethnic Germans lived in Central and Eastern Europe. They constituted a significant minority far into Soviet Russia. The Nazi regime popularized the term *Volksdeutsche* and also exploited this group for their own purposes. They were heavily recruited to serve in every arm of the *Wehrmacht* and the *Waffen*-SS.

Wehrmacht: The umbrella term for the armed forces. This included the three major groupings of the German military: the *Heer* (Army), *Luftwaffe* (Air Force) and *Kriegsmarine* (Navy), as well as the *Waffen*-SS, which – although commanded by Himmler – was tactically a part of the *Wehrmacht*.

LIST OF ABBREVIATIONS

BK: *Balli Kombetar* (Albanian National Union party)
BSRN: *Boyevogo Soyuza Russkaya Naroda* (Fighting Union of Russian Nationalists)
DAF: *Deutsches Arbeits Front* (German Labour Front)
DNL: *Den Norske Legion* (Norwegian Legion)
DNSAP: *Danmarks Nationalsocialistiske Arbejder Parti* (Danish National Socialist Workers Party)
GSSN: *Germanske SS Norge* (Norwegian SS organization established by the Germans)
HSSPF: *Höhere SS-Polizei Führer* (Higher SS and Police Commander – the highest German police authority in a region)
KONR: *Komitet Osvobozhdeniya Narodov Rossii* (Committee for the Liberation of the Peoples of Russia)
LAF: *Lietuviu Aktyvistu Frontas* (Lithuanian Activist Front)
LVF: *Légion des Volontaires Français* (French Volunteer Legion)
MSR: *Mouvement Social Revolutionnaire* (French collaborationist party)
MVSN: *Milizia Voluntaria Sicurezza Nationale* (Italian Fascist militia – the 'Blackshirts')
NCO: non-commissioned officer
NS: *Nasjional Samling* (Norwegian National Unity Party)
NSUF: *Nasjonal Samlings Ungdomsfylking* (Norwegian NS Youth Organization)
NSB: *Nationaal Socialistische Beweging* (Netherlands National Socialist Movement)
NKVD: *Narodnyy Kommissariat Vnutrennikh Del* (Soviet 'Peoples' Commissariat for Domestic Affairs' – the Secret Police)
NSKK: *Nationalsocialistische Kraftfahrkorps* (Nazi party motor transport organization)
OKH: *Oberkommando des Heeres* (Army High Command)
OKW: *Oberkommando der Wehrmacht* (Armed Forces High Command)
POW: prisoner(s) of war
PPF: *Parti Populaire Français* (French collaborationist party)
RAD: *Reichsarbeitsdienst* (Reich Labour Service)
RFSS: *Reichsführer-SS*
RNNA: *Russkaya Natsionalnaya Narodnaya Armiya* (Russian Nationalist Patriotic Army).
RNP: *Rassemblement National Populaire* (French collaborationist party)
ROA: *Russkaya Osvoboditelnaya Armiya* (Russian Army of Liberation)
RONA: *Russkaya Osvoboditelnaya Narodnaya Armiya* (Russian National Army of Liberation)
RSHA: *Reichssicherheitshauptamt* (Reich Main Security Office)
SA: *Sturmabteilung* (Nazi 'Brownshirts')
SD: *Sicherheitsdienst* (SS Security Service)
SS: *Schutzstaffel* ('Protection Squad')
STO: *Service du Travail Obligatoire* (French forced labour service)
USSR: Union of Soviet Socialist Republics
VDB: *Volksdeutsche Bewegung* (Luxembourg national socialist party)
VT: *Verfügungstruppe* (armed SS units that were the forerunners of the *Waffen*-SS)
WKB: *Wehrbezirkskommando* (Military District Headquarters)

BIBLIOGRAPHY

Abbott, Peter. Men-at-Arms 131. *Germany's Eastern Front Allies, 1941–1945*. London: Osprey, 1983.

Ailsby, Christopher. *Hitler's Renegades: Foreign Nationals in the Service of the Reich*. Washington, DC: Brassey's Inc (USA), 2004.

Anders, Wladyslaw. *Russian Volunteers in Hitler's Army*. Bayside, NY: Axis Europa Books, 1998.

Forbes, Robert. *Pour L'Europe: The French Volunteers of the Waffen-SS*. Self-Published, 2000.

Jurado, Carlos Caballero. Men-at-Arms 147. *Foreign Volunteers of the Wehrmacht, 1941–1945*. London: Osprey, 1983.

Kleinfeld, Gerald R. and Lewis A. Tambs. *Hitler's Spanish Legion: The Blue Division in Russia*. Carbondale,

IL: Southern Illinois University Press, 1979.

Littlejohn, David. *Foreign Legions of the Third Reich, Volume 1: Norway, Denmark, France*. San Jose, CA: Bender Publishing, 1979.

Littlejohn, David. *Foreign Legions of the Third Reich, Volume 2: Belgium, Great Britain, Holland, Italy, Spain*. San Jose, CA: Bender Publishing, 1981.

Littlejohn, David. *Foreign Legions of the Third Reich, Volume 3: Albania, Czechoslovakia, Greece, Hungary, Yugoslavia*. San Jose, CA: Bender Publishing, 1985.

Littlejohn, David. *Foreign Legions of the Third Reich, Volume 4: Poland, Ukraine, Bulgaria, Romania, Free India*. San Jose, CA: Bender Publishing, 1987.

Munoz, Antonio J. *Hitler's Eastern Legions, Volume 1: Baltic Schutzmannschaft*. Bayside. NY: Axis Europa Books, 1998.

Munoz, Antonio J. *Hitler's Eastern Legions, Volume II: The Osttruppen*. Bayside. NY: Axis Europa Books, 1997.

Munoz, Antonio J. *Forgotten Legions: Obscure Combat Formations of the Waffen SS*. Boulder: Paladin Press, 1991.

Nafziger, George F. *German Order of Battle in World War II, Volume 7. Foreigners in Field Gray: Russians, Croats, and Italians*. West Chester, Ohio: Nafziger Collection, 1995.

Rikmenspoel, Marc. *Soldiers of the Waffen-SS: Many Nations, One Motto*. Winnipeg: J.J. Fedorowicz, 1999.

Thomas, Nigel. Men-at-Arms 363. *Germany's Eastern Front Allies (2): Baltic Forces*. Oxford: Osprey Publishing, 2002.

Weale, Adrian. *Renegades: Hitler's Englishmen*. London: Pimlico, 2002.

Williamson, Gordon. *Loyalty is my Honor*. Osceola MI: Motorbooks International. 1995

Websites

Axis and Foreign Legion Militaria
axis101.bizland.com

Axis History Factbook
www.axishistory.com

www.feldgrau.com

Waffen-SS Order of Battle
www.wssob.com
www.gutenberg-e.org

INDEX

INDEX

INDEX

INDEX

THE INTERPET ENCYCLOPEDIA OF
KOI

Kin Matsuba

A timber bridge provides an oriental atmosphere and the perfect place from which to view koi.

THE INTERPET ENCYCLOPEDIA OF

KOI

A comprehensive introduction to keeping and displaying these magnificent ornamental fish, from choosing healthy stock to installing a fully equipped koi pond. Plus a full-colour survey of all the major varieties.

An **INTERPET** Book

Published by Interpet Limited

An **INTERPET** 🐟 *Book*

©1999 Interpet Publishing
Vincent Lane, Dorking,
Surrey, RH4 3YX.

ISBN 1-902389-73-5

Credits

Editor: Anne McDowall
Design: David Jones and Stonecastle
Graphics
Colour reproductions: Scantrans Pte.
Ltd.
Filmset: SX Composing Ltd.
Printed in China

A stone wall will screen the pond and enable children to watch koi safely.

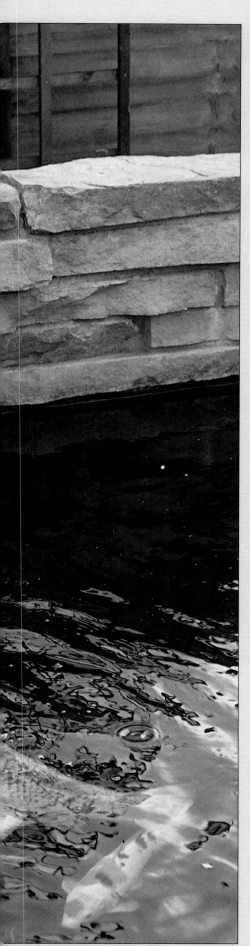

寄稿者
CONTRIBUTORS

This encyclopedia embraces the experience of a team of professional koi dealers, the insight of enthusiastic hobbyists and the expertise of specialists in associated fields. The main contributors are as follows:

Bernice Brewster
(Koi anatomy, Water quality and filtration, Health care)

Nicky Chapple
(Buying koi, Koi varieties)

John Cuvelier
(Pond and filter construction)

Mark Davies
(The history of nishikigoi, Feeding koi, Breeding koi)

Deri Evans
(Pond and filter construction, Seasonal care)

Glyn Evans
(Pond and filter construction)

Keith Phipps
(Showing koi)

Yvonne Rees
(Landscaping and water gardens)

Peter W. Scott MSc., BVSc., MRCVS, MIBiol.
(Health care consultant)

目 次
CONTENTS

PART ONE
PRACTICAL SECTION   8

PART TWO
KOI VARIETIES   122

Greenery, rockwork and Japanese artefacts create a restful, oriental setting for these koi ponds.

PART ONE

PRACTICAL SECTION

A fascination with koi often develops into an obsession, but enthusiasm for collecting and showing these beautiful fish must be coupled with a clear understanding of what makes them 'tick' and how you can provide the ideal environment for them. The chapters in this practical section of the book reflect and enhance these priorities.

After a brief introduction to the history of koi, our attention turns to the anatomy and basic physiology of koi as members of the carp family. The next two sections offer guidelines on providing the most appropriate physical environment for koi – with practical advice on designing and constructing suitable ponds and filters – and an all-important look at the biochemical aspects of maintaining water quality. These are followed by three chapters that consider in turn the subjects of buying, feeding and seasonal care. In these sections, you will find essential guidance on how to look after your koi on a day-to-day and season-by-season basis.

Since a koi pond can be a decorative addition to your garden, the next chapter takes up the challenge of landscaping and water gardening in the widest sense, with practical suggestions that embrace both Western and Oriental influences. It is a sad fact, however, that even in the best systems koi are prone to ill-health from time to time. How do you cope? This is the subject addressed in the chapter on health care, which includes a detailed survey of all the common pests and diseases that could affect your koi, together with sensible advice on prevention and cure. The final two chapters provide basic information on breeding koi – a pursuit rapidly spreading from the exclusive domain of professionals into the growing world of enthusiastic hobbyists – and offer a 'behind-the-scenes' look at showing koi.

Selecting prize-winning koi at a national koi show.

錦鯉の歴史

THE HISTORY OF NISHIKIGOI

The many beautiful koi varieties we know today are, in fact, all descendants of the black fish known as Magoi. Although early records of koi (i.e. common carp) date back some 2,500 years, their farm cultivation is much more recent. Colour mutations first appeared some two hundred years ago and by the end of the 19th century many of the varieties we know today had been established. However, it was not until the 20th century that koi-keeping as a hobby began to flourish. The development of road and rail links and, more particularly, the advancement of air travel, facilitated the transportation of koi, and these beautiful fish soon attracted a huge following in other parts of the world, particularly in the USA and UK. Since the first days of the culture of nishikigoi – as fancy koi came to be known – many farmers have invested much time and effort in developing new varieties. Although Japan still leads the world, other countries are now producing koi for their own home markets, and it is probable that the most beautiful nishikigoi are yet to be seen.

A tea house, strong green foliage and large boulders create the Japanese atmosphere in this water garden.

THE HISTORY OF NISHIKIGOI

Contrary to common belief, koi are not indigenous to Japan. They originate from eastern Asia – in the Black, Azov, Caspian and Aral Seas – and from China, where the earliest written record of these fish is found. At his birth, the first son of the great Chinese philosopher Confucius (551-479? BC) was presented with a koi by King Shoko of Ro. Confucius named his son after this fish because it was considered to be a symbol of strength; allegedly, it was the only fish able to swim up the falls of the Yellow River. In 533 BC, a Chinese book entitled 'Yogyokyo' set out methods of breeding koi. At this time, colour variations were limited to red and grey. Since koi at this time were cultivated solely for food, however, such variations were not considered seriously in the ornamental sense.

Koi were introduced to Japan with the invading Chinese, and the first account of them being kept in Japan, apparently by an Emperor, dates back to AD 200. From here, the story moves forward to the 17th century, when rice farmers of Yamakoshi go, a village in the Niigata prefecture on the northwestern coast of mainland Japan, introduced carp into their irrigation ponds to supplement their diet of rice. The area is situated high in the mountains, where snow fall of up to six metres made access difficult, if not impossible, during the winter months. Such an isolated position forced the inhabitants of Yamakoshi go·to rely on the resources they had, and the attention they devoted to breeding carp led to the Niigata region becoming established as the centre of the growing koi 'industry'.

Colour mutations were first noticed between 1804 and 1830. These mainly involved red koi, white koi and light yellow koi (the latter being improved to become the first single-coloured Kawarimono) and, later, the tortoiseshell-patterned koi – all mutations from the black common carp, known as Magoi. Around 1830-50, cross-breeding of red with white carp produced what could be described as the first Kohaku. Early koi varieties, such as Asagi, Higoi and Bekko, were cross-bred until, in the 1880s, many of the varieties we know today were fixed. Certain varieties consistently reached high standards of quality over a period of several generations and, in this way, lineages became established.

Asagi and Ki Utsuri were first produced in 1875. These varieties were highly prized and began to exchange hands for very large sums of money. This led to a temporary ban on the industry, as the local authorities thought that such carp breeding bordered on speculation. Fortunately, as the local villagers had no other means of livelihood or pastime, the ban did not last long.

Meanwhile, in Central Europe, a mutation arose in the late 18th century that was to exert a striking influence on koi 'design'. The mutation affected the scales, resulting either in scaleless, so-called 'leather' carp or 'mirror' carp with large shiny scales along the dorsal line. These fish, which became known as 'doitsu' from their Germanic/Austrian origins, were originally bred for the table, being easier to clean than fully scaled fish. Some doitsu carp were introduced to Japan in 1904 and from these individuals the first Shusui (which are doitsu Asagi) were produced in 1910.

Breeding fancy koi was restricted to the Niigata region until the beginning of the 20th century. Indeed, it was not until

Below: *The many beautiful koi varieties we admire today are all descendants of the black common carp, known as Magoi, shown in this old illustration. This fish, which is still in existence, has a history of some 2,500 years, and originates from the seas of Eastern Asia and China.*

1914 that koi were introduced outside this area, when Hikosaburo Hirasawa, the Mayor of Higashiyama Mura (now Yamakoshi Mura), sent 27 koi to the great Tokyo Exhibition to promote the economic circumstances of the poverty-stricken people of the Niigata region. These koi were awarded a second prize at the exhibition and eight of them were presented to the Emperor Taisho's son. This marked the beginning of the flourishing koi industry as we know it today.

Unfortunately, after several good years, during which the Kohaku and Sanke varieties were stabilized, an economic depression in 1920 caused the koi industry to fall to a low ebb. During the period up to the Second World War, several more varieties, including Shiro Bekko and Showa, were successfully established, despite another depression in the industry, this time caused by food shortages. Koi breeding continued to thrive in Niigata, and the industry grew as the area became more accessible, with the building of the Shin-etsu Railway and the National Highway Route 17.

Above: *The bright colours and patterns of these beautiful koi are the result of nearly two centuries of selective breeding. Today, there are hundreds of different varieties in existence and new and unique koi are continually appearing, principally in Japan.*

To a certain extent, the boom in the breeding of koi that took place at the end of the Second World War was made possible by the commercial development of air travel. Transportation of koi all over the world was then possible and a huge international market developed. For example, koi were first shipped to San Francisco in 1938, to Hawaii in 1947, to Canada in 1949 and to Brazil in 1953.

Koi-keeping outside Japan has increased dramatically, particularly during the 1980s, and many koi are now being produced in other countries for their own home markets. Although at present Japanese varieties outshine those produced in other parts of the world in terms of range and quality, it is conceivable that new varieties will eventually appear for the first time outside Japan.

Above: *It was here, in the Niigata prefecture of Japan, that koi were first bred, initially for food but later for their beautiful colours and patterns. The region remains at the heart of the koi-breeding industry.*

KOI ANATOMY

Before considering any health-related problems to which koi may be subject, it is vital to understand a little bit about their basic anatomy. After all, few people would consider tackling a faulty car engine without having some idea of how an engine is put together. In the same way that understanding the structure of an engine and how it works enables a mechanic to detect and repair any faults, so appreciating how koi are 'built' and 'what makes them work' is a necessary first step in tackling any problems associated with their health.

This section considers the body shape of koi and then the very basic anatomy in two natural categories: the external anatomy, which includes all the visible parts of the body; and the internal anatomy, which embraces the organs and tissues and the systems that 'connect' them inside the body.

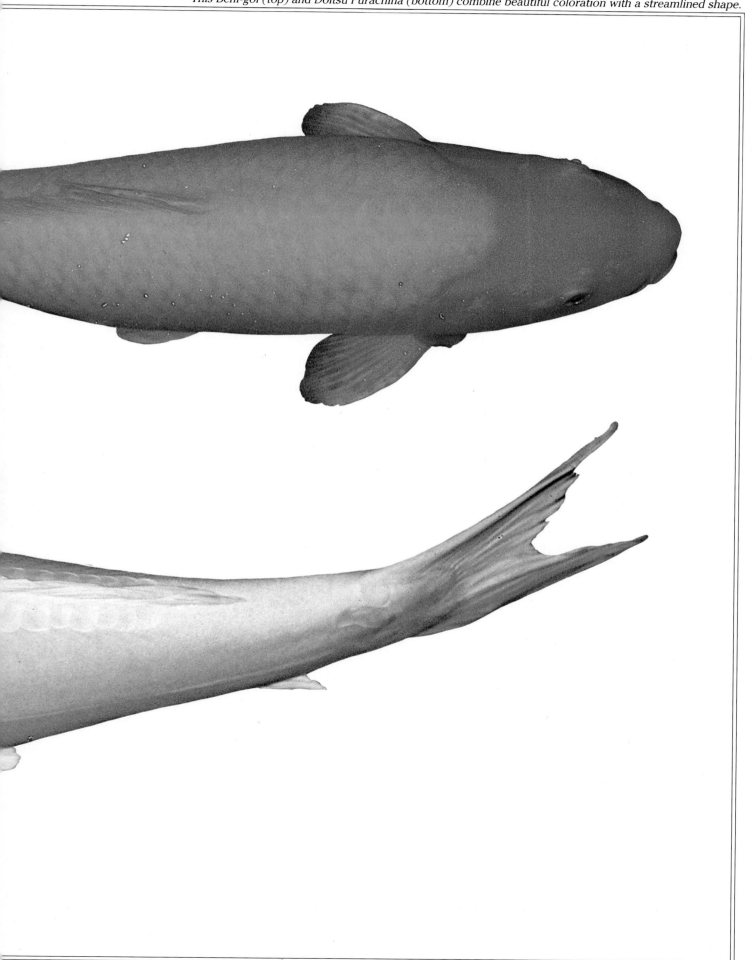

KOI ANATOMY

Body shape

In common with most fishes, koi are broader at the front than at the tail end. Such a shape streamlines the koi and minimizes turbulence as it moves through the water. If a cone is placed with the pointed end turned into a current of water, the water swirls at the rear flattened surface, creating turbulence, or drag. If the cone is reversed, so that the flat surface meets the current, the flow of water around it is less turbulent and actually assists its passage through the water. The movement of koi through the water is similar to that outlined for the second cone.

The external anatomy

The external anatomy of koi includes the scales, fins, operculum (gill cover), vent, eyes, nostrils, barbels and lateral line.

Scales These form a lightweight, pliable suit of armour over the surface of the fish. Each scale is an extremely thin but flexible plate of bone-like material. The front end of the scale is inserted into a deep pocket of skin; the back is quite free and overlaps the front of the scale behind, just as roof tiles overlap. There are two distinct types of scale pattern found on koi: completely scaled, and the so-called doitsu, in which the scales are enlarged and arranged along the midline of each side of the body and, usually, at the dorsal and anal fin bases. The scales of doitsu koi are entirely embedded in the skin. (We look more closely at scalation, and, in particular, at the various types of doitsu scalation, in the varieties section on page 125.)

Covering the scales and, indeed, the whole body of the fish, is a layer of mucus. This mucus is mildly antiseptic and is secreted by special cells in the skin. It gives fish their characteristically slimy feel and literally 'lubricates' the body as the fish moves through the water, helping to maintain a 'slippery', hydrodynamic shape.

Fins Koi have five sets of fins: the dorsal, anal and caudal (or tail) fins, which are single, and the pectoral and pelvic fins, which are paired. Fish swim using the body muscle, (as explained on page 18), and the fins play an important role in maintaining stability in the water. When erected, the dorsal and anal fins prevent rolling and yawing, and the pectoral and caudal fins control pitching. The pectoral and pelvic fins also control fine movement by counteracting the propulsive forward motion caused by the exhalation of water from the gill covers, thus enabling the koi to remain motionless.

Operculum (gill cover) This is a large bony plate that protects the delicate gills (see page 20). It is free at the rear and lower edges and acts as a one-way valve, allowing water to leave the gill chamber but preventing any backflow of respired, oxygen-deficient water to re-enter the gills. It articulates with the skull and the large hyomandibular bone. (In fishes, this bone forms part of the suspension for the lower jaw; in humans, it is tiny and forms the stapes in the inner ear.)

Vent Just in front of the anal fin is a large pore, usually termed the vent. The gut and the ducts from either the testes or ovaries terminate at this point. This is not a cloaca, which is a term used to describe a common opening for the digestive, urinary and genital systems. Just in front of the vent there is a smaller opening, which receives the urinary ducts from the kidneys.

Eyes Koi have fairly good eyesight for fish. The position of the eyes on the head gives them almost total 360° vision, enabling them to see above and behind, as well as in front and below themselves. The ability to see above and behind is particularly important because it enables koi to watch for the approach of enemies while they are feeding.

Nostrils On either side of the snout are a pair of nostrils, i.e. four in all. In cross

External features of koi

The streamlined shape of a koi is typical of the carp family of fishes to which it belongs. The strong, high-backed body and well-developed fins give the fish speed and manoeuvrability in the water. Note the two pairs of sensitive barbels.

Operculum (gill cover)

Nostrils

Barbels (two pairs)

Pectoral fins

section, the nostrils are seen to be joined by a U-shaped tube. The water flows in through the front nostril and out through the rear one. The floor of the tube is folded into a series of ridges, which are then arranged in the form of a rosette. The ridges are coated in a skin that is peppered with olfactory, or 'smelling', cells. These cells are able to detect extremely small quantities of dissolved substances in the water, even from quite distant objects. In fact, the sense of smell is more important to the koi than eyesight for finding food.

Barbels Koi have one pair of barbels on each side of the mouth, a small barbel on the side of the upper lip and a larger one

more or less at the corner of the mouth. These fleshy structures are moved by muscles that once operated parts of the jaw and palate and are covered with taste buds that literally allow koi to taste anything the barbels contact. Like their ancestors, the wild carp, koi are bottom feeders, using their barbels to locate grubs, insects, crustaceans, worms and water plants in the substrate. (Koi-keepers generally feed koi with floating pellets and sticks, but this is simply to enjoy seeing their spectacular livery as they surface to feed). Thus, koi use their sense of smell to locate an area where food is to be found, and then detect the individual particles of food using the very sensitive taste buds on their barbels.

Lateral line organ Along the middle of each side of the body there is a row of scales, each pierced by a small pore that connects by way of a small tube to a canal that lies in the skin beneath the scales. This system of canals and tubes forms part of the lateral line organ. On the head, the lateral line organ runs beneath the eye to the snout, its passage being marked by conspicuous pits. In some doitsu koi (see page 125), the lateral line may be seen as a conspicuous line that runs along the middle of the fish, from just behind the operculum to the tail. Although the sensory cells of the lateral line are similar to those found in our internal ear, it is difficult to interpret precisely the sensation these cells impart to

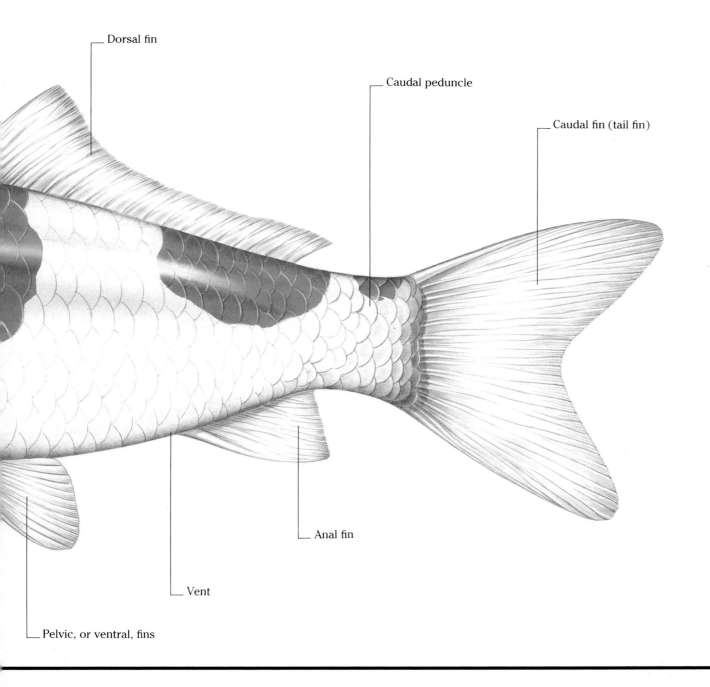

Dorsal fin

Caudal peduncle

Caudal fin (tail fin)

Anal fin

Vent

Pelvic, or ventral, fins

KOI ANATOMY

the fish. It seems that they are sensitive to water movement, waves and disturbances in the water, enabling koi to avoid other fishes, objects and the pond walls.

The internal anatomy
The internal anatomy is more complex than the external anatomy, not only because of the number of different organs involved, but also the way these various organs interact.

Skeleton One of the most important features of the internal anatomy, but one which receives the least consideration, is the skeleton. Koi are members of a group of fish known as teleosts, literally meaning 'bony skeleton'. The skeleton has several major functions: it forms a protective and supporting framework for the internal organs and tissues, and enables the fish to move by providing a series of flexible joints and attachment

points for muscles.

Parts of the first four vertebrae of the backbone are modified to form the Weberian ossicles, a system of tiny bones that link the swimbladder to the inner ear. Sounds travelling through the water cause the swimbladder to vibrate and the ossicles amplify these vibrations and transmit them to the sensitive hair cells within the liquid-filled semicircular canals of the inner ear. With such an apparatus, koi can undoubtedly 'hear'.

Teeth Koi, like all other members of the cyprinid family, lack teeth in the jaws. Their few teeth are large grinding devices on plates of bone in the throat.

Muscle The bulk of the koi body is formed from four large blocks of muscle, two on either side of the body. These blocks are subdivided into V-shaped muscle segments. The muscle segments

of the throat and gill arches are very well developed to control respiratory movements. The jaw muscles cover most of the cheeks and exert their force in closing the jaws. The muscles of the paired fins are simple in construction, although those controlling the pectoral fins are very extensive.

Heart The heart, situated just behind and below the gill arches, is a large muscular pump consisting of four consecutive chambers. The first chamber is simply a thin-walled sac with very little muscle. The second chamber, or atrium, is also thin walled, but expandable. The third chamber, or ventricle, has thick muscular walls and is largely responsible for the pumping action of the heart. The fourth chamber is also thick walled and has special non-return valves in it, preventing blood flowing back into the preceding chambers.

Koi skeleton

This skeleton, drawn from life, clearly shows how it forms a framework to support and articulate the body of the fish. The vertebral column is literally the central axis of the koi's skeleton, providing attachment points for the major blocks of muscles that give koi their power and agility.

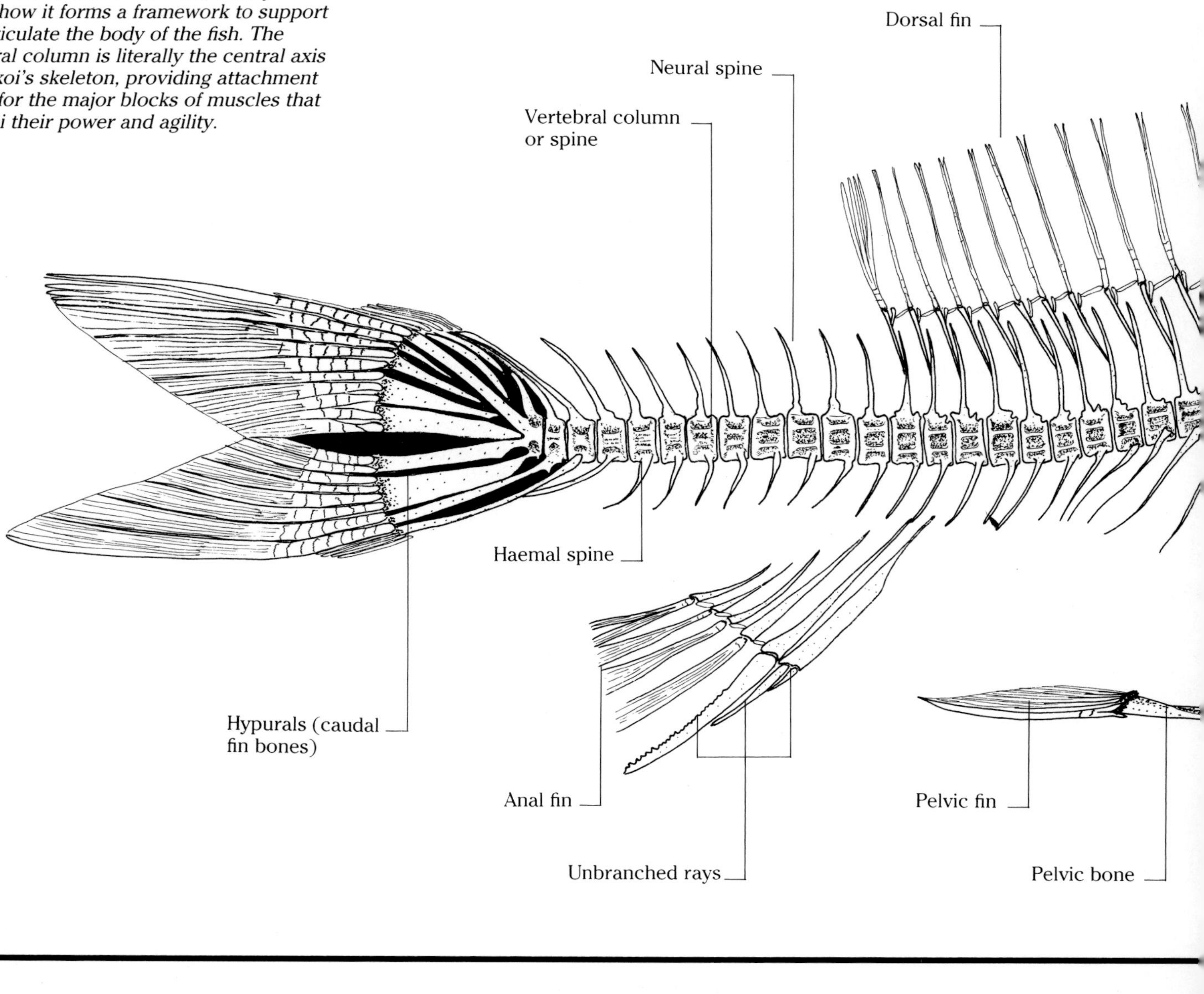

Dorsal fin

Neural spine

Vertebral column
or spine

Haemal spine

Hypurals (caudal
fin bones)

Anal fin

Unbranched rays

Pelvic fin

Pelvic bone

The circulatory system

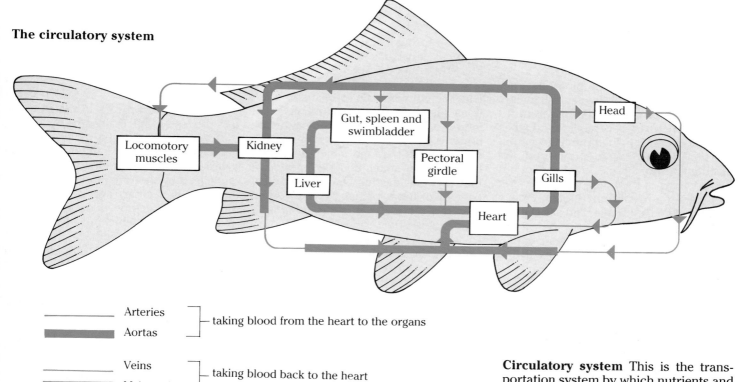

Arteries
Aortas
— taking blood from the heart to the organs

Veins
Major veins
— taking blood back to the heart

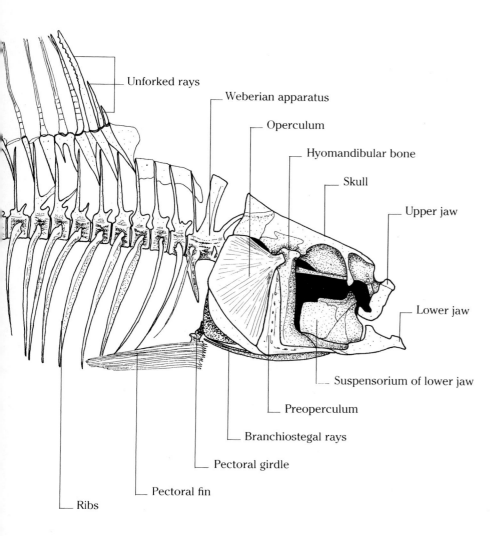

Unforked rays

Weberian apparatus

Operculum

Hyomandibular bone

Skull

Upper jaw

Lower jaw

Suspensorium of lower jaw

Preoperculum

Branchiostegal rays

Pectoral girdle

Pectoral fin

Ribs

Circulatory system This is the transportation system by which nutrients and oxygen reach the cells of the body and waste products are removed from them. It is an embracing term that includes the blood, plasma and vessels through which these body fluids flow. The heart provides the pumping force to move the blood through these vessels, first to the gills and then to the brain and the remaining parts of the body, before returning once again to the heart. The vessels that carry blood to and from the gills, to the brain and then body are arteries; those that return the blood to the heart are veins. (See the diagram shown above.)

Generally, the most important function ascribed to the circulation is transporting oxygen from the gills to the tissues and removing carbon dioxide from the body via the gills. However, it also supplies a constant stream of food materials from the gut or liver to the tissues. As the tissues process the foodstuffs, they produce nitrogen-containing waste products, which are poisonous to the tissues. Some of these nitrogen products, together with any excess water, are transported in the blood to the kidneys, where they are extracted and 'processed' into urine. As in other bony fish, most of the nitrogenous wastes leave the body in the form of ammonia, which diffuses into the water from the gills.

Blood The blood consists of three main elements: the plasma, red blood cells and white blood cells. The plasma is a watery fluid of complex structure. The red blood cells contain haemoglobin, a red pigment that binds with oxygen. Thus, the red blood cells flowing from the gills carry oxygen to the tissues, where they ex-

KOI ANATOMY

change their oxygen for carbon dioxide, the waste gas produced during the process of metabolism.

The white cells in the blood have an equally important role to play, but mainly in terms of protecting the fish from infection. There are several different types of white blood cell, their precise function varying according to their type. All accumulate in injured, inflamed or infected areas of the body, where they repel bacterial or viral invasions, remove dead or damaged tissue, and assist in repairing damaged tissues.

Blood cells have a short lifespan, new ones being produced primarily in the spleen and kidneys.

Gills The gills are the equivalent of our lungs; they provide a large surface area of tissue where carbon dioxide is exchanged for oxygen. In addition to carrying out this process of gaseous exchange, they are an important site for osmoregulation (i.e. controlling the salt/water balance and excretion).

To the naked eye, the gills appear as rows of very fine, finger-like projections arranged on a series of curved arches. There is a double row of delicate filaments in a V-shaped arrangement along the posterior surface of each arch. The surface of the filaments is highly folded, enormously increasing their surface area, and the skin is extremely thin, allowing intimate contact between the blood and water. As water flows over the gill filaments, oxygen is extracted and carbon dioxide released – a process of 'external respiration'.

The osmoregulatory role of the gills is made possible not only by their large surface area but also by an outer layer of special cells that absorb salts from the water. (Salts is used here in the chemical sense, rather than simply referring to sodium chloride, or common salt.) Since the body tissues and fluids of a koi contain a higher concentration of salts than the surrounding fresh water, there is a tendency for water to be absorbed and salts lost through the gills. (The processes at work here are osmosis and diffusion. Osmosis is the process by which water passes through a semi-permeable membrane – in this case, the gill membrane – from a weaker to a stronger solution. Salts move by diffusion in the opposite direction. Water and salt movement stops when the solutions are equally concentrated on either side of the membrane.) The excess water absorbed through the gills is excreted in copious amounts of dilute urine produced by the kidneys. The special cells in the gill membrane selectively absorb salts back from

the water, thus helping to maintain the correct salt balance within the blood and body tissues of the koi.

Gut The gut performs three major functions: physical breakdown and mixing of food (i.e. by the teeth); chemical breakdown (i.e. by digestive enzymes); and absorption of the food materials. In koi, there is no stomach; food is digested in the very long intestine. Once the nutritive content of the food has been absorbed into the bloodstream, the remaining solid, undigestible material is voided.

Spleen The spleen, a compact purple-red organ, lies very close to the gut and liver. It is important for the formation and storage of red and white blood cells.

Liver The liver in koi is very large and consists of several lobes. Its main function is to store glycogen – a stored form of glucose – and, to a lesser degree, other food products. As glucose and other simple sugars are used up by the working tissues and organs of the body, the liver releases the stored glycogen, which is broken down into glucose and 'fuels' the working cells.

The liver also breaks down old and damaged blood cells. The product is known as bile and collects in the gall bladder. From here it drains through the bile duct into the intestine, where it is mixed with the solid waste.

Pancreas The pancreas is a soft tissue, similar in appearance to the liver, that produces a number of digestive enzymes, which it releases into the intestine to chemically break down food.

Kidneys The kidneys are paired organs that lie in the dorsal (upper) region of the body cavity on either side of the vertebral column, or backbone. Each kidney is basically a construction of tubules, closely surrounded by a network of tiny blood vessels, called capillaries. The tubules are connected to a system of ducts that merge into a single one, the ureter, which runs from the kidneys to a pore just in front of the vent, where the urine is voided.

The intimate contact between the capillaries and the kidney tubules allows waste products to pass from the blood into the tubules in a continuous filtering process. The waste products involved are simple nitrogen compounds formed in the tissues during the metabolism of proteins. These compounds would prove poisonous to the cells if they were not carried away in the bloodstream and removed by the kidneys (and via the gills).

The kidneys also regulate the water content of the body – urine is largely water – and control the type and quantity of salts retained by the koi.

Reproductive organs In males these are the testes; in females, the ovaries.

The testes tend to be rather compact and more regularly shaped than the ovaries and, although subject to seasonal change, they show no marked difference between the resting and breeding condition. The testes produce sperm cells, many millions of which may be released during the breeding period.

The ovaries are relatively large and irregularly shaped organs in mature female koi. Eggs may be found in the ovaries throughout the year but the number of mature eggs present is very low when the fish is not in breeding condition. When the female is ready to breed, the ripe eggs burst into a central cavity in the ovary, then pass into the oviduct and are shed at the vent.

Swimbladder As its name suggests, this organ helps the koi to swim by providing buoyancy in the water. It is an elongated oval sac that lies along the top of the body cavity, just beneath the vertebral column and kidneys. It is almost sub-

Internal anatomy of koi

This generalized view shows how the major organ systems lie within the body cavity. Note the long kidneys that lie close to the swimbladder near the spine.

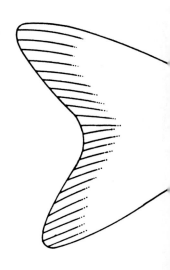

divided into two parts by a narrow constriction. At this point there is a duct, which connects the swimbladder to the gut. Indeed, in embryo koi the swimbladder develops as a minute outgrowth from the gut. This connecting duct enables koi to 'top up' the swimbladder by gulping and swallowing air at the water surface. The air bubble passes into the gut and is 'pumped' into the swimbladder by a duct. The mixture of gases within the swimbladder is more or less the same as air.

Brain The brain is a very soft, pink organ encased by the bony skull. During the development of the embryo in koi, the brain and spinal cord are formed as a tube. The front portion subsequently enlarges to form the brain, the hollow within the tube persisting as fluid-filled cavities, or vesicles. The brain consists of three regions: the fore-, mid- and hindbrain.

At the front of the forebrain are the olfactory lobes, one lobe for each pair of nostrils on each side of the head. They receive the nervous impulses from the nostrils and interpret them as smells. The forebrain also incorporates the light-sensitive pineal organ and hormone-secreting pituitary gland. During the development of the embryo, part of the forebrain is responsible for forming part of the eyes, their associated nerves and the pineal organ. (Interpreting optic nerve signals as sight is a function of the midbrain.) The pineal organ, located on the upper surface of the forebrain, is light sensitive and is thought to represent the remnant of a second pair of eyes on top of the head in some remote ancestor of vertebrate animals. In koi, the pineal organ senses changes in daylength and stimulates the release of reproductive hormones during the breeding season. The pituitary gland produces hormones that stimulate growth and reproduction as well as activating other glands, such as the thyroid.

The main function of the midbrain is to interpret messages relayed to it by the nerves, particularly those concerned with movement and the attitude of the body in the water. The midbrain also acts as the 'seat' of memory, learning and intelligence, although it is very difficult to assess or quantify degrees of learning and intelligence in koi. On top of the midbrain are two oval optic lobes that interpret nervous signals from the eyes and thus provide the sense of sight.

The function of the hindbrain is unclear, although it appears to act as a coordination centre for movement, equilibrium and posture.

Spinal cord The spinal cord is the posterior continuation of the brain, its fluid-filled central canal being the vestigial remnant of the embryonic tube from which the brain develops. The spinal cord extends almost the entire length of the body and is connected to many of the major nerves. As in other vertebrate animals, its main role is to act as a 'through route' for nervous impulses travelling between the body and the brain (see also below).

Nervous system Apart from the brain and spinal cord, which can be considered as the central nervous system, a complex network of nerves extends throughout the body of the koi. This system relays sensory information, such as touch, taste and smell, to the brain and activates the tissues, glands and muscles. There are two quite clearly defined types of nerve systems: the autonomic system and the motor system. The autonomic nervous system controls the 'unconscious' activity of organs such as the gut, gills and certain glands. In effect, the fish is unaware of their 'background' functioning. The motor nerves, on the other hand, carry signals to initiate conscious activities, such as the contraction of muscles to achieve movement.

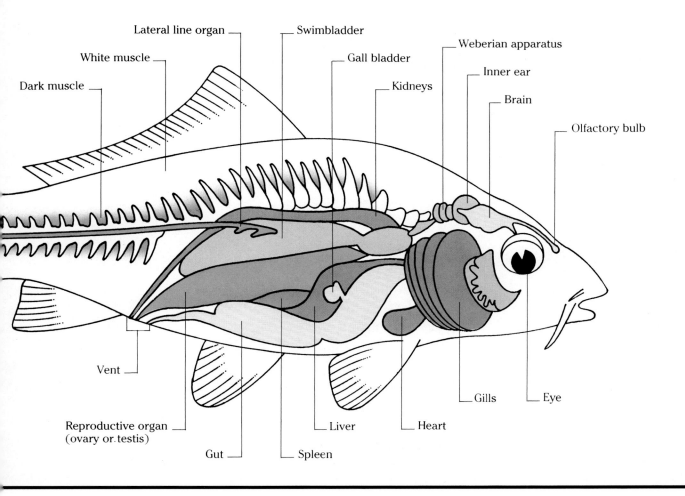

Lateral line organ

White muscle

Dark muscle

Swimbladder

Gall bladder

Kidneys

Weberian apparatus

Inner ear

Brain

Olfactory bulb

Vent

Gills

Eye

Reproductive organ (ovary or testis)

Liver

Heart

Gut

Spleen

POND AND FILTER CONSTRUCTION

Once you have decided to build a koi pond, your first task must be to give a great deal of thought to just what type of pond you require, both from your own point of view and, even more importantly, from the point of view of its future inhabitants. Whatever your circumstances and capabilities as a builder (if you are doing the job yourself), constructing a pond pleasing to the eye, that is easy to maintain and, last but not least, provides a safe and permanent home for your koi, is a considerable feat of civil engineering and should certainly not be entered upon lightly. Bear in mind that creating a pond that consists of a stark rectangular hole in the ground, perhaps surrounded by boulders or even a brick or stone wall, intended solely for the purpose of displaying koi, requires exactly the same degree of care in its design and construction as does the more informal pond intended to blend in with the rest of the garden, complementing the dry land plants with its display of waterborne flora. In this section, we explore first the design and logistic decisions involved in planning a koi pond and its filter system. Then we concentrate in more detail on the basic construction techniques involved in building a pond and a simple multichamber external filter.

POND AND FILTER CONSTRUCTION

Initial planning

Sitting down to design a koi pond is probably the most important aspect of the whole operation. If you do not get it completely right or forget to make allowances for some vital component or aspect, the actual construction could become a nightmare rather than a pleasure – in addition to increasing the expense of your pond out of all proportion! The secret of avoiding such disasters lies in checking and double checking at each successive point in your design, both at the drawing stage and during the actual construction.

Before you become absorbed in detailed design considerations, you will need to think about, firstly, how much space you have available for the pond and its filtration system and, secondly, your financial budget for the project. Be careful not to set your sights too high – these things have a habit of growing in size and, consequently, in cost! Remember that the time that you spend at this stage on the initial planning, and later on more detailed pond and filter design, will save you time and money both during the construction process itself and, subsequently, in maintaining the completed system on a day-to-day basis.

Working out a budget

Should you be in a financial position to be able to have your pond constructed by a professional firm, you would be wise to insist upon a written estimate for the job, then add, say, 10 percent for contingencies. Also, ask for details of other ponds your selected company has built, bearing in mind that the custom building of pools specifically intended for koi-keeping is a relatively new industry. And remember that house builders, or even landscape gardeners, are not necessarily professional koi pond builders.

If you are taking the DIY route, working out the cost of your proposed pond should be relatively easy, even if the result is frightening! The supplier of items such as liners will provide exact costings according to your measurements (accuracy is essential), be it in sheet or box-welded form. A building supply company will be able to provide delivered prices for concrete blocks, bricks, cement, sand, etc. It is in the area of 'sundries' that your problems can really start! Plumbing can run away with a great deal of money, for example, and here you must make the crucial choice between using 'domestic' or high-pressure pipe for the bottom drains and associated filter network (see page 31). The difference in cost can be substantial.

In costing your pool, you should also take into account all the mundane things like the hiring of a skip or a cement mixer. In fact, it could be more profitable to buy a small electric cement mixer outright; if you look after it properly and clean it regularly during your building operation, you could re-sell it and lose less than the cost of hiring one.

Also consider the cost involved in preparing drawings. If you have no knowledge of how to lay out your ideas, then find somebody who understands the principles and detail and can translate your plans into a set of drawings you will be able to work from. Money spent at this stage will save you a lot more in the long run. Starting to construct a new koi pond without a full set of drawings can be a costly mistake.

Which style to choose?

Obviously, your first decision must be the type and style of pond you wish to build and, unfortunately, this is where many prospective koi-keepers fall at the first hurdle. Having seen koi displayed at various retail outlets, usually in plain, un-relieved display tanks, naturally enough all attention is focused on the dramatic colours and patterns of the koi, with scant attention being paid to their surroundings. Your first question to yourself must be: Will such a tanklike pond be in keeping with my garden, or should I aim for a more informal and decorative style?

Thus, choosing the style of your pond is probably the most important, and yet one of the most difficult, decisions to make. Before deciding on whether to build a formal or informal pond, first consider how it will look in your garden. Although the finished pond will undoubtedly form the centrepiece of your garden, do make sure that it blends in with your surroundings. Consider as many aspects as you can and take the time to study as many garden and landscape books and magazines as possible before you begin to plan the style of your pond. These will give you new ideas to add to any thoughts you may already have.

Try to choose materials that blend or contrast with any rockeries, walls or

Above: *A rectangular pond is relatively easy to design, construct and maintain. It creates a formal shape in the garden, but its hard edges can be effectively softened with suitable rockwork and planting.*

Below: *This is a fine example of an informal koi pond, complete with wooden decking over the filters, planted borders, pebble beach and Japanese stone lantern.*

paths already in your garden. Bear in mind, however, that very ornate finishes can be difficult and extremely costly to produce, and are also difficult to maintain. Try, therefore, to keep your designs and finishes as simple as possible – as the Japanese would say, 'simple is beautiful'.

Should you wish to concentrate solely on building up a collection of exhibition-class koi purely for the pleasure of viewing them in isolation, then the clinical 'hole-in-the-ground' type of pond should suit you admirably. However, while it might please you, consider the feelings of your future charges! Will your koi feel at home swimming around hour after weary hour in gin-clear water, unrelieved by any other form of life, lacking shelter from the sun, unable to rest for a while in the shade of water lily leaves, or to browse among the stalks of irises and other marginal plants? Before you make your final decision, contrast this scenario with the natural habitat of the carp family, to which koi belong. Their idea of heaven would be a muddy, heavily planted pond in which they could happily grub around searching for those succulent morsels of plant, crustacean and insect life which abound in that type of natural aquatic environment!

Obviously, for the hobbyist, such a 'natural' pond is totally impractical, but a semi-formal, planted pond with clear water does at least strike a happy medium, pleasing to the viewer as well as to the koi. Many people believe that koi and plants cannot live together satisfactorily, a belief which is quite incorrect. It is perfectly true that koi are extremely efficient plant destroyers, capable of uprooting well-established plants in their never-ending search for food but, provided that plants are correctly installed in koi-resistant planters, there is no reason why both should not flourish together in a well-organized koi pond.

What shape is best?

Having decided on the general style of your pond, the next question is: What shape should it be? Here, of course, a great deal depends on the space available and the surroundings that will form a backdrop to the finished pond. In addition, choosing a specific type of construction material will raise some immediate limitations on your options concerning shape. If you opt for one of the liner materials, the pond shape will be restricted to one in the range of square, rectangular, elliptical, oval, or round. The square and rectangular shapes can be ordered 'box welded', thus obviating the unsightly and dirt-gathering folds that bedevil liner ponds.

If you aspire to a more intricate shape of pond, then you will need to select an alternative method of construction. However, try to avoid designing a pond that is too complicated in shape. Although a pond of very irregular outline might look very attractive and natural, you could well run into difficulties with areas of 'dead' water, which will allow dirt to collect, encouraging the growth of anaerobic bacteria and the proliferation of disease organisms. Such stagnation can occur very easily in a very irregularly shaped pond, where it is difficult to ensure that water returning from the filtration system is mixed sufficiently with the water in the pond. This type of pond will also be more difficult to maintain and, more importantly, could create prob-

lems if and when you need to catch the koi – for disease treatment, for example.

A surprising omission on the part of the majority of pond designers, particularly of larger ponds, is the use of an island in their design. Properly constructed, an island can really add the finishing touch to an otherwise very ordinary pond, especially when a nicely constructed bridge is incorporated. With a little thought and a tiny amount of extra plumbing, it is even possible to incorporate a small rockpool which cascades water back into the pond. An island should be located off centre in the pond, thereby creating a channel of faster flowing water that koi seem to enjoy. Of course, it is important to avoid making this channel an area of stagnant water.

Suitable pond shapes

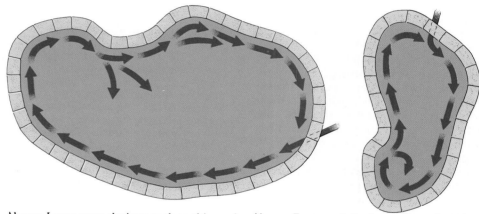

Above: *Large open designs such as this, and more formal squares and rectangles, are ideal for koi ponds. Sensibly placed, this design could include an island, as long as it does not create areas of 'dead water'.*

Above: *Even a relatively small pond can be fine for koi, as long as the water is deep enough and its flow is unobstructed. Even in rectangular ponds it is advisable to 'round' the corners for this purpose.*

Unsuitable pond shapes

Good
Water flow

Stagnant
areas

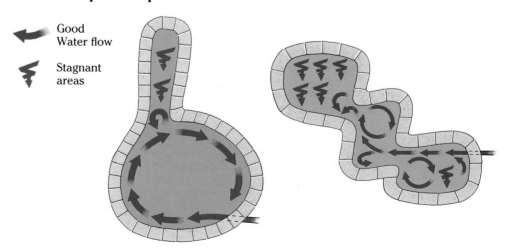

Above: *The narrow neck in this otherwise suitable design will invariably become an area of stagnant water 'marooned' from the water flow. This will ultimately affect the environmental quality of the whole pond.*

Above: *Complex shapes like this may look impressive in the garden but the dead ends and narrow channels create areas of stagnation and prevent thorough mixing of filtered water returning to the pond.*

POND AND FILTER CONSTRUCTION

Surface area of the pond

There is one golden rule to follow when deciding on the surface area of the pond; irrespective of shape, always aim for as great a surface area as possible. In so doing, you will obtain maximum air/water interface and oxygen absorption, oxygen being the life force in any water ecosystem. As an example, compare two ponds each with a surface area of $10m^2(1076ft^2)$, one of which is 2m(6.6ft) deep and the other 1m(3.3ft) deep. The first pond contains twice as much water as the second, yet both ponds are only able to absorb the same amount of oxygen from the atmosphere via the water surface. Thus, pond surface area is an extremely important consideration, and providing a larger volume of water is of no benefit without adequate surface area. (But consider this in relation to the advice on depth that follows.)

Depth of the pond

There are many differing opinions on the correct depth of water for successful koi-keeping, most of which have been based on empirical reasoning. Some koi-keepers have had resounding success with ponds only 1m(3.3ft) deep, but these are the exceptions rather than the rule, with climatic conditions and straightforward luck often playing a part. The majority of enthusiasts have ponds 2m(6.6ft) deep, and even 3m(10ft) deep, in some cases. In order to fully promote growth through exercise gained by swimming, deep water is certainly essential for koi, but just how deep is deep? Generally, you should consider 1.5m(5ft) as the minimum depth and 2.4m(8ft) as the optimum depth for a koi pond. (If you live in a climate that is not subject to lower temperatures, i.e. below 5°C(41°F), then such a deep pond may not be essential.) Any depth between 1.5 and 2m(5-6.6ft) is probably an acceptable compromise in most circumstances; depths in excess of this merely make life difficult during the excavating process and after completion, when pond maintenance and/or catching your koi can become problematical.

Another important consideration when deciding on the depth of your pond is that of temperature fluctuations. If there is one thing likely to distress koi, it is rapid changes in environmental temperature. The deeper your pond is in proportion to its surface area, the less susceptible it will be to temperature

Right: To calculate the volume (and therefore water capacity) of your pond at the design stage, consider it in terms of simple shapes and follow these guidelines.

Calculating approximate pond volume

Simple rectangular shapes

Calculating the volume of a square or rectangular pond is simply a matter of multiplying the length x width x depth (in metres) to produce the volume in cubic metres (m^3), which is equivalent to the weight of water in tonnes. To convert the volume into litres, multiply this figure by 1000. To convert litres to US gallons, multiply by 0.26; to convert litres to Imp. gallons, multiply the figure by 0.22.

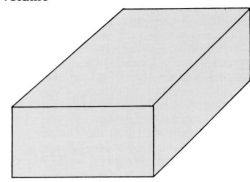

Ponds with shelved areas

The easiest way to calculate the volume of a pond with a shelf is to treat the shelf section and the remaining pond section as two separate portions. Thus, use the above formula to calculate the volume of each of the rectangles and add the results together.

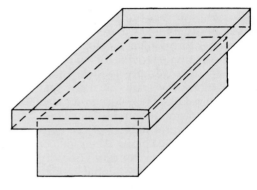

Shapes with a benched bottom

Here, we consider ponds with angled sides in the bottom section. Let's assume for simplicity that the angle is 45°. Calculate the volume of the main rectangular body of the pond using the formula in the first example. Next, consider the centre section along the bottom as another rectangle and treat it in the same way. Then, add the two opposite triangular sections together as a long thin rectangle and add the volume of this to the volume of the other two sections. Also, do the same for the triangular sections running across the width of the pond at each end – not shown here. For simplicity, these calculations do not include the small triangular sections at each bottom corner.

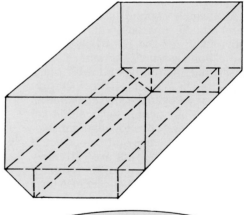

Straight-sided circular shapes

Here we need to introduce a new formula to calculate the surface area. This is radius squared (i.e. half the diameter multiplied by itself) x 3.14 (which is an approximate value for π). If the pond is straight sided and has a constant depth, multiply the surface area by the depth to calculate the volume.

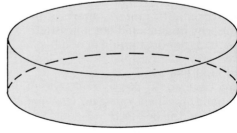

Conical shapes

Tapering sides are found on many koi ponds and so it may be necessary to estimate the volume of a conical shape. The shape shown here is not a cone but simply has a bottom area smaller than the surface area. In this case, calculate the average radius of the two circles by adding them together and dividing by two and use this in the calculation given above.

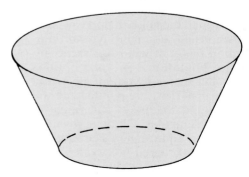

fluctuations. Bear in mind that, even in warm climates, temperatures can fall dramatically overnight, severely chilling shallow ponds, and this may be followed by a rapid rise to very high temperatures the following day. Koi should not be subjected to fluctuations of more than 1-3°C(2-5°F) in a 24-hour period. The larger the volume of water, the slower the dissipation of heat loss into the surrounding ground, but remember that heat loss will be higher if the surface area is larger. Thus, the chill factor of a 1m-deep pond will be twice as great as that of a 2m-deep one, even if both hold the same volume of water. At a water depth of 1.5m(5ft) or more, temperature changes are insignificant, whatever the ambient air temperature. During a hot spell of weather, the temperature in a deep pond will rise, but only slowly, causing no distress. The reverse applies in cold weather, again with no ill-effects.

In very deep water, such as is found in natural lakes, a phenomenon known as a thermocline develops. This is the level below which no variation of temperature takes place whatever the surface air temperature. To a lesser degree, a similar state of affairs exists in a koi pond, where temperature changes reduce as depth increases. (The exception to this rule is the situation when water is being removed from the pond bottom for filtration, when surface and bottom temperatures will eventually almost equalize.) A simple way of appreciating the impact of ambient temperature upon a pond is to consider it as a giant storage heater, being slow to both gain and lose heat in response to external influences.

Shallow ponds not only offer an unstable environment in terms of temperature, but they can also affect the koi's security, preventing them from escaping from a potential threat. How often have you seen skittish koi in confined shallow ponds darting about and probably damaging themselves in the process? Shallow ponds, especially those with ledges, also create a perfect feeding place for the domestic koi's largest predator – the heron. Try to avoid building such inviting feeding haunts into your design; if they have easy access to a food supply, herons and other predators will continue to visit a pond until the supply runs out. If, however, the pond creates dangers for them and they are unable to take food easily, they will soon move on to easier opportunities, leaving you and your koi in peace.

Koi, like most animals, need exercise to maintain their muscle tone and body shape. They achieve this by swimming vertically in the pond, not horizontally.

Where vertical swimming is restricted, koi become fat, and such effects are often seen in koi that have been kept in shallow ponds for long periods. The higher water pressure found at depth is also important to koi for maintaining their shape.

Pond and filter capacity

Working out the surface area, volume and capacity of your pond is essential to enable you to choose the correct size of filter, set stocking levels and establish effective dosages for treating the pond against disease and parasites. The formulae and estimating techniques described in the panel will help you to arrive at these figures before you start work on constructing the pond. Of course, deviations will occur in the building process – even minor changes will alter your initial results – but getting close to the final expected capacity will at least enable you to arrive at the all-important figure for the capacity of the filter system that you will be planning in parallel with the pond.

We will be considering the selection and design of filters later in this chapter.

Right: *With the cover removed, it is clear that the capacity of this filter is at least one third the size of the pond it serves. This is the ideal minimum ratio between filter and pond, and applies for either internal or external filters. A filter cannot be too big.*

Below: *The same pond photographed from a different angle with the filter covered up with wooden decking. This rectangular koi pond measures 5.2x2.4x1.5m deep (17x8x5ft) and contains about 30 koi of various sizes. Its capacity is about 19m³.*

At this point in the planning process, it is a good idea to apply the general rule of allowing space for your filter equivalent to one third of the surface area of the proposed pond. In other words, a pond with a surface area of 15m² requires a filter with a surface area of 5m². This general rule applies equally for external and internal filters and should be regarded as a minimum. In Japan, some hobbyists actually go as far as having filter systems as large as the ponds they serve. Certainly, you need not be concerned over building too large a filter; quite the opposite as, where koi pond filters are concerned, big is beautiful!

Confirming how much water your pond and associated systems hold on completion is a simple matter of hiring a flowmeter when you first fill them up.

POND AND FILTER CONSTRUCTION

Selecting a site

Having finalized the design of your pond, your next objective must be to choose a suitable site in which to install it. Deciding on a position will depend on several factors, including its proposed size and style, and the decision must be a balance between common sense and prudence. Be prepared to compromise, because it is only very seldom that what you want and what you can have will coincide. The chances are that on the very spot that you would like to locate your pond there is a sewer inspection cover, a telegraph pole, or even a block of concrete supporting your washing line! Such things are sent to try you! And when you start digging, also be prepared to find that your chosen site also proved attractive to the builder of your house as a dump for all his surplus materials and rubbish! Forewarned is forearmed!

Also consider the safety angle when planning the position of your pond, particularly where young children are concerned. You may need to put up a strong fence and a gate with a substantial lock to keep inquisitive children at bay (see the pond shown on page 27). It is worth noting here that a shallow pond is not necessarily any safer than a deep one, as children can fall in and knock themselves out on the hard bottom of a shallow pond. And remember, too, that small children who can swim are just as much at risk when they instinctively panic.

Above: *This square pond enjoys an open setting with a boundary along one edge. A planting scheme based on low-growing conifers allows easy access to the pond, an unobstructed view and few problems from leaves, making maintenance an easy task.*

Buildings, walls and fences

Ideally, your pond should be easily viewed from the house but should not be located closer than 3m(10ft) to the building to avoid disturbing the integrity of the property. If you do want to build nearer than this, you should take professional advice. In fact, consider this 'safety margin' as applying to any wall or fence near the pond. This distance will also allow ample 'walking round space' for maintenance of your pond, something often overlooked until it is too late.

If you cannot avoid siting your pond in a position where the full force of the prevailing wind strikes it, then do consider installing some form of windbreak, such as a trellis fence or screen block wall, or even a row of slow-growing conifers upwind of, and not too close to, the pond. A solid wall type of barrier, such as a close-boarded fence, would be quite useless, as this would simply create turbulence on its leeward side and not break up the wind pattern and reduce its velocity as would pierced blocks or a hedge.

Trees

Consider carefully before building a pond close to trees. Trees have various types of root structure, and siting a pond close to a tree with spreading roots could cause considerable problems. The classic and graceful weeping willow, for example, loves water and its rooting system can travel 20m(65ft) or more, and will break through the side of a pond with the greatest of ease! Not only may tree roots affect the finished pond, but if you damage an existing tree's roots during the construction process, the tree may become unsafe and fall into your pond or, worse still, onto your house or an adjoining property. So, if you are obliged to build close to an existing tree, be sure to establish what sort of root structure it has before you start digging.

If you are starting with a bare site, the best advice is to avoid planting trees close to the pond from the outset. Everyone has a mental picture of a garden pond surrounded by lawns and with a tree or two languorously dangling over the limpid water. After a few sessions of clearing leaves, branch tips – even cones – from the water, plus dredging out grass clippings every time the lawn is cut, this idyllic picture quickly loses its attractions! Compromise must be the order of the day; you will be just as happy with a few less vigorous shrubs and a garden seat strategically positioned on a 'buffer zone' of patio slabs. Needless to say, there are certain circumstances where leaf fall simply has to be tolerated, such as when your neighbour has several

trees, the leaves of which inevitably blow in the direction of your garden. In such cases, all one can do is to grin and bear it rather than start a mini-war by requesting the removal of the offending objects!

Surveying the site

Once you have decided on the style and size of your new pond and its position in the garden, you will need to carry out a detailed survey to establish the levels and actual position of the pond and any external equipment, such as filtration systems and standpipe chambers.

While marking out positions is a simple operation, establishing levels may be an unfamiliar and somewhat daunting task. If you are unsure about this aspect, take professional advice to avoid difficulties later on. If you are using the services of a pond builder, they will have all the necessary levelling equipment and will carry out the survey for you. If you intend to do the job yourself, you should be able to pick up what you need from a local hire shop.

Whatever levelling technique you use, you will need an accurate, long tape measure, a club hammer and a supply of wooden stakes (say 38mm/1.5in square) of various lengths from 30cm(12in) up to 1m(39in). Mark out and measure the pond shape and size using the wooden stakes; you may find that you need to do this a few times before you position the stakes correctly. Then do the same for any externally sited equipment. Once you have completed this procedure, stand back and make sure you have created what you had in mind. If you are considering an informal pond, it will help to trace out the shape on the ground using a length of hose.

If you want to be absolutely precise, when you are 'staking out' your pond, measure the distance between your first stake and a convenient fixed point (technically known as a datum), such as the edge of a wall, and then record the positions of the remaining stakes in relation to each other. Making a note of this will enable you to reposition any stakes that become misplaced.

The next stage is to establish the levels of the ground. If you have an extensive site and you contemplate building a large pond, you may consider doing this the 'professional' way by using a surveyor's level of some kind. A dumpy level is ideal. This consists simply of a bubble tube (for levelling the device) and a telescope (for sighting). A calibrated staff will be supplied with the equipment and you can use this to read off different heights. To carry out the survey, first set up a tripod in a suitable position, where you can see all areas of the pond and other sited equipment, and mount the levelling device on top. Use the bubble tube to set the device level. The first task is to establish a datum height. This can be the first marker, but a fixed object, such as a wall, would be better, just in case a peg is accidentally moved or knocked out of the ground. Sight through the lens towards the staff (held vertically by a willing assistant) and establish the reading to give you your datum height. Use a chalk to mark this datum position on the staff for future use and write it down on a table. Make sure you keep the staff upright when taking these sightings, otherwise you will obtain false readings. You can now proceed to establish the heights at all your peg positions and record the difference compared to your datum height. Keep this data sheet safe – you will need it when you are drawing up the detailed design of the pond system and to establish levels during construction.

A simpler method of establishing levels over long distances is to use a hosepipe with a funnel attached to each end. Fill the hose with water and adjust the funnels until the water reaches the brim of each funnel, indicating that they are level with each other. Then measure the distance from each funnel to the ground below. Ensure that one funnel stays in the same position (as a datum) and only move the other funnel, otherwise you will obtain a false reading. (Alternatively, use a clear plastic hose so that you can see the water level inside and align the meniscus with a mark.)

The most (literally) 'down to earth' way of establishing levels, and one which is ideal at the building stage, is to use an accurate spirit level and a straight edge (or a series of both) to check the level between the tops of pegs driven into the ground short distances apart. We will see how this technique works in practice on page 38, under *Preparing to build*.

The basic principles involved in the above surveying processes are reflected in the panel shown below. This has been a very brief explanation of what is an extremely important stage in designing and installing a koi pond. If you have any doubts about your own abilities in this respect, be sure to seek expert advice rather than make unfortunate errors.

Establishing ground conditions
Before you decide on the type of construction, you will need to establish the ground conditions. These vary considerably; the ground may be clay, flint, sand, rock, or a combination of two or more of these natural substrates.

A high water table can also be a problem; you may dig down just a few centimetres and find water. This can become an almost impossible hurdle to overcome. If you have a stream or natural pond in your garden or close by, you can assume that the water table is fairly high

Using a surveyor's level

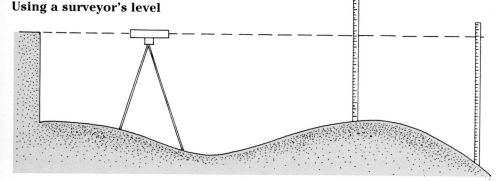

Using surveying equipment to establish levels may seem complex, but the general principles involved are very simple. To use a dumpy level – literally a sighting telescope levelled on a tripod – establish a datum height on a nearby fixed object, such as a wall, by holding up the calibrated staff and sighting through the telescope. Mark this height on the staff using chalk and then ask someone to hold the staff vertically at various locations and mark the staff at the line of sight. The difference between the datum and each location height shows how the levels vary. Keep a table of results.

Using a water-filled hosepipe

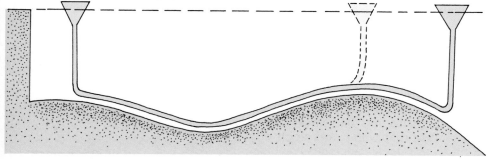

This method makes use of the purely physical property of liquids finding their own level. You can use a clear hosepipe and check the level against a mark on the pipe or, as here, fit funnels at each end and check for these being full up to the brim. The method again involves setting up a datum height and keeping one end of the hose in a fixed position while the other end is taken to various locations around the site. Measuring the distance from the brimming funnel to the ground provides a series of comparative heights around the site.

Using pegs, spirit levels and straight edges

Using a spirit level is perhaps the most familiar way of checking levels. Try to buy or borrow a good-quality, long spirit level (ideally two) of the type builders use and arm yourself with an assortment of sturdy wooden pegs of various lengths, plus some straight and true pieces of hardwood. Drive in the first peg with its top at the desired height, and using the straight edges and spirit levels, set out a series of pegs with their tops at the same level as the first. Allow for a peg every 30cm(12in) for accuracy. You may need to flatten bumps.

POND AND FILTER CONSTRUCTION

(i.e. close to the surface), although this may vary at different times of the year. If you live at the top of a hill, however, it is highly unlikely that ground water will cause you any problems. In any case, it is best to assume nothing until you have checked the ground conditions yourself and are satisfied that you are safe to proceed with the excavation.

The best method to ascertain the ground conditions is to use a hand sampler, or auger, (basically, a large 'corkscrew' device that removes a plug of earth for examination). These are normally available from a plant hire shop. Alternatively, just make sample excavations near the centre of the proposed pond. Removing two or three spadefuls of earth from around the site gives a better knowledge of the conditions prevailing, preferably to the full planned depth of the pond, but this is not always possible.

If you do find a high water table, coping with it will create extra cost, since you may need to use special equipment in order to prevent the excavation continuously filling up with ground water. The cheapest, and easiest, method of removing ground water is to hire a large mechanical pump that can cope with sludge. Connect this to a pipe and discharge the water as far away from the excavation as possible. This method has its disadvantages, however. If the flow is fairly fast and the ground is of a light substrate, such as sand or gravel, or very heavy, like clay, the side walls of the excavation may collapse, which will create further problems and may be dangerous. A second, though considerably more expensive method, is to freeze the ground. This is achieved with a compressor and spiked probes, which are driven into the ground around the pond edges and act in a very similar way to a domestic refrigerator. Once the ground has frozen, a barrier is created to inhibit the flow of water into the excavation.

Providing services

You will need to allow in your design for the provision of services, such as electrical power, mains water and drainage. (Of course, you will also need to discover the location of existing services before you start excavating.) While you can be flexible with regard to the route taken by electricity supply cables and mains water pipework, the positioning of the pond and filter drain plumbing must be governed by the accessibility of your nearest sewer inspection chamber. To ensure that pond bottom drains operate at maximum efficiency, the outlets must enter the sewer at the lowest point pos-

sible, i.e. at the base of a sewer inspection chamber. Should you not have an inspection chamber or sewer within easy distance of your proposed pond, you have a problem. In that case, do not be tempted into thinking that a rubble-filled sump will suffice as an alternative; it won't! A surprising amount of 'muck' is washed out of a pond each time a bottom drain is operated, and this would quickly render a sump useless. You would be well advised to omit a bottom drain(s) and to rely on a vacuum system for cleaning the pond. The waste can then be piped to wherever there is access to your sewer system.

With regard to pipework, nothing detracts from the overall visual impact of a pond than a conglomeration of visible pipework and cables. In a properly designed pond, there should be nothing visible in the way of pipework, apart from the vertical air intake of a venturi and the overflow/skimmer outlet.

When considering a supply of mains water for pond cleaning and topping up purposes, it is much more acceptable to have a dedicated separate supply permanently installed, which can usually be obtained by plumbing a 'tee' into the supply for an outside tap. This type of installation has the benefit of being easily fitted with a de-chlorination cartridge, together with a spraybar injection system to 'gas off' any small amount of residual chlorine remaining. Such a system is much neater and much less trouble than using a hosepipe for every maintenance. Do check with your local water supply company to ensure that you comply with local byelaws, and there will probably be a small annual fee to pay.

Unless you are suitably qualified or experienced, do not tackle the electrics yourself. It is much safer to consult an electrician in the early stages, who will advise on suitable cables and assist with planning a route for your cable. Do not be tempted to merely plug your pond electrical apparatus into the nearest socket. Remember that water and electricity form an extremely dangerous combination. It is important – and legally required in many countries – to fit a residual current circuit breaker to the electrical circuit. Such a device will automatically switch off the current in a matter of milliseconds should anyone touch a live part of the circuit. (We look at this aspect again at the building stage.)

Choosing building materials

Possibly the most important decision you will make during the design stage is the choice of building material. Every material has advantages and dis-

advantages, depending upon your point of view. If at all possible, do not be influenced by the question of cost. Far better to spend a little more and take slightly longer over the construction, and end up with a pool that delights you, rather than to go for a lower cost option that will always be a cause for regret! As for the materials, all you can do is read the following descriptions, make comparisons, weigh the pros and cons, and come to your own conclusions.

Precast ponds

Probably the simplest, although not the cheapest, size-for-size pond you can 'build' can be obtained ready made in glass-reinforced plastic. These are available in a range of sizes and shapes, and, can be installed at ground level, partially above or fully above ground level. They come fully finished apart from the fitting of services. They are excellent in their own way, but, of course, you are limited to the chosen shape of pond. Where space is limited, one of these precast ponds could well fill the bill. Be sure to choose one that is deep enough for keeping koi (see the recommendations about depth on page 26).

Liners

The liner is far and above the most popular material used in the construction of ornamental ponds. The principal advantage in using a liner is undoubtedly the time factor; a liner pool is quite capable of being completed over a weekend – if sufficient labour is available.

What liner materials are suitable? Polythene sheeting is not suitable, as many would-be builders have found to their regret! Not only is polythene fragile, it also degrades rapidly under exposure to sunlight. It is fine for use as an underlining 'skin', but nothing else. There are a

Above: *This is a sample of the butyl rubber sheeting widely used to line ponds. This example is 0.75mm(0.030in) thick and will provide a service life in excess of 20 years. Black is an ideal colour for koi ponds.*

number of proprietary liner materials available, most of them based around PVC (poly vinyl chloride), some of which have woven nylon reinforcement and offer colour variations. These are reputed to have a service life of between five and ten years, which is a relatively short timespan.

Butyl rubber is undoubtedly the best material for use as a liner, but, of course, it is much more expensive. For a square or rectangular pond, butyl liners can be supplied 'box welded' to fit the buyer's measurements, which must be accurate. The heavier grades of butyl have a reputed life of up to 50 years, even the standard grades being good for 20 years.

This material is ideal for the type of pond desired by koi-keepers who are not interested in the idea of incorporating plants or interesting contours into their ponds. Butyl can be used for informal ponds, but suffers from the disadvantage of being unable to accommodate curves without forming pleats and folds, which can be a nuisance by collecting dirt and mulm at a remarkable rate, in addition to being unsightly. Fitting service outlets and flanges, etc., is relatively simple, although it is vital to take great care to ensure that the various holes are accurately positioned.

Once filled, a butyl liner pond will not take kindly to any stress the weight of water might place on the material around an inaccurately positioned pipe flange. It can be most offputting to find the liner has torn through this cause! There have also been cases where the family dog has fallen into the pond and, in its panic-striken struggle to escape, has literally shredded the liner. Another disadvantage with liner ponds is that the inevitable growth of algae or blanketweed cannot be scraped off, and vacuuming is also a problem, as the liner tends to be sucked onto the end of the vacuum tube in the process. Nevertheless, despite all its apparent shortcomings, the liner remains in the forefront of a long list of pond building materials and is certainly worth considering.

Fibreglass

Well known among the pleasure boats and yachting fraternity, fibreglass is being increasingly used as a finishing coat on concrete ponds. Unfortunately, it is appallingly messy to apply, and one can only recommend that the application be left to a professional company! Successive layers of glass matting and resins are applied, building up to a thickness of approximately 5mm(0.2in), with a final coloured gel coat, preferably black, finishing the job. Correctly carried out,

Above: *Applying resin to a layer of fibreglass matting in a large commercially built koi pond. The resulting layer of bonded fibreglass provides an excellent, if expensive, lining. The final coloured coat should be black or dark green.*

the fibreglass pond is probably the ultimate attainment, giving infinite durability, colossal strength and, in the event of a crack developing in the concrete, simple to repair by means of patching.

As it is apparently so good, why don't we all use it? The short answer is that it is expensive, being more than double the price of the concrete pond to which it is applied! However, an ingenious technique may well signal the end of the price barrier! Specialist companies are now able to spray simultaneous jets of fibres and resins straight onto a suitable excavation, thereby eliminating the pre-coating building work. Using this system, the most exotic pond shapes are obtainable and the fibreglass pond is well worth consideration!

Concrete

For the average DIY builder without funds available for the more exotic materials, concrete must be the best choice. It has to be admitted that, in the past, concrete ponds have gained a bad reputation for springing leaks and developing cracks. Nowadays, however, thanks again to advancing technology, these problems are a thing of the past. The secret lies in the use of tiny plastic fibres added to the concrete and rendering mix which enable the mix to contain a much higher proportion of cement powder.

Once the chemical reaction with water has taken place, cement alone is a very strong material but, in drying, tiny hairline cracks develop, weakening the finished product. Sand is added in various proportions in order to reduce

the shrinkage as the concrete dries, but the result is a fairly porous and relatively weak product. By adding fibres, the proportion of sand can be reduced dramatically and the concrete or rendering has incredible strength once it has dried. It is impermeable to water and, most important for pond use, is highly resistant to damage by frost.

Building a concrete pond now merely consists of laying a floor of lean concrete, erecting dense concrete blockwalls and rendering the whole thing with a 5mm(0.2in)-thick coat consisting of two parts sand and one part cement plus the fibres mixture. The resulting pond is long lasting and very cost effective when compared to other methods. Coupled with the fact that almost any shape and contour is possible in concrete, this type of building material must be a very strong contender!

Choosing pipework

The suppliers of high-pressure PVC/ABS pipe are likely to advise you that only this pipe will withstand the continuous pressure of water remaining within it i.e. rather than simply flushing through it. They may dissuade you from using domestic-grade plastic pipe because it simply isn't up to the job. Even encasing in concrete may not guarantee its integrity, since the concrete may crack and allow water leaking from a fractured pipe to escape. The conclusion of this line of reasoning is that, yes, pressure pipework and its associated fittings are expensive, but so are your koi. Something you may reflect upon when you discover them high and dry in an empty pond.

The converse argument weighted from the DIY point of view is that in the average pond and filter pipework arrangement, the head or pressure encountered will be well within the handling capabilities of ordinary domestic soil pipe, which is available in 10cm and 15cm (4in and 6in) diameters, the orange-brown variety being suitable for in-ground use. The rubber seals which are an integral part of the fittings used with this piping form a leaktight union and have the advantage of being easily removable should you find during assembly that your measurements are incorrect. With solvent-welded, high-pressure pipe, getting it wrong can be an expensive mistake.

The golden rule is to ask around for advice. What you hear may save you spending out unnecessarily on expensive pipework or, conversely, persuade you that saving money in the short term will only lead to inevitable disaster in the future. (In the building section, we explain how to use both types of pipework.)

POND AND FILTER CONSTRUCTION

Designing for water

Here, we look at the design aspects concerned with water and the movement of water, starting, appropriately enough, with bottom drains.

Bottom drains

Bottom drain filtration is probably the most underestimated of filtration and pond cleaning systems. Remember that your pond is the biggest settlement chamber you have and a considerable amount of debris will collect on the bottom, including leaves from surrounding trees, dust, fish waste and uneaten food from within the system.

Bottom drains take the heavier, 'dead' water and debris from the bottom of the pond to a separate chamber, where it is either passed through the filtration system or discharged into the main drainage system. Recirculating bottom water through the filter is only recommended when the stocking level of the pond is low and you want the nitrifying bacteria in the filter system to obtain as much 'food' i.e. nitrogenous wastes, as possible. When stocking levels are high, the water should be released through a valve or standpipe to a drainage system.

To be really effective, it is essential to scallop the bottom of the pond and position the drains in the centre of these dished areas, which help to guide dirt and mulm into the drains. Many people make the mistake of installing bottom drains on a flat surface, and even drains installed above the lowest point in the pond are not unknown!

How many bottom drains should you install? Here, again, the answer is influenced by what is financially and/or practically acceptable to you. In practice, the more bottom drains you install, the better your overall filtration/cleaning will be. On a 'money-no-object' basis, you should aim to incorporate a bottom

Using valves to switch filter feeds

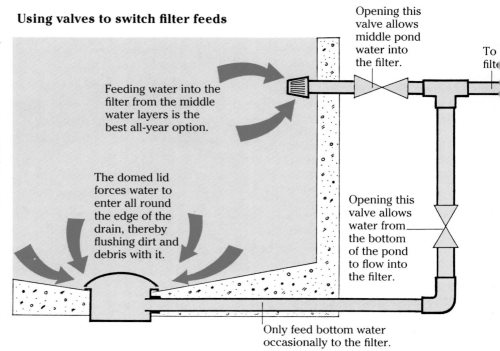

Feeding water into the filter from the middle water layers is the best all-year option.

The domed lid forces water to enter all round the edge of the drain, thereby flushing dirt and debris with it.

Opening this valve allows middle pond water into the filter.

To filter

Opening this valve allows water from the bottom of the pond to flow into the filter.

Only feed bottom water occasionally to the filter.

drain every 1.5-2m (5-6.6ft), i.e. the centres of each dished area should be this distance apart. By this reckoning, a koi pond measuring 6x3m(20x10ft) should have eight bottom drains. Obviously, this is not always possible. In financial terms, it would add a very large amount to the cost of your pond, as each bottom drain requires a dedicated length of pipe and a separate 'pull tube' or ball valve. (If you connect two drains to a common outlet, remember that the effective suction 'pulling power' of each drain is halved.) A more 'economical' suggestion would be to avoid having bottom drain centres more than 3m(10ft) apart. On this basis, in an average pond of $14m^3$ capacity (approximately 3080 Imp. gallons/3640 US gallons), one bottom drain should be adequate, with an additional drain recommended for each further $10m^3$(2200/2600 gallons) of planned pond capacity.

If you do not install bottom drains, or have not installed enough to cope adequately with your pond, you will need to vacuum the bottom of the pond regularly to avoid build-up of waste, using either a hand vacuum or electric pump with vacuum attachments. You will also need to make regular water changes – in practice, a daunting and very time-consuming task.

Helping water flow

When deciding on the shape of your pond, you will need to think about how water flows within it. Water will flow in a straight line until either it loses momentum and velocity and becomes stagnant,

Above: *How a system of valves can be used to divert either middle or bottom water into the filter. Opinions vary, but it seems advisable to use middle water most of the time, with the occasional use of bottom water when the filter is bacterially 'low'.*

Below: *Bottom drains and their associated high-pressure pipework in place during the construction of a large commercial koi pond. Each drain has its own dedicated pipe leading to the standpipe chamber.*

or until its direction is changed by other influences, such as other moving water currents or a fixed structure, such as the pond wall. Obviously, if it hits a flat wall at 90°, its momentum and velocity are reduced significantly, as the water is displaced in 360° from the point of impact. If, however, it strikes the pond wall at a shallow angle then the water is deflected in the same direction as the flow, albeit at a reduced velocity. Therefore, if all corners of the pond are radiused, or 'faired out', velocity losses will be greatly reduced. (There are frictional losses as

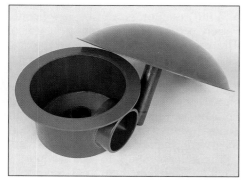

Above: *A bottom drain fitment suitable for a concrete or fibreglass pond. The drain is set into the concrete foundations and rendered or fibreglassed up to the lip. The domed 'lid' shown alongside fits into the recess in the base, leaving a gap around the edge.*

Above: *The radiused, or 'faired', corners of this koi pond help to promote good water flow – an important design feature that pays dividends when the pond is fully stocked and operational. Such shapes mimic the rounded contours of natural watercourses.*

Right: *In the sides of this professionally built koi pond under construction, the filter feeds are positioned at different heights and locations, providing a variety of options for taking pond water into the chambers of the external filter system, shown on page 35.*

the water rubs along the wall of the pond and as it shears on slower moving water, but we will ignore these.) So, when designing your pond, always allow for 'faired corners'.

Vertical movement and pond returns

As we saw earlier, ponds with narrow necks are unsuitable, as they inhibit water flow and create eddying currents, leaving stagnation points. Vertical motion of the water is also important. Most ponds are constructed with shallow water returns (pumped water is returned either at the surface or just below it). But where ponds exceed 1.2m(4ft) in depth, deep water returns are advisable if there are no waterfalls to create downcurrents. This is because water returning to the pond at, or near, the surface will shear, leaving deeper water reliant on movement from bottom drains. A deep-water return will allow control of water movement deeper in the pond.

The number of returns to a pond should be proportional to its volume and surface area. For example, a pond measuring 3x1.5x1.5m deep (10x5x5ft), with a capacity of $6.75m^3$, would need only one return, while a pond 9x4.5x2.4m deep (30x15x8ft), with a capacity of $97.2m^3$, would need two or three surface returns plus a waterfall, or one or two deep-water returns. You should be able to control these by using a valved bypass. This would be used to turn off the deep water returns in winter, when pond temperatures drop and koi become inactive. (Any fast-flowing, deep-water returns would disturb the koi and use up their reserve energy, weakening them when they are unable to feed, see also page 78.)

Filter feeds

Filter feeds must be considered during the pond design stage, since, depending upon the type of filter feed you choose, you must allow for the pipe runs in the plan. There has been much argument as to the various advantages and disadvantages of using pond middle water or bottom water for feeding a filter. There can be no doubt that the optimum solution is to have the option to use either, exerting control by means of valves. In order to accommodate the necessary valves, etc., be sure to allow for a suitably sized valve chamber and consider carefully the layout of piping needed to make the system operate efficiently. During the cold winter months, feed middle water to your filter, thereby avoiding any chilling of the deeper parts of the pond. During the summer months, you can choose to valve off the middle water outlet and feed bottom water to your filter. In line with our comments under *Bottom drains* on page 32, however, we recommend that water from the bottom drain is only fed to the filter occasionally when the nitrifying bacteria population is low. In effect, it is quite acceptable to use middle water all year round.

Of course, you may wish to consider using a vortex chamber as the first stage in your filter chain. Feeding water from the bottom drain into the top part of such a chamber sets up a spinning current that allows the sludge to fall to the base, where it can be run off to waste, while the 'cleaner' water in the uppermost layers is fed into the filter proper. Such chambers, although expensive, do offer a solution to clogging problems that may arise when using bottom drain water as a filter feed.

Watercourses and waterfalls

One of the most attractive features of a properly designed koi pond is undoubtedly the spectacle of moving water. If space permits, consider fitting a watercourse between your filter outlet and the point of re-entry to the pond. In addition to the visual impact of a stream, the ecological benefits to the natural balance of the pond are considerable. Planted out with suitable plant life – watercress is ideal – the stream becomes an extension of the filter system, finishing off the purification process carried out in the filter. A waterfall is also a very important part of any water ecosystem, adding as it does much needed oxygen to the water. But beware of creating excessive noise; complaining neighbours may compel you to switch off a noisy waterfall at night, at the very time when oxygen demand is at its highest! (See page 51 for more details.)

Above: *In a small corner of a grander scheme, a waterfall not only provides a focal point but also helps to keep the water aerated as it flows from one pond to another. Such an attractive and beneficial water feature should be part of every pond.*

POND AND FILTER CONSTRUCTION

Filter design

Many newcomers to koi-keeping imagine that the function of filtering the koi pond is merely to obtain clear water in which to view the fish. In fact, the clarity aspect is of secondary importance. The primary object of filtration is to enable the pond to support a greater number of fish than would be possible in an unfiltered pond, by removing the toxic end products of the natural bodily processes that take place within the fish. Even a dozen large koi occupying a relatively small pond will, in the course of 24 hours, excrete a considerable amount of waste. Ammonia and other toxic chemicals will quickly build up to a point where the fish will suffocate on their own waste, unless these toxins are continuously converted into less harmful products.

We discuss filtration from the biochemical point of view in *Water quality and filtration*, starting on page 48. Here, we look at the 'nuts and bolts' of filter design, including both ready-made systems and the DIY alternatives.

Internal (undergravel) filtration

Although very popular at one time, undergravel filters are no longer regarded as an efficient means of filtration and should only be considered as a last resort when lack of space precludes the use of external types. In its simplest form, an internal filter consists of a matrix of pipework laid on the floor of the pond and covered with a layer of gravel ranging from 25 to 50cm (10-20in) deep depending upon the size and type of gravel used. (As a rough guide, use 25cm of 6mm(0.25in) gravel or 50cm of 15mm(0.6in) gravel.) A pump attached to

one end of the pipe matrix pulls water down through the media, where debris is trapped and biological action strips the toxins from the water before it returns to the pond.

When first matured, this type of filter is undoubtedly very efficient, but it suffers from the inescapable drawback of area 'blocking' caused by a build-up of heavy solid waste products and the formation of colonies of anaerobic bacteria. Raking the gravel surface is only a short-term remedy, as the dislodged solids will merely settle elsewhere and start the process all over again. After perhaps two years in service, an internal filter will also prove disappointing because continual digging by koi leads to heavily 'coloured' water loaded with suspended solids. In most cases, your only option will be to remove your fish to a holding tank while you dig out and wash perhaps a couple of tonnes of extremely dirty gravel – a back-breaking and unpleasant task that will do you and your koi no good at all, thanks to the upheaval involved.

Should you be unable to avoid using an undergravel filter, then ideally your pond should be flat bottomed or, preferably, the filter can be contained within a walled-off area of the pond. In either case, the filter area should be approximately one third the pond surface area.

Use piping of a minimum diameter of 38mm(1.5in) – plastic domestic plumbing pipework is fine – and construct the matrix of pipework in such a way as to ensure maximum drawdown through the media. Once the matrix is assembled, drill 5mm(0.2in) holes throughout the length of the matrix at approximately 40mm(1.6in) centres along the piping.

Above: *A hobbyist's pipe matrix in place on the filter bed section of a liner pond. It is important to design the grid so that water is drawn down evenly over the whole area. This will prevent channels developing in some parts of the gravel bed.*

Ideally, drill these holes on the underside of the pipes at the 4 o'clock and 8 o'clock positions. Put the matrix in position and cover it with a sheet of plastic mesh with 12mm(0.5in) apertures – this will slow down the clogging process – and then spread gravel to an even depth over the whole area. You can use either 'sharp' or 'smooth' gravel, but ensure that the particle size does not exceed 15mm(0.6in).

As with any filter, do not switch off an undergravel filter for more than 12 hours, otherwise the oxygen-dependent nitrifying bacteria will start to die and you will end up with a serious pollution problem.

External filters

Although external filtration systems are considerably more expensive to build and more complicated in their construction, they are far more effective and maintainable. Although they, too, may be

A typical undergravel (internal) filter

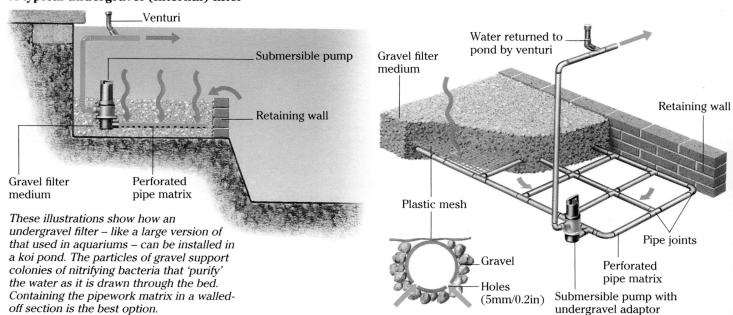

These illustrations show how an undergravel filter – like a large version of that used in aquariums – can be installed in a koi pond. The particles of gravel support colonies of nitrifying bacteria that 'purify' the water as it is drawn through the bed. Containing the pipework matrix in a walled-off section is the best option.

Venturi — Submersible pump — Retaining wall — Gravel filter medium — Perforated pipe matrix

Water returned to pond by venturi — Gravel filter medium — Retaining wall — Plastic mesh — Gravel — Holes (5mm/0.2in) — Pipe joints — Perforated pipe matrix — Submersible pump with undergravel adaptor

Right: *This represents a typical example of a single-chamber, external filter fed with water from a submersible pump. In some designs, the water flows upwards.*

susceptible to blocking, the time involved in back-flushing to clean them is minimal in comparison to the internal system. Draining debris is simple and analyzing water quality and condition is easy. Taking all things into consideration, an external filter is by far the best option, and it is worth considering this type of system, even if you have to opt for a smaller pond to keep within your original budget limits.

External filters fall into two main groups, those which are pump fed and those fed by gravity.

Pump-fed external filters

There are a number of small, single 'tank' filters available commercially which use a variety of systems and medias to achieve the same aim, that of producing pure water. You should be prepared to accept the premise that when a large body of water requires filtering, there is no way that a small tank containing media of whatever type will be capable of doing the job properly. Having said this, there is every possibility that a system using multiples of these miniature units could be assembled into an effective system. Problems may arise with the plumbing, however, as the majority of these types of filter are pump fed, the water entering at the top and percolating down through the medium (or having reached the bottom, percolating up through the medium). Rather than tackling the filtration in such a piecemeal manner, however, it would be more advisable either to opt for a larger commercial 'modular' filter or to build a suitable filter from scratch.

Pump-fed external filter

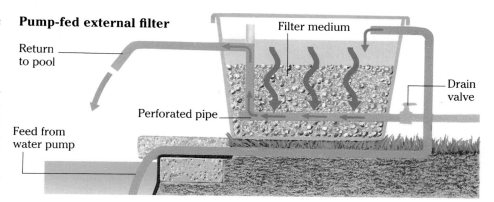

Filter medium

Return to pool

Feed from water pump

Perforated pipe

Drain valve

Gravity-fed multichamber filters

There can be no doubt that the most popular and proven system of filtration is that of the gravity-fed, multichambered variety. With this system, the filter body is constructed or installed at the same physical level as the pool so that the water level in both is identical. Therefore, if water is drawn from one end of the filter, gravity carries a fresh supply to the filter. Irrespective of how many chambers are used, water will flow from chamber to chamber, passing through successive 'blocks' of media as it progresses. (This is why it is so important to establish correct levels throughout the system during the design and construction phases.)

Water is transferred from chamber to chamber via transfer ports, and these must be of sufficient size to ensure there is no restriction of flow. The larger commercial modular filters use full-width transfer ports, which are greatly superior to those using, say, 10cm(4in) piping. These larger commercial filters are usually constructed in glass-reinforced plastic and are truly excellent, being provided with drain ports (for cleaning the media) and the correct size of inlet and outlet piping where required. Unfortunately, their excellence is reflected in

their relatively high cost. Here, once again, DIY design can come into its own; anyone capable of laying concrete blocks accurately can design and build an equally effective filter system at a fraction of the cost, as we shall later when we consider how to build one on page 46.

Above: *Part of an extensive multichamber filter system serving a large koi pond. These are commercial units that can be plumbed together in various configurations to suit any type and size of koi pond. They are expensive but highly effective.*

Below: *This schematic cross-section shows the working principles of a basic DIY multichamber filter system, featuring two settlement chambers and four media chambers. This design is featured in the construction phase, starting on page 46.*

Basic multichamber filter design

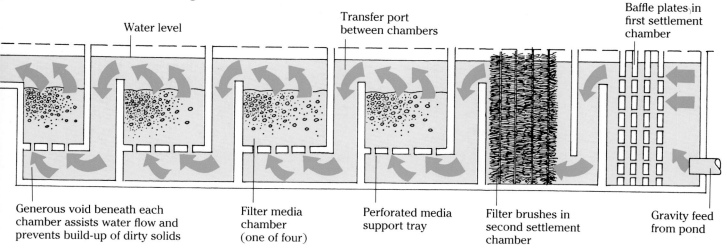

Water level

Transfer port between chambers

Baffle plates in first settlement chamber

Generous void beneath each chamber assists water flow and prevents build-up of dirty solids

Filter media chamber (one of four)

Perforated media support tray

Filter brushes in second settlement chamber

Gravity feed from pond

POND AND FILTER CONSTRUCTION

Filter design parameters

If you are thinking of building your own multichamber external filter, consider the following design parameters and interpret them in the light of your own requirements.

Pond to filter ratio

It is obviously important that your filter is large enough to cope adequately with the demands of your pond. There are many different formulae for calculating the designed pond to filter ratio, but the most commonly used are related to the surface area of the pond and filter system, and the rate at which water passes through the filter – which is a function of contact time and turnover rate.

Surface area As we have seen, the general rule is that the surface area of the filter should be one third of the pond surface area. You can regard this as a minimum, however, because there is no

upper limit to the size of a filter. Literally, the filter could be as big as the pond – it's just a question of space and finance!

Contact time This is the time taken for a given volume of water to pass through the filter system from the point of entry to exit. The contact time of filter water should be between 10 and 15 minutes.

Turnover rate This is the number of times that the total pond capacity should pass through the filter per day. The turnover rate through the filtration system should be 8-12 times the total pond capacity per day. Remember, however, that pump outputs are affected by the length of pipe runs, bends in pipes, and the height at which the water leaves pipes. Venturis may also affect turnover rate. If you are unsure of the effect of these factors on your designed system, consult your local dealer or the pump manufacturer for guidance.

Water flow through the filter

When considering water flow through your filter, your primary objective should be to set up obstruction-free flow paths. An important aspect in achieving this is the sizing of transfer ports, which should occupy about one fifth of the chamber volume. Another way of promoting freedom of flow is to limit the depth of media in each chamber. There is no point in having a media depth of greater than 50cm(20in). There is no evidence that biological efficiency improves with more media; the bacterial population responds to the nitrogenous loading.

Below: *A basic configuration of a koi pond and external filter system. The set-up is simplistic and is intended to highlight how the various elements fit together. The scheme is shown in plan view on the righthand side, with cross-sections through the standpipe chamber, pump chamber and settlement chamber of the filter arranged down the lefthand side.*

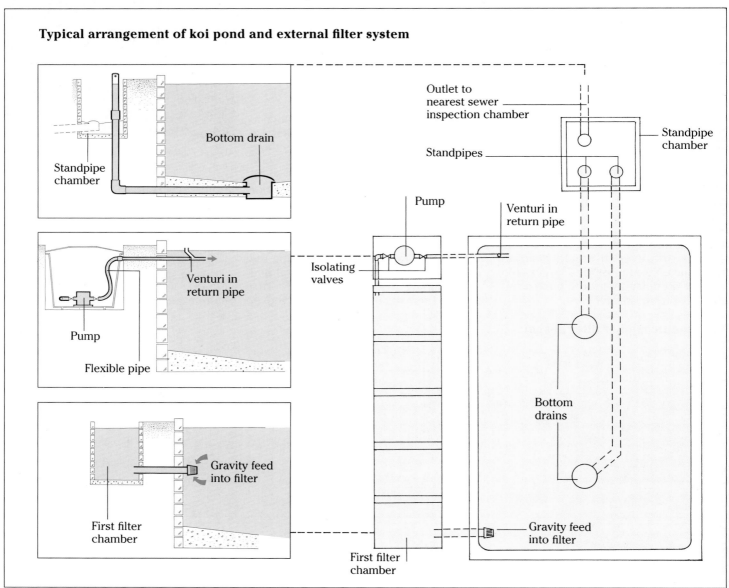

Typical arrangement of koi pond and external filter system

Whichever type of media you decide to use, it will require some means of support in the chamber. Here again, the correct choice of media support will ensure freedom of flow. Possibly the simplest media support is perforated PVC sheeting, which is available from dealers. Whatever you decide to use as a media support tray, mount it in the chamber in such a way that a void of at least 20cm(8in) is left underneath the media. The purpose of having a void is twofold: to assist freedom of water flow, and to prevent pockets of dirty solids gathering, which could encourage the growth of unwanted anaerobic bacteria.

Water levels
In gravity-fed systems, the top water level in the filter must equal that in the pond. Achieving this in practice relies on careful planning and surveying at the initial design stage (see page 28) and following these plans through accurately during construction.

Maintenance
You will need to clean the void spaces in your filter on a regular basis, particularly if your design does not incorporate a bottom drain system. Inserting a vacuum pipe down through the transfer port and under the void space is quite effective, which is another good reason for having large ports and voids.

Settlement chambers
It is vital to provide adequate settlement areas in your design. It might appear to be a waste of space having two or three empty chambers apparently doing nothing, but after seeing just how much solid waste will collect at these points rather than proceeding into the filter proper, the benefits of settling chambers will quickly become obvious. It is also an advantage to fit two or three baffle plates in the first settling chamber to reduce the natural turbulence of the water as it enters the chamber. A few rows of long filter brushes should also be fitted as an additional means of trapping solids.

Vegetable filtration
If your pond design does not include an area devoted to a stream for watercress or similar plants to flourish, you might like to consider adding a chamber at the end of your filter chain for this purpose. Since your filtered water will be very rich in nitrates, a bed of 'greedy' aquatic plants will consume a great deal of this before the water returns to the pond.

Type of pump
It is important to decide at an early stage in the design process on the type of pump to use. The choice comes down to submersible or external. (We will be considering the practical aspects of installing pumps on page 43.)

Submersible pumps, although simpler to install, are usually rather more expensive to both buy and run and are certainly not as reliable in the long term as external pumps. Should you elect to use a submersible pump in a multichamber external filter, install it in the final chamber of your filter chain, and conceal the return outlet pipework leading back to the pond. In this configuration, the pump effectively 'pulls' water through the filter system by gravity as it continuously pumps water from the final chamber into the pond.

External pumps are designed to pump water rather than to pull it, and so they must be installed at as low a level as possible relative to the level of water in the filter. This will ensure that a constant positive head is available – 'head' being the term used to denote the height of water above the pump inlet point. You will need to build a dry, but well-ventilated, chamber to house an external pump. The ventilation is essential to dissipate the condensation caused by the heat of the motor windings; otherwise the motor would soon burn out. Also allow space in the pumping chamber for isolating valves, so that you can turn off the water flow through the system in order to service or replace the pump.

Above: *A view looking from the last chamber of an external filter (at the bottom of the photograph) along the mazelike channels of a vegetable filter that ultimately leads the cleaned water back into the pond. The aquatic plants growing in the channels absorb excess nitrates from the water.*

Below: *A multichamber filter system next to a koi pond, with the pump chamber clearly visible in the foreground of the photograph. Note the isolating valves fitted on either side of the pump to enable it to be serviced or replaced. Good design speeds maintenance.*

POND AND FILTER CONSTRUCTION

Preparing to build

Whatever type or style of pond you have elected to build, you'll need a basic 'kit' of tools and equipment to complete the job. Make sure everything is to hand before you start; there is nothing worse than having to stop while you track down a vital piece of equipment. Therefore, make a list of what you will need and be sure to obtain everything in good time! If you are fortunate enough to be able to engage a professional builder to construct your pond, such mundane matters need not concern you as your contractor will doubtless know just what is required. For the DIY builder, however, there is quite a formidable list of equipment to consider.

In the majority of cases, most of the spoil from your excavation will need to be disposed of, and for this you'll need to hire a skip. Don't run away with the idea that your proposed rockery or landscaping will swallow up all you dig out; spoil from an excavation has an almost magical ability to more than double in bulk once removed from the hole! You'll also need a good wheelbarrow to get the spoil into the skip, which itself will require some means of access in the form of a very strong ramp from the ground up to the edge of the skip, which can be as high as 1.2m(4ft). Make the ramp as long as possible; a barrow load of soil can be extremely unwieldy, both to push to the top of a ramp and then to lift and tip. If at all possible, get a helper to do the barrowing while you do the digging and filling, and then take it in turns to relieve the monotony.

The only other large item of equipment you need worry about is a concrete mixer. If you are hiring one, then preferably choose a petrol-driven model, as it is not unknown for a power failure to occur just when a mix has been started, leaving a rapidly solidifying mess to be cleared from a 'powerless' electric model. If you feel confident about your electricity supply then it could be worthwhile to buy an electric mixer and re-sell it after the job is complete, as we mentioned earlier on page 24.

An assortment of chisels for working stone and brick is an absolute must, as you will find during construction that bricks and blocks will always need trimming. If you have access to one, a disc cutter (like a hand-held electric circular saw with a stone-cutting disc) will prove very helpful. A disc of 12.5cm(5in) diameter being adequate for most jobs. Be sure to use goggles when using a disc cutter; no pool, however impressive, is worth damaging your eyes for!

Perhaps the most important items of equipment you will be using are spirit levels – ideally, a 30cm(12in) and 120cm(48in) level – plus an assortment of straight edges (lengths of straight and true hardwood). For establishing very long levels, you can use a length of clear plastic hose filled with water, as we have described on page 29. Depending upon the size of your proposed pond, you will need a number of wooden pegs when setting levels out. Preferably, make these from 38mm(1.5in)square hardwood, pointed at one end to make them easy to drive into the ground. Allow for a peg at not more than 30cm(12in) intervals to ensure accuracy when setting out. The ideal length of the pegs will vary according to the type of ground; for solid clay a length of 30cm(12in) will be fine, whereas crumbly and friable earth requires double this length.

Should you be unfortunate enough to strike a layer of stone when excavation is underway, an electric jackhammer (a portable pneumatic hammer drill) will be essential. You can hire this from a plant hire company, but, again, be sure to wear goggles when you use it.

Building a liner pond

Here, we look in detail at the sequence of steps involved in building a liner pond. Starting on page 45, we will review the basic differences involved in building a concrete pond.

Installing a concrete collar

The first step is to install a concrete collar, or 'ring beam', which will form the 'skeleton' of your pond. The simplest method of visualizing this collar is to imagine it as a large concrete 'washer' lying in the ground, the inside of which represents the finished diameter of your pond. Be sure to check your plans!

You can use a length of hose to mark out the shape of your pond, pinning it in position temporarily with wire hooks driven into the ground. Dig a trench along the outside of this area approximately 45cm(18in) deep and 30cm(12in) wide, removing the spoil as you go, otherwise you will quickly find yourself working in a quagmire! Your trench should have vertical sides and a clean, debris-free base. You will find it an advantage to check the level of the trench base as you go along, rather than wait until you've finished.

Before pouring any concrete, and assuming the trench base is level, install lengths of hardboard around the inner edge of the trench, smooth side facing outwards. This will ensure a smooth surface for the liner to rest against. Hold these hardboard strips in position with transverse lengths of wood. Remove these when you pour in the concrete and tamp it down in the trench.

Drive a series of pegs along the base of the trench, following the centre line at approximately 30cm(12in)-intervals, setting the first peg to the depth of the finished collar. Follow this level all the way round with subsequent pegs. Take your time; a mistake or a little carelessness at this stage can ruin the completed job! Provided that you have adjusted these pegs to the correct height, your finished collar, and consequently the pond, will be exactly level. (You can leave these pegs in position when pouring concrete, or you can drive them into the ground after the collar has set and fill the holes with wet concrete.)

Below: *The first stage of constructing a concrete collar to establish a firm edge around the pond. Here, work has started on digging the trench to receive the concrete.*

Having finished preparing the trench, you can now begin the actual construction. Start mixing the concrete early on in the day so that you can finish filling your collar trench before dark. Spreading this operation over two days will result in a weak collar, because concrete does not bond to itself very effectively. Make the mix from one part cement to six parts by volume of mixed aggregate (sand and gravel). Add water carefully. The ideal mix should be quite 'stodgy', with no tendency to 'slump' or run; too wet a mix will dry weak and be prone to cracking. Shovel the mix into the trench, working it well into the bottom and sides. Treading it in with heavy boots can be quite effective, the object being to expel as much air as possible from the mix. If it makes you feel happier, hire a vibrating poker for this job.

Having filled the trench and tamped it down, you can now begin the task of obtaining a smooth, level surface, using the tops of your pegs as guides. A large plasterer's float is an excellent tool for this purpose. Once this task is completed, go away and forget about it for at least 48 hours to give the initial 'set' a chance to take place undisturbed. (It will take anything up to a month for the concrete to cure fully, so be warned and tread carefully during the next operation.) If your concrete has been mixed to the correct consistency without too much water, now is a good time to remove the sharp edge from the inside rim of your collar in order to prevent later damage to the liner. This is easy to carry out by running the point of a trowel along the line of the hardboard shuttering, removing a little concrete and leaving a slight chamfer along the edge.

The main excavation

Following the initial 48-hour setting period of the concrete liner, you can now begin the task of digging out. There is a right and a wrong way to tackle this job; the following suggestions employ a little logic but still require the same muscle power! Start your digging in the centre and work in straight lines, progressing a spade's width at a time but leaving a spade's width all round the edge. Having removed the first layer of topsoil and stacked it somewhere for later use, now remove the last spade's width from around the edge. Do this carefully, avoiding any undercutting of the collar and ensuring that the excavation sides remain vertical. Carry on in this manner until you have reached the required depth, bearing in mind the recommendations about optimum depth made on page 26. Eventually, you will reach a point at

Left: *Smoothing off the surface of the wet concrete collar with a plasterer's float. Try to do the whole concreting operation in one day; new and old concrete will not bond very well if you split the job over two days. Let the concrete set for at least 48 hours before digging out the pond.*

Below: *Digging out the soil from inside the collar. Dig in straight lines, starting at the centre and working outwards, removing one level at a time. Be very careful to keep the sides of the excavation vertical and avoid any undercutting that may cause collapse.*

which it is physically impossible to lift the spoil out of the excavation. At this point, enlist the assistance of a helper armed with a couple of buckets suspended on ropes – slower, but most effective!

At this point, we should introduce a few words of caution on the question of safety while digging. If the terrain is at all crumbly, do be aware of the danger of slippage; the sides of an excavation can collapse inwards without warning, with dire consequences. Should you suspect that this could happen as you dig deeper, be sure to change your plans, not only for your own safety while digging but also to preserve the stability of the finished pond. The best way to cope with this is to incorporate brick or block walls. It will be too late to embody these after the liner is installed and filled with water. Unprotected in this way, the walls of an unstable pond could subside during a very wet spell. (This can happen even to long-established ponds.)

Installing bottom drains

Having excavated the hole to your liking, the time has arrived to install your bottom drain(s). While it is possible and quite common practice to install these devices straight into the ground, do consider laying a concrete base with the bottom drain encased in it. Not only is this a much more workmanlike method, but it also has the advantage that should you, as many others have done, decide that a liner pool is not for you after all, you have a sound base all ready for laying blocks to construct a concrete pond (see page 45). Either way, the installation procedure for the bottom drain is identical, apart from the height difference depending on whether a concrete base is used.

Together with its associated pipework, a bottom drain is a very expensive item and any mistake made during its assembly is uncorrectable, so take a long look at all the components and carry out a 'dry run' before attempting the installation proper. The best-quality components are moulded from PVC/ABS plastics and are intended to be solvent welded together. This technique involves coating both mating surfaces with a solvent cement and inserting one piece into another. As the name implies, the cement welds the two surfaces together – virtually instantaneously. Theoretically, there may be five seconds in which to make any adjustment of position but, to be on the safe side, you should assume that there will be no time at all!

POND AND FILTER CONSTRUCTION

Cut all the pipework and fittings to exact size and assemble them 'dry', marking them to ensure that they will fit together accurately at the cementing stage. The easiest way to mark your components is simply to scratch a series of lines on each component where it meets its partner. Do this once everything is assembled 'dry' and when you have checked that each length of pipe is truly horizontal and vertical. Due to the moulding process, it is not unknown for some components to be unacceptably tight at the dry-fit stage. To avoid assembly problems once the solvent cement has been applied, check each joint for fit and, if necessary, 'dress' the surfaces with the finest grade of abrasive paper until an easy slide fit is obtained.

Having cut everything to size, assembled the various components 'dry' and propped them in position as necessary to take measurements, you can now begin the task of trenching the ground for your pipe runs. By now you should know exactly where the termination point for the waste pipe will be and will have dug out the chamber ready to receive the standpipes, etc. Dig the trench from your standpipe chamber so that it terminates about 30cm(12in) from the pond wall. Then make the final breakthrough from within the pool to minimize damage to the soil under the collar. Where a change in direction occurs, allow for the larger diameter of any bends or elbows. Also allow for the vertical run of pipe from the bottom drain during trenching.

Once the trenching is complete, assemble the drain and pipework 'dry' *in situ*, just as a final check, placing blocks under the drain and pipework as necessary to achieve the correct positioning. All being well, you can now begin the jointing process. To carry out this task properly and without undue mental stress really requires two or three pairs of hands, so don't be tempted to go it alone, however much you want to get on with the job. A hasty mistake could spell disaster! Assembling solvent-welded systems involves cleaning each male and female connection with solvent cleaner, applying solvent cement to each jointing face, lining up your marks and inserting one component into the other with firm pressure. Provided you have applied the solvent cement generously, there is no need to insert them with a twisting motion; this may lead to positioning problems for the 'first-timer' using plastic jointing technology. Having made the joint, just run a finger around the outside of the joint to spread any surplus cement and form a small fillet. Within the space of five minutes or so, the integrity of the

Fitting the bottom drain pipework together

Side view

Standard bottom drain fitting

Vertical pipe to standpipe chamber

Blocks to support the pipework in position while you check fit and measurements

Plan view

Ensure that your marks on the pipe and elbow match

A length of standard 10cm(4in) high-pressure PVC/ABS pipe

joint will be sufficient for you to manipulate it within reason while making the next connection.

Once the assembly is complete, you can now manoeuvre it into its final position within the pool, temporarily securing it with a collection of odd bricks, blocks, etc. Then you can fix it permanently by placing a stiff mix of concrete in the trench around the piping and leave it for a couple of days to set. If you are intending to use a separate filter feed, say for middle water, you will need to repeat the whole exercise in order to install the pipework, but by now you should be feeling something of an expert!

Concreting the pond base
Having completed the pipework, the next job to tackle is laying the pond floor. First and foremost, set your level around the outer edge of the pond excavation, once again using wooden pegs set at about 30cm(12in) centres. Aim for a minimum concrete depth of 15cm(6in), this depth being constant right across to the bottom drain. If you did not allow for a slight slope towards the bottom drain during excavation, it is quite acceptable to incorporate this now by returning some of the removed spoil as necessary and compacting it into position before driving in the level pegs.

Whatever size of pool is involved, you will need a considerable quantity of concrete for the floor and, as with any concreting, this is best completed in one working day. Should you have any doubt about achieving this timescale, you might wish to consider taking a delivery of ready-mixed concrete. There are cer-

Above: *It is vital to 'dry-fit' the pipework components together before you solvent weld them; mistakes can be impossible to rectify later! Use blocks to support them.*

tain advantages to this method; for instance, when placing the order, you can ask to have a waterproofing additive in the mix. The only major problem with bulk concrete delivery is one of time. Most delivery drivers expect to simply drop and depart, although some are prepared to unload the mix into a wheelbarrow, as long as there is a rapid turnround made possible by, perhaps, three helpers each with a barrow. As concrete can become unworkable quite quickly, especially in warm weather, the ready-mixed option also requires extra help with the pond for laying the stuff, so some organization is called for.

Use the same laying technique as for the collar, but on a somewhat larger scale. Shovel the concrete into position and work it well in with the shovel, particularly in any areas around exposed pipework, then tread it in with large boots and finally smooth it off with a plasterer's float. Of course, you will reach a stage when you are trapped in the excavation with the part under your feet waiting for concrete. Exit by means of a pair of steps or small ladder and complete the concreting from outside the pool, if necessary, by being held by the feet over the edge.

Positioning the liner
The moment has now arrived when the liner can be offered up to the excavation – better known as the moment of truth!

Even for a modestly sized pool, a folded liner can be incredibly heavy, so don't bank on being able to cope singlehandedly, quite apart from the danger of abrading or tearing your liner by dragging it across the ground.

Depending upon the size of liner involved, you should have at least four people to place the liner in position. If you are installing a box-welded liner, do ensure that you have the thing the right way round; if you get it wrong, it can prove quite difficult to lift out and turn. Lay the flat sheet type of liner across the excavation, ensuring that there is an equal amount of overhang around the edge. The easiest way to get the liner into its hole is simply to run water into it but, as the weight begins to pull the liner down, do ensure that the overhang does not become unbalanced, resulting in a lopsided configuration.

The weight of water will eventually pull the liner down until it touches the floor. At this point, the procedure to follow is identical for both box-welded and flat-sheet liners, and involves a volunteer going for a paddle, preferably barefooted to minimize the risk of damaging the liner. Whatever grade of liner being used, there will be a certain amount of stretch in the material but not enough to prevent pleats and folds developing. All that can be done is to manually persuade the liner to take up a position as free from pleats and folds as possible. Since this can only be done while filling is in progress, someone has to get wet! The more water you can get into the pond, the better will be the final lie of the liner, even though you will need to empty the pond when you make the various pipe connections.

With the pond as full as possible, lay the surplus liner flat around the edge and weight it down with heavy blocks; leave these in position until the pipefitting work is complete. Avoid placing any tension on any part of the liner that is still exposed, as this could lead to later problems, such as tearing. You simply have to endure any wrinkles that are visible, although many of these will not be seen once you have added the finishing touches. Leave the water in the pool overnight to allow the liner to settle into its position ready for the next operation.

Fitting drains and pipes to the liner
You are now about to enter the area of most risk when building a liner pond, that of attaching the liner to the various drain and pipe flanges. This is risky because any error in positioning may lead to the liner tearing due to the stress placed upon it by the weight of water.

Pump out the water from your pond down to a depth of perhaps 30cm(12in) and place three or four concrete blocks broad-face down around the site of the bottom drain. This will prevent any movement of the liner relative to the bottom drain while you are paddling around carrying out the fixing operation. When these are in position, pump out the remaining water before you start to cut and attach the liner.

You are probably now wondering how to set about cutting the liner accurately so that the centre hole and all the screw holes are correctly aligned? This is where the concrete blocks show their worth! After completely drying the area of liner around your bottom drain, take a piece of chalk, preferably the type used by tailors, and rub briskly around the face of the bottom drain flange, which you should be able to feel through the liner. This will leave an imprint of the centre hole and screw holes on the liner. Carefully cut around the centre with a sharp knife and expose the bottom drain sump. To make this task easier, hold the liner flat against the flange and cut with downward strokes, using the inside of the sump as a guide. Remove the circular section of liner and perforate the screw holes using either a leather punch or a small soldering iron, but be careful!

Clean all the mating surfaces carefully and assemble the flange using the appropriate mastic compound, if required by your particular bottom drain. (This should have been supplied with the drain.) Now tighten the screws in an even manner, ensuring that none is tightened more than the others. It might be helpful at this point to call it a day, run some water into the pond and mark the level, ready to check for leaks the next morn-

Fitting a liner to a bottom drain

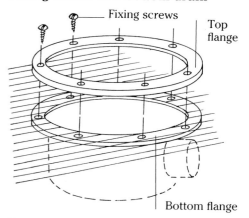

Above: *Cutting and fitting the liner around a bottom drain demands a good deal of care. Mark the position of the hole and flange screws using chalk, cut out the centre, perforate the screw holes and tighten the screws evenly to ensure a secure seal.*

Above: *Placing the liner in the excavation is a tricky operation needing lots of willing help – at least four people for a large liner. Try to arrange an even overlap around the edge of the pond, with plenty to spare.*

Right: *Running water into the hole is the best way to bed the liner into position. If necessary, get into the water and manually sort out pleats and wrinkles.*

POND AND FILTER CONSTRUCTION

ing. If you have followed the above sequence of instructions to the letter, there should be none!

Mark out, cut and fit the filter feed pipe connection in the same manner. If you are using one of the threaded types of connection here, wrap some PTFE tape on the threads to ensure a watertight seal. (Plumbers use this kind of tape.) When fitting these attachments, it is vital to ensure that the weight of water in the finished pond will not stress the liner at these attachment points. Otherwise, there is a real risk of a tear developing.

However impatient you might be to get on with the job, pause at this point and take stock. Fill the pool yet again and leave it overnight to check for leaks.

Finishing off the edge
You have now reached the exciting part of your project, finishing off the edge of the pond. Whether you intend building an ornamental wall around the pond or just placing large rocks around the perimeter, the requirements are identical. In broad terms, you should lay the excess liner flat around the outside of the pond, set your wall or rockwork on top and cement it into position. The weight involved will hold the liner in place, but be sure to let the mortar set before continuing, otherwise all your good work could be undone!

The object is to fold the liner up behind the wall or rockwork in such a way that the liner remains watertight far above the proposed top water level. The aim is to hide the edge of the liner from view by arranging for the water level to be above the point at which the liner changes from the vertical to the horizontal axis.

If you are constructing a wall, make this double-skinned and run the liner between the two layers. Achieving the same effect with rockwork can be a little more difficult. With very large stones, you can still fold the liner up, cement it and hold it in position with a gravel path or paving stones. If you fancy something slightly different, consider fitting sections of tree log around the edge as shown below. Do

Left: Sawn logs provide a natural-looking edge to a koi pond. Do ensure that the wood preservative used is not toxic to fish. This type of edging is just one of the many options for finishing off your pond.

beware of using any materials which have been treated with preservatives, however, as these chemicals are invariably toxic to fish! You may wish to incorporate a shelf for marginal plants, but do try to avoid any sharp edges on which the koi can damage themselves when swimming, particularly at spawning time. All that now remains is to remove any excess liner with a sharp knife and to leave the pool filled to allow any cement in contact with the water to lose its alkalinity and harden off completely (see also page 46 for more on alkalinity).

Building the standpipe chamber
The standpipe assembly normally used on koi ponds is a commercial assembly consisting of a sleeve and socket with a neoprene 'O' ring for sealing purposes. A pipe long enough for the top end to be above the top water level in the pond is inserted into the sleeve; a cross piece, or 'tommy bar', allows the pipe to be withdrawn. With this pipe in position, the pool water finds its own level by gravity. Pulling out the pipe (with a twisting motion) causes a difference in level be-

Variations on edging a liner pond

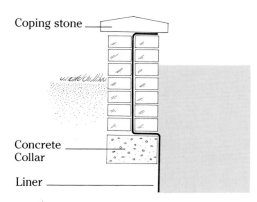

Coping stone

Concrete Collar

Liner

These are a few ideas for finishing off the edge of a liner pond. The aim is to secure the liner above the water level and hide it from view. Sawn and treated sections of log are particularly effective and will fit in well around an informal pond. If you build a marginal planter, either leave the pond edge low enough for water to splash onto the soil or, better for koi, build up the edge but leave out the occasional perpendicular joint to allow water to reach the roots. Slope any paving or turf slightly away from the pond to prevent pollution from the garden.

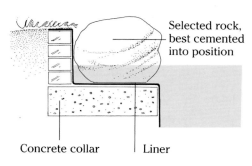

Selected rock, best cemented into position

Concrete collar | Liner

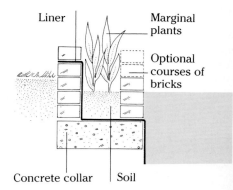

Liner | Marginal plants

Optional courses of bricks

Concrete collar | Soil

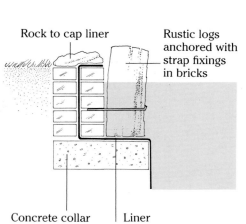

Rock to cap liner

Rustic logs anchored with strap fixings in bricks

Concrete collar | Liner

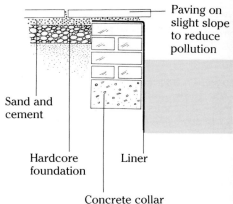

Paving on slight slope to reduce pollution

Sand and cement

Hardcore foundation

Liner

Concrete collar

tween the pond and the standpipe chamber and water flows by gravity into the chamber. The flow comes from the bottom drain and carries with it any debris within the suction area around the drain. This rush of water is propelled by the head of water in the pond and will continue to flow until either the standpipe is replaced or the water level in the pond falls to the level of the standpipe socket. The pond cannot be completely emptied via a bottom drain unless the standpipe socket is at the same level as the bottom drain itself.

You can build the standpipe chamber either from concrete blocks, and then render it, or from engineering-quality bricks. Do not use ordinary house bricks, as these will quickly deteriorate under the action of water. In addition to an entry point for the pipe from the pond, there must also be an access out of the chamber to your main sewer, which means breaking into the nearest sewer inspection chamber. (You may need to seek advice on this, depending on your local building regulations and byelaws.) Ideally, use standard clay sewer piping from the standpipe chamber to your sewer inspection chamber, as it is much easier to achieve a watertight seal with cement, this being a drawback with plastic piping. Arrange for the entry into the inspection chamber to be as low down as possible to ensure that the maximum head of water is available from the pond.

From a technical point of view, the standpipe is a rather crude device. A much more efficient and reliable method of releasing waste water from the pond is to use an industrial ball valve of the same diameter as the bottom drain pipework. Needless to say, these valves are very expensive, particularly the motorized versions. But what price perfection for the committed enthusiast?

Attaching the filter feed
By now, attaching the filter feed pipework should seem to be child's play. If you are using the same industrial-quality piping as on the bottom drain, this will merely be a matter of fixing a flange at the point of entry into the filter and cementing a suitable length of pipe into position. You might find it easier to cut the pipe to length and cement the flange on the end of it first. Then you can adjust the position and height of the filter carcass before drilling the holes for the flange-fixing screws.

If you have elected to build your own filter system from cement-rendered concrete blocks (see page 46), you could run into difficulties obtaining a watertight seal at the flange connection, as cement does not adhere very well to plastic pipe, even if the surface is roughened. Various methods have been used to overcome this problem, their success rate depending upon the skill and perseverance of the individual. One method is to make a hole in the blockwork large enough to accommodate the feed pipe, then to liberally coat the flange-bearing surface and the inside of the hole with fibreglass. Once this has all dried and been checked for flatness (most important), attach the flange using a suitable mastic compound as a seal. Then cement a short length of pipe from the inside of the filter so that it butts up to the inside of the flange, and spread a fillet of gap-filling cement on the inside of the pipe where it touches the flange. Finally, paint the whole area with a waterproofing paint. It might seem rather clumsy but it does work! If you like spending money, you could attach a flange at both sides of the blockwork, thus reducing the risk of seepage.

A more economical alternative to using industrial pipework and fittings for the feed pipe – and one which has worked successfully on many ponds – is to use domestic drainage systems. These consist of 10cm(4in)-diameter plastic tubes, fitted together with push-on units sealed with neoprene gaskets. Once assembled, these systems can withstand quite a considerable head of water without seepage. Connecting this class of pipe to a concrete construction poses no problems at all; adaptor sleeves can be used to couple the plastic pipe to the unglazed clay pipe, to which cement adheres readily. For the pool end, one of the complementary ground boxes and screens can be easily fitted to the liner and will work quite satisfactorily.

A cautionary word about electricity
Your pond and associated systems are going to require a source of electricity and you should think seriously before tackling this yourself. Electric current and water form an extremely dangerous alliance and on no account should you tackle this job unless you are really confident or suitably qualified.

Do not expect one domestic socket to serve the needs of your pond. A little thought should tell you that your pump will need one, a vacuum pump will need another and, during winter, you might well wish to run a heater to keep a small area of water free of ice. As an absolute minimum, you should aim for a double socket or even two doubles, of the switched variety and of the 'metal clad' construction. These should be housed in such a position that rainwater cannot drip upon them and they should prefer-

ably be hidden from the view of the casual visitor. Consider housing your electrics in a lockable metal cabinet, for example, for safety and security.

Statutory regulations governing the installation of external electrical circuits vary from country to country, but all are designed to protect you and yours from a lethal electric shock. Where appropriate, the most important of these regulations requires the fitting of a residual current circuit breaker to any new outdoor circuit, a device that shuts off the supply instantaneously in the event of a circuit, or equipment connected to that circuit, developing an earth fault and becoming 'live'. If you already have an outside electrical supply to a greenhouse or garage, for instance, do seriously consider fitting such a circuit breaker; it could save your life! There are also regulations governing the depth at which outside circuit cables can be buried in the ground, as well as the type of cable and methods of installation. Taking all these factors into consideration, there really is a good case for calling in an electrical contractor and having this part of the job carried out professionally.

Installing pumps
At the heart of any koi pond is a pump. Unfortunately, there is an absolutely bewildering assortment of pumps available, and buying an unsuitable one can be both frustrating and expensive. As we have seen on page 37, the pumps with which you will be concerned can be divided into two groups: the submersible type for direct immersion into the water to be pumped, and the external pump intended to be installed remotely.

Taking a look firstly at the submersible type, you might be forgiven for thinking that, on the face of it, nothing could be more simple than dropping such a pump into your pond, coupling it up, switching it on and running the system up to full

Above: *A typical pump chamber located close to a koi pond, showing its associated pipework. Properly installed in a dry, ventilated chamber, external pumps are preferred over submersible ones for long service life and ease of maintenance.*

POND AND FILTER CONSTRUCTION

power. So what are the snags? Firstly, submersible pumps are more expensive to buy, usually more expensive to run, and, finally, may not prove extremely reliable. The higher purchase price can be explained by the fact that the electrical and mechanical components need to be well insulated from contact with the water, which entails the motor windings, bearings and internal connections being contained within a sealed pot that is usually filled with oil to cool and lubricate the motor. Another drawback is that the perforated screen fitted in order to prevent debris from entering and clogging the impeller (the part which actually moves the water) can quickly become matted with blanketweed, etc., necessitating frequent removal of the pump for cleaning, which can become a most boring chore! From an aesthetic point of view, the pump, its cable and its outlet piping are virtually impossible to conceal, and will certainly detract from the visual pleasure of your pond.

Some submersible pumps can be purchased complete with an adaptor plate that fits over the inlet screen, allowing direct connection to pipework associated with undergravel filters. The one place where a submersible pump can be used with advantage, however, is in the final chamber of a filter chain, where, of course, it is invisible, along with its cable and piping. When used in a filter chamber, this type of pump is sometimes simply placed on the surface of the final layer of gravel that gives the filtered water a last 'polish'. Here, you must take precautions to prevent fine grains of gravel being sucked into the pump, where they will play havoc with the bearings. It could well be an added advantage to buy the type of submersible pump fitted with an automatic switch that shuts the pump down in the event of a disaster with your plumbing which could result in your pool being pumped dry, with obvious consequences for your koi. (An example of this would be a fracture occurring in the return pipe from the filter to the pond, allowing water to leak away. An 'automatic' pump has a sensor that shuts it down when the water level drops by a certain amount, thereby preventing the pump from completely emptying the pond.)

The externally mounted pump undoubtedly has a number of advantages over the submersible variety. The most important of these must be that of purchase and running costs. The water in a great number of koi ponds is now circulated by central heating pumps, better known in the plumbing industry as 'circulators'. The difference in cost can be quite staggering; three small central heating circulators can be bought for the same cost as one submersible pump, for example. Some of these circulators have a variable speed control, which can be useful during the winter months, when full circulation is not really necessary – thereby saving on running costs.

The only real drawback with external pumps is that they need to be properly housed in a dry, well-ventilated chamber if you are to avoid condensation problems. However, once properly carried out, these precautions will pay for themselves over and over again in that your pumps will give years of trouble-free service. One relatively simple method of housing an external pump is to use a domestic polypropylene water tank placed in the ground. Use 38mm(1.5in) diameter plastic piping for your pumping circuit. (This is an internationally accepted standard, making spares always easily available.) Connect the inlet and outlet pipes by means of 'tank connectors' used with domestic plumbing systems. Screwed pump connections are also easily available using the same size and type of piping. When deciding on piping sizes, always remember that even a small reduction in the diameter of pump pipework can have a serious effect on the efficiency of a pump, quite out of proportion to the reduced diameter.

Selecting the most suitable size of pump can be difficult, as the information given in pump literature can be misleading. For instance, the pumping output figures provided for a given pump and head are based on the unit pumping against an open end; such parameters as pipe size and any change of pipe direction are not taken into account. As an example, a pump rated at, say, 4500 litres (approximately 1000 gallons) per hour at 1.2m(4ft) head may only deliver 80 percent of that when connected to pond pipework with perhaps a venturi connected at the outlet end. Therefore, when selecting a pump, always consider both the pipe size and the number of pipe bends used in the system. To maximize pump efficiency, always try to limit the number of bends in the output pipework by sensible location of your pumping chamber (see the scheme on page 36).

Above: *The smaller of two ponds in an extensive koi pond complex at the block wall stage. Note the three standpipes for the bottom drains set in the base.*

Above: *The same pond after the walls have been rendered into smooth curves and fibreglassed. The base around each bottom drain has been dished to aid water flow.*

Above: *Part of the multichamber filter system under construction that will serve both this relatively small pond and the larger informal koi pond featured at various stages on the opposite page.*

Right: *The small pond on completion and stocked with fish. Brick, stone and log edging complement each other and blend in well with the overall style of the garden.*

Take care when comparing the running costs of various pumps, as the figures quoted for power, whether expressed in watts or horsepower, invariably relate to the output power rather than the actual energy consumed when pumping. Thus, a pump whose data plate quotes a power figure of, say, 60 watts, could use anything up to twice this figure in electrical consumption.

When installing your pump or pumps, do remember the advice given on page 37 regarding the fitting of isolating valves to enable the pump to be removed for servicing or replacement. A point to remember when siting your pump is that pumps are designed to propel water rather than suck it, so any pump must be installed at the lowest point possible relative to the normal top water level. This will ensure a constant positive head of pressure is available at the inlet, or suction side, of the pump.

Building a concrete pond
Constructing a concrete pond generally follows the same techniques as for a liner pool, the excavation and laying of the base, as well the installation of bottom drains, being identical.

If you have laid your base level, then it is merely a matter of building a wall from concrete blocks. If the terrain is heavy – solid clay, for example – you can erect these block walls flush with the sides of the excavation. If the terrain is at all crumbly, however, it will be better to leave a gap that can be backfilled with hardcore or even concrete as the work proceeds. When building in solid terrain, use dense concrete blocks measuring 45x23x10cm(18x9x4in), and in loose terrain, use hollow blocks measuring 45x23x23cm(18x9x9in). As you lay each two courses of blocks, backfill as necessary, but only up to the halfway point of the last block laid so that the layers of backfill do not coincide with the weaker mortar joints. To cope with acute corners, cut the blocks into smaller segments and work mortar well into the joints, particularly at the rear. Tackle the inlet and outlet points for pipework in the same way as for a liner pond, using unglazed clay pipe with adaptors for plastic pipe where appropriate.

Rendering a concrete pond
The traditional method of finishing a concrete pond was to apply two separate rendering coats, each approximately 20mm(0.8in) thick, containing a high proportion of sand to reduce cracking. Unfortunately, the result was inherently weak, with a high porosity and extremely vulnerable to frost damage. The modern

Above: *An early stage in building a large informal pond. The concrete base is underway and metal rods are already in place to reinforce the block walls.*

Above: *Bottom drains and connecting PVC/ABS pipework in place before the floor is built up around them. Each drain has its own pipe to the standpipe chamber.*

Above: *Making the dished areas around each bottom drain involves shaping the concrete within these circular templates. The aim is to avoid areas that will not drain.*

Above: *The block walls are now in place and both these and the base have been contoured and rendered. The smooth curves will promote water flow in the pond.*

Above: *The interior of the pond after it has been fibreglassed and painted. This dark green colour is ideal for koi ponds and will show off the koi colours well.*

Above: *Now the attention turns towards finishing off the edges of the pond, with brickwork, stonework and a shallow pebble beach in preparation in the foreground.*

Above: *The newly finished pond, with new areas of planting just beginning to get* established. *It will be several months before the pond fully 'matures' in all aspects.*

POND AND FILTER CONSTRUCTION

method involves applying just one coat of 5mm(0.2in)-thick rendering made from a 2-to-1 sand/cement mix with the addition of the plastic fibres mentioned on page 31. Where there is any uneveness, such as at the corners, you can apply the rendering material as thick as necessary to give a smooth contour, there being no tendency for it to slump or fall away. Cover the whole pond, including the floor, in one continuous operation. Spreading the job over two days is not recommended, as the material is so impervious to water once dry that successive coats will not bond. If you render the pond in very hot weather, take precautions to prevent it drying out too rapidly, either by providing a cover over the pool or by spraying it periodically with a fine mist of water. After a couple of days, fill the pond. Concrete cures much more evenly under water, it being a little known fact that concrete continues to cure for many weeks after laying.

If you intend to coat the pond with a fibreglass skin, you can carry this out without further preparation, but be sure that it is completely dry before you start. As we mentioned previously, this is really a task best left to the professionals.

Coping with alkalinity

For a normal concrete-finished pond, there are just a couple more points to consider. Firstly, with such a high level of cement being used in the rendering, the level of alkalinity will also be proportionally higher and this could make the pool uninhabitable for fish if it is not neutralized. This is possible by chemical means or even by repeated washing with clean water, but the end result will be a pond of a most unnatural appearance, as the rendering will be almost white in colour. Painting is the best solution.

Painting the pond

The most popular method of finishing off a concrete pond, and at the same time affording protection against alkaline pollution, is to paint it. Here again, cost must be the controlling factor in your choice of which paint finish to use. The best – and the most expensive – option is to use a two-part, water-soluble epoxy paint. This is a completely non-toxic product that has a texture very similar to emulsion paint and was first developed for sealing drinking water reservoirs. It dries with a hardwearing and slightly glossy finish that, to some degree, discourages the growth of algae. Applying a thinned-down coat, followed by two full-strength coats, produces a virtually everlasting finish, which even resists the action of a scraping and cleaning operation! An

alternative and much cheaper option is to use a suitable bitumen-based paint. This contains a high percentage of sand, so the finish is not up to the standard of the previous material, and applying it is quite a messy operation. On no account be tempted to use one of the many paints advertised for use as roof repair mediums; most of these are highly toxic to fish. Check and double check before buying paint for your pond!

Before starting to paint, you must overcome the problem of surface fibres. The rendered surface will contain many of the reinforcement fibres and these will 'peak' when paint is applied, resulting in lots of needle-sharp points just waiting to gash any passing fish. The remedy is simply to pass a blowlamp over the rendered surface to dissolve any stray fibres. After applying the first coat of paint, carefully go over the whole surface of the pond with the flat of your hand to find any fibres you have missed. As the paint will have hardened these, a quick rub with sandpaper will remove them. Be sure to carry the painting up as far as is necessary to cover any mortar used to secure ornamental rockwork around the edge of the pond.

What colour paint should you use? Black is the best choice. Avoid light colours; it is a well-known fact that the colours of koi do fade against a light-coloured background. In the epoxy paint range there is a clear variety available which is ideal for coating any cement work that is not underwater and visible to the viewer. This is a useful precaution against rainborne alkaline runoff from ornamental rockwork, and for protecting the joints in waterfalls, cascades, etc. from leakage.

Building an external filter

If you are installing a ready-made module, the procedure couldn't be more straightforward; simply excavate the site, arrange the pipework and drop the carcass into position. When budget considerations preclude the use of such a 'luxury', one alternative option is to build a simple multichamber filter in concrete. Here, we look briefly at the steps involved in building such a filter.

Building the carcass

To build the filter carcass, use the same techniques and materials as for the concrete pond. Excavate the hole, making the sides as vertical as you can, and create a flat, level floor. Break through the walls of the excavation in the appropriate positions to accommodate the pipework, not forgetting to allow for the thickness of the base and walls.

Above: *Another view of the 32,000-litre (7000-gallon) pond shown on page 86, this time with the covers taken off the filtration system, cleverly positioned beneath the pavilion. The multichamber filter system includes a sand filter at extreme left.*

Using a set of level pegs as before, lay a 15cm(6in)-deep concrete base of 6-to-1 aggregate/cement mix and allow it to set. Once the base will bear standing on without damage, build up the walls using dense concrete blocks suitable for the terrain. Use your spirit level constantly to ensure correct levels throughout. Leave gaps in the blockwork to accommodate the pipework, and make these good with a strong concrete mix after the piping has been installed. Ensure that the walls extend 10-15cm(4-6in) above the planned top water level.

Render the inside in one operation with the 2-to-1 sand/cement mix with fibres added, to a uniform thickness of 5mm(0.2in). Carefully seal around the piping with the rendering mix and apply the same rules as for the pond with regard to premature drying.

Making and fitting the partitions

Providing and installing backwash and drain valves in a concrete filter is such a difficult business that it is best to omit these in favour of making extra wide transfer ports that enable a vacuum pipe to be passed down and under the media support trays for periodic cleaning. (If you use ring media in the filter, such as plastic hair rollers or similar, this material is easy to lift out and clean anyway.)

Make the partitions within the filter body by casting them from a fibre-reinforced mix of 1-to-1 sand/cement. The extra strength provided by the higher proportion of cement is necessary because the flat sheets you will cast will only have a nominal thickness of 12mm(0.5in). These concrete sheets will be used to form two kinds of partitions within the filter body: those fixed off the base to allow water to flow beneath them and equivalent ones on the upstream side that rest on the base with water flowing over the top. To avoid any confusion, let us call the first type 'partition sheets' and the second type 'transfer port sheets'. (The diagram opposite clearly shows how these are arranged.)

Cast these parts in a simple, one-sided mould made from a flat sheet of exterior-quality plywood with a framework made from lengths of 12mm(0.5in)-square timber screwed onto the face. The inside measurements of this removable frame should be identical to the size required for your partitions. You can afford a little latitude in this measurement, but avoid making them too big; the method of fixing will cater for any slight undersizing.

Casting your sheets involves applying a quantity of the cement mixture onto the mould frame, taking care not to leave any spaces around the edges or in the corners, and scraping off any surplus cement with a straight edge to leave an even surface. It is a good idea to lay the mould on a hard, flat surface, such as a garage floor, and to rest a concrete block or two on the edges of the framework while the cement is setting. This will discourage any tendency for the mould to warp. After three days, unscrew the framework and carefully remove the cement sheet from the backing plate. Stand it on edge to allow it to dry completely. Depending on the size and number of chambers in your filter, casting the partitions is obviously going to be a lengthy task and so you might prefer to make a number of moulds in order to speed the job, bearing in mind that this type of plywood will always be useful in the future and not just be wasted.

Fixing the partitions into the filter carcass is quite straightforward, but does require careful use of a spirit level. First establish at what height the underside of the partition sheet is to be above the base; 15cm(6in) is ideal, with the top of the partition being level with or slightly below the top edge of the filter carcass. Find something to lay on the filter base to act as a temporary support, two pairs of house bricks laid side by side will provide the correct height, and lower the partition into position until it rests on the support. Check it for level and compensate for any discrepancy by inserting thin packing material between the sheet and the support.

Now tap small wooden wedges into place between the sides of the sheet and the filter wall; these will effectively hold the sheet in position while you complete the next operation. Mix a quantity of cement mortar of a fairly dry consistency and apply a fillet of this to all four corners of the partition in contact with the filter wall. You can leave the wedges in posi-

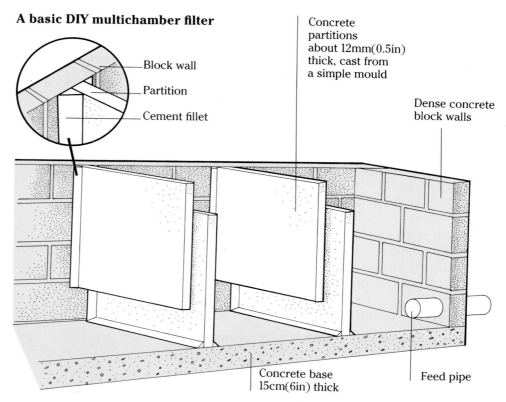

A basic DIY multichamber filter

Block wall
Partition
Cement fillet

Concrete partitions about 12mm(0.5in) thick, cast from a simple mould

Dense concrete block walls

Concrete base 15cm(6in) thick

Feed pipe

Above: A cutaway view of the DIY concrete multichamber filter featured in the text and shown in 'functional' cross-section on page 35. At this stage, the partitions and transfer port sheets are being installed. Be sure to allow sufficient time for the concrete to set at every stage. Site the filter system so that the water level matches that in the pond.

tion and cover them with the mortar. Repeat this operation for each partition in the filter. After about three days, gently tap out the supporting bricks.

Since the transfer port sheets rest on the base of the filter, no temporary support is required, but you might find that a little packing is required to get them level, depending on how good your building skills were! Don't forget that these sheets are located at the upstream side of the partitions you have just installed, i.e. towards the pond inlet end. Leaving a gap of 15cm(6in) from each partition sheet, fix the second sheets with wooden wedges and fillet them with cement as before. In this case, however, also apply cement along the sheet at base level to prevent unwanted leakage of water between the chambers.

Adding supports for media trays
Once all these have dried to your satisfaction, you must provide some means of holding up the media support trays. Two courses of engineering-quality bricks laid around three sides of each chamber, leaving the opening free to the transfer port, is probably the easiest strategy. You can lay these bricks dry, if you prefer but, for the sake of a little time, it is better to cement them into position. If you are using a rigid tray for the filter media, the lack of support at the front end will not be a problem, particularly if you intend using lightweight plastic ring media. If you use more flexible support trays with perhaps gravel media, then you will need

to provide additional support along the fourth side – a couple of bricks laid longitudinally should be fine.

Adding baffle plates
Should you decide to fit some baffle plates in the settlement chamber(s) you can make these using the same 1-to-1 sand/cement mix in the moulds. Use a short length of plastic pipe like a pastry cutter to make holes in each sheet before it sets. Since these baffle plates do not require permanent fixing in the chamber, wooden wedges alone will hold them in position quite satisfactorily.

Finishing and painting
The final stage of construction consists of painting the filter using the same materials and sequence as with the pond. As fish will not be in contact with the filter surfaces, there is no need to remove the fibres, but do be careful when setting up and maintaining the filter as the upstanding painted fibres can be rather sharp.

Although the above may appear to be a rather daunting marathon of work, the finished result will be a superb filter, every bit as efficient as its commercial equivalent but at a tenth of the cost.

水質と濾過

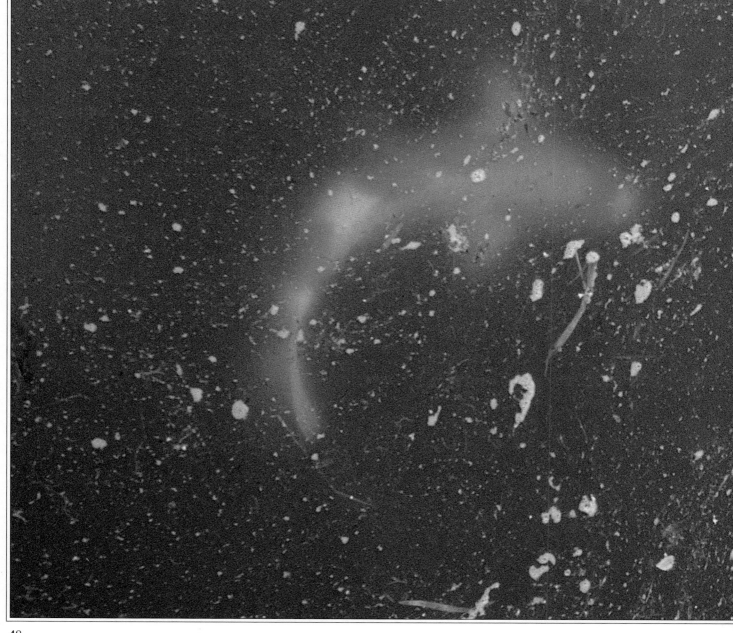

WATER QUALITY AND FILTRATION

Of all the pets we may choose to keep, fish are among the most demanding; in addition to feeding them and caring for their general well-being, we must also closely control the environment in which they live. Water is an alien medium to us and it is not easy to know whether the water in the pond is of the right quality to keep our koi in the best of health. Clear water is not always an indication of purity; it may contain colourless dissolved impurities, such as ammonia and nitrite, that are harmful and may even kill our koi. In this section, we explore the vital subjects of water quality and filtration, with special emphasis on the nitrogen cycle and the underlying principles of biological filtration. We also review the common types of filter media used in koi ponds, including those that exert a chemical influence on the water. For the application of filtration processes in practical terms, including how to build a simple multichamber design, see *Pond and filter construction*, starting on page 22.

Excessive protein waste in the water can cause an obvious scum, but even clear water may not be pure.

WATER QUALITY AND FILTRATION

Water quality

Water is one of the earth's most abundant compounds; more than two-thirds of the surface of the world is covered in water and it is essential for all living organisms. Koi, like their wild ancestors, are freshwater fish, and we need to understand the quality of their natural environment in order to simulate it as nearly as possible in the pond.

Water quality embraces a number of parameters, such as temperature, pH value (degree of acidity or alkalinity), hardness (and salinity), oxygen content, and the levels of ammonia, nitrite, nitrate, chlorine and chloramine. Water may also be contaminated by algae and/or by pollutants, such as pesticides and herbicides. Here, we look briefly at these important parameters.

Temperature

Koi are basically extremely hardy fish, being able to survive a temperature range of 2-30°C(36-85°F). In their native Japan, the winters are cold but relatively short. In Northern Europe and North America, the severe conditions experienced in very long winters may cause problems. Ambient temperatures are obviously not easily within the koi-keeper's control, although it is possible to influence the water temperature in the winter more than in the summer. Water heaters added to the system in winter can keep filters operational and the fish slightly more active.

The pH value of water

The pH scale is used to register the degree of acidity or alkalinity of a body of water. It ranges from 0 (extremely acid) to 14 (extremely alkaline) and is based inversely on the concentration of hydrogen ions (H^+) in the water in relation to hydroxyl ions (OH^-); the more hydrogen ions, the more acid the water and the lower the pH value. At the neutral point, pH7, the concentrations of hydrogen ions and hydroxyl ions are in balance. As hydroxyl ions outnumber hydrogen ions, the water becomes more alkaline and the pH value rises. It is extremely important to remember that the scale is logarithmic, i.e. each step represents a ten-fold change. Thus, pH6 is 10 times more acidic than pH7, and pH5 is 100 times more acidic than pH7. You can keep a check on pH values by using simple test kits (as shown on this page) or sophisticated electronic meters.

For koi, the ideal pH value is between 7 and 8, i.e. neutral to slightly alkaline. In the majority of koi ponds, the pH value rarely falls below 7 (i.e. becomes acidic), unless there has been some accidental

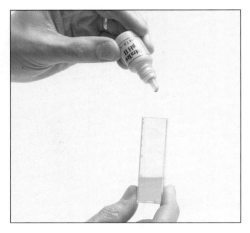

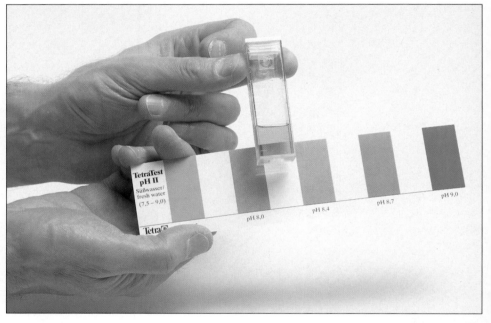

Left: Using a test kit to check the pH value of the water is simply a matter of adding the required amount of a reagent to a measured sample of pond water in the container supplied with the kit. Shake the container gently to ensure complete mixing.

Below: Very quickly, the water sample changes colour and it is then an easy matter to compare the result with a pre-printed chart to read off the pH value. All test kits are based on the same basic principle. Be sure to keep the charts out of the sun to prevent colour fading that may give misleading results. Try to take tests at the same time of day and water temperature.

pollution of the pond. Slight fluctuations in pH value are quite normal and should not cause any problems. In ponds with green water (i.e. with an algal bloom), the pH value may fluctuate between 7 and 11 during a 24-hour period. Although this sounds drastic, these temporary fluctuations will not prove serious to fish that have acclimated to such conditions.

Water hardness

Natural fresh water carries a host of dissolved substances, including both inorganic and organic compounds that are picked up from the soil and rocks over which the water flows and that enter as run-off from the land along the banks of rivers and lakes. The mains water that you use to fill your koi pond is neither sterile nor distilled, and so retains this natural mix of dissolved compounds so essential for life (plus some others that the water supply company add, as we shall see later on). Many of these dissolved substances are present in extremely small amounts – literally 'trace' elements – while relatively few account

for over 95 percent of the total concentration. These major substances are chlorides, sulphates, carbonates, bicarbonates, calcium, magnesium, sodium and potassium. Among the characteristics they contribute to water are its hardness and salinity.

In fresh water, the salinity (i.e. the level of total dissolved salts) is relatively low (compared to sea water, for example), while the hardness varies quite considerably and depends mainly on the concentration of calcium and magnesium salts. In terms of hardness, koi can cope with a wide variation, although typically 'hard' water from chalky regions may be slightly beneficial simply because the calcium compounds it contains help to bind up toxic metals (such as lead) in the water.

Water hardness has two important influences on aquatic life and these are relevant to koi. First, it influences the osmoregulation system. In practice, hard water reduces the workload on the koi's osmoregulatory system, while koi living in soft water must have a more efficient osmoregulatory system to maintain their internal salt/water balance. In this connection, adding salt to the pond water benefits ailing or stressed koi by reducing their osmotic workload.

Secondly, water hardness influences alkalinity. In effect, a high degree of temporary hardness (caused by bicarbonate ions) increases the alkalinity of the water. Thus, it is important to view hardness and pH value as interrelated parameters when judging water quality in overall terms. Test kits, as well as electronic meters, are available for monitoring water hardness.

Oxygen content
The amount of oxygen dissolving in water is temperature dependent; as the water temperature increases, the maximum amount of oxygen that will dissolve into it decreases. As a koi-keeper, it is vital to understand this physical relationship between water and gas, and to be aware of the conditions that can cause oxygen deficiency and hence stress the koi in your pond.

Koi require at least 6mg/litre of oxygen in the water. In order to achieve this, the water should be pumped continuously in the pond 24 hours a day for 365 days a year. It is surprising how many people turn their pumps off at night or during the winter months (see *Seasonal care*, pages 78-79 for cold-weather strategy).

Since warm water can hold less oxygen than cold water, the summer months are the most vulnerable period for low oxygen levels, and the level at night is the most critical of all. During the day, water plants use carbon dioxide and release oxygen into the water during the process of photosynthesis. At night, the cycle is effectively reversed, with plant (and animal) respiration using up oxygen and producing carbon dioxide. It is not surprising, therefore, that warm summer nights can result in dangerously low levels of dissolved oxygen. This situation is often worsened during humid, thundery weather, when low pressure effectively reduces the amount of atmospheric oxygen available per unit surface area of water. Accumulated organic debris, either from uneaten food or faeces, will further reduce the oxygen content of the water and so it is vital to remove this from the pond and not allow it to form an organic silt.

During the summer months be sure to check the oxygen content of your pond water on a regular basis. You can use test kits or an electronic meter to obtain a reading. The ideal time for testing the water is between 6.0am and 7.0am, when the oxygen content will be at its lowest.

Below: *The principle of the venturi tube, a simple device for introducing air into the stream of water returning to the pond from the filter. The name arises from the Italian physicist who devised it.*

Above: *A venturi in full flow in a koi pond. The vertical tube (with cap) is clearly visible on the left and the oxygenating mass of air bubbles can be seen 'boiling' just beneath the surface of the water on the right.*

How a venturi works

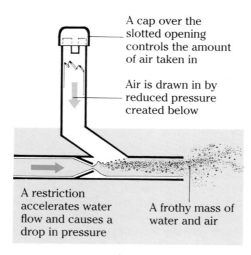

A cap over the slotted opening controls the amount of air taken in

Air is drawn in by reduced pressure created below

A restriction accelerates water flow and causes a drop in pressure

A frothy mass of water and air

Ammonia, nitrite and nitrate
The level of these three nitrogenous compounds in the water is a critical indicator of water quality conditions. Ammonia (NH_3) is a highly toxic gas produced from the decomposition of organic wastes and as a metabolic waste product by the koi, most of which is excreted from the gills. It is lethal in very low concentrations; depending on species and levels of other water conditions, 0.2-0.5mg/litre will kill fish fairly rapidly. Over long periods, a tenth of this concentration can cause increased susceptibility to disease and a hundredth

can produce gill irritation. Other water quality conditions can affect the toxicity of ammonia; rising temperatures and pH values increase ammonia toxicity, while increasing salinity lowers it.

· To prevent koi mortalities, it is vital to monitor water quality for the build-up of ammonia. Various test kits are available that make this a straightforward task; most involve adding a measured amount of reagent to a small sample of pond water and comparing the intensity of the colour change against a graduated scale to read off the ammonia level as mg/litre nitrogen. If ammonia levels are too high, make partial water changes of up to 20 percent of the pond water to dilute the ammonia. Until the level subsides, you may need to make such water changes every day.

Nitrites (NO_2^-) are produced as a breakdown product of ammonia as part of a naturally occurring sequence of biochemical reactions that has become known universally as the 'nitrogen cycle'. (The 'motive force' for this cycle is provided by various kinds of bacteria, and we shall be considering their action more closely under *Biological filtration*.) Nitrite is highly poisonous; it disrupts the haemoglobin in red blood cells and produces listlessness and oxygen starvation. Raised nitrite levels can prove fatal to koi less than 15cm(6in) in length; larger koi become lethargic and may lie on their sides at the bottom of the pond, although they will still swim to the surface to feed. As we shall see later, nitrite commonly causes a problem in new

WATER QUALITY AND FILTRATION

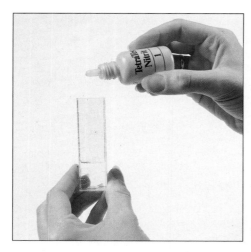

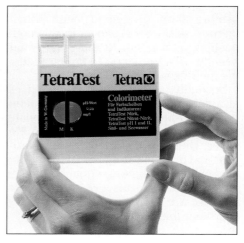

Above: *This is the first stage in a three-step sequence for determining the level of nitrite in the water using a test kit. First add seven drops of reagent 1 to a 5ml water sample and shake the vial gently to mix them together. It is important to be accurate.*

Above: *Then add seven drops of a second reagent to the sample and allow up to five minutes for the colour change to develop fully. Using this kit, the colour produced at this stage will range from yellow through orange to deep red.*

Above: *Place the vial into a comparator and turn the wheel until the 'window' colour matches that of the sample; the appropriate nitrite reading is displayed alongside. The colour gel is viewed through a 'control' of untreated water to improve accuracy.*

ponds, and so it is important to monitor the level using a suitable test kit. While the nitrite concentration is more than 0.15mg/litre, make regular partial water changes of 20 percent.

As with ammonia, increasing the level of dissolved salts in the water decreases the toxic effect of nitrite. Thus, adding 3gm/litre of cooking salt to the water (to make a 0.3 percent solution / approximately equivalent to 0.5oz per gallon) helps to counteract the effects of nitrite.

The third nitrogenous compound in this biochemical sequence is nitrate (NO_3^-), which is much less harmful to koi and other aquatic creatures than the preceding two compounds. In fact, koi can probably tolerate nitrate concentrations up to 500mg/litre, but these levels are very unlikely to occur in the average koi pond. Eggs and fry are more sensitive to nitrate than are adult koi, however. Since nitrate is used as a fertilizer by algae and other plants in the pond, high levels precipitate algal blooms ('green water'), particularly during the summer, when warmth spurs rapid plant growth.

Chlorine and chloramine

In addition to dissolved minerals and organic molecules, natural fresh waters also contain a wide range of microscopic living organisms, from tiny larvae and protozoans to bacteria and viruses. The majority of these are non-pathogenic, but some can cause disease in both humans and other animals. To render such waters fit for human consumption, water supply companies treat it with suitable disinfectants, the most widely used being chlorine. This is forced into the water as a gas and most combines chemically with water to form, among

other compounds, hypochlorous acid, which acts as the disinfectant. A small part of the chlorine remains as 'free chlorine' and is relatively unstable in water and will readily diffuse into the air. Although the usual amounts of chlorine and chlorine compounds added to domestic water supplies are not harmful to humans, they can be highly toxic to koi and other fish, with respiratory distress being the most obvious sign. The degree of toxicity depends not only on the total amount of chlorine present, but also on the temperature, pH value, oxygen content and pollution/organic loading of the water in the pond.

With these facts in mind, it is obviously important to check the chlorine content of your local water supply using an appropriate test kit. And bear in mind that chlorine levels may rise in the summer, when water supply companies increase chlorination to cope with expected seasonal rises in pathogenic bacteria in the water. Adding domestic water directly to your pond can be particularly hazardous at this time of year.

Since free chlorine readily evaporates from water, it is relatively easy to drive this off during water changes by spraying the new water into the pond or splashing it from a reasonable height to maximize the mixing of air and water. When you are filling a new pond with water from the mains, it is best to fill it completely and allow the pond to run with maximum aeration for 7-10 days to dechlorinate the water before adding the koi.

A disturbing slant on the chlorination story is the use of chloramines for disinfection of domestic water supplies. Chloramines, complex organic derivatives of chlorine, are formed from the combina-

tion of chlorine and ammonia, and are particularly effective because they are more stable than chlorine in water and release twice as much hypochlorous acid over a longer period. Chloramines can also form naturally when chlorinated water mixes with nitrogenous compounds such as nitrate fertilizers. The dilemma for the koi-keeper is that chloramines are even more difficult to eradicate. If you think your water may be affected in this way, fill your pond and run the water through the filters with maximum aeration for a period of 10-14 days before adding the koi.

Filtration

Like most animals, koi excrete urine and produce solid wastes (faeces), both of which are voided at the vent. The urine consists largely of water and a small amount of urea; the main nitrogenous waste product from the breakdown of proteins is ammonia, and this is excreted through the gill membranes. Faeces are largely the remnants of undigested food. In the wild, such waste products and the results of their decomposition are diluted and/or removed by the relatively large volumes of, usually, moving water in which the fishes live. In the enclosed environment of the pond, it is the job of the filtration system to perform this natural cleansing role.

Whatever form a filter system takes, the principal filtration processes involved can be divided into mechanical, biological and chemical. In practice, these processes often occur at the same time, but it does provide a convenient way of looking at what can be a complex and sometimes overlapping series of physical and biochemical reactions.

Mechanical filtration

Most filter media have a mechanical function. (See the photographic review of the most widely used filter media on pages 54-55.) In fact, the most basic forms of mechanical filters simply allow gravity to 'drag' solids out of suspension by taking the pace out of the incoming water flow. Such 'settlement chambers' invariably form the first part of a filter system and as such they prevent the second and any subsequent chambers of a filter from being clogged with solid particles, which would ultimately result in a build-up of sediment in the filter. This would eventually block the water flow and allow the pond water to become foul. If this happens, you will need to take the media out of the filter and remove the sediment from it before replacing it in the chamber. Some filters have a drain fitted at the bottom of each chamber so that you can draw off any sediment without needing to remove the media.

In addition to 'baffles' to slow down the incoming pond water, koi-keepers also use a variety of mechanical filter media to 'strain' the incoming water, including brushes, aquarium filter wool, matting, scouring pads (but not impregnated with soap or detergent) and even hair rollers.

Biological filtration

Biological filtration relies on the activity of specific bacteria cultured in the filter to break down toxic waste products into less harmful substances. These bacteria occur naturally and are used to break down domestic sewage in special treatment plants. Water treated at these plants is so clean that it is often recycled for domestic use. In effect, a biological filter on a koi pond is really a small sewage treatment unit, exploiting the natural sequence of biochemical reactions that occurs in the nitrogen cycle.

There are two stages in the breakdown of ammonia in a biological filter system, each stage involving different types of bacteria to 'power' the detoxification process. In the first stage, ammonia is broken down to nitrite by a number of different nitrifying bacteria, the most important of which is *Nitrosomonas*. A second group of nitrifying bacteria, principally *Nitrobacter*, converts the nitrite to nitrate. (These two stages, and how they relate to other steps in the nitrogen cycle, are clearly shown in the diagram on this page.)

Both these groups of bacteria are aerobic, i.e. they need oxygen to thrive and thus purify the water. The nitrifying bacteria require an oxygen level of at least 1mg/litre in the water continuously flowing through the medium. Sediment

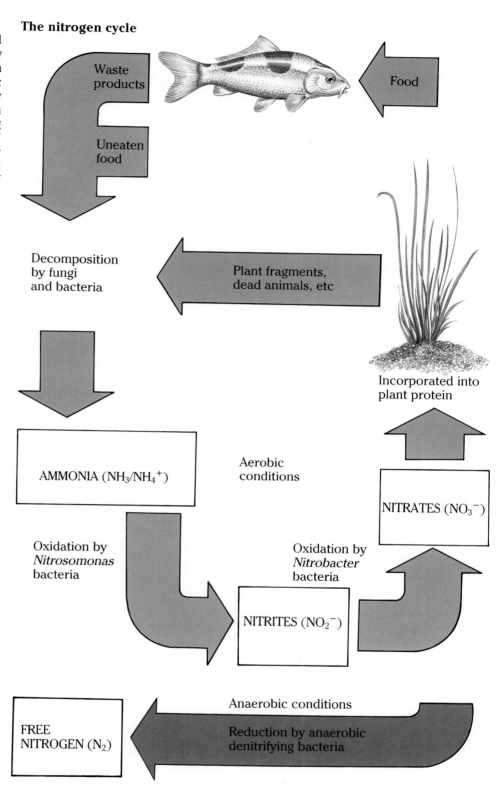

The nitrogen cycle

Food → [fish] → Waste products / Uneaten food → Decomposition by fungi and bacteria

Plant fragments, dead animals, etc

AMMONIA (NH_3/NH_4^+)

Oxidation by *Nitrosomonas* bacteria

Aerobic conditions

NITRITES (NO_2^-)

Oxidation by *Nitrobacter* bacteria

NITRATES (NO_3^-)

Incorporated into plant protein

Anaerobic conditions

FREE NITROGEN (N_2)

Reduction by anaerobic denitrifying bacteria

building up in the bottom of the filter can deplete oxygen levels in the water and encourage the growth of anaerobic bacteria (those that thrive in the absence of oxygen), rendering the filter ineffective. It is vital, therefore, to keep sediment to a minimum in the filter.

The second chamber in a filter system is usually the biological filter and contains a medium that will provide a large surface area on which the nitrifying bac-

Above: *These are the main steps in the nitrogen cycle – a naturally occurring sequence of biochemical reactions that keeps nitrogen circulating. The aerobic nitrifying bacteria play a crucial role.*

teria can grow. Again, a variety of different, and equally effective, media is available. It really does not matter what type of filter medium you use, provided that the system is capable of breaking

WATER QUALITY AND FILTRATION

down the poisonous waste products into harmless ones. (The biological value of certain filter media is explored further in the captions on these pages.)

Installing a biological filter system to a pond does not guarantee an immediate improvement to the water quality; ammonia and nitrite levels are likely to fluctuate in a new filter and it may take from six months to a year before the filter has finally matured. You may notice that the concentration of ammonia in the water increases dramatically, sometimes to dangerous levels, once you introduce koi into a new pond. These high levels of ammonia may take only a matter of days to subside in the summer, but up to several weeks during the winter months. This is because these filters are biologically active and thus their efficiency is affected by external parameters, such as the weather, water temperature and pH value, and the number and size of fish in the pond. The growth and reproduction of bacteria are inhibited by the cold, for example; both will cease at temperatures below 5°C(41°F). With these fluctuations

in mind, it is important to check pond water quality regularly, particularly after installing a new filter system. Get into the habit of taking ammonia and nitrite readings every week and recording these analyses on paper. If you run into difficulties with koi health, it is always useful to have a record of any preceding water quality problems.

Both freeze-dried and live cultures of nitrifying bacteria are available; adding one of these preparations to the biological filter on a new pond, or to an established pond in the spring, will boost the filtration process. Early evening is the best time to add these bacterial cultures to the pond, as water temperatures are then at their highest.

Chemical filtration

As the term implies, chemical filtration media remove impurities from the water flow by chemical means. In practice, chemical filtration media are often used in the second chamber of a non-biological filter system, the first one containing a purely mechanical medium to strain off

suspended particles. A typical combination would be filter wool as a mechanical medium and activated carbon as a chemical filter medium. Activated carbon removes ammonia and other organic waste products from the water by a process of adsorption. This means that the adsorbed substances became loosely linked to the surface of the filter medium.

The process of 'activating' the carbon granules – by heating them to a very high temperature – opens up millions of pores that present a large surface area for chemical adsorption. When the surface area becomes 'full up', you will need to replace the activated carbon. In fact, because of their limited lifespan, both filter wool and activated carbon are really only suitable for smaller ponds (i.e. with a capacity of not more than 500 litres/ approximately 110 gallons).

For larger ponds, it is more practical to use zeolite, a chemical filter medium that also removes ammonia and nitrite from the water. Zeolite consists of the hydrated silicates of calcium and alumi-

Filter media commonly used in koi pond systems

Filter brushes are ideal for removing sediment and large particles from the pond water. The individual brushes can be taken out of the filter and allowed to dry, then the dirt will come off easily.

Nylon pot scourers are also used as filter media, both in a mechanical and biological sense, because they also provide a large surface area for bacteria to colonize. They are durable and easy to clean.

Filter wool (usually manmade fibres, such as dacron floss, nylon floss, etc.) is ideal as a mechanical filter but only in smaller systems, as it eventually becomes blocked. Unfortunately, it is not easy to clean.

This commercial filter medium consists of pieces of plastic pipe, very similar to the hair rollers, although the latter have more perforations. Again, you will need to use a large amount of such medium in the filter.

Canterbury spar is prepared from natural flint pieces baked until they split into sharp-edged stones permeated with fissures. It acts as a mechanical filter and also offers a huge surface area for nitrifying bacteria.

These spherical granules of baked clay also provide crevices for bacteria to colonize but they are much lighter than the equivalent amount of Canterbury spar. The granules are also used to grow plants in water.

nium, sometimes with sodium and potassium. It looks like off-white or pale brown stone chippings and is available in various grades. As with most other filtration media, the larger the surface area of zeolite exposed to the pond water, the more effective it will be in removing

Above: *A commercial filter chamber with a venturi fitted on the water inlet, six rows of brushes in the main compartment and zeolite chippings in the final section. Such basic boxes are available in a range of sizes and configurations to suit most systems.*

waste products. While small grade chippings theoretically offer a relatively large surface area, in practice, they tend to compact down and become less efficient. The ideal grade to use is a particle size of about 10cm(4in). In any event, you will need a large quantity; filter systems that rely on zeolite alone need approximately 1kg per 5 litres (about 2.2lb per gallon) of pond water.

One of the advantages of using zeolite in preference to activated carbon is that it can be 'cleaned' and re-used. The chemical bond between zeolite and ammonia is very weak and can be broken by adding salt water to the 'tired' chippings. As the ammonia is released, the zeolite becomes effectively 'recharged' and ready for use again. To do this, remove the zeolite from the filter and replace it with new or 'recharged' zeolite. Put the used zeolite into a container and add a salt solution made up with 6gm of cooking salt per litre of water (approximately 1oz per gallon) for 24 hours. Wash the zeolite thoroughly in fresh water before using it in the filter again.

Unfortunately, using zeolite as the principal filter medium does have several disadvantages. For a start, considerable quantities are required, making it an expensive option for ponds with a capacity greater than 2500 litres (550 gallons). Also, recharging the zeolite can become an onerous and time-consuming task; in the summer months, when koi are most active, it will need recharging every week. Finally, using zeolite prevents you from using salt as a treatment, simply because ammonia and other toxins will be released from the zeolite back into the pond, creating detrimental water quality conditions that will only aggravate any prevailing health problems.

Many koi-keepers use zeolite in conjunction with a biological filter, adding the mineral rock to the final chamber of a multichamber filter. This is particularly beneficial in new pond systems and during the spring, when numbers of bacteria are low in the biological filter and using zeolite will help to keep the concentration of ammonia/ammonium compounds in the pond down to a minimum.

Filter matting consists of latex-coated fibres; it is easy to handle and clean and should not need replacing if regularly maintained. The coarse nature of the matting provides a large surface area for nitrifying bacteria.

Filter foam is usually placed in three layers in the filter chamber. The texture allows this medium to be cleaned easily and it is fairly durable in use. The foam tends to hold back particles and supports nitrifying bacteria.

Ordinary plastic hair rollers can make a very useful filter medium. They are easy to clean and provide a good surface area for nitrifying bacteria to colonize. Large numbers of hair rollers will be needed.

Use this freeze-dried preparation to seed the filter system with useful bacteria. Mix it with warm water and allow it to stand to 'reactivate' the bacteria. Some preparations contain live bacteria for immediate use.

Zeolite is an alumino-silicate mineral used to remove ammonia from the pond water. It is available in small, medium and large-grade chippings; the latter are best as they are easier to handle and do not pack down.

These granules of activated carbon soak up wastes by adsorbing the molecules on the extensive surface area. Activated carbon cannot be recharged once 'full' and must be replaced, making it rather expensive.

WATER QUALITY AND FILTRATION

Continuous flow filtration

In a continuous flow system the water is not recirculated, but passes through the pond to waste. The supply of water must therefore be spring fed, or a diversion of part of a small river system, which passes through the pond before returning once again to a natural water source. Although this type of system is favoured by trout farmers, it is not practical for the majority of koi-keepers. Firstly, a continuous flow system requires a great deal of land. Secondly, while spring-fed water will be fairly free of pathogens (disease-causing organisms), river water may well contain pathogens and/or parasites, such as fish leeches (*Piscicola geometra*) or snails acting as intermediate hosts for spiny-headed worms (*Acanthocephala*), that are detrimental to koi health. Finally, and most importantly, the majority of koi are imported and may be infected with diseases and/or carrying various parasites, which can be spread to wild fish in the untreated water returning to the river, with serious and even potentially devastating results for natural fish populations in these waters.

Sand filters

Some koi-keepers use a sand filter as a final stage in the filtration of pond water. The water is pressurized to 0.85-1.0kg/cm^2 (12-14 lb/in^2) as it passes into the filter, where it is filtered through sand contained in a pressure cylinder. The sand filter removes fine solid particles from the water, so that on returning to the pond it is almost entirely free of solids. There is a great deal of evidence that bacterial activity takes place inside the sand filter to further the breakdown of toxic wastes produced by the koi. Without doubt, sand filters are a very beneficial addition to a pond's filter system.

On extremely rare occasions, however, a sand filter may draw in air with the pond water. When this happens, the air is forced by the pressure of the sand filter into solution in the water, leading to supersaturation. The supersaturated water builds up in the pond, giving the water a 'fizzy' appearance and coating the surface, plants and anything else in the pond with a fine layer of bubbles. This leads to a clinical disorder known as 'gas-bubble disease' (see *Health care*, page 111), in which gas bubbles form in the fins and beneath the fin bases, as well as in the blood and among internal organs.

Right: *A sand pressure filter with its associated pipework. The whole affair looks complicated, but the large multiport valve is clearly visible on the left. This has various settings, including one for backwashing.*

How a sand pressure filter works

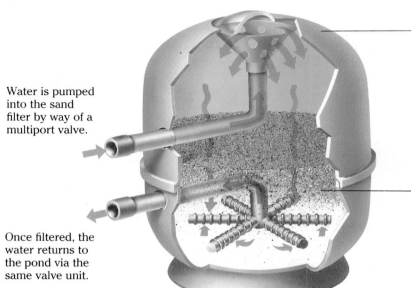

Water is pumped into the sand filter by way of a multiport valve.

Once filtered, the water returns to the pond via the same valve unit.

The sealed ve is domed in s to withstand internal press

The body of t filter contains special grade coarse silica that strains o any suspende solids as the water is force through it.

Should such a situation arise, by-pass the sand filter and seek immediate advice from the supplier. The excess air in the pond will 'gas off' over some hours as the water passes through the filters and aeration system. Koi suffering from gas-bubble disease may take several weeks to recover completely as they 'decompress'.

Controlling algae

Green water is caused by a bloom of microscopic algae that contain the green photosynthetic pigment, chlorophyll. Pond water containing these microscopic algae is usually free of both ammonia and nitrite, quite simply because these tiny organisms thrive on the final breakdown product of the nitrogen cycle, namely, nitrate. Nitrate is a powerful fertilizer for plants, and so as the filter unit becomes established and the quantity of nitrate in the pond increases, the algae thrive in the abundance of this nutrient.

Green water is not harmful to koi, but positively beneficial; koi feed on the tiny animals that eat the algae and in this way green water is one of the best colour enhancers of koi available. In Japan, many koi enthusiasts keep their koi at home in their ponds through the winter months but return them to the farms during the summer so that the koi can benefit from spending several months in green water. The disadvantage of green water, of course, is that you are unable to see the koi. Not only will this spoil your enjoyment, but koi that have injured themselves or are suffering from parasites, such as anchor worm, will remain hidden from your attention.

Green water can be very persistent and may take many months to clear from a newly established pond. The water may periodically go green in an established pond, depending on the aspect of the pond and the climatic conditions. During hot, sultry spells, algae will use essential oxygen during the hours of darkness and it is worth running an external pump, such as an aquarium pump, with an airline and airstones in the pond to ensure maximum aeration of the water.

Some koi-keepers have started to use ultraviolet (UV) light as a means of controlling algae. (UV light is very harmful; never remove the bulb from its protective casing while the light is switched on.) UV light damages the tiny algal cells internally, and thus kills them. The UV unit

is usually placed at the end of the filter system, before the water is returned to the pond.

One of the major myths concerning this form of light is its ability to kill bacteria and render the pond sterile. Although this is true in part, the water passing through the unit would have to be almost motionless for the UV light to kill most of the bacteria. In practice, the flow of pond water through an UV light system is too fast to seriously reduce the number of bacteria present in the pond water. Be sure to replace the UV tube every six to nine months if you are using it continuously; after this period it ceases to be effective even though it appears undimmed.

It is also possible to control algae using ozone. Ozone (O_3) is a highly unstable form of oxygen (O_2), which has strong disinfectant properties. (It occurs naturally in the upper atmosphere, forming the so-called 'ozone layer'.) It is created for aquarium and pond use in a device known as an ozonizer, in which dried air is passed through an electrical discharge to 'weld' one extra oxygen atom onto each normal molecule. Since it is toxic to all life forms, it is vital to use it correctly and carefully. Ozone units are usually fitted in the return water plumbing, where the ozone gas effectively breaks down the algal cells. It is import-

Above: *Summer brings light and warmth to the pond, which, together with an abundance of nitrates, can cause algal blooms, especially in new ponds. If you need to control green water, do it with care.*

ant that the ozone does not reach the fish and plants in the main pond. (Vigorous aeration or filtration over activated carbon will remove ozone from treated water.) The effective dosing rate of ozone is reduced by high levels of organic matter in the water.

Surprisingly, algal blooms can be controlled by magnetism; small electromagnets placed on the return water pipe will disrupt microscopic cells internally, either killing them outright or preventing their reproduction.

Many chemical products are available to clear algae from ponds. When using these algicides, be sure to follow the manufacturers' directions and never exceed the recommended dosage or frequency of treatments. There is always the possibility that, used incorrectly, such chemicals can harm the fish and aquatic plants. And remember that a sudden die-back of dense concentrations of algal cells can cause water quality problems. In such cases, consider using some mechanical method of removing the bulk of the algae, such as high-rate mechanical filters, before dosing the water.

鯉の購入

BUYING KOI

Buying koi should be a pleasurable experience, but keeping them is a responsibility not to be undertaken lightly. Never buy a koi on a whim, and make sure that you have the capacity, without stretching the limits of your pond, to look after them properly. Having decided to buy, there are several things you will need to think about. When you buy will be dictated, in part, by the calendar of the koi-keeping industry – most dealers import koi in November and December and hobbyists generally stock their ponds in the spring. Think carefully, too, about where to buy your koi and, having found a reputable dealer, spend time watching any that interest you; the checklist on page 63 will remind you what to look for. In the second half of this section, we look at how to avoid stressing and damaging koi while transporting them and, finally, we examine the much-debated subject of quarantining newly purchased koi.

BUYING KOI

Sources of koi

The main countries that now export koi are Japan, Israel, Singapore, and the United States of America.

Japan is the home of the koi and those produced here are of top quality in terms of colour definition and availability of varieties in different sizes. If you are interested in showing your fish, then Japanese koi are the ones to buy, but they are generally more expensive than those from other countries.

Koi from America and Singapore tend to be of indeterminate variety, and colours are often indistinct. As they get older they seem to lose their body shape and may become fat and dumpy.

Israel tends to produce extremely pretty, small koi, which become more plain in appearance as they get older. Over the last two years, however, the number of koi imported from Israel has increased dramatically and it is expected that the quality will continue to improve.

When to buy

The best quality koi tend to be exported from Japan in November and December. There are two reasons for this; firstly, the growing-on ponds in Japan are harvested in October. Secondly, as the water temperatures are lower, water can contain higher levels of dissolved oxygen, and this, combined with the fact that the koi are less active and demanding on their environment at lower temperatures, makes the transportation of them less risky. Koi are also imported in March, April and May, but high-quality speci-

Above: *These fish are waiting to be sold by auction. In Japan, such events take place twice a month from April to October. Here,* many dealers buy young koi from breeders to grow on in their ponds over the winter before selling them the following year.

mens are not available for sale any later in the year as they are returned to growing-on ponds until October. 'Ordinary' quality koi are available throughout the year in most places, however.

Most enthusiasts buy koi to stock their ponds in the spring, when the water is beginning to warm up and the fish are becoming more active. Obviously, the majority of koi-keepers do not have indoor pools in which to house koi, recently arrived from Japan, throughout the winter, and you will find that most dealers will happily hold the koi until the spring. It is a good idea to buy your koi in time to allow them a generous settling in period before their first winter.

Where to buy

Having decided on when to buy, and from which country, the next decision you will need to make is where to buy. Try to visit a reputable dealer who has a sound knowledge of koi and their environment. It is best to avoid garden centres at busy times, such as the weekends, unless they have specialist staff. A good dealer will want to know that his koi are going to good homes and so will be happy to explain anything that is necessary to help you maintain your new koi in the best of health.

When you arrive at a dealer, the first thing to look for is the state of the pond

Left: *If you are setting up a pond for the first time, choose young koi such as these. Small fish in the size range 7.5-10cm(3-4in) are ideal for the new koi-keeper.*

water; it should be well filtered and clean, not only so that you can view the fish but, more importantly, because koi kept in poor water are prone to disease and infection. Bear in mind that clear water is not necessarily 'good' water – your nose will be as useful as your eyes in assessing its true condition. However, even the smell of the water may not be a guarantee of its cleanliness – the dealer may have just discharged his bottom drains – nevertheless, it should provide some indication. If there is a strong 'fishy' smell and the koi appear distressed, it may be worth bypassing that particular dealer.

Choosing your koi

Spend time watching a prospective koi; watch the way it swims – its movements should be fluid, not jerky – and see how interested it is in its surroundings. Pay particular attention to its gill movements, which should be slow and regular, using both gills. The gill plates of a healthy fish are close to the body, so avoid fish whose gill plates are proud of the head and that seem to be puffing hard or hanging near the surface of the water. Look out for a white bloom on the skin of the fish (similar in appearance to the bloom on grapes), which may indicate *Ichthyobodo* (previously known as *Costia*) or *Trichodina* parasites. Also look for raised scales or holes, as these, although common, can sometimes be difficult to treat. Avoid fish with cloudy eyes, fin rot, or bumps on either side of the gill plate or on the head. The cause of these bumps is not yet known, but they may burst, leaving holes in the gill plate that can take months, if not years, to heal. (See also *Health care*, starting on page 98.)

Once you have found a fish that appears to be healthy, ask the dealer to 'bowl' it for you so that you can examine it more closely. Watch the way that this is done – fish can be damaged if badly handled. The dealer should use a shallow pan net to catch the fish, and then encourage it to swim into the tilted bowl. Ideally, the dealer should not lift the koi out of the water.

Once the fish is in the bowl you can examine it for any redness on the body or fins. Such signs may suggest that the fish has been recently imported, but could indicate a developing internal problem. Watch out, too, for parasites on the fins, such as fish lice (*Argulus*), or anchor worms (*Lernaea*) around the dorsal and tail regions. Neither create serious problems but, even so, you should ask the dealer to remove any parasites. You should also treat your own pond, to prevent any further disturbances.

Ask the dealer to outline the good and

Above: *Always ask the dealer to 'bowl' a koi for you so that you can examine it carefully before you decide to buy. Note how the* dealer uses the edge of the net to dip the side of the bowl, so that the koi can swim in without leaving the water.

bad points of your selected fish and to tell you its variety name; this will give you a clearer understanding of what to look for in future purchases. Do not be influenced by merely snobbish considerations; look at the fish as a whole and respond to the impression it makes on you. Too many new hobbyists tend to spend hours evaluating all the bad points on an otherwise very impressive koi. Listen to the dealer's advice, of course, but don't be afraid to rely on your own judgement as far as personal preference is concerned.

Transporting koi

Once you have selected the fish and inspected it carefully, the dealer will bag it for you to take away. Be sure to tell the dealer if you have a particularly long journey home; he may be able to accommodate your special needs by providing extra bags or a special box in which to carry the fish, for example, or by packing

ice around the bags in hot weather. Normally, fish are placed in a bag with one part water to two parts oxygen. There only needs to be enough water to cover the koi's gills; oxygen is much more important to the fish than water, especially on long journeys or if the water is warm. Unless you live locally, be sure to avoid dealers who do not oxygenate their fish bags.

When buying larger koi, make sure that the bags are long enough to contain the fish properly, without the risk of causing bent tails and broken fins. Koi are usually double bagged, or even triple bagged in the case of larger fish, to avoid accidents and leaks. In fact, it is a good idea to box larger fish, and to ensure that there is as little movement as possible between the box and the bag. Since moving a fish can be a very traumatic experience for it, it is vital to avoid undue stress during the process. As far as

BUYING KOI

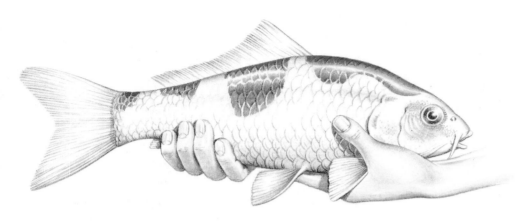

Above: *It is important that you handle koi correctly to avoid damage and undue stress. Hold the fish's head towards you with one hand underneath its jaw and the other behind the pelvic fins. This will give you a firm hold without inhibiting its movement.*

Below: *Once you have selected your koi, the dealer will bag it for you to take home. A double or triple layer of plastic bags are normally used and these should be filled with one part water – just enough to cover the koi's gills – to two parts oxygen.*

intact. It is less stressful for a fish to go from cold water to warm water than vice versa – imagine how you would feel diving into cold water on a hot day!

Quarantining
Newly imported fish are normally quarantined by the dealer, not because they are necessarily diseased on arrival, but to rest them. They will be stressed and will, therefore, be prone to disease and parasites in the same way that a person who is run down or has had a traumatic shock is prone to illness.

On their arrival in the country, the dealer will usually salt dip the koi and then rest them in a separate pond or quarantine tank, to which has been added a mild antiseptic solution to ward off infection while the fish are at their lowest ebb. Here they will be left for at least a week, without being disturbed. Koi that are highly stressed may be left longer; rest and recuperation are the best 'medicine' for the majority of fish. If, during this time, the dealer notices evidence of para-

possible, avoid sudden fluctuations in temperature, flashing lights, and loud noise, which may disturb the koi.

You will probably be transporting your koi home in the car. Avoid carrying the fish bag on your lap, as your body heat will increase the temperature of the water quite rapidly. For the same reason, do not place the bag in the front footwell of the car, where warm air from the heater will have the same effect. The best place to carry the fish bag is in the boot of the car. Tuck a blanket around it to prevent it rolling about or wedge it between objects that will not pierce it. If the car does not have a boot, place the bag in the footwells behind the front seats, preferably out of the way of anyone's feet. You can reduce stress to the fish by covering the bag with a blanket to cut out light. Drive steadily, trying to avoid bumps and holes in the road and remember not to take corners too quickly. This will help to prevent banged noses and split fins.

On arriving home, remove the bag from the car and float it on the surface of the pond or quarantine tank (see below) for an hour or two. If there is oxygen in the bag, this delay need not cause any problems. While the bag floats, the temperature of the water in the bag will gradually equalize with that of the pond or tank. (Check with the dealer the temperature of the water in his pond.) If the temperature of the bag water is very close to that of the pond water, you may remove one of the bags straight away. If the difference is more than a few degrees centigrade, leave both (or all three) bags

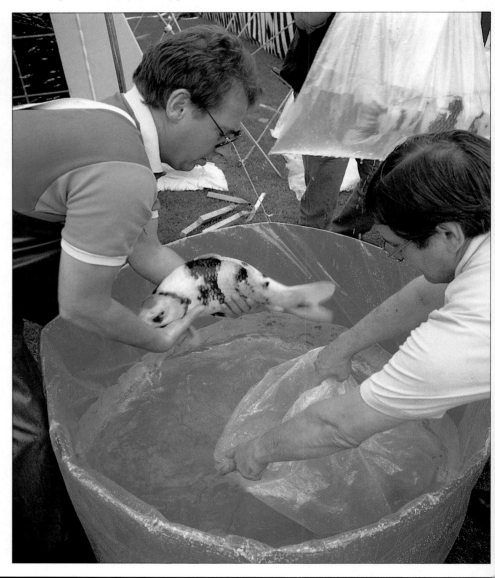

sites, such as anchor worm, he will be able to deal with the infestation before mixing these newly purchased koi with the rest of his stock.

Many koi-keepers are opposed to quarantining newly purchased fish themselves, however. Their arguments are that it increases, rather than diminishes, the stress because it involves moving the fish twice – to the treatment tank and then to the pond. Other possible causes of this increase of stress could be that koi are shoaling fish and do not like being kept on their own.

It is important to point out, at this stage, that the results of stress may take several weeks to become apparent and that the incubation period of some diseases can be as long as several months, or even years. Many fish diseases and problems can result from something that happened in the past; the symptoms of gill rot, for example, may appear approximately three weeks after the pump in the pond was turned off for a few days. Therefore, although some fish-keepers maintain that fish in quarantine develop the symptoms of any virus or bacterial infection they may have before they are mixed with other stock, this is not, in itself, an adequate reason to support additional quarantining of newly purchased koi.

If you do decide to quarantine new fish, make sure that the treatment tank or pond is large enough. Few hobbyists have adequate quarantine facilities and many people, to their cost, have quarantined fish in small, cramped ponds with inadequate filtration. When you consider all the stress-inducing factors involved, it is hardly surprising that the koi have died on being moved to the pond.

In the majority of cases, it is better to place the fish straight into your pond. You should, in any case, keep an eye on the progress of newly acquired koi for the first six weeks or so, particularly at, and just after, feeding times. Make sure that each fish actually swallows any food that it takes. Many fishkeepers find that fish 'sulk' after being introduced to a new pond; isolating themselves from other fish, seeming disinclined to feed and lying at the bottom of the pond. Do not panic – some fish respond better than others to being moved. Watch a particular fish carefully for a week to ten days, but do not touch it. If after this time it still takes no interest in its surroundings, you may need to administer a salt bath. This will kill parasites, such as *Ichthyobodo* and *Trichodina* (see *Health care*, page 102), which tend to multiply rapidly on stressed fish. Such a treatment will normally be sufficient to rouse the koi.

Bagging a koi

Koi will normally be bagged, and larger fish boxed, for you to carry home. It is important that these bags are large enough and that they are oxygenated; oxygen is more important to the fish than water.

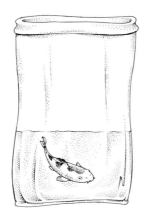

Place the koi in a bag with just enough water to cover the gills.

Holding the top, squeeze out any air trapped inside the bag.

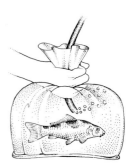

Fill the bag with oxygen, holding the top firmly against the hose.

When there is enough oxygen in the bag, twist the top tightly.

Secure the top of the plastic bag with an elastic band.

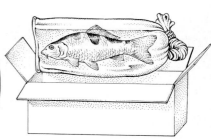

Larger koi should be boxed to prevent bumped noses and split fins.

What to look for when buying koi

Choosing your dealer
● How did you hear about the dealer?
● How far away is it from your home?
● What condition are the ponds in? Does the water appear well filtered and clean?
  Is there a strong 'fishy' smell?
  Do the koi appear distressed?
● How does the dealer handle and bowl the fish?
● Does the dealer oxygenate the bags?
● What sort of quarantine facilities are there?

Choosing your koi
● How does the fish swim? Are its movements fluid or jerky?
● How interested is it in its environment?
● How steady are its gill movements? (They should be slow and regular.)
● Is the koi using both gills?
● Do you *like* the fish? (Don't be persuaded by a pushy dealer!)

Koi to avoid
Avoid koi with any of the following:
● Parasites (such as fish lice on the fins or anchor worms around the dorsal or tail regions)
● Gill plates that stand proud of the head
● Bumps on the side of the gill plates or on the head
● Redness on the body or fins
● A white bloom on the skin
● Raised scales or holes
● Cloudy eyes
● Fin rot
● Also avoid any koi that seem to be puffing hard or that are hanging near the surface of the water.

鯉の餌

FEEDING KOI

Good body shape is the single most important feature that judges and breeders look for in koi. It should also be the priority of the fishkeeper, who should aim to provide a well-balanced diet that will build up the muscle, but not the fat, in the koi, and enhance their colour. The Japanese say that a healthy koi is a hungry koi, even after feeding. This is certainly true; koi will always accept more than they can comfortably eat, and often become too fat, with potentially fatal results. Overfeeding also leads to an increase in the volume of waste products excreted by the koi into the water and this, together with pollution resulting from decaying uneaten food, creates a new problem: poor water quality, that is, high ammonia and nitrite levels. 'Little and often' is a good rule to follow when feeding koi; in this way the koi, although receiving enough food, are kept hungry and will tend to feed from your hand.

Lettuce is a favourite treat for koi, and large fish, like these, will happily tear leaves from a whole one.

FEEDING KOI

Feeding and growth rate

The feeding pattern, and thus the growth rate, of koi depends on many factors, such as water temperature, water quality, stocking density and genetic background. Koi feed most actively at temperatures in excess of 15°C(59°F), thus sexually immature fish can grow rapidly during the summer months when the temperature is warmer (see below). Once koi are mature, their growth rate slows considerably; in sexually mature fish, most of the food eaten is utilized in producing eggs or sperm in preparation for breeding. However, unlike many other vertebrates, fish continue to grow throughout their lives and it is easy for pampered koi to reproduce and continue to grow because of their artificially high feeding rates. The cycle of rapid growth in summer and retarded growth in winter produces rings on the fish's scales (much like the growth rings of a tree) and a koi's age can be determined by counting these rings. Some koi-keepers, however, who heat their pools in the winter, continue to feed their koi throughout the year. If a koi has continued to feed during winter its rings will not be clearly defined and it will therefore be difficult to age.

Water quality affects the rate of growth because koi lose their appetites and may even stop eating if their environment is poor. Poor water quality can also affect the fish's metabolism, thus hindering digestion of food.

The stocking density of the pond can

Below: Koi can become quite tame. Encourage hand feeding with prepared foodstuffs or give your koi a treat with prawns, brown bread or lettuce.

also have marked effects on koi growth rate. In a lightly stocked pond, koi will become sexually mature while still of a relatively small size (25-30cm/10-12in) and once mature, growth is retarded (see above). Although koi in a densely stocked pond will mature at a much larger size (50-60cm/20-24in), competition for food will slow the growth rate, food will be scarcer and the 'battle' for it can stress some koi. You will have to decide on optimum stocking levels for your own koi pond bearing this in mind. In fact, these considerations are really most important for koi farmers.

The genetic background, too, influences the size to which koi will grow; as the children of tall parents tend to be tall, and short parents produce small children, so the same is true of koi. This is obviously a simplified view of gene action, however, because of the significant role the environment plays in influencing size.

Water temperature affects fish more than any other single factor. Fish are ectothermic – their body temperature fluctuates in accordance with the temperature of their environment, usually remaining 1°C higher (see page 72). As the temperature drops, the ability of the koi to digest and assimilate food decreases. In the winter months, therefore, at temperatures below 10°C(50°F), it is a good idea to feed cereal diets that the koi can digest quickly and easily and that do not stay in the gut too long. High-protein diets linger in the gut and can cause severe problems; the bacteria found in the fish's gut, which play a role in breaking down some less readily digestible substances, such as cellulose,

may become pathogenic if food is retained in the gut too long. As the water temperature rises, however, the koi need protein for growth, repair of damaged tissue and injuries, and for reproduction. In the summer, koi will benefit from a high-protein diet containing 35 to 40 percent of fishmeal-based protein. (See also *Seasonal care*, pages 70-79.)

Nutritional content of food

Food contains various elements, such as proteins, fats, carbohydrates, vitamins and minerals, which are essential for all animals to maintain healthy bodies, grow and reproduce. Here we explain what these elements are and why they are important components of food.

Proteins are made up of amino acids. Thirteen essential amino acids should be included in any fish diet, although there are about 20 found in natural proteins. An adequate diet contains sufficient quantities of both essential and non-essential amino acids to allow the koi to grow, repair damaged tissue and produce either eggs or sperm. Deficiency of protein or any of the essential amino acids causes koi to grow more slowly and, if this dietary problem continues, can result in a deformation of the spine. (Spine deformities may have a number of other causes, such as disease, however).

Fats provide a source of energy to koi; their important role is in providing fatty acids (see below), such as triglyceride and phospholipids; vital components of membranes surrounding all cell walls. Koi can make almost all of the fatty acids they need with the exceptions of linoleic and linolenic acids, which are essential and must be provided in the food. Linolenic acids are required for growth.

All fats are made up in a similar way to proteins, but of fatty acids, rather than amino acids, bonded together with glycerol. If essential fatty acids are omitted from the diet, symptoms of fin erosion and heart and liver problems may result. Fats have a low melting point and are thus more easily digested by koi. They are found in fish, soya and corn oils and in high concentrations of wheatgerm. Fatty acids become rancid on exposure to air - a chemical process known as oxidation. In koi, the liver is the chief organ for storing fats and if stale food is fed to them it can result in disease and death. Unfortunately, rancid food has no outward appearance of having 'gone bad'. It is, therefore, worth buying smaller packs of food, rather than a large quantity which is utilized slowly, and never keep food from one year to the next.

The function of some vitamins in the koi diet

Vitamin	Source	Function	Consequences of deficiency	Notes
Fat-soluble vitamins				
Vitamin A (Retinol)	Greenfood	Important for skin and sight	Poor growth; haemorrhaging; blindness	An excess of Vitamin A can lead to liver, spleen and skeletal problems
Vitamin E (Tocopherol)	Wheatgerm	Anti-oxidizing agent in food to stop fats turning rancid	Skeletal disorders; fatty degeneration of the liver (the latter probably caused by fats turning rancid)	An excess of Vitamin E may lead to clinical disorders
Vitamin K	Green plants	Aids blood-clotting	Internal haemorrhaging in the muscle and gut; excessively long blood-clotting time; anaemia	
Water-soluble vitamins				
Vitamin B complex				
Thiamin (B1)	Yeast and wheatgerm	Nerve function; digestion; reproduction	Disturbed swimming behaviour (skittishness); poor coloration; haemorrhaging at fin bases; paralysis of the fins	Koi have an enzyme that can destroy this vitamin but, fortunately, some is absorbed. It is not clear whether koi can make thiamin themselves
Riboflavin (B2)	Liver, kidney, heart of various animals; milk	Assists the absorption of oxygen in muscle and tissues that have a poor blood supply	Formation of blood vessels in the cornea; cataracts; bleeding inside the eyes; sensitivity to light; bleeding from the nostrils and gills; loss of appetite; retarded growth; anaemia	
Nicotinic acid	Mainly meats	Aids growth (particularly important in fry and young koi)	Stunted growth	
Choline	Meats, egg yolk, cereals, legumes	Aids metabolism of fat	Fatty liver degeneration	
Pantothenic acid	Liver, kidney, egg yolk	Aids metabolism of fat and carbohydrate	Loss of appetite; abnormal mucus production; gill problems	The gill filaments become clubbed and fused, leading to respiratory distress
Pyridoxine (B6)	Meats, wheat, yeast	Aids metabolism of protein	Can be fatal; rapid ventilation of the gills; skittishness; retarded growth; internal haemorrhaging; pop-eye disease	Absence of pyridoxine has caused high mortalities in koi
Inositol		Function in metabolism unknown	Ulceration and haemorrhaging in juvenile koi; anorexia; reduced growth and anaemia	
Folic acid	Some leafy plants; liver and kidney	Important for cell formation	Anaemia	
Cyanocobalamin (B12)	Animal meats, especially liver and kidney	Aids blood cell formation	Possible reduced appetite, otherwise none	
Vitamin C (Ascorbic acid)	Leafy vegetables; fruits	Development of cartilage and collagen	Deformed spine and gills; internal haemorrhaging	Particularly important in the diet of young koi

FEEDING KOI

Carbohydrates also form a source of energy for koi but fish metabolize them less readily than omnivorous birds or mammals. Too much carbohydrate is very bad for koi health, resulting in either degeneration of the liver or an excessive storage of these substances as glycogen, leading ultimately to heart failure.

Vitamins are essential for the normal metabolism and growth of koi, and requirements of some are increased during spawning. Vitamins are complex-structured substances, needed in only small amounts in the diet, but deficiencies can cause clinical disorders.

Vitamins are divided into two categories: fat soluble and water soluble. Fat-soluble vitamins are found in a variety of forms, all of which are metabolized slowly and can be stored in the body fat. An excess of fat-soluble vitamins can lead to a condition known as hypervitaminosis, which, depending on the vitamin, can lead to clinical disorders.

Water-soluble vitamins are easily absorbed and are not usually excreted.

All essential vitamins are supplied in more than adequate quantities in proprietary koi foods and it would be unusual for the hobbyist to meet clinical symptoms associated with deficiency.

Minerals, too, aid basic metabolic functions, as well as performing their own duties, which include building skeletal structures, osmoregulation, building of nerves, and maintaining the efficiency of gaseous exchange in the blood system. Little is known about mineral deficiencies in fish, probably because most minerals are absorbed from the surrounding water. Normally 12 percent of the diet is made up of minerals, being contained in fish food in the form of ash.

Nutritional requirement of koi
The type of food you give your koi and the quantity you offer them will vary according to their size. The majority of

proprietary koi foods have a cereal base (see table) with different ingredients added either to enhance colour or aid digestion. Choose a food size that is small enough to be eaten by the smallest fish in the pond, otherwise they may die of starvation. If you keep very small koi with larger ones, offer a mixture of large and small foodstuffs, but always make sure that young fish are adequately fed.

Most koi food comes in two forms: floating and sinking. Koi are bottom-feeding fish and are, therefore, better suited to sinking food. This is made by compressing the meal through a die at high pressure. The meal is held together with fats and, again, takes a long time to be dissolved by cold water. The disadvantage with relying on this type of food is that you will be deprived of seeing your koi feeding. Fortunately, koi will take food from the surface – indeed, you can even tame your koi to feed from your hand – and special expanded (hollow) foods have been formulated for this pur-

A selection of foods suitable for koi

Koi sticks
Koi sticks contain all the essential nutrients for a balanced diet, together with additives to enhance colour.

Colour enhancer pellets
Feed these pellets in the summer to enhance colour. Choose the size of pellet to suit the smallest fish in the pond.

Wheatgerm pellets
Wheatgerm, which has a high cereal content, should form an essential part of the koi's diet in the spring and autumn.

Pond sticks
Often mixed with koi sticks to add variety, pond sticks are ideal when the water temperature exceeds 10°C(50°F).

High-protein pellets
High-protein pellets promote maximum growth during the summer. Feed when the water temperature exceeds 20°C(68°F).

Staple pellets
Many koi-keepers like to mix staple with colour enhancer pellets to provide variety in the diet, particularly in the summer.

pose. These are steam cooked to create an outer shell, which protects the food particle from saturation for a while. (Once the pond water has dissolved the shell, the food will sink.) Another advantage with floating food is that it is easy to see when the koi have eaten enough. Take care when feeding sinking types – uneaten food can easily pass unobserved, particularly in murky water.

Provide just enough food so that after five minutes it has all been eaten. On koi farms in summer, smaller koi (i.e. below 15-20cm/6-8in in length) are fed five percent of their body weight per day, whereas large mature koi (i.e. over 20cm/8in long) are only fed two percent. The nutritional value of koi food is calculated by weight and not by volume. Normally, 1kg(2.2lb) of fish food will increase koi growth by 500gm (1.1lb) or even 700gm (1.5lb) in favourable conditions.

In the winter, provide wheatgerm-based diets on a maintenance basis, in order to keep the body functions ticking over, since it is too cold for the koi to grow. Wheatgerm is also a good source of Vitamin E (see table).

Feeding to enhance colour

Koi are highly valued for their colour and certain additives can be included in the diet to maintain and enhance the fish's natural coloration. Carotene affects the red pigmentation, but if used at too high a concentration, even the white pigment on the koi will turn pink. *Spirulina platensis* also enhances and fixes the red pigment, but does not turn the white to pink to the same extent. It is a type of algae found and cultured in Mexico and eaten by the people, since it contains a high level of protein. Initially, it was fed to koi on account of its nutritional value and not because of its colour-enhancing characteristics. Now that these have been established, it is fed to koi for only one month each year, usually during September, but can be given at any time, even during colder periods, at temperatures of 10°C(50°F), but no lower. Some koi farmers feed it for the month before the fish go to market to bring out the best colours in the koi.

Good coloration is not only enhanced by good feeding, however. Healthy fish tend to have much brighter colours than diseased ones. To bring out the colour in koi, particularly the white, you must provide good living conditions. Strong red and yellow pigments develop well in waters rich in green phytoplankton (single-celled plants). Because koi are difficult to see in green water, it helps to feed a diet that will enhance the red pigmentation. Black pigment is enriched in hard water with a pH level of 7.5-8.5. Remember, however, that changing the pH and hardness of the water can affect the toxicity of ammonia and nitrite.

Livefoods

Koi will relish a variety of livefoods, including cockles, worms and prawns. Earthworms can be fed to the fish all year round and, like prawns and cockles, are high in protein and soon become a favourite treat – a sure way to gain the affection of your koi. Tadpoles from frogs are another great treat in spring and, in summer, silkworm pupae, imported from Japan, are an excellent source of protein. Feed these pupae only as an occasional treat, however, as they have been shown to cause a diabetes-like disease in koi. Chironomid larva (bloodworms) and mosquito larva are a popular diet for small fish, though not easily available. Daphnia ('water fleas'), plentiful in earth ponds, are one of the first foods for koi fry but tend to be too small for adult koi. Maggots are not recommended as they can carry harmful bacteria from the decaying flesh. Do not rely on livefoods to form the staple diet for koi, however, but offer them as a supplement to the regular diet. If koi are fed on these titbits alone, there is a risk that nutritional diseases will set in as the result of a lack of vitamins or amino acids.

Other foods

Koi will accept many foods thrown to them in their pond, but many of these are of little or no nutritional value and may even harm the fish. Brown bread is acceptable, but white bread contains a mild form of bleach, which does the koi no good at all. Do not offer beans, peas or corn, since koi are unable to digest the hard outer casing of these foods.

Koi will take lettuce leaves and may also eat duckweed and other plants around their pond (with the exception of blanketweed, which is too coarse for them to pull off the sides).

Flake food
Ideal for small koi (less than 15cm/6in long), each colour flake represents a different nutritional ingredient.

Brown bread
Brown bread is another good treat for koi. Roll the soft dough into pellets of a size suitable for the smallest fish.

Prawns
Prawns are an ideal, if expensive, treat. Whole prawns are best; the red pigment in the shells is a very good colour enhancer.

Lettuce
Lettuce is a favourite with koi; large fish will tear pieces off a whole lettuce, but smaller koi will require individual leaves.

季節ごとの世話

SEASONAL CARE

Unlike most other pets you may choose to keep, koi are generally kept outside. Although some koi-keepers have an additional pond built into a garage or conservatory for overwintering their fish, the majority have only a single pond in their gardens. Here, koi are subject to the whims of the changing seasons, which may include wide fluctuations in temperature, flower fall (from flowering cherry trees, for instance) and leaf fall. Caring for koi and maintaining them in a healthy condition therefore requires certain adjustments to pumps, filters and routine pond maintenance, as well as changes to the koi's diet, at various times of the year. In this section we chart the progress of the year from spring through summer and autumn to winter, outlining the steps you should take to ensure that your koi enjoy the best possible water quality and remain in peak condition throughout the year. Checklists provide a quick reminder of tasks for each season.

The red foliage of a Japanese maple provides a colourful focal point to this koi pond in autumn.

SEASONAL CARE

Spring

Spring marks the beginning of an active time for the koi-keeper. The air temperature gradually rises but may be subject to wide variations, with warm, sunny days followed by cold, even frosty, nights in many parts of the world. Water takes much longer than air or land to warm up and, consistent with this, tends to maintain slightly more constant temperatures than air.

Spring is probably the most hazardous season of the year for koi. Like most fish, koi are ectothermic, that is they have little ability to physiologically maintain a constant body temperature. Their body temperature is usually fractionally higher than the water in which they live due to muscle activity and metabolic functions, both of which generate a small amount of heat. The koi's immune system is more or less inoperative at temperatures below 10°C(50°F) and becomes effective quite slowly as the temperature rises. However, with the advent of warmer days, many species of bacteria and protozoa quickly become very active and, as the temperature approaches 10°C(50°F), begin to reproduce rapidly. It is therefore imperative that you pay close attention to routine maintenance work, such as cleaning the pond and adding proprietary brands of bacteria to the pond filter system to give the koi every opportunity of surviving the hazards that spring brings with it.

Feeding

As the pond water gradually warms up, koi start to look around for food. When the water temperature first reaches 10°C(50°F), feed the koi very sparingly, in the mornings only. The reason for this cautious approach is that the fish's metabolism (i.e. their entire bodily function) is governed by the surrounding water temperature. Overnight frosts in early spring can chill the water, and food in the digestive tract moves very slowly when the water is cold. As a result, undigested food decomposes inside the gut, leading to internal bacterial problems (see *Health care*, particularly pages 108-110). To minimize this risk, avoid high-protein foods in early spring and instead offer a readily digestible laxative food, such as wheatgerm pellets.

Once water temperatures stabilize at around 10°C(50°F) and above, start to introduce a balanced diet of carbohydrate wheatgerm, protein and trace elements, often marketed as 'staple' food. Once temperatures stabilize above 15°C(59°F), you can begin to offer them a higher protein food.

Resist the temptation to rush for last

Above: *A small koi pond in spring, with petals from a cherry tree settling on the water's surface, but these few should not cause any real problems for the fish.*

year's leftover food, as any opened pack may have oxidized and deteriorated or, worse still, grown microscopic moulds that are highly toxic to koi.

Pond management

If you have not installed bottom drains in the pond (see page 32), it will benefit from a thorough clean with a good vacuum pump to remove all the detritus and debris that have accumulated over the winter months. The filters will also benefit from a good backwash; since the growth of bacteria is retarded in cold and cooler weather, there is no risk of seriously damaging the activity of the filter. However, always try to avoid using tapwater to clean your filters, particularly during late spring and summer, as it contains chlorine to control bacteria that are pathogenic to humans. The chlorine can have an equally destructive effect on the bacteria specifically cultivated in the filter media to break down fish waste.

Use pond water to wash through the filter, and then top up the pond with mains water using a mist spray to 'gas-off' the chlorine added by the water authorities. The chlorine evaporates readily, so by spraying water into the pond, the chemical will have effectively 'gassed off' by the time it reaches the 'friendly' bacteria in the biological filter.

As the koi become more active, you should take steps to increase the flow rate of the pond water. Cooler, dirtier water at the bottom of the pond is thus filtered more positively and more water is exposed to the warming atmosphere and to the aeration system. The near-freezing water will have retarded the growth of the bacteria in the filter chambers. Now that the flow of waste products from the

Above: *As the water warms up, so algal blooms are likely to turn the water green. Here, small koi gasp at the surface in the competition for oxygen.*

koi is increasing, the biological filter must be restored to full activity. Freeze-dried or live-cultured bacteria are particularly beneficial in the spring to colonize new filters and to reactivate an established system. Subject to temperatures, freeze-dried or live bacteria can help to make the filter more efficient. If water temperatures, oxygen levels and nutrients are favourable for bacteria to flourish, they will multiply at a prodigious rate.

Controlling algae

In spring, microscopic algae often flourish, giving rise to green water. Green water offends the pride and spoils the enjoyment of many fishkeepers, who may turn to biological filter starters to clear the algae. However, by far the largest constituent of algae is chlorophyll, which oxygenates the water in the presence of light but de-oxygenates it in the dark, sometimes leaving insufficient oxygen for the filter bacteria before dawn. Presumably for this reason, some manufacturers warn that their filter starters are ineffective in green water. Nevertheless, experience has shown that a reduced dosage of either the freeze-dried or live bacteria preparations applied to the filter system every morning when dissolved oxygen levels are rising can clear a pond in 10-14 days. By continually replacing the bacteria after a few hours of warmth during daylight hours, they will gradually become established.

Interestingly, however, green water is usually indicative that the filters are functioning perfectly, the algal bloom being caused by the presence of a large quantity of nitrate, the final product of nitrifi-

cation (see below and page 53). Green water can be very beneficial to koi, enhancing the colour patterns of small koi and providing essential nutrients to newly hatched fry. On Japanese koi farms, green water is positively encouraged in the fry ponds with the addition of large quantities of manure!

Nitrogen cycle

Remember that the nitrification process that recycles fish waste in the biological filters is a two-stage transaction. Koi produce ammonia as waste, and *Nitrosomonas* and other bacteria increase in response to the increasing ammonia concentration to convert it to nitrite. This in turn encourages other bacteria, principally *Nitrobacter,* to multiply and change this lethal byproduct to nitrate. All biological filters undergo these unavoidable stages in their early development and even a mature filter will do so during the spring.

Nitrite poisoning is probably responsible for more mysterious disease and deaths than any other disturbance. Symptoms are often observed about three weeks after the koi have been subjected to this toxin; large koi may respond to excess nitrite in the water by lying on their sides and are generally lethargic, although they will continue to feed; small koi usually die.

Testing water conditions regularly while new filters are becoming established, after the winter when mature filters are becoming fully operational once again, or following some other disruption, will enable you to monitor any potentially dangerous increase in nitrite levels. Reducing, or even withholding food from koi in order to limit the ammonia production is one way of minimizing potential damage, while adding zeolite to the filtration system will extract surplus ammonia.

In the case of high nitrite levels you may need to change as much as 30-40 percent of the water daily. If the nitrite level is extremely high, you can neutralize it to some extent by adding cooking salt to the water at the rate of 3-6gm/litre (0.5-1oz per Imp. gallon) of pond water. This will discourage many parasites and inhibit bacterial growth, while gently encouraging the production of protective mucus on the fish's skin. (Do not add salt to the pond if you have zeolite in the filter, since this will release ammonia back into the water.) Many koi-keepers like to treat the pond against bacterial and parasitic problems in the late spring. (See the table on pages 112-113 for advice on suitable chemicals; always follow the supplier's directions for use.)

Seasonal checklist:

SPRING

POND MANAGEMENT

- Clean the pond thoroughly with a vacuum pump if you have not installed bottom drains.
- Top up the pond with mains water, using a mist spray to 'gas off' any chlorine in the water.
- Increase the flow rate of the pond water as koi become more active.
- Give filters a good backwash (but avoid using tap water).

WATER QUALITY

- Restore biological filters to full activity and add proprietary freeze-dried or live-cultured bacteria to reactivate them.
- Test water conditions regularly to monitor ammonia and nitrite levels.
- If nitrite levels are high, carry out daily water changes of up to 30-40 percent of the pond water.

FEEDING KOI

- Feed koi sparingly once the water temperature reaches 6°C(43°F).
- Feed readily digestible laxative foods, such as wheatgerm, while temperatures are low.
- As temperatures stabilize at 10°C(50°F) and above, start to add 'staple' food to the diet.
- Offer higher protein foods only once temperatures consistently reach 15°C(59°F).
- Avoid using up food remaining from last year; it may have oxidized or, worse, become mouldy during storage.

HEALTH CARE

- Treat the pond against bacterial and parasitic problems in the late spring. Use treatments according to the manufacturer's instructions.

SEASONAL CARE

Summer

Summer is the zenith of the koi-keeper's year, when koi are active and may breed. This is also the time of year when koi develop formidable appetites. As summer progresses, offer the koi larger amounts of food, but stick to the general principle of giving them only as much as they will consume in five or ten minutes, feeding them little and often. Always remember that while you are feeding your fish, you are also feeding the filter; be careful not to feed beyond its limitations or you will poison your koi.

Water changes

The question posed most often in summer by the fishkeeper with a newly established pond and filter system is 'how much and how often should I change the water?' It does seem that the longer a pond has been established, the less water changing goes on. This is not just because the koi-keeper gets lazier, but because the water quality improves as a filter matures. Where a new filter is still allowing high concentrations of ammonia and nitrite in the pond water, a water change will not necessarily dilute these contaminants, but may incur the risk of introducing other toxic substances, principally chlorine, and will probably reduce the pond temperature at the same time. A good compromise is to run off just enough water to flush the bottom drains, or to vacuum pump the detritus off the bottom and occasionally service the filter system. (Remember to keep the hose pipe away from your biological filters at all times.)

Water flow and aeration

While you should take care not to pump water too fast through the filter, it is essential to keep the water continuously well aerated, particularly during hot, thundery weather and overnight, and especially so if you have plants, blanketweed or green algae in the pond. Before becoming dedicated fishkeepers, many water gardeners enjoy an array of fountains, waterfalls and gushers, and turn pumps off at night, believing them to be unnecessary. Unfortunately, when they put koi into their ponds, they continue to turn off the pumps nightly and are distressed when fish that were perfectly healthy one evening are dead the next morning. This immediate evidence of a problem is followed a few weeks later by outbreaks of fungus, fin rot, gill rot and all manner of parasitic infestations that take advantage of fish stressed by living in oxygen-deficient water with, perhaps, an excess of carbon dioxide.

Chlorophyll – the substance that

Summer set-up for water circulation

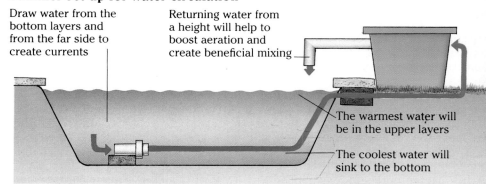

Draw water from the bottom layers and from the far side to create currents

Returning water from a height will help to boost aeration and create beneficial mixing

The warmest water will be in the upper layers

The coolest water will sink to the bottom

makes plants green – is responsible for photosynthesis, a process by which carbon dioxide and oxygen are chemically converted to sugars used for plant growth or storage. This formation of sugars is a two-stage process; the first stage takes place in daylight and the biochemical process causes oxygen to be released and carbon dioxide absorbed. When the light fades, carbon dioxide is released and oxygen absorbed, increasing the amount of carbon dioxide in the water. The plants are thus competing with fish for oxygen at night. The more greenery there is in the water, the greater the oxygen consumption and carbon dioxide production, which will in turn lead to overnight asphyxiation of the koi.

In addition to these processes, we must also consider that the capacity of

Above: *The brilliant light and warmth of summer herald the most productive period for the koi pond. Properly planted, these water lilies provide welcome shade against the harsh rays of the sun.*

Left: *It is very important to maximize the water flow and aeration during the summer months. This simple configuration of submersible pump and external filter shows how bottom water should be cycled.*

the water to absorb dissolved oxygen decreases as the temperature rises. Furthermore, warm water induces greater activity in many animals, including fish, thus placing even greater pressure on the dissolved gas content of the water. Clearly, any disturbance and rippling effect created as water returns from the filter will also increase the surface area in contact with the atmosphere. The surface of the pond is where the greatest gaseous exchange takes place, i.e. it is here that carbon dioxide and other volatile toxins evaporate and oxygen dis-

solves into the water. However, this process can be inhibited by any surface film, such as undigested oily products or dust.

Most experienced koi-keepers have some sort of device to skim off this film from the surface of the pond. Ideally, such a device might consist of a floating weir falling into a basket to catch leaves and large pieces of debris, before feeding a pump to a high-pressure sand filter, which runs continuously. If you are not fortunate enough to have a skimmer, it is worth fitting an overflow onto the pond and using this occasionally, even though it will necessitate running precious mature water to waste.

One further piece of summertime advice: if your pump is submerged in the pond, check it regularly and unblock the inlet, which often sucks in pieces of debris or detritus. Throughout the summer and autumn months, the filter can be supplied with water pumped from near the bottom of the pond.

Spawning

In late spring and early summer, koi measuring 38cm(15in) or more may spawn. This usually takes place early in the morning following warm days but cold nights. A 'naturalized' pond, with shallow edges and marginal plants, is an ideal area for koi to spawn. In the summer, be sure to walk around such a pond every morning in case any females have been driven out of the water by energetic males, as spawning is extremely frantic. Stranded fish can often survive out of water for a considerable time and it is well worth returning them to the water even though they may appear to be dead.

Koi are very bad parents; as soon as they have finished spawning, they will return to the eggs and eat them! If you intend to rear the fry from the koi eggs, it is vital that you remove the spawning ropes from the pond as soon as the koi have finished spawning. Even if you do not want to rear the fry, it is advisable to remove the eggs from the pond, as the adults often damage themselves raking through the weeds and gravel to eat the eggs. The dead eggs may grow fungus and the spores can infect any of the females damaged during spawning.

After koi have spawned, it is worth checking ammonia and nitrite levels in the pond for a week or so, as these are often higher at this time. During spawning, the excited koi produce more urine, and this, together with the decomposition of dead or unfertilized eggs, causes the ammonia level to increase quite dramatically and the population of nitrifying bacteria in the filter may be unable to degrade it into less harmful substances.

Seasonal checklist:

SUMMER

POND MANAGEMENT

- If a new filter is still allowing high concentrations of ammonia and nitrite in the pond, run off just enough water to flush the bottom drains, or vacuum pump the detritus off the bottom.
- Remove debris from the surface of the pond with a skimmer, or fit an overflow and use it occasionally.
- If your pump is submerged, check it regularly for blockages.
- Place spawning ropes in the pond during late spring and early summer, check them regularly and remove them as soon as the koi have spawned, to prevent egg-eating.
- Walk around the pond every morning to ensure that no females have been driven out of the water during spawning.

WATER QUALITY

- Service the filter system occasionally to ensure that ammonia and nitrite levels are minimal.
- Take care to avoid over-pumping filters, but ensure that the pond water is continuously well aerated.
- Keep a check on ammonia and nitrite levels for a week or so after koi have spawned; they are likely to be higher at this time.

FEEDING KOI

- Offer the koi more food in summer but give them only as much as they can consume in five or ten minutes.
- Feed little and often; any uneaten surplus will only cause pollution.

HEALTH CARE

- Check for infections and parasites; they develop faster in warm water.

SEASONAL CARE

Autumn

Autumn can be a very unpredictable season in many temperate parts of the world, with temperatures occasionally soaring above those recorded for the preceding summer months, followed by increasingly cooler days. With regard to water temperature, autumn is the reverse of spring; the water remains warmer for longer than the air and cools more slowly. For the koi, this is the last opportunity to fatten up in anticipation of the onset of winter and, for you, the time to make preparations to help your koi overwinter as healthy fish.

Feeding

During early autumn, koi will continue to feed as energetically as during the summer, in preparation for the winter. As the water cools, koi become less active and their appetites decrease. Start to introduce a little wheatgerm to their diet and gradually increase this element until early winter, simultaneously phasing out the dietary pellets, which contain high proportions of protein. Wheatgerm pellets, which have a high cereal content, are readily available from most koi dealers or aquarist shops.

Pond management

Throughout the summer, the management and maintenance requirements of your pond will change very little. However, with the advent of autumn, falling leaves may become a problem and, if you have not fitted an adequate skimmer to the pond, you should put nets in place to catch falling leaves. Once they sink to the bottom, leaves readily decompose, aided by bacteria. The bacteria that cause decompostion of organic debris, such as leaves, are 'opportunist' organisms, feeding from dead or damaged tissue. If koi have any damaged scales or dead anchor worm on their bodies, these bacteria will start to feed on them, gradually eating their way into the living tissue and giving rise to ulcerous lesions or septicaemia (blood poisoning). Allowing dead leaves to decompose on the bottom of the pond causes the numbers of these bacteria to increase and form a potential problem to the koi. Some trees even produce natural insecticides that become activated as the leaves are damaged or decay and these can make koi very ill. A net over the pond might also usefully serve to deter herons, cats, foxes and other potential predators.

Right: The shorter days of autumn bring a cooling influence to the koi pond. Be sure to keep the water clear of leaves and check your koi for parasites and disease.

Autumn is also a good time to clean out the filters. If you have a multichamber system, clean out one chamber at a time, waiting a week or so before cleaning the next. This will give the nitrifying bacteria an opportunity to re-colonize the chamber and minimize any adverse effect on water quality (see page 53). Remember to keep the hosepipe away from filters at all times and *never* scrub filters clean with detergent or disinfectant, which will kill the bacteria in the filter and endanger the koi by causing the water quality to degenerate.

Health care

The autumn is a good time to ensure that the koi are free from parasites, such as fish lice and anchor worms (see page 104), particularly if you have added new stock during the summer. Anchor worms and fish lice can cause lesions to develop on the skin of the koi, which if left can become ulcerous. Wounds on koi heal very slowly, if at all, below 12°C(54°F). As the autumn temperatures cool the water, the koi's immune system starts to become less effective, and at temperatures of 10°C(50°F) and below, ceases to work altogether, while most bacteria are active down to 2°C(36°F). It is vital that koi with any wounds or lesions recover during the autumn period and it is worth setting up a treatment pond for any koi with unhealed wounds. Ideally, you should prepare this treatment pond in advance and use healthy fish to start up the filter and overcome the problems of intitially high ammonia/nitrite levels that occur with any new filter system (see page 51). Sick fish cannot tolerate the fluctuations in water quality of a newly installed filter system and will die. Once the treatment pond is ready, place the sick koi into it with some healthy fish to keep them company. ('Ordinary' hardy goldfish are generally much more resilient to disease than koi, being less highly inbred!) The water in the treatment pond should be maintained at a minimum temperature of 16°C(61°F).

There are many preparations on the market that will kill fish lice and the free-swimming stages of anchor worms. (You will need to remove adult female anchor worms with a pair of tweezers.) However, although they are safe for use with koi, many of the preparations on the market designed to kill these parasites are highly dangerous to some other fish species. (It takes about seven days for the chemicals in these preparations for killing fish lice and anchor worm larvae to degrade into an innocuous form.) If you keep species such as orfe, tench or rudd, you must remove them from the pond before treating it. Place them in a suitable container, ideally another pond, and remember to aerate the water. If the container does not have a filtration unit, then test the water at least daily for ammonia. If the ammonia content in the water starts to rise, either add zeolite to the final chamber of your filter or, alternatively, carry out 20 percent water changes daily until the fish can be returned to the pond. If you are treating the pond for fish lice, remember to check the other coldwater species to ensure they are not harbouring any of these parasites before returning them to the koi pond.

Below: This simple holding tank is ideal for treating koi with unhealed wounds or any health problems before the winter 'recess'.

Seasonal checklist:

AUTUMN

POND MANAGEMENT

- Use a skimmer, or a net over the pond, to catch falling leaves. A net will also discourage herons from raiding your pond to build up their own fat reserves for the winter.
- Give the filters a thorough clean. Leave a gap of a week or so between cleaning each chamber of a multichamber filter and, of course, never use detergents or disinfectants in the process.

WATER QUALITY

- Use a thermostatically controlled heater (in the filter) to stabilize erratic water temperatures.

FEEDING KOI

- Continue to feed koi little and often during early autumn.
- As water temperatures decrease and koi become less active, start to introduce a little wheatgerm to the diet and gradually increase amounts until early winter, simultaneously phasing out high-protein foods, such as most dietary pellets.

HEALTH CARE

- Keep the pond clear of fallen leaves; any that decompose on the bottom of the pond may cause harmful bacteria to proliferate.
- Check koi thoroughly for parasites, such as fish lice and anchor worms, particularly if you have added new stock during the summer.
- Set up a treatment tank for any koi with unhealed wounds. Maintain a minimum temperature of 16°C(61°F).
- Remember that fish such as orfe, tench and rudd can be killed by some remedies used in the pond.

SEASONAL CARE

Winter

As temperatures drop, koi move into the deeper parts of the pond and become more reluctant to feed, and below temperatures of 6°C(43°F) cease feeding altogether. As the water continues to cool, the koi tend to lie huddled together on the bottom of the pond with all fins except the tail fin clamped tightly against their bodies. This conserves some body heat, as each fin is supplied with a tiny network of blood vessels through which heat escapes if the fish lie with their fins outspread. One of the major areas of cooling of a fish's body is through the gills, where the warm blood is cooled by the water passing over the gill filaments. You may have noticed that koi seem to breathe more slowly in winter – this is a method of conserving body heat. At temperatures between 2°C and 6°C (36-43°F) koi are described as being in a 'torpid state'. Their senses such as smell and taste are inoperative but they can still see and respond to some external stimulation, such as touch, or water movement below the surface.

Temperatures below 2°C(36°F) are critical to koi, as there is an increasing risk of ice crystals forming in the delicate gill membranes. Because water expands when it freezes, these crystals break the tiny cells in the gills and the koi die.

Winter filtration and aeration

Like many other materials, water expands when it warms and contracts as it cools. Because water is a liquid, warm water is light and therefore rises. (If you feel your hot water storage tank, you will notice that it is hotter at the top than at the bottom.) Logically, you might expect, therefore, that freezing water (ice) should lie at the bottom of exposed water but, as we all know, this is not the case. In fact, a reversal of this principle occurs at temperatures just below 4°C(39°F), when colder water rises to the surface and warm water sinks. This is the salvation of most underwater life. Water is a poor conductor of heat, so the cold water and ice form an insulating layer that retains the heat of the warmer water below it. As we have seen in the section on pond and filter construction, the pond should be at least 1.5m(5ft) deep; depth will aid the temperature stability of the warmer water below the ice and the water will also absorb heat from the ground.

Keep all biological filters running throughout the winter. It is important that the water continues to ventilate so that oxygen can diffuse into the water and harmful carbon dioxide (the byproduct of respiration) does not become sealed in by total ice cover. If the pump is

Winter set-up for water circulation

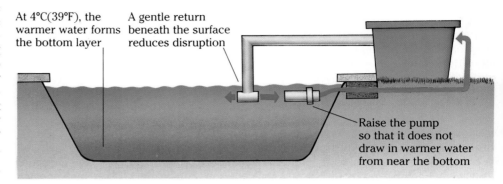

At 4°C(39°F), the warmer water forms the bottom layer

A gentle return beneath the surface reduces disruption

Raise the pump so that it does not draw in warmer water from near the bottom

turned off, the fish will suffer and the plumbing will corrode or freeze if the pump is then left in the water. If a variable flow pump is fitted in the pond, turn it down to its minimum output. If your system enjoys the versatility of two or more pumps, then using one should be sufficient at this time of year in all but the very largest ponds. This will give you the opportunity to service any pumps not in use. (Most pumps are now sealed units and you need only clean them and check the strainers, cables and switches.)

You may have a submersible pump in the pond or a variable level gravity feed pipe, if so, you can vary the level from which the filter is fed. As the water temperature drops towards the critical 4°C(39°F), raise the pump or filter feed to 15-23cm(6-9in) below the surface. This will avoid disturbance and chilling of bot-

Above: *This is how the simple set-up shown in the summer section on page 74 should be rigged for winter. The vital change here is that circulation is reduced and the bottom water is thus left undisturbed.*

tom water and allow the koi to rest, while preventing the pond from completely icing over.

You may decide to moderate the water return to the pond. Restrict the air flow on your venturi, bypass waterfalls and turn off fountains, since all these means of aeration are no longer necessary, as cold water is usually rich in oxygen, and, if left on, will excessively chill the water. If your water return is via a straight pipe from a filter above pond level, terminate it with a 'T' piece or elbow pipework to prevent disturbing the lower water.

It is not a good idea to use rubber balls,

Above: *Beneath the crisp whiteness of this winter scene, the koi are in a state of torpor. It is vital that you keep one area of the pond free of ice and maintain a continuous but gentle circulation to ventilate the water.*

Right: *Yes, this smart koi pond is in the foyer of a public building, but it does show what can be done for koi indoors. You may wish to consider this strategy during the colder months of the year.*

hammers or kettles of boiling water to prevent or break up ice formations. Although the koi are torpid (see above), they can sense any water movement, and breaking ice sends violent shock waves through the water, which can severely stress, and even kill, koi. (It is a sensation probably similar to someone suddenly crashing a loud drum close to your ear while you are sleeping and waking you with a start!)

Heating outdoor ponds

A growing number of enthusiasts are installing heating systems in their outside pond to keep their koi active and feeding, and thus growing, throughout the year. Avoid placing heaters in the bottom of the pond, however, as they can set up convectional currents that lift the warmer water, which chills as it rises towards the surface or towards a layer of ice, thus returning cold water to the koi. (You should also remove any airstones from the bottom of the pond in winter for the same reasons.) Instead, place small heaters in the filter system, preferably in the settling chamber or transfer ports. Any heating unit should be thermostatically controlled and capable of maintaining the water temperature at a minimum of 10°C(50°F), even through the severest of winters. Rapidly fluctuating temperatures are highly undesirable and temperatures sufficiently high to activate the fish but too low for safe feeding can

have a debilitating effect. Furthermore, between 0°C and 10°C(32-50°F) the koi's immune system does not operate, but bacteria in the water are still active. If your heater cannot maintain an adequate temperature throughout the winter, use it only to help stabilize autumn and spring temperatures.

Indoor ponds

An alternative to heating outdoor ponds that is favoured by some koi-keepers is the installation of pond systems in the garage, greenhouse or conservatory, and some enthusiasts even have permanent fish houses. Such pond systems are usually smaller and may be used at certain times of the year, for quarantine purposes or for raising baby koi, or they may be rested throughout the summer and used only during the colder months, to protect koi from the chill of winter.

Use mature water from the existing pond rather than tapwater to fill the inside pond. In this way, you avoid subjecting the koi to a change in temperature and water quality when you move them inside. In addition, you could move a small portable filter to the inside pond when you transfer the fish, having matured it with established pond water. Alternatively, by transferring some of the media from the active outdoor filter, you can overcome the ammonia/nitrite problems associated with new filters and pond systems (see also page 54).

(see also page 54)

LANDSCAPING AND WATER GARDENS

Your pond should, of course, be planned to provide an ideal environment for your koi, but water is also an excellent design element and, with a little forethought and flair, will greatly enhance the layout and general impact of your garden. Its movement and light-reflecting properties can play interesting visual tricks, producing the illusion of space in a small area, for example, rather like a mirror indoors, while streams and watercourses and the shape and position of ponds can appear to lengthen and widen the plot. Modern materials offer more scope for creativity with shape and design and enable you to produce a formal or informal focal point, or a complete water garden complex employing a wide range of water-based effects. The pond's primary role will be to show off your koi to best advantage, and so it is important that you plan it in relation to your total garden design. You should consider not only its position and setting, but also your choice of surrounding features and plants. This way your water garden will look completely natural and you can successfully capture exactly the atmosphere you want – whether that be Oriental minimalism or the lusher, more colourful Western style of landscaping. For it to look good and work well, you should consider the style of a pond as carefully as its construction details.

Here, the combination of water, plants and rockwork demonstrates what can be achieved in a water garden.

LANDSCAPING AND WATER GARDENS

Siting the pond

There are several points you will need to consider when deciding on the position of a pond (see also page 24). It should always be sited away from deciduous trees or large shrubs, where dropping leaves, and sometimes fruits, seeds and insects, quickly pollute the water or make regular dredging a difficult but necessary chore. A sunny spot is important for healthy water and fish and flourishing plants, although a little shade should be provided for your koi in summer. The position should not be too shady, but it must be well sheltered, both for your comfort and for that of your fish. An evergreen hedge, fencing or screening between the pond and prevailing winds should be sufficient and their filtering effect is far more efficient than a solid barrier, such as a wall. Bamboo screening or brushwood is equally effective and gives the area a distinctly Oriental atmosphere.

It makes good practical and financial sense to be close to services such as electricity and drainage, and a site near to the house is often ideal. A koi pond, large or small, can make the perfect patio feature, offering plenty of opportunity to enjoy the koi at close quarters. Proximity to the house is also convenient for feed-

Above: *A small, stone-slab retaining wall around a koi pond is suitably informal and yet adds an essential safety feature.*

ing and general maintenance. In Japan, koi ponds are traditionally installed near the house, and in some cases the pool even runs under the foundations and reappears indoors. You can imitate this effect in various ways without embarking on major constructional alterations: a timber-decked patio running from the

house to overlap a pond will give the impression that the water runs right beneath it and you may wish to emphasize this effect by setting a smaller pool in the decking itself. Alternatively, butt the pond up to the house and install a corresponding small pool inside the living room, conservatory or sun room extension. Patio doors across the width of the wall, or a large floor-to-ceiling window will provide plenty of light for your indoor pond and will enable you to see both indoor and outdoor ponds, making them appear undivided.

If a position close to the house is impractical, you will have to consider other likely spots in the garden. Incidentally, your pond need not be at the rear of the house; sometimes converting the whole of the front garden into a large formal pond with a bridge across to the front door looks stunning and makes a spectacular approach to the house. Elsewhere, any low spot or hollow is ideal for a pond. Following the natural contours of the garden will give the best effect and avoid any feeling of incongruity, so do walk around it at leisure and get an idea of the lie of the land. This will also help you get an impression of how your water garden will look from every vantage point – from nearby paths and corners

Below: *Informal ponds are easier to blend into the natural contours of your garden site. A corner position (left) affords an*

excellent backdrop and screening using the garden boundaries. Often a site nearer the house is more convenient, however (centre

and right). Remember to check the shape and position of the proposed pond site from inside the house as well as in the garden.

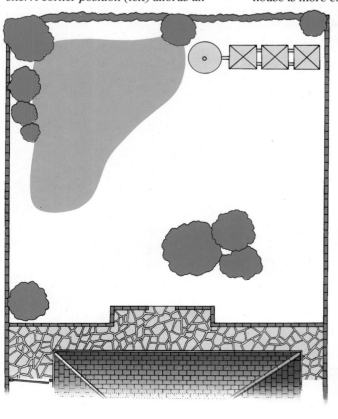
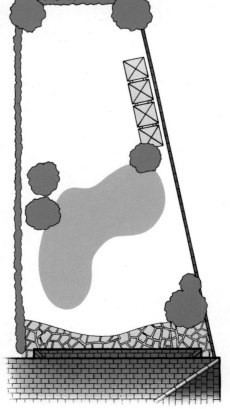
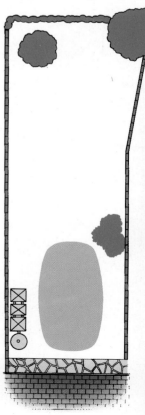

and from the opposite end of the site as well as from the house. Remember, you enjoy the garden all around you, not just as a stage from the back door. You may find it helpful to sketch out the rough shape and position of the pond in the garden, using a hosepipe or stakes and string. This will enable you to view it not just from every angle, but also, if appropriate, from the upstairs windows of your house, to see how it fits the general layout of your garden.

While a formal pond can be excellently integrated into a patio design, an informal style makes a fine focal point in the lawn or landscaped into a break of slope where you can make the most of a sunny aspect. Bear in mind that your pond's position should facilitate easy and comfortable observation of your koi, so access must be good and remain dry underfoot in wet weather. Ideally, you should be able to sit and laze at the waterside in fine weather. If you have a summerhouse at the opposite end of the garden, a water feature within sight of the verandah may be the ideal spot.

Other practical points to consider when planning the position and layout of your water garden include proximity to boundary hedging or fencing, which might inconvenience neighbours and make construction and maintenance difficult (see page 28). It is also worth digging down a little way with your spade within your proposed site; if solid rock is only inches below the subsoil or you have a particularly high water table, you may have to opt for building a raised pond. Consider, too, who will be using the garden. Young children under five years will be at risk unless you can arrange for the pond area to be fenced or gated off until they are older (something grandparents may forget). Where there is an elderly or disabled member of the household, a raised pond may again be the best option, with seats or wheelchair bays integrated into the design so that the water and its occupants can be more easily appreciated.

Size and shape
The size and shape of your pond must be kept in scale with the rest of the garden, although it is usually better to err on the large side, especially if you are hoping to create an eye-catching focal point. Large areas of water, if carefully planned and well integrated with good background landscaping, look stunning even in small gardens and provide plenty of room for fish. A pond that is too small will look cramped and insignificant.

Shape and style will depend on your own preference and the general scope

and atmosphere of your garden or pond area. If you wish to maintain an Oriental feel, the Japanese prefer an informal-style water garden, but with the right materials and surroundings it is possible to create a similar atmosphere around a more formal koi pond, particularly a simple square or rectangular shape within a small courtyard or patio complex. Generally, simple shapes are best, even for formal ponds, where a combination of squares, rectangles and hexagons produce the best effects. This style lends itself to a series of ponds, maybe on different levels and linked by timber or paving, and offers the opportunity to display different varieties of koi in separate ponds. Most popular, particularly for a simple Japanese-style patio or back yard, is a formal L shape which emphasizes the sense of seclusion and enclosure away from the hurly-burly of life outside the

Left: A formal square or rectangle butted up to the house is a popular Oriental koi pond design, here reinforced by background planting of dwarf conifers and interesting foliage plants among stone and rock.

Below: Twin ponds with a path between offer plenty of opportunity to wander through the garden and observe your fish at close quarters. The central position of these ponds has been softened by their irregular shape and varied foliage planting.

garden; essential to the Oriental philosophy of gardening.

More informal ponds, usually edged with stones or boulders, should also be restricted to simple shapes, such as ovals, irregular circles and kidney shapes. A pond whose shape is too intricate – with narrow necks, for example – will be difficult to construct, will inhibit adequate water flow and cause maintenance problems later (see page 25). It is particularly important to get a feel for the natural contours of the land if you want an informal pond, so that it looks as natural as possible when completed.

When considering a liner for your pond (see page 30), remember that the preformed type will limit you to a particular shape and size and that, while the choice is reasonably large, some koi-keepers prefer to use butyl or concrete for the greater creative scope they offer.

LANDSCAPING AND WATER GARDENS

General landscaping

To tackle your pond or water garden as a complete landscaping project, you will have to plan in detail the background area and surrounding plants and materials. The best way to do this after you have mapped out your prospective features on the ground with stakes and string, is to draw it up roughly to scale on a piece of graph paper. Now you can start adding the other elements, aiming for a good blend of hard landscaping – boulders, stones and paving; and soft – plant material and maybe timber. You will also want to achieve a good variety of shapes and colours and plan for something of interest right through the year for all-seasons appeal. This is where you can reinforce your desired style, restricting your hard landscaping to natural stone or gravel and choosing plants with bold architectural shape and form (rather than bright flower colour) to create an authentic Japanese feel.

Ponds need a good backdrop to set them off, preferably something with a bit of height; use carefully selected trees or shrubs guaranteed not to drop too much plant matter into the water – maybe a bamboo or rhododendron, or carefully contour the plot, making use of the subsoil and rubble saved from excavating the pond. You need not attempt anything too exaggerated; a gentle slope, planted with alpines between the boulders or with a small waterfall installed, can make all the difference, providing not just shelter and dappled shade, but also interesting reflections in the water's surface. If more shelter is required, plant trees or shrubs, but not too close so that they won't shade too much of the pond. Those species that love a damp location and that have light foliage, producing only a dappled shade, look the most natural; the sort of trees you see growing beside streams and ponds in the wild are ideal (but avoid invasive weeping willows!). For smaller gardens or patio ponds you may need to resort to screening. Build it no higher than you need to for privacy and shelter and choose a sympathetic material, such as timber, wattle hurdles or bamboo. Plants in containers can be used to soften their outline. (This is a useful planting device around ponds where you need to keep soil and other vegetable matter out of the water.) Hedging, screening, shrubs and trees will make your water garden seem more secluded, the foliage plants adding a sense of coolness and lushness; vital to both Oriental and Western schemes.

While your plans are still in this experimental stage, consider extending your water garden with other features, such as

Above: *Hard and soft landscaping around the pond will help it blend with the rest of* the garden, particularly if you choose a more formal style like this simple square.

a wide shallow stream to link one pond to another or to other parts of the garden; you could even incorporate a simple bridge or stepping stones. A waterfall makes interesting use of a rocky outcrop and, like the stream, adds the delightful sound of moving water to your garden. Both streams and waterfalls require a pump to recycle the water and this must be carefully chosen to suit the volume of water you wish to move (see page 37). You can achieve a similar effect with watercourses and cascades; both are constructed in a similar manner to ponds and can be finished with brick, stone or timber to match the style of the main pond. They are a popular device in the Japanese-style water garden where an informal, natural effect is preferred. The Japanese have also developed a form of water gardening without water: the dry stream, complete with weirs at every break of level, following the general course and shape of a natural stream and crossed by low timber bridges or large flat stepping stones, but filled only with rocks and stones. With water-loving, streamside plants along the dry banks, the effect can be remarkably realistic, without all the effort and expense involved in lining and pumping an elaborate moving water feature.

Water garden style

Before you begin choosing specific plants and hard landscaping materials and plotting them in on your plan, you should have a clear idea in your mind of the kind of atmosphere and the style of water garden you are trying to create.

A Japanese or Oriental flavour is often popular with koi-keepers, not only because koi are traditionally associated with Japan, but because the architectural, more spartan style of an Oriental pond, which uses shapes rather than colours, serves to show up the koi to best advantage. A subtle setting will enhance, rather than distract the eye from, their shape, colour and movement. It is a structured but essentially informal style, ideally suited to small town gardens or a secluded corner of a larger site. The Japanese garden is a peaceful retreat from the stress and hubbub of everyday life, and uses natural forms, such as water, rock and sand, to imitate mountains, lakes and seas. This gentle feeling of harmony is created with subtle foliage effects rather than bright flowers; a pattern of greens and greys relying on leaf shape and size for variety. There are usually a lot of evergreens for year-round interest and a mixture of informal woodland plants, such as rhododendrons, along with more formal clipped shapes. There may be mounds of box or azalea, simulating the rolling countryside, contrasted with strong shapes, such as bamboo and *Enkianthus*.

The Japanese water garden looks good all year round, but is particularly striking in spring and autumn, when it blazes into colour and provides special dazzling reflections in the water's surface. Japanese varieties of small trees, such as *Acer* (maple) and *Prunus* (plum and cherry) are often grown for their beautiful blossom in spring and glorious foliage colour in autumn, and a single tree is often placed strategically to provide a special focal point in the pond setting.

The surrounding area of your pond (or ponds, stream or waterfall) is an essential element of the total design of the Japanese water garden, a resting place where the lazy perambulations of the fish can be observed at leisure, either from the comfort of a waterside stone slab or seat, or from a low bridge or stepping stones just skimming the surface of the water. The pond itself is likely to be surrounded with stones or boulders, or, for a formal pond, bricks or stained timber decking (see *Surrounding surfaces,* page 86). These, combined with a few Japanese-style plants, such as bamboo or a small *Acer palmatum,* (plant them in pots or Chinese 'ginger jars' for small patio gardens) will instantly create an Oriental atmosphere. This type of water garden could be adapted to either a small patio pool or a large informal pond landscaped in the lawn.

Since the starker, rather controlled style of Oriental water gardening isn't to everyone's taste, there is nothing to stop you adapting the basic principles of Japanese design and softening or extending your plans to suit a more Western ideal of the perfect water garden. This type of garden will contain more plants and brighter colours, particularly around the pond itself – something hardly ever seen in Japanese water gardens. Hard landscaping – usually of stone or brick – tends to be semi-concealed by foliage and a lush combination of flowering plants chosen to create a dense display of colour. It is a good idea to enforce some kind of discipline on your choice of plants or the effect can look too garish – thriving moisture lovers and pond plants can range from pinks and purples to bright yellows and blues. You will create a more interesting and pleasing water garden if you devise a basic framework of interesting foliage shapes and colours (the choice here is wide) and then add more colourful elements sparingly, in clumps of maybe one or two shades only. Thus East can meet West harmoniously.

If you intend to grow marginal plants - species that will grow with their roots in the boggy or waterlogged soil at a pond's edge – you should incorporate a shallow shelf (see *Pond and filter construction,* page 42) and contain the plants in tubs or with a stone or brick retaining wall for protection. Koi delight in uprooting these marginal plants, which is one of the reasons why you do not see them very often in strictly styled Japanese koi ponds. This is also a problem should you wish to plant aquatic species (those that float on or in the water) in your pond, as these, too, will usually be eaten or scattered by the koi. Aquatic plants also tend to reduce the oxygen levels in the water. You must be content, therefore, with more interesting and varied marginal planting and, if you must have plants or flowers on the water's surface, try one or two of the more vigorous forms of water lilies. They will naturally have to be of a deep-water variety and supported so that their leaves and flowers are just level with the surface of the water.

Your choice of surrounding surfaces and features such as ornaments, pots and containers, even garden furniture and screening materials, will also influence the look of your pond, as well as your planting scheme. If the water garden is quite large and ambitious, you could maybe create an Oriental corner with a few large boulders and tub of bamboo or grasses, and develop a lusher, more Western-style planting further round the pond.

Above: *In a larger garden, you can afford to be more ambitious, making your pond a* major feature. Here, a change of level allows for an informal waterfall linking two ponds. The design also incorporates a rustic bridge and small viewing platform.

LANDSCAPING AND WATER GARDENS

Surrounding surfaces

It would be foolish to try to economize on pond construction materials, but for the surrounding surfaces, the less expensive options are often the most exciting and successful. Local stone, for example, costs far less than good manufactured paving or something carrying heavy transportation charges, and will look far more natural and in keeping with most pond styles. Similarly, second-hand timber gives an instantly mature look, while cheap timber treated to a coloured stain or varnish offers all kinds of exciting creative possibilities you wouldn't think of with a more expensive pre-treated type. For formal ponds, second-hand bricks are worth looking out for. To soften or age the effect of new brick or stone, chop moss stems in yoghurt or buttermilk and spread over the surface, keeping well watered until established. A special 'antiquing fluid' is also available to prematurely age stone should your pond look rather raw and new. (Of course, if you are going to use it on stone that comes in contact with the pond water, do check first whether it is toxic to fish and plants.)

You will need some form of flat paving or timber effect such as this to hide your pond construction, but you may also want large, sculptural pieces of rock and stone, to disguise the pool edges, to form a backdrop, or maybe an artificial beach, or to position in the water as a decorative

Above: *A pebble 'beach' makes a beautiful informal edging if allowed to run right down into the pond shallows. Contrast with larger boulders and some spiky plants.*

feature. This is particularly important in Japanese-style water gardens where large boulders – sometimes weighing several tonnes – are used to represent mountain ranges or surrounding hills. Ideally, the boulders should be water-worn, with smooth facets or natural, craggy outlines. You can buy these from a specialist supplier or quarry, but remember: large pieces are going to be expensive and difficult to transport and position, so make sure you know exactly what you need beforehand. It helps to make a rough model of the pond area or water garden and experiment with stones and pebbles to see the kind of effect you want and how many rocks and of what size you need. It is important to keep these larger elements to scale and, again, local stone will look most natural.

Rock varies considerably in colour, form and performance according to type.

Above: *This delightful pond complex divides up an otherwise boring suburban strip. A timber-decked platform follows the shape of the pond and leads naturally across a small bridge to create circular walks of the garden and good views of the water.*

Pebbles are frequently used in Oriental-style water gardens, to make shingle 'beaches', to mix with boulders at the edge of the pond or to construct dry streams. They are ideal for creating contrasting effects among other surfaces. Use them to cover the bare soil below plants to conserve moisture – an excellent plan beneath trees where nothing will grow in the shade – or below plants in tubs and containers to reinforce an Oriental look in the garden.

Sand and gravel are also popular in Japanese-style water gardens, for paths and seating areas, beneath trees and shrubs to maximize the impact of foliage and flowers, or to create special effects, such as dry streams or ponds, maybe mirroring the real thing. The Japanese use a special type of sand that comes in a wide choice of colours and large grains, up to 2mm(0.08in) in diameter. These may be raked into swirls and ripples to imitate water, and surrounded by boulders and dwarfed trees and bushes to simulate mountains and forests. Areas of sand or gravel are worth incorporating around your pond as they make an interesting change of texture and, like many other Japanese features, require little maintenance.

Timber is equally useful in the water garden providing it is well treated and maintained. A hardwood, such as redwood or red cedar, is costly but long lasting; relatively inexpensive softwoods, such as larch or spruce, will need annual treatment against rot. The beauty of timber is its soft mellow appearance – a welcome change of surface from stone or paving – and its flexibility – it can be built around any shape or size, or formed into integrated seating or planting areas. Its big advantage over paving is that it is less expensive and easier to install over large areas, especially on a sloping site. You can lay it in all manner of decorative patterns, from vertical and horizontal planking to diagonal herringbone and elaborate weave patterns.

Decking can be used to create an excellent patio area, overlapping the pond like a jetty and making the perfect spot from which to observe or feed your fish. Secure a platform from the house using steel or timber ledger strips and strong bolts, or support freestanding decking on joists and beams set in concrete footings high up or only just off the ground, according to your needs. You could use timber walkways instead of paths to link your decked area to other parts of the garden, or to build low bridges over streams and ponds. Position these almost level with the water's surface so that you can observe the koi at close

Above: *Blending a variety of materials around the pond can be very effective. This informal koi pond is balanced between a* curving planting bed edged with boulders and a timber-decked viewing platform to provide a change of level and textures.

Above: *Raked sand or gravel and rough stone provide a traditionally Oriental setting for a koi pond. Keep plants to a minimum;* here a collection of miniature Bonsai trees are the perfect companions. Stepping stones allow access to the pond across the gravel.

quarters. Decking is ideal for concealing filters and service areas; a hinged hatch will allow access.

Planting areas can be incorporated in decking surrounding a pond to accommodate bamboos, lush foliage plants or simply areas of pebbles, with no risk of polluting the water. Alternatively, use tubs and containers for your plants. The Japanese are equally fond of timber's design potential and low maintenance benefits. In Japan, timber is simply treated and varnished, or stained a dramatic black walnut or deep red for extra impact. Stains and coloured varnishes are readily available for outdoor use:

white and grey produce an attractive weathered look, while blue looks surprisingly good in both Western and Oriental settings. The more coats you apply, the deeper the colour.

Don't be afraid to mix materials – turf with boulders, timber abutting paving, or areas of larger and smaller stones – for variety within your scheme. (Never mix rock types though, as this tends to look confusing and incongruous if the contrast is too striking.) Remember, too, to incorporate a built-in seating area or flat slab for sitting right at the water's edge – koi can be trained to come to a certain point and feed from your fingers.

LANDSCAPING AND WATER GARDENS

Planting

As we have seen, planting can affect the whole shape, nature and theme of your water garden. Certain types, such as bamboo and *Acer,* produce an instant Oriental atmosphere, while rampant *Lysimachia,* ferns and primulas can be used to create a woodland effect. Moisture-loving plants tend to grow quickly, so don't plant too many different types; it is better to aim for a good variety of foliage shapes rather than to concentrate on flowers. You can blend giant-leaved marginal plants, such as *Gunnera manicata* or *Petasites japonicus,* with spiky bamboos and grasses, the thick, deeply veined leaves of hostas, the arrow-shaped *Saggitaria* or feathery ferns and *Astilbe.* Marginal plants tend to have strong dramatic shapes, so choose them carefully to ensure that they blend well. Japanese water gardens prefer a strong framework of evergreens and a mixture of architectural shapes balanced with the more formal domes of clipped box or mosses: mix these with plenty of rocks and boulders and you should achieve the right effect around your pond.

Acers, particularly *A. palmatum,* the Japanese maple, make a beautiful focal point close to water with their lovely

Below: *These illustrations show a variety of marginal and water-loving plants that will flourish in and around the koi pond.*

Above: *Dwarf conifers and heathers are ideal pondside plants. They offer endless combinations of shape and colour, and here effectively disguise filter pipework.*

shaped foliage and superb autumn colour. Some forms have interesting bark for winter interest, too – *A. griseum,* the paperbark maple, has a bright orange-coloured trunk. They are a popular element of Japanese gardens, particularly the smaller cultivars.

Azaleas are grown mainly for their beautiful spring flowers but the Japanese have also developed evergreen forms, which they clip into formal shapes. They are all lime haters, i.e. need acid soils.

Bamboos are dramatic evergreen grasses with a decided Oriental appearance. They like a rich soil and plenty of sunshine, forming dense groves of ornamental stems topped with fluttering foliage in the right conditions. Stems may be bright green, yellow or striped with black. *Sasa palmata* is a useful hardy form; *S. veitchii* grows only to about 1m(3.3ft) and tolerates shade.

Ferns love cool, damp shady spots and are the perfect companions for pond or stream edges. Their bright green feathery foliage is familiar enough and makes a welcome contrast to large-leaved or spiky marginal plants. There is an interesting choice of different shapes and forms including the glorious Royal Fern, *Osmunda regalis,* which is hardy and has good autumn colour; and the Hart's Tongue Fern, *Phyllitis scolopendrium,* which has more crinkly, less divided fronds than the Royal Fern.

Iris are among the few flowering plants you might see in the Japanese water garden. They are prized for their sword-like foliage and delicate, exotic-looking blooms. Most species are hardy and flower in summer.

Mosses enjoy shady, moist areas and produce a dense mat or mound of tiny foliage that is popular ground cover in Japanese gardens. You can collect them from the wild or encourage them to grow on rocks and boulders as described earlier on page 86.

Rhododendrons (the family group includes Azaleas) come in a very wide choice of sizes and varieties, grown primarily for their evergreen foliage and breathtaking spring blooms. Their exotic shape and colour make them a popular shrub for Japanese gardens, where their relatively brief burst of glory in spring and dependable glossy green foliage all year round are valuable in background planting for a garden pond.

Right: *Many lush marginal plants will thrive in pots arranged at the water's edge, making them easier to maintain and ideal for enclosed formal ponds.*

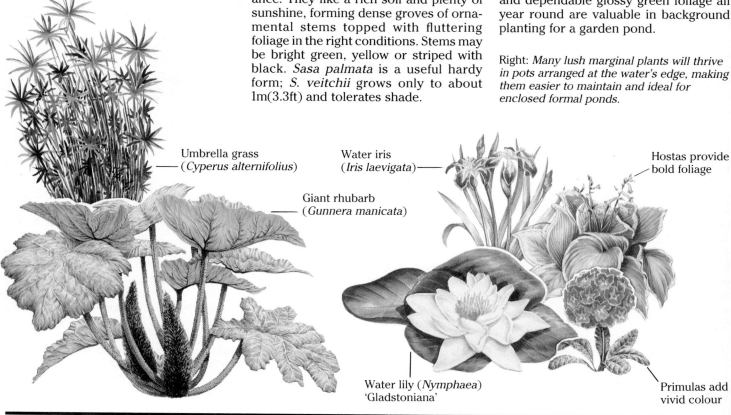

Umbrella grass
—— (*Cyperus alternifolius*)

Water iris
(*Iris laevigata*)——

Hostas provide
bold foliage

Giant rhubarb
—— (*Gunnera manicata*)

Water lily (*Nymphaea*)
'Gladstoniana'

Primulas add
vivid colour

LANDSCAPING AND WATER GARDENS

Above left and right: An Oriental-style bridge looks best in larger gardens where it can span a large pond and be softened with foliage and surrounding shrubs. The strong red colour is traditional but you will need to choose nearby leaves and flowers carefully to avoid a garish effect. Here, soft lilacs and strong greens complement the bridges without competing with them for attention.

Water lilies in the koi pond are restricted to vigorous, deep-water types, such as most forms of *Nymphaea*. These include the white-flowered Gladstoniana, pink *N. tuberosa rosea,* or yellow *N. marliacea chromatella,* which can be planted with up to 120cm (48in) of water above the crown. Planting the tubers in solid containers, rather than mesh baskets, and topping the rich loam soil with coarse gravel, will help discourage the koi from disturbing the soil.

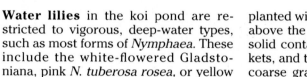

Above: Simple bridges are often the most effective and the closer they are to the water, the better you will be able to observe your koi. This shingle path is contained by rustic logs, travelling across the koi pond and around the garden.

Other features

Other, more ornamental, features will also set the tone and style of your pond and you can choose these to reflect an Oriental or more Western theme. It is important not to overdo the effect with too many ornaments or too large a bridge, for example. Keep any additions in scale and take care they do not detract from the pond itself. Most of these features tend to serve a practical as well as an ornamental purpose.

Bridges create an obvious crossing place but are also a means of enjoying the water mid-pond, as it were. Large, oriental, arched bridges, usually painted red, are for large gardens only; smaller water gardens are better equipped with a small, simple timber-planked design, preferably just skimming the water's surface, and which will lose no points on style if you are trying to recreate a Japanese atmosphere. Alternatively, install a series of staggered timber walkways straight across, or changing direction to zigzag over, a wide stretch of water for equal Oriental panache.

Stepping stones are another popular Japanese device for getting from A to B at a leisurely pace. These large, flat, waterwashed stones or slabs of timber were originally used to lead across grass, moss or gravel, through the garden to the tea house for a formal tea ceremony. They impose a careful, relaxed pace and wider stones encourage a rest and the chance to appreciate a particular focal point or feature. Securely positioned, they make an informal crossing and resting place in the larger water garden.

Other features from the traditional Japanese tea garden have survived as ornamental features: the little stone lanterns, once a means of lighting the garden so that it could be enjoyed at night; the stone buddha enshrined on a stone slab among ferns or leafy evergreens, and the charming *shishi odoshi* – a length of hollow bamboo on a pivot. As water drips through this bamboo tube, the stem is forced downwards to pour its contents into a small stone trough or basin before springing back to hit a strategically placed rock with a distinct 'dock' noise. Frequently employed as a small ornamental water feature, the *shishi odoshi* was once as important as the scarecrow – its purpose to frighten deer away from tasty foliage plants.

If you are hoping to create a water garden with a more Western influence, you should be keeping your eye open for interesting statuary or sculpture to make a special focal point or extra feature. Even plant tubs and containers on the deck or patio should be chosen with a certain

Below: *The* shishi odoshi *is an ornamental Japanese water feature, originally designed to scare animals away from foliage. As the bamboo drains, it springs back with a noise.*

Above: *Used with restraint, Oriental ornaments can look effective beside a koi pond. These stone lanterns are best arranged singly among rocks and foliage.*

emphasis in mind: Versailles tubs for elegance; cut down barrels for rustic charm; terracotta for a Mediterranean feel, or glazed Oriental pots for your bamboos and small *Acers*.

Lighting the water garden

When installing electricity for filters and pumps, don't forget to make provision for lighting, too. Subtle use of outdoor lamps will make a stunning feature of your water garden by night as well as day, to be viewed from the house or enjoyed from the patio when entertaining or indulging in an al fresco dinner. Forget all those garish underwater coloured lights and instead use outdoor spotlights and lamps to highlight trees, shrubs or bold marginal planting whose reflected form in the water's surface will be far more effective. Lamps used to light paths, walkways and bridges are not only functional but also look quite charming beside a reflective pond. Alternatively, string lanterns or fairy lights in the trees, or above a bridge, for party nights. Special features, such as waterfalls, a piece of sculpture, or a particularly fine rock or boulder, can all benefit from being highlighted with a spotlight. You may find some lights are supplied with optional coloured filters; white light is best in most instances, although a blue or green cast is sometimes effective when highlighting foliage plants, for a softer, more subtle effect. Avoid red and yellow filters, however, which add a garish grotto atmosphere to the night scene.

鯉の品種改良

BREEDING KOI

Whether you are an experienced koi-keeper, keen to understand and implement efficient methods of breeding and rearing koi, or simply enjoy watching these beautiful fish in your garden pond, seeing the results of your koi spawning will bring a sense of pride and excitement. Left to themselves, koi will naturally spawn in summertime, and if any of the resulting eggs are to hatch and fry survive, you will need to know what to do. In this section, we look at how to differentiate between the sexes, collect koi eggs without damaging them and successfully incubate them, and how to raise the fry. Later in the section, we examine various methods used in farm culture of koi, including those where man interferes with the koi's biochemistry to dictate where and when the fish releases its eggs.

In these mud ponds in Japan, koi are farmed in huge numbers for an international market.

BREEDING KOI

Sexing koi

It is impossible to sex koi smaller than about 25cm(10in) in length, because they are sexually immature. Once the koi exceed this size, the testes (in males) and ovaries (in females) begin to develop. The ovaries are much larger organs than the testes (see *Koi anatomy*, page 20). Females are usually easier to spot, as the belly of a mature female koi is generally plump, whereas males remain streamlined and more 'torpedo' shaped.

When males are ready for spawning, they develop breeding tubercles on the head and pectoral fins, principally along the bones of the fin rays. These breeding tubercles appear as fine raised spots and could be mistaken for white spot (*Ichthyophthirius*, see *Health Care*, page 102). The tubercles are most profuse on the pectoral fins, where they are quite rough to the touch and arranged in fairly regular rows. They are used during breeding, when the male nudges the female with his head and fins to induce her to spawn.

Spawning

Koi will naturally spawn in the hobbyist pond in the early summer. A water temperature of 20°C (68°F) is ideal, although koi will occasionally spawn at a temperature of 17°C (63°F). As the water in the pond warms, the koi will try to spawn 'en masse'. This is known as flock spawning and, although it can produce very healthy offspring, the quality of the patterns and colour are generally poor.

The female koi deposits her eggs – approximately 100,000 per kilogram of her body weight – over the pond walls, floor and on any plants. Unfortunately, it is very difficult to collect eggs deposited in this random manner in order to incubate them in an environment where they will not be eaten by their parents or attacked by parasites. If left to their own devices, a few of the eggs will hatch and you can then collect the offspring and raise them in an aquarium.

You can, however, ensure the survival of a greater number of eggs by placing artificial spawning ropes in the pond. The koi will deposit their eggs on these in preference to using the hard pond wall. To make these spawning ropes, cut 10cm(4in) lengths of 10-15mm (0.4-0.6in) thick nylon-fibre rope and thread these between the strands of a 120cm(4ft)-piece of the same sort of rope.

As the koi prepare to spawn, you will notice males chasing a female, nudging her side with their mouths. The female will occasionally stop and suck at the sides of the pond in an attempt to clean an area on which she can deposit her

Mature female koi

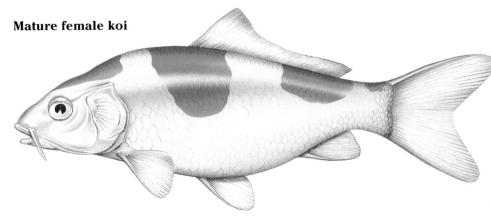

Above: *The pectoral fins of a female koi tend to be smaller than those of a male. During the months of April and May in the second year of life, a female koi develops* ripe ovaries and begins to show secondary sexual characteristics. Her abdomen swells with the egg-filled ovaries, and her vent reddens, becoming slightly swollen.

Mature male koi

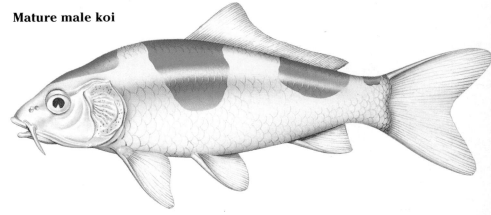

Above: *Secondary sexual characteristics also appear in the male in the second year of life, with the development of long pectoral fins and a rough texture to the gill* covers. (It is vital to distinguish these 'spots' from the signs of white spot disease.) However, there are no outward signs of the testes developing within the fish.

eggs. This is the time to gently lower the spawning ropes into the pond. Spread out the coils of rope into a fanlike shape and anchor them to the side of the pond.

Try to avoid disturbing the fish before and during spawning, but keep a careful eye on them, as the males may bully some females. If this happens, remove the female and place her in a separate pond. Koi may prefer to spawn around dawn but they may also spawn throughout the day. When they have finished spawning, the females hang head down, respiring heavily, and the other fish will become less excited. Gently remove the spawning ropes and carefully place them in a vat for incubation. Koi are not good parents and unless you remove the eggs from the pond quickly, they will begin to eat them. Immature koi may also eat the eggs, so if you want to rear them, you should separate the spawning koi from others in the pond.

Incubating koi eggs

The incubator should have a reasonable capacity – a household water storage

Above: *Spawning ropes are easy to make using a 120cm(4ft) long, stranded nylon rope and several 10cm(4in) lengths. Untwist the strands of the longer piece and thread the shorter lengths through the loops, fraying out the fibres to give as large a surface area as possible on which the thousands of eggs can attach themselves.*

tank (about 450 litres/100 gallons) is ideal – and should, of course, be made of non-toxic materials. It will need a valve-operated water inlet point, and an outlet with as large a surface area as possible, screened with a fine (0.3-0.5mm) stainless steel or plastic mesh. Fine nylon stockings may provide an adequate alternative, although they are less robust.

Lay the ropes out in the vat with 0.2mg/litre malachite green solution to stop fungus (*Saprolegnia*) from attacking dead eggs and spreading infection to living eggs. Place three lengths of string across the vat to keep the ropes 5cm(2in) below water level. Do not add any more water at this stage, but place an airstone on the floor of the vat to gently and continuously aerate the water, as developing eggs need plenty of oxygen. When you begin to see the growing koi's eyes in the egg – after one or two days – run a fine trickle of water into the incubation vat. The day before the koi hatches, the eyes in the egg will have a shine to them. Soon afterwards, the young koi will begin to wriggle then, gradually, over the next few hours, it will break out of its 'shell'. It will take three to four days for the koi eggs to develop and the fry to hatch at temperatures of 20-22°C(68-71°F). Koi fry can develop at temperatures as low as 17°C(63°F), in which case their incubation will take five or six days, or as high as 25°C(77°F), which will decrease their hatching time. However, there is a greater chance of the fry being deformed at such extreme temperatures.

An incubator for koi eggs

Below: *A household water storage tank (with a capacity of approximately 450 litres/100 gallons) is easily converted into a suitable incubator for koi eggs. Transfer the spawning ropes, on which the eggs will have attached themselves, into this tank as soon as spawning has taken place, as adult koi are prone to eating their own eggs.*

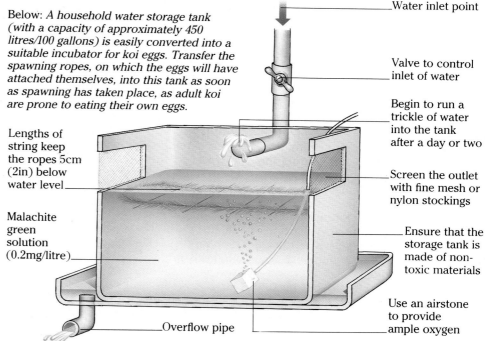

Water inlet point

Valve to control inlet of water

Begin to run a trickle of water into the tank after a day or two

Screen the outlet with fine mesh or nylon stockings

Ensure that the storage tank is made of non-toxic materials

Use an airstone to provide ample oxygen

Lengths of string keep the ropes 5cm (2in) below water level

Malachite green solution (0.2mg/litre)

Overflow pipe

Development and growth of fry

When the fry have hatched, they will instinctively seek shelter and hide in any cover they can find. The spawning ropes are ideal for this. Using a special sticky pad on their heads, the fry attach themselves to the ropes' fronds, or to the vat wall. At this stage in their development, the young koi have no swimbladder, mouth or vent. They breathe by absorbing oxygen through the fine blood capillaries that surround the yolk sac, which is still attached to the gut. It is essential that there is plenty of oxygen entering the water at this stage, as a reduction in the quantity of dissolved oxygen in the incubator could lead to mass mortality.

The koi fry have only one fin, which encircles the posterior end of the body. As the koi grow, feeding on their yolk sacs until all the yolk is utilized, they develop paired fins, a mouth and other organs. After two or three days, the young koi swim up to the surface and take two or three gulps of air, which they force into their swimbladder. They then start to swim freely in mid water, usually congregating around the airstones – a sign that they are ready to be fed.

First feeding

Koi fry at the 'swim up' stage do not have any developed taste buds and so must detect their food by sight. Therefore, they need to have food all around them. Hard-boiled egg yolk is an ideal food for the first day or so – this has very little dietary value, but will increase the size of

Left: *This sequence shows the stages of development of the koi egg and young fry, from the newly laid egg to the three- or four-week-old fry, ready for release into growing-on facilities. The eyes first become apparent after one or two days (5) and a day or so later will develop a shine (6). Shortly after this, the fry will break out of its 'shell' and attach itself to the spawning rope, using a sticky pad on its head.*

The development of the koi egg and fry

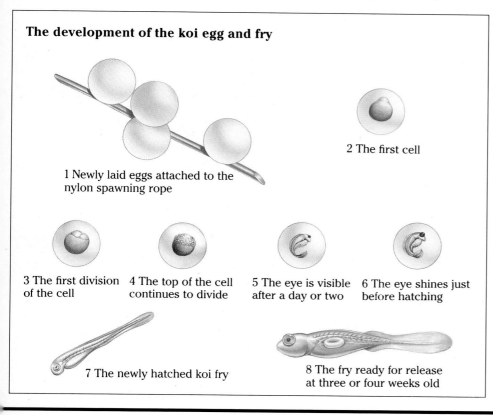

1 Newly laid eggs attached to the nylon spawning rope

2 The first cell

3 The first division of the cell

4 The top of the cell continues to divide

5 The eye is visible after a day or two

6 The eye shines just before hatching

7 The newly hatched koi fry

8 The fry ready for release at three or four weeks old

BREEDING KOI

the stomach. Newly hatched brine-shrimp (*Artemia salina*) larvae are also a good food source for young koi fry. Start feeding the brineshrimp when the koi are about one week old. After another week or so, the koi will be ready for a mash diet (the powder dust that is left after the manufacturing process of fish food). From this time onwards, feed the koi food of a size that can be taken by the smallest fish in the vat.

You will need to remove accumulated debris and waste frequently during this first feeding stage. A siphon made from aeration tubing is ideal for removing settled and suspended waste from the incubator, and an old toothbrush is useful to clean the outlet screen. You should also add fresh water regularly to the vat to remove nitrates and ammonia. Tap water, which contains high concentrations of chlorine, should be aerated before it is added to the vat, to allow the chlorine to evaporate. After three or four weeks, the fry will have grown to 5-10mm(0.2-0.4in) in length and will be starting to take larger quantities of more generously sized foods.

Growing on

At this stage, move the koi to a growing-on facility, such as an aquarium, tank or pond. Watch the young koi carefully, as cannibalism is not uncommon. If you suspect this, remove any larger fry to another tank. You can heat this to 20-25°C(68-77°F) to provide faster growth rates, but be careful; if koi grow too fast, they lose their colour. One-month-old koi need about five percent of their body weight in food and should be fed little and often. As they grow, koi need less food – about two percent of body weight at 15cm(6in) or larger. The size of pelleted food is critical; not all fish grow at the same rate and it is too easy to look at the larger koi and select the pellet size to suit them, forgetting the smaller fish. Unfortunately, koi that are nearer to the common carp in appearance grow faster than the prettier koi. This is because nishiki-goi are highly inbred – that is, they are mated with other koi to which they are closely related, such as either parents or siblings – and, as with any highly inbred animals, nishikigoi are not as hardy as their wild counterparts.

Right: Although not generally favoured in Japan, these ponds are commonly used for breeding koi elsewhere in the world. Both the Dubisch and Hofer types rely on the cultivation of grass as a spawning medium on the elevated section of the pond. The koi are introduced to the pond when the water is 45cm (18in) deep and the level is then raised to induce the koi to spawn.

Farm culture of koi carp

Koi have been grown for food for over 2000 years in China, where they were cultivated in earth ponds and became a vital source of protein in the leaner winter months. Interestingly, similar breeding techniques have developed in Asia and Europe (the native home of carp) and, indeed, wherever koi have been artificially reared. Over the last century, culture methods have progressed remarkably with the discovery and use of hormones and induced spawning. In the rest of this section, we look at methods of breeding koi that are used by professional koi-breeders throughout the world. Some of these methods are only practical where large numbers of koi are being spawned. Other methods rely on the use of hormones, and such techniques are best left to experts, as the drugs used will interfere with the metabolism of the treated fish and misuse may result in the death of the parent, or malformed offspring.

Dubisch and Hofer ponds

These small ponds, about 100m² and 0.3m deep (1076ft² x 1ft) were devised in the 19th century for spawning and rearing carp. The original design by Dubisch was later modified by another fish farmer, Hofer. Around the edge of the Dubisch pond is a ditch, 15cm(6in) deeper than the rest of the pond, which allows the fish swimming space. The Hofer type has a ditch only along one side, and the elevated section slopes gently towards the ditch. Both types of

pond use the same drainage system, known as a 'monk' after the monastic people who invented it centuries ago. This is a three-sided box, open at one end and with a pipe at the lowest point of the middle wall. A series of boards, placed in the open end, regulate the water level, and vertical metal bars in front of the boards prevent the fish from swimming out of the pond.

Both systems rely on the cultivation of grass, used by the fish as a spawning medium, on the elevated section of the ponds. Before flooding, the drained ditch is cleaned of all debris. The pond water, which is checked for purity, is continuously aerated to saturate it with oxygen. Koi are very sensitive to rapid changes in temperature, so the time at which the pond is filled and the adult koi introduced is critical to reduce the possibility of such fluctuations. The adult fish are placed in the pond when the water has reached a depth of 45cm(18in) and a temperature of between 18°C and 22°C(64-72°F). The water level is then raised gradually in an attempt to induce the koi to spawn. The water level should be maintained at a height just covering the grasses, with a constant trickle of water flowing through the pond.

After a few days, the koi will be triggered to spawn, and the parents are removed from the pond a day later to prevent egg-eating or spreading of disease to the fry. Under favourable conditions, about 50 percent of the eggs will hatch. At temperatures of 18-20°C(64-68°F), the eggs take two to three days to 'eye up'

Dubisch breeding pond

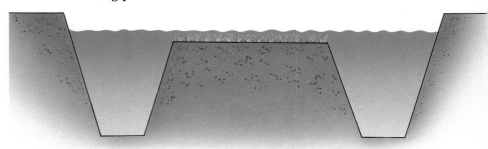

Hofer breeding pond

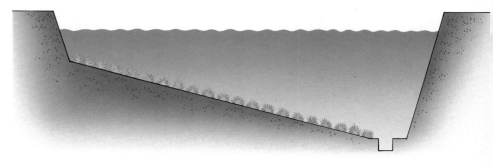

and four to six days to hatch, and at 21-25°C(70-77°F), about one to two days and three to four days respectively. After another two to four days, the fry are ready to be moved to growing-on facilities. The water level is slowly lowered so that the fry gather around the ditch. Here, the farmers can collect them easily using a fine net. Rough handling at this stage can cause damage, which may deform the koi or even kill them.

Dubisch and Hofer ponds are not generally favoured by koi farmers in Japan, probably because of the higher water temperatures there.

Using spawning ropes
This method has been used for many years and is the main technique employed by the Japanese for the propagation of koi. Spawning nets are suspended in the pond, which is usually 30m^2(330ft^2) and 90cm(3ft) deep, is filled with water to a depth of 25-30cm(10-12in). Airstones are used to provide maximum saturation of oxygen. The female koi and then two males are placed in the pond, together with 10 spawning ropes (or 15 for a large fish), placed evenly over the pond.

Usually the fish begin spawning at about four o'clock in the morning and they may spawn again at the same time the following day. The female will suck at the ropes to prepare them for laying her eggs and the males will nudge her abdomen, inducing her to release the eggs. She will then rush through the pond, with the males in pursuit, leaving a green cloud of eggs, which the males will fertilize with a white cloud of sperm.

When the fish have finished spawning, the ropes are removed and placed in a pond of water containing a 0.2mg/litre malachite green solution. The parents are then removed from the pond, malachite green is added at 0.2mg/litre, and the spawning ropes are replaced. The aeration is kept on, but the water supply is turned off. As soon as the eggs start to 'eye up', a gentle trickle of water is added to remove the ammonia and nitrates, which will be produced as a byproduct of the developing eggs.

The eggs hatch after three to five days and the fry gather around the spawning ropes. Once all the fry have filled their swimbladders – two or three days after hatching – they will crowd around the airstones. They are then placed into growing-on facilities.

Using pituitary hormone injections
This modern method is not recommended for use by the inexperienced hobbyist as it interferes with the fish's

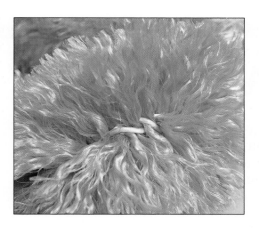

Above: *Spawning ropes are used by amateur and professional koi-breeders. This is a commercial one, but they are easy to make.*

natural hormone levels. Spawning is induced with an injection of a hormone called gonadotropin, which is extracted from the pituitary gland of a donor fish's brain. The pituitary gland stores the gonadotropin hormone and this acts as a messenger between the gonads (ovaries in females and testes in males) and the brain. Release of the hormone is triggered by increasing day length and rise in temperature. In females, the hormone will only stimulate the ovulation and release of the eggs if they are in a ripe condition. In the wild state, a koi is able to regulate its own level of hormone and release it at the right time. Unfortunately, it is hard for the koi-breeder to regulate the precise time of spawning, and the usual time – about four o'clock in the morning – is not ideal for the hobbyist. With hormone-induced spawning, it is possible to determine both the time of year and the hour at which the eggs are released. However, the koi farmer will have to 'strip' the koi of eggs and milt

(sperm), as explained below.

The koi are removed from the pond and placed in a tank containing water at the same temperature. The temperature is then raised 1°C every day until it reaches 22-25°C(71-77°F). The fish are then kept in water at that temperature for 1000°C days, that is, at 25°C(74°F) for 40 days. The male and female are then injected with a solution of pituitary hormones, each fish receiving 0.3mg of acetone-dried pituitary per kilogram of body weight. (Each whole pituitary weighs on average 2.5-3mg.) Twenty four hours later, the female only is given a decisive dose of 3mg per kilogram of body weight, and ten hours after this the koi are ready to be stripped.

It is advisable to have the fish anaesthetized before hand stripping; this relaxes the koi and helps the eggs to flow. The fish is wrapped in a slightly damp towel, leaving the vent clear. Holding the anal fin against a clean dry bowl, a gentle pressure is then applied to the abdomen to release the eggs from the vent. No excess pressure should be applied to force the eggs out. Sperm from the male fish is collected in the same way, and spread over the eggs. A fertilization solution made up of urea and sodium chloride dissolved in distilled water is then added to the bowl and the eggs are gently agitated, either by stirring the solution with a feather or by aerating it gently for three to five minutes. About 40-45 minutes after the koi have been stripped, milk is added to the solution to prevent the eggs from sticking together and the eggs are placed in a glass jar, where they hatch in water at 23°C(74°F). The jar is then emptied into a tank. When the fry have filled their swimbladders with air, they are ready for release into growing-on ponds.

Above: *Netting koi from a growing-on lake after the summer season has*

finished. The best fish selected from these are destined for dealers' ponds.

HEALTH CARE

During the course of its life, a koi may receive an injury, act as host to any one of a number of parasites, or fall ill. With a basic understanding of koi anatomy and some knowledge of health care, you will be equipped to treat some of the misfortunes that may occasionally befall your fish. In this section, we consider the subject of health care in five areas: first-aid and injuries, anaesthetics, parasites, diseases, and environmentally related disorders – including stress in general.

Before starting to consider health care practices, however, we should offer a few words of caution. Although there are no hard and fast rules governing when to treat koi or when to leave them alone, it does far more harm than good to keep netting koi to check them over for possible problems. Sometimes, however, they do require medical attention. If in doubt, consult someone with experience in fish health to come and see the koi in your pond; it is often more beneficial to see the afflicted fish in its own environment rather than trying to determine whether a highly stressed fish in a plastic bag is ailing. Like any other animal, a sick fish is best treated at home if possible; moving it around will only stress it further and reduce its ability to fight off illness. Finally, before rushing off to consult someone about a sick fish, check the water quality in the pond; it is always possible that ammonia or nitrite levels are too high.

A koi losing buoyancy in a treatment salt dip; it should recover quickly on being returned to the pond.

HEALTH CARE

First-aid and injuries

A first-aid kit is essential to treat any injuries that koi are likely to incur. Ideally, this should include a sharp pair of scissors, a pair of tweezers with rounded tips, cotton buds, an antiseptic cream or lotion, and a towel in which to wrap the koi when treating it. You should be able to treat koi up to 30cm(12in) long without resorting to the use of anaesthetics; larger fishes are difficult to hold and treat and so usually need to be anaesthetized (see below). Always wrap koi under treatment securely in a towel dampened in pond water. Make sure that your hands, too, are wet before handling koi – dry hands stick to the scales, pulling them out and leaving ugly scars until new scales grow.

Many brands of antiseptic cream are available, all equally effective in the treatment of wounds, but it is best to select one with an oil base since this will not dissolve so easily when the koi is returned to the pond. Several antiseptic lotions are also used in treating wounds. These include malachite green, povidone iodine, potassium permanganate, methylene blue and mercurochrome. Koi-keepers usually have their own preference, but it is worth noting that mercurochrome, which has a mercury base, is highly toxic to humans. Wear protective gloves when using this treatment and wash off any splashes immediately with plenty of water.

As a caring koi-keeper, you should go to great lengths to ensure that there are no sharp projections or obstructions in the pond on which your fishes could damage themselves. Despite these precautions, some fishes will still sustain injuries. Koi use the lateral line organ (see page 17) to detect any projection or obstruction in the pond, but they will periodically rub themselves against submerged objects, an action known as 'flicking'. This behaviour is frequently seen after feeding and is probably associated with cleaning their bodies. It may also be seen when the fish has some skin irritation, such as that caused by a parasite. As you might imagine, flicking can easily lead to a superficial cut on the body. Similarly, koi will jump from time to time, either from sheer 'joie de vivre' or from irritation caused by a parasite. Such blind leaps can end in disaster, since the koi may leap into a projection above the pond, or even out of the water and onto the surrounding area.

Damage is usually superficial, but it is better to take some simple first-aid precautions to prevent the koi suffering a secondary bacterial infection. If the wound is on the body, clean the area with a cotton bud and apply antiseptic cream or lotion. Lotions are best applied by dipping a cotton bud into the solution and painting it, neat, onto the affected area. If the wound is in the region of the head or gills, use cream; antiseptic lotions are more likely to run into, and damage, sensitive areas such as the gills, eyes and nostrils.

If the koi only bruises itself, this is seen as blood beneath a number of scales, which may also be raised. If the bleeding has been slight and the scales are not raised, it is best to leave the injury to heal on its own. Should the bleeding be heavy enough to raise the scales, be sure to treat the fish, since such bruising can become a focus of infection, resulting in a hole developing. Express the blood by carefully raising the scale with a needle and, keeping it in close contact with the scale, gently puncture the skin of each one that is affected. Using slight pressure on the affected area, squeeze the congealed blood through the perforation made by the needle. Finally, treat the whole area with an antiseptic lotion. Bruising may also occur if koi are badly netted or handled. If the bruising is severe, treat it as described above. Take great care not to worsen existing injuries or create new damage when catching koi and removing them from the pond.

Occasionally, koi will jump right out of the pond onto the surrounding area. If the fish has recently jumped out and is still actively thrashing, simply return it to the pond. If it is still breathing but slightly laboured, it is worth treating it to a 10-minute, well-aerated salt bath before returning it to the pond. Make up the salt bath by dissolving 20gm of cooking salt per litre of pond water in a separate container. This makes a 2 percent solution. (On a larger scale you can dissolve 1kg of salt in 50 litres of water, or approximately 2.2lb in 11 gallons). As a result of stress, and a prolonged exposure to an alien environment (i.e. being out of the water), the fish will be susceptible to secondary fungal and/or bacterial infections. The salt bath should help to prevent any fungal spores or bacteria from colonizing the koi's protective mucus.

These photographs show basic first-aid and treatment techniques. Do not attempt any of these procedures unless you are qualified or experienced. The top row from the left shows an anaesthetized koi about to be wrapped up in a wet towel, cleaning the damaged area with a cotton bud and then applying mercurochrome lotion. Always use mercurochrome with care and, ideally, wear gloves. The bottom row shows the application of a waterproof ointment to protect and further sterilize the area, and then attending to another lesion.

Above: *Salt baths can be a very effective way of controlling parasites such as* Ichthyobodo *and* Trichodina. *(See the table on pages 112-113 for concentrations). Note the use of an airstone to aerate the water.*

Koi can often be successfully resuscitated, even when they appear to be dead. Before casting the 'corpse' away, take a close look at it. Look for the slightest movement of the skin surrounding the operculum, or gill cover, turn the fish upside down and watch the eye closely to see if it rolls, and check the mouth – it may gape in a last desperate attempt to breathe. The koi is literally suffocating when it is out of water. In the water, the delicate gill filaments are able to absorb oxygen because they are separated as they literally 'float' in the respiratory current. Out of the water, the gill filaments stick together, immediately reducing the respiratory surface, and as they start to dry out, the mucus on them congeals. This damage to the gills is a problem which may need to be resolved after the fish has been resuscitated.

The heart continues to beat even for some hours after a koi stops showing any sign of life. To resuscitate the fish, take hold of the section of the body between the caudal fin and the dorsal and anal fins – known as the caudal peduncle – and pull the koi firmly but gently backwards not more than about 30cm(12in). This action forces water under the opercula, over the gills and out through the mouth. Then push the fish forwards so that the water forces the opercula closed. Ideally, resuscitate the koi where air is being pumped into the pond, such as alongside a venturi. Continue this action until the fish can breathe regularly on its own.

This could take two or more hours, depending on the size of the fish.

Once the fish is able to breathe on its own, place it in a floating basket or bowl containing pond water, with an air supply from an aquarium pump and leave it. At this stage, the koi will be on its side. When the koi is upright, which may take several hours, release it into the pond. Over the next few days, pay particular attention to this koi. The fish may still succumb to a fungal infection but, hopefully, will make a complete recovery.

Anaesthetics

Anaesthetics are drugs whose effect is to produce insensibility to touch and pain. The only purposes for anaesthetizing a koi should be to inject it, treat it or to perform surgery. Anaesthetics have also been used to subdue koi when transporting them, but this is an inadvisable and risky practice, since the fishes are likely to become comatose and die. If all possible preparations and precautions are taken (see *Buying koi*, page 61), there should be no need to anaesthetize koi when transporting them.

The range and availability of anaesthetics varies from country to country, as do the regulations about their use. The chemicals used as fish anaesthetics include benzocaine, quinaldine and ethyl-m-aminobenzoate (MS 222). If you are not qualified and/or experienced in using anaesthetics, always consult a veterinarian or qualified expert. The following notes are offered for general guidance only and must be interpreted in the light of your local situation and regulations, plus your own qualification and/or experience of dealing with fish.

While the use of anaesthetics is some-times necessary, none of them is completely safe; even at the recommended doses, it is extremely easy to over anaesthetize a koi, from which recovery is rare. Occasionally, you may find a koi that is allergic to the chosen anaesthetic. Unfortunately, there is no way of knowing before immersing the fish whether it will be sensitive to the drug. A sensitive koi will respond instantly by losing all mobility, and this can have fatal results unless you remove it immediately.

Before mixing the anaesthetic with the pond water (in a separate container), ensure that you are prepared for treating the koi; have the first-aid kit immediately to hand and the wet towel ready to receive the fish. If you have never anaesthetized a fish before, it is a good idea to watch over the shoulder of someone experienced with the technique before trying it for yourself. If the fish is very large (over 45cm/18in long), use a large, floating bowl. Place it in the pond, fill it to the required level with pond water and add the necessary amount of anaesthetic. Once the koi has been netted, 'swim' it towards the bowl and tip it to receive the fish. You will probably need to lift the koi over the inclined edge of the bowl, to avoid tipping any of the anaesthetic into the pond. You can net smaller fishes into a floating basket and then lift them (with wet hands) into the receptacle containing the anaesthetic. You can also anaesthetize a koi in a plastic bag, but it is difficult to get it out quickly if it reacts adversely to the anaesthetic.

Having placed the koi into the anaesthetic, watch it all the time. At first, it will open and close its mouth rapidly, as though it has swallowed something distasteful, and may well thrash about for a minute or so before becoming subdued. Gently push the fish over onto its side and hold it there; if it struggles, leave it in the anaesthetic until it stops pushing against your hand, then lift it out of the anaesthetic and wrap it in the wet towel.

Above: *Koi being anaesthetized. Once on its side, remove each koi and wrap it in a towel moistened with pond water. Do not attempt this if you are not experienced and never leave fish unattended in an anaesthetic.*

HEALTH CARE

Once the fish is anaesthetized, the opercular movements are greatly reduced although still discernible. A lightly anaesthetized or sedated koi will still be slightly responsive; wrapping it in the towel will help to hold it still and also prevent any further injuries should it struggle while it is out of the water.

Once you have completed the treatment, bring the koi round by placing it in a floating basket in the pond. Usually, the anaesthetic-free water is sufficient to revive the fish, but sometimes you may need to place it in the air flow from the venturi to aid its recovery. Not all fishes react in the same way to anaesthetics – some will 'go down' very rapidly, while others take an exceptionally long time to react and then recover more slowly.

Parasites

A parasite is an organism that lives on or inside another organism, termed the host, and benefits from the association, usually by feeding off the host. The host does not benefit and, indeed, the presence of a parasite is usually harmful. Koi can be host to a wide variety of parasites, ranging from tiny single-celled organisms (protozoans) to large, visible ones, such as fish lice, leeches and 'worms'. As there are so many different parasites to consider, we examine them here according to their biological category, starting with protozoans.

Protozoan parasites

Protozoans are tiny, single-celled organisms, the very largest of which is less than 1mm(0.04in) across and just visible to the naked eye. There are many different types of protozoans, most of which are free living in damp and watery environments, where they feed on dissolved nutrients or tiny particles, including bacteria. The parasitic protozoans infect a variety of hosts, including fishes, where they can reproduce rapidly and form large populations, either remaining in or on an individiual fish or spreading to the remainder of the stock. Of the many protozoans detrimental to fish health, some affect a wide range of fish species while others are host specific, i.e. they occur only on one type of fish. Here, we look at a number of conditions caused by protozoans that can affect koi.

Sliminess of the skin

The common name of this condition aptly describes the chief sign of infection, a greyish white film of excess mucus on the body. This is the skin's reaction to the presence of a range of irritating protozoan parasites, notably *Ichthyobodo*, *Trichodina* and *Chilodonella*.

Above: *A tancho koi suffering from an infestation with* Ichthyobodo. *These flagellate protozoans feed on skin cells and cause a whitish grey film as the fish produces excess mucus as a response. The skin also becomes slightly inflamed.*

Ichthyobodo (formerly known as *Costia*) is a very small, bean-shaped protozoan parasite that moves around using long whiplike threads called flagella. It moves around the body and gills of the fish, feeding on the skin cells. In the early stages of infection, *Ichthyobodo* invades the pockets of skin at the bases of the scales. As their numbers increase, the parasites move onto all parts of the body, including the gills. In addition to the whitish film on the body, the signs shown by koi infected with *Ichthyobodo* include scratching and leaping, followed by failure to feed and lethargy. *Ichthyobodo* has a wide temperature tolerance of at least 2-29°C(36-84°F), although recent reports show that it has a much higher temperature tolerance than this, being able to reproduce at 38°C(100°F). Like other protozoans, *Ichthyobodo* is particularly active in the early spring, increasing in numbers while koi are still recovering from the winter. Because it infects the scale pockets, it is difficult for the koi to eradicate. The main problems associated with an infection by this organism are the secondary bacterial and fungal infections that invariably occur as a result of the damage caused.

Trichodina and other trichodinid parasites are probably among the most familiar protozoans to the koi-keeper. These saucer-shaped organisms have distinctive rings of tiny hairs (cilia) around the body which enable the cell organism to move. (These cilia are clearly visible at a magnification of x100-200 through a microscope.) Koi infected by *Trichodina* develop the familiar grey film over the body in response to the infestation. This excess mucus simply encourages the *Trichodina* to reproduce at a faster rate. Trichodinids are found on even the most healthy koi, but if the fish is diseased or in poor condition, they reproduce unchecked and allow secondary baterial infections to occur. Trichodinids can also

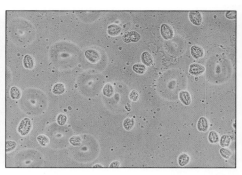

Above: *A microscope view of* Chilodonella, *a common cause of sliminess of the skin. It is particularly common on injured or weakened fish. Each of these ciliate protozoans is about 50 microns across. (A micron is a thousandth of a millimetre).*

infect the gills, where damage to the delicate filaments makes the gills susceptible to bacterial infection. In the early stages of infection, koi repeatedly scratch themselves and leap out of the water. As the infection progresses, the fish stop feeding and hang at the surface, usually where air enters the pond. They may be seen to gasp and frequently gulp air at the surface. At this stage, there is very little chance that an infected koi will survive, even with treatment.

The protozoan *Chilodonella* looks rather like a tiny gooseberry and is found on the fins, body and gills, where it feeds on skin cells. *Chilodonella* reproduces very rapidly in the early spring, when the koi are still rather lethargic, allowing the infestation to become well-established before the fish can groom them off. Koi affected by *Chilodonella* have the usual signs of a grey-white film on the body, plus the typical behaviour pattern of scratching, leaping, followed by lethargy. Left untreated, affected koi will die. *Chilodonella* is usually associated with fish that are already weakened by stress or disease and is often found together with bacterial and fungal infections.

White spot (Ich)

White spot is familiar to everyone who keeps fish. It is caused by a protozoan with the scientific name of *Ichthyophthirius multifiliis*, hence the alternative common name of 'ich'. White spot has a very complicated life cycle and spreads rapidly through a fish population. The white spots on the skin, fins and gills are individual protozoan cells that become enclosed between the epidermal cells of the fish and feed on the body fluids and cells. They 'mature' at about 1mm(0.04in) across and 'punch' out of the skin and fall away from the fish. Within a few hours, they settle in the pond, form into a cyst and inside begin dividing to produce a thousand or more

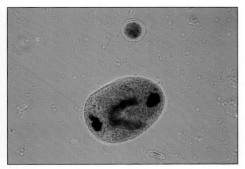

Above: *A single mature cell of the protozoan parasite* Ichthyophthirius multifiliis *that causes white spot disease in koi and a wide range of other fish. Special staining clearly reveals the characteristically curved nucleus. Each cell matures at 1mm (0.04in).*

Right: *1 Individual cells beneath the skin. 2 Mature parasites 'punch' out and swim away. 3 Parasites become enclosed in a gelatinous capsule. 4 Each cell divides to form 1000 or more infective stages. 5 'Swarmers' must find a host in 24 hours.*

White spot disease cycle

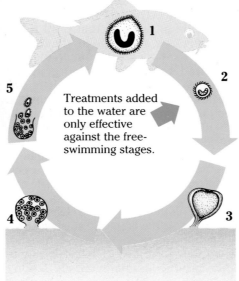

Treatments added to the water are only effective against the free-swimming stages.

tiny infective stages. When these free-swimming 'swarmers' break out of the cysts, they must find a fish host within about 24 hours in order to survive. They are well equipped to penetrate the skin or gills of any fishes on which they settle and quickly establish themselves to start the infection cycle again.

As well as showing the typical white spots, infected koi tend to scratch and swim into the water inlet. As the infection progresses, they stop feeding, become lethargic and often discoloured. Left untreated, white spot is fatal. Fortunately, effective commercial white spot remedies are widely available.

Nodular disease
The last strictly parasitic protozoan included here is *Myxobolus*, the most important feature of which is that it produces spores, which are very resistant to chemical treatment. *Myxobolus* infects

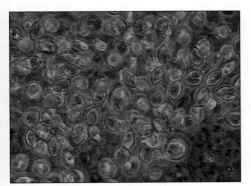

Above: Myxobolus *spores collected from an infected fish and photographed at a magnification of x200. These spores are released from nodules that form within the tissues. The infection can spread between fish in a number of different ways.*

koi internally, where the parasites invade the gut or muscle. Thousands of tiny spores form inside cysts and, once released into the water (in a number of ways, including from the decomposed bodies of dead fish), it is these that spread the parasites to other koi, although the precise details of the life cycles of these parasites are poorly understood. Koi suffering from nodular disease (named from the 'nodules' that the cysts produce) lose weight and become lethargic, showing symptoms very similar to those produced by the bacterium causing tuberculosis (see page 109). There is no cure for infected koi and those fish known to be suffering from heavy infestations of this parasite are best disposed of humanely before the infection spreads throughout the remaining fish.

Opportunistic protozoan infections
A number of protozoans colonize koi without being strictly parasitic. Notable among these are the so-called 'bell animalcules', scientifically known as the Peritrichida (literally meaning 'hairy mouthed'). Around the mouth there is a fringe of tiny hairs that waft microscopic food particles into the hungry bell animalcule. The food particles are usually bacteria or tiny pieces of organic debris, so these protozoans are very common in biological filters. When affecting koi, the bell animalcules are found near ulcers or damage on the body, where they feed on bacteria infecting the wound. Alternatively, they may also be found on the fins, busily feeding on the bacteria responsible for causing finrot (see page 109).

Protozoans of this type include *Vorticella*, *Epistylis*, *Carchesium* and *Apiosoma*. *Vorticella* has a bell-shaped 'body' on a long spiral stalk. When feeding, the stalk is very long as the organism 'stretches out' to reach food particles. It is a solitary organism but occurs in large groups of individuals. *Epistylis* and *Carchesium* are both colonial organisms. Their bell-shaped bodies are able to lengthen or shorten and are located at the tips of branched, twiglike stalks. *Apiosoma* is rather more funnel-shaped and sits on a short, fat stalk. Like *Vorticella*, it is solitary but occurs in groups of large numbers. In addition to bacteria, *Apiosoma* also feeds on other protozoans smaller than itself.

Thus, these bell animalcules are not truly parasitic but opportunistic, appearing as whitish patches (often tinged green with algae) on koi that are already damaged or infected by bacteria.

Above: *Groups of* Apiosoma *protozoans clinging to a gill filament. Each cell reaches about 100 microns (thousandths of a millimetre) long. In large numbers, these opportunistic ciliates can block the gills and cause respiratory distress.*

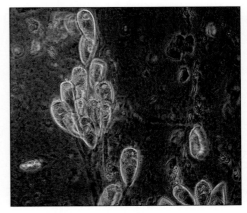

Above: *These* Scyphidia *are very similar protozoans to* Apiosoma. *This microscope view clearly shows the typical flask shape of these cells, each with a terminal ciliated 'mouth' that strains out organic debris and microorganisms from the water.*

HEALTH CARE

Crustacean parasites

Crustaceans are jointed-limbed invertebrates that encompass a huge range of creatures, from crabs to 'water fleas' (*Daphnia*). Many are free-living aquatic species that pass through several larval stages during their reproductive life cycles. The majority are harmless to koi and other fish, but some species have developed a specialized parasitic way of life and can pose serious health problems if they occur in large numbers. Here, we look at the most common of these crustacean parasites.

Anchor worm

One of the most notorious crustacean parasites that infest fish is the anchor worm, *Lernaea*. There are several species of anchor worm, all of which are parasitic on fish. The complete life cycle of the anchor worm takes 17-33 days, depending on the temperature. At 20°C(68°F), for example, the cycle takes 25 days; below 15°C(59°F) it may not complete at all. The newly hatched anchor worm, or nauplius, is elliptical in shape and free swimming in the pond water. The nauplius moults into a second stage (the metanauplius), which is also free swimming. Subsequent juvenile stages are parasitic and must find a fish host, where they settle on the gills. When these juveniles mature into adults, the males mate with the females and then become nonparasitic and leave the host.

The fertilized females leave the gills and settle on the body of the koi, where they continue to grow, gradually losing their crustacean features and becoming

Anchor worm life cycle

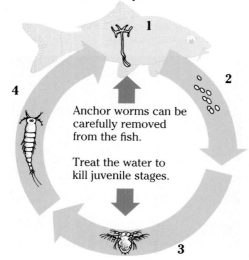

Above: *1 Adult female anchor worm embedded in skin. 2 Eggs released into the water from mature egg sacs. 3 First free-living juvenile stage. 4 Later juvenile stages are parasitic. When mature, the adults mate and the female develops a wormlike shape.*

elongated and 'wormlike' in shape. At the same time, they burrow deep into the skin and underlying tissues, developing anchorlike processes that hold them firmly in place. At this point, the mature anchor worms are clearly visible attached to the fish, being up to 20mm(0.8in) long, depending on species. Digestive juices secreted by the anchor worms enable them to draw in and feed on dissolved body tissues. The nutrients received from feeding on the koi are used to produce eggs, visible as twin white egg sacs at the posterior end of the mature female. A single female can produce several thousand eggs in her lifespan. As these eggs are released into the water, so the life cycle starts again.

Anchor worms are usually seen on koi when they have been feeding for some time, producing characteristic bloody spots that are highly prone to secondary infection by bacteria or fungi. And if an anchor worm dies while still attached to the koi, bacteria and/or fungi will readily invade the dead parasite's tissues and then spread to the koi. In fact, anchor worms are probably one of the biggest culprits in causing holes on the body.

Fish lice and gill maggots

The fish louse, *Argulus*, is yet another type of parasitic crustacean familiar to fishkeepers. Both male and female fish lice are parasitic on the body and gills of koi. Up to 10mm(0.4in) across, the fish louse has a distinct round shape, with two prominent, disc-shaped suckers on the underside. (Looking at microscope views of fish lice, these suckers appear at first glance like two eyes, but the eyes are smaller black dots located further forward on the head.) Each sucker is hard, being made of a substance very similar to the exoskeleton of insects. They allow

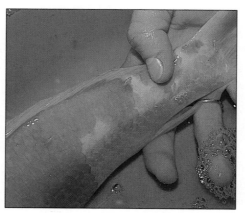

Above: *An anchor worm is clearly visible clinging to the tail region of this koi. These crustacean parasites can be quite deeply embedded in the body wall and underlying tissues, causing wounds that often become secondarily infected with fungi and bacteria.*

Fish lice life cycle

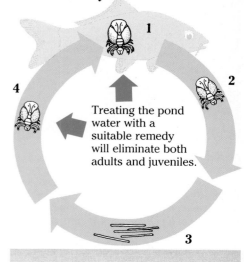

Above: *1 Adult lice clinging to skin by means of suckers. 2 Mature females leave fish to lay eggs. 3 Eggs are laid in long gelatinous capsules. 4 Juveniles pass through several stages before becoming adult.*

Above: *This close view of the underside of a fish lice* (Argulus) *clearly shows the feathery crustacean legs and the two prominent suckers, with the smaller, darker eyes further forward. These parasites grow to a maximum size of about 10mm(0.4in).*

the fish louse to stick onto the koi's body and help it to glide around on the layer of mucus. Fish lice are very adept swimmers; when brushed off the surface of a koi, they simply swim around until they find another fish. Between the suckers are needlelike mouthparts that the fish louse inserts through the koi's skin. Glands produce a toxin that flows down the hollow 'needles' and the louse breaks up the affected tissue using a sawing action of the mouthparts. Where a fish louse has been feeding, a prominent red welt develops on the koi's body.

Not surprisingly, fish lice cause intense irritation to koi, and they may show outward signs similar to those resulting from infestation with protozoan parasites, i.e. scratching followed by jumping. Affected koi may also show weight loss, since they

Gill maggot life cycle

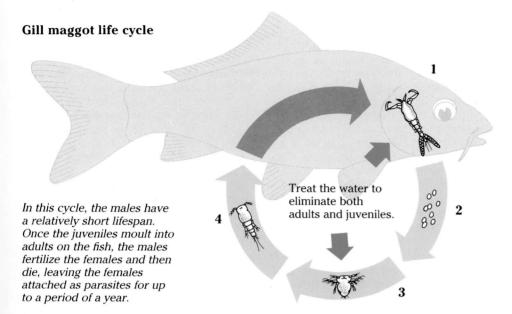

In this cycle, the males have a relatively short lifespan. Once the juveniles moult into adults on the fish, the males fertilize the females and then die, leaving the females attached as parasites for up to a period of a year.

Treat the water to eliminate both adults and juveniles.

Above: *1 Parasitic females attached to the gills. 2 Eggs are released into the water from the prominent white egg sacs. 3 Eggs hatch into free-living juveniles. 4 Later juveniles must find a host fish to survive.*

are distracted from feeding by the fish lice and, left untreated, the presence of these parasites will retard the growth of the fish. The damage caused by fish lice is often a prime target for secondary infection by bacteria or fungi. If they infect the gills, the damage they cause is very severe, resulting in respiratory distress and often leading to secondary infection by bacteria. Fish lice can also transmit disease from fish to fish in a population, including protozoan parasites, various bacterial infections and spring viraemia of carp (see page 108).

The term 'gill maggots' refers to the mature females of the parasitic crustacean *Ergasilus*, with their distinctive maggotlike, white egg sacs. (The males are not parasitic, dying very soon after mating.) The females are found on the body and fins, but principally on the gills of affected fish. The first pair of legs are modified into grasping organs, with prominent hooks that enable the parasites to grasp the gill filaments and feed on the tissues. Heavy infestations can cause severe damage by eroding the filaments and allowing secondary infections with bacteria and fungi to develop. Although not a very common problem with koi, it is advisable to check new fish, since it is only on affected fish that such parasites can be introduced into the pond.

Insect pests
A wide range of flying insects pass through larval stages in an aquatic environment. Some of these insect larvae are predatory and can pose a hazard to baby fish. Dragonflies, for example, lay their eggs in or close to water, either on the water surface or inside the tissues of water plants. The nymphs that emerge from these eggs have large, pincerlike jaws which they use to catch and eat

Above: *These gills are clearly infested with gill maggots* (Ergasilus). *The term 'maggots' aptly describes the appearance of the long, white egg sacs produced by the mature female parasites, first during the spring. Heavy infestations can damage the gills.*

small fish up to about 3cm(1.2in) long. Similarly, the larvae of great diving beetles, *Dytiscus*, are armed with a formidable pair of jaws and can easily devour baby koi up to their own size of about 5cm(2in). Both these and dragonfly larvae are harmless to fish larger than about 10cm(4in).

Skin and gill flukes
Most koi-keepers are aware that koi are host to flukes. They are just about visible to the naked eye, but being translucent are difficult to see without the aid of a microscope. There are two kinds usually found parasitizing koi: *Dactylogyrus*, which is usually known as the gill fluke (and has two pairs of eyes); and *Gyrodactylus*, the skin fluke (which does not have any eyes). Despite these common

names, both may be found on the body and the gills, feeding on the koi's mucus. *Dactylogyrus* lays eggs that hatch to produce free-swimming larvae, while the young of *Gyrodactylus* develop within the body of the parent, which 'gives birth' to live flukes. Both types of fluke have an array of hooks by which they grasp the surface of the koi. It appears that the irritation they cause stems from the use of these hooks as grapples to move around on the gills and skin.

Flukes are present on all koi; they are the fish equivalent of fleas on cats, dogs and wild mammals. Healthy fish can keep the numbers of flukes to a minimum, by scratching them off and expelling water with force through the gills to wash them away – an action that looks as though koi are yawning. Koi that are stressed or

Above: *A portion of dissected gill tissue with several gill flukes* (Dactylogyrus) *attached to the filaments. Each fluke may grow up to 2mm(0.08in) long. The life cycle of such flukes involves the release of eggs that hatch into free-swimming larvae.*

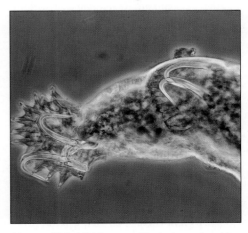

Above: *This highly magnified view of a skin fluke* (Gyrodactylus) *shows the 'grappling hooks' of the adult and also those of an unborn juvenile within its body. Such flukes are the fish equivalent of fleas.*

HEALTH CARE

diseased, however, are less able to cope with these grooming activities and the flukes may increase to large numbers. Sometimes, sick or stressed fish may have literally hundreds of flukes on the gill filaments. In the spring, flukes can be a nuisance, as they respond to rising temperatures more quickly than the koi. This is an evolutionary adaptation that enables parasites to increase their numbers before their unwilling hosts can effectively remove them. It is not known whether flukes can transmit viral or other disease agents.

Parasitic worms

It is very uncommon for koi to be infested with worms, but if they do occur, they are usually parasitic in the gut, feeding on the koi's food as it passes through the intestine. The worms that parasitize fish are either flatworms, tapeworms or threadworms. Koi infested with worms tend to be thin and rather sickly, but show no other outward signs. In most cases, worms in the intestines of newly imported or wild fish will die and reinfection will be unlikely because of the absence of the intermediate hosts in their complex life cycles.

Leeches

The leech most commonly found parasitizing koi is the fish leech, *Piscicola geo-*

Fish leech life cycle

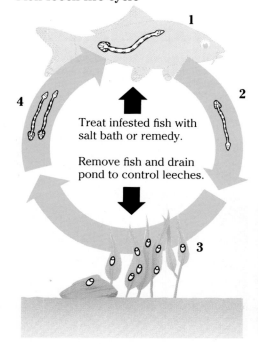

Treat infested fish with salt bath or remedy.

Remove fish and drain pond to control leeches.

Above: *1 Adult leeches feed on fish blood for 2-3 days at a time. 2 They leave the fish to digest their meal or to lay eggs. 3 Leech eggs laid in oval cocoons attached to rocks and plants. 4 Newly hatched leeches must find a fish to feed upon.*

metra. It is slender and up to about 5cm(2in) in length, with prominent ridges and pale yellow hoops at regular intervals around the body. It moves by a characteristic looping action and, when not feeding on a fish, is found among the pond plants or substrate. A hungry fish leech stretches out from the plant or substrate and waits for a passing koi to brush against it, when it will grasp the fish. Once on the fish, it moves around with a looping action until it finds a suitable place to feed.

Once attached to the koi, fish leeches can pierce the skin to feed on the fish's blood. They will attach anywhere on the body, but particularly where the skin is soft, such as around the fin bases, vent, mouth and gills. The amount of blood each leech takes from the fish is very small, but heavy infestations can reduce the health of a koi, causing it to become anaemic and laying it open to other infections. Leeches can transmit some protozoan parasites and spring viraemia of carp to koi, and there is some evidence that they can also transmit certain bacterial infections.

The leeches that parasitize koi produce eggs in a cocoon with a hard, leathery coating that is resistant to most chemicals with the exception of lime (calcium hydroxide). Where leeches are a problem in a pond, the only remedy is to remove those on the koi and place the fish in another pond while you drain down the affected pond and then treat it with lime. This will kill the adult leeches in the plants and substrate and also destroy the egg-filled cocoons. When setting up the pond again, be sure to wash everything well and use new plants.

Leeches are usually introduced on wild fish or plants – so it is worth checking any aquatic plants carefully before putting them in the pond. Few retail outlets would have access to plants infected with leeches or their cocoons, but beware of taking plants from the wild!

Above: *A single fish leech,* Piscicola geometra, *full of blood after feeding. The suckers at both ends of the elongated body are powerful attachment organs. The 'head' end has sharp cutting mouthparts and the slightly smaller of the two suckers.*

Fungal diseases

Fungi are plants that lack the pigment chlorophyll, which enables green plants to harness the sun's energy to form essential nutrients in the process of photosynthesis. Fungi obtain nutrients from organic sources, either from dead plants or animals, or, in the case of entirely parasitic fungi, from living tissues. The most familiar types of fungi consist of long, branched threadlike filaments (hyphae), that tangle together to form a matted structure called the mycelium. Since fungi need to live in damp or wet conditions, they are always present in the koi pond. Dead fish are an ideal growth medium for fungus, so be sure to remove them immediately from the pond. Fungus also infects koi eggs, which are rich in nutrients and an ideal target for attack. Always remove contaminated eggs and dispose of them as soon as you discover them. Both eggs and koi infected with this type of fungus show grey, woolly patches. Here, we consider two fungal infections that fall into this category, *Saprolegnia* and *Branchiomyces*.

Saprolegnia

One of the most common fungal infections of koi is caused by *Saprolegnia*. As part of its complicated life cycle, *Saprolegnia* forms fruiting bodies that release spores into the water. These are the 'infective agents' that germinate on koi tissue already damaged by pests, parasites, other disease organisms, accidental damage (such as caused by careless netting), water quality problems or stress. The fungal spores will grow anywhere on the body, including the gills, initially ger-

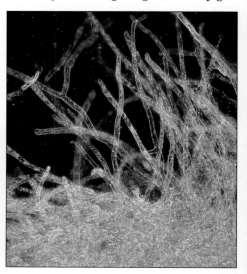

Above: *The individual strands, or hyphae, of* Saprolegnia *fungus intertwine to form a white fluffy mass, or mycelium, that can be seen on the surface of severely affected fishes. Each of these strands is 20 microns (thousandths of a millimetre) across.*

Above: *Whitish tufts of fungus erupting from between the scales show that these threadlike growths have become established in the underlying tissues. Such outbreaks often start from spores germinating on dead tissue around wounds or other damage.*

Above: *A particularly severe case of Saprolegnia fungus allied with scale erosion on a young koi. The fungal growths are tinged green with algae. Prompt treatment with a suitable remedy is essential to contain such infections.*

minating on areas of dead tissue. The threadlike hyphae produced by the spores invade the dead tissue, releasing juices that dissolve the tissue and create a nutrient-rich 'soup' on which the fungus feeds. As the fungus grows, these digestive juices start breaking down living cells, thus enabling the hyphae to invade other areas of the body, until the fungal growth becomes easily visible on the surface. Infected gills are not so easy to see, but if your koi become lethargic, cease feeding and show signs of respiratory distress – hanging at the water surface, breathing hard and often gulping air – examination of the gills may show them to have the characteristic grey cotton-wool-like growths of *Saprolegnia* fungus. (Take care, however: these signs are not exclusive to fungal infection.)

Branchiomyces

Branchiomyces is a fungus that contaminates the gills. It is spread through the water and thrives in areas where the water is slightly acidic (pH 5.8-6.8). It has a life cycle similar to *Saprolegnia*. Spores released into the water either remain in suspension or sink to the bottom of the pond, where they are sucked in by koi grubbing around for food. On contact with the gill filaments, the spores germinate and begin to form hyphae that invade and kill the gill tissues. This dead gill tissue is still infective and under laboratory conditions will produce fungus very quickly. Because of the close proximity of the blood supply to the gill tissue, some spores may enter the bloodstream, and *Branchiomyces* has been found in the liver and spleen of infected fish.

The disease caused by this fungus is called branchiomycosis. Koi suffering from the infection initially become lethargic, cease to feed and hang at the surface of the pond, usually near the water inlet, respiring heavily and showing signs of respiratory distress. (Unfortunately, these symptoms are common to many other diseases.) Examination of the gills will show the characteristic cotton-wool-like growths. Before panicking that all the koi in your pond will succumb to branchiomycosis, it is worth remembering that this fungus must be introduced into the pond; it is not part of the natural flora of the water. If there is a history of *Branchiomyces* in your pond then it is likely that your koi may become infected, otherwise it is more likely to be the fungus *Saprolegnia* causing the problem.

Viral diseases

Viruses are probably among the most successful organisms ever to have evolved and, apart from other viruses, can infect all other living organisms, including bacteria. Their structure is one of elegant simplicity, consisting essentially of a protein coat surrounding a core of genetic material. The life cycle might also be described as simple compared with other organisms that must recreate whole cells or whole bodies in the process. The infecting virus literally 'injects' its own genetic material into a single cell of the host. Once inside the cell, the viral genetic material takes command of the cell's genetic material and causes it to produce more viruses. Very simply, it may proceed in one of two ways. The virus may cause the host cell to mass

produce other virus particles that are released when the host cell ruptures, allowing the virus particles to infect other cells and organisms. Alternatively, the virus can incorporate itself into the host cell's genetic material and may have an initial infective stage causing more virus particles to be produced. The virus then enters a non-infectious state during which the particle remains in the host cell's genetic material but is inactive. Stress or other diseases can then cause this type of virus to become infective again. A classic example of this type of viral infection is the herpes virus which causes cold sores in man.

One of the sinister aspects of any virus is that its genetic material is not very stable; it mutates very easily, giving rise to 'new' viral strains. The perfect example of this are the viruses that cause influenza, with different types appearing apparently each winter to plague us!

There is no treatment or cure for any viral disease. Prevention of viral disease using vaccination is the only method currently available. With respect to viral fish diseases, there are a few vaccines that have been shown to be effective, but most of these are used by commercial fish farmers with stock destined for food. The study of viruses that infect fish is still in its infancy. Many scientists are investigating this area of fisheries science but it will be many years before they can establish all the diseases caused by viruses.

Here, we look at two viral diseases known to occur in koi.

Carp pox

Carp pox produces solid waxy lumps, usually on the fins but also on the body, and is caused by the type of virus that incorporates its own genetic material into the host cells (i.e. the second of the two strategies outlined above). Carp pox will

Above: *The typical waxy growths of the viral infection carp pox are clearly visible near the head of this koi. These are often seen on infected fish during the spring as the water warms up. They are quite firm and may change colour with age.*

HEALTH CARE

Above: *Here, carp pox has produced unsightly growths on the 'lips'. These may not necessarily interfere with the fish's ability to feed and live normally, and such symptoms may fade away on their own.*

Above: *Smooth growths of carp pox on fin rays. This viral infection cannot be treated in any reliable way, but it does not usually pose a serious threat. It seems to be spread by contact, but is not highly infectious.*

not kill koi, but in severe cases the lumps it produces can look very unsightly. It is not clear how the virus is transmitted, although it is clear that koi develop carp pox by contact with other koi already infected with the virus. Koi-keepers may notice that koi often develop the characteristic waxy lumps during the spring, when rising temperatures 'warm up' the virus before the fish's immune system becomes fully effective. Koi infected with the carp pox virus also develop the signs when they are stressed.

Spring viraemia of carp
As the name implies, spring viraemia of carp (svc) commonly occurs in the spring, when the water temperature starts to increase. (Studies of outbreaks have shown maximum mortalities at 13.5-15.5°C/56-60°F.) The typical signs of infection are a bloated body (as in dropsy, see page 110), pale gills and sometimes bleeding under the skin on the body and around the vent. Internally, the body fills with a either clear or brown fluid. The blood vessels around the swimbladder are often ruptured and the liver and spleen become enlarged.

Young koi are highly susceptible to this virus and few survive it. Those that do survive will have developed immunity to the disease but are potential carriers of the virus. The virus is released into the water with the faeces of an infected koi. It appears to infect a new host via the gills and from there enters the bloodstream. The virus can also be transmitted between koi by direct contact with infected fish, through mucus, contaminated equipment and water, and by the fish louse, *Argulus*, and the fish leech, *Piscicola geometra* (see pages 104 and 106).

There is no cure for svc. The best preventative measures are to buy fish from reputable sources, quarantine new introductions, disinfect equipment, maintain your koi in the best possible water conditions and check them regularly for any signs of ill-health.

Bacterial diseases
There are many different types of bacteria, the majority are not harmful and may even be useful – such as nitrifying bacteria in biological filters – but that still leaves a large number that are potentially harmful, or pathogenic. Most pathogenic bacteria will cause disease in many different species of fish, including koi, while some are more discriminating and infect just a few species.

So what are bacteria? They are single-celled microorganisms, with an average size of 0.5-1.0 microns (thousandths of a millimetre). There are three basic shapes of bacteria: spherical (cocci), rodlike (bacilli), and spiral (spirillum), and these can be arranged singly, in chains or in clusters. Some bacteria have tiny threadlike flagella which they use to move themselves around with surprising speed and agility.

Bacteria absorb food materials through their rigid outer cell wall and can be grouped according to whether or not they require oxygen for growth. Thus, aerobic bacteria can only grow in the presence of oxygen, while anaerobic bacteria will grow only in the absence of oxygen, since this gas is toxic to them. (Just to confuse matters, there is a third group of bacteria that will grow in the absence of oxygen but, if oxygen is present, will utilize it readily.) Bacteria usually reproduce by simply splitting

into two (binary fission) and, in ideal conditions, some bacteria may divide every 15-30 minutes. Bacteria also have a form of sexual reproduction, during which genetic material is exchanged between two cells.

The size, shape and colour of the colonies that bacteria form are useful pointers to their type, although accurate identification involves a complex procedure of taking swabs and incubating the bacteria on plates of nutritive gel. Further incubation on different gels may be necessary and then treatment with stains, such as those that classify bacteria into Gram-positive or Gram-negative types. These procedures are carried out at specialist laboratories and are not within the scope of hobbyists.

Here, we consider briefly the most common bacterial infections known to affect koi, starting with fish TB.

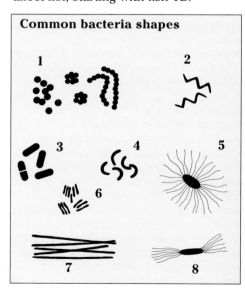

Common bacteria shapes

Above: **1** Cocci *(spheres) singly, clusters or chains.* **2** Spirillum *(spiral).* **3** Bacilli *(rods). Variations on this theme are:* **4** Vibrio *(comma shaped)* **5** Peritrichous *(flagella all round)* **6** Mycobacterium *(very small rods)* **7** Flexibacter *(long thin rods)* **8** Lophotrichous *(flagella at each end).*

Fish tuberculosis

Fish TB is caused by bacteria such as *Mycobacterium*. (A very similar disease is caused by *Nocardia* bacteria.) Infected koi become progressively thinner and hollow bellied, the eyes bulge, the skin is inflamed and often open wounds develop on the body. Tiny tubercular nodules also usually appear within the internal organs. To prevent the infection of other koi in the pond, it is vital to separate affected fish and humanely dispose of them if they do not improve. Although certain antibacterial drugs are available from veterinarians, successful treatment is far from guaranteed. In short, when the fish develop full-blown signs of fish TB, the condition is invariably fatal. Accurate diagnosis relies on identifying the clinical symptoms of the disease and subsequently confirming the presence of the bacteria by examining prepared and stained sections of tissue under a microscope, and also by culturing bacteriological samples (as outlined above).

These bacteria are transmitted from fish to fish by way of contaminated food or debris. The bacteria are voided with the faeces and can also be picked up from skin tubercles and from dead fish. Thus, it is important to remove dead or dying fish from the water to prevent the spread of infection.

Finrot, ulcers and septicaemia

A number of bacteria, notably *Aeromonas* and *Pseudomonas*, are associated with finrot, skin lesions and internal haemorrhaging. The bacteria are common in fresh water and may cause disease at temperatures as low as 10°C(50°F) and so they can be particularly problematical in spring and autumn. They often cause infections in fish weakened by stress, physical damage or poor water conditions, and so providing the best possible environment in the pond goes a long way towards preventing these problems arising in the first place.

Carp erythrodermatitis, a skin disease caused by one species of *Aeromonas*, results in ulcerous lesions developing in the skin of affected koi. (In salmon and trout, this disease is often termed 'furunculosis'.) The condition usually starts at the site of an injury, and the damage caused by this aeromonad infection often suffers secondary fungal infections. Left untreated, aeromonad infections will invade the body, leading to internal lesions and septicaemia (blood poisoning). If diagnosed in time, this condition should respond to antibiotic treatment, although there may be some problems of antibiotic resistance where these drugs have been misused (see below).

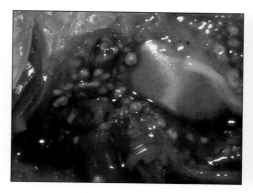

Above: *These whitish nodules among the internal organs are typical of a severe TB infection. At this stage, treatment (difficult at the best of times) is not likely to be effective. Remove dying or dead fish to block the spread of infection.*

'Hole disease' is probably the term used by many koi-keepers to describe the ulcerous lesions that may appear on the body surface as a result of bacterial infection. Such holes invariably lead to osmoregulatory problems. In a healthy fish, there is a balance between the amount of water entering the body (mainly by osmosis through the gills) and that excreted as urine by the kidneys. In koi that have holes in the body, water enters freely through the damaged skin and creates an extra burden on the kidneys, which can lead to their failure. In these circumstances, it is worth adding salt to the water at a concentration of 3gm per litre (approximately 0.5oz per gallon). This 0.3 percent solution helps to restore the osmotic balance at the site of the wound and reduces the workload placed on the kidneys.

Salt treatment is often used to help stressed koi recover their equilibrium, since stressed koi are more prone to bacterial infection. Salt is a powerful antiseptic and will often kill any pathogenic bacteria before they have a chance to cause any problems. On receiving shipments of koi from Japan, for example, the majority of dealers allow a period of time for the fish to recover by leaving them in a pond that may contain up to twice the above concentration in the water! It is in the koi-keeper's interest to have a large bag of salt constantly available and at the first sign of a problem add some to the pond water. (The salt concentrations recommended in this book for use with koi are generally lower than those usually quoted. In effect, we are being cautious; using too much salt and/or not diluting it with water before adding it to the pond can easily produce 'salt burns', as shown in the photo on page 111. If you are experienced in keeping koi, then you may already be using slightly more salt than we recommend.)

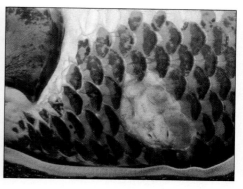

Above: *Abscesses can arise very quickly in fish and cause extensive swelling. Sometimes, an abscess may burst, as shown above. It is best to seek expert advice immediately in such cases. Treatment may involve antibiotics or other antibacterial.*

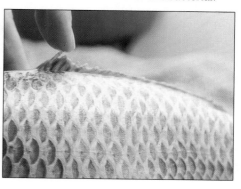

Above: *Chronic finrot can lead to the total erosion of the affected fish. In this case, almost the entire dorsal fin has rotted away, making effective treatment very difficult. Good environmental conditions should forestall such bacterial infections.*

Above: *Ulcers of the belly region can lead to further complications, as shown above, where the gut is protruding through the infected muscle wall. Such cases are usually fatal. Adding salt to the water can provide some help in less severe examples.*

Cotton-wool disease

This is another bacterial infection that is most likely to strike when koi are kept in poor conditions or when a sudden change in water quality stresses the fish. The common name originates from the whitish tufts that typically develop first around the mouth (hence the alternative, but misleading, name of 'mouth fungus')

HEALTH CARE

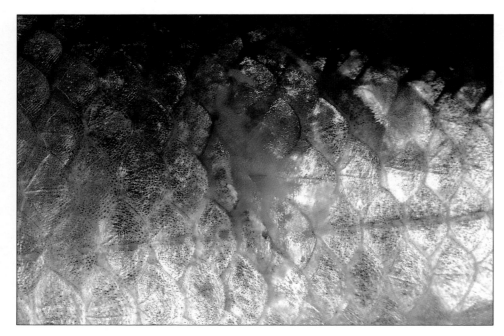

Above: *These are the characteristic growths of cotton-wool disease caused by the Flexibacter bacterium. At first sight, they can be confused with a fungal infection. In fact, the term 'mouth fungus' is often used.*

and then spread to the body and fins, often leading to ulcers and an overall thin appearance. The bacterium involved is *Fexibacter*, which has a characteristic appearance under the microscope, a colony consisting of relatively long, thin rods that move with a smooth flexing motion. *Flexibacter* is especially common in warm, organically rich water, and will spread rapidly from fish to fish in these conditions. Treatment with antibacterial drugs is usually effective.

Bacterial gill diseases

The gills are open to invasion by many different types of bacteria, the signs varying according to the kind and severity of the infection. In many cases, microscopic examination of the gills shows the tips of the filaments to be clubbed or, in severe cases, fused together. Alternatively, the filaments may become eroded, leaving only the central cartilage rod. It is important to note that bacteria are not always responsible for producing these signs, and many diseases of the gills remain undocumented.

Bacterial diseases of the gills are not easy to treat; if diagnosed in the early stages of infection, the koi may recover, but all too often, by the time the signs are noticed the damage is irreversible.

Dropsy

The signs of 'dropsy' are unmistakable; the eyes bulge out from the head (often referred to as exophthalmia, or 'pop-eye') and the scales are raised and stand out from the body rather like a pine cone. It is very important to note that dropsy is a sign of a number of possible health problems; it can be caused by kidney failure or congestive heart failure, for example, but may also be caused by bacterial invasion of the body. In fact, it is extremely difficult to differentiate between the possible causes of dropsy; ultimately, infection by bacteria may only be confirmed by the development of the signs in more than one koi. Bacterial dropsy is infectious and so it is best to isolate affected individuals. Treating the pond water with a suitable antibacterial may help to stop the disease spreading to other koi, while those koi that have developed the symptoms of bacterial dropsy are best treated in isolation with a broad-spectrum antibiotic or similar drug (see the table on pages 112-113).

Bacteria and antibiotics

Without doubt, the discovery of antibiotics is the most important medical and veterinary advance this century. Within the last 30 years, more and more drugs with antibiotic properties have been discovered (including synthetic antimicrobials) and this has led us to become very complacent about their use. Antibiotics are powerful drugs, and should only be used under strict veterinary supervision. Using antibiotics where they are unnecessary or as a prophylactic (i.e. to prevent a disease occurring) is misuse and leads to bacterial resistance.

Bacteria are rather unusual in that their genetic material is free inside the cell rather than contained in a nucleus. This enables bacteria to freely exchange genetic material with each other, including species that are totally unrelated or even dead individuals! By adding antibiotics to the pond water, resistance can be induced in the 'beneficial' bacteria that break down fish waste in the biological filter and then these bacteria can pass on resistance to pathogenic bacteria. This not only causes problems for koi-keepers, but also has wider implications, since some of these bacteria are pathogenic to humans and it is quite feasible for us to become infected with drug-resistant strains.

Another dilemma for koi-keepers is that few veterinarians are willing to prescribe drugs for fish, usually because many lack experience in this field. Many koi dealers, however, work in close conjunction with the few veterinarians that

Below: *Exophthalmia, or pop-eye, is one of the symptoms that may be associated with dropsy. The causes of dropsy may be many and varied, but the result is usually an excess of body fluid that causes swelling.*

are experienced in fish disease and are willing to obtain the necessary information about antibiotic treatment of fish.

Environmentally related disorders

Like other fishkeepers, koi-keepers are under an obligation to ensure that the water quality in their ponds is as near perfect as possible. If the water quality is poor, the fish become stressed and are more likely to become diseased. As we have seen on pages 48-57, water quality embraces a number of different (and often interacting) physical, chemical and biochemical parameters. Here, we consider these briefly in terms of their impact on koi health.

Temperature In addition to the close correlation between temperature and oxygen content (see page 51), the main health problems involving temperature concern the activity of parasites, spawning, and the immune response.

In the spring and autumn, many parasites are actively reproducing and the koi may be too drowsy to cope with their large numbers. Usually, treating the pond water with a suitable remedy can solve this problem.

In temperate regions, the increasing hours of daylight from early spring onwards induces the maturation of eggs inside the female koi. Spawning is triggered by temperatures in excess of 20°C(68 °F). If these temperatures are not realized, female koi can become highly stressed by their inability to spawn, and fall prey to disease. Temperature can also affect the development of eggs and baby koi. Sudden temperature fluctuations, for example, can cause various abnormalities, usually of the skeleton and particularly of the spinal column.

Temperature has a great influence on the immune system of koi. Below 12°C(54°F), koi do not produce antibodies (the special cells that seek out and destroy pathogens), but many bacteria and viruses are still active at this temperature. Similarly, koi subjected to a substantial increase in temperature of, say, 10°C(18°F), will take a week for their immune system to become more active. For bacteria, on the other hand, a temperature rise of half that amount is sufficient to stimulate their growth rate, bearing in mind that a single bacterium can produce a colony in excess of 25 million in 24 hours in ideal conditions. So, it is vitally important that any temperature changes are undertaken gradually. In normal circumstances, koi are protected from rapid temperature changes simply by the physical characteristics of the watery medium in which they live. On a

hot day, for example, while air temperatures soar rapidly, it takes many hours for the water to increase in temperature significantly.

pH value Slight daily fluctuations in pH value around the usual range of pH7-8 should not cause any health problems. As we have mentioned on page 50, in ponds with green water, the pH value may fluctuate between 7 and 11. Although these higher (more alkaline) peaks may cause some stress, the resident fish will be acclimated to these variations and should be able to cope. But do not introduce new fish to such conditions; they will surely succumb. Of course, it makes sense to check the pH value of your pond water on a regular basis to avoid any health problems related to this aspect of water quality. A continual reading above pH9, for example, demands swift investigation and a suitable response.

Oxygen content Insufficient oxygen in the water causes koi to stop feeding and become lethargic, with stressed fish often seen at the surface, respiring heavily. Such stress not only has direct physical effects but also makes the fish more susceptible to 'opportunistic' parasites and disease organisms. In a pond with low oxygen levels, the morning after a humid summer night may see the largest fish floating lifelessly on the surface. (The largest individuals always die first in these circumstances because their oxygen needs are greater than those of small fish.) To redress the oxygen balance in vulnerable ponds, it is vital to keep plant life down to a minimum and to add a second or larger pump to the system to boost the aeration of the water entering the pond.

Ironically, too much aeration can supersaturate the water with gases and possibly cause so-called 'gas-bubble

disease', with bubbles of gas appearing in the skin and fins. It is not necessarily dissolved oxygen that causes this problem; it is the total dissolved gases that create gas-bubble disease, and as 80 percent of air is nitrogen, the result of saturating water with air can produce behavioural signs equivalent to those of 'the bends' in human divers. Unless this supersaturation is remedied, koi can die from gas bubbles forming in the blood vessels and in delicate tissues such as the gills and eyes. Supersaturation with oxygen can arise in well-planted ponds (through excessive photosynthesis) or from the over use of venturis.

Ammonia and nitrite Even the most well-maintained ponds and filter systems may be subject to fluctuations in ammonia and nitrite levels. Some pond treatments, for example, can disrupt the action of biological filters by killing the nitrifying bacteria they support. The result is that ammonia excreted by the koi as a toxic waste product (mainly through the gills) is not broken down into nitrites and, in turn, these highly poisonous nitrites are not converted into less harmful nitrates. Raised levels of ammonia and nitrite can have devastating effects on koi health, including severe gill irritation and malfunction, reduced oxygen uptake by the blood, destruction of mucous membranes of the skin and intestine, external and internal bleeding, and damage to the nervous system and organs such as the liver, spleen and kidney. Following pond treatments, therefore, it is vital to monitor the levels of these two chemicals once a day for 7-10 days (see page 52 for test kits).

Chlorine As we have seen on page 52, excessive amounts of chlorine and chloramines in treated tap water can cause respiratory distress as the chlorine

Above: *During the warm summer months, large numbers of aquatic plants, together with insufficient aeration in the pond, can cause major tragedies, as the largest fish die from lack of oxygen. These koi are victims of just such an episode in their pond.*

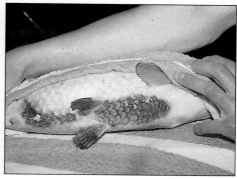

Above: *While common salt is a very useful medication and supportive treatment, it is vital to ensure that the required amount is completely dissolved before adding fish to strong dips. Otherwise, the belly and fins may be severely damaged, as here.*

HEALTH CARE

attacks the gill membranes. The level of chlorine needed to have lethal effects varies with a number of water quality parameters, including the dissolved oxygen content, the presence of pollutants, the pH value and temperature. In general, 0.2-0.3mg/litre of so-called 'residual chlorine' will kill most fish species fairly rapidly, while concentrations 100 times lower can cause chronic toxic effects. Fortunately, clearing chlorine from tap water is not difficult, by aeration for several days. It is worth asking your local water supply company if it adds chloramines to the water, however, since these take a little more effort to eradicate successfully.

Algae Microscopic algae are responsible for a phenomenon termed 'green water'. In most cases, green water is not harmful to koi, but the fluctuations in pH caused by the algae can stress fish that have not become gradually acclimated to such conditions (see page 111). Some koi may suffer respiratory distress caused by clogging of the gills by the algal cells, but this is very rare. Like other plants, algae deplete oxygen at night and this may cause a problem in the summer months, when dissolved oxygen levels are relatively low. At such times, it is worth checking the dissolved oxygen content of the pond water regularly.

Pollutants In most ponds, the only likely source of pollution is from treatment applied to nearby lawns and gardens. It is difficult to advise on the course of action to take if the pond becomes polluted. The most sensible first step is to make a water change and then contact the manufacturers of the product to ask for their advice on the best course of action.

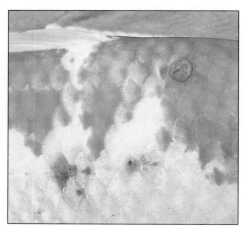

Above: *The damaged scales on this koi could have been caused by accidental injury and will be a prime site for fungal and bacterial attack. The small tumour could be caused by environmental pollution, but may not necessarily cause any lasting problem.*

Guidelines for using chemicals

Chemical	Concentration mg/litre (ppm)	Dosage range per 100 litres
Benzalkonium chloride	Bath: 1-4	0.2-0.8ml
Chloramine T	Bath: 2.2 Pool: 0.5	0.2gm 0.05gm
Ethyl-m-aminobenzoate (MS 222) Anaesthetic	Bath: 25-100	2.5-10gm
Formalin (A solution containing approx. 37% formaldehyde)	Bath: 24 Pool: 13.5	2.4ml 1.3ml
Formalin and malachite green mixture	Pool: Formalin 15 and malachite green 0.05	1.5ml of mixture
Levamisole	Bath: 10	1gm
Malachite green	Bath: 0.4 (*1) Pool: 0.2 (*1)	2ml 1ml
Methylene blue	Bath: 2(*2)	8ml
Nifurpirinol	Bath: 1-4 Pool: 0.25	0.1-0.4gm 0.025gm
Nitrofurazone	Bath: 1-3	0.1-0.3gm
Oxolinic acid	5gm per kg of treated food	Give treated food at rate of 1% of fish body weight per day
Oxytetracycline	Bath: 13-120 In food: 50mg per kg of fish	1.3-12gm
Para-chloro-phenoxyethanol	Bath: 20	1.8ml
Phenoxyethanol	Bath: 100 Food: Soak in 1% solution (10gm/litre)	9.1ml
Sodium chloride (Common salt)	Bath: 30,000 (3%)	3kg
	Bath/Pool: 10,000 (1%)	1kg
	Pool: 3,000 (0.3%)	300gm
Trichlorphon (Dimethyltrichloro-hydroxyethyl-phosphonate)	Bath: 22 Pool: 0.3	2.2gm 0.03gm

(*1) Parts per million (ppm) based on solid. Dosages based on 2% solution in water.
(*2) ppm based on solid. Dosages based on 2.5% solution in water. To convert dosages for 100 Imperial gallons and 100 US gallons, multiply figures in 'Dosage range' column by 4.55 and 3.79

Treatment time	Other details	Effective against
60 mins	Dosage based on liquid formulation containing 50% active ingredient	Cotton-wool disease, finrot, tailrot and other external bacterial diseases
60 mins Continuous until cured. Repeat after 3 days	Available as powder. Maximum of 3 consecutive treatments	Slime disease, white spot, skin flukes, myxobacterial gill disease, external bacterial diseases
1-3 mins, depending on pH, temperature, size and condition of fish	Requires care. Consult veterinarian or other skilled person. Ensure preparation is suitable for fish anaesthesia	Used as anaesthetic. MS 222 is a water-soluble form of benzocaine
30 mins Continuous until cured. Repeat after 7 days	Rarely used alone. Normally used with malachite green, see below. Aerate water	Combined with malachite green; fungus, slime disease, white spot, skin and gill flukes
Continuous until cured	Use 3.3gm of malachite green solid in one litre of formalin	Fungus, slime disease, white spot, and skin and gill flukes
12-24 hours		Intestinal worms
30 mins Continuous until cured. Repeat after 7 days	Use with formalin or sodium chloride	Fungus, slime disease, white spot, other parasites, such as skin flukes
Continuous until cured	Do not use with biological filters; it will disrupt their action	Traditional treatment for fungus, protozoan parasites. Commercial remedies better
60 mins Continuous until cured	If difficult to obtain, consider using para-chloro-phenoxyethanol	Cotton-wool disease, finrot, tailrot, plus other bacterial and fungal diseases
60 mins	If difficult to obtain, consider using para-chloro-phenoxyethanol	Cotton-wool disease, finrot, tailrot, plus other bacterial and fungal diseases
Use for 10 days	Available ready mixed with food; take advice from veterinarian	Dropsy, ulcer disease, plus other bacterial diseases
Continuous until cured. Use for 7 days	Antibiotic. Use lower concentration unless hard water reduces effect	Bacterial diseases
Continuous until cured	Take care to dissolve and disperse thoroughly	Fungus, finrot, tailrot, and other bacterial diseases
Continuous until cured. Use for 7 days	Supplied as oily liquid. Take care to dissolve and disperse thoroughly	Fungus, cotton-wool disease, finrot, tailrot. Use soaked food against nematode worms
Up to 10 mins	Remove fish immediately if it shows distress	Cloudy eye and parasites. (Increases mucus flow)
1-2 weeks	Use with malachite green or phenoxyethanol	Supportive for various diseases and wounds/ulcers
Continuous until cured		General protection, e.g. against nitrite toxicity
60 mins Continuous until cured. In hard water repeat after 7 days	Maximum 3 consecutive treatments. Take great care with bath treatments. Kills tench, orfe and rudd	Fish lice, anchor worms and other parasites, such as skin and gill flukes

respectively. Internationally accepted chemical names used where possible. Local regulations affect the availability of drugs. Seek veterinary advice.

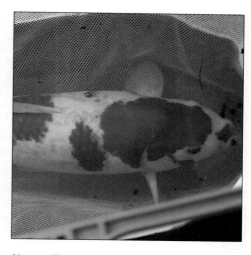

Above: *The reddening of the white areas on this koi are caused by stress. Netting a koi too frequently can cause stress, as can unsuitable changes in a wide range of environmental parameters, including temperature, pH value, oxygen content and levels of ammonia and nitrite. A stressed fish is more likely to succumb to disease.*

Stress

One word that appears repeatedly in this section on health care is 'stress', but what does this word really mean? For the majority of people, stress implies a psychological or emotional disturbance. Indeed, stress can be induced by an emotional disturbance but it is not just our minds that react to the situation; changes also occur in our body chemistry. Some of these changes help to prepare the body to cope with the situation, such as the release of hormones that break down fat reserves and mobilize them for energy production, while others effectively close down some of the body systems, such as the immune and digestive systems (hence feeling 'sick with worry'), to focus the body's resources. The result of these changes is that when the crisis has subsided, our bodies are weaker than before and our immune system is not able to fend off any opportunistic infection. Similarly, if we are physically stressed by heat, cold, over exertion, injury or tiredness the same physiological responses occur in our bodies.

While it is difficult to measure emotional stress in koi, it is certainly true that physical stress produces the same reactions as it does in us. Thus, in stressed koi the immune system is less effective, digestion is interrupted and important hormonal changes take place. In short, it is easy to see why stressed koi are more vulnerable to disease than are those kept in ideal conditions. Which brings us neatly to the constant realization that good health stems from preventing problems rather than simply curing them.

SHOWING KOI

Showing koi is a popular, if somewhat controversial, subject among koi-keepers. Although some may disapprove of the stress of transporting koi to shows and the sometimes unsatisfactory conditions under which they are kept throughout the period of the show, few would deny the virtue of koi shows in increasing the hobbyist's knowledge and appreciation of koi. Certainly, a well-run koi show is an exciting day out for all koi enthusiasts, whether they are competitors, or just spectators, and everyone enjoys the opportunity of seeing so many top-quality koi at such close hand.

Koi shows are organized on many levels, from huge extravaganzas, such as the All Japan Show (see page 119), held annually in Tokyo, at the top end of the scale, to small local events. Competitive spirit runs high in shows of all sizes, and show organizers, dealers and hobbyists spend a great deal of time in preparation. The beautiful koi you see at a show will be the result of much hard work on the part of their owners.

Large national shows, such as this Western-style one, are the climax of the koi-keeping year for many hobbyists.

SHOWING KOI

Koi shows and societies

Most hobbyists interested in showing their koi start at local shows organized by koi societies. In some countries, national koi societies have local sections where hobbyists meet periodically for talks, visits to members' ponds and to discuss various koi-keeping issues.

Koi societies usually hold shows, and these may be either closed or open. Only members may enter their koi in a closed show. At such events, benching, judging, and public viewing tend to take place on a single day. Open shows, on the other hand, are accessible to any member of the public who wishes to enter their koi in the competition. When run by local sections, these shows may be either one or two day events, depending on the projected attendance and the venue. Larger open shows are often organized by national societies. Professional shows, run by and for koi dealers, are open to the public for viewing.

Koi shows are usually advertised in koi magazines, national fishkeeping magazines and by dealers, and local koi societies generally have information on events taking place in their area.

Preparing for a show

An unhealthy koi is not going to look at its best no matter how good its pattern or body shape. In the same way that dogs have wet noses and a shiny coat when they are well, a koi that is in good condition will have a healthy looking shine on the skin, which enhances its pattern and general appearance. A koi whose skin lacks this healthy lustre will not be considered by judges. You should therefore do everything in your power to ensure the best possible conditions in the pond so that your koi will be in peak condition ready for showing.

As well as taking all the usual precautions and carrying out regular checks to ensure that ammonia and nitrite levels are acceptable, and that the level of debris in the pond is low, you can improve the mineral content of the water by adding a special supplement (ask your dealer for advice). This will help improve general health and vitality, as well as enhancing colours on the koi and aiding digestion. The fine, claylike powder gives the pond a muddy appearance for approximately 48 hours. During this time, the koi swim through it and it passes through their bodies, binding up their waste and causing it to sink to the bottom of the pond along with any other suspended debris, leaving the water sparkling clear.

A healthy diet is also of paramount importance, particularly in the build-up to a show. Feed the koi a well-balanced diet, incorporating colour enhancers with other foodstuffs to help improve the depth of colour and sharpness of pattern and to guard against shimis (black flecks) on the skin. It is a good idea to stop feeding koi a few days before the show so that they produce a minimum amount of waste while travelling to and from the show and while they are in the show vats. This will help to protect your koi by preventing poor water quality.

Below: Benching in progress at a koi show. This is the first critical stage in the day's proceedings. Here, show officials are sorting the koi according to their size and variety. To keep track of each individual fish, all the koi that pass this initial stage are photographed. The main reason for rejection at this stage is on health grounds; any koi that show signs of disease or parasite infestation are withdrawn from the show.

Shade is important, especially during the summer months, as koi can suffer from sunburn if their pond is exposed to direct sunlight. This normally exhibits itself as a reddening of the skin along the dorsal and will make the koi unshowable.

Disturb your koi as little as possible in the months preceding a show. The more the koi are disturbed, the more nervous they become and the more prone to parasites or infection caused by knocks and bumps. In the week preceding the show, examine the koi for any knocks or abrasions, split fins, fading colours or any sign of disease.

In Japan, koi are kept in 'mud' ponds in the months preceding a show. These natural ponds are full of green algae and minerals, providing a perfect food source for koi and promoting their growth and colour. Japanese dealers generally have their own mud ponds and keen hobbyists often pay to keep their koi outside in these mud ponds for the summer, when maximum growth can be achieved. The koi are taken from the mud pond a month or so before the show and any parasites and abrasions are dealt with so that the koi are in peak condition. This facility for growing on koi in mud ponds is currently rare outside Japan. Elsewhere in the world, hobbyists would be reluctant, on the whole, to part from their precious koi; many are more interested in their koi as pets than as potential show winners.

Benching koi
On the morning of the show you will need to catch and bag your koi ready to transport them to the show. Take great care not to damage the koi at this late stage or they will be unshowable. The way in which you transport the koi is important, not only to reduce stress, but also to avoid bumped noses and split fins.

On arrival at the show ground, show officials will 'bench' your koi, that is, they will sort them into the appropriate variety and size ready for judging. Normally, koi are exhibited in large blue vats, which have airlines running into them to supply oxygen. Show officials carry out regular water tests on each of the vats and attach small filters to the airlines in vats containing larger koi, which obviously create more waste.

In Japanese-style shows, koi of the same size and variety are exhibited in the same vat, irrespective of owner. This makes life simpler from the judges' point of view because it enables them to directly compare koi competing against one another. However, many hobbyists are concerned about the risk of infection or parasites if their koi are mixed with others. In some shows, therefore, all the

koi owned by one person are exhibited in the same vat. The risk of transmission of disease is thus reduced, provided that nets, bowls and hands are sterilized and equipment is not transferred between vats. Judging, however, is made more difficult as direct comparison between koi of the same variety is not possible.

Fourteen different variety classifications are currently recognized in most of the koi-keeping world. These are:

Kohaku
Taisho Sanke
Showa Sanshoku
Bekko
Utsurimono
Asagi
Shusui
Koromo
Kawarimono
Hikarimono (Ogon)
Hikari-Utsurimono
Hikarimoyo-mono
Tancho
Kinginrin

These classifications are explained on pages 122-201, where the various varieties included in each are illustrated, listed and described.

The koi are then separated into different sizes. The number of size groups will depend on the extent of the show.

Above: *An early stage in the first round of judging. Here, the judges vote on the merits of an individual koi 'bowled' into a plastic floating basket to allow closer inspection. The judges work as teams, each team being responsible for judging different size groups throughout the day. At this point, decisions are arrived at by open majority with a show of hands; from the second round, voting is carried out by secret ballot.*

Outside Japan, koi are generally divided into six size groups for judging purposes. These are:

Size one – up to 15cm(6in)
Size two – 15-25cm(6-10in)
Size three – 25-35cm(10-14in)
Size four – 35-45cm(14-18in)
Size five – 45-55cm(18-22in)
Size six – over 55cm(22in)

After its classification and size has been established, each koi is carefully scrutinized for any form of disease, such as fin-rot, anchor worm, fish lice, carp pox, white spot, bacterial infections or any evidence of damage or deformity. Any koi found to have such faults is automatically withdrawn from the contest.

Each koi is then photographed in colour and its variety, size and owner's name are recorded before it is moved to the appropriate variety and size show vat ready for judging.

SHOWING KOI

Judging koi

Koi shows have gradually changed their format over the years. Since 1987, shows in most parts of the koi-keeping world have followed the Japanese style (see page 119). The judges – there may be as many as 24 – group into teams and draw lots to decide which sizes each will judge. The teams then select first and second place koi in each of the 14 classifications and six sizes and these koi are moved into the best in size vats. From these koi the judges select a first, second and third in each of the six sizes, irrespective of variety. This second stage of judging determines the best 18 koi from which the three supreme champions are singled out. The supreme champion baby koi is chosen from sizes one and two, the supreme champion adult koi from sizes three and four, and the supreme champion mature koi from sizes five and six. The grand champion of the show is chosen from these three winners. All decisions from the second stage onwards are by secret ballot.

Awards are then presented for 'tategoi' – the koi that shows most potential for the future, whether or not it has already won a prize. The judges decide on first, second and third place tategoi in group discussion. Decisions on awards for the best home-bred koi, the best koi in the dealers' section and the best jumbo koi (awarded to the largest koi in the show) are also made on majority open ballot.

Right: *A typical scene from a national koi show, with a vat of koi awaiting the judges' attention once they have finished their deliberations around the vat in the background. Judging the koi is a serious business and nothing must be allowed to interfere with this day-long process.*

Below: *This diagram shows the logistic sequence of judging and prize giving at a typical national koi show (but not the All Japan Show). The circles represent vats, with the arrows reflecting physical movement of koi as well as status attained after judging. The cup and rosette are used merely as symbols to highlight some of the major prizes awarded at a show.*

The judging sequence at a typical koi show

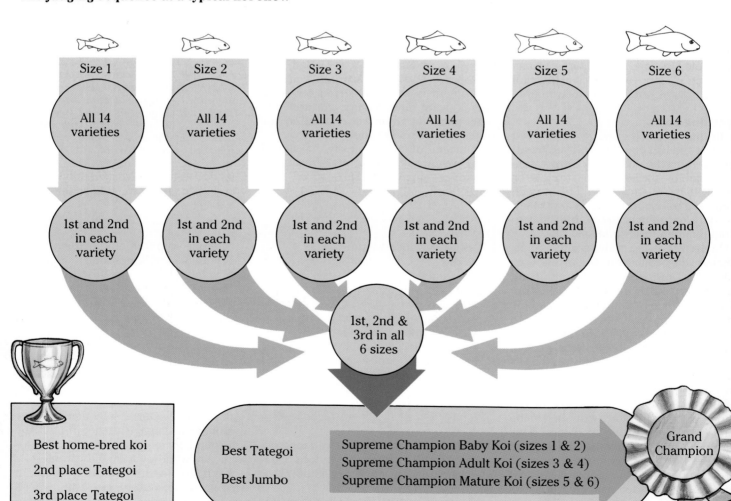

The All Japan Show

The All Japan show, which takes place each January in the capital city of Tokyo, Japan, is the climax of the koi-keeping year for dealers, breeders and hobbyists all over the world, and in many respects is, therefore, the 'blue-print' for the many koi shows, which are held throughout the world.

The show is organized by the All Japan Nishikigoi Dealers Association with the help of the Zen Nippon Airinkai (the koi-keeper society with a worldwide membership). The show is open to both professional and amateur koi-keepers (although all the koi must be entered by dealers). The show takes place over five days; the koi are benched on the first day, judged on the second, and on general view to the public for the rest of the period of the show.

Each dealer collects koi from his customers and keeps them in his own ponds to rest before beginning what is, for many, a long journey to Tokyo. On the morning of travel, the dealer measures each koi and takes four photographs of it, which he attaches to the paperwork required for benching and entry to the show. (See *Benching koi*, page 117).

On arrival at the show, which is held indoors in a very large hall about 5km(3 miles) south of Tokyo city centre, the dealers are met by the show officials and directed to the various benching areas. Over 1200 vats will be ready to receive the 5000 or so koi that are entered each year from all parts of Japan, with entries, too, from the USA, Taiwan, Korea, Thailand and the UK. Each vat has its own air supply line coming down from the roof and many of the vats containing larger koi have their own filter systems. (These are necessary since the koi will be swimming in the vats for up to five days.) There are also reservoir vats where koi can be deposited before being transferred to the main exhibition vats.

Officials check each koi with its paperwork and photographs and examine it for any damage that may have been caused during the journey to the show. Benching, that is, sorting the koi into the appropriate variety and size groups, is the responsibility of the dealers, but in the event of a dispute, officials will adjudicate.

The koi are currently divided into 16 variety groups for judging purposes. These include the 14 listed on page 117, along with a further two groups – Goshiki (see page 166) and Doitsu (see page 125) – which have been judged independently only since 1988. Although, at present, these two classifications are recognized only in Japan, it seems probable that eventually they will be adopted internationally.

Because of the huge numbers of koi entered in this and other Japanese shows, each variety is divided into 15 size groups. Male and female koi of sizes 10 to 15 inclusive are judged separately and so there are 21 groups in all. These are as follows:

Size 1 – under 15cm(6in)
Size 2 – 15-20cm(6-8in)
Size 3 – 20-25cm(8-10in)
Size 4 – 25-30cm(10-12in)
Size 5 – 30-35cm(12-14in)
Size 6 – 35-40cm(14-16in)
Size 7 – 40-45cm(16-18in)
Size 8 – 45-50cm(18-20in)
Size 9 – 50-55cm(20-22in)
Size 10 – 55-60cm(22-24in) males
Size 10 – 55-60cm(22-24in) females
Size 11 – 60-65cm(24-26in) males
Size 11 – 60-65cm(24-26in) females
Size 12 – 65-70cm(26-28in) males
Size 12 – 65-70cm(26-28in) females
Size 13 – 70-75cm(28-30in) males
Size 13 – 70-75cm(28-30in) females
Size 14 – 75-80cm(30-32in) males
Size 14 – 75-80cm(30-32in) females
Size 15 – over 80cm(32in) males
Size 15 – over 80cm(32in) females

The organization room is split into two sections; on one side are the 150 or so helpers, and on the other the judges, press, and important guests. There are around 100 judges, about 90 percent of whom are members of the All Japan Nishikigoi Dealers Association.

Before judging begins, the show chairman calls all the judges to a meeting, where they are divided up into small groups. They then draw lots to determine which three or four sections each group will judge. Each group of judges nominates a leader who will have the casting vote in the event of a tie.

The judges look at one, two, or three vats (depending on the size of the show) of a particular variety of a given size and ask the helper to lift any that warrant a better look into a fibreglass vat on a trolley nearby. They choose the best koi by a show of hands count and it is then moved to a separate vat. The second best koi is also chosen and the award pinned onto its photograph above the vat. If two koi of a particular variety and size impress the judges equally, they may decide to nominate one as a winner and award a special prize (between the first and second place awards) to the other koi they have chosen.

After each variety winner has been selected in a particular size, it is taken to join the other winners of that size in a separate vat. The judges then move on to the next size group they are judging, and the same process takes place. Finally, after all the size groups have been assessed, the judges select the winner of each size, independent of variety, known as the 'Kokugyo'. All judges then reunite to group these Kokugyo into classes to select the following size group champions. This is done by secret ballot and the count takes place under strict supervision.

Grand prize in the Yogyo section (Baby koi) sizes 1-3Bu*

Grand prize in the Wakagoi section (Young koi) sizes 4-6Bu*

Grand prize in the Sogyo section (Adult koi) sizes 7-9Bu*

Grand prize in the Seigyo section (Mature koi) sizes 10-12Bu*

Grand prize in the Kyogoi section (Jumbo koi) sizes 13-15Bu*

These winning koi are all transferred to one vat and the judges then select the Grand Champion of the All Japan Show. It is interesting to note that, although breeders, dealers and hobbyists all compete against one another, this highest award is almost invariably won by a private hobbyist. Of course, the breeder of the winning koi and the dealer will also be important figures on the day.

*Bu is the Japanese abbreviation for 'size'. This term is frequently used in shows throughout the world.

SHOWING KOI

Judging criteria

To lay down criteria for the perfect koi is no easy matter; beauty, as we all know, is in the eye of the beholder. Until recently, there have been hard and fast rules about what constitutes a 'good' koi, but over the past few years, this attitude has softened as new varieties have been introduced and many beautiful and unique koi have been produced.

What is important is the overall impression that a koi makes on the eye – how imposing is it? Its shape, balance of colour and pattern and the lustre of its skin are all qualities that the judge has to consider critically, concentrating as much, if not more, on a koi's positive attributes as on its negative aspects.

In this section, we look at the qualities a judge will be looking for in a show-winning koi of any variety. (In Part Two of the book, we examine in more detail the particular colours and patterns that are considered ideal in the many different varieties.) There are approximately four main aspects that a judge will be considering in examining your koi. These are: shape, colour, pattern and overall quality, lustre and shape.

Shape The koi's body shape is of primary importance; even a koi with good coloration and a perfect pattern will lose points if its shape is poor. The body should be symmetrical on either side and the backbone straight. Although koi are bred to be viewed from above, the shape of the body seen from the side is also important; the abdomen should be more rounded than the dorsal line.

The judge will also be looking at the way a koi moves in the water; it should swim straight through the water without twisting its body. A koi that swims awkwardly will be disqualified.

Volume and imposing appearance are important attributes to be assessed. A striking aspect may compensate for a lack of strong colour and pattern, and a large impressive koi will always be selected in preference to an equally outstanding smaller one. Apart from the fact that a large koi of high quality is very majestic, it is far more difficult to maintain good body shape and skin quality in a large mature koi than it is to produce a baby koi, or a relatively young one, with the same qualities. This is the reason why the Grand Champion of a show is nearly always a jumbo koi.

The koi's fins should be in proportion to the rest of its body and should enhance the overall movement and elegance of the koi. A female's pectoral fins are often slightly smaller and more rounded than the males'. Ideally, the dis-

Above: *Obviously, this particular koi is causing quite a stir among the judges. It is important that they take their time and arrive at a well-considered opinion, especially in the final stages of the show. The judges will be looking at the shape of each koi and assessing its colour, its pattern and its overall quality. They will give more credit to a larger koi with the same good points exhibited by an equivalent small fish, since it is much harder to retain good quality in more mature koi.*

tance between the dorsal fin and the tail should be one third of the distance between the first ray of the dorsal fin and the head region. A koi whose dorsal fin is too close to the tail – a common fault – will appear unbalanced.

The elegant beauty of the head is much easier to appreciate in a mature koi. The head should be in proportion to the rest of the body and should not be too rounded or pointed. There should be no pit marks or indentations on the head and, on jumbo koi especially (sizes 5 and 6), the cheeks should be solid and round. The round black or red marks often found just under the skin on young koi are not, in fact, colour pigmentation, but the internal organs showing through the skull of the koi. As the koi grows, its skull will skin over and these marks will eventually cease to be visible. Minute bubbles may also be apparent on the head of a small koi. These are a sign of good skin quality but tend to disappear when the koi is two years old.

Colour The clarity and depth of the koi's coloration is of obvious importance in judging. All colours should be of an even hue over the koi's body and unblemished by any other pigmentation, unless these markings form part of the pattern.

The white should be snow white, without flecks – known as 'shimis' – of red ('hi') or black ('sumi'). Unfortunately, the head, in particular, can appear yellowish in colour on some koi.

The hi (red) markings should be of a uniform shade, well defined and free of sumi (black) shimis. Bright hi of an orange-brown hue is preferred to purplish hi (see *Kohaku*, pages 128-135).

As a general guide, round sumi markings are favoured in preference to uneven, angular ones, but this depends on the particular koi concerned. Sumi should be ebony in colour, and shiny, like chinese lacquer.

Pattern No two koi are alike and, although each variety has its own pattern characteristics, unique patterns are now often preferred to standard traditional ones. All the markings must be well balanced, however, and the pattern should normally be consistent over the body of the koi to give a pleasing aesthetic effect. For example, hi markings on a Kohaku should normally be balanced along the length and breadth of the koi. The edges of a marking ('kiwa'), such as the border between hi and white markings on a Kohaku, for example, should be crisp and well defined.

Overall quality

The quality of the skin is an important factor in the koi's overall appearance. The skin should have lustre, that is a shiny finish, so that the koi looks as though it has been lacquered with a clear varnish and may appear to be slightly metallic. Such skin quality is quite common in young koi, but jumbo koi that retain this lustre are much admired. Judging quality in koi is a skill that is mastered only after years of experience. Essentially, the quality of a koi can be defined as the sum of its shape, pattern, colour and overall elegance.

Right: *This five-year-old Taisho Sanke has a near perfect body shape, balanced beautifully by superbly shaped fins. The skin quality is excellent, being snow white with no yellowing, flaws or discoloration. The hi is intense and even in colour and creates an interesting pattern, with a breaking design over the shoulder and dorsal area complemented by smaller hi markings near the tail. The sumi is very strong and clean edged, with two small, but attractive, markings on the shoulder. A fine example.*

PART TWO

KOI VARIETIES

All koi belong to one species, Cyprinus carpio, of which about one hundred colour varieties have been developed. However, these are not genetically fixed, which means that spawning one variety produces offspring of other varieties. Those currently in existence are the result of much cross-breeding (i.e. breeding together closely related types) to produce stable varieties, and new ones are appearing all the time.

On pages 124-5, we show how the many (and, at the outset, confusing) variety names are made up of Japanese words that describe the colour, pattern, lustre or scalation of a particular koi. Learning to recognize the different varieties is made simpler when you understand the various classifications into which they are grouped. Some of these, such as Kohaku, feature only one variety, while others embrace several varieties; Hikarimono, for example, includes all single-coloured, metallic koi. On pages 126-7, we explain and review the classifications, with illustrations of some of the more popular varieties or those most typical of their group. Appreciating the different patterns and becoming familiar with the Japanese names will come with practice. Meanwhile, most dealers will be happy to help you by telling you the correct names of any koi that take your eye.

The broad sweep of Part Two (pages 128-201), looks in detail at over one hundred different koi varieties, including all the classic 'favourites' as well as many of the more unusual ones. The wealth and range of patterns involved are shown in the form of symbol-like illustrations of a large number of the varieties. Of course, every koi is unique and, although certain criteria will have to be satisfied on a prize-winning koi, a diversity of different patterns are acceptable in most varieties. Therefore, these illustrations are representative as well as stylized. The photographs show real koi and here the captions point out any shortcomings as well as celebrating their finer qualities.

The variety of colour and pattern on these graceful koi justifies their universal popularity.

KOI VARIETIES

The ever-increasing number of koi varieties and their seemingly arbitrary classifications are apt to confuse the new koi-keeper, and the abundance of Japanese names, too, can be bewildering. Unfortunately for the new koi-keeper, no 'Westernized' names and groupings have been devised and so we have adhered to the traditionally accepted Japanese variety names and classifications.

Over the next few pages, we will try to unravel some of the mystery that surrounds these variety names. Most, in fact, are made up of Japanese words that describe a single aspect of a koi. If you understand the meaning of some of these words, you will find it easier to learn the different variety names.

We have chosen to look at these terms under the four headings of colour, pattern, scalation and lustre. As we saw in the section on *Showing koi* (pages 114-21), these are all aspects that a judge will be looking at during the evaluation of a koi in a show. There is a more comprehensive glossary of Japanese and other 'koi' words on page 202.

Colour

There are several Japanese words associated with colour that are used to describe koi. For example, red markings are usually called 'hi' markings, but there are also other words for red, such as 'aka' and 'beni', which are generally used to describe an overall red colour. The same is true of black; sumi is the word for black markings, while 'karasu' (literally, 'crow') is the name given to a totally black koi. The list of colour-associated words below will help you to begin to understand how koi names are built up.

Ai	blue
Aka	red (as a base colour over the body)
Beni	orange-red (usually as a base colour over the body)
Cha	brown
Gin	silver (metallic)
Hi	red (markings on the body of the koi)
Karasu	black (as a base colour. Literally, 'crow')
Ki	yellow
Kin	gold (metallic)
Midori	green
Nezu/nezumi	grey (literally, 'mouse')
Orenji	orange
Shiro	white
Sumi	black (markings on the body of the koi)
Yamabuki	yellow (literally, a Japonica bush with pale yellow flowers)

Above: **Sumi-goromo**
The dark edges to the red scales are clearly visible on the body of this koromo koi. On Sumi-goromo the 'robed' pattern is combined with solid sumi markings.

Pattern

Many variety names incorporate a Japanese word that describes the pattern. An understanding of some of the more common ones will help you to appreciate the patterns and learn the variety names of your koi.

Budo Literally, 'grape'. In fact, this word refers as much to the colour as to the pattern of the koi, being used to describe the purple, grapelike cluster pattern on Budo Goromo and Budo Sanke, both from the Koromo classification (see pages 158-9).

Kage Literally, 'shadow' or 'phantom'. The word kage refers to the blurred, reticulated sumi, or black, pattern that appears on certain Utsuri and Showa. These koi are classed as Kawarimono rather than Utsurimono and Showa.

Kanoko Literally, 'fawn'. This word is used to describe the dappled 'hi', or red, markings found on certain Kohaku, Sanke and Showa. These Kanoko koi are judged in Kawarimono (see pages 166-9).

Koromo Literally, 'robed'. Koi in the Koromo classification have a hi pattern that is outlined (or 'robed') in a darker colour (see pages 156-9).

Inazuma Literally, 'lightning strike'. Used particularly with reference to the hi pattern on some Kohaku, where 'inazuma' describes a zig-zag marking stretching from head to tail.

Matsuba This word describes a black pattern in the centre of the scales, commonly described as a 'pine-cone' pattern. Non-metallic Matsuba koi are classed in Kawarimono, metallic ones in Hikarimono (see pages 163 and 178-9).

Tancho Literally, 'red spot on the head'. Tancho koi have only one hi marking, which is on the head. These Tancho Kohaku, Sanke and Showa are judged in a separate Tancho class in shows.

Utsuri Literally, 'reflections'. Actually, the name of a group of koi (the full classification name is Utsurimono), utsuri describes the pattern on these koi, where the sumi markings are often mirrored by the second colour (white, red or yellow, depending on the variety) on the opposite side of the dorsal.

Above: **Tancho Sanke**
Tancho koi, with their striking red head marking, are understandably popular with koi-keepers all over the world.

Above: **Gin Matsuba**
The matsuba pattern in the scales, which creates a latticelike effect, shows up particularly well against the metallic white skin of this impressive variety.

Scalation
Most koi are fully scaled over the body. Such normally scaled koi are called 'wagoi', but this term is rarely used. Other Japanese words used to describe the scalation of koi include:

Doitsu Koi that are only partially scaled are known as doitsu koi (see page 12 for their history). If a koi has doitsu scalation, the word doitsu is used as a prefix to its variety; for example, Doitsu Hariwake, Doitsu Purachina. There are a few exceptions to this when a doitsu koi becomes a separate variety; for example, a doitsu Asagi is a Shusui. Although variations are not generally differentiated in shows, there are, in fact, three separate types of doitsu scalation:

Leather koi have no scales along the lateral line and only very small scales along the dorsal line. This is the normal type of doitsu scalation.

Mirror doitsu koi have large scales along both the lateral and dorsal lines.

Yoroi or Ishigaki doitsu koi are partially scaled koi that have scales other than along the lateral and dorsal lines, in jumbled patterns. ('Yoroi' means 'armour', and 'ishigaki' means stone wall scales.) These koi are not considered to be of high enough quality to be worth entering in competitive shows.

Kinginrin This term, often abbreviated to ginrin, refers not to the extent of scalation but to a certain type; kinginrin scales are highly reflective, sparkling when they catch the light. Although any koi may have some kinginrin scales, only a koi with about 20 or more would be classed as Kinginrin. Until 1988, all Kinginrin koi were judged independently from normally scaled koi of the same variety. Now only Kinginrin Kohaku, Sanke and Showa are judged in a separate Kinginrin class (see pages 198-201).

Fucarin A term adopted only in the late 1980s, fucarin describes the area of skin between the scales rather than the scales themselves. Fucarin is usually associated with good metallic koi. It is generally considered that the smaller the scales, the better the lustre on the koi. The diagrams below show the difference between fucarin and normal scalation.

Normal scalation

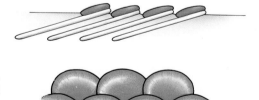

Fucarin scalation

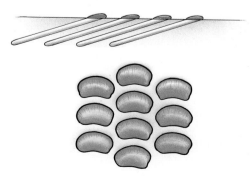

Above: *Good metallic koi have smaller scales that allow the skin to show between them (bottom). Such scalation is known as fucarin and the effect is to improve the quality of lustre, or shine, on the koi.*

Above: **Kinginrin Showa**
The sparkling deposit on nearly all the body scales of this beautiful koi differ from the all-over metallic lustre of, for example, the Gin Matsuba shown in the opposite photo.

Lustre
Lustre is a word sometimes used to describe the shine that should be present on the skin of a healthy koi. However, it can also be used to differentiate between metallic and non-metallic koi. The two principal words that are used to describe the lustre on a koi are:

Hikari Used as a prefix to a classification name, hikari indicates that all the koi in that group are metallic. Hence, Hikarimono denotes single-coloured metallic koi, for example. Of the fourteen classifications, the three containing truly metallic koi are all prefixed 'Hikari': Hikarimono, Hikari-Utsurimono and Hikarimoyo-mono. (Kinginrin koi have a number of sparkling scales rather than being truly metallic, see above).

Kawari This word, normally used as a prefix, means non-metallic. It is used primarily in Kawarimono, which is probably the largest group of koi. This classification contains all non-metallic koi not included in any other group.

KOI VARIETIES

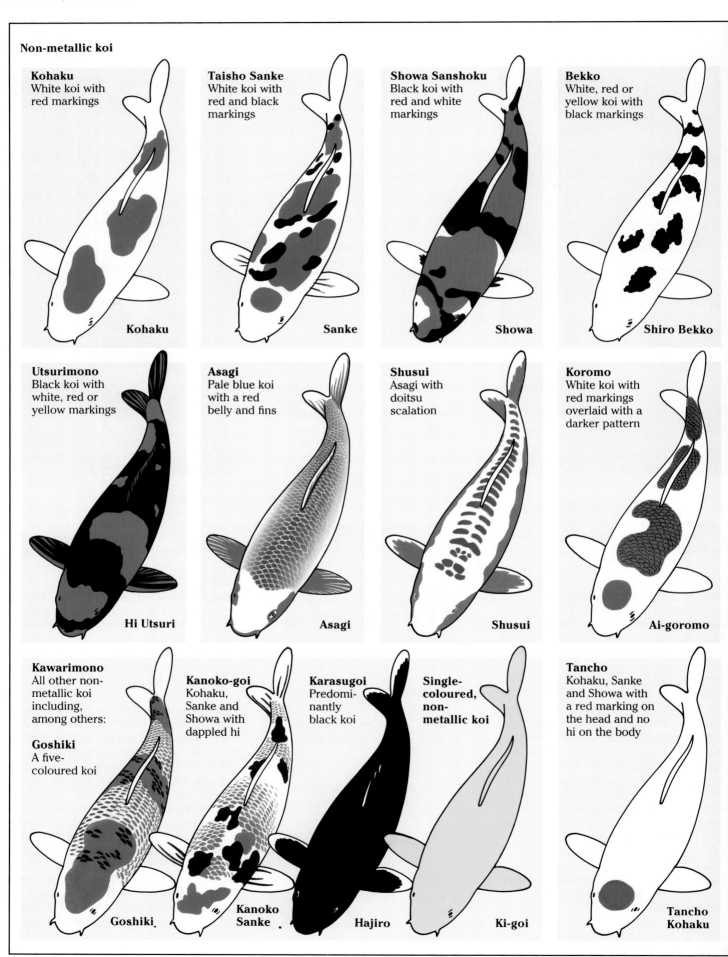

Non-metallic koi

Kohaku
White koi with red markings

Kohaku

Taisho Sanke
White koi with red and black markings

Sanke

Showa Sanshoku
Black koi with red and white markings

Showa

Bekko
White, red or yellow koi with black markings

Shiro Bekko

Utsurimono
Black koi with white, red or yellow markings

Hi Utsuri

Asagi
Pale blue koi with a red belly and fins

Asagi

Shusui
Asagi with doitsu scalation

Shusui

Koromo
White koi with red markings overlaid with a darker pattern

Ai-goromo

Kawarimono
All other non-metallic koi including, among others:

Goshiki
A five-coloured koi

Goshiki

Kanoko-goi
Kohaku, Sanke and Showa with dappled hi

Kanoko Sanke

Karasugoi
Predominantly black koi

Hajiro

Single-coloured, non-metallic koi

Ki-goi

Tancho
Kohaku, Sanke and Showa with a red marking on the head and no hi on the body

Tancho Kohaku

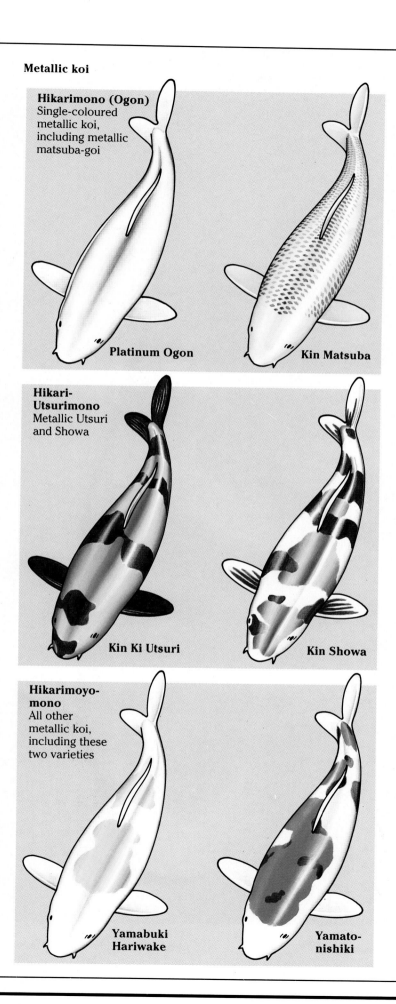

Metallic koi

Hikarimono (Ogon)
Single-coloured metallic koi, including metallic matsuba-goi

Platinum Ogon

Kin Matsuba

Hikari-Utsurimono
Metallic Utsuri and Showa

Kin Ki Utsuri

Kin Showa

Hikarimoyo-mono
All other metallic koi, including these two varieties

Yamabuki Hariwake

Yamato-nishiki

As you might imagine, many koi are produced that do not fit easily in the confines of a specific variety. The Japanese, in particular, are adept at accepting new and interesting koi (and thinking up new names) and their classifications for showing purposes reflect this. So, although your koi may not have a specific variety name, you should be able to place it, however tenuously, in one of the classifications that we review briefly here and consider in more detail in the following pages. These are:

1 Kohaku
2 Taisho Sanke
3 Showa Sanshoku
4 Bekko
5 Utsurimono
6 Asagi
7 Shusui
8 Koromo
9 Kawarimono
10 Hikarimono (Ogon)
11 Hikari-Utsurimono
12 Hikarimoyo-mono
13 Tancho
14 Kinginrin

The Japanese system of classification is designed to accommodate not only the specific variety groups (1-8 and 10 above), but also the following, more flexible, classifications:

Kawarimono This group includes all non-metallic koi that do not appear in a more specific variety.

Hikari-Utsurimono. These are metallic Utsuri and Showa.

Hikarimoyo-mono All metallic koi that do not fall in any other classification are included in this group.

The remaining two classifications, Tancho and Kinginrin, both include Kohaku, Sanke and Showa with, respectively, specific markings or type of scales. (Kinginrin koi are not illustrated here because their markings are the same as those of Kohaku, Sanke and Showa; they differ only in their scalation.)

Two other classifications have been recognized in Japanese shows since 1988:

Goshiki This five-coloured koi is still judged in the Kawarimono classification elsewhere in the world.

Doitsu koi Doitsu koi of any variety (except Shusui, which is a variety in its own right) are now judged in a separate classification in Japan.

KOHAKU

One of the most quoted phrases in koi-keeping is that the hobbyist begins with the Kohaku and ends with the Kohaku. In fact, many new hobbyists overlook the Kohaku in preference for the brightly coloured Ogon (see pages 174-9) and other metallic koi because they feel that Kohaku 'look too much like goldfish'! However, as they begin to appreciate the colours and patterns of koi, hobbyists often turn to Kohaku because of their simplicity and elegance.

Not only do Kohaku share the red and white colours of both the Japanese flag and the symbol of that country, the Tancho crane (a white bird with a red head), but it is much more difficult to find a prize Kohaku than a show winner of any other variety. In Japan, to own a good Kohaku is the ambition of every koi-keeper.

The history of Kohaku

Red and white koi first appeared in Japan between 1804 and 1829, when the offspring of a black carp was found to have red cheeks. She was called Hookazuki and her white offspring were bred with a Higoi, a red fish, to produce koi with red stomachs. By 1829, a koi with red gill plates called Hoo Aka had been produced, and between 1830 and 1849 several different patterns appeared, including Zukinkaburi (red forehead), Menkaburi (red head), Kuchibeni (red lips) and Sarasa (red spots on the back).

The breeding of Kohaku continued and varieties were improved, especially in the Niigata region, now considered the birthplace of koi-keeping. In about 1888, a gentleman called Gosuke bought a Hachi Hi, a red-headed female, and bred it with his Sukura Kana, a cherry blossom patterned male. It is believed that the modern Kohaku was developed from the offspring of these koi.

Between 1949 and 1952, Gosuke's koi were inherited by Tomoin and at least two distinct lineages resulted from these fish. Two of Tomoin's koi were sold to Buketa, who developed Kohaku with a very fine skin of transparent white, occasionally prone to yellowing, and with a purplish hi (red marking). This lineage has a particularly good body shape.

The second line evolved in about 1944, when a Tomoin female was bred with a Monjiro male, and between 1950 and 1960 the Yagozen line was created. These Kohaku also have good shapes but the hi is of a vermillion hue, which tends to splatter. However, markings are usually well defined and the white opaque.

These are the two principal lines that have been developed; there are others, but most hobbyists would find individual lineages difficult to identify.

Above: **Kohaku**
This impressive female Kohaku displays a voluminous, well-shaped body. Excellent colour and definition add precision to the well-balanced pattern, which extends from the head to the tail of this particular koi.

Maruten Kohaku

Left: **Maruten Kohaku**
This a well-shaped male. Note the hi marking on the head, known as the maruten spot, which is distinct from the pattern on the rest of the body. Definition between the colours is good on the whole, although the pattern is slightly smudged on the shoulder.

KOHAKU

Kohaku colours

Kohaku are white koi with red, or hi (pronounced 'he') markings. Ideally, the hi should have a good depth of colour but, more importantly, the colour should be of a uniform shade and the edges of the hi pattern should be well defined. This definition between hi and white markings is known as 'kiwa'. There appear to be two types of hi coloration. The purplish red hi is dark but does not fade easily. This colour is considered to lack elegance and tends to splatter over the koi. Brownish red hi can produce a very fine, almost translucent, colour but tends to fade easily. The Japanese tend to prefer this colour hi, which they consider more elegant than the purplish hi.

The white should be the colour of pure snow and free from blemishes. A poor white, which can be dirty yellow in appearance, will spoil an otherwise good Kohaku because the hi pattern does not stand out well against it. Small black specks can sometimes appear on Kohaku. These are known as 'shimis' and are detrimental to the koi's appearance. They may be caused by poor nutrition or water quality and will often disappear if the koi is kept under better conditions.

The unity and balance of colour and pattern on a Kohaku are of utmost importance. As a general guideline, the hi should cover between 50 and 70 percent of the koi and the white between 30 and 50 percent. If there is more than 50 percent of white on a Kohaku, the koi may be bland in appearance. It is the hi, complemented and emphasized by the white, that creates the impression on the eye.

Kohaku patterns

Because Kohaku appear such simple koi in terms of coloration, the criteria by which they are judged are severe. The pattern on a Kohaku is the last factor to be considered when the koi is being judged but is probably the most discussed. Balance over the whole of the koi's body is the key to any pattern.

Head

On any Kohaku the hi pattern begins on the head. Kohaku without hi on the head are considered worthless in terms of competition. The traditional head pattern for the hi is a large U shape, which should reach down as far as the eyes. Hi that extends over the eyes is considered a defect, however. If the hi does not reach the eyes, the pattern may be compensated for, or balanced by, 'kuchibeni' or lipstick-like markings. In Japan this throwback to the original carp is frowned upon, but elsewhere it is considered charming and is greatly admired by hob-

Below: **Kohaku head patterns**
A variety of hi patterns are acceptable on the head of a Kohaku. The traditional pattern is the U shape. The menkaburi pattern, which extends over the head and face of the koi, is generally unpopular.

Kuchibeni

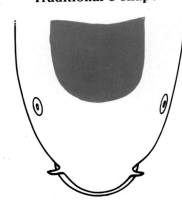

Traditional U shape

Hanatsuki

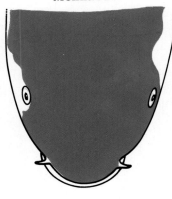

Menkaburi

byists. A hi marking that reaches the mouth is known as 'hanatsuki', and a pattern that spreads over the face is called 'menkaburi'. Both these patterns are generally unpopular as they are considered to lack refinement or elegance.

Recently, however, koi-keepers have begun to appreciate Kohaku with interesting or irregular-shaped markings on the head; for example, Tancho Kohaku with a diamond-shaped mark (see page 194). Such markings can add character to the fish and their aesthetic appeal may override any preconceived ideas as to what constitutes 'good' markings. A koi whose hi reaches the nose may, therefore, be redeemed by other markings, such as a blush on the cheek.

There are two varieties of Kohaku that are named in connection with their head markings. These are:

Tancho Kohaku This is a white koi with a red spot on the head. In a show, Tancho Kohaku would be judged in the Tancho classification (see pages 194-7), rather than with other Kohaku.

Maruten Kohaku This koi has a separate red spot on the head along with other hi markings on the body.

Body

Large hi markings, known as 'omoyo', are preferred to small hi markings (komoyo) on Kohaku as they create a stronger impression against the white. This is especially true of markings behind the head since this is the part of the Kohaku pattern that most attracts the eye. A break in the hi pattern is preferred between the back of the head and the shoulder. Variation is also important, however; an interestingly patterned koi is more highly prized than a Kohaku with a straight hi pattern. A continuous pattern without variation from head to tail is known as 'ippon hi' (see page 132) and is a valueless pattern in terms of showing.

Koi grow from the abdomen, so when selecting young Kohaku, look for patterns with large hi markings as they will stretch and may even break up. The small hi markings on a young Kohaku will also stretch but will rarely cover the body

Inazuma Kohaku

Right: **Inazuma Kohaku**
*This cigar-shaped male koi shows good,
even coloration and excellent definition of
pattern. Unfortunately, the hi pattern is
rather heavy and the final hi marking
extends into the tail. The slightly yellow
coloration on the head is also a flaw.*

KOHAKU

sufficiently to make a good impression.

Smaller hi markings, resembling splatters of paint, are known as 'tobihi' (which literally means hi that has 'jumped away') and are considered detrimental to appearance. If such markings appear on the lower half of a large koi they do not represent a serious defect as they are not too conspicuous. If, however, they appear on the shoulder they break up the homogeneity of the pattern and are considered a more serious flaw.

Another thing to look for when choosing Kohaku is secondary hi, known as 'nibani', which suggests the koi is of a poor quality. This hi will appear and disappear depending on such factors as the amount of colour enhancer that is incorporated in the koi's diet.

Balance of pattern over the body of the koi is most important. A Kohaku that has most of its hi pattern at the front of its body, for example, lacks balance and elegance and is of no value for showing. Patterns should begin at the head and end at the tail. On larger koi, the hi pattern should, ideally, wrap around the body below the lateral line to add elegance. This type of pattern is called 'makibara'. On smaller koi, the hi should extend only to the lateral line.

Kohaku patterns can be divided roughly into two categories:

1 Continuous patterns that extend from the head to the tail are known as 'moyo'.

Inazuma Kohaku This is a continuous pattern, extending from the head to the tail, but with variation. Inazuma literally means 'lightning strike'.

2 Stepped patterns are known as 'dangara' or 'danmoyo' and are much more highly valued by the Japanese than continuous patterns because they are more obviously balanced. Dangara patterns are described by the number of markings down the body of the koi.

Nidan Kohaku Nidan means two and a Nidan Kohaku has two hi markings.

Sandan Kohaku This is a Kohaku with three hi markings.

Yondan Kohaku This is a Kohaku with four hi body markings.

The hi pattern on either the continuous or dangara-patterned Kohaku should be balanced not only down the length of the koi, but also on either side of the dorsal fin. A pattern on only one side of a koi's body is called 'kata moyo'.

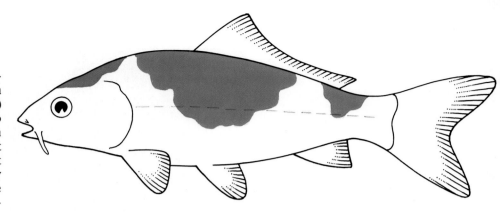

Above: *A hi pattern that wraps around the body below the lateral line on the koi is especially important on a large Kohaku. This pattern is called 'makibara'.*

Below: *On this Kohaku, the hi pattern does not extend below the lateral line. Judges generally prefer this pattern to the makibara pattern on smaller koi.*

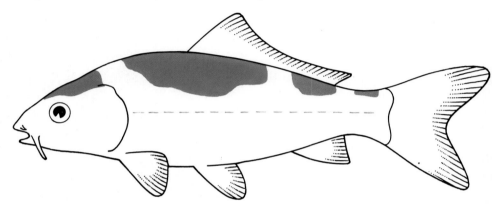

Ippon hi   **Kata moyo**

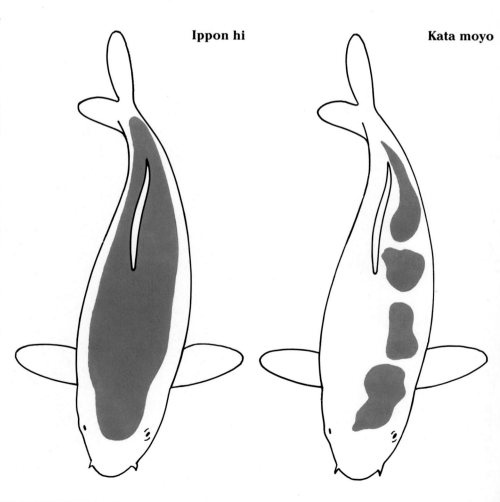

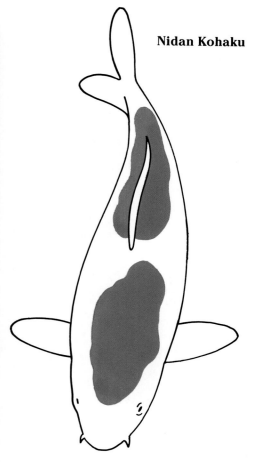

Nidan Kohaku

Left: **Nidan Kohaku**
This male Kohaku has a good balanced shape, although it lacks volume. The pattern and colour are excellent; note in particular the break in the hi near the front of the dorsal fin. A weakness is the head hi pattern, which moves into the eye.

Other varieties of Kohaku include:

Goten-zakura Kohaku This koi has a pattern more commonly known as a cherry-blossom pattern. The hi is dappled and looks like clusters of grapes.

Kanoko Kohaku
   See *Kawarimono* (pages 166 and 168).

Tail
The end of the pattern is as important as its beginning and continuation along the body. On a perfectly marked Kohaku, the hi pattern ends just before the tail joint. A hi marking that spreads into the joint of the tail gives the pattern a heavy and unfinished appearance and is considered a defect. Likewise, if there is no hi marking near the joint of the tail, there will be an area without pattern, known as 'bongiri', which will also be considered a flaw if the koi is entered in a show.

Fins
Snow white fins are the perfect accompaniment to the red on white pattern of a

KOHAKU

Sandan Kohaku

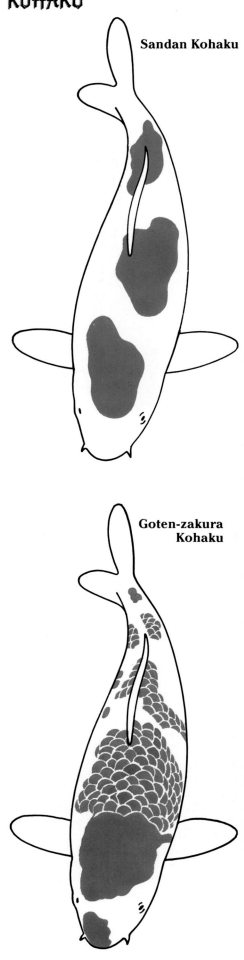

**Goten-zakura
Kohaku**

Yondan Kohaku

Left: **Sandan Kohaku**
The white fins show off the deep even hi of this koi. The head pattern is the traditional U shape but, unfortunately, the hi marking moves slightly into one eye.

Right: **Yondan Kohaku**
This is a young koi, probably male, with a long, thin, but symmetrical, body shape. The hi pattern on the body is good, but the head marking is messy and unfinished.

large Kohaku. As a general rule, hi extending into the fins is considered detrimental to the koi's markings. Hi in the pelvic fins is not a problem because it cannot be seen when a koi is judged, while hi in the pectoral and caudal fins devalues the koi. If the hi wraps round the body of the koi, hi in the joints of the pectoral fins may be permissible. Kohaku occasionally have black in the fins and this is obviously unacceptable.

Scalation
Scalation should be even all over the body of the koi. The Japanese prefer hi that is strong enough to disguise the individual scales. Scales that are visible because the hi is thin are known as 'kokesuki'. Scales with 'shadows' under the skin are known as 'madoaki'. A Kohaku of any pattern with scales only along the dorsal and lateral lines is known as a Doitsu Kohaku (see *Scalation*, page 125).

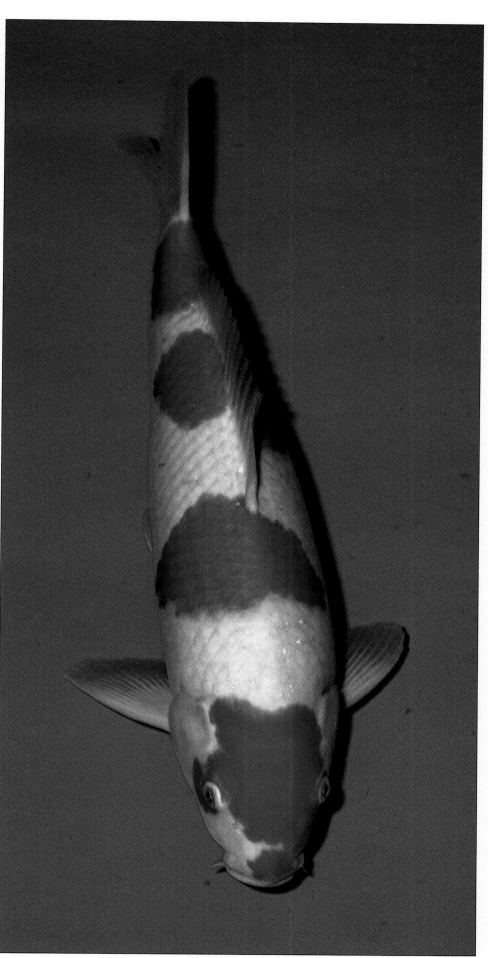

TAISHO SANKE

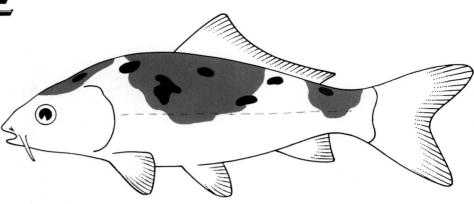

Sanke are extremely popular with hobbyists in all countries and, along with Kohaku and Showa, are among the major prize winners in competitions. Their wide variety of patterns can give them a more individual appearance than Kohaku at first glance.

The word Sanke literally means tri-colour, the three colours being red, white and black. In Japanese characters the word Sanke is also read as Sanshoku, the term used in early works on koi.

The history of Sanke

The word Taisho refers to the period in Japanese history when the Sanke was first recorded, that is, between 1912 and 1926. Sanke were among the first koi ever exhibited. A male Sanke, owned by a man called Gonzo Hiroi from Shoiya, was shown at the Tokyo Exhibition in 1914, where the Emperor's son saw koi for the first time. The names of the first breeders of Sanke were not recorded, but, as this koi was approximately 15 years of age at that time, the first Sanke were probably produced at the end of the nineteenth century (or between 1868 and 1912 – the Meiji era of Japanese history).

Among the first Sanke recorded were those from Ojiya City, in Niigata, where Heitaro Sato found them among Kohaku fry in 1915. These were bought by Eizabura Hoshino from Takezawa who then crossed one with a male Shiro Bekko (see pages 144-5), so forming one of the first distinct Taisho Sanke lines.

Over the past 60 years the markings of the Sanke have changed quite dramatically. The first Sanke were very striped in appearance but today's show-winning Sanke is a beautifully balanced koi whose sumi, although deeper in shade, is more delicate in appearance than that of its ancestors. Many distinct lineages have been developed. Among the better known is the Sadazo Sanke bred by Sadazo Kawakami, which has bright hi markings with small sumi markings that do not overlap the hi. This koi differs greatly from a Sanke from the Jimbei lineage, where both the hi and the sumi are dark in colour, but whose large, shiny sumi markings resemble those of Showa.

Sanke colours

The Sanke is a three-coloured koi with hi (red) and sumi (black) markings on a white base. As with the Kohaku, the depth of these colours is very important. The white should be the colour of snow – a yellowish white does not give a good background for the pattern to stand out against, gives the koi a dull appearance, and generally lacks the visual impact of a pure, opaque white.

The hi should be of the same quality as on a good Kohaku, that is, it should be of a deep hue and of uniform shade. The proportion of red to white should, again, be the same as on a good Kohaku. The base of any good Sanke pattern is a good Kohaku pattern; Sanke are basically Kohaku with Bekko markings.

The sumi (black) of a Sanke, like all other koi colours, should be fine, uniform in shade, and with a good depth of colour. It should be shiny in appearance, like Japanese lacquer. As sumi should overlay the Kohaku-style pattern, the markings need to be clearly defined in order to stand out. They should also appear in a balanced pattern.

Sumi can appear and disappear over the lifetime of a koi, and sumi of a poor quality may be affected by water quality, temperature and change of environment. A koi with poor sumi will obviously never make a good show koi because the pattern may fade when it is bowled, giving it the appearance of only a second-rate Kohaku. Sumi that is apparent in fry and remains in the adult koi is known as 'moto', or original sumi, and that which appears later is called 'ato', or late sumi. It is as well to bear in mind, when buying young Sanke, the fact that a Sanke's sumi can change in quality throughout its life. Good sumi in baby koi, for example, can deteriorate as the fish grows; it is rare for a Sanke with good sumi markings as a baby to keep in that condition above size 4 (see *Showing koi*, page 117). A Sanke that has underlying sumi markings – known as 'sashi' – as a baby, on the other hand, becomes more stable with age.

Sumi markings on Sanke are also described by their position on the pattern of the koi, so sumi that appears on the white skin is known as 'tsubo' sumi, while sumi that appears on the hi is known as 'kasane' sumi. Tsubo sumi is believed to be more stable than kasane sumi, but appreciation depends on the quality and position of the sumi as a whole. (Note the solid, deep kasane sumi on the Aka Sanke on page 139.)

Above: *The basis of a good Sanke pattern is a Kohaku pattern. Hi may extend below the lateral line but sumi rarely does so.*

Right: **Taisho Sanke**
A stunning aspect of this impressive Sanke is its skin quality; the translucent appearance of its skin enhances the clear coloration and interesting pattern. Note the break in the hi behind the head.

Sanke patterns

Although Sanke differ from Kohaku in that they have three colours, the criteria by which the two varieties are judged are very similar. As we have mentioned, the balance of colour and pattern is of the greatest importance on koi. Very simply, if the sumi were removed from a well-marked Sanke it would be a good Kohaku, whereas if the hi were removed, it would make a good Shiro Bekko.

Head

There should be no sumi on the head of a Sanke. The head pattern required is the same as on a Kohaku; that is, a large U-shaped hi marking, which should not extend down over the eyes, the face, or as far as the mouth. Unusually shaped head markings are not so easily tolerated as on Kohaku, possibly because there is an extra colour on the fish and a 'busy' pattern lacks elegance and visual impact. This does not mean that a blush on the cheek or 'kuchibeni' lips are necessarily detrimental to a Sanke, however; it all depends on the particular fish.

Body

Large hi markings are preferred down the length of the Sanke's body, complemented by sumi markings, which should also extend the length of the body. Sumi markings should start on the shoulder, along with a hi marking, giving a balanced pattern down the body.

Sumi markings should be small in number – an excessive amount of smaller sumi markings gives the koi an untidy appearance – and should not extend below the lateral line of the koi.

TAISHO SANKE

Hi markings should be similar in pattern to those of Kohaku and balanced on either side of the koi. These may be stepped or there may be one large hi marking down the body of the koi. If the hi markings are concentrated at the front of the body, the koi will lack balance.

Aka Sanke This is a Sanke whose hi marking extends the length of the body.

Maruten Sanke This is a Sanke with a separate hi marking on the head.

Fuji Sanke Not a variety as such, this is the name given to a Sanke with a highly metallic lustre on the head, visible as minute bubbles. Such markings tend to disappear when the koi grows.

Tail

Sanke tend to suffer with too much sumi towards the tail, and this can be detrimental to the fish's appearance. As with Kohaku, the pattern over the body of the koi – of both sumi and, even more importantly, hi – should end cleanly just before the tail joint.

Maruten Sanke

Above: **Maruten Sanke**
This is a young adult koi, probably male. The head spot is symmetrical and well placed and the hi pattern on the body is traditional, though rather heavy. The sumi is not yet fully developed.

Aka Sanke

Fins

Striped sumi is preferred in all the fins, but especially in the caudal and pectoral fins of the koi. Sumi in the fins is a sign of stability in the sumi over the body of the koi. Too large a number of sumi stripes can lead to a loss of gracefulness in appearance, however. Solid sumi in the joint of the pectoral fins, and hi in any of the fins, is also considered detrimental. Sanke may have no colour in their fins. This is not frowned upon; again, it depends on the overall balance of pattern on the koi. Such Sanke have normally derived from Kohaku lineage.

The following Sanke appear in other classifications:

Koromo Sanke
See *Koromo* (page 159).
Kanoko Sanke
See *Kawarimono* (pages 166 and 169).
Sanke Shusui
See *Kawarimono* (page 169).
Yamato-nishiki
See *Hikarimoyo-mono* (pages 184-5).
Tancho Sanke
See *Tancho* (page 194).

Above: **Aka Sanke**
The hi extends from the nose to the tail on this young koi and the small, deep sumi markings are well balanced along the body. Note the charming, clownish head marking, which ends with a dot on the nose.

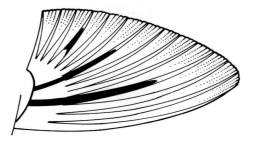

Right: *Traditional sumi stripes in the pectoral fins of the Sanke complement the sumi pattern on the body. Alternatively, the fins may be white (see page 137).*

SHOWA SANSHOKU

Here we look at Showa, the last of the big three. Like Sanke and Kohaku, this variety is very popular. Showa have much more sumi in their pattern than Sanke and are very imposing.

The history of Showa
This is a relatively new variety, first produced by Jukichi Hoshino in 1927, when he crossed a Ki Utsuri (a black koi with yellow markings, see pages 146 and 149) with a Kohaku. On the original Showa the hi was yellowish brown in colour, but this has been improved by crossing with Kohaku until the Showa we know today was produced, in about 1964.

Showa colours
Although Showa, like Sanke, are three-coloured koi, they differ from Sanke in that they are predominantly black koi with red and white markings, while Sanke are white koi with black and red markings. As with both Sanke and Kohaku, the depth and uniformity of colour are very important, and the white should be the colour of snow. A traditional Showa should generally have about 20 percent of white over its body, but this is not always the case (see Kindai Showa). The large sumi markings should be ebony in colour and the hi blood red. All colours should be clean and well defined.

Showa patterns
Not only do Showa have more sumi than Sanke, but on a Sanke the sumi markings are roundish and appear above the lateral line, while on a Showa they are larger, encompassing the body of the koi. The most obvious difference between the two varieties, however, is the sumi head marking on a Showa, which a Sanke lacks. Sumi should also appear in the joints of the pectoral fins of a Showa.

Head
The hi on the head of a Showa should be similar in pattern to that on a Kohaku except that it may extend much further down the head, over the nose, cheeks and jaws on the former.

The sumi head marking of Showa is one of the most important features of the pattern of this variety. The two most common head patterns occur where either the sumi divides the hi on the head in two (this is the traditional pattern and is known as 'menware'), or the sumi draws a V shape behind the head, with another sumi marking on the nose. This V-shaped marking is a modern pattern, which is very impressive because it so beautifully defines the head.

Body
A bright, well-defined pattern over the body of the Showa is very important. The sumi often appears as a lightning strike - 'inazuma' - over the body of the koi (see Kohaku, page 131), or may be highly patterned and distinct, producing a 'flowery' effect. Sumi markings tend to be large and can often produce asymmetrical patterns very similar to those found in Utsuri (see pages 146-9). The white and hi of a Showa emphasize the delicate or elegant pattern of the sumi by producing a distinct contrast. The hi pattern on the body of the Showa should be similar to that on a Kohaku; that is, balanced down the entire length of the koi on both sides of its body, being complemented by the white. Balance in colour is again the key factor in the pattern of a Showa.

Hi Showa This is a predominantly red Showa, that is, with a straight hi marking from nose to tail. The hi tends to be more orange in colour than on other Showa varieties (see page 142).

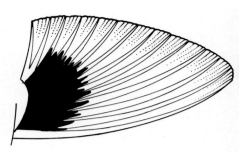

Above: *Traditionally, Showa have sumi in the base of their pectoral fins. Markings should be even in both fins and of a symmetrical shape in the base.*

Kindai Showa This modern Showa has a predominantly white pattern, with significantly more white on its body, therefore, than the 20 to 30 percent found on most traditional Showa.

Boke Showa The sumi on this Showa is blurred and indistinct, more grey than black in appearance. This variety is becoming very popular.

Tail
Although the requirements for tail patterning in Showa are not as clearly defined as for Kohaku and Sanke, the pattern, nevertheless, should be balanced and should not extend into the tail. A white tail gives a clean finish.

Fins
The markings in the pectoral fins on Showa are very important to balance and offset the pattern of the koi. Sumi should be found in the base of the pectoral fin and should be the same on both sides.

Other varieties of Showa appear in other classifications:

Koromo Showa
    See *Koromo* (page 159).
Kage Showa
    See *Kawarimono* (page 164).
Kanoko Showa
    See *Kawarimono* (pages 166 and 167).
Kin Showa
    See *Hikari-Utsurimono* (page 180).
Tancho Showa
    See *Tancho* (pages 194 and 197).

Below: **Menware head marking**
This traditional Showa head pattern is called 'menware'. Here the sumi divides the hi marking on the head, often with an 'inazuma', or 'lightning strike', pattern.

Below: **V-shaped head marking**
On this modern Showa pattern the head is defined by a sumi marking on the back of the head. This may be balanced with a sumi marking on the nose or jaw.

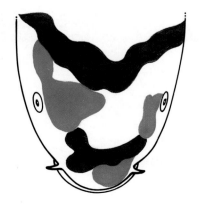

Right: **Showa**
The solid sumi in the base of the pectoral fins sets off the markings on the body of this beautiful koi. The sumi pattern on the head is heavy and deep in colour but balances with the hi, which is even and extends along the length of the koi. The body shape is symmetrical and elegant.

SHOWA SANSHOKU

Right: **Hi Showa**
The superb body shape and colour of this koi are balanced by large pectoral fins with solid, even sumi in the base. The sumi markings are deep and evenly spaced along the length of the body and are complemented by the hi. The colour and pattern on the head are particularly good and the skin quality is excellent.

Hi Showa

Kindai Showa

Boke Showa

Above: **Kindai Showa**
This interesting young koi has a large
proportion of white on its body. The sumi
overlaps the hi marking and is well spaced
down the body. Unlike most Showa, this koi
has clear, white pectoral fins.

BEKKO

Bekko are mat (that is, non-metallic) white, red or yellow koi that have a distinctive set of sumi markings over their body. They are often mistaken for Utsuri, which are similar but are predominantly black koi with white, red or yellow markings. Their simple coloration and pattern ensure that the criteria by which they are judged are severe.

Bekko are a derivative of the Taisho Sanke family. In simple terms, a Shiro Bekko, for example, is a Sanke with no hi pattern on its body. These koi are not produced in great numbers and good Bekko under size 4 are very hard to find.

Bekko colours
The Bekko's sumi markings should be jet black and solid in appearance.

Shiro Bekko This is a white koi with sumi markings. The white should be pure and the colour of snow. A yellowish head is detrimental as it lacks elegance and gives the fish a dirty appearance. The colour should be even over the body of the koi. Doitsu Shiro Bekko can also be very attractive, particularly when the markings are clearly defined. Large doitsu scales, however, can complicate the elegant simplicity of the pattern.

Aka Bekko This is a red koi with sumi markings. (Aka is another word for red). Often the red is of an orange hue; Aka Bekko with a deep red coloration are rarely seen, especially as the colour seems to fade as the koi grows in size.

Ki Bekko This koi has a yellow base colour with sumi markings. The yellow should be of the same hue over the whole body of the koi. Like Aka Bekko, this is a very rare variety.

Bekko patterns
The pattern on Bekko is very simple and elegant, with small sumi markings spread evenly over the body.

Head
The head of a Bekko should be free of any sumi markings and the same shade of colour as the rest of the koi. It is difficult to find a Bekko that is 'bald' of any pattern on the head; any blemishes are obvious through the skin on the scalp. However, a small sumi marking on the head, for example, may be acceptable if it complements the pattern on the body. A black tancho marking is sometimes considered attractive on a Bekko, although a koi with this type of marking would not be classed as a traditional Tancho because Tancho markings have to be red (see *Tancho*, pages 194-7).

Body
A large sumi marking on each shoulder of the Bekko is desirable, as are small clusters of sumi balanced along the length of the koi's body (as on the Aka Bekko, below). Small, isolated spots of sumi, resembling freckles, are not favoured, however, although they often appear, to the detriment of Ki Bekko, in particular.

Tail
The pattern of sumi markings should finish just before the tail in the way that the pattern on a Sanke ends.

Fins
A Bekko's fins may be either white or have sumi stripes in them, similar to those of the Sanke.

Aka Bekko

Below: **Aka Bekko**
The colour of the hi is even over the body of this young koi. The deep sumi markings are relatively evenly spaced. The pectoral fins are unusual in that instead of striped sumi there is hi in the joints of the fins.

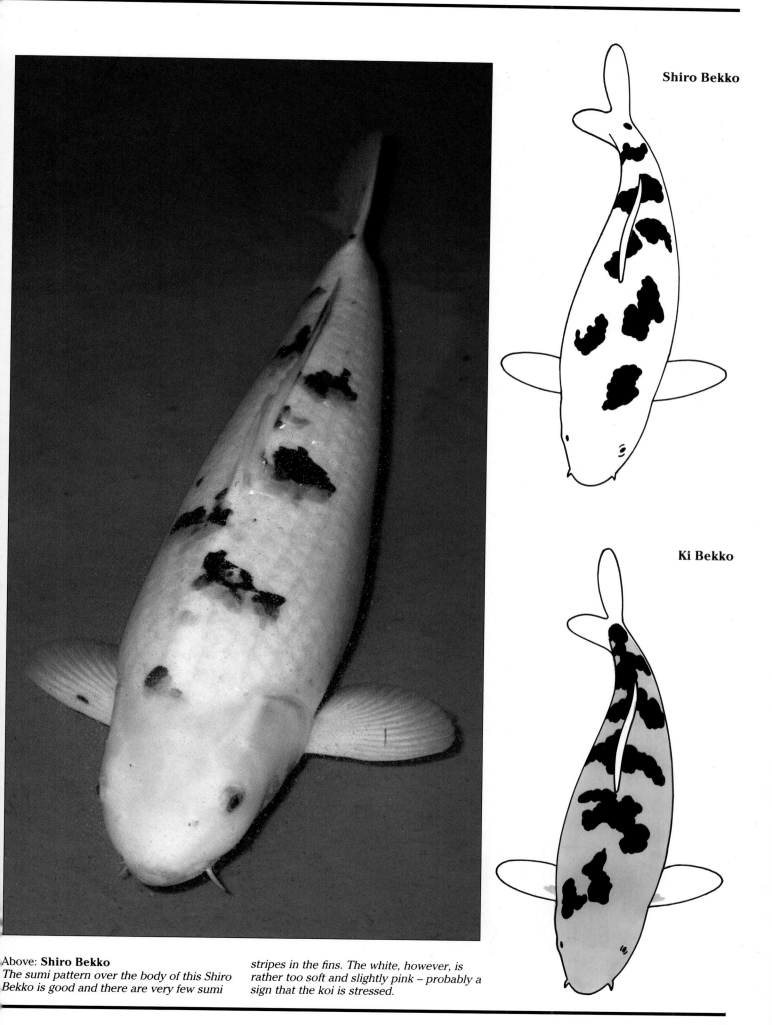

Shiro Bekko

Ki Bekko

Above: **Shiro Bekko**
The sumi pattern over the body of this Shiro Bekko is good and there are very few sumi stripes in the fins. The white, however, is rather too soft and slightly pink – probably a sign that the koi is stressed.

UTSURIMONO

Koi in the Utsurimono group are often confused with those in the Bekko classification (see pages 144-5) because of their similar coloration. The main difference between the two is that Utsuri are black koi with white, red or yellow markings, whereas Bekko are white, red or yellow koi with black markings. A further distinction can be made in the head markings of these two groups - unlike Bekko, Utsuri have a sumi marking on the head that reaches down to the nose.

In Japanese, 'utsuri' means reflections. This refers to the sumi pattern on the koi, which is often mirrored by the second colour on the opposite side of the dorsal.

The history of Utsurimono
The history of this variety is unclear. It is believed that Shiro Utsuri are of Magoi lineage and were first produced in around 1925 by a gentleman called Kazuo Minemura. However, it is known that Ki Utsuri appeared quite early in the history of koi, possibly at the beginning of the Meiji era (in about 1875), and were originally known as Kuro-Ki-Han, which literally translated means black with yellow markings. They were renamed Ki Utsuri in 1920 by Eizaburo Hoshino.

Utsurimono colours
Utsuri have striking, heavy sumi, which should be jet black in colour and of uniform shade. The second, and contrasting, colour of any Utsuri should emphasize the sumi pattern.

Shiro Utsuri This is a black koi with white markings. The white should be pure and unblemished by a yellow tinge or small black specks or 'shimis'. The cleaner the white, the more the black pattern stands out on the koi.

Hi Utsuri This is a black koi with red markings. The hi should be uniform in shade, which is difficult to achieve in this variety. Often the hi on the head is much darker than that on the body, and this

divides the pattern on the fish and detracts from the sumi pattern. It is hard to produce a good Hi Utsuri because these koi are not as stable in coloration as many of the other varieties. Black specks in the hi, which detract from the basic symmetry and simple elegance of the koi, often mar this beautiful variety.

Ki Utsuri This is a black koi with yellow markings. Ki Utsuri are rarely found but can be quite exquisite and delicate. Unfortunately, they often suffer from the same problem as Hi Utsuri, that is, black specks in the markings.

Utsurimono patterns
The Utsuri pattern owes much to the Showa Sanshoku with regards the sumi, which is the most striking aspect of this koi. In the same way that the sumi pattern on a Bekko resembles that of a Sanke, the Utsuri pattern can be described as that of Showa without the extra colour.

Head
The sumi pattern required on the head of an Utsuri is the same as that on a Showa; that is, a lightning strike sumi that divides the face, or a V shape. Whereas in Showa the modern V shape is more popular, on the Utsuri the sumi marking that divides the face is favoured.

Body
The sumi pattern required on the body is, again, similar to that of the Showa. Large, imposing sumi markings in a reflective pattern (black reflecting white) are preferred to a smaller chequered pattern. If the pattern is highly reflective, it is often described as 'flowery'.

The sumi on an Utsuri should wrap around the body below the lateral line, (while on a Bekko the sumi pattern remains above the lateral line). The sumi markings should extend from the nose to the tail and be balanced down the length of the body and on both sides of the dorsal line of the Utsuri.

Shiro Utsuri

Fins
The fins should have sumi in the pectoral joints. The striped fins of Bekko are not favoured on Utsuri, however.

Below: *The traditional pectoral fin pattern of Utsuri resembles that of Showa, but on the former stripes shoot out from the solid sumi in the base of each fin.*

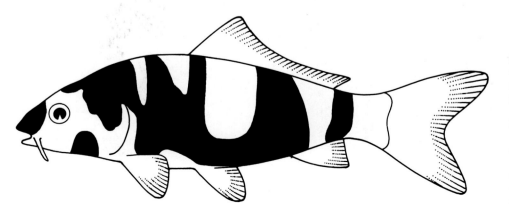

Left: *The Utsuri is a black koi with red, white or yellow markings. The sumi wraps itself around the body, extending the pattern below the lateral line.*

Right: **Shiro Utsuri**
This modern Utsuri has a larger proportion of white on its body than is usual on Utsuri. The solid sumi pattern is even down the body and less 'flowery' than many patterns. Unfortunately, the head is slightly pointed and the body rather thin.

UTSURIMONO

Above: Kinginrin Hi Utsuri
The bright colours and distinct pattern of this Hi Utsuri are complemented by kinginrin scales (see page 125), which lighten the colours of the body. The solid sumi of the fins beautifully highlights the koi's predominantly orange body. The pattern is of a modern type, that is, with less sumi than the traditional Utsuri.

Hi Utsuri

Ki Utsuri

Above: Ki Utsuri
This is a very rare koi, so slight inconsistencies in the eveness of the ki (yellow) pattern are forgivable. Note the hi spots on the left side of the body and the irregularity of colour in the fins.

ASAGI

Asagi are plain koi compared with other varieties; they are non-metallic and lack the bright coloration of many koi, being mainly grey-blue in colour with hi along the sides, cheeks and in the fins. However, a first-class Asagi is a quiet, elegant fish, with a delicate pattern of scalation and fine colour.

It is as well to remember that koi are usually viewed in a group and their value to the hobbyist depends as much on the impression they make juxtaposed with other koi in the pond as on their individual appeal. A pond full of bright metallic koi, for example, would be less striking than one of different varieties, including 'lowlights', such as Asagi.

The history of Asagi

Asagi are one of the original types of nishikigoi and their history has been documented for 160 years. These koi were developed from one of the three types of Magoi – the black carp, which is the ancestor of all modern nishikigoi varieties. One of these fish, the Asagi Magoi, has a blue back with a light blue or white pattern definition around the scales, and hi on the cheeks, sides and pectoral fins. Two types of Asagi have developed from the Asagi Magoi. The first is the Konjo Asagi, which is dark blue and very similar to the Magoi. This is a valueless form in terms of showing. The second variety, and the one from which modern Asagi are developed, is the Narumi Asagi. This koi is lighter in colour, and its scales have a dark blue centre, paling towards their edges. Its name comes from a similarly patterned tie-dyed fabric made in Narumi, Japan.

Asagi colours

The blue coloration of the Asagi varies in shade but a lighter blue is preferred. The pattern of the scalation is distinct; darker blue in the centre, lighter blue at the edges. The hi on the head, sides and pectoral fins should be strong in colour, but often tends to be orange. In colder waters, Asagi tend to become very dark, even black, in colour. This is undesirable and makes the koi worthless with regard to showing. Black specks often appear over the head and body of the koi and these are also detrimental to the appearance of this variety.

Asagi patterns

The head should be light blue-grey in colour with no inference of black or speckling. There should be hi marking along the cheeks, reaching the eyes, and the markings should be symmetrical on both sides of the face.

The markings on the body of the Asagi

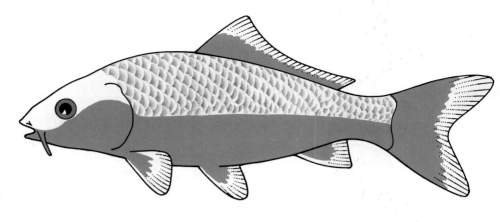

Above: *The hi marking on an Asagi normally extends from the belly up to the lateral line. There should also be hi on the jaw and in the base of all the fins.*

Below: *A good Asagi will have a deep orange (hi) marking in the base of its light grey-blue pectorals, similar in pattern to the sumi on a Showa's fins.*

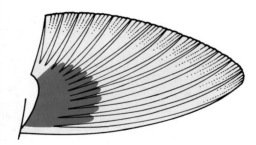

should also be symmetrical, hi should extend beneath the lateral line, and the belly should be white. The pattern on the back of the Asagi should be even over its entire length and the scales should be outlined clearly. The contrast between the centre of the scale and its edge should also be clearly defined.

Hi should extend into the base of the fins, particularly the pectorals.

Scalation

Regularity of scalation is of paramount importance. The scales should evenly cover the whole body from head to tail and the light edges of the scales should be of equal length on all scales.

Above: *The deep blue centre of each scale should be juxtaposed with a light blue edge. The eveness of the scalation over the body of an Asagi is of paramount importance.*

Narumi Asagi This is the typical light-blue patterned Asagi.

Konjo Asagi This very dark Asagi is almost black in colour.

Mizu Asagi This is a very light Asagi.

Asagi Sanke This Asagi has a pale blue back, red head and sides.

Taki Sanke The blue body of this Asagi is divided from its red sides by a white line.

Hi Asagi The hi marking of this Asagi extends over the lateral line – sometimes up to the dorsal.

Narumi Asagi

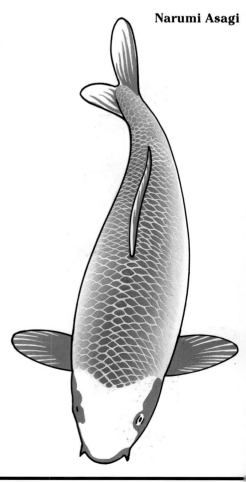

Above: Asagi
This large koi is an impressive example of an Asagi. Note the evenness of the hi markings along the jaw line and on either side of the head, which is a perfect blue-grey in colour, with no hint of black. The fins, too, are even in coloration. However, it is the uniform scalation over the body of this koi that is its most striking feature.

SHUSUI

Their unusual coloration and doitsu scalation have made Shusui firm favourites with koi-keepers, particularly those new to the hobby. They are basically doitsu Asagi and, like Asagi, have a tendency to go very dark in colder waters. As dark Shusui are worthless in terms of competition, it is not advisable to keep too many of this variety. Unlike the majority of other varieties, good Shusui are more common at size 1 than at size 4 and above, because of their tendency to darken with age. The coloration of bright young Shusui can, however, be quite startlingly beautiful.

Shusui were first produced in 1910 when Yoshigoro Akiyama crossed an Asagi Sanke with a doitsu mirror carp. Until 1986, both Asagi and Shusui were judged in the same classification but, because the lack of scale pattern on Shusui changes its appearance so dramatically, they are now regarded as separate classifications.

Shusui colours
The colour of the Shusui is basically the same as that of the Asagi. The head is blue-grey with hi on the jaws and the scales along the lateral and dorsal lines of the koi are darker blue than the rest of the koi. Because the scale pattern of Asagi is lacking, the skin on the back of the Shusui is an unusual pale sky blue, more delicate in shade than on Asagi.

Shusui patterns
The pattern on the pale blue-grey head of Shusui is the same as that on the Asagi, namely a hi marking on the jaw. The head should be free from any other markings.

Below: *The striking blue and red colours of Shusui contrast beautifully with other koi. This group includes two Shusui with Kohaku, Utsuri, Yamato-nishiki and Sanke.*

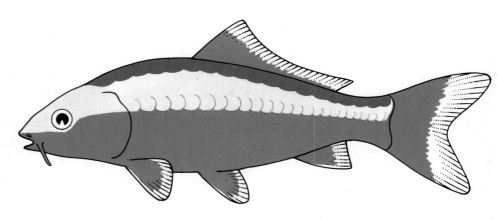

Above: *As on Asagi, the hi on Shusui should extend from the belly up to the lateral line. The evenness of the doitsu scalation is particularly important on this variety.*

The blue of the Shusui's body should be of an even shade over the length of the koi, extending from just below the lateral line up to the dorsal line on either side of the body. There should be two parallel stripes of hi reaching from behind the gills to the tail on either side of the dorsal.

Hi should extend into the base of the fins, particularly the pectorals.

Scalation
Scalation is an important aspect of the pattern of Shusui, as it is on Asagi. The scales along the dorsal line (and lateral line, if present here) should be neatly aligned. Rogue scales on the body will devalue this koi in terms of competition.

Hana Shusui This koi, also known as a flowery Shusui, has hi markings between the abdomen and the lateral line and between the lateral and dorsal lines.

Hi Shusui The hi on this Shusui spreads up from the belly and covers the back.

Ki Shusui This very rare Shusui is yellow with a greenish dorsal.

Pearl Shusui This is a Shusui with silver scales. It is very rarely seen.

Other varieties of Shusui appear in other classifications:

Sanke Shusui
　See Kawarimono (page 169).
Showa Shusui
　See Kawarimono (page 169).
Goshiki Shusui
　See Kawarimono (page 169).
Kinsui/Ginsui
　See Hikarimoyo-mono (page 190).

Right: **Shusui**
This is not a perfect example of a Shusui, although the blue coloration is good. Note the irregular scalation along the dorsal, the thin, rather poor, body shape, and the uneven hi markings in the fins.

Shusui

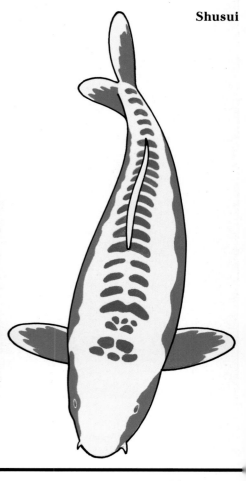

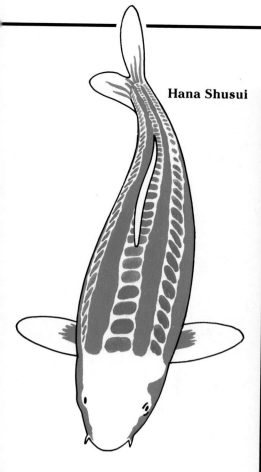

Hana Shusui

Left: **Hana Shusui**
The coloration is particularly striking on this voluminous koi; note the way the hi covers the blue to give a deeper colour. The head and fins are particularly impressive.

Hi Shusui

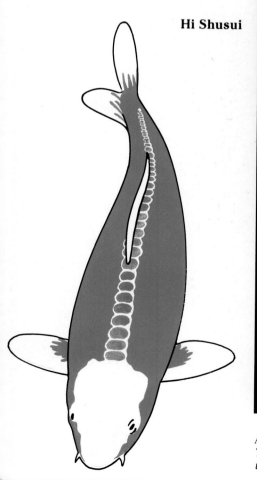

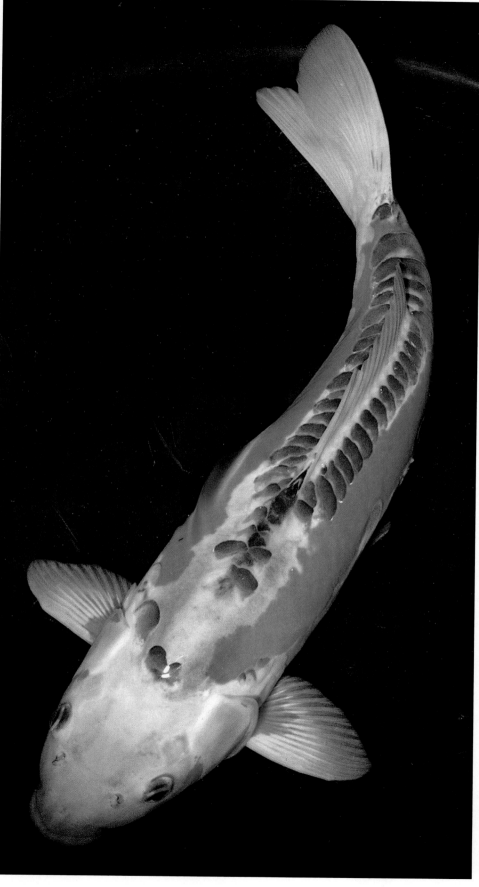

Above: **Hi Shusui**
The hi on this Shusui is strong and even but, unfortunately, the blue is nearer to grey in colour and suggests that the koi may eventually turn black. The scalation along the dorsal line is rather uneven.

KOROMO

Koi found in the Koromo group are much admired by collectors. Koromo literally means 'robed'. This describes the hi pattern, outlined in a darker colour, which varies with the particular variety. Although they tend to be insignificant as young koi, large specimens are very impressive, with an elegance to match that of Kohaku. A Koromo very rarely appears 'finished' as a young koi. If the patterns are complete when the fish is still small in size, the sumi is likely to overdevelop and become unbalanced as the koi grows. The chances of achieving a good Koromo are small compared with most other koi varieties.

Koromo koi are bred from Kohaku crossed with Narumi Asagi (see page 150). All the koi in this group have been in existence only since about 1950.

Koromo colours
The most important aspect of the Koromo is the basic Kohaku pattern with a very deep hi. This depth of colour is

Right: **Ai-goromo**
One of the most impressive features of this male Ai-goromo is the even scalation. Note the lack of sumi (or any darker markings) on the head and the interesting shape of the hi marking – a traditional Kohaku pattern.

Ai-goromo

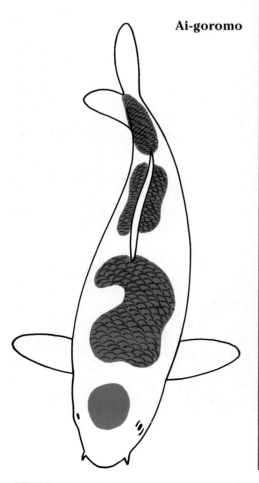

even more important than in Kohaku because a pale orange will appear 'washed out' with the overlay of Koromo.

The white should be the colour of snow and the same quality all over the koi. The white is very important in Koromo as it should offset the lace or 'robed' pattern on the hi. The colour of the lace pattern depends on the variety.

Ai-goromo This is the most common of the Koromo group. The literal translation of Ai-goromo is 'blue robed' ('Ai' means blue) and the Ai-goromo is basically a Kohaku whose hi scales have blue semicircular borders, giving the koi a reticulated pattern.

Below: *The blue-edged hi scales, shown here in close-up, are responsible for the elegant pattern of Ai-goromo. The reticulated scales should appear regularly on the hi markings over the body.*

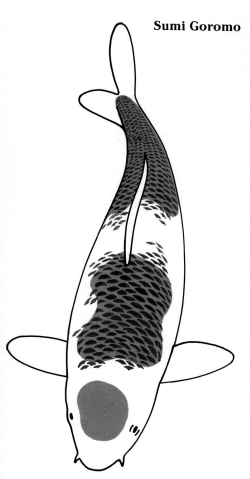

Sumi Goromo

Above: **Sumi Goromo**
The basic koromo pattern on this koi is excellent and the interesting hi marking has plenty of movement. The solid sumi markings in front of the dorsal and near the tail complement the rest of the pattern.

KOROMO

The head pattern on the Ai-goromo should be the same as that on a Kohaku. A U-shaped head marking is preferred, but more unusual head markings are more easily tolerated than on Kohaku, as perfectly marked Ai-goromo are rare. The body of the Ai-goromo should have the same hi pattern as that of the Kohaku, with the Koromo blue reticulated overlay pattern. This should be evenly spread over the hi, and should not extend to the edge of the hi or into the white. On young Ai-goromo, the blue overlay is rarely fully defined, but develops with maturity. If the blue is clearly defined on a young koi, it tends to deteriorate as the koi grows.

Male Ai-goromo tend to mature younger than female koi, whose pattern does not generally develop until size 4 or 5, so what is thought to be a baby Kohaku can sometimes develop into an Ai-goromo.

The fins of an Ai-goromo are either white, or have hi in the pectoral fins. There should be no sumi.

Sumi-goromo These koi, as the name implies, have sumi on the hi pattern, which creates an impression of dark elegance. This sumi is solid (unlike the overlaid blue on the Ai-goromo), but does not overshadow the hi pattern, which is the same as that on Kohaku.

Above: **Budo Goromo**
The snow-white base colour and elegant white fins of this well-shaped koi highlight the deep maroon pattern over its body. Note that the sumi does not extend into the white base, but is confined to the hi.

Sumi-goromo lack the neat reticulated patterns of Ai-goromo and the sumi, which is present only on the hi pattern, appears irregularly in the scales. Unfortunately, Sumi-goromo are prone to over-large sumi spots, which spoil their otherwise elegant appearance. The fins, as on an Ai-goromo, should either be white, or have hi in the base.

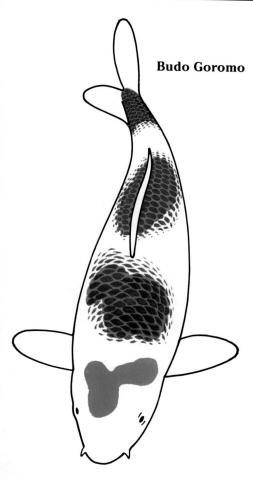

Budo Goromo

Budo Goromo These koi were, until about 1986, extremely rare, but now seem to be appearing in larger numbers. Good specimens of this variety are still exceptional, however.

The word 'budo' is literally translated as grape. This refers to both the pattern and the colour of the koi. The snow white quality of the base colour is very important as a background to the purple grape-like cluster of colour which constitutes the pattern over the body of this koi. The sumi overlays the hi, giving a purple appearance to the markings, and the delicate pattern is similar in its position to the hi pattern on a Kohaku. The clarity of the pattern on a good Budo Goromo can be startling; often it is as though the very light sumi has slipped slightly on the deep hi to show red at the front of the scale and deep purple at its base.

There may be no head markings on a Budo Goromo (that is, the head may be clear white with no markings beneath the skin), or the koi may have a head pattern similar to that of a normal Sanke or Kohaku (see pages 130 and 136 respectively). Ideally, the fins should be white and clear of any colour.

Budo Sanke The Budo Sanke is called a Sanke because both the pattern and colours of the Sanke are evident but in a different form. That is, it has sumi overlaying the hi to give a purplish effect, like the Budo Goromo, combined with solid sumi markings, placed as on a normal Sanke. A good specimen is highly prized.

Koromo Sanke The Koromo Sanke is bred from an Ai-goromo and a Taisho Sanke. It has the Koromo reticulated pattern over the hi markings along with the sumi markings of a traditional Sanke. The Sanke sumi is called the 'hon' sumi, which means 'genuine', and the overlay on the hi is called the Koromo sumi.

This variety is extremely rare and is considered a connoisseur's koi because of its sometimes complicated pattern, which is not always appreciated by newcomers to the koi-keeping hobby.

Koromo Showa This koi is the result of crossing Ai-goromo and Showa. As on the Koromo Sanke, the hi pattern of the Koromo Showa is overlaid with the reticulated Koromo pattern. This koi is sometimes referred to as Ai-Showa.

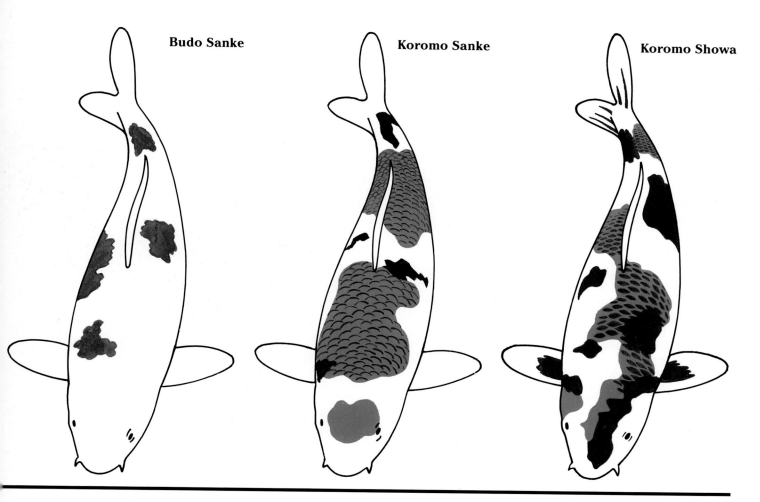

Budo Sanke   **Koromo Sanke**   **Koromo Showa**

KAWARIMONO

The Kawarimono classification accommodates all non-metallic koi that do not fall into the other varieties and is, therefore, a constantly expanding group. It includes koi that are the result of a cross between different varieties and others whose exact lineage is uncertain. Some, such as Kage Shiro Utsuri (see page 164), have been developed beyond the confines of their original classification, although their lineage is certain.

Although the Kawarimono group includes many different types of koi, the criteria by which they are judged is no less vigorous than for other varieties. All should have definite, clear-cut patterns and colours, and should be aesthetically pleasing. Larger Kawarimono can rival Kohaku, Sanke and Showa for major prizes in shows because of their subtle coloration and understated elegance.

Buying baby Kawarimono can be difficult because small Kawarimono are rare and can be singularly unimpressive. Judging how a pattern will develop with age comes only with experience, as does the confidence to appreciate 'different' varieties. Distinctive koi often appear in this classification because Kawarimono are not limited to the same variety specifications as Kohaku, for example.

Here we examine Kawarimono koi from various lineages: Karasugoi, Matsuba-goi, Kage Utsuri and Showa, Goshiki, Kanoko-goi and those of Shusui lineage, as well as other varieties whose lineages are less clearly defined. Some Kawarimono, such as Hajiro and Kumonryu, are very popular, but many are quite rare and some have not been seen, as yet, outside Japan.

Karasugoi

Some of the most sought-after koi in the Kawarimono group come from the Karasu lineage. Karasugoi are black koi with white or orange bellies. (Karasugoi literally means 'crow' fish.) The Karasugoi sumi, which is ebony in colour and darker than that of a Magoi (see pages 12 and 150), should be of the same dark hue all over the body or the koi will be worthless. Most Karasugoi are not generally admired by hobbyists because their black bodies do not show up well in the pond. However, some people like to keep one black koi in a pond because of the startling impression it makes as it suddenly breaks the surface to feed.

Right: **Kumonryu**
Note the striking contrast between the black and white markings over the body and head of this koi. The pattern on this variety is complemented by large doitsu scales along the lateral and dorsal lines.

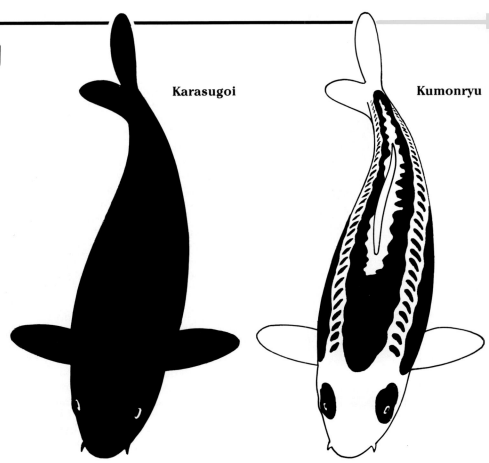

Karasugoi

Kumonryu

Sumi-nagashi

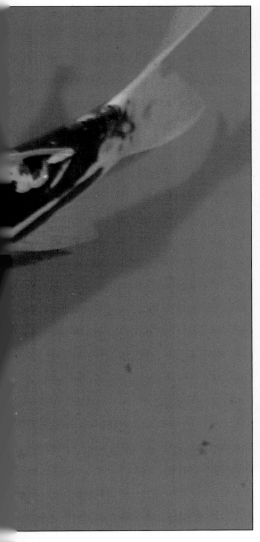

Above: **Sumi-nagashi**
The delicate pattern of black scales outlined in white is surprisingly complicated on this elegant koi. Patterns vary considerably in this variety; compare this koi with the illustration shown at above right.

KAWARIMONO

Hajiro This is a black koi with white tips to its caudal and pectoral fins. It is greatly admired by hobbyists because of the way that its white fins define its black body and make the koi visible in the pond.

Hageshiro This koi has not only white tips to its caudal and pectoral fins, but also a white head and nose.

Yotsushiro (Literally, 'five whites'.) This relatively rare koi has a white head and white pectoral and caudal fins.

Matsukawa-bake The pattern of this black and white koi changes with the time of year and water temperature.

Kumonryu Its black and white pattern, complemented by large doitsu scales, has given this koi its name, which literally means 'dragon fish'. Kumonryu is a doitsu koi with white markings on the head and fins and additional white on its body. Unfortunately, this variety has a tendency to go either completely white or black. However, the clarity of contrast between the white and black on the body of a good koi of this variety can be very beautiful. Kumonryu have become very popular since the mid 1980s and are appearing in increasing numbers.

Sumi-nagashi This is a very subtle koi whose black scales are outlined in white, creating an effect very similar to an Asagi pattern. In Japan it is sometimes known as Asagi Sumi-nagashi.

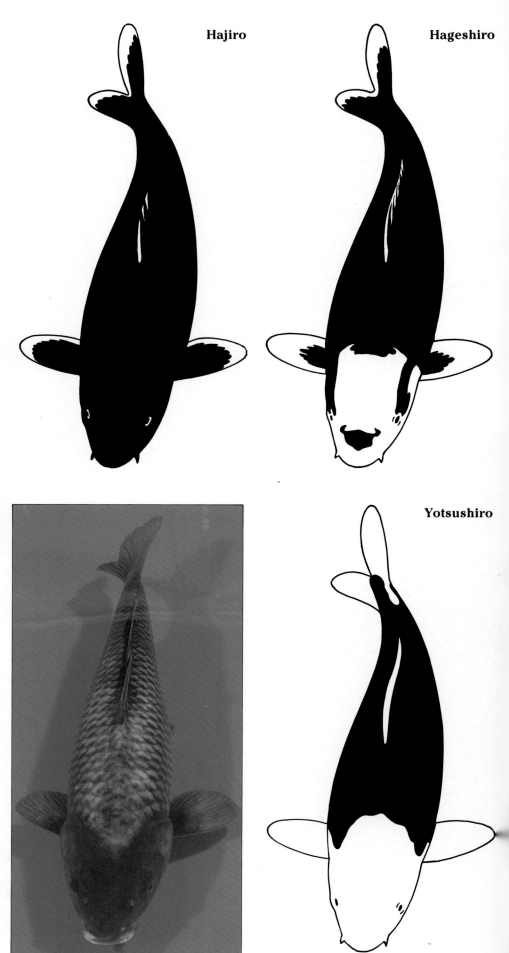

Hajiro

Hageshiro

Yotsushiro

Right: Matsukawa-bake
The patterns and coloration of this unusual koi change quite dramatically depending on such factors as water temperature and level of stress. In other conditions, the scales may be white with black centres.

Matsuba-goi

Matsuba-goi that are included in the Kawarimono classification are single-coloured, non-metallic koi with a matsuba (or 'pine-cone') pattern in the scales along the back.

Aka Matsuba This is a red koi ('aka' means red) with black markings in the centre of the scales. The red head of the Aka Matsuba should have no black markings or speckling. Although not as rare as Ki or Shiro Matsuba, this koi has become less common in recent years.

Ki Matsuba This is the yellow-based equivalent of the Aka Matsuba and is an extremely rare koi.

Shiro Matsuba This white koi has a black pine-cone patterning in the scales. Like Ki Matsuba, it is a very rare variety.

Aka, Ki and Shiro Matsuba also appear with doitsu scalation. These rare koi have black matsuba scales along the dorsal and lateral lines, which contrast with the single-coloured, non-metallic skin of the rest of the koi.

Ki Matsuba

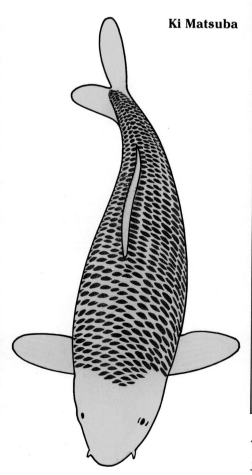

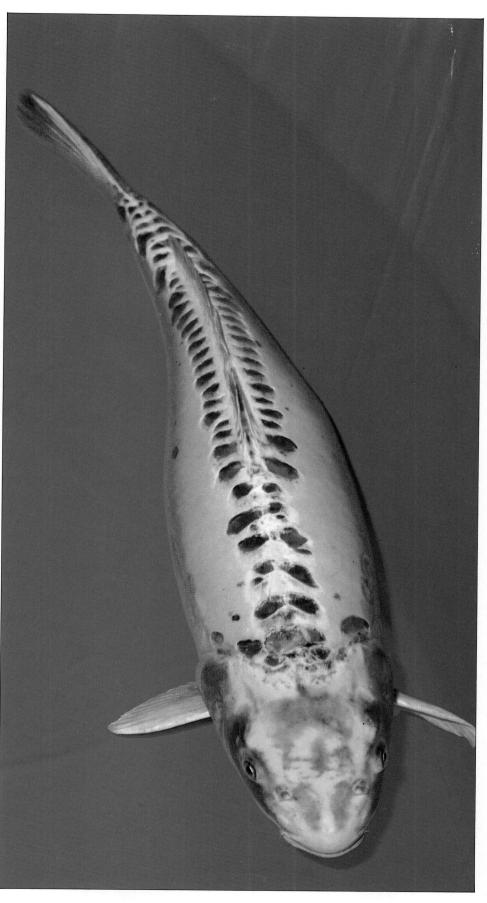

Above: **Doitsu Ki Matsuba**
The impressive scalation, body shape and yellow skin are responsible for the commanding appearance of this koi. The rarity of this variety vindicates the hint of black coloration on its head.

KAWARIMONO

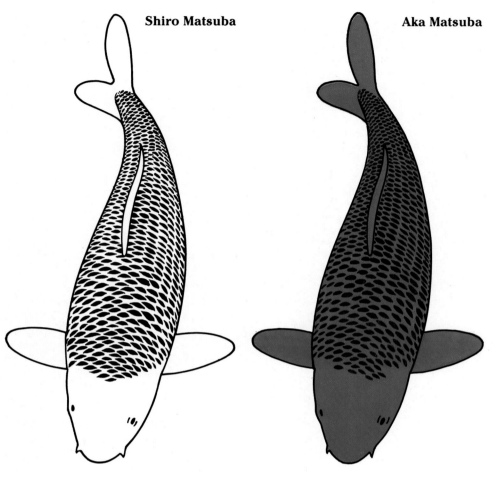

Shiro Matsuba

Aka Matsuba

Kage Utsuri and Showa

Kage varieties of koi include both Utsuri and Showa that have a blurred, reticulated black pattern over the white or hi of the koi. (The word kage literally means 'shadow' or 'phantom'.) These koi should also have a solid sumi pattern, complementing this 'shadowy' Kage pattern.

Although they are still comparatively rare, Kage koi are beginning to appear in greater numbers. Their quiet, elegant pattern is greatly admired, particularly by 'connoisseur' koi-keepers.

Kage Shiro Utsuri This variety has the basic black and white utsuri pattern with the Kage, shadowy, reticulated pattern over the white of the body.

Kage Hi Utsuri This koi has the red and black pattern of the Hi Utsuri (see pages 146 and 148) with a Kage pattern over the hi. It is especially important that the sumi pattern should be solid on this variety.

Kage Showa The Kage Showa has the basic showa markings with the Kage pattern over the white of the koi.

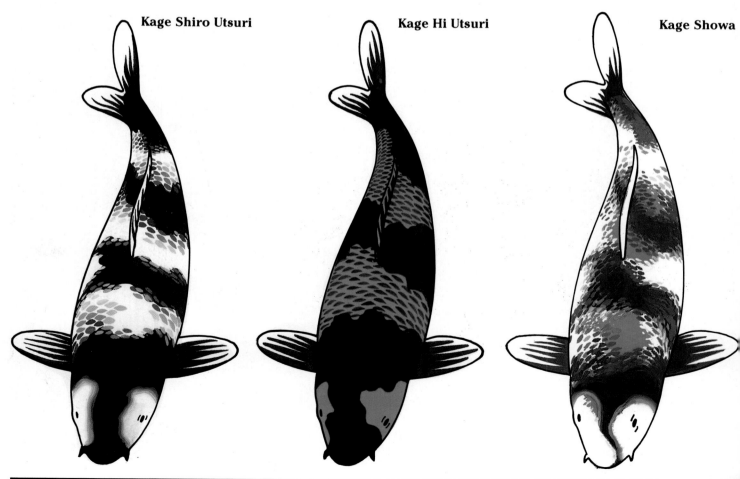

Kage Shiro Utsuri

Kage Hi Utsuri

Kage Showa

Above: Kage Showa
This koi needs a little more volume to be truly impressive. The sumi pattern is especially interesting on the head but is also balanced down the length of the body. The hi markings, also well placed, are even in hue. The 'kage', or 'phantom', sumi does not extend over all the white on this koi, but, where it is present, it is even.

KAWARIMONO

Goshiki
Goshiki means five colours. These colours are white, red, black, blue and dark blue, but since they are mixed together on the body of the koi, they often give a purplish appearance.

Goshiki were originally bred from a cross between an Asagi and a Sanke and are popular with hobbyists because of their flowery patterns. They should be kept in warm water as cool water makes the colours darken and, indeed, may cause the koi to turn almost black.

Kanoko-goi
Kanoko means 'fawn' and refers to the dappled pattern of hi found on some koi. Koi with this type of marking are classified with Kawarimono rather than in their original variety groups.

Kanoko Kohaku The hi markings on this Kohaku should be Kanoko (or dappled) but the hi marking on the head almost always remains solid.

Kanoko Sanke This is a Sanke whose hi markings are dappled rather than solid.

Kanoko Showa It is rare indeed to find good dappled hi markings on this Showa.

Goshiki

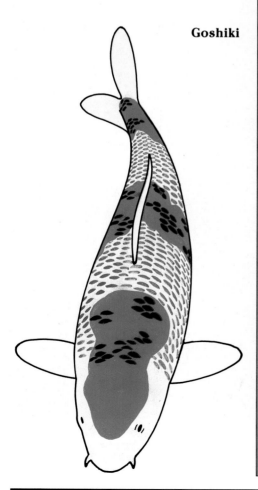

Kanoko Showa

Left: **Goshiki**
This young adult koi shows stunning coloration and pattern. The deep, clear hi shines through the grey-black pattern on the body with surprising brightness and is well balanced down the length of the koi. The rest of the pattern is reticulated, each scale having a lighter edge.

Right: **Kanoko Showa**
The good, strong sumi pattern on this Showa is particularly apparent in the menware stripe across the face. The white is clear and the hi is of a good even hue. The kanoko, or dappled, pattern is not fully developed but its clear definition shows promise for the future.

KAWARIMONO

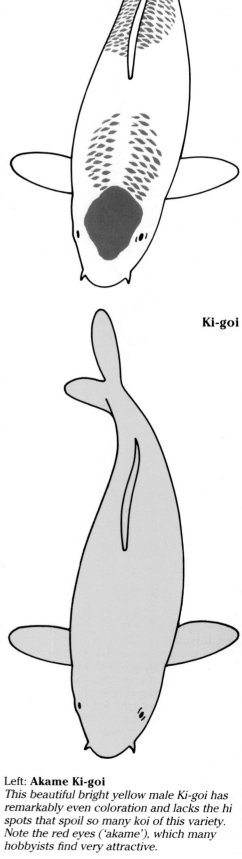

**Kanoko
Kohaku**

Ki-goi

Left: **Akame Ki-goi**
*This beautiful bright yellow male Ki-goi has
remarkably even coloration and lacks the hi
spots that spoil so many koi of this variety.
Note the red eyes ('akame'), which many
hobbyists find very attractive.*

Kanoko Sanke

Shusui hybrids

Other Kawarimono are derived from other crosses. One important group includes the following varieties, which have Shusui lineage, that is, they all have the basic blue coloration of the Shusui on the body, on which the markings of another variety are superimposed.

Sanke Shusui The pattern on this doitsu Sanke is underlaid with the blue back of the traditional Shusui.

Bunka Sanke This is a blue Sanke with shiny pectoral fins. These koi are only seen as babies because they lose this sheen in maturity.

Showa Shusui This koi should have the strong sumi and pattern of a Showa but with the underlying blue of a Shusui.

Goshiki Shusui As its name suggests, this is a doitsu non-metallic blue Goshiki.

Single-coloured koi

The following varieties are single-coloured, mat (non-metallic) koi. They tend to acquire volume in body shape more easily than other varieties and larger specimens can be quite beautiful.

Ki-goi This is a non-metallic single-coloured, bright yellow koi, whose colour should be of an even hue all over. Large Ki-goi are very impressive. A Ki-goi with pink eyes (albino) is called Akame Ki-goi (see far left).

Cha-goi (Cha means brown.) This is a single-coloured, non-metallic koi of a light brown or saffron colour. (The young Cha-goi is brownish green in colour.) It is also one of the most easily tamed of all koi, and exceedingly fast growing. Although Cha-goi appears quite plain at first glance, its faintly reticulated scalation is very attractive and this koi gains in appeal with association.

Cha-goi

Right: **Cha-goi**
This non-metallic, coffee-brown variety is not to everyone's taste and often suffers from black pigmentation spots. The elegance of Cha-goi lies in its simplicity, however, and, in this particular case, in its beautiful body shape.

KAWARIMONO

Sora-goi

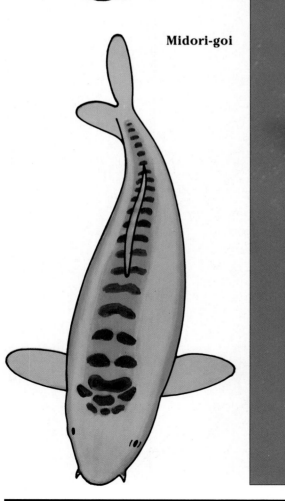

Midori-goi

Sora-goi This is a single-coloured, non-metallic, grey-blue koi. Like Cha-goi, it is a very fast growing variety.

Midori-goi (Midori means green.) This variety is so rare that it has an almost mythological reputation. A doitsu Midori-goi was produced by Tacho Yoshioka in 1963 – the result of a cross between a female Shusui and a male Yamabuki Ogon. This bright green koi with black or silvery scales has a tendency to go black, because of its Shusui lineage, or a very light green. It is unlikely that

Below: **Midori-goi**
This is a very young Midori-goi, which is not yet fully developed. The illustration, at below left, shows the bright green coloration that this extremely rare variety should obtain when it is mature.

anyone would try to specialize in breeding these koi, as in a spawning of 50 or 60 thousand young, probably only five or six Midori-goi would result.

Shiro-muji This non-metallic white koi is derived from Kohaku. Such koi are normally culled out or discarded, but large unstained Shiro-muji can be surprisingly impressive.

Aka-muji This is a non-metallic red koi. (The name derives from 'aka' meaning red, and 'muji' meaning skin.)

Beni-goi This attractive koi resembles Aka-muji but is deeper red in colour.

Aka Hajiro This is an Aka-muji with white tips to its pectoral and caudal fins.

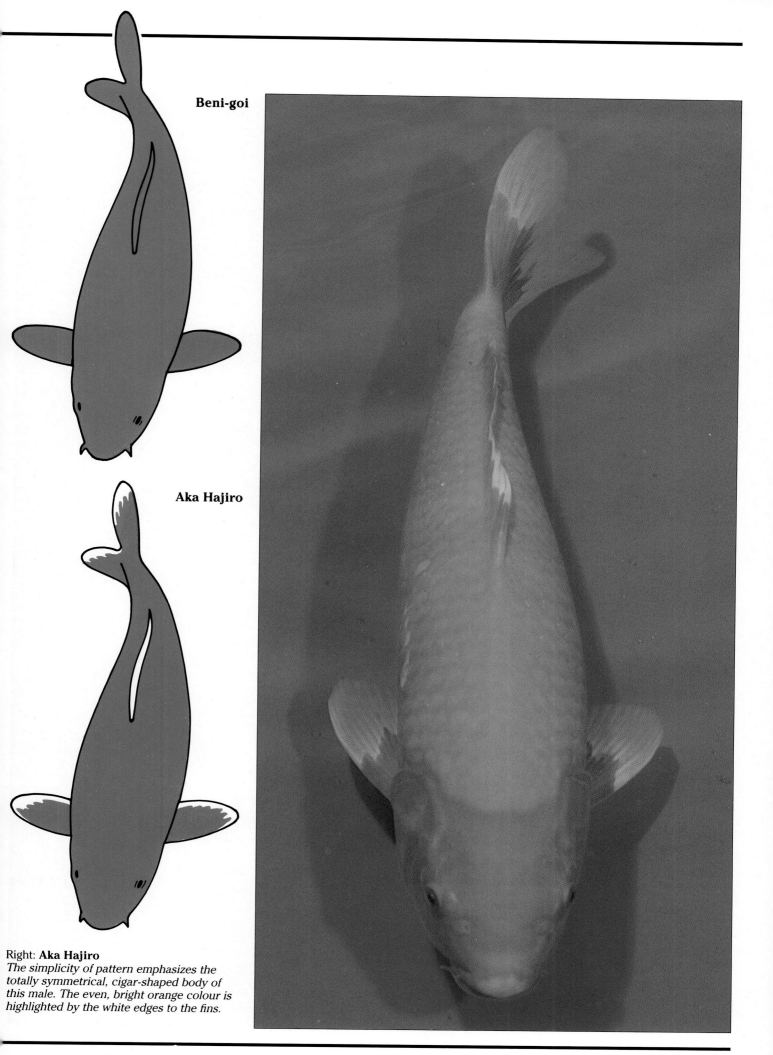

Beni-goi

Aka Hajiro

Right: **Aka Hajiro**
The simplicity of pattern emphasizes the totally symmetrical, cigar-shaped body of this male. The even, bright orange colour is highlighted by the white edges to the fins.

KAWARIMONO

Other Kawarimono include:

Hi-botan This koi is derived from Utsuri lineage and has a pattern that resembles Bekko. There are no sumi markings on the head but those on the body are much larger than on a Bekko.

Ochiba-shigure This koi is blue-grey in colour, with a brown pattern. The literal translation of Ochiba-shigure is 'autumn leaves on the water'. This is another variety for the connoisseur.

Right: **Ochiba-shigure**
This is another unusual variety, whose patterns and shades of colour vary considerably from one koi to another. Many patterns are more delicate than those of the fish shown here. Note the way that each scale on this koi is defined, as though it had been drawn with a pencil.

Ochiba-shigure

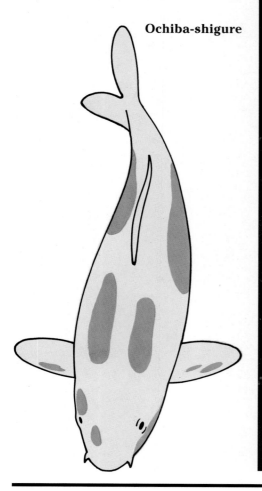

Above: Asagi (patterned)
Although this koi has the basic pattern and coloration of an Asagi, it would be classified in Kawarimono (the group containing all non-metallic koi not belonging to any other classification) rather than with other, *traditionally marked, Asagi because of the way that the hi is highly patterned and irregularly placed over the body.*

HIKARIMONO (OGON)

The category Hikarimono ('hikari' meaning metallic, 'mono', single colour) includes one of the most popular varieties of koi, particularly with new koi-keepers – the Ogon. Ogon are highly metallic koi, normally silver or golden yellow in colour, and contrast beautifully with other koi varieties. Indeed, it is generally agreed that the hobbyist should keep at least one Ogon in a pond for this reason. However, since they are such simple koi, the more experienced koi-keeper and breeder may miss the challenge of developing such patterns as are possible in Sanke, for example.

Because of their popularity, Ogon are bred in huge numbers, but the competition in shows is fierce. As with Kohaku, the deceptive simplicity of these single-coloured koi means that the criteria by which they are judged are severe.

Also included in this variety are Gin and Kin Matsuba; the metallic, and more common, counterparts of Shiro and Ki Matsuba (see Kawarimono, page 163).

The history of Hikarimono
The history of the true, gold Ogon began in 1921 when a gentleman called Sawata

Aoki took a koi with gold stripes along its back and selectively bred from it and its offspring, choosing those with the most gold coloration on their bodies. After about five generations, the koi known as Kin Kabuto, Gin Kabuto, Kinbo and Ginbo were developed.

Kin Kabuto and Gin Kabuto These koi, now considered rejects of the Ogon variety, are black koi whose scales have gold or silver edges. Their heads are gold or silver with a black marking, sometimes described as a helmet.

Kinbo and Ginbo These koi, which are black with either a gold (kin) or a silver (gin) metallic sheen, are also considered by modern koi-keepers to be valueless.

The Ogon lineage was stabilized in about 1946 when two entirely gold Ogon were produced. The development of Ogon has done much for the development of koi generally; Ogon have been cross-bred with other varieties to produce many fine koi in the Hikari-Utsurimono and Hikari-moyo-mono varieties, for example (see pages 180-3 and 184-93 respectively).

Originally Ogon were rare, and therefore expensive, koi, but due to very successful breeding they are now more common and have, consequently, decreased in value. As with all koi, a good Ogon can still command a high price, but these koi rarely win top prizes in shows.

Colour
Although Ogon are traditionally gold koi, colours vary depending on the variety. Whatever the colour, it should be of the same hue all over, from head to tail and down to the tips of the fins.

Pattern
Ogon are single-coloured metallic koi and should have no markings. Be particularly careful when buying young koi to avoid any with marks underneath the skin or on the head; these are likely to become more noticeable with age.

Right: **Platinum Ogon**
This beautifully shaped female koi has even coloration, although there are a few red stress marks on the head and a slight black tinge in the scales. Normally, Ogon have more metallic lustre than this.

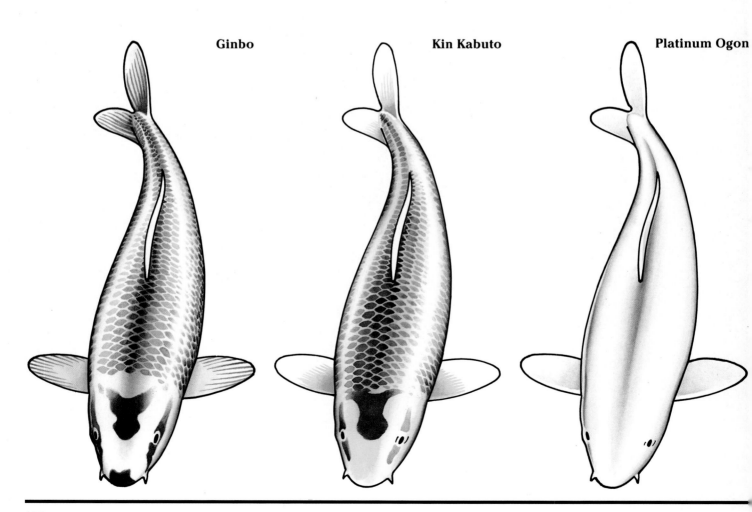

Ginbo   Kin Kabuto   Platinum Ogon

HIKARIMONO (OGON)

Lustre

The lustre (or metallic quality) is the most important factor of Hikarimono koi and should extend all over the body, head and fins. The head should be bright and the fins highly metallic. Ogon are frequently spoilt by fins that are unbalanced or that are small in comparison with body size. Large fins are highly desirable on Ogon to offset the plain body.

Scalation

The scalation of these koi is very important; the scales should, ideally, spread into the abdominal region, and their edges should be trimmed with gold. An Ogon that has lost scales (through damage or disease) is valueless because it lacks regularity of scalation.

Matsuba koi (see below) have black centres to each of their scales, giving an attractive pine-cone effect to the body.

Platinum Ogon This is a metallic white Ogon. The first Platinum Ogon was bred in 1963 by Mr Tadao Yoshioko as a result of pairing a Ki-goi (see page 169) with a Nezu Ogon (see below). This variety was originally called Shirogane, which means white gold. Another commonly used name is Purachina. As with the traditional gold Ogon, the head should be bald of all markings, and the lustre and scalation should be even over the whole koi.

Nezu Ogon This Ogon is silver grey in colour. The word 'nezu' is an abbreviation of 'nezumi', meaning 'mouse' or grey. This koi has a dull metallic lustre, clear head and even scalation.

Yamabuki Ogon This yellow-gold Ogon ('yamabuki' means yellow in Japanese) is now one of the most common of all Ogon. It was produced in 1957 from the cross between a Ki-goi and an Ogon.

Orenji Ogon As its name implies, this Ogon is a deep metallic orange in colour. First produced in about 1953, it is becoming very popular with hobbyists because of its brilliant coloration.

Fuji Ogon This is the name given to any Ogon with a highly metallic head.

Left: **Yamabuki Ogon**
The even scalation, bright colour and clear lustre of this voluminous female koi would cause her to stand out in any pond.

Right: **Orenji Ogon**
This is another Ogon with impressive scalation and coloration, lacking black shimis on the head or in the scales. Ideally, the body should be plumper and the head a little less pointed, however.

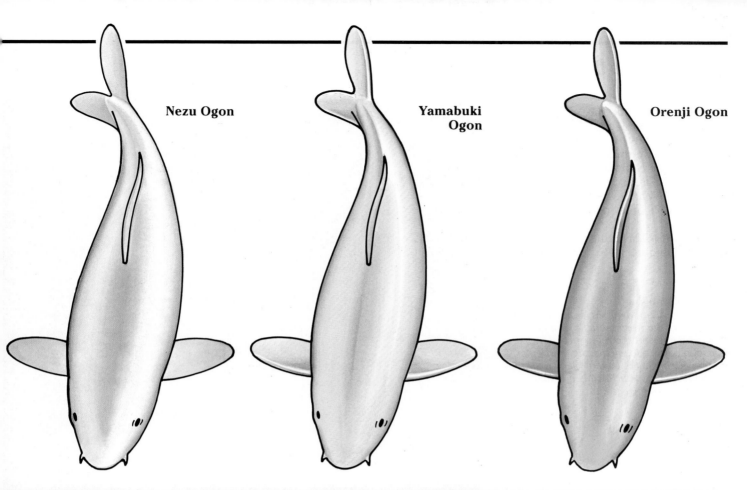

Nezu Ogon

Yamabuki Ogon

Orenji Ogon

HIKARIMONO (OGON)

Kin Matsuba (Matsuba Ogon) Each scale of this metallic gold or yellow koi has a black centre, giving the body a 'pine-cone' pattern. The head is clear of any hint of black on a good koi.

Kin Matsuba was first produced in 1960 by Eizaburo Mano, when an Ogon and a Matsuba were bred together.

Gin Matsuba This is the silver version of the Kin Matsuba.

Right: **Kin Matsuba**
A stunning, full-bodied koi. Note the evenness of the deep metallic orange of the body and fins and the regularity of the matsuba pattern in each scale. Particularly commendable is the lack of black markings on the head – a clear head is unusual in a Kin Matsuba of this size.

Kin Matsuba

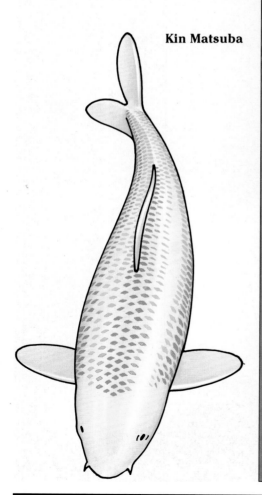

Right: Gin Matsuba
This is the silver counterpart of the koi on the opposite page. The matsuba pattern is less clearly defined on this koi, although it is of an even hue all over the koi, as is the base colour. Unfortunately, there is a slight trace of yellow around the nose and eyes.

Gin Matsuba

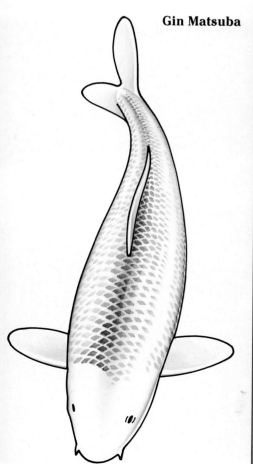

HIKARI-UTSURIMONO

Hikari-Utsurimono, like Hikarimoyo-mono, have arisen from an Ogon cross, in this case with Utsuri or Showa. Koi in the Hikari-Utsurimono group are basically metallic Showa and Utsuri and the same criteria for appreciation apply, for example head pattern and pectoral fin markings (see pages 140 and 146).

These very beautiful koi are living proof of the far-reaching effect that the Ogon has had in the breeding and classification of nishikigoi over the past 25 years. The one drawback with these elegant koi is that the strong metallic lustre can make the colours appear to fade, so that the hi becomes brownish and the sumi grey and blurred. However, this is not always the case and fine-quality koi in this classification are imposing, attractive and elegant in appearance.

Kin Showa and Gin Showa
Kin Showa and Gin Showa are both the result of Showa and Ogon crosses. Kin Showa have a golden lustre while Gin Showa are predominately silver. The name Kin Showa now tends to be used for both varieties, however.

Gin Shiro
This koi is a metallic Shiro Utsuri (see page 146); the sumi markings on its silver body should form the same patterns as on a Shiro Utsuri. This variety was, until

Kin Showa

recently, quite rare and, although it is now appearing in greater numbers, larger Gin Shiro are still uncommon.

Kin Ki Utsuri
This variety occurs from the cross between the Ki Utsuri and the Ogon. These are beautiful koi with bright colours, clear sumi and a metallic gold lustre. Again, they can be appreciated in the same way as Utsuri.

Kin Hi Utsuri
This is a metallic Hi Utsuri, the result of a cross between a Hi Utsuri and an Ogon.

Right: **Kage Gin Shiro**
The rather faint sumi and underlying hi on the nose and body are vindicated by the very even and balanced pattern over the head and body of this koi. The slight shadow of sumi over the silver – described as 'kage' (see page 164) – would group any such non-metallic koi with Kawarimono, but there is no such group for metallic koi.

Below: **Kin Showa**
This is a highly metallic koi with a good lustre. The fins are beautifully matched, with sumi stripes down to the base. Often, as here, the sumi on a metallic koi loses depth, and the pattern of both the sumi and hi could be more evenly spaced down the body of this koi. Nevertheless, this Kin Showa is an attractive fish.

Gin Shiro

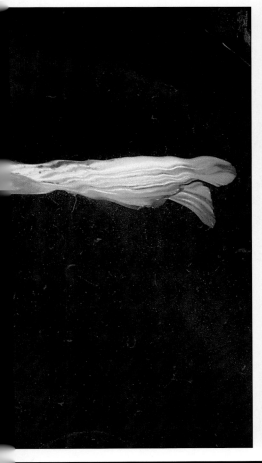

Gin Showa

Kin Ki Utsuri

Left: **Kin Ki Utsuri**
The beautiful Utsuri pattern over the body of this stunning metallic koi is enhanced by its warm gold coloration, which is even in hue from nose to tail. Note that the sumi is paler than it would be on a non-metallic koi.

Below: **Kin Hi Utsuri**
The metallic red counterpart of the Kin Ki Utsuri opposite, this koi, too, has superb colour and lustre and a good Utsuri pattern, although there are a few black marks along the dorsal fin and on the head.

HIKARIMOYO-MONO

Metallic koi that have more than one colour but are not of Utsuri lineage generally fall into the class of Hikari-moyo-mono. (Note, however, that Gin and Kin Matsuba belong to the Ogon category, see page 178.) The koi in this classification are extremely popular because they are highly metallic, appear in many colours and are immediately attractive to the eye. Koi-keepers, especially those new to the hobby, are very attracted to baby koi in this classification because they are so bright. However, when buying one of these young koi, make sure that its head is clear of a black helmet-like marking. Although this is not unattractive on a young koi, it becomes more noticeable as the koi grows and will be a serious defect if you wish to show your koi. In fact, such a koi would be ruled out immediately by the judges.

The koi varieties in the Hikarimoyo-mono classification have arisen from two sources. The first group includes koi that have resulted from crossing a Platinum Ogon with any other variety except Utsuri. These crosses have produced such varieties as Yamato-nishiki (also known as a metallic Sanke), Gin Bekko and Kujaku. These koi all have a metallic base overlaid with coloured patterns.

The second group consists of varieties known collectively as Hariwake, and includes Orenji Hariwake, Hariwake Matsuba etc. These koi all have two colours; platinum, and metallic orange or gold.

Yamato-nishiki

This variety is the result of the cross between a Taisho Sanke and a Platinum Ogon and was first bred in 1965 by a gentleman called Seikichi Hoshino. In fact, there were originally two distinct varieties; Yamato, which was the direct result of a cross between a Sanke and a Fuji Ogon (see page 176), and Koshi-nishiki, which was the result of a cross between a Sanke and an Ogon. However, the differences between the two were so minimal that Yamato-nishiki became the accepted name for both varieties.

The very attractive Yamato-nishiki is basically a metallic Sanke, with a platinum (metallic white) or silver skin with hi and sumi markings. The sumi markings on Yamato-nishiki are often pale and blur into a metallic grey, while the hi tends, more often than not, to be pale orange in hue instead of the blood red normally associated with Sanke. This is because the red pigment is transparent and the silver lightens the red, like the sun shining through a stained glass window. Yamato-nishiki with good hi and sumi do exist however, and can be very startlingly beautiful in appearance.

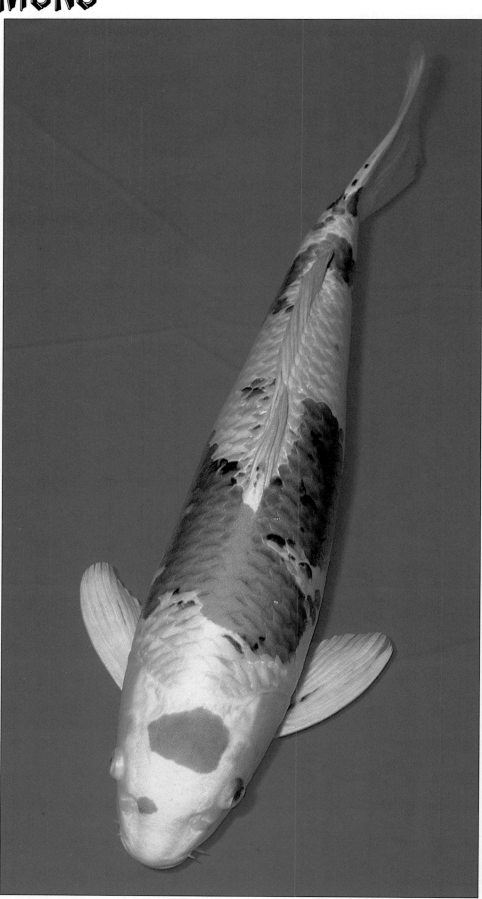

Above: **Yamato-nishiki**
A male koi with the excellent lustre of a good Hikarimoyo-mono. Both hi and platinum are strong and although the sumi is slightly blurred, it is well balanced and deeper than on many metallic koi.

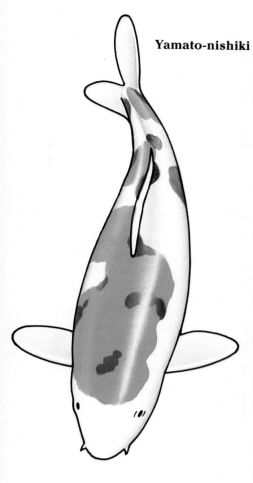

Yamato-nishiki

Kujaku

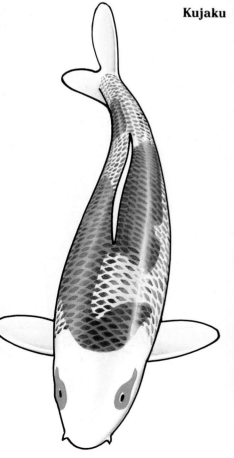

Above: **Kujaku**
Excellent body shape and large fins are responsible for the impressive quality of this koi. The regular matsuba pattern in the scales complements the metallic gold coloration. Note the unusual head marking.

HIKARIMOYO-MONO

Platinum Kohaku

Kujaku

(Also known as Kujaku Ogon) Kujaku are platinum koi with hi markings that normally cover a large proportion of the body. The scales are overlaid with a matsuba (or black pine-cone) pattern, which is said to resemble peacock feathers. The most prized Kujaku have heads that are red with no black markings. These koi look especially impressive in a pond of non-metallic varieties, and good specimens, which are appearing in larger numbers, are highly sought after.

Kujaku were first produced in 1960 by Toshio Hirasawa from Ojiya and are derived from Shusui, Matsuba and Hariwake. Many of the original offspring were doitsu, but fully scaled Kujaku are generally considered to be more impressive and are now produced in greater numbers than their doitsu counterparts.

Beni Kujaku This is a Kujaku with hi markings all over the body. It is a rare, but beautiful variety.

Doitsu Kujaku This is a platinum koi with hi markings over its body and sumi markings only in the scales along the dorsal and lateral lines.

Platinum Kohaku (Kin-Fuji)

This koi, which is quite rare, is derived from the Kohaku and the Platinum Ogon. The skin is platinum with an overlaying hi pattern that tends to be of a brownish orange hue rather than scarlet. There should, ideally, be no hi on the head and the fins should be glossy platinum in colour and lustre.

Kikisui

(Literally, 'water chrysanthemum'.) This doitsu platinum Kohaku is highly sought after by hobbyists. The Kikisui has a deep gold or orange wavy line along the length of the body on either side of the pattern. Its head should be platinum.

Gin Bekko

This koi is the result of a cross between the Shiro Bekko and Platinum Ogon. It should have platinum skin with sumi markings as those on a Shiro Bekko. Good sumi is rare on a Gin Bekko.

Right: **Doitsu Kujaku**
The lustre on this koi's body is good and the hi pattern is well defined. Unfortunately, the thin body shape makes the head appear disproportionately large and there are traces of black coloration on the head.

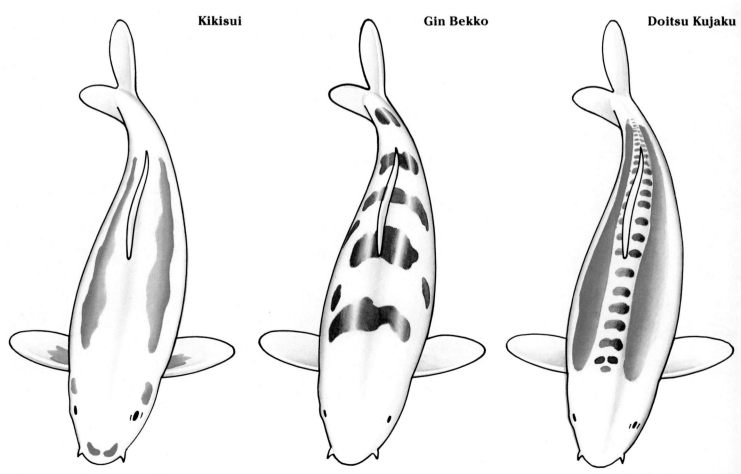

Kikisui   **Gin Bekko**   **Doitsu Kujaku**

HIKARIMOYO-MONO

Above: Kinginrin Sakura Ogon
This young koi is an excellent example of its variety with a good body shape. The pattern is varied and interesting; note particularly the markings on the head and the 'inazuma' pattern on the body. The coloration, too, is impressive; it is unusual to find such a deep red on a metallic koi. The kinginrin scales cover most of the body.

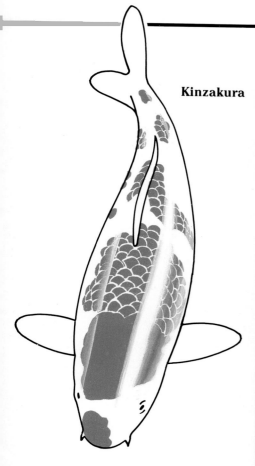

Kinzakura

Right: **Shochikubai**
This metallic Ai-goromo is a very rare variety. The pattern down the body is evenly spaced and well defined on this koi. Because of the good metallic lustre, the hi appears slightly brown in colour.

Sakura Ogon

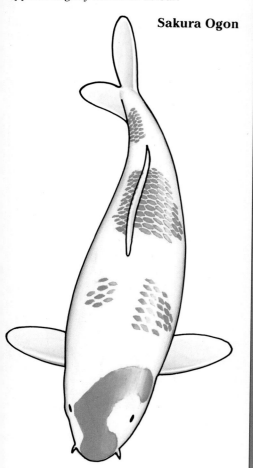

189

HIKARIMOYO-MONO

Sakura Ogon
In simple terms, a Sakura Ogon can be described as a metallic Kanoko Kohaku (see pages 166 and 168). It is often mistaken for the Orenji Hariwake because of its similar coloration. Unlike the markings of the Orenji Hariwake, however, those of the Sakura Ogon are dappled.

Kinzakura
This is a metallic Goten-zakura (see *Kohaku*, pages 133 and 134) and the name Kinzakura is seldom used. It is an extremely rare variety.

Shochikubai
This is a metallic Ai-goromo and should have a metallic lustre all over the body. It is a rare and very highly prized variety.

Kinsui and Ginsui
Both these koi varieties are metallic Shusui. The lustre of both varieties is good on young koi but tends to grow dull with age. Kinsui have a greater number of hi markings than Ginsui.

Tora Ogon
(Tora means tiger.) This Ogon with black markings is basically a metallic Ki Bekko. Good specimens in large sizes are rare.

Hariwake
Hariwake have two metallic colours; platinum and either orange or gold. They fall roughly into four categories:
1 Fully scaled   3 Matsuba
2 Doitsu   4 Doitsu Matsuba

Doitsu Hariwake tend to be the most popular because of the beautiful metallic lustre of their skin.

Yamabuki Hariwake (Yamabuki means bright yellow.) Yamabuki Hariwake is a silver koi with metallic yellow markings, which should be balanced over its body. On a fully scaled Yamabuki Hariwake the edges of the scales should be visible in relief. The head should, ideally, be free from colour (that is, it should be silver). However, a yellow pattern on the head is usual and is not a severe defect. These attractive koi are very popular.

Orenji Hariwake This variety is the orange equivalent of the Yamabuki Hariwake. The orange markings on the platinum body should be deep and metallic.

Hariwake Matsuba This is a silver and yellow metallic koi with a matsuba pattern of sumi in each of its scales.

Right: Yamabuki Hariwake

Although it is young, this koi has a good body shape. Both the yellow and platinum are clear and of even hue over the body, and the lustre is excellent. The head pattern and fins are also commendable. The rather uninteresting pattern of the yellow will probably break into a more appealing one as the koi grows in size.

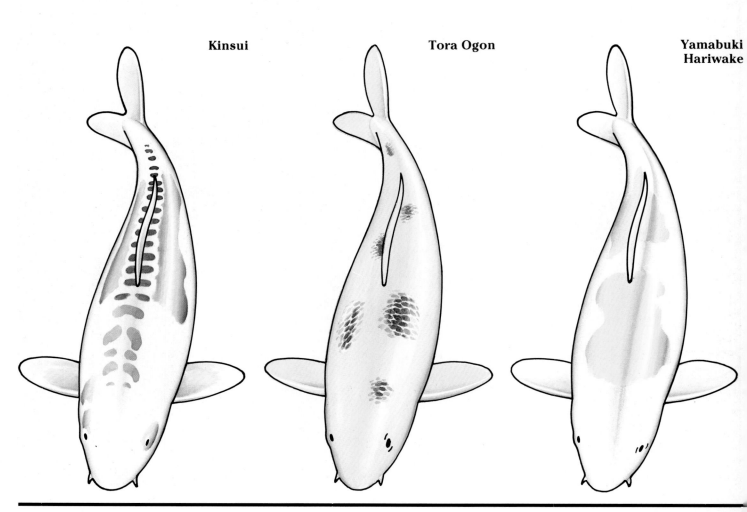

Kinsui

Tora Ogon

Yamabuki Hariwake

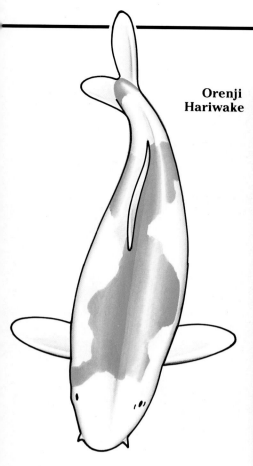

Orenji Hariwake

Left: Orenji Hariwake
An engaging aspect of this koi is its white nose, which has an excellent lustre. The platinum on the fins enhances the fish's deep orange colour. More pattern and volume would be desirable, however.

Matsuba Hariwake

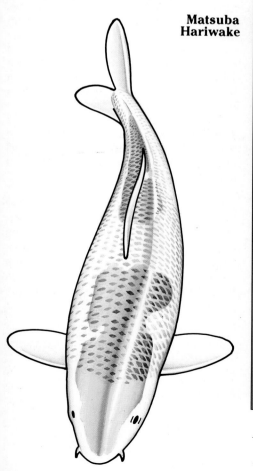

Above: Matsuba Hariwake
This is a beautifully coloured koi with interesting markings. The matsuba pattern is faint but evenly distributed in the scales. The pectorals are particularly attractive, with yellow in the base of each fin.

TANCHO

Tancho koi are among the most popular of all koi varieties and it is quite common for hobbyists to have more than one Tancho in a pond. Tancho Kohaku, in particular, are simple koi and yet it is obvious that a great deal of effort has taken place in their development.

The name Tancho is derived from the national bird of Japan, the Tancho crane (*Grus japonensis*), which has one round red marking on its head, and the word tancho literally means 'red spot on the head'. These koi are highly prized in Japan because of their similarity with the Japanese flag. The Tancho classification differs from others in that it contains koi from different varieties – namely, Kohaku, Sanke and Showa – that have one distinguishing feature – a red mark, or tancho, on the head.

Tancho colours
The hi marking should be of a deep, even red. The white on any Tancho is very important because it provides the background for a very startling pattern. (This is particularly true of the Tancho Kohaku.) Sumi markings on both the Tancho Sanke and Tancho Showa should be deep ebony in colour.

Tancho patterns
The distinguishing factor about the Tancho's pattern is the hi marking on the head, combined with a lack of hi elsewhere on the body.

Head
The hi marking should be on the centre of the head and should not cover the eyes, or extend back onto the body of the koi. The edges of the marking should be clearly defined. There are variously shaped tancho markings. In terms of judging, the most highly prized are the perfectly round spots, but hobbyists enjoy collecting other markings, such as oval, heart shaped and diamond, which add an element of uniqueness to the koi.

Body
The body pattern varies depending on the variety concerned.

Tancho Kohaku The hi marking on the head is the only marking that should be visible on this Tancho. Its body should be snow white from head to tail and there should be no hi in the fins.

Tancho Sanke The only hi marking allowed on a Tancho Sanke is on the head; the rest of the body is black and white. Many koi-keepers are confused as to why this variety is classed as a Sanke and not as a Tancho Bekko, as it is basically a Bekko with a red spot on its head. (Sumi markings on a Sanke are similar to those on a Bekko.) There are two things to remember that will help to clear up this confusion. Firstly, a Tancho of any variety lacks any other hi on the body and, secondly, it is not possible to have a Tancho Bekko because there is no hi on a Bekko. (However, a Bekko may have a black tancho marking, see page 140.)

Tancho Showa This koi combines the black and white pattern of a Shiro Utsuri over its body and head with the tancho hi marking on its head.

Fins
Fins should be as for the different varieties; that is, on a Tancho Kohaku the fins should be pure white, on a Tancho Sanke they should be white or have black stripes in them, and on a Tancho Showa there should be a sumi at the base of the pectoral fins (see pages 139 and 140).

Left: **Tancho head markings**
The tancho should be central on the head. The round marking is the traditional one, but other shapes are also popular.

Right: **Tancho Sanke**
This is a beautiful, large koi with a strong tancho marking placed squarely on the centre of the head. The sumi markings down the body are accompanied by very impressive sumi stripes in the fins.

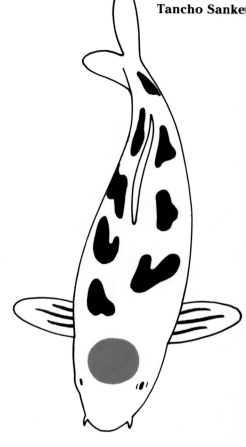
Tancho Sanke

Oval tancho

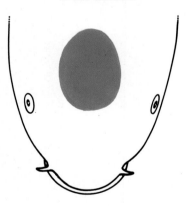

Traditional round tancho

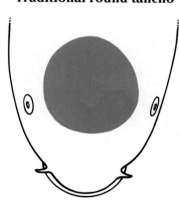

Heart-shaped tancho

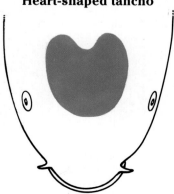

Diamond-shaped tancho

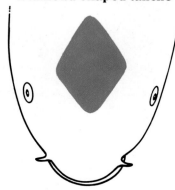

TANCHO

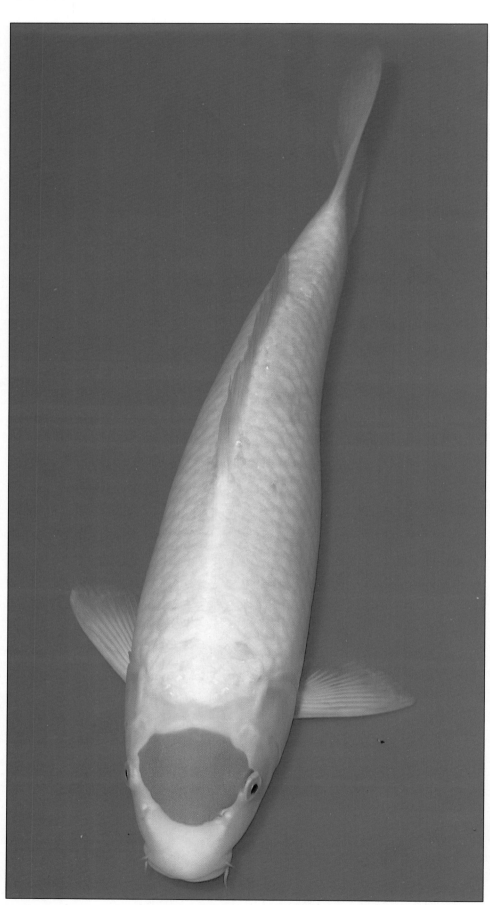

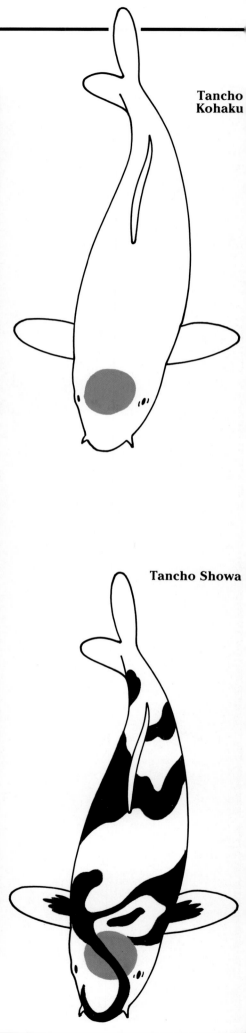

**Tancho
Kohaku**

Tancho Showa

Above: Tancho Kohaku
The traditionally shaped oval tancho of this koi is generally good although it moves slightly over one eye. Pure white fins complement the clear coloration and elegant body shape of this male.

Above: Tancho Showa
This koi has an unusual pattern; the tancho is well placed but unsymmetrical in shape and the sumi markings on the head and body are less extensive than on some other Tancho Showa. The pectoral fins are the most striking feature of this koi, with solid sumi over the entire fin except for a thin white stripe along the front edge.

KINGINRIN

Kinginrin literally means 'golden silvery scales' and refers to the sparkling effect of the scales, which appears golden over hi and silver over white and sumi. The impression is of an iridescence in individual scales rather than the overall metallic lustre of koi in the Hikarimono group, for example. A koi may have any number of such scales on its body but if there are less than about 20, the koi will not be described as Kinginrin.

These koi, which first appeared in 1929, are highly prized by hobbyists because of the way they shimmer in the sunshine and stand out from other koi. Kinginrin has sometimes been considered a weak point as it can blur the edge of sumi and so spoil the pattern, but this is now not always the case, and kinginrin scales can add an impressive dimension to the colour and pattern.

Until recently, Kinginrin of all varieties were entered and judged as a separate group. This changed in Japan in 1988 and it is expected that the rest of the world

Pearl Ginrin

Beta-gin

Diamond Ginrin

Kado-gin

will follow Japan's example. Now only Kinginrin Kohaku, Sanke and Showa are judged in this separate, Kinginrin group. Kinginrin koi from other varieties are entered in their normal variety groups.

Kinginrin scale forms

Kinginrin appears in different forms and affects different parts of the scales. These types, which do not alter the koi's classification, can be divided into two groups:

Pearl Ginrin (also known as 'tsubu-gin' or 'tama-gin'). On this type of Kinginrin there is a solid sparkling area on each scale, giving the koi the appearance of being covered with tiny pearls, as the name suggests. Its iridescent centre makes the scale stand out in relief. Although Pearl Ginrin koi are very attractive when young, they become more dull as they grow larger and it is rare to find good Pearl Ginrin koi larger than size 2.

The second type of Kinginrin has three variants. In all these forms, the effected scales have a flat appearance, lacking the solidity, or lumpy appearance, of the Pearl Ginrin scales.

Beta-gin Here, the whole of the surface of the scale sparkles. Beta-gin is considered the finest type of Kinginrin. However, these shimmering scales are often uneven over the body, being most prominent on the sides of the koi.

Above: **Types of kinginrin**
These illustrations show the various forms that the shiny deposit, or kinginrin, can take on a koi's scales. In reality, these types are rarely differentiated in koi shows.

Diamond Ginrin This koi was first produced in Hiroshima in 1969. The brilliant scales, which sparkle like diamonds, are greatly admired outside Japan but are generally unpopular among Japanese koi-keepers, who consider that their brilliance lacks elegance.

Kado-gin Here, only the edges of the scales are iridescent ('kado' means edge). Kado-gin koi are not generally admired in Japan because the amount of shiny deposit on each scale can be variable and uneven and, as on the Diamond Ginrin, is often missing from the scales along the dorsal line of the koi.

Although these different types of Kinginrin exist, koi with kinginrin scales are generally divided only into Pearl Ginrin and other Ginrin types. Most hobbyists would neither need, nor be able, to distinguish further between them but would agree, nevertheless, that these koi are the living jewels of nishikigoi.

Left: *This Kohaku displays exquisite kinginrin in its scales. However, the white is rather pink in tone and the hi pattern is fragmented and badly defined. The hi markings at the tail joint and on the eyelids would also be considered defects.*

Right: **Kinginrin Kohaku**
A stunning example of a Kinginrin Kohaku. The kinginrin is especially noticeable along the dorsal of the koi, particularly on the white, where it shows up as a silvery 'mother-of-pearl' deposit on each scale. The colour on this koi is superb; the depth of the hi is normally lightened by kinginrin scalation but this is not the case on this koi and the vivid hi pattern is well balanced along the length of the koi's body.

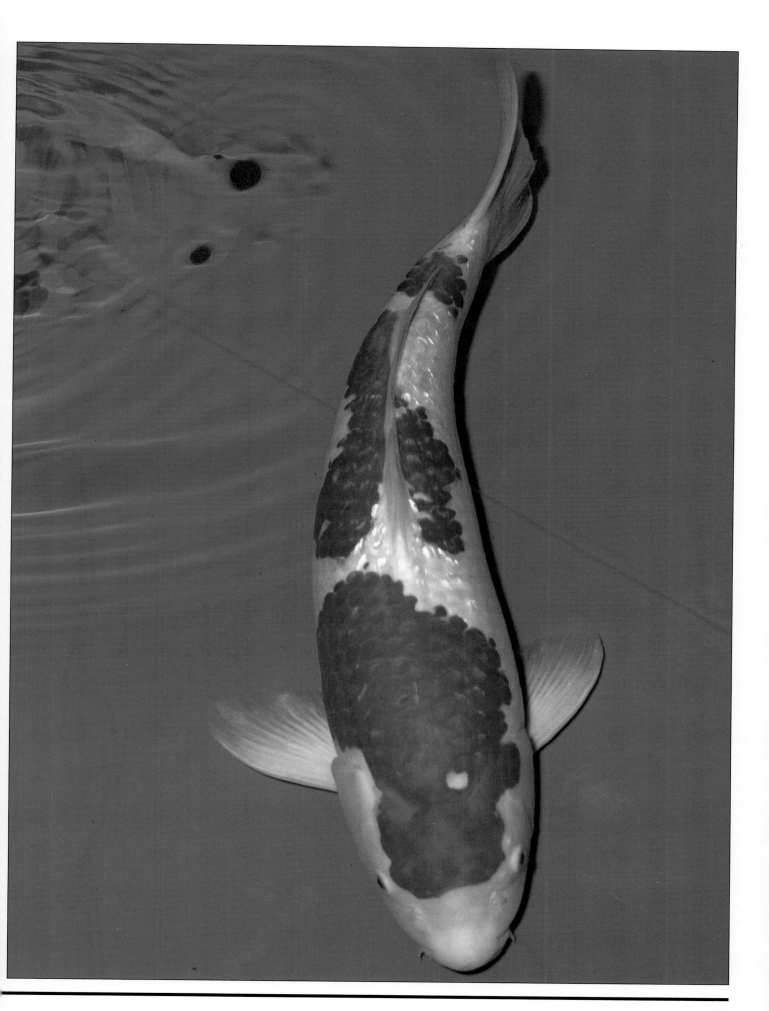

KINGINRIN

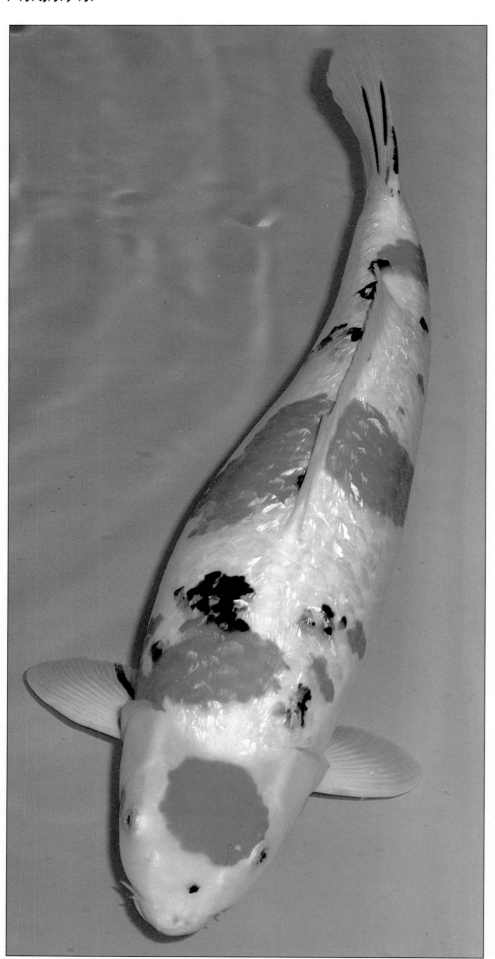

Left: Kinginrin Sanke
This koi shows excellent, even kinginrin scalation along the dorsal. The lightening effect of the kinginrin scales is clearly visible on both the sumi and the hi markings over the body of the koi. The pattern is interesting, with a particularly charming maruten marking to one side of the head.

Right: Kinginrin Showa
This koi is probably one of the most famous of its variety ever, having won many major competitions in Japan. The excellent silver lights in the white, and gold lights in the hi, markings are the perfect accompaniment to the balanced pattern, both on the head and, more particularly, on the four hi markings, which are evenly spaced along the body.

用語解説
GLOSSARY

A

Ai-goromo Basically a *Kohaku* whose red scales have blue semicircular borders, giving the koi a reticulated pattern. *(Koromo)*

Ai-showa See *Koromo Showa. (Koromo)*

Aka Red (usually as a base colour over the body of a koi).

Aka Bekko A red koi with black markings. *(Bekko)*

Aka Hajiro A red koi with white tips to the pectoral and caudal fins. *(Kawarimono)*

Aka Matsuba A red koi with a black 'pine-cone' *(matsuba)* pattern in the scales along the back. *(Kawarimono)*

Aka Sanke A *Sanke* whose red marking extends the length of the body. *(Sanke)*

Aka-muji A non-metallic red koi. *(Kawarimono)*

Akame An eye with a red iris. Most often seen in *Ki-goi.*

Asagi A grey-blue koi with red along the sides, cheeks and in the fins.

Asagi Magoi An early ancestor of the modern *Asagi.*

Asagi Sumi-nagashi A koi whose black scales are outlined in white. More commonly known as *Sumi-nagashi. (Kawarimono)*

B

Bekko Mat white, red or yellow koi with black markings.

Beni Red (usually as a base colour over the body of a koi).

Beni Kujaku An orange-red *Kujaku* with red markings all over the body. *(Hikarimoyo-mono)*

Beni-goi A non-metallic red koi, resembling *Aka-muji* but with a deeper red coloration. *(Kawarimono)*

Beta-gin Probably the finest type of *Kinginrin*, where the whole surface of each scale sparkles.

Boke Showa A popular form of *Showa*, with blurred, greyish *sumi. (Showa)*

Bongiri An area without pattern near the tail joint, considered a flaw.

Budo Literally 'grape'.

Budo Goromo A koi with a purplish, grape-like pattern on its white body. *(Koromo)*

Budo Sanke A koi with a pattern resembling that of *Budo Goromo* combined with solid black markings. *(Koromo)*

Bunka Sanke A blue *Sanke* with shiny pectoral fins. Seen only as a baby koi. *(Kawarimono)*

C

Cha Brown.

Cha-goi A non-metallic light brown koi. *(Kawarimono)*

D

Dangara A stepped pattern on the body of a koi, also known as *Danmoyo.*

Danmoyo A stepped pattern on the body of a koi, also known as *Dangara.*

Diamond Ginrin A form of *Kinginrin* where the scales sparkle like diamonds.

Doitsu A koi with scales along the dorsal and lateral lines only.

Doitsu Kujaku A platinum koi with red markings over its body and black markings in the scales along the dorsal and lateral lines only. *(Hikarimoyo-mono)*

F

Fucarin The area of skin around the smaller scales of good metallic koi. The smaller the scales, the greater the lustre.

Fuji A highly metallic lustre on the head of a young koi, visible as minute bubbles. Most often seen in good young *Sanke* and, occasionally, *Ogon* and *Kohaku.*

G

Gin Bekko Basically a metallic *Shiro Bekko: (Hikarimoyo-mono)*

Gin Kabuto A black koi whose scales have silver edges. Now rejected as a poor *Ogon.*

Gin Matsuba A metallic silver koi with a black 'pine-cone' *(matsuba)* pattern in the scales. *(Hikarimono)*

Gin Shiro A metallic *Shiro Utsuri. (Hikari-Utsurimono)*

Gin Showa A metallic *Showa* with a silver lustre. *(Hikari-Utsurimono)*

Ginbo A black koi with a silver metallic sheen. Now considered valueless.

Ginrin The more commonly used term for *Kinginrin*, referring to sparkling scale types.

Ginsui A metallic *Shusui* with a silver lustre. *(Hikarimoyo-mono)*

Goi Fish.

Goshiki A five-colour koi, on which white, red, black, and light and dark blue are mixed to give a purplish appearance. *(Kawarimono)*

Goshiki Shusui A *doitsu*, non-metallic blue *Goshiki. (Kawarimono)*

Goten-zakura Kohaku A cherry blossom patterned *Kohaku. (Kohaku)*

H

Hachi Hi An early ancestor of the modern *Kohaku.*

Hageshiro A black, non-metallic koi with white tips to its pectoral fins and a white head and nose. *(Kawarimono)*

Hajiro A black koi with white tips to its pectoral fins. *(Kawarimono)*

Hana Shusui A form of *Shusui*, also known as a flowery Shusui. *(Shusui)*

Hanatsuki A hi pattern that reaches the mouth.

Hariwake Koi with two colours, one of which is platinum, the other metallic orange or yellow. *(Hikarimoyo-mono)*

Hariwake Matsuba A silver and yellow metallic koi with a black pattern in each of its scales. *(Hikarimoyo-mono)*

Hi Red (markings).

Hi Asagi An *Asagi* whose red marking extends over the lateral line. *(Asagi)*

Hi Showa A predominantly red *Showa. (Showa)*

Hi Shusui A *Shusui* whose red pattern spreads up from the belly and covers the back. *(Shusui)*

Hi Utsuri A black koi with red markings. *(Utsurimono)*

Hi-botan A koi resembling *Bekko*, derived from *Utsuri* lineage. *(Kawarimono)*

Higoi A red koi, an early ancestor of the modern *Kohaku.*

Hikari Metallic.

Hikari-Utsurimono Metallic *Utsuri* and *Showa.*

Hikarimono The classification for single-coloured metallic koi.

Hikarimoyo-mono A classification including all metallic koi with two or more colours, except metallic *Utsuri* and *Showa.*

Hon sumi Literally, 'genuine *sumi*', referring to the black *sumi* markings on a *Koromo Sanke.*

Hoo Aka A koi with red gill plates. An early ancestor of the modern *Kohaku.*

Hookazuki A black carp with red cheeks. An early ancestor of the modern *Kohaku.*

I

Inazuma A zig-zag pattern.

Ippon hi A continuous pattern, without variation.

Iromono The collective name for all metallic koi.

K

Kabuto A cap or helmet, referring to koi with a head colour different from that on the body.

Kado Edge.

Kado-gin A form of *Kinginrin* where only the edges of the scales are iridescent.

Kage Literally, 'shadow' or 'phantom', referring to koi with a blurred, reticulated black pattern over the white or red.

Kage Hi Utsuri A koi whose red and black *utsuri* pattern is complemented by a *kage* pattern over the red. *(Kawarimono)*

Kage Shiro Utsuri A koi with the basic black and white *utsuri* pattern and *kage* pattern over the white. *(Kawarimono)*

Kage Showa A koi with the basic *showa* pattern and *kage* pattern over the white. *(Kawarimono)*

Kanoko Literally, 'fawn', referring to the dappled red pattern found on some koi. *(Kawarimono)*

Kanoko Kohaku A *Kohaku* with dappled red markings.

Kanoko Sanke A *Sanke* with dappled red markings.

Kanoko Showa A *Showa* with dappled red markings.

Karasu Literally 'crow'. Black (overall colour).

Karasugoi Black koi with white or orange bellies. *(Kawarimono)*

Kasane sumi *Sumi* that appears on the *hi*. (As opposed to *tsubo sumi*, which appears on the white skin.)

Kata moyo A pattern on only one side of the body.

Kawarimono A classification of all non-metallic koi not included in any other group.

Ki Yellow.

Ki Bekko A yellow koi with black markings. *(Bekko)*

Ki Matsuba A yellow koi with black 'pine-cone' *(matsuba)* markings in the centre of the scales. *(Kawarimono)*

Ki Shusui A yellow *Shusui* with a greenish dorsal. A very rare variety. *(Shusui)*

Ki Utsuri A black koi with yellow markings. *(Utsurimono)*

Ki-goi A non-metallic bright yellow koi. *(Kawarimono)*

Kikisui Literally, 'water crysanthemum'. Basically a *doistu* platinum *Kohaku. (Hikarimoyo-mono)*

Kin Metallic gold.

Kin Hi Utsuri A metallic *Hi Utsuri. (Hikari-Utsurimono)*

Kin Kabuto A black koi whose scales have gold edges. Now considered valueless.

Kin Ki Utsuri A metallic *Ki Utsuri. (Hikari-Utsurimono)*

Kin Showa A metallic *Showa* with a gold lustre. *(Hikari-Utsurimono)*

Kin-Fuji See *Platinum Kohaku.*

Kinbo A black koi with a gold metallic sheen. Now considered valueless.

Kindai Showa A *Showa* with a predominantly white pattern. *(Showa)*

Kinginrin A normally scaled koi that has gold or silvery mirror-like deposits on each scale.

Kinsui A metallic *Shusui* with a gold lustre. *(Hikarimoyo-mono)*

Kinzakura A metallic *Goten-zakura. (Hikarimoyo-mono)*

Kiwa The definition between *hi* and white markings.

Kohaku White koi with red markings.

Kokesuki Scales that are visible because the colour is thin.

Komoyo Small *hi* markings.
Konjo Asagi A dark blue fish. An early ancestor of the modern *Asagi*.
Koromo Literally 'robed', referring to a group of koi whose *hi* pattern is outlined in a darker colour.
Koromo Sanke A koi with the *koromo* reticulated pattern over the *hi* marking, and the *sumi* markings of a traditional *Sanke*. *(Koromo)*
Koromo Showa A koi with the markings of a *Showa* overlaid with the *koromo* pattern. *(Koromo)*
Koshi-nishiki The result of a cross between an *Ogon* and a *Sanke*. Now known as *Yamato-nishiki*.
Kuchibeni Red, lipstick-like markings.
Kujaku A platinum koi with *hi* markings covering a large proportion of the body and with *matsuba* patterning in the scales. *(Hikarimoyo-mono)*
Kujaku Ogon Another name for *Kujaku*.
Kumonryu Literally, 'dragon fish'. A black *doitsu* koi with white markings in the scales on its head, fins and body. *(Kawarimono)*
Kuro-Ki-Han The original name for *Shiro Utsuri*

M

Madoaki Scales with 'shadows' under the skin.
Magoi A black carp, an early ancestor of modern *nishikigoi*.
Makibara A red pattern that wraps around the body.
Maruten A koi with a separate red marking on the head (e.g. *Maruten Kohaku*). Also used to describe such a head marking (i.e. maruten spot/maruten).
Maruten Kohaku A *Kohaku* with a separate red marking on the head and additional red on the body.
Maruten Sanke A *Sanke* with a separate red marking on the head and additional red on the body.
Matsuba A koi with black markings in the centre of the scales on the body. This *matsuba* pattern is also known as a pine-cone pattern. Non-metallic Matsuba koi are classed in *Kawarimono*, metallic ones in *Hikarimono (Ogon)*.
Matsuba Ogon Another name for *Kin Matsuba*. *(Hikarimono)*
Matsukawa-bake A non-metallic black and white koi whose pattern changes with the time of year and water temperature. *(Kawarimono)*
Meija era A period in Japanese history, 1868-1912.
Menkaburi An early *Kohaku* with a red head.
Menware The traditional *Showa* head pattern, where the black pattern divides the red marking on the head.
Midori Green.
Midori-goi A very rare koi, bright green in colour, with black or silvery scales. *(Kawarimono)*
Mizu Asagi A very light *Asagi*.
Mono Single.
Moto Or 'original *sumi*', i.e. black markings that are apparent in fry and remain visible on the adult koi.
Muji Self-coloured (literally, 'nothing else').

N

Narumi Asagi The typical light-blue patterned *Asagi*. *(Asagi)*
Nezu Grey.
Nezu Ogon A silver grey koi with a dull metallic lustre. *(Hikarimono)*
Nezumi Grey.
Nibani Secondary *hi*, which appears and disappears depending on such factors as water condition and temperature.
Nidan Two.
Nidan Kohaku A *Kohaku* with two hi markings on its body. *(Kohaku)*
Niigata An area on the northwest coast of mainland Japan, the birthplace and pillar of the koi-breeding industry.
Nishikigoi Fancy or coloured koi (from 'nishiki', a beautiful, coloured linen, and 'goi', meaning fish).

O

Ochiba-shigure A blue-grey koi with a brown pattern. *(Kawarimono)*
Ogon Single-coloured metallic koi. *(Hikarimono)*
Omoyo Large hi markings.
Orenji Orange.
Orenji Hariwake A silver koi with metallic orange markings. *(Hikarimoyo-mono)*
Orenji Ogon A deep orange metallic koi. *(Hikarimono)*

P

Purachina A white metallic koi, also known as a *Platinum Ogon*. *(Hikarimono)*
Pearl Ginrin A solid sparkling area on each scale, also known as *Tsuba-gin* or *Tama-gin*.
Pearl Shusui A *Shusui* with silver scales. *(Shusui)*
Platinum Kohaku A metallic white koi with an overlaying *hi* pattern. Also known as *Kin-fuji*. *(Hikarimoyo-mono)*
Platinum Ogon A metallic white koi, also known as *Purachina*. *(Hikarimono)*

S

Sadazo Sanke One of the better-known *Sanke* lineages, with bright *hi* markings and small *sumi* markings that do not overlap the *hi*.
Sakura Ogon A metallic *Kanoko Kohaku*. *(Hikarimoyo-mono)*
Sandan Three.
Sandan Kohaku A *Kohaku* with three *hi* markings. *(Kohaku)*
Sanke Literally 'tri-colour'. White koi with red and black markings. (Referred to in early literature as *Sanshoku*.)
Sanke Shusui A *doitsu Sanke* whose pattern is underlaid with the blue back of the *Shusui*. *(Kawarimono)*
Sanshoku See *Sanke*.
Sarasa Red spots on the back.
Sashi The underlying black or red markings on a koi. These markings often stabilize when the koi is mature.
Shimis Small black specks, which sometimes spoil the appearance of the white or red markings of koi.
Shiro White.
Shiro Bekko A white koi with black markings. *(Bekko)*
Shiro Matsuba A white koi with a black 'pine cone' *(matsuba)* pattern in the scales on the back. *(Kawarimono)*
Shiro Utsuri A black koi with white markings. *(Utsurimono)*
Shiro-muji A white non-metallic koi. *(Kawarimono)*
Shirogane An early name for *Platinum Ogon*.
Shochikubai A metallic *Ai-goromo*. *(Hikarimoyo-mono)*
Showa Black koi with red and white markings.
Showa Shusui A koi with the strong *sumi* and pattern of a *Showa* and the underlying blue of a *Shusui*. *(Kawarimono)*
Shusui *Doitsu Asagi*.
Sora-goi A grey-blue, non-metallic koi. *(Kawarimono)*

Sui Water (rippling effect).
Sumi Black (markings).
Sumi-goromo An *Ai-goromo* whose *koromo* pattern is overlaid with solid black markings. *(Koromo)*
Sumi-nagashi A koi whose black scales are outlined in white.

T

Taisho era A period in Japanese history, 1912-26.
Taisho Sanke The full name of *Sanke*, which are white koi with red and black markings.
Taki Sanke An *Asagi* whose blue body colour is divided from the red markings on its sides by a white line. *(Sanke)*
Tama-gin See *Pearl Ginrin*.
Tancho A red spot on the head. (Used when the koi has no other red on the body, in contrast to 'maruten'.)
Tancho Kohaku A white koi with a red spot on the head. *(Tancho)*
Tancho Sanke A *Sanke* whose only red marking is a head spot. *(Tancho)*
Tancho Showa A *Showa* whose only red marking is a head spot. *(Tancho)*
Tobihi Small red markings, resembling splashes of paint.
Tora Ogon (Literally, 'tiger' Ogon.) An *Ogon* with black markings. *(Hikarimono)*
Tsubo sumi Black that appears on the white skin (as opposed to *Kasane sumi*, which appears on the red markings.)
Tsubu-gin See *Pearl Ginrin*.

U

Utsuri See *Utsurimono*.
Utsurimono Black koi with white, red or yellow markings.

Y

Yagozen A *Kohaku* lineage, developed in the 1950s.
Yamabuki Literally, a Japonica bush with pale yellow flowers.
Yamabuki Hariwake A silver koi with metallic yellow markings. *(Hikarimoyo-mono)*
Yamabuki Ogon A yellow-gold *Ogon*. *(Hikarimono)*
Yamato The result of a cross between a *Sanke* and a *Fuji Ogon*. One of the two varieties now known collectively as *Yamato-nishiki*.
Yamato-nishiki A metallic white koi with red and black markings, (basically a metallic *Sanke*).
Yondan Four.
Yondan Kohaku A *Kohaku* with four red body markings.
Yotsushiro Literally, 'five whites'. A black koi with white head, pectoral, dorsal and caudal fins. *(Kawarimono)*

Z

Zukinkaburi An early *Kohaku* with a red forehead.

総合索引
GENERAL INDEX

種別索引
INDEX TO VARIETIES

Page numbers in **bold** indicate major references to classifications. Page numbers in *italics* indicate captions to illustrations. Other text entries are shown in normal type.

写真提供
PICTURE CREDITS

Artists

Copyright of the artwork illustrations on the pages following the artist's name is the property of Salamander Books Ltd.

Bernice Brewster: 18-19(B)

Rod Ferring: 103, 104, 105, 106, 108

Bill Le Fever: 16-17, 19(T), 20-21, 25, 53, 62, 63, 74, 78, 82, 88, 94, 95, 96, 118, 125-198

Janos Marffy: 34, 35(T), 56

Ian Stead: 26, 29, 32, 35(B), 36, 40, 41, 42, 47, 51

Stuart Watkinson: 73, 75, 77, 79

Photographers

The publishers wish to thank the following photographers and agencies who have supplied photographs for this book. The photographers have been credited by page number and position on the page: (B)Bottom, (T)Top, (C)Centre, (BL)Bottom left etc.

Chris Andrews: 57, 73, 102(TR), 103, 105(C,B), 106(BR), 109(TC)

Heather Angel/Biofotos: 79

Bernice Brewster: 98-9, 101, 102(TC), 109(TR,C,B), 110(B), 111, 112

The British Museum: 12

James Chubb: 104(C), 105(CR), 106(CB), 107(TL), 108, 110(T)

Eric Crichton © Salamander Books: Endpapers, Title page, Copyright page, Contents page, 8-9, 22-3, 24, 27, 28, 30, 31, 32, 33, 35, 37(B), 42, 43, 44, 45, 46, 48-9, 51, 54(BL),

55(T), 56, 61, 62, 72, 76, 80-1, 82, 83, 84, 85, 86, 87, 88, 90(TR,B), 91(T), 97(B), 100, 114-5, 116, 117, 118, 120, 122-3

John Cuvelier: 37(T), 70-1, 74-5

Mark Davis: 13(B), 60(T), 92-3, 94

Garden Picture Library: 10-11(Elizabeth Wilkinson), 78(Derek Fell), 89(Ron Sutherland), 90(TL, Marijke Heuff)

Ideas into Print: 14-15

Jonathan Kelly © Salamander Books: 13(T), 54-5, 58-9, 60(B), 64-5, 66, 68-9, 77, 97(T), 139, 144, 147, 152, 153, 155, 158, 160-1, 161, 162, 165, 166, 167, 170, 172, 177, 180-1, 181, 187, 189, 192

Kent Koi Ko: Half title page, 104(B), 121, 124, 125, 128, 129, 131, 133, 134, 135, 137, 138, 141, 142, 143, 145, 148, 149, 151, 154, 156, 157, 163, 168, 169, 171, 173, 175, 176, 178, 179, 182, 183,

184, 185, 188, 191, 193, 201

M. R. Lewis: 34, 38, 39, 41

Peter W. Scott: 107(TC,BR), 113

Harry Smith Horticultural Photographic Collection: 91(B)

Stonecastle Graphics: 50, 52

Acknowledgements

The publishers wish to thank the following individuals and organizations for their help in the preparation of this book:

Chris Ball, Mrs Barret, Nigel Caddock, Stuart Craik (indexes), Philip Edwards, Brian Garner, G.A. Grant, Brian Harman, Kent Koi Ko., Graham Lowe, Alan Mann, Mitaka (Japanese typesetting), Panache (headline setting), Gregory Peck, Mary Riddoch, Peter Tebby, Ken Waterhouse, Helga Watson, World of Koi.